HOSPITALITY

IN

HEALTHCARE

HOSPITALITY

IN

HEALTHCARE

How Top Performing Practices Boost
Team Happiness and Give the Best in
Care to Their Patients

Debbie Boone, CVPM

Published by Press 49, a division of BMH Companies LLC, Chandler, Arizona

This book is brought to you with the support of CareCredit® and Pets Best. Synchrony and its affiliates, including CareCredit® and Pets Best, share this information solely for your convenience. All statements are the sole opinions of the author, and Synchrony makes no representations or warranties regarding the content.

Limit of Liability/Disclaimer of Warranty: While the publisher and author have used their best efforts in preparing this book, they make no representations or warranties with respect to the accuracy or completeness of the contents of this book *and* specifically disclaim any implied warranties or merchantability or fitness for a particular purpose. No warranty may be created or extended by sales representatives or written sales materials. The advice contained herein may not be suitable for your situation. Neither the publisher nor the author shall be liable for any loss of profit or any other commercial damages, including but not limited to, special, incidental, consequential, or other damages.

Some names have been changed to protect individuals' privacy.

The views expressed in this publication are those of the author; are the responsibility of the author; and do not necessarily reflect or represent the views of Press 49, its parent company, its owner, or its partners.

Volume pricing is available to bulk orders placed by corporations, associations, and others. For bulk order details and for media inquiries, please contact Press 49 at info@press49.com or 833.PRESS49 (833.773.7749).

FIRST EDITION

Library of Congress Control Number: 2023908427
ISBN: 978-1-953315-30-4 (Hardcover)
ISBN: 978-1-953315-32-8 (Hardcover Special Edition)
ISBN: 978-1-953315-29-8 (eBook)

BUS070170 BUSINESS & ECONOMICS / Industries / Healthcare
REF004000 REFERENCE / Business Skills

Printed in the United States of America.

DEDICATION

This book is dedicated to my parents, Ralph and Mildred Huey, who believed in offering the best in hospitality to everyone who dined with them. Thankfully, they taught their children their "farm kid" work ethic, an uncompromising desire for quality, and true Southern hospitality.

Special thanks go to Dr. Steve Cobb who gave me my first job in a veterinary clinic and who taught me how to successfully run a practice.

To the many veterinary professionals, veterinary technicians, assistants and client service representatives I have had the pleasure to work beside and teach, your commitment to the animals in your care and their people inspire me daily.

Thank you also to all those in the profession who gave me so many wonderful opportunities to share my message.

To the multitude of animals that have shared my life, especially my dogs who show hospitality to friends and strangers alike with a wagging tail and a jump for joy greeting. We can learn a lot from them.

To my much-loved Football Girls and Hens—these women are my "sisters by choice." Everyone needs a posse, and you are mine.

To Brenda Andresen who took a casual conversation over coffee and turned it into a reality and to CareCredit's team who supported the idea, I am infinitely grateful.

Finally, to my husband, Mike, who is my rock through all of life's ups and downs. He encouraged me to take the big leap of starting my business. He supports my passion for my work by keeping my home life on track, and he keeps me centered. He is my sounding board, my cheerleader, my editor, and my in-house business guru. He makes me laugh every day. He has been the love of my life since we met in high school, and each year together just gets better. Growing old with you is my deepest desire.

Contents

Advance Praise
for Hospitality in Healthcare

"*Hospitality in Healthcare* gives veterinary clinics the keys to unlocking extraordinary experiences for veterinary clients. In this exceptional work, veterinary practice consultant Debbie Boone, CVPM reveals the transformative power of excellent customer service in the world of animal care.

With unrivaled expertise and a passion for both animals and their human companions, Debbie takes readers on a captivating journey, revealing the untapped potential within every veterinary hospital. Seamlessly blending practical strategies with heartwarming anecdotes, she demonstrates how a culture of hospitality can redefine the veterinary experience.

Through the pages of this enlightening book, you'll discover the profound impact of a warm smile, a comforting word, and a genuine connection with clients. Meticulous insights provide invaluable guidance on improving communication, cultivating empathy, and fostering trust—a recipe for creating and offering an exceptional environment where pets and their owners feel welcomed and cared for.

Hospitality in Healthcare is a testament to the importance of exceptional customer service in veterinary medicine, a must-read for veterinary professionals and animal lovers alike."

Dr. Ernie Ward
Author of "Creating the Veterinary Experience"
Author of "Creating the Veterinary Appointment"
Award-winning practice owner and veterinarian, impact entrepreneur, and business consultant

"Debbie has taken her extensive wisdom and accumulated knowledge shared with countless audiences over the years and put it all here for the veterinary world to benefit from. As one of the world's most respected voices in veterinary client care, Debbie's insights are sure to make the team stronger, the culture brighter, and the pet parents happier. Whether you're struggling to make a major shift or working near the top of your game and looking to take things to the next level, this book has gems for anyone looking to be just a little extra. A must-have for the discerning practice management bookshelf!"

Jessica Vogelsang, DVM
American Animal Hospital Association Chief Medical Officer
Author of *All Dogs Go To Kevin*

"Every time your team delivers veterinary medical care, the client is there (and returns) because of the experience. Sorry to burst your bubble, but their choice to return is rarely about the medicine. From the initial contact (whether on the phone or on your website) to conversations in the consult/exam room and the outcome, it's the hospitality received (or not) that bonds the client and their pet to your team and practice. In usual fashion, Debbie Boone, CVPM, does an eloquent job of supporting veterinary teams in communicating and creating an extraordinary experience. Take a deep dive with your team to learn more!"

Rebecca Rose, RVT
Certified Career Coach

"There's something truly special about the way Debbie opens up and shares her life experiences with vulnerability and clarity. It's a kind of honesty that's admirable and also incredibly valuable. There's an old saying that 'Clients don't care how much you know until they know how much you care.' Debbie perfectly communicates that sentiment in *Hospitality in Healthcare*.

She skillfully communicates essential workplace concepts like the importance of mattering, emotional intelligence, and psychological safety. Her storytelling and insightful observations really hit home.

Debbie focuses on creating a positive, memorable experience for our patients and clients. It's not just about providing a service; it's about making a difference. By doing this, she gives us powerful tools to enhance the meaning and purpose behind our work. I would recommend this read to any veterinary professional."

Philip Richmond, DVM, CAPP, CPHSA, CPPC, CCFP
Founder and CEO
Flourishing Phoenix Veterinary Consultants, LLC

"In businesses throughout every industry, success of any kind relies on the whims of people. The services and products we offer are less important than how we offer them. People who feel good in a purchase tend to repeat that purchase. With her distinctly unique voice, amplified by her expansive knowledge and thoughtful approach, Debbie Boone has given us a gift in *Hospitality in Healthcare* that provides us approachable tools to transform the client experience in our practices. Her approach to hospitality won't just benefit clients; it will elevate the care we're able to provide the patients we serve and, in turn, improve the wellbeing of the people of veterinary medicine. By the last page, you'll be inspired not only to serve your whole community better but by the natural hospitality that oozes from Debbie's words."

Josh Vaisman, MAPPCP
Founder and Lead Positive Change Agent
Flourish Veterinary Consulting

"Southern charm meets the business of veterinary medicine. Debbie shares how to make clients feel welcome, important, and respected. As a result, team members are happier, clients become fans, pets live longer, and the bottom line thrives."

Bob Lester, DVM
Co-founder and Chief Medical Officer
WellHaven Pet Health

"Veterinary medicine is a service industry that provides healthcare!! You may not like this statement, but you better get used to it. Our clients are having higher and higher expectations and we are delivering lower and lower value and service. The place to start in a service business is ... SERVICE. Client service!! Why not look to other industries to learn from? The hospitality industry survives on service. Debbie Boone has taken her knowledge and experiences as a consumer and combined them with her knowledge of the veterinary profession to create a tome that will lead your practice from being doctor-centric to being client savvy. Long term success in veterinary medicine requires putting the client (and patient) first and by emulating successes from other client-focused industries, and as Debbie demonstrates, you can do that."

Peter Weinstein, DVM, MBA
PAW Consulting
Simple Solutions 4 Vets, Inc.

"There are lots of social media tricks of the trade these days, but as Debbie Boone points out, the oldest and most persuasive PR remains the same as it's been forever, and that's word of mouth. While providing excellence in veterinary medical care is clearly important, even more significant is the way in which the entire staff makes clients and their pets feel. Customer care is more than a phrase; it's about empathetic action, demonstrating that each and every person in the practice truly cares about their clients and their patients. And when clients feel that you sincerely care, they will return for life and likely tell their friends and family. There's no real trick here, as Debbie points out in *Hospitality in Healthcare*; try to put yourself in the client's shoes and never think "it's us versus them.""

Steve Dale, CABC
Program host, WGN Radio and national radio programs
Speaker at veterinary meetings around the world
www.stevedale.tv

Introduction

The goal of this book is to revolutionize the lives of patients, clients, medical care professionals, and these professionals' teams by sharing how lessons and skills learned from the hospitality industry can transform the pre-visit, visit, and post-visit experience for all the participants.

I acknowledge that this is a bold statement, but having lived a life of providing hospitality to others, it is also something I know, from firsthand experience, that it works. It worked for the restaurants I grew up in and for the fabric shop and veterinary practices I managed. It works for the practices with which I consult. It will work for you, too. Every weekend, the restaurants had lines of patrons waiting to be seated, and even though it has been more than fifteen years since the last one closed, people still remember them and speak fondly of the food, the service, and the memories created. The fabric shop thrived on a loyal customer base and was one of the most prosperous in the chain. Using the skills of hospitality in a medical environment built our veterinary practices to be the most successful in our area. Our reputation in the community was stellar. We retained our team members for years, saw loyal clients whose kids then became loyal clients, our staff enjoyed their work, drama and client complaints were almost nonexistent, and we had a compliance rate on preventive care that was 30 points above the national benchmarks. The team was well compensated, and profits were at the high end of the industry standard. Other local practice owners wondered what the "magic formula" was that made our practice so unusual. It was hospitality!

Anyone who ever hears me speak instantly knows I am from the South. Born and raised in North Carolina, I was taught Southern hospitality from birth. Add to that the fact that my parents were successful restaurateurs who believed in teaching their kids to meet and serve the public from a young age, and you have the formula for my belief that learning to anticipate, personalize, and observe people's needs is the key to a happy team and a happy life. How do I know the employees were happy? Because they stayed even in tough times.

In 1973, my father committed suicide. He was a well-loved and well-respected person in our community, and everyone was shocked at his death. My mother was a thirty-nine-year-old widow with two teenagers to raise and multiple restaurants to manage. A few days after the funeral, my mom held a staff meeting and laid it all on the table to her employees. She needed their help to keep the business going, and she needed their expertise. Every single person stayed and pulled together to keep the business running without my father, and within a brief period of time, it was flourishing as never before.

As a child, I would observe the waitstaff find their "regulars" waiting in line to be seated. They would hurry to clear a table, get them seated, and serve those customers their usual beverages without them even having to ask. They remembered what the guests usually ate, confirmed their choices, reminded them when the special cobbler they liked was going to be on the menu and watched unobtrusively for a cue that the coffee needed a refill or when the plates were ready to be removed. They chatted and joked with those who enjoyed interaction or discreetly served those who preferred a quiet meal. This level of customer care extended into the kitchen where the cooks also knew the customers' preferences and cooked the fish a little browner or the steak a little rarer for certain folks. They would even prepare and slice homegrown tomatoes that some of the before-work regular breakfast crowd would bring to share with their revolving group of business buddies at our largest table in the front of the dining room. This was beyond ordinary service, but in our restaurant, it was the norm. That is why every Sunday after church let out, the lines to get in would often wrap around the building. Great service paired with great products is worth the wait.

In today's world, people are rarely served well. We go through our days with silent, unsmiling people shoving bags out a drive-through window at us, being ignored by retail workers who are afraid we may ask them a question, and being talked at by medical professionals who are speaking jargon and using terminology we don't understand. Then those same ineffective and discourteous workers wonder why the public is being so difficult. In retaliation, these inattentive employees spend their time complaining about the rude customers and non-compliant patients with whom they are forced to interact, sometimes even to the point of firing them as clients rather than taking any ownership in their part of the communication breakdown.

Hospitality changes all that.

Will some customers be challenging? Of course. You will always serve someone who is having a difficulty you know nothing about, yet they bring that to your table. But utilizing superior communication skills, having emotional self-control, and diagnosing how to resolve a challenge can turn that "grump" into a fan. The result? A better workplace where clients trust you, listen to your recommendations, and become avid supporters for years to come. When this happens, coming to work becomes enjoyable, *especially when we use the same hospitality skills to care for each other.*

Hospitality is not just "being nice." People who are not naturally nice can still be hospitable, and extremely nice folks can still serve poorly. Hospitality is a mindset and a skill. This book is a guide into developing this mindset for your own wellbeing and the success of the business you own or in which you work. Hospitality can also help in your personal life as the skills learned work on all humans and not just customers, clients, or patients.

I hope you enjoy the book as I share the lessons learned from a lifetime of joyfully and successfully serving others.

Debbie Boone, CVPM

1

Know Your Purpose

It may seem odd to begin a book on hospitality with a chapter on purpose, however, humans are put on earth to accomplish things. We evolved as part of a tribe that collaborated to undertake tasks that allowed us to survive. If we worked together sharing our individual skills, we thrived. Alone, we died. *Purpose* in Neanderthal days was simple. Food, water, reproduction, and safety were the goals. As man evolved, our goals became more elaborate. Humans still desire to eat and drink, but now it may be a sumptuous dish from a top chef and well-crafted wine from a five-star restaurant. We certainly want to feel safe physically, but also mentally. Much of good hospitality focuses on creating psychological safety for those we serve. Similar to animals, most bad behavior by humans is based in fear. Hospitality allows fear to subside and trust to thrive.

Simon Sinek is best known for shining light on the importance of knowing our purpose. His explanation of the Golden Circles in *Start With Why: How Great Leaders Inspire Everyone to Take Action* is one of my favorite tools to share when training. He says most people define themselves by "what" they do, then advertise "how" they do it when instead they should start with "why" they do things, then move outward to what they do and how they do it. WHY matters to our soul and keeps us focused, especially when the "how" part gets difficult.

As someone who has spent more than thirty-five years in veterinary medicine, I can attest that it is a purpose-driven profession. Yet, when asked "What do you do?" those same animal health advocates will say "I am a doctor" or "I am a technician" when what they really do is partner with pet owners to help provide a healthy life for their patients with preventive care and owner education and to save animal lives in times of crises. That is BIG! Too much emphasis is placed on *what* we do over *why* we do it. Focusing on the *task* of our work diminishes the higher purpose of our jobs. The medical field, whether animal or human, requires hours of rigorous education, training, and developing proficiency of task. But when we lose sight of the true reason for performing those tasks, they become a burden to be borne rather than the means to a higher end.

Over the years, I have observed team members go above and beyond the call of duty in volunteer jobs. My veterinary assistants and technicians carried neonatal kittens home to bottle feed them every couple of hours day and night. They fostered unwanted animals and worked a network of connections to find them good homes. All this work was done without pay, on their own time, and with the only reward being the satisfaction of helping those animals.

> **Purpose surpasses money in the human psyche.**

This is not to say that appropriate pay is not important, but choosing work that satisfies the soul and allows us to pay our bills is far superior to a job that we feel is "just working for a paycheck." That type of job is usually reflected in our attitude towards it. Dread overtakes joy, and we grind away doing the minimum we can to avoid getting fired.

When we work for purpose, we make the effort to go beyond the job description. Rather we take that base and build on it to create an experience for those we serve that is memorable, positive, and connected.

> **It is the duty of the leaders of any business to define the higher purpose of the work, hire people who desire to demonstrate that purpose, and put systems in place that allow them to accomplish their goals of doing good in the world.**

You can always tell when an employee enjoys their job. Their attitude is engaged in performing their tasks with excellence and creativity. They connect with the patient, client, customer, and fellow staff members in a genuine and caring manner. They also flourish in environments where extra effort, positive attitude, and genuine commitment are acknowledged and rewarded. Even the most purpose-filled employee can be ruined by a poor leader. If this occurs, you will find these workers leave for better cultures, or they wither away to become below average or, on occasion, even toxic employees.

Serving the public is not always easy. People can be difficult, unreasonable, and even frightening. Knowing that serving them well and having the skills to overcome all those negatives can lead to accomplishing your purpose and makes the discomfort more tolerable. Sometimes conquering the ornery customer makes us feel more victorious than when we serve the easy ones. It is in those situations we get to show off our hospitality talents and think, "Damn! I am good!" We give ourselves a mental high five when that cranky patron leaves with a smile. Surprisingly, those well-managed grumps can turn into some of your most loyal fans.

Learning hospitality skills can help us accomplish the aspirations of our work, which go beyond getting a paycheck. When we achieve our goals, we feel better about our lives, and even on difficult days filled with challenging cases and demanding humans, we can walk out the door and feel we made a positive mark on the world.

EXERCISE: Consider what your personal purpose is at work. Does it align with the business purpose? If not, what can you do to become more aligned?

2

Know Your Brand

Several years ago, I consulted with a veterinary practice in Pennsylvania. This was a highly successful five-doctor hospital, but they were having some issues. As I interviewed the doctors and staff, I discovered an inconsistency between the practice owners and the team regarding the position of the hospital in the community. The practice was accredited by the American Animal Hospital Association (AAHA), and it practiced to a high standard of care. The facility itself was slightly dated but immaculately clean and uncluttered. There was a combination of longtime employees and several fairly new ones. After interviewing the staff, I felt like many of the newer employees did not understand the practice's origin story nor did they have a strong belief in the brand of the practice and how it was different from others in the town.

Branding is a marketing term. According to Oberlo, a Shopify platform, "Branding is the process of creating a strong, positive perception of your company, and its products in your customer's mind." This statement is accurate; however, it leaves out an important aspect of branding, which is the employees must also have a strong positive perception of the company and be engaged in the creation of a superb customer experience. Every business has a story to tell, and the team should all know and appreciate the story. They must feel like what they offer the patrons they serve is unique and special. If it can be done with coffee, it certainly can be done in medicine.

International best-selling author and keynote speaker, Kindra Hall has made a name for herself by telling stories and helping businesses discover and fine tune their brand story. In her book, *Choose Your Story, Change Your Life: Silence Your Inner Critic and Rewrite Your Life from the Inside Out,* she offers a list of questions to help people recall important moments that bring out the real narrative behind the company. My favorite is "Whose life is different because of your business?" What an amazing reflection about the effect our most routine efforts make in the lives of others.

As I began my training session with the Pennsylvania practice, I asked them, "What is your favorite memory of a moment in practice?" **Two stories stood out.**

The first. One of the senior veterinary technicians recalled the time she got to help treat a bald eagle. She said the grandeur and magnificence of this bird was breathtaking. Her heart started to race just from its presence. The very fact that she got the opportunity to touch this incredible animal and help it back into the sky was a moment that she would remember the rest of her life. You could see the memory come back to her and the power of working to save the bird made her remember the reason for all her education and training.

The second. The practice owner was on call for after-hours emergencies when he received a page. One of the local canine officers had been hurt protecting his handler during an arrest and was gravely wounded. The doctor rushed to the practice, calling for his support team to meet him there. All worked frantically to save the dog, but unfortunately, the damage was too severe and the patient was lost. Except the memory wasn't really about the dog but rather about the community of fellow officers who appeared at the hospital to support their canine comrade during his surgery. When they were made aware of the death of their comrade, they ordered appropriate transportation for the body, then all the officers followed their fallen canine teammate in a police honor guard as he was driven to his final resting place. The practice owner said, "It was then I saw the impact of the human-animal bond. Even for these tough law enforcement officers who saw the worst of humanity on a daily basis, that dog was more than a working tool—he was a companion and respected ally, and they honored him as such. I felt the importance and impact of my work on that night."

Both stories helped clarify the purpose behind the work. As we continued the meeting, other staff members told stories of helping animals and humans and the feelings behind the reactions they received. They were able to define their brand story as a company that was there in times of need for two- and four-legged creatures, all while acknowledging the value of their services to sustain the joy and importance of those human-animal bonds. They realized that it was because of their AAHA accreditation, the superior medical care, years of experience, and modern equipment they boasted that these opportunities came to them. So, the brand became about progressive medicine leading to exceptional opportunities to help in unique situations. They were special because they were prepared for the routine as well as the uncommon.

EXERCISE: Recall a moment in your work that is your favorite memory. Did it help identify your purpose?

Once you clarify your brand, you begin to look for ways to exhibit it to the community. We all understand the difference between Walmart and Nordstrom. They each serve a different customer population, and as such, they set up their stores in ways that are appropriate to a targeted demographic. Walmart focuses on low price and carries everything from clothing to cleaning supplies. Customers go to Walmart for bargains. Nordstrom focuses on higher quality merchandise for a shopper who values and can afford designer brands and who seeks top-quality materials and garment construction. Nordstrom is also known for superior customer service, which is a match for its brand. Walmart shoppers generally do not expect to have clothing selections carried to a dressing room for them and personal attention given as they try on outfits. Nordstrom customers do.

Obviously, hospitality plays a part in both experiences. The question being posed by all consumers is "How will I be served?" Customers visiting a bargain-branded business usually have lower experience expectations than those visiting more expensive ones. Therefore, giving a better-than-expected experience in a low-priced store is usually easy and a delightful surprise to the customer. Case in point—there was a Goodwill store near my former home, and the bookworm in me frequented it often, searching for bargain business books. The staff members were always friendly and helpful with pleasant greetings for every customer. Even Goodwill can show hospitality.

We have all been through the fast-food drive-through window and had our order taken by a person who attempts to rush us through our selections, mumbles a price total over the microphone, and tells us to drive up to the next window. When we arrive and pay, a bag is handed over with a scripted but meaningless *"thank you,"* and we only hope the food order is correct and that maybe we have a few napkins. Then there is the Chick-fil-A experience. Some protest their religious policies, but no one can dispute they are the outstanding customer service title holders of fast food. In his book, *How Did You Do it Truett?: A Recipe for Success,"* Truett Cathy, the founder of Chick-fil-A, said it was about "creating a culture that sets, expects, and rewards high standards and performance." Every business should follow this advice and build this type of culture. One of Truett's long-time employees, Zelma Calhoun, worked for him for forty-five years. When asked what made her so loyal, she said, "I've never heard Mr. Cathy raise his voice. I don't remember him arguing with anybody. I've never heard him tell somebody to do something. He would ask ...."

> **It's about creating a culture that sets, expects, and rewards high standards and performance.**

In today's high turnover employee market, perhaps leaders should follow Mr. Cathy's lead. It certainly seemed to work. Truett Cathy understood hospitality and used it for customers and his team. If we expect our staff to serve our clients to high standards, we must remember that leaders model the behaviors that are acceptable for everyone who works there. If snide remarks and shouting at each other are allowed within the ranks, expect no better behavior when those same employees are facing your clients. As the old saying goes, "Shit rolls downhill!"

Other companies have strong brand recognition. Starbucks has the green mermaid, but they also write the customer's name on each cup of coffee so that they soon come to learn their regulars. Target has a brand known for reasonable pricing yet unique design not to mention the bright white of the floors and walls accented by big red targets that make us feel we are in a well-organized, immaculately clean space. My husband loves to visit Bass Pro Shops. Their buildings house areas for camping, hunting, and fishing with their well-known aquarium filled with multiple kinds of fish at center stage. When you enter Bass Pro Shops, you expect and see lodge pole beams, flannel shirts, fishing poles, and camping stoves. They don't sell silk pajamas as that would be off brand. Their staff are hired for their knowledge of outdoor sports, and they offer guidance when customers are purchasing goods. Being outdoorsy is their brand.

What do your clients picture when they think of your business? For a veterinary office or a medical or dental office, the first impression should be "immaculate cleanliness" with only pleasant odors detectable. Smell is a powerful trigger of memory and emotion for animals and humans alike. Animals react to them at the veterinary practice if they trigger memories of discomfort and will balk at the door. As a breast cancer survivor, I recall fanatically washing my hands during the months of my chemo treatments. The Cancer Center at Duke had a very particular handwash in the bathrooms called Steris. It had a medical smell, and twenty years later, if I smell it, I get a nauseating grab in my gut because it brings me into that chemotherapy room once again.

As the hospital administrator of a top tier veterinary practice, I made sure that the facility was clean and smelled pleasant when clients walked in the door. The staff were well-dressed, and the parking lot was maintained without potholes and was freshly striped on a regular basis. One small touch that also stayed on-brand were our magazines. Everyone has been to the doctor's office that offers dog eared five-year-old *People* and *Time* magazines. I made sure that was never the case in our practice. Our magazines reflected the interests of our clients. *Veranda, Southern Living, Architectural Digest, Vogue, Time, Reader's Digest,* and *Newsweek* were all fresh and on the wall rack. One of our clients even took the time to find the practice owner and comment, "You always have the BEST magazines." Though it seems insignificant, those magazines made a statement about our brand. If a client was really enjoying a magazine, we would offer to gift it to them. If you are a veterinary office, don't make the mistake of having only animal magazines in your lobby. Your clients have pets, but they have many additional interests so provide variety in your selection.

The devil really is in the details when shaping your brand and the customer experience that accompanies it, those subtle nuances matter more than you know.

EXERCISE: What small touches or fine details help define your office brand? What could you add to make your brand stand out from the crowd?

3

Clients Want an Experience, Not Just an Appointment

Every time we walk into the door of a business, we receive an experience. On occasion, the experience is negative. For the most part, our experiences are nondescript. They're not particularly good nor are they particularly bad. They leave us with no emotional response at all. It's unfortunate that the majority of our experiences are like this. Except on occasion, we encounter someone who completely transforms our standard experience and leaves us with a smile on our face and a glowing opinion of the company for which they work. Because we are so accustomed to mediocre service, small improvements can make big impressions.

One of the biggest complaints in both veterinary and human medicine is wait time. As a patient, my longest wait time beyond my scheduled appointment was two hours. Because I was waiting for one of the top oncologists in the United States, I was willing to accept the delay, but if I had been waiting for my dental hygienist I certainly would have rescheduled or found another provider.

Medical care providers tend to forget that they must provide a positive experience for their client or patient. In fact, it was the poor customer service experience I had with the first oncologist I visited after my breast cancer diagnosis that ended up costing that hospital more than a million dollars in lost revenue. More on how I arrived at that figure later.

In truth, my experience with my cancer diagnosis had multiple hospitality flaws. I had noticed a lump on my breast and because of a history of cysts, I casually visited my friend's plastic surgery practice to have it checked. She immediately became alarmed when she was unable to draw fluid from the lump and sent me to a well-respected local radiologist. She happened to be out of the office that day, so I saw her associate.

I was prepared for a mammogram then an ultrasound, and as I lay there on the table wondering if I had cancer, this doctor and her assistant stood above me and talked about an imminent visit from the doctor's in-laws and the stress that she was under. At first, I was certain they would quickly finish their personal conversation and concentrate on me. But that never happened. I laid there feeling like an inanimate object, secondary in their focus. There was no attempt to connect with me. Empathy was never shared. I was a "chore" to be performed and quickly sent out the door so as to not bother the doctor who had other more important things to think about. I felt like an unwelcome distraction rather than a valuable patient whose health mattered.

The ultrasound was inconclusive, so I was sent away to return in three weeks. Once again, the ultrasound was unable to be read, and once again, I was to return. Finally, on the third trip, the mass was biopsied, and when I returned a week later for the results, a different doctor was there. I remember distinctly being called into the x-ray room and seated on a rolling backless stool and having a stranger I had never seen say, "I am sorry, Mrs. Boone, but you have breast cancer." I couldn't believe that a conversation this important and heavy was to be conducted in a working area full of equipment rather than while seated in a private location. This was life-changing news, and it deserved a better plan for delivery. Because of my familiarity with medicine, I quickly asked, "What kind?" This doctor gave me a bewildered look and answered with "the normal kind." I asked to see my pathology report.

Most women know that there is not a "normal" kind of cancer, especially when it is your cancer. Some types are certainly more common, but others are aggressive and difficult to treat. There are plenty of television commercials to teach us those facts. We all have someone in our circle who has been through cancer treatment, so we know enough to recognize bad news from *really bad news*. Some assurance that mine was a non-aggressive type would have definitely eased some of my fear as it would for anyone in my shoes. Needless to say, I was less than impressed with this entire event because it not only made me feel uncared for, but it also made me question the competence of the group. In an appropriate scenario, with concern for my feelings, I would have been taken to a doctor's office with the door shut, spoken with someone I had actually seen before, given an empathetic statement by the doctor who could have said, "I am sorry to share that you have cancer, however, it is adenocarcinoma, which is the most common type of breast cancer and usually successfully treated." I know I could have found some relief and hope in that statement as would anyone in my circumstances.

My next visit was to a surgeon whom I knew from a previous surgery. It was at his office that I felt the first true empathy on this terrible journey. After hearing his advice, my husband and I moved on to see the recommended oncologist. This doctor had stellar credentials having formerly been on the transplant team at Duke. However, after a brief visit where he looked at my chart—rarely at me—offered a plan without my input, and seemed completely unconcerned about the possible outcome of my treatment, I left.

My husband looked at me as we crossed the parking lot and said, "This man will not be your doctor because to him you are not a person—only a chart."

And that is exactly what I felt like. I was a medical problem to be solved, not a human who was starting a fight for her life and who needed an ally and a guide.

Thanks to serendipity, connections, and a few phone calls, I became a patient at Duke University Cancer Center. My experience with this group was 180 degrees different. I was fortunate that I had the opportunity to have this world-class hospital just forty miles from my home not only because of the exceptional medical skill residing within its walls but because of the equally excellent hospitality of my medical care team. I particularly remember one of the receptionists in the oncology clinic who treated every patient like she truly cared about them. As nerve-racking as those visits were, she was always kind and engaged. It's been twenty years, and I still remember her. And I still return to Duke once a year for routine mammograms and exams, driving four hours from North Myrtle Beach, South Carolina to Durham, North Carolina because I trust them so deeply.

My good friend, Pamela, and I are both cancer survivors who were treated at Duke. We started a breast cancer survivor group at our very large church. As women came into the group, we advised them to have treatment at the Duke Cancer Center rather than at the local hospital, and I certainly steered them away from the oncologist I first encountered. Over the next few years, I personally sent at least fifteen other women to my doctors and to the Duke facility. Pamela did the same. By the time my treatment was finished, my hospital bills totaled more than $150,000. And if you calculated each of the referral's treatment at only $100,000, you can see how my single, less-than-stellar patient experience ended up costing the original hospital in excess of a million dollars in lost revenue.

Like a stone falling into a pool of water, the ripples of my positive service experience moved outward to create a patient referral group of my making, and we can most certainly add to the tally the patients that those women referred after they got an equally excellent experience. The repercussions are infinite.

What could those initial providers have done to make my experience better?

First, the radiologist could have recognized that the most stressed person in the room was me, not her, regardless of *anything* she may have had going on in her life. My visit should have never been about her anxiety about a visit from her in-laws. It should have been a time where my concerns were addressed and details given about the need for my return, and upon the second visit, action should have been proactively taken to biopsy the lump. She delayed almost another month because she assumed my friend's attempt to aspirate the mass created blood in the area. Yes, she threw her under the bus with this assumption—a whole other issue. Second, it appeared the uncomfortable conversation with me about my positive diagnosis had been pawned off on the intern who was obviously poorly or inadequately trained to hold it. My diagnosis was given to me in a room with little privacy while sitting on an uncomfortable rolling stool in an x-ray room. If I had broken down into tears, I don't think there was even a box of tissues available. When a patient asks an obviously informed question like I did when I asked the type of cancer, it should register with the provider that they are working with a person with some degree of medical knowledge. The conversation should then be tailored to their level. Offices ask patients and clients to fill out forms that ask where they work or their profession. Providers should use this information to tailor how they speak with the people they serve, conversing in terms and on levels that are equally respectful to and informative for the patient.

What about the first oncologist? He could have changed his greeting from the typical handshake and generic "*Nice to meet you*" to something more in alignment with the gravity of the situation. Perhaps saying "*I know this is frightening and I am here to help*" would have been more appropriate before he flipped through the two pages in my brand-new chart in order to avoid eye contact with me. This was a person that I could have spent many hours with while going through treatment. As a patient, I wanted someone by my side who cared about me as a human.

Conversely, when I went to Duke and met my oncologist, he spoke with me and my husband about what this journey would look like for both of us. He understood how stressful it was and even allowed me to record our initial conversation so I could play it back when I got home. He took my hand, touched my forearm, and looked me in the eyes with great empathy. That was when I knew I had found the team that would save my life.

Understand that the experience is not limited to interactions with the doctors but encompasses the entire staff. An impatient remark by the person answering the phone can begin a downward spiral that continues into the facility visit. Often a poor encounter on the phone when attempting to simply schedule an appointment can lead that potential client to change their mind or merely be a "no show" for their scheduled time because they called another provider and got a friendly voice and a genuine connection.

Poor experiences also occur when there's a lack of follow-through and consistency. On a recent annual visit to my general practitioner, my bloodwork showed an elevated A1C. The doctor wanted to repeat the test in three months. I scheduled the lab appointment for three months later and returned as planned. However, when my test results came back, my A1C test was not listed in the results. Upon calling back to find out why, I was told not to be concerned, that it wasn't high enough to matter. You can see there was an inconsistency between what the doctor told me in the exam room the day she reported it was elevated and what I was told three months later over the phone after returning for additional testing at her request. Did she really not mean to order the test, or did someone drop the ball and then tell me it was unimportant just to cover up a mistake? This confusion has me questioning whether I need to search for a new doctor.

When I managed veterinary hospitals, hospitality was one of our major focuses. If you bought a bag of food, there was a likelihood the practice owner would carry it to the car for you and if not him, certainly one of the staff members. Even over client protests, this small courtesy was performed. Clients' names were remembered as were their kids' and pets' names and were used in conversation. Connections were made whether it was a comment about a cute pair of shoes they were wearing or the novel they had in hand. Our team observed our clients and found ways to build relationships. Those relationships kept our clients loyal and formed a referral network for us beyond what any paid advertisement or marketing plan could possibly provide. Client retention was high and often multi-generational. Understand that this practice was in a large city, not a small town. We just gave folks that small town feeling and showed them that they mattered regardless of the size of the city or the practice.

One day, one of our former competitors attended my class on customer service. He was the regional medical director for a large corporate practice group. At the break, he came up to me and said, "Debbie, every veterinarian in town wanted to know what the hell you people were doing at that practice. I used to get some of your boarding overflow during the holidays, and try as we might, even though we were less expensive, we could not get those people to change to us. Now I understand that it wasn't the medicine but the hospitality that keep those clients so loyal."

I just smiled.

There are a lot of wonderful veterinarians and doctors out there, but since clients are not usually medical professionals, they make judgments based only on how they feel when visiting the office. We worked to make clients feel welcome, important, and respected. The team was also well-trained, and systems were in place to make sure things like my A1C snafu didn't happen. This positive energy was returned to us in trust, compliance, and referrals. Since we measured where all our new clients came from, we knew that well over 80 percent came from referrals from our existing clients.

Care for your health or for your pet's health is an emotional event. Just consider how someone's blood pressure will rise simply from the sight of a white coat at a doctor visit. For animals, they smell the odors of the hospital and pheromones of other fearful pets and become reluctant to enter the door. When we consider the emotions at play in a trip to the practice and train our team on how to influence them in a positive way, it is a win for all stakeholders.

The real payoff when clients and patients have a great experience is the wellbeing of the team. Happy people don't get angry and upset and give employees a hard time. Animals who are not fearful because staff acknowledge their fear and overcome it with treats and low-stress handling better tolerate and even like their veterinary visits. This makes everyone's job easier and much more enjoyable. When trust is built and maintained with those we serve, they become more amenable to our offerings and directives. "Yes" becomes the norm as opposed to "You only care about the money" or "You are in bed with the drug company and get kickbacks." I always laugh when I hear this because the rules are so stringent—pharma reps can't even give away ink pens without scrutiny, and veterinarians certainly don't get big bonuses from pet food manufacturers. I know because I see their books.

I once received a call from one of my favorite practice managers. She asked me to help with some team training because she said, "Our team is spiraling into negativity and the client has now become our ENEMY." I was seeing the same murmurs online. Acknowledge that this is happening in your practice and address it expediently and appropriately.

Recognize that the pandemic exacerbated this poor behavior, but social unrest, politics, too much time disconnected from others, and social media echo chambers are all damaging the fabric of our humanity. Dehumanization of others causes otherwise normally kind and ethical people to go against their core beliefs. As an example, the Nazis called Jews "vermin and rats." Slaveholders justified their acceptance of slavery by stating that those they enslaved were "subhuman." Native Americans were deemed "savages" in order to feel no remorse in stealing native lands. So, when we dehumanize our clients by calling them "idiots, assholes, or fools," we are doing the same thing, and if allowed to continue, it will poison our business, our culture, and our very souls.

For now, just being aware of how client bashing is damaging our own mental health is a strong incentive to change. Negativity is an energy suck. Neuroscience research studies show that our brain seeks what we tell it to find. So, if we look for negative things, we will find them and dwell on them to our own detriment. That is why mindfulness and gratitude are so valuable in retraining our brain to seek the positive.

As a service industry, team members can never forget that clients are the source of our livelihood. They are the decision-makers for the pet that we want to treat. They also have a lot of choices where to spend their money. There were five good quality practices within a two-mile radius of my first practice, so I grew up in veterinary medicine dealing with a lot of competition. To top it all, our practice was probably the most expensive in town and one of the most successful because of the bond we built with our clients and each other.

During the COVID-19 pandemic, clients became a faceless voice—often a rude one. We missed out on the chit-chat, small talk, and personal encounters that make us human to each other. Now when our conversations are all limited to business and medical transactions, we are missing something vital for our clients and ourselves—connection with others.

How do we regain connection?

Communication training can help people understand their own reactions and those of their clients. When we have emotional intelligence, we can more easily navigate the choppy waters of human anxiety and stress. This goes for your external customer—the client—and your internal customer—the staff. Treat them both with kindness and empathy and support their goals; and trust me—life will improve for everyone. When you treat people well, gain their trust, and build a base of raving fans, your business will be successful and a wonderful place to work.

> **EXERCISE:** Reflect on a medical visit for you or your pet. Did you feel the providers cared about you as a person? How did they show you they cared? Or did you experience lack of caring? What could have been improved?

4

The Story: Who is the Hero? (Hint ... It's Not You)

Being from the South, I think I was born to be a storyteller. My father's side of the family was particularly good at spinning a yarn and certainly fabricating a tall tale. Still, true stories are always the best to share when moving people to action. Stories are powerful, especially in business. I mentioned earlier the value of storytelling in sharing your purpose and understanding your brand. But stories can go much further. They make training engaging and dramatically improve retention. They help people visualize and express goals and dreams. They can be used as cautionary tales of what not to do. They can inspire us to do things beyond our comfort zone. They can make us see others as more human when we walk in their shoes through their story.

In the book *Building a Story Brand: Clarify Your Message So Customers Will Listen* by Donald Miller, Miller does an exceptional job showing his reader how to define and create the story of their customer's journey. As an avid reader, I have whiled away many hours engrossed in a good book. I identify with the heroine, aspire to be the wizard who knows all, and embrace the joy of a happy ending by living vicariously through the characters. According to Miller, this framework is required for any successful novel, movie, or play. We must always have the main character who is our hero. They must be faced with some sort of challenge that they cannot solve on their own. Along comes the wise counselor (think Merlin from *Tales of King Arthur*) who guides them along the path. The storyline continues with the hero moving through the quest or journey and the wise counselor guiding them along the way. Problems are solved and decisions are made. The goal is resolution of the challenge resulting in a positive outcome. The end. When the final outcome is negative and the hero loses, we are dissatisfied and don't care for the story.

In medicine, a mistake is often made in identifying the hero. Doctors regularly go into medicine with the idea that they will be saviors of their patients and gain adulation from them or, in veterinary medicine, from their patient's owner. Consequently, the storyline in those practices revolves around the practitioner. The websites and marketing content tell stories about the doctor's accomplishments, degrees, and awards. In veterinary medicine, the animal is often deemed the hero. Patients and clients are inconvenienced to accommodate the whim of the practitioner. Inadequate appointment times are allocated because time management overrides the needs of the customer. Practices chronically run behind, making clients wait. Arrogance replaces respect.

I once performed some consulting in a veterinary teaching hospital. On the day of my visit, multiple complex surgical cases had been scheduled. The evening before, several of the veterinary specialists who were scheduled to perform these surgeries decided, without notice to their boss or team, to go to a conference a couple of hours away. This caused their patient care coordinators to have to call the pet owners, apologize for the late notice, cancel the surgeries, and attempt to reschedule them. These doctors gave absolutely no consideration to the anxiety or stress of the pet owners who had already mentally, physically, and logistically prepared to bring their pet to the specialty hospital. It is likely that the clients had asked to be off work, had to arrange childcare, or make some other kind of plan to enable them to transport their ailing pet to the hospital. No consideration was given to fellow team members such as the patient care coordinators who were on the frontline with the clients. They had to make those calls; finagle the surgical schedule; and field the irritation and, quite likely, the wrath of these disrespected pet owners. In this scenario, it is obvious that these doctors considered themselves to be the hero. Their own self-interest and self-importance led their decision-making. Because they were tenured, the employer had little recourse to reprimand this selfish behavior. I'm sure you are thinking, "*That would never happen in my practice.*" But sometimes the slights are not as egregious as in this story, but they are still present. For instance, when service providers schedule appointments for 8 a.m. and show up to work at 8:30, causing patients to have a longer wait before they are seen, the same self-centered mentality is manifested. Thoughts of "self" have superseded respect for others.

Wise counselors are there for the heroes. They support, guide, and coach with empathy, respect, and knowledge. They desire the hero to win, and they offer their skills to make that happen. That is not to say the councilors should not set boundaries. They should. Even wizards take a break to rest, study their craft, and renew their powers.

> **"The purpose of life is not to be happy. It is to be useful, to be honorable, to be compassionate, to have it make some difference that you have lived and lived well."**
> —Ralph Waldo Emerson

When we focus on hospitality, we realize the medical team's position is to be the educator and knowledgeable guide to solving the hero's problem, which can be their own illness or an issue with their pet. When we realize our focus needs to shift, then our communication manner will change from authoritarian dictator to empathetic collaborator. If we want to live a life with purpose and accomplishment, we must focus on serving others well. Never being subservient but instead being helpful, empathic, and giving others grace when they are not at their best. The goal is to look back on your day and know you left the world a little better than you found it.

EXERCISE: Review your company website, social media posts, and internal focus. Who is front and center? Is it the client, or is it the medical staff? How would you edit the "story" so it is properly focused on the real "hero"?

5

Appearance and First Impressions

I have a photograph from my family's archives of the opening of our first restaurant. The waitresses were all dressed in white starched uniforms with white nurse's shoes. The kitchen staff wore white chef's coats, black pants, and white aprons. The equipment in the photograph gleamed. Everything about this picture spoke of cleanliness, quality, and attention to detail. Over the years, the business grew and the uniforms changed, but the attention to detail, cleanliness, and quality never wavered.

We certainly live in a more relaxed society when it comes to clothing than we did in the 1950s. Nevertheless, first impressions still matter.

Neuroscience teaches us that our brain is an energy hog, and therefore, it creates shortcuts in order to conserve calories. One of those shortcuts is snap judgments. Accurate or not, the instant we meet a new person our brain and our biases go to work to quickly place them in a category we understand. We are judging the person in front of us as someone we can trust or distrust. We determine if they are competent. Maybe they look like someone we didn't care for, and we transfer that dislike over to a stranger. Perhaps they make a remark that goes against our beliefs, and we never give them an opportunity to show us their entire self. The brain likes to "sort." The problem is many times our brain is dead wrong!

Not only are we judging the people in front of us, but we are also judging their surroundings. If there is clutter, we assume they are disorganized.

If their area is too Spartan, we assume they are too rigid. We look at hair, makeup, hands, nails, shoes, clothing, jewelry, cars, homes, and even their kids and make decisions about where to mentally place these people on our trust or respect scale. We can't ignore our nose in this decision making. Smell is an additional factor in "sorting" people as smell evokes memories.[1] It is neither fair nor accurate, but it is human nature and must be considered.

My husband and I live in North Myrtle Beach, South Carolina. One night, we decided to go to an impersonator show. This show released around 10 p.m., and there were few choices of restaurants available. We decided to grab a late dinner at the Hard Rock Café. When we were seated, our server, a young woman, approached. She was a beautiful girl, but she was covered from the neck to her chest and from her shoulders to her wrists in tattoos. In addition, she had piercings in her nose, eyebrow, and a multitude in her ears. I admit that our first thought was "We are never going to eat," but it turns out she was one of the best servers I have ever had.

Growing up in the restaurant business, I am a tough critic. She did an excellent job, and we enjoyed her personality tremendously. Still, I had to talk to myself about my immediate reaction and understand that as a person who grew up when tattoos were considered inappropriate, styles have changed, and I need to recognize my bias. Now, if this young woman had dirty hair, half-chipped-off nail polish, and a uniform that looked as if she had slept in it, no amount of self-talk would have overcome the impression that my food was being served by someone who was less than "food service clean." In fact, I may have left the restaurant.

EXERCISE: Think back about the people you see at work, on the street, in shops you frequent, or even celebrities. Consider what instant judgments you make about these strangers. Are they based on fact or a stereotype? Now think about what those same people are thinking about YOU!

Like it or not, our patients and clients are judging us, and that first impression is incredibly important. My wonderful waitress had to "dig herself out" of my mental hole. We have about ten seconds to hit the mark, and if we miss, it can take years to overcome the initial disappointment *if we are even given the opportunity*. It is here that company dress codes come to play.

Dress codes set clear expectations on what attire, jewelry, hair styles, shoes, and overall appearance are acceptable for work. Dress codes are not universal because your brand is not universal. The attire of the team should complement the brand you envision. The majority of our clientele were business executives, doctors, attorneys, and other affluent members of the community which made my first hospital like the "animal country club," so for the North Carolina summers, our team had embroidered tee shirts and for the winter, sweatshirts emblazoned with our logo. The customer service representatives (CSRs) wore business casual and were instructed to dress like bank tellers with white embroidered lab jackets over their clothes. The doctors wore light blue front zip smocks and business casual clothes with the men in ties. While other practices have a much more relaxed dress code with scrubs as the norm, the formality of our dress worked well for our clientele. Many studies have been done on dress codes in medical offices with some that tout white coats for doctors and newer ones stating that scrubs are more trusted. My thoughts are decide *your* brand, and let it dictate your dress code. One tip I would suggest: Incorporate your brand and logo colors into your dress code. The point? Starbucks' green is so imprinted on our psyche that we would know it if it was a big green dot instead of the full image of the iconic mermaid.

Digging a little deeper, what does it look like to drive up and walk inside your practice? Often team members park in the employee lot, enter through an employee door, clock in, and begin to work. Because we live and work in our office every day, we no longer notice the wear and tear on our furnishings and even our parking lot. It is always a good idea to drive up to the practice as a client would and to get an idea of your client's view. The same goes for the lobby and waiting areas.

I once visited a veterinary practice with one of my friends who was a sales representative. We drove into the parking lot, dodging enormous potholes. What was left of the parking space striping was faded. The shrubbery had overgrown to the point that it had narrowed the opening for the front door sidewalk down to a width of approximately three feet. To get inside, we had to squeeze past two gigantic unkempt bushes. Upon entering the lobby, we were hit with an odor that was a mix of cat urine and pine cleaner. Every chair had a rip in the upholstery. The walk-off mats at the entry were covered in fur.

Upon approaching the front desk, we were greeted by a CSR whose hair and scrub top were equally dirty. The staining on the scrub top looked suspiciously like poop. There were mounds of paper charts piled behind the desk. The framed pictures on the wall were yellowed with age and covered in fly specks. The posters taped to the wall were long out-of-date with curled and torn corners. The baseboard radiator was rusted from years of a multitude of dogs lifting their legs upon it. When we announced ourselves, the CSR stared at us as if we were aliens and turned away to ask someone else what to do with us.

As we waited in the lobby, I overheard some pet owners discussing how bad their dog's breath was and that they hoped the doctor would offer some solutions. They were eventually called back, and since the doctor never closed the exam room door, I observed the visit and saw to my disappointment that the dogs were not examined but were merely given a couple of vaccinations, and their teeth were never addressed. It was hard to hold my tongue and not say, "There is an excellent practice 3 miles down the road and they will help your dogs." My first impression in this case ran true—this practice was not only shoddy in appearance but equally shoddy in medical care.

Attention to detail shows in all we do. Consider a trip to Disney's Magic Kingdom. Every detail is considered, including the doorknobs and the manhole covers imprinted with images of Mickey Mouse. One of Disney's core values is "show." Walt Disney knew that when guests entered the theme parks, the first impression would be imprinted on their minds. Visitors will find no chipped paint, immaculate bathrooms that are checked every thirty minutes, no overflowing trash bins, not a single piece of trash on the streets, and you will never see a character from one themed area walking in another because Disney has designed a system of underground tunnels for employees to use after they are costumed. They never break character. Even the trees and flowers are chosen based on their appropriateness to the area and the theme.

Periodically drive into your client parking lot, enter into your lobby, and sit down for fifteen minutes, then look around. Find the dirt, the rips, the marks on the walls, the old magazines, and make corrections so the first impression you give is a great one.

First impressions are not limited to our first visual impression, but it is also our first verbal or even digital impression.

In today's tech savvy world, practices are utilizing many digital tools to communicate with clients. These tools are extremely helpful and leverage our capacity to serve people by taking over routine and redundant tasks. That being said, the first impression given by these communication tools should be that they are easy to use, enable us to quickly understand how to respond, and provide an immediate result to the task we are trying to accomplish.

This is certainly not a book about digital marketing, but having a website that is customer-friendly; ADA compliant, inclusive of all ages, races, and genders; logical to navigate; and displaying the exact information that the client seeks is an important first impression. If half of your doctors have retired and their pictures are still on the site and the photographs of your building are from 1995, it is more than time to update. As a new client, I want to be able to fill out and submit paperwork online. I also do not expect to have to repeat this process in-person. I want to be able to receive text confirmations of my appointment. I expect to be able to conveniently see my patient records via a secure portal accessible via my personal device. I want to text my provider a question, and I want to request a medication refill or an exam without having to call. If these services are not provided, my impression is of a practice that is way behind the times in customer service and possibly in current trends in medical care. At the same time, it is important that we remember our elderly who may not be comfortable with technology and continue to provide the face-to-face and pen and paper encounters they prefer. It is never appropriate to abandon a segment of your clientele because you find it inconvenient or more expensive. In hospitality, all are served in the way **they** desire and are comfortable.

6

You Had Me at "Hello"

Phones are still a vital part of our communication toolbox; not everything is done online. Training proper phone etiquette is essential to giving a great first impression.

In my early days as a CSR, I was trained to answer the phone by the third ring. The rule has now changed to answer on the first and have a plan by the third for someone else to answer if you can't.

We live in a world where the average person has the attention span of a goldfish. We are used to instant gratification when we Google a topic or message a company. Our expectations are even higher when we make the effort to call. Receiving a multitude of rings or a phone tree that offers no helpful or understandable choices immediately sets a negative tone. My suggestion is if you have a voicemail system, that you periodically use it to get through to your own office. Even better, have a friend or family member who does not work there run this exercise and report back to you on their experience.

EXERCISE: Find out how many hoops your clients are jumping through to make an appointment or to ask a simple question. Be a harsh critic, then fix what you don't like. I have yet to find a customer who said, "I love getting trapped in voicemail!"

My rule has always been to serve the person in front of you and have a backup for the phone. To me, the person who made the effort to drive to my office has status over the one who is calling. That is not to say the caller is less important—just don't break service with a person who is physically in your building to get the phone. And NEVER take a personal call from your cell phone when serving a client! This is incredibly disrespectful. You are showing that person they are not important or valued by you or your company.

If you have no other person who can answer the phone, it is appropriate to say to the person you are working with, "I apologize. I am the only person here today. Would you mind if I pick up the phone?" When met with this request, people are usually understanding and will graciously say they do not mind. Then answer the phone and ask the caller's permission to place them on a brief hold after first confirming it is not a medical emergency. (Over the years, I have discovered that the practice's definition of a true emergency and the client's definition can vary greatly.)

Speak slowly and distinctly when you identify yourself and your business and when you request permission to place the caller on hold. People are calling with a plan on what to say, and when you respond in a manner different from their expectations, they often don't listen, or they don't fully hear what you said. You may need to repeat your request to place them on hold.

Smile. It seems silly to smile when the caller can't see your face, but the caller can *hear* your smile; a smile changes the tone of your voice. Our first impression to our caller should always be that we are happy to have the opportunity to serve. People can pick up on your emotion by listening to the

> **TIP:** Place a mirror near the telephone and check your smile and facial expression when you speak with your clients.

tone of your voice. Impatience, aggravation, and frustration all transmit over the phone as does kindness, empathy, and pleasure in serving. Make sure your tone matches the message you want to convey. When we answer, "Thank you for calling ABC Practice. "This is Debbie!"—they shouldn't hear in your voice the sound of "What a bother you are. I don't have the time or the patience to serve you." One simple tip I have shared is before you pick up the telephone, take in a deep breath. If you begin to run out of air in your lungs, you tend to speed up your greeting, and running through your greeting at a rapid pace gives the impression you are too busy to help your caller. Breathing also helps you center yourself mentally before collaborating with the caller.

Always identify your company and yourself by name. This is how we begin to build a relationship. I once called a practice who answered the phone with "Animal hospital." *How special and unique was that practice portrayed?*

We all love to have that special person on the inside of the businesses we frequent—the one we know will recognize us, know about us, and help us. It gives us a sense of security that we have a personal guide and someone to call on if we need assistance. Your goal is to become "that" person for many of your clients.

One of the most unique marketing tools I have seen employed in a practice involved the use of a large postcard with a group photograph of the team. When any member of the hospital worked with a new client over the phone, they circled their picture on the card, wrote their name under it, and mailed it to the new client with a statement that read, "Mrs. Jones, it was a pleasure helping you today. Remember my name is Toni, and if you need anything in the future please call and ask for me." Now, Toni was no longer a faceless voice on a telephone call; she was an inside connection that the client could call and even recognize when they walked in the door. Brilliant! In today's world, we can text a photo and a digital greeting instead.

When speaking with clients on the phone, you should not engage in multitasking. In fact, the ability to multitask is a myth. We are biologically incapable of multitasking. Instead, what we do is called "task switching," which is typically very inefficient. The brain cannot do two complex things simultaneously and do them well. However, we can perform an established habit (like brushing our teeth) and simultaneously think a complex thought.[1] If you have ever driven to work while trying to solve a problem in your mind and arrived with no memory of how you got there, you have experienced complex thought paired with a well-established habit. Attempting to multitask when serving others only leads to distracted work and unhappy clients who feel they are playing second fiddle to the other tasks you are attempting to perform. Focus on the person. Leave the other tasks until you are finished.

One challenge you will experience when attempting to put the concepts of hospitality in place will be overcoming your current habits. It is uncomfortable and takes mental effort to overcome your old patterns and create new ones. If you have ever changed jobs and found yourself mistakenly driving to your old job while lost in thought, you understand. Habits are neuropathways our brain creates to conserve energy. Unfortunately, the bad habit paths are permanently embedded in our brain, so we have to be wary of them popping up when we let down our guard. This is why smokers struggle to quit. Even though they desperately want to stop, they are pulled into old habits when they engage in activities where they habitually smoked, like drinking in a bar, after a meal, or on work breaks with other smokers. Their subconscious neuropathway is reactivated, and they pick up a cigarette. Support from others is helpful when you are working on building a new improved habit. I call this the Weight Watchers theory of habit change. We allow others to help hold us accountable until our new path is so ingrained that we no longer backslide. Great cultures do this for each other using kindness, humor, and forgiveness when we fail. Change is hard, but the results are worth it!

True confession time. I was terrible at remembering names. The famous Dale Carnegie quote "Remember that a person's name is to that person the sweetest and most important sound in any language" was trained in me at an early age, but there are many distractions at the front desk and names often got lost in the midst of finding a solution for a pet's or person's problem. Life got easier when client records could be searched by phone number, but that really isn't helpful when you meet them in the grocery store. Somehow, I could usually remember the pet, and it saved me embarrassment on many occasions. In his book, *How to Win Friends and Influence People,* Dale Carnegie writes a tip for how to remember names; it's called LIRA, which is the acronym for Listen, Impression, Repetition, and Association.

> **The first step in any conversation is to intently focus on the person with whom you are speaking.**

We often only half listen while we are distracted with the next task or planning our response. Instead listen as if you were playing the children's game Simon Says. The laser focus required to follow the Simon Says "Pat your head" type command is the gift we should give anyone with whom we are speaking. If your mind starts to wander, be aware of this, and mentally pull it back into the conversation. Other than being respectful, active listening is important[2] when seeking cues to diagnose an illness. It also stops us from making mistakes of omission. Distracted listening can cause us to miss important information pertaining to symptoms, medications, and even services requested. Practice active listening, and it will pay off in many ways.

Next, take a mental photograph or form a mental impression of the person. Keep in mind the location where you met them and the situation. Link them together in your mind. In veterinary medicine, we often link owners with their pets. I personally have been caught many times in a restaurant greeting a client whose name I do not remember but whose pet I absolutely did. Did they come in with someone you know? If you draw a blank, you can quietly ask that person to refresh the name of their acquaintance for you.

Find a way to repeat a person's name. I recently met one of my new neighbors while out walking my dog. We chatted for a few minutes, and as I walked away, I looked back and said, "Tonia, right?" And she said, "Yes, and you are Debbie, right?" This repetition and confirmation made sure we will both remember each other's names in the future. By the way, her dog's name is Fez, which I instantly remembered. If you are on a call with a client, it is a good idea to use their name at least three times in the conversation and especially when ending the call. If you didn't catch the name the first time, just apologize and say, "I am sorry. I missed hearing your name. Do you mind repeating it for me?" At this point, you should also reintroduce yourself so the caller can remember who they spoke with. When speaking with new clients, I used to end our call with, "Mrs. Smith it was my pleasure speaking with you. Remember my name is Debbie, and if you have any other questions or need something else, just call and ask for me."

Often, we are embarrassed to ask a person's name again, but forgetting someone's name in a conversation is universal and human. If we take the time to ask again the name of person we just met, they know we feel they are important, that we value them, and want to honor that by knowing their name. If a name is challenging to pronounce, it is also okay to ask if you are pronouncing it correctly. I would say, "It is important to me to get this right. Will you help me pronounce your name correctly?" It is also okay to practice it with the person. If someone has an unusual name, they know people struggle. Rather than butcher it, move into the discomfort, confess your difficulty, and get it perfect. People appreciate a genuine effort. In this moment, we also share our vulnerability, which makes us more likeable.

I met another neighbor who has an unusual name. I asked if it was a family name, and she told me she was actually named after a TV producer for *The Bob Newhart Show*. Her parents were watching it one night shortly before she was born and liked the name. Knowing the story behind her name makes it "sticky." We also connected by laughingly recalling the brothers Larry, Daryl, and Daryl from the show. I now easily recall her name when I see her. She had just adopted a new puppy named Harbor, and her older dog's name is Rocket. I recalled the dog's names because we live on the water, so "Harbor" made sense in that context; and Rocket made me visualize a dog with the zoomies running like a rocket. *(See what I mean about remembering pets' names.)*

> **EXERCISE:** Use the acronym LIRA (listen, impression, repetition, and association) or another tool to go through your day and make a conscious effort to remember people's names that you meet. Then at the end of the day try to recall all the names and faces. How successful were you?

One tip I have shared over the years has been when working, keep a pen and small pad handy, and the minute someone shares their name, write it down. (If you want to sneak and try this at a party, feel free.) I understand that the client's name is usually up on a computer screen, but writing it down is a memory prompt. It sticks better when more of our senses, like touch and sight, are involved in creating the memory. As I went through conversations with clients, I would often flip screens from appointment check-in to medical chart notes to boarding reservations. Keeping that name in front of me made sure no matter what I was looking at, and even if I needed to walk away, the name was available at a glance. It also reminded me to use that name in the conversation and especially when I was ending the call. When you use someone's name, it personalizes the call for them and for you. They become an appreciated human rather than a chore to be checked off a task list.

In veterinary medicine, sometimes our calls are urgent. Managing a caller whose pet has been hit by a car can be challenging. The pet owner is distraught, the pet is critical, and the CSR or technician has to guide this conversation while maintaining a calm yet empathic tone. Acknowledge the distress of the owner by saying, "I know this is frightening, and I am going to help you." Then move forward with instructions for transport, first aid, and directions to the practice if needed. Practice empathy first! Always get a call back number. On occasion, clients will call, an emergency situation is determined, and the medical staff is alerted, but the client and patient never show up. If you give them a reasonable amount of time to arrive and they are not at the hospital, call to see if they are lost, if the pet expired, or if they need instructions on handling the pet because it is uncooperative.

If you are not sure what the protocol is for various types of emergency situations, find out. To this day, I still remember the first "hit by car" case I participated in admitting. I had no training on what to do or who to call to help. I am sure that client received no comfort in having me attempt to check her in at the front desk. Fortunately for the dog, it was just a slight bump, and he was fine; but as a new employee, I was still left hanging out to dry because of a lack of a formal training plan.

Once the caller is on the way, you may need to take a short personal break. These calls are not routine unless you work in an emergency room (ER) so taking time to calm your mind and release the tension is a good idea. A simple box breathing exercise will help you relax. (See insert on page 44.) Then you can move back into serving other clients with a smile once your adrenaline has shifted back to a normal level. This also works with the client who is belligerent. Take that time to return to a calm state.

EXERCISE: Consider any urgent or emergent case you have seen. What could you do to improve the protocol to help give the client a better service experience? What training do you need to do so?

BOX BREATHING

Box breathing is known to help us bring our energy down to a normal level after a stressful event. The technique is simple:

- Breath in deeply to the count of four.
- Hold it for a four count.
- Release it to the count of four.
- Hold it for another four count.
- Repeat at least three times.

It is easy to remember if you envision the steps like the sides of a box with each set of four-count breathing as a side.

In busy practices, it is inevitable that we must place callers on hold. If you must, ask permission first. Don't be surprised if the caller continues speaking. Over the years, I have discovered that people who call a business plan their conversation ahead of time. When the team member answers the phone and the conversation doesn't go as expected, the client is frequently caught off guard. When you veer off routine, often they are not actively listening and, instead, continue their conversation. At that time, you will probably have to repeat your request to be allowed to place them on hold. Usually, they apologize and comply. Sometimes they continue to press their need. If so, you must decide if you can manage the call in a brief time then quickly continue serving the client in front of you. If not, you may once again insist about the hold.

If you do place a caller on hold, that call is your responsibility until another team member engages that client. The perception of hold time by the caller is vastly different than the perception of time by the busy person who answered the phone. Two minutes can seem like an eternity, especially if there is no music or messaging on hold. If someone has been on hold more than two minutes without getting a response from the person they asked to speak with, get back on the call, and ask if they would like to continue to hold or if they would prefer a call back, a text or an email instead. This way, if the caller chooses to wait, you made the offer. If they choose a different route, make sure you follow-up. Remember, this is still *your* call and your responsibly to manage. Just as if you were the host of a party where you would escort a guest in your home from one room to another, you must be a good host to this caller. You are their escort from the call to the intended party, and you should never abandon them to chance.

Perhaps the caller decides to leave a message instead. Do not assume the person they asked to speak with has all the person's information—no matter how familiar they appear to be. I can't tell you how many clients called my practice owner by first name, yet he had no idea who they were when they called. Clearly write the caller's full name; time of call; subject of call or question; best time to return the call, and in veterinary medicine, the pet's name they are concerned about. Always put your initials or an identifier to indicate who wrote the message, and have a designated area for messages to be placed. You can also take digital messages if you use internal message boards. Again, follow-up and make sure the person you took the message for has received it. If the person is not in the office the day the call comes in, give the caller an idea of when the call will be returned. Don't leave people in limbo!

When clients call us, they are looking for a solution to a problem. It can be as simple as they need a bag of pet food or as complex as a medical issue that needs to be addressed by the doctor. Our job is to guide that conversation in a way that is mutually agreeable.

> **Our job is to guide conversations with clients in a way that is mutually agreeable.**

Appointment scheduling is a place where untrained team members fail to be good "tour guides." Typically, in general practice veterinary hospitals, Mondays and Fridays are very busy. Animals become sick over the weekend, and pet owners are reluctant to visit the emergency hospital; so, they wait until Monday. Friday appointments are usually dominated by owners trying to get in before the weekend for problems they have been monitoring all week, or that is the day they get paid and have the available funds to make the visit since most pets in the US do not have pet insurance. Well-trained CSRs understand this and can steer clients away from those heavily scheduled days while also smoothing the schedule for the medical team.

Once it is determined if an appointment is needed, we can ask a preference of morning or afternoon by the client. Then we look at the schedule for the entire week and find our slow day and offer no more than two appointment slots on that day. If neither work, offer one more. Never ask the client what time they want to come. They cannot see our appointment schedule and playing a guessing game where they hope to hit an open slot is unreasonable. The reason we limit offers is to avoid decision gridlock.

When humans are tasked with deciding between too many options, they shut down and opt-out. Make the choices simple and few. Guide them to a spot on your schedule that makes your work go smoothly and helps you stay on time while it also accommodates the client's needs. It is always smart to sprinkle routine wellness visits in between sick patient appointments. Sick patient visits are unpredictable and are frequently the reason our doctors get behind. By giving them routine visits before and after sick visits, we allow them to have some "catch up time." Stacking sick patient after sick patient is a recipe for disaster. The number one complaint of all human and veterinary clients is waiting. Strategic scheduling may not solve wait times 100 percent, but it can certainly reduce the chances for doctors to get behind.

My advice to practices is to perform time and motion studies on their appointments and gather data on the true amount of time a certain kind of appointment takes. (See the Time and Motion Study template in Appendix A.) For example, a wellness visit typically takes approximately twenty minutes, a geriatric patient visit takes approximately forty, new client and new patient takes forty to sixty minutes if you add in a hospital tour, and a new puppy booster or a nail trim on a compliant pet takes only ten minutes. By using differentiated appointment times, we can avoid the stress of walking into an exam room and getting blasted by an angry client because they had to wait. Differentiated appointment times position us to better serve our clients and simultaneously keep our team happier. Today's practice management software can be set up with drop down lists that have preset time lengths for different types of visits. Take advantage of the tools you have to make your day more pleasant for all.

EXERCISE: Use the Time and Motion Study template from Appendix A to perform a study on your exam room flow for one week. Then average the times for each appointment type. This will give you a more accurate idea of the correct amount of time to allocate for each appointment.

Always keep in mind that our initial contact with a person leaves a lasting impression. The goal is always to make our client feel that we respect their time, that we understand and empathize with their needs, and that we are there in partnership to help them. When clients begin their experience with our practice on a positive note, they become more cooperative and are more enjoyable to work with. Working with clients who view us favorably certainly influences the enjoyment of our own work. It is human nature to want to be liked. Great hospitality can make that a strong possibility.

7

Active Listening: Observation, Anticipation, and Personalization

You may have noticed by now that I have not given you a lot of specific verbiage. That particular training is certainly important, and there is plenty out there to utilize. Rather than teach you what exact words to say, my goal is to teach you how to "think hospitality" and to use your people skills and imagination to create communication that connects.

In my mind, great customer service is like a three-legged stool. Without employing each of the legs, the stool becomes useless. The three legs are observation, anticipation, and personalization.

Observation

Human beings evolved in tribes. They are meant to work in collaboration and to be able to read each other's body language. In fact, we are so good at reading body language that newborn babies can differentiate and understand the nonverbal expressions of their mother's faces.[3] However, as instinctive as this is, the multitude of distractions in today's society often causes us to miss important cues into what others around us are thinking and feeling. This is why it is so important for us to minimize our distractions and to intently focus on the people around us. If you have ever felt uneasy when walking alone in the vicinity of a stranger, you understand how observation plays a role in personal safety. Devices like cell phones have certainly reduced the utilization of one of our greatest safety measures—reading the body language of other humans.

In a personal safety class I attended, the police officers stressed that in order to remain safe while traveling, always utilize situational awareness. In today's world, with the rise in mass shootings, it is even more important that we are paying attention to the people around us. Another important point was to always know where the exits are and to never hide in a place where you may end up trapped. Also, consider and take out-of-the-ordinary exits like a window if you are ever in a dangerous situation. For more information about how to best be safe, visit the Federal Emergency Management Agency (FEMA) website.[4]

Just like any other muscle we desire to build, the ability to read non-verbal cues can be exercised. The study of body language requires greater depth than is possible in this book. Many textbooks on the subject will be more complex than necessary when training client service. My favorite reference is *What Every Body is Saying: An Ex-FBI Agent's Guide to Speed-Reading People* by Joe Navarro. Navarro is an ex-profiler for the FBI and made his living deciphering the body language of criminals. His books are easy to read, and the photographs are extremely helpful. It is well worth your time to read and study his books.

For now, let's discuss helpful observations that will enable you to provide better service.

The first goal is to observe the person when you initially encounter them and gain a baseline for what is probably a neutral emotional position. At least, we hope they enter in either neutrality or in pleasant anticipation of a positive encounter with our team. It is immediately evident when an upset person approaches us. We read the tension in their face and in their body posture. This observation takes nanoseconds. Often, our reaction is defensiveness or flight. In these situations, it is important to control your own mental dialogue and understand that this person needs your help. Being empathetic and actively listening will help you succeed more easily than preparing for a fight. We will get into more detail about conflict resolution later, but for now, let's talk about the neutral or positive person.

People who are in a neutral emotional position usually have relaxed facial expressions and their lips are also full and lack tension. Shoulders are typically relaxed, and arms hang by the person's side. The eyes are soft, and the eyebrows and forehead are smooth. Everything in their body posture says they are comfortable. Ideally, you want your customer to remain in this posture or, even better, to begin to feel pleasure and start to smile. Happy people smile with not just their lips but also with their eyes. The eye corners will crinkle with smile lines and the ends of the lips turn up. You may even notice a slight bounce in their step.

> **A simple rule is when humans are happy, things move up, and when humans are unhappy, things move down.**

If you have ever been in the position to tell a client that their bill was significantly less expensive than they anticipated, you may have seen that little "jump for joy" in their step. The greatest example of these body posture differences is to watch sports teams leave the field. The winners are all jumping, smiling, and have their arms waving in the air while the losers bow their heads, drop their shoulders, and move slowly with great sadness to the locker room.

Nonverbal cues exhibit themselves at the direction of the limbic part of the human brain. The limbic brain is responsible for keeping us out of danger. It reacts in milliseconds when it feels we need to respond to a threat. The common limbic brain responses are fidget, freeze, flee, and fight.

When people feel uncomfortable, as they often do in a healthcare facility, they may begin to fidget. You will often see women fidget with their necklace, twirl a lock of hair, or hold an object like their purse in their lap in front of their chest. Men will rub their face, smooth a tie, or pull on the neck of their shirt as if it's too tight. All people will perform what is called a leg cleanse by rubbing their hands up and down their legs from hip to knee as if they were cold. When we observe these "tells" we can intervene and help soothe whatever is distressing them. Commonly, clients will not tell you they do not understand medical terminology because they do not want to appear ignorant. But their body will show you that they are uncomfortable or confused. By observing these movements, you know you need to restate your information in a more user-friendly manner along with asking the client if they would like additional questions answered. As a general rule, medical professionals should always avoid medical jargon unless they are speaking with another medical professional. I occasionally catch my own veterinarian talking over my head because he assumes I know a lot about medicine due to my many years in veterinary practice management. I am familiar with common matters, but complex issues are beyond my scope of knowledge so I will ask him to clarify them for me. Most clients won't do that. Keep the language and explanations simple.

Too often, we allow clients to leave our practice confused. It is then that they return home to ignore or improperly perform our instructions for their own or their pet's care. I will always remember the client whose poor dog received his antibiotic pill as a suppository!

Or the person departs feeling disrespected and gouged for money just because they were being asked to pay for services with benefits they really never understood. Compliance is always one of a medical provider's greatest challenges, and if we learn to observe humans for signs of confusion and if we clarify our message, chances are great that they will follow instructions as we desire.

Impatience is another common nonverbal cue that we can manage. When we observe clients who are checking their watch, rapidly wiggling or kicking their foot with their leg crossed, sighing heavily and pacing, we want to run for cover. Rather than avoiding them, we can approach them with empathy and information. As mentioned earlier, waiting past scheduled appointment times has historically been the greatest complaint of human patients and veterinary clients. Medicine is not always predictable, and urgent and emergent patients will occasionally be discovered during a planned routine visit. These situations often disrupt workflows and certainly appointment schedules.

When we observe clients becoming impatient, it is important to inform them of approximate wait times and make an offering such as allowing them to leave to run an errand or to reschedule. Some practices have even been known to give out gift cards to nearby coffee or donut shops to waiting clients. People appreciate when you respect their time. They also enjoy being cared about enough to have their emotions read, recognized, and acted upon *before* they have to say anything. Good observation skills will enable you to avoid having situations escalate into conflict simply by intervening when the person has shown minor aggravation but has not reached a highly distressed emotional level.

Another helpful observation skill is seeing deception. Medical personnel agree that people are not always truthful about their behaviors. I recall a visit to a large specialty hospital outside of Philadelphia. While I was there, a teenager and her mother presented their family dog for what appeared to be intoxication. The mother had just come back into town after leaving the teenager home alone for a couple of days. As the veterinary technician questioned the pair, she noticed the young girl's body language. When she directly asked if the dog could have ingested an intoxicating substance, the young girl fidgeted in her seat, refused to make eye contact, and turned her body slightly away. This experienced technician knew enough to continue to press the question, and soon the truth was revealed. The child had a party while the mother was away, and the dog had eaten some marijuana-laced brownies. The mom immediately okayed the necessary medical treatment, looked at her daughter, and said, "We will discuss this further when I get you home." The truth was revealed because of this astute technician's skills, and the dog recovered.

EXERCISE: Think of a time you knew a person was upset before they even spoke. What cues did their body give? How did you react?

In 1972, psychologist Paul Ekman suggested that there are six basic human emotions: fear, disgust, anger, surprise, happiness, and sadness. Later, in 1999, he expanded his list to include a number of other basic emotions, including embarrassment, excitement, contempt, shame, pride, satisfaction, and amusement.[5] Every one of these emotions can be observed in the body language of humans, and as we learn to fine tune our observational skills, we can easily come to read those around us and react appropriately.

Observational skills can and should also be utilized within the team itself. It is a common occurrence for staff members to catch a doctor in the middle of a case to ask a question about a different client, to okay a prescription refill, or attend to some other minor need. This is often not a problem; however, we should observe our doctor for signs of deep concentration or hurriedness. In those situations, it is inappropriate to interrupt to ask your question. It breaks concentration and causes the doctor to have to mentally restore their thought processes pertaining to the case on which they are presently working. These distractions could certainly cause possible harm to a patient if they result in the doctor being delayed in providing care, inadvertently excluding an important finding in a chart note or mistyping a patient prescription. While getting your question answered may seem an efficiency, what you have in fact done is made your doctor inefficient by forcing them to restart the mental process of case management. Remember that humans are incapable of multitasking, so you are forcing your doctor to task switch. These interruptions can cause a task to take much longer just because of the need to regroup.[6] If you approach the doctor and they open their stance to welcome you into their circle, then asking your question is appropriate. If they are standing or sitting and you approach and they do not swivel their hips, shoulders, or head to look at you but continue to focus on their task, you should not interrupt but rather wait until their body signals they are open to your approach. It must be incredibly annoying to have your work interrupted multiple times a day, so no small wonder some medical professionals get a reputation for being snippy.

> **EXERCISE:** Count how many interruptions you receive at work in a two-hour period of time. Have other members of your team do the same. Discuss this at a team meeting, and work to create a system to reduce interruptions.

As important as nonverbal cue reading can be when serving others, one of its most important aspects is observing mental distress. Human and animal medical care will always have dire outcomes that, no matter how much skill resides in our practice, cannot be overcome. Most people, although they may be upset, manage to move through the sadness and grief. However, working daily with terminal patients in emergency, oncology, or assisted living takes a toll. In veterinary medicine, we will occasionally have what we call "death week" where it seems all our favorite elderly patients come in for euthanasia. Unfortunately, this usually occurs near the holidays because it's the typical time of year when families gather, and as such, it is considered a perfect opportunity to have everyone visit their old furry friend before saying a final goodbye.

Our observation skills should be used to monitor those around us for changes in their baseline behavior. Appropriately intervening with compassion and concern when a fellow human is struggling can mean the difference in that person getting needed help. A wonderful resource for pet loss and grief is the University of Tennessee Veterinary Social Work website.[7] They offer multiple resources to help pet owners through the grief process along with a telephone hot line manned by veterinary social workers. Post the new 988 Suicide and Crisis Hotline number in your practice.[8]

Always keep several books on pet loss and grief available for distressed clients, and don't overlook books for children of varying ages. Many local funeral homes have licensed grief counselors available. Contact them and offer to share the names with clients. Many times, in the twenty-three years I managed veterinary practices, clients have called me for support because the non-pet owners in their circle did not understand the very real emotional toll losing a pet creates. They were met with comments like "It's just a cat. Why are you so upset?" Animal lovers know that losing a beloved pet can be devastating, especially when the death is unexpected. Veterinary teams have the opportunity to demonstrate true hospitality in these situations.

> **Understand your limitations. Mental health counseling is a specialized skill set. We can certainly be knowledgeable, empathic, and supportive, but we should share professional mental health resources with those people who seem to be showing signs of overwhelming distress rather than attempting to counsel them.**

The American Veterinary Medical Association has a free resource on suicide prevention and mental health for veterinary care providers.[9] For human healthcare workers, the American Medical Association offers an extensive website focused on identifying mental health issues in physicians and in patients.[10] Fortunately, veterinary social work education is becoming more available, and professional social workers are being hired in many veterinary hospitals to support clients and staff with the emotionally taxing events common in caring for animals.

Anticipation

I have always thought that this was one of the truly fun aspects of client service—figuring out what people might need, enjoy, and be delighted by. In the realm of medicine, a comfortable and inviting lobby with pleasant lighting, nice artwork, and attractive and comfortable furnishings with some groupings that allow for individual privacy and others for family groups is advised. The Cancer Center at Duke University Hospital has certainly done a beautiful job in this aspect. When you walk into the entry you are greeted with a lovely thirty-foot marble fireplace. The desk and wood of the stairwells are a pleasing midtone color that looks as if it belongs in a high-end spa. The floor contains a meditation pattern with inspiring messages from some of the volunteers who founded various support groups for cancer patients. When you visit radiology for mammograms, the spa theme continues with beadboard wooden walls, iridescent tiles the colors of light green foliage, seating that seems to wrap you in a hug, and carpet containing subtle leaf patterns continuing the theme of a forest meadow. There is a refreshment station for coffee, tea, and water. Even though all the women in this room are draped in hospital gowns, waiting for a cancer screening or to get their results, they seem to be calm and relaxed while waiting to be called back.

> **Not everyone has the funding to create this type of Zen space, but everyone can do something to anticipate the needs of our human and animal patients. Simple acts of thoughtfulness will fill the bill.**

For years, we kept inexpensive reading glasses in a jar at the front desk for our clients to use. A jar of candy was aways full to give "people treats" just like we gave treats to our animal patients. Before coffee bars in offices were the norm, our practice brewed pots of coffee and served it to our clients in the exam rooms. We knew that pet owners who were leaving for vacation were in a hurry to get on the road, so we called them two days prior to their reservations to review the requests for play times, special foods, medications, and any other instructions for their pet's stay. Airlines even anticipate delays and have small bags to give patrons with a toothbrush, comb, toothpaste, razor, and shaving cream for the unexpected overnight stay. A student told me a story of a trip to a Ritz Carlton Hotel with her mother. They took a long walk in the garden, and when they returned to the hotel patio, an employee was there with two bottles of chilled water for them. He said, "I thought you might be thirsty after your walk so I brought you water." Anticipation of need!

An important anticipation of need in medical care is having tools in place to help a client afford care. In human health, we have uninsured and under-insured patients, and in veterinary care, we have a majority of patients with no pet insurance. We should work with payment providers to help clients pay for the services we offer. There are many options. Some are banks with credit cards specific for medical care like the CareCredit® health and pet care credit card that allows clients to pay over time for all their pets' care. Others are auto drafting companies that auto-draft payments from checking or savings accounts similar to how we remain current with our gym memberships. Still, others will split the bill over several months on the client's existing credit card while the financial institution remits to the practice the total amount due. Anticipate that people may, at some point, need these services and set systems in place to inform clients of your payment options. I keep a list of charities and ideas for how people can raise funds to help them pay for their pet's medical care. This list has expanded and still lives on my website, and you are free to download it to help clients, family, or friends.[11]

Anticipation can be used when we design our offices. We can opt for wider parking spaces for people with pet carriers. It is difficult to get carriers out of the back seat without hitting the car in the next space if they are too narrow. Add an automatic door that's operated with the push of a button or a sensor for when owners have sick animals in their arms, and provide a covered area for rainy and snowy days that allows people with non-ambulatory pets to drive up to the front door and stay dry while transporting them in for care. A favorite small touch is to add a place to hang a leash when checking out at the front desk. Even better, check people out in the exam room so they are not being pulled by the dog or holding the cat while trying to pay. Plan on seating for all sizes of people in the lobby and in the exam room. According to a report from the Centers for Disease Control, on average, both men and women gained more than twenty-four pounds between the early 1960s and 2002. During the same time period, mean height increased approximately one inch.[12] If you are still using chairs that look like they belong in elementary school, it is time to invest in the comfort of your clients.

Let's face it—filling out forms is necessary, but we can anticipate and innovate. Instead of requiring an existing client fill in a form with their name, address, and other identifiers, give them a digital pre-populated form that they only need to edit or confirm the details therein. For this, you can use digital tools to have them fill out client questionnaires in a more efficient and private manner. There is no reason these forms can't be texted or emailed to clients to complete in the comfort of their homes and returned to the office before their visit. I would certainly prefer the CSR to spend time greeting and welcoming clients rather than handing them a clipboard or an iPad and sending them to the lobby.

And with these forms, anticipate that not every patient who visits your practice does so with the same knowledge of their familial background. To this end, ensure your patient intake form includes an option in the family history section for the patient to indicate they have no information pertaining to their family medical history due to being adopted. While conversations among parties associated with adoption are certainly more open now than they were in generations past, this is not the case for everyone, and not having this option on the form can be triggering for the adoptee who struggles with or who has no communication with their biological family. One friend, who's an adoptee and whose biological family doesn't even know she exists, shared with me there have been times when she's angrily marked a huge strike-through over the entire family medical history section of a form and scribbled the word "adopted" on it because she found, at best, the practice was inconsiderate to assume all patients are in touch with their family and, therefore, privy to such medical history. At worst, with no option to specify she is adopted, she felt overlooked or not even seen. To include on the form an option for the patient to indicate they are adopted demonstrates your practice understands that not everyone is the same and that this is a reality you respect and is one for which you have anticipated.

Other areas of anticipation are accommodations for disabled or diverse people. In Greensboro, North Carolina where I first managed practices, there is a well-known school for the deaf; as a result, many hearing-impaired people permanently relocated to our area. We had on staff a person who was fluent in American Sign Language who we would call upon to help. Sure, we could communicate with these clients in writing, but accommodating them with someone who easily spoke their language was so much friendlier. If you live in a community with a large contingent of people who speak a foreign language, then hire multilingual employees. Our bilingual team members often interpreted medical instructions for our non-English speaking clients. This saved their bilingual children from having to learn difficult news of a poor prognosis for their pet, then having to translate it for their parents.

> **EXERCISE:** Go room by room throughout your practice, and brainstorm as a team what needs you anticipate clients may have and how you can accommodate them. For example: In the restroom, you might offer lotion, mouthwash, a magnifying mirror, and tissues. From what other conveniences or accommodations will your practice and clients benefit?

Let's take this a step further and anticipate our employees' needs. Anticipate a need for your new moms who need a private and sanitary place to pump. Plan refrigeration for your team so they can bring healthy foods and snacks. Some days are filled with unexpected challenges, so keep food that is filling, healthy, and portable in the break room for times when meal breaks are impossible. Have personal lockers for everyone. Ask your team what they would like to have. We did and our group chose a picnic table outside so they could get a break in the fresh air.

Personalization

How annoying is it to you to go to a place of business and be greeted by people who are using a script? It is obvious that a customer service trainer has been in, and all the employees are now required to use this specific script on every person who visits. To make sure this is happening, cameras are recording the staff's client interactions.

My husband used to go to the drive-through at our bank every day to make a deposit for his business. He was a well-known customer, yet every day, he was greeted with the same words and asked the same question mostly by the same teller. After a few days of responding that he did not have an interest in whatever loan they were selling, he simply quit answering and ignored the person waiting on him. Instead of greeting a well-known customer with something personal, he was treated as if he was a stranger driving up for the first time. Rather than promoting a positive interaction with the bank personnel, he, instead, left so aggravated that he came back to his office complaining. I am sure, when budgeting for and investing in customer service training, this is not the outcome the bank wanted to achieve.

In the exact opposite direction, my good friend's mother, Jackie, was a teller at a local bank for many years. She had a memory for people and a genuine concern for their well-being. She also had a great sense of humor and was a joy to be around. Even if there were three or four teller stations open, Jackie always had a line. The bank manager would often try to direct people to another line, but the customers would decline and patiently wait for their turn to be waited on by Jackie.

I have seen this repeated in restaurants, clothing shops, garden centers, and certainly in veterinary hospitals. Clients find "their person" and become regulars because these customers appreciate the individualized care and attention they receive. People NEVER like to be treated as if they are interchangeable. Humans are not cookie-cutter and should be served as the unique individuals they are.

According to an April 2020 survey by the world's largest strategy consulting firm by revenue, McKinsey & Company, "a positive customer experience is hugely meaningful to a retailer's success: it yields 20 percent higher customer-satisfaction rates, a 10 to 15 percent boost in sales-conversion rates, and an increase in employee engagement of 20 to 30 percent."[13] Doctors don't consider themselves retailers, but the fact is that humans judge us on how we make them feel no matter the business.

How can we make a visit to our practice personal? A simple first step is to remember and use their name as already discussed. But, digging deeper into personalization, we can remember specific things about the person we serve. If they have children, an inquiry about how they are enjoying college or their new elementary school is a good start. Maybe we expand on that topic and ask what their favorite subject is or who is their favorite teacher. Are they wearing a sports team logo on their clothing? We can ask how their team is doing this season. Are they reading a book? Ask about the title and author and if they like the book so far. Over the years, I have discussed jewelry, shoes, jackets, pet collars, books, nail polish, haircuts, new grandbabies, new jobs, retirement, new cars, classic cars, good restaurants, the price of groceries or gas, and the pain of moving or building a house. And with clients I knew well, I've discussed divorce, the loss of parents and children, cancer, heart attacks, and arthritis just to name a few. In fact, I even helped one of my long-time clients figure out why her husband had no appetite after finishing his cancer treatment. When she mentioned that Ted complained that food was unappealing because he couldn't taste it, I remembered my own issue with the same problem. I had thrush after receiving some heavy-duty antibiotics for a post-surgical infection. Everything I ate tasted like I had a mouthful of dry cornmeal. I suggested that Ted have his doctors check his throat, and it turns out I was correct. He started eating again after being treated. I couldn't have helped if I hadn't paid attention and known these clients beyond them being dog owners.

Keeping it personal doesn't mean asking invasive questions. It merely means that you actively listen to the clients, sincerely take note of what makes them unique, then you care enough to remark or act on those observations. People will tell you surprising things when they feel you care. Know the patient's history and age before entering the exam room. If they have family who are also clients or patients or have other pets, make an inquiry about them before you jump into "business." One of the joys of working in my first practice for nineteen years was watching children grow up to become clients and often seeing them become parents. How rewarding it was to have three generations of humans and multiple family pets returning to our practice over the years. Hospitality pays in retention!

One of the challenges all medical professionals face is getting people to actually administer prescribed medications and carry out at-home regimens. Paying attention to people can be an important aspect of getting them to comply with directives. For instance, when my mother's cat, Charlie, was diagnosed with diabetes, I was concerned that the severe arthritis in her hands would create a problem with administering his insulin. Fortunately, Charlie is a very chill kitty and will simply jump up on the table, get his shot and a treat, jump down, and move on with his day. My Mom and Charlie have a fine-tuned system. But, when he was found to have arthritis that caused him too much pain to be able to jump onto his perch, he was given a nutraceutical. He has always been a very picky eater, so he refused to eat his food that was now laced with the supplement—not a good thing for a diabetic cat. If the veterinarian had listened to my mother about Charlie's very particular eating habits, she would not have wasted her money on a product that the cat wouldn't eat, Charlie would not have almost crashed from missing meals, and all would have been better off. But back to my Mom's hands—her pharmacist filled her prescriptions yet never explained how to flip the cap of the childproof bottle so she could more easily open her medications. One day, I visited her, and while in her dressing room, I noticed all these open pill bottles. When I asked her why, she explained that she couldn't get them open with her hands, so she simply left the lids off. I flipped the caps to show her how to cap the bottles and easily screw them off. She couldn't believe no one ever told her. Me either. Paying attention to people matters.

One of my favorite stories comes from a famous New York City restaurant. The restaurant owner and chef, Will Guidara, walked the dining room one evening, greeting his guests. He stopped by a table of men and asked them if they were enjoying their meal. They all agreed that the food was exceptional and told him they were on a foodie weekend where they were dining at all the most famous restaurants in the city. They were leaving early the next morning and expressed regret that they had missed getting a real NYC hotdog from a street vendor. The owner thanked them for dining with him and immediately sent one of the staff to buy a couple of hot dogs from a nearby vendor. He took them into the kitchen, plated, and garnished them to his standards, then took the dish to the table. He explained to the gentlemen that he couldn't let them leave without this last NYC culinary experience. The customers were so surprised and delighted that even though they had just consumed one of the finest meals the city had to offer, all they could talk about was the hotdog.[14] That is personalized service! That is true hospitality.

> **EXERCISE:** Think of a time that a service person truly personalized your experience. How did that make you feel? Are you likely to return to that business? Are you likely to recommend that business to your friends and family?

Again, perform this same personalization for the team. Leaders should know their staff and spend time understanding their life goals and needs. Can you offer specialized training to a person who desires to learn a skill outside their normal duties? If it will help the practice, then there is no reason why not. At one point in time, I had multiple assistants taking online classes to become licensed veterinary technicians. Our doctors agreed to mentor and teach as did our already certified technicians. Not only did this increase job satisfaction for these folks, but we were growing our own experts—experts who were extremely difficult to find in our area.

Flexibility is another way we can personalize work for our staff. Rotating holidays, understanding family needs, and allowing the group to swap days off are all simple things that can make life better. I used to tell my team, "I can't pay you what other jobs pay, but I can make it fun and enjoyable to work here." Staff retention was record-breaking with many team members working in the practice for well over twenty years. Hospitality works for all.

8

Training for 7-Star Service

As important as giving great service is, setting up systems that enable it to happen is even more important. Credit goes to Dr. Cody Creelman for his 7-star service goals. When Cody opened his new practice, FenVet, he had a vision of what it would be like to come into his hospital. He wanted people to know immediately that they were in a special place with special people dedicated to caring for special humans and their pets. A few months before he opened, he asked me to facilitate communication and client service training to his team. Then, he proceeded to engage those team members in building the workflows and the systems that would allow them the time to fulfill the vision. The architect designed the spaces to be open and to offer the transparency Cody envisioned. Clients watch through glass walls as their pets receive treatment. There is no formal reception area as clients are greeted by technical team members upon entry to the building. The lobby area is even specially designed for training classes.

Cody knew that giving great service requires appropriate spaces and tools along with enough properly trained staff to have time to serve clients to the best of their ability. Technology plays a significant role in Cody's 7-star service model. His business is an unprecedented success with him showing a profit after only nine months in business. In addition, he built such an excellent reputation that he had eleven doctors waiting in line to come work for him. Now, he is opening an additional practice to accommodate the demand by both clients and potential team members to be served by or to work in an environment like FenVet.

Too many times new employees are thrown into the fire without proper training. Some sink, some swim, but all suffer. No one wants to work in a position where they are set up to fail. Improper training does just that.

The first step in training starts with a job description. We should never hire people without informing them of the tasks and behaviors we expect of them. Creating job descriptions where there are no clear tasks or expected behaviors already defined can be daunting, but over the years, my suggestion has always been to let the people who are doing the work build the job descriptions. Start a digital document, or if you prefer low-tech, put a notepad in the area where the work is performed and ask your staff to write down all the things they do in a day, a week, and a month. Then simply review the document and organize the tasks. Quite often, we find job duties being performed in the wrong department. This gives us an opportunity to make strategic adjustments and to put better systems in place.

Keep in mind that you can have wonderful, kind people and a fantastic culture but still have lousy systems in place that make it difficult for the team to perform at their best. The best way to create good systems is to allow the team to develop them. Outline the goals for service, then build the pathway that positions everyone on the team to know their role in accomplishing the goals.

A good place to begin is with technology. I once was the chief operating officer of a large mixed animal and emergency practice. When I began working there, my goal was to vastly improve the service that clients received. I discovered that the software program slowed down the ability of my CSRs to enter new clients into the system without a multitude of tedious steps. It was just as difficult to invoice and accept payment. You know you need new software when a client looks over the front desk and says "I can't believe how many keystrokes it takes you to do this task. That is ridiculous!" So, we changed to a new software provider and invested in training.

A piece of advice I typically give practices that are bringing in any type of new technology is to utilize the on-site trainer to train the team in enough basic knowledge to be able to work the system. Then, six months later, invest in bringing in an external trainer to fine-tune the team and the workflows.

When learning a new technology, people find a path that works best for them. The problem is that is not necessarily the fastest or easiest way to perform that task. Bringing a trainer back after the team is familiar with the new technology; has a list of tasks they would like to perform better; and is knowledgeable enough to understand the windows, tabs, task names, and other features is a wise investment in next-level competency. Making this investment actually increases the return on investment made in purchasing new technology. On its own, cutting a key stroke or two may seem insignificant, but when we multiply that by ten, twenty, thirty, or more people performing that task twenty or thirty times in a day, you realize a dramatic savings of time—time that can be better utilized caring for patients and caring for people. Today's practice management software has capabilities that most practices rarely utilize. Investing in training allows us to leverage this amazing tool to grow our business, educate our clients, and support our teams by helping them with templates, formularies, reminders, and integrations that make their work easier and that allow them to go home at the end of the day with all their charts complete. It can even set-up roadblocks to medical errors by not allowing someone to invoice a product to the incorrect weight or species.

As a minor but irritating example, I picked up my dog from the boarding kennel after his first stay. When I got home, I noticed I had been charged for a twenty-pound dog rather than a twelve-pound dog. Tucker's weight was in his record, and since I am very familiar with the software in use at the kennel, I know for certain that the invoice codes can be set up to reference patient weight and give an alert when an incorrect code is invoiced. This mistake caused me a phone call, and it took time away from the CSR with whom I spoke so she could make the correction at the kennel checkout desk and so she could make another call to me to inform me about the credit being issued to me. Correctly utilized software saves employee time and client aggravation.

Each department should have a list of duties ranked from beginner to intermediate to proficient (pro). Accompanying these duties should be a system of pay grades that parallel the skill levels. Often a challenge in small businesses is lack of advancement. People come in with entry-level skills and start at beginner wages but have no knowledge of how to advance themselves to earn more income. By developing a skill-based training list, a brand-new employee can see what skills they need to develop to reach the pro level. Keep in mind that these skillsets are not all physical duties like placing catheters or running the end-of-day reports. Behavior and communication skills can also be trained and advanced. A brand-new CSR certainly is not ready to take on the highly disgruntled client, but the lead CSR should unquestionably have those conflict resolution skills. **Never tie raises to performance reviews or employee anniversaries**. Instead, tie them to your practice's performance levels and personal growth milestones. I have encountered people who have worked in a practice for years, yet their skills do not go beyond an intermediate level because they didn't make any effort to be or do better. They were coasting for a paycheck.

> **Reward growth and increased responsibility, not merely longevity.**

When training new employees, it is important to not only have them work with an official trainer, but it is also essential that they are partnered with a mentor. There is a difference. A trainer is available to teach tasks, systems, and the proper use of equipment. A mentor is available as a go-to person when the new employee feels overwhelmed or struggles with their trainer or any other employee. The mentor can give valuable information about special clients, a doctor's preferred way of working, and even some background on fellow employees so the new person can avoid committing an avoidable faux pas.

Training requires planning. I have worked with practices that close for two hours every Monday to hold a staff meeting and offer team training. Other hospitals do this monthly, and yet others look upon training as a random free lunch provided by sales representatives. Schedule and engage in team training. It is as important to the success of your practice as scheduling patient blood work or surgery, and you can certainly make time for one if you make time for the other. It is a matter of priorities.

My last practice had eleven veterinarians and approximately forty staff. We were open twenty-four hours a day, and naturally, the large animal doctors were often out on farm calls. By January, staff and training meetings were scheduled and posted for the entire year. Departments met to discuss their specific issues. Each department received specialized training. The leads of each department attended all the department meetings so a cross-pollination of information and ideas occurred. It was our commitment to team communication and ongoing learning and professional development.

For new employees, start with an orientation to the building, a review of the employee manual (I give a test on it because people don't read it thoroughly), the rules about parking, tardiness, dress code, history of the practice, bios of the principles, who is their direct supervisor, who to go to if there is an issue with that supervisor, and then the most basic tasks associated with their job. Have a checklist. See Appendix B for an example.

People need to see they are accomplishing things, and managers need documentation of what has been taught and that the employee has demonstrated proficiency in their work. "Follow them" training is not a plan. Once the new employee has demonstrated an understanding of and comfort with a beginner task, the trainer can sign off that they are ready to move forward. We then move into our next list. These tasks build and expound upon the basic task list. Some new employees may quickly move through the basics and the intermediate lists and be ready for the pro task training in a short amount of time. Others may need to stay at the basic level longer before moving to the second tier. Trainers, mentors, and supervisors should determine if someone struggling with basic tasks should be kept and worked with more diligently or dismissed as a hiring error. A common mistake is to keep working with someone who will never be the right person for the job. It wastes the trainer's valuable time and is not fair to the employee who is a poor fit for your practice but may be perfect for a different opportunity. Even great hiring managers make mistakes.

When team members become proficient at all the training levels, remember to keep reinforcing your standards. If you don't use a skill frequently, it is often forgotten like algebra or a foreign language. You must keep practicing. Experienced new employees come in with their own way of performing their job duties. On occasion, these tasks may be inconsistent with your workflows and the employee needs to be retrained. Or, if it appears they have a better way to perform a task, consider integrating it into your training regimen. Systems need constant evaluation as medicine and technology change.

Hospitality, as mentioned before, is about making people feel important and safe. When several people on our team are inappropriately performing job tasks, it creates confusion, especially when new staff members are coming on-board and observe multiple ways of doing a certain task. This is not to say that the way someone performs the task is incorrect; it *is* to say that we should consistently train all of our team members to perform to your standards. This also goes for setting standard protocols for procedures performed by doctors.

As a personal example, I have visited a couple of physicians in a local general practice group, and I have experienced a range of different protocols for my routine physical exams. The fact that my nurses and doctors seem to be jumping around in no particular order leads me to believe that this practice is disorganized and chaotic. Unfortunately, this disorganization has greatly reduced my confidence that I can get adequate care in this practice, and I will certainly be seeking a new medical care provider. Not only am I looking, but in random conversations with my neighbors, they have also noted that they had the same experience and also left the practice. Lack of consistent team training is causing this practice to lose clients daily.

In veterinary medicine, routine care, like vaccinations, exams and spays or neuters, are items often shopped by phone. Without standards set by the medical team for the vaccination schedule, proper vaccines for location-based risk, and protocols involved in surgical services, the team is unable to accurately give price quotes to callers. Medicine is an art and a science. Doctors do not work exactly the same for complex-case care based on where and when they were trained. However, for these extremely routine services, a practice must have all the doctors and the team on the same page. The doctors must work with a medical director to establish protocols and fees and then train the team to adhere to these protocols. When clients ask a question of any staff member about these services, the answers must be consistent or confusion occurs, and trust is reduced. The more doctors on staff, the more confusion is created unless standards of care are set.

Once routine training at all three levels is accomplished, a manager should work with individuals to discover their areas of specific interest (provided that it is of benefit to the practice) and invest time and resources into advanced training on these topics. A CSR may want to learn about social media management, or an assistant may desire to go to school to become a licensed professional. The manager could learn advanced bookkeeping, inventory management, or take leadership training. Constant training helps your team reach excellence. Sometimes you can even train them "out the door" when they are ready to advance beyond your practice. That is an acceptable risk. I have always believed it is better to have someone wonderful for a year than someone terrible or unengaged for ten.

9

Personality Styles: Customizing Communication

Many years ago, I was fortunate enough to take a class called "Dealing With Difficult People."[15] Even though I had been serving the public since I was twelve years old, I felt that this training could be beneficial because my new boss was certainly challenging. He had a strong personality, with definite opinions about how things should be done, and he was also very tall, which made him even more intimidating. I felt that any tips I picked up in this class would be helpful. I was right. Learning about different communication styles based on personality profiling was one of the most helpful continuing education courses I have ever taken. I used this knowledge when managing staff and when serving clients.

Personality profiling is certainly nothing new. Documentation of the different profiles can be found as far back as 444 BC and credited to Hippocrates. William Marston, in his 1928 book, *Emotions of Normal People*, described four basic personality types: Dominance, Inducement, Submission, and Compliance. These personalities styles have been expanded on in a multitude of ways, including Colors,[16] Myers-Briggs,[17] and even in Enneagrams.[18] As a fun aside, Dr. Marston also invented the lie detector and the comic book character Wonder Woman.

All these personality tests accomplish the same goal. They help us understand ourselves and those around us. People are usually a combination of the personality types. Typically, one personality style takes precedence over the others, with the secondary style being utilized in specific situations. As an example, someone with the Inducement personality as their primary and Dominance as their secondary will first attempt to charm the person they are interacting with into complying with their wishes. If charm has no effect, then they will attempt force by raising their voice and then using sarcasm or, finally, threats to get their way. The main thing to remember is that each of us is unique, but each of us has tendencies that are predictable if we know what to look for.

Let's start with the Dominance style.

If this personality style had a tag line, it would be "Get 'er Done!" In my mind, folks with the Dominance personality style are, or at least attempt to be, the ruler of their world. They have a strong need to be in control. As customers, they tend to want to dictate their service experience to suit their need for speed. Above all things these people hate wasted time, so getting them into an exam room and seen very close to the appointment time is a key to a smooth start. Think *efficiency!* Allow them to fill out paperwork ahead of time if possible, and don't spend lots of time on idle chitchat. Get to the point. Chances are good that any conversation will be more about them attempting to teach you how you should be doing things more efficiently rather than you instructing them on healthcare. You can recognize this personality style by their direct and often blunt speech patterns. They are decisive, so you won't have to be concerned that they waver over difficult decisions. They make up their mind quickly and move forward to the next task at hand. These people have a lot of self-confidence, often to their detriment because they want to jump ahead. Training staff members of this personality type can be challenging because they think they are ready for the next step before mastering the step you are teaching. Patience is not one of their strengths. Sometimes, if it won't cause harm, it is good to just let them learn by failure. Let them discover for themselves that they are not yet as skilled as they assumed they are. Then, they are easier to teach.

The Dominance style has a lot of good qualities. As clients, they are on time (ten minutes early is late). They are not overly emotional, so there are no histrionics when they get bad news. They are stoic until they are angry. Then, they are the most likely to push, yell, be sarcastic, and attempt to bully to get their way. They have an uncanny ability to see processes when it comes to organizing workflows. They like order, systems, and direct communication. You will often find these people in positions of leadership because they are not afraid to take a risk and direct others in their work. If we remember that under their pushy exteriors, they usually have good hearts and are willing to help others by using their skills to make tasks more efficient, we are better able to give grace when they get frustrated and begin to bark orders.

To help you begin to recognize these clients, I'll tell you about John. John was a longtime client of my first veterinary practice. He was a contractor with two beautiful golden retrievers. Every weekend John traveled to his beach house and boarded the dogs in our kennel. One day John called me to explain that he would no longer be bringing his dogs to our practice because it took too long to get them checked-in. Keep in mind that because we knew these dogs so well, we would fill out their boarding sheets in advance, have their records ready when John walked in, and, when we saw him drive in the driveway, we immediately called for a kennel attendant to be waiting at the door to take his dogs back. It was pretty efficient. However, because our boarding kennel was large and always full during holidays, John had gotten caught in the crowd and felt that we had become too big. I told John that I appreciated his candor and that, try as I might, I could no longer shrink our practice back to the two-doctor practice it used to be. But I said, "John, if you ever need anything in the future, all you have to do is call, and I am happy to help you." You see, John's only complaint was about speed. Ironically, only three months later, John, in his direct manner, once again called me to ask if he could return to the practice because the new hospital didn't know him or his dogs and he preferred to take the chance of being slowed down slightly rather than go to a practice that did not give him personalized service. I welcomed him home.

Our next personality style is Inducement.

If you have ever met someone who immediately engaged you in conversation, has never met a stranger, and is so charismatic that everyone wants to know them, you have been around a person with the Inducement style. This style has also been called "the influencer" and "the entertainer" because the person often enjoys being the center of attention. They are people oriented, while the Dominance style is task oriented. However, they love having people as an audience more than being supportive of others, as you will learn about with the Submissive style. You will recognize the Inducement personality style by their elaborate and often dramatic communication. There is a lot of laughter, hand-waving, and gestures used to punctuate their sentences. You may find this personality style in many of your sales representatives. It is certainly a positive attribute to be able to connect quickly with a stranger when you are visiting practices and attempting to bypass gatekeepers.

As clients, these folks are often some team favorites because they are typically fun, upbeat, and engaging. Frustration steps in when we attempt to educate or give detailed instructions about patient care because this style is certainly not detail oriented. In fact, details are often considered quite boring for these big-picture thinkers.

As team members, duties best suited to their style involve creative thinking. They flourish with posting on social media, taking photographs, and creating content that is interesting and appealing. These are the perfect people to work on the theme for your next open house or practice event. Whatever you do, don't give them a task that requires attention to meticulous detail, such as counting and managing inventory. They will be incredibly bored, and chances are good that they will become distracted mid-count and never finish—especially if they are doing it alone. In a veterinary practice, they make wonderful exam-room technicians. They have the ability to make connections quickly and a flare for explaining the need for services and getting agreement from clients.

When training this personality style, visuals and hands-on practice typically are more effective than reading. If they must read to learn, present content in short segments and test incrementally. They won't shirk from role-playing, and you will often find that giving them public praise is very motivating, much like the applause from an audience.

My client, Ruth, is the perfect example of the Inducement personality style. Ruth didn't just walk into the practice; Ruth made a grand entrance into the practice. You could hear her laughing in the parking lot, and we all recognized her deep, throaty laugh. She was boisterous upon entry, instantly greeting all our CSRs, then turning to any waiting client in the lobby to see who she knew. She always had a story or joke to tell as we checked-in her pet for its medical care. We rarely bothered putting her in the exam room to wait for the doctor because, within seconds, she would be back out at the front desk for a chat. Remember, the Inducement personality style hates to be alone. If the CSRs were busy, Ruth would visit with other clients, whether she knew them or not. Our doctors knew to first peak in her assigned room and, if she wasn't there, come up to the lobby to retrieve her. When it was time to check out, she left with as much enthusiasm as she had entered, and once she was gone, the hospital felt slightly diminished. I'm sure you have some "Ruth's" in your practice.

Submission is our third personality style, often called "steadiness" or a "relator."

When I think of this personality style, the word that comes to mind is "aww" because they are highly empathetic, relate to others' suffering, and "aww" is the first thing they say when they hear a sweet or sad story. Many people have this personality type in the medical field. Similar to Inducement types, Submission types are people oriented. They have a deep need to be liked by others and, because of that, will often fail to stand up for themselves, even when circumstances warrant that they should. They are agreeable and love to be helpful and supportive. In my training classes, I ask leaders to pay special attention to these kind hearts as they can be subjected to bullying by stronger personality styles.

As clients, people with this personality style are usually patient, understanding, and kind to those serving them. They pay compliments and, on occasion, bring cards or small gifts to people who regularly care for them. They ask a lot of questions beyond the medical reason that they are in the office because they love to build personal relationships with others. They have amazing memory for details about casual acquaintances that most people would instantly forget. Submission styles do tend to be very talkative. Busy team members have been known to avoid answering a call from these clients just because they know how long they will be tied up chatting. Submission styles are very patient and understanding when the medical team is delayed. When they do lose patience or feel hurt by an unfeeling comment, their communication is rarely confrontational, often passive-aggressive, and manifested in a negative social media review or an email to the boss after they leave the office.

If you have forgotten someone's name, this is the coworker to ask because they will certainly know. Submission types make exceptionally good CSRs because of their interest in people and building strong bonds with others. Their kindness is, on occasion, negative when people sense that they can be taken advantage of. *Never have a Submission type as your collection agent.* Their highly empathetic nature makes them fall easily for a sob story. They will take their training seriously, particularly when it focuses on the benefit to pets or other people. They will struggle when confronted with a difficult client because tears come easily, yet they are so nice that it is hard to be angry with them. Dominance and Submission personality styles often have tension. Submission types dislike blunt, direct, and unfeeling behavior, and Dominance types dislike emotional, touchy-feely expressions and long, drawn-out stories. It is best to separate these coworkers if each is strong in their personality style because they will get on each other's nerves.

My client with a Submission personality style was Candy. We loved seeing her come in the door because she was always so sweet and cheerful. We knew her well because she had a lot of pets and was a "frequent flyer." We also knew to give our doctor an extra ten minutes in the appointment slot because he was going to chat with her about many things other than just the animal she had in front of her. We made sure that we asked about Candy's family, her other pets at home, and even the horse that we did not treat. No matter how busy, we spent time chit-chatting about her day, and we never rushed her into an exam room because taking time to have conversations with the four or five CSRs at the desk was part of a positive customer experience for her. She felt so close to our team that we were some of the first people to learn of her cancer diagnosis, and we supported her journey until she unfortunately lost her battle.

Our final personality style is Compliance.

For this personality type, think details! This personality style is task focused and excellent at fact-finding and organizing. Label makers, folders, and lists are the tools likely found in this person's workspace. Skilled at data collection and itemization, Compliance-style employees are the perfect candidates for managing inventory, creating standard templates, bookkeeping, and organizing information and supplies. They communicate indirectly and include lots of details and facts. Questions are part of their approach to any action, and they contemplate the answers deeply before they react. They are slow to decide because they require a lot of time to gather information before feeling that they can make a well-informed choice. Getting things right is of paramount importance, and often they will struggle with decision gridlock and perfectionism. They will not be pushed into a speedy decision, no matter how hard you try. In fact, pushing slows them even more. Planners to their core, they hate surprises, especially changes to their schedule.

These are your clients who come with reams of Google printouts because they have investigated their problem online. They will clam up when confronted with information they don't like, and they can be very stubborn when you need them to make a necessary adjustment. To get them to change, you must use facts and present your case with logic and in a step-by-step format. Be patient; they really hate change.

Staff training for this type requires systems, lists, and reading materials—the more, the better. The need to be correct means that they will follow training protocols to the letter, and when asked to change to something new, they will struggle. Remember their love of details, so assign them tasks that require accuracy. Often, they will build a system that works better than a current protocol.

One of my Compliance clients was an older lady, Mrs. Mason. She was nice but reserved. I recall one Saturday morning when she brought her small dog in for a vaccination appointment. We had just launched our Total Quality Health Program, and I shared the information and benefits of additional diagnostics for her pet as I checked her in. Mrs. Mason refused the additional service but still seemed curious. Rather than give up, I placed her in an exam room and offered her a brochure detailing all the tests and the reasons for them. I suggested that she take a look at the brochure while she waited for the doctor to come. Sure enough, after she had time to read the details, which reinforced my earlier education, she was ready to say "yes" when the doctor arrived.

Keep in mind that these personality styles are generalizations and are meant to illuminate how people tend to react to the world they live in.

Humans are never all or nothing; they are a wonderful and unique blend of all styles and should be treated as individuals.

The personality styles are helpful as guides to serving others and in developing a better understanding of people on our team. Managers can use this knowledge to place employees in work tasks that they enjoy and in which they will flourish and grow. Service providers can use knowledge of personality styles to help clients get the experience they desire while providing information in the correct fashion for the person they are serving. Outcomes improve when communication and service experiences improve. Everyone wins!

EXERCISE: Have you determined what your main personality style is from the descriptions? Consider your family members or well-known clients. How would you categorize them? If you would like to take a DiSC personality profile at no cost, visit www.discpersonalitytesting.com, or find the link under the Resources tab on my website, www.debbieboonecvpm.com.

10

What Does "Great" Look Like?

As previously mentioned, it is rare in today's world that people receive a truly remarkable service experience. Companies like Disney, The Ritz-Carlton, and Nordstrom are famous for providing great experiences. Each has spent time defining what their ideal customer experience should be. In veterinary or human medical care, how do we define what a great experience looks like, and who is a great employee? The truth is the team builds and sustains the experience, so defining our experience goals and training our team to give that level of service are the keys to success.

I think the place to start is with the superstars on our team. We all have one or two people who seem able to manage the most difficult client, gain compliance from the most stubborn patient, and get rave reviews from the people they serve and their coworkers. Look at those people and define "great" for your workplace. You can even use former standout employees as your "North Star."

Here are the things I have always looked for in great team members:

First, great employees show up. They are 100-percent present mentally and physically, ready to do their very best to care for their patients, and ready to help others on their team. They bring ideas to the table about how to work better, smarter, or faster. They want to leave at the end of the day knowing that they did their best and left the practice and their world better than it was. The exceptional staff member doesn't rely on the leadership team to formulate all the improvement ideas, but instead they put thought into their work and seek ways to make it better. I always looked for smart people to hire who demonstrated the qualities of forward thinking and commitment to superior work. Great team members *care*.

Second, great team members are understanding of others. They give others grace and assume positive intent until proven otherwise. Sometimes hurtful remarks made on busy days mean nothing more than someone is hungry, frustrated, exhausted, or feeling overwhelmed. The great team member is mindful of this. They do not text their coworkers or manager at ten o'clock at night because it is convenient to them. They understand that in the few hours that coworkers are off work, they would prefer to enjoy their family rather than answering a question that could have easily waited until the next workday. A great team member understands that your client wants to care for their pet, their child, or themselves, but perhaps they are battling a personal or financial crisis you don't see. Empathy for others is the core of being a good human. Great team members are considerate and non-judgmental.

Third, great employees communicate. They respectfully speak up and act with curiosity in situations in which stress or conflict occurs. They acknowledge that all stories have three sides: yours, theirs, and the truth. Great employees seek the truth without telling themselves a story that makes others the bad guys and themselves the victim. You are only a victim if you allow it. Don't accuse—ask. Great team members communicate and don't ruminate.

Fourth, great employees are lifetime learners. They don't stand back and wait to be taught; rather, they actively seek to learn new skills. If education is not offered at work, they find resources on their own. Then, they live by the premise that knowledge not shared is wasted, and power comes from generously sharing what you know so others can learn. The great employee learns and shares.

Fifth, great people choose to live with a positive attitude. Neuroscience informs us that the brain seeks what we train it to find. If we look for negativity, we will find and dwell on it, but if we intentionally seek positivity in our day, we will train our brain to look for uplifting events. Great employees smile. Not only does a smile make others feel better, but it also releases endorphins in the brain that makes us happier. Smiling can set off a chain reaction of smiles, just like a yawn sets off other yawns. A compliment can do the same. Humans mirror the behaviors of those around them. Great team members seek to be happy and spread happiness with intention.

Finally, great employees have pride. They believe that their actions are the signature they put on their work, and they want to be proud of what they sign. Not every task is something they love, but they still do it to the best of their ability. In every business, there are fun tasks we love, tasks we are okay performing, and tasks we must do to keep the practice running. Personally, I disliked writing payroll. It was tedious and boring, but I wrote it early in the day so my team could take their checks to the bank at lunch. I was careful not to make mistakes because this was their livelihood. I accurately tracked the benefits because I wanted everyone to get the full measure of what was promised to them, and I did this every other week for nineteen years and never missed a payroll. I did it well because it mattered to my team, and I took pride in looking after them. Great employees care to do things well.

In a business, success rests on the performance of the people who work there. If you get the people right, success shows up. Only the employees have control of the culture. It is up to the leaders to find the right people, embrace and teach the core values of the business, and then allow the team to create the systems and culture to sustain greatness. Leaders must value people over profit. Profit certainly is important to keep a business running and paying its people, but it cannot be the only reason for a business to exist. The best leaders place employees first, customers next, and investors after that. Business is a long play, and it's a bad strategy to shortchange staff and customers or not invest in upkeep, team training, and quality equipment in order to show short-term gains.

Now, let's look at what a great experience involves.

Earlier in this chapter, I mentioned Disney and the experience it works hard to develop in its parks. One component that is stressed in the book *Be Our Guest* by the Disney Institute is the importance of process.[19] The writers equate process with the engine of a train. No matter how kind the conductor is or how beautiful the passenger cars are, if the train doesn't run, people won't pay to ride it. Processes include policies, tasks, and procedures that are involved in delivering service.

Having visited a multitude of veterinary hospitals and been a patient in several human healthcare practices, I can attest to the importance of having good processes in place to be able to deliver an experience worth recommending.

Wonderful experiences start with proper staff training as referenced in Chapter 8. Nothing is more frustrating to a client than to have someone who is clueless attempt to help them or, even worse, misdirect them. But beyond training is having a set of standards, core values, and a mission that the whole team understands and accepts. It is often surprising to people to learn that one of Disney's core values is safety, which is ranked first above courtesy, show, and efficiency. If a guest will be harmed by an action, the staff knows that keeping someone safe ranks above courtesy in that moment.

> **Every medical practice should build and rank their own core values list and then discuss with the team how they will be demonstrated in the business in daily interactions.**

Over the years, I have helped many practices build their core values. Sometimes this is challenging because it involves some deep emotional exploration with the leaders as to why the business exists. However, parsing out four to six core value words and then having the team discuss how they will live out the values and what actions they will put behind them helps get everyone paddling in the same direction. For an example of a core values statement, visit Appendix C for a list that I helped one of my clients develop for their practice. Their practice had been in existence for many years, so don't think it is too late to create this list for your practice.

As a consultant and professional writer, I helped develop the language for this document. The ideas and thoughts came entirely from the team. You can see that the values cover almost every aspect of the practice, from keeping a neat and clean workplace to never gouging clients with unnecessary services or products.

If you don't feel that your writing skills are up to this task, engage a professional content creator who can put into words the emotions evoked by your core value words and then utilize that language to reinforce the core values that your practice chooses to live by. Keep these and your mission statement at the front and center of each staff meeting and training session. They are meant to be used, not filed away in an employee handbook.

I think we could all agree that if a team demonstrated the core values from Appendix C, they would offer an exemplary client experience in their practice. However, this team also has a solid set of processes and standards of care that are written and taught to all new employees. Over the years, I have discovered that few hospitals take the time to formalize their workflows. Single-doctor practices have an advantage because there is only one way—and that is the owner's way. When the practice owner retires and a new doctor comes in, the staff is often pulled between how they have always worked and the preferences of the new owner. As hospitals grow and add more doctors and more staff, systems and workflows become more complex and often muddy. Taking the time to write out how the work is to be done is a good use of time, but it can also be intimidating to think of all the details.

A favorite tool I recommend is the exercise from Tom Wujec's TED Talk, "Got a Wicked Problem? First, Tell Me How You Make Toast."[21] This is an exercise in systems thinking. If you take the time to view the video, and I highly recommend that you do, you will see that a process as simple as making toast can be broken down into a very complex system. When I use this system in veterinary practices, I will typically take a common procedure, for example, a dog spay, and ask the team to start from the incoming appointment request and use Post-it Notes to create a step-by-step workflow for each department until the dog leaves the practice. You may think that this is as simple as the following: we answer the phone, we book the appointment, the technician checks in the dog on the day of the appointment, the doctor performs the surgery, the technician calls the client to confirm that their pet is fine, the client comes to pick up the dog and gets take-home instructions, and the client pays and goes home. But once you start developing this system, you find many branches to the tree as possibilities occur. For example, the appointment request is from a new client who was moving from another practice to yours. Now medical history has to be requested, and the client and the patient entered into the practice management software. Or, what if you discover that the dog is in season or its pre-surgical blood work is abnormal; you now have a new branch to the tree and more processes to be documented. This is an excellent exercise to utilize because it involves all the members of the team who take part in these workflows. It also reveals glitches.

In a recent visit to a new consultation, we were performing this exercise with the team. It was here that we discovered that two doctors insisted on a specific pre-surgical blood test and the other two doctors did not. This was a source of confusion for the technical team as they built estimates for their clients. Thanks to this exercise, we were able to confirm that the correct process was that all pets undergoing an anesthetic procedure would be required to have this pre-surgical test. Now the team is all on the same page, and they will all share with clients the same education about the surgical procedures performed in their practice.

> **Good systems create consistency of performance. Consistent performance helps build trusting client relationships.**

Clients like to know that when they visit a practice, the team is confident in exactly how care is to be administered. They want to have a reliable experience that creates a sense of safety and certainty in the competence of their care providers.

The final step in creating a great care experience is to engage the team in building what they would consider to be an ideal customer visit. Most of us have been on the other side of the exam table as a client or a patient. Reflecting on those experiences, work together as a group—even if it is seemingly impossible to do—to create a visit to your practice that would leave you walking away feeling like you discovered a diamond mine.

A common practice of all superior customer service providers is that they allow their team the autonomy to create a delightful moment. I was training a class in the Atlanta area several years ago when a doctor told me a wonderful story. His family had arranged to take him to dinner at The

Ritz-Carlton hotel for his birthday. They were finishing a fabulous meal when the waiter returned to see if he could serve them in any other fashion. Jokingly, the doctor said, "Yes, my kid has a rash on his arm. Got anything for that?" The waiter smiled and disappeared. About ten minutes later, he returned to the table and handed the doctor a tube of hydrocortisone cream. He said, "I went across the street to the pharmacy, and they said this was good for a rash."

This server was not only empowered to leave the dining room, go to a pharmacy, and spend money on a customer, but he was trained from day one to do so. The Ritz-Carlton earmarks a certain amount of money for every employee every year to use as they see fit to create these amazing service moments. They don't have to ask their supervisor. They are trained to think "over-the-top service" and are given the autonomy to provide it.

Over the years, my veterinary teams have hand-delivered medications to someone's house. They used our van to pick up skunked dogs and bring them to the practice for baths. My doctors made house calls to euthanize a special patient when we did not normally make house calls. They have entertained generations of children with everything from ice pops to showing them X-rays of puppies in the womb. They have celebrated the birth of children and grandchildren with "oohs" and "ahhs" over pictures and handwritten cards. They have shared the grief of the loss of a spouse by lending a well-timed tissue, a shared tear, and a shoulder to cry on.

Being great at customer service is not just what you say, it's what you do and how you connect.

> **EXERCISE:** As you go through your day at home or at work, think about how you could provide a little "magic" to the people you care for. It doesn't have to cost anything to bring joy. Try to create at least two moments a day that delight others. Note how this makes you feel.

11

Going Above and Beyond

There are a multitude of definitions of hospitality, but they all come down to how one provides service and cares for those they serve. I like this quote from Wikipedia: "Hospitality is the relationship between a guest and a host, wherein the host receives the guest with some amount of goodwill, including the reception and entertainment of guests, visitors, or strangers. Chevalier Louis de Jaucourt describes hospitality in the Encyclopédie as the virtue of a great soul that cares for the whole universe through the ties of humanity."

> **Hospitality is the virtue of a great soul that cares for the whole universe through the ties of humanity.**

Typically, we think of medical care providers as scientists and their teams as support for the science. But I discovered a long time ago that we are a service industry with medical care as our product. It behooves us to be good at both hospitality and sales. People are often shocked when I mention this, but we are working with people and their emotions. Both superior hospitality personnel and sales professionals have a deep understanding of how people tick and how to approach them in ways that build productive two-way relationships. Traveling and teaching enabled me to gather a multitude of good "above-and-beyond" ideas in addition to the ones my teams used. Hopefully, sharing them will inspire you to create your own. Remember that hospitality is a creative process, and once we begin thinking of inventive ways to delight others, the ideas just keep coming.

Above-and-Beyond Ideas

Welcome Letter. All new clients receive a welcome letter signed by the doctors. This letter comes as "snail mail" because it is a formal welcome and similar to a wedding invitation in that it deserves formality. It is written on the company letterhead. Tip: It is difficult to have multiple doctors sign these letters, so I used to have my doctors sign their name with a permanent marker in very large letters on a plain sheet of paper. Then, I scanned them into my computer and pulled them into my Microsoft Word document, shrinking them to normal-size signatures. This gave them a crisp, handwritten look. Just be sure that the signatures are password protected! We don't want those out in the world. See Appendix D for an example of a welcome letter.

Certificate of Bravery. I heard about this from a student and loved the idea, but more than that, the story she shared. She said they had a client who was a professional groomer. The client owned multiple dogs and was an excellent pet owner. Over the years, the client had brought all her pets to be altered at the veterinary hospital. Each pet had received its own certificate of bravery after its surgery. One day, a team member visited the grooming shop and on the wall, hung proudly, were seven certificates of bravery, one for each pet. Obviously, this small gesture meant a great deal to the client but also what a wonderful passive marketing tool for this hospital.

The certificate was a Word document with the pet's name, the type of procedure (surgery or dentistry), the doctor's signature, and the date. It was branded with the company logo, of course. It was given to the owner upon the pet's discharge. I remember as a kid going to the dentist and getting a certificate for an ice cream cone that I could redeem at the local drugstore down the street. It was a positive reinforcement for my dental experience.

Teddy Bears for Comfort. This idea was shared by my friend Emma, a Certified Veterinary Practice Manager. Emma was running a large ER and specialty practice, and she noticed that children would often cry when leaving their pet for treatment. She arranged to purchase a bunch of teddy bears that had been donated to the local Goodwill, and she used them to "make a trade." When the kids would cry as their pet was hospitalized, she would offer to trade the teddy bear for the length of the pet's stay, then trade it back when the pet returned home. This worked wonders for the tears, but she did note that often the teddy bears did not return. In another use, she would have the pet owners choose a teddy bear to comfort their sick pet (just so long as it was not there for ingesting teddy bears!). They were instructed to hold it while the team discussed the treatment plan and then they all walked back to the kennel area and "tucked in" the pet with the teddy. It smelled like the owners, and the pets seemed happier, as did the clients. Perception of caring was shown in this gesture of kindness.

People and Pet Treats. For years our hospital kept a candy jar at the front desk filled with chocolate, mints, gum, and other assorted wrapped candies. The jar was labeled "People Treats," and clients knew to help themselves. If the jar didn't have much candy left or it got down to the low-value candy, our clients would remark that we needed to make a trip to the store. This little bite of happiness was so well-known by our clients that, one day, a mom came to get her dog, and, before she left the car, her kids said, "Don't forget to get us some candy." We also kept cat and dog treats in envelopes for clients and our team to share with our patients. Everyone got a treat! Small surprises can make big impressions.

Keep Memories in Scrapbooks. In my twenty-three years as a manager, the number of cards, photos, and letters of gratitude and appreciation received by my practices were innumerable. This is not uncommon when clients perceive that they are truly cared about. I kept two different scrapbooks. The first contained the letters and notes of appreciation. On the hard days, anyone could look through this book and see the impact on families that our team had made over the years. It could be a real ego boost after a difficult client encounter or the death of a patient. The second scrapbook contained photos that our clients had sent over the years in cards. Because we were a long-established practice, it was possible to see children and pets grow up before your eyes in these pictures. There were photos of many of our favorite people and patients, some of whom were no longer with us but who still lived fondly in our memories. These scrapbooks were available for clients to view. Clients were always delighted that we cared enough to archive the pictures they had sent. Memories connect us. You can also use digital frames, but make sure to unplug them after closing because they tend to be a fire hazard.

Give Practice Tours. One hard-and-fast rule in my practice was to be prepared to give a tour of the entire facility at any and all times ... without warning. And we did. Cleanliness, order, and organization increase efficiency and are mentally less stressful than working in a cluttered mess. The mind appreciates having few things to view, sort, and ponder. It is amazing that a client can frequent a veterinary practice for years yet never have seen the working area. If you are ever a little behind in your appointment schedule, giving a hospital tour is a great way to occupy a waiting client and share how impressive your practice is from the technical side. As clients toured through the treatment area, grooming room, boarding kennels, X-ray room, and surgical suite, they were astounded at the complexity of the equipment used to provide care for their animal. One client exclaimed, "This is like a hospital on TV!" The perception of value is greatly increased when they understand that you work with more than a stethoscope, thermometer, needle, and syringe.

Follow-Up Check-Ins. When we discharge a patient and never call to see how they are doing at home, we lose a prime opportunity to show that we genuinely care. Practice management software can be set up to automate a list of calls, texts, or emails generated by particular service codes. It is typical in some practices to call the next morning after a procedure, but are we taking the next step by calling to find out how that ear medication is working three days into treatment? Or if a diet change is causing any gastrointestinal distress? Or if an eye ointment is even possible to administer? I will always remember how impressed my husband was with his endodontist when the doctor called him at nine o'clock the night after his root canal. It was a WOW moment.

Holiday and Birthday Cards to Clients and Pets. In veterinary medicine, getting a pet's birth date is a standard part of medical record keeping. I believe it is the same for human medicine. Every year our hospital sent out more than 500 holiday cards thanking our clients for their support in the past year. Since we can't know the religious beliefs of all our clients, a card of thanks and well wishes for a new year is better than a traditional Christmas or Hanukkah card. Your practice management software can generate a list by sales, date of first visit, or any other criteria you choose, or you can decide to send one to all your clients. Some businesses choose to send

Thanksgiving cards in November. Keep a list of all the clients who send you cards and make sure that they are on your list. Many of the reminder-provider companies offer birthday cards as an option. I enjoy getting cards from my bank, my dentist, and my vet.

Weather Prep. Being located in upper North Carolina, our practice experienced all types of weather. Rain, hail, snow, sleet, ice, hurricanes, tornadoes, thunderstorms—we got it all. On those cold snowy or rainy days, we kept big golf umbrellas in a stand and walked our client and their pets to the cars. Occasionally, if it was snowing a lot, we would bring warm towels from the clothes dryer up to the reception desk to offer to clients as they came in shaking off the snow. There is really nothing that feels more comforting than a warm towel when you are chilled to the bone. We kept nice towels for this—not the ones with bleach holes and stained with silver nitrate or ... well, you can guess the possibilities. When I was working on planning my last practice building project, I insisted on a porte cochère so clients could drive up and be covered when transporting injured animals from their vehicle. We also added an automatic door with a button (similar to a handicap button) that you could push with a hip if your arms were full.

Playing Doctor. As old-school X-ray machines are replaced by modern digital units, many practices have leftover X-ray viewer boxes. One of the most delightful uses that I have seen of these outdated pieces of equipment was hanging them at child height in examination rooms with a toy stethoscope, a child's doctor lab coat, and a pretend medical chart. An old X-ray is hung on the viewer, and the child is allowed to play doctor while the parents are educated about health issues. I have also seen these viewers used outside of exam rooms with welcome notes, written on the screen with an erasable marker, to the client and patient who will be entering.

First-Visit Keepsakes. Whether a child, a puppy, or a kitten, the first visit to the doctor is a memorable event. Arrange to take pictures of these new additions to your practice to share with the parents. In fact, how much fun is it to take pictures on recurring visits as these little ones grow? Share these photos privately with parents, ideally utilizing the client's cell phone to capture the moments for privacy's sake. In the animal world, these are wonderful photographs to share and celebrate on social media (with the owner's permission, of course). You can also do this for the first grooming— just like baby's first haircut—and save a few locks of hair for the scrapbook.

Farewell Keepsakes. Saying goodbye to our pet family member is always hard, but having a thoughtful keepsake acknowledges the human–animal bond. Many veterinary hospitals create clay paw prints for their clients. Kits are available in craft stores and also through veterinary distribution companies. But one of my favorite keepsakes is the nose print. Similar to a fingerprint, a pet's nose is unique. People spend much more time looking at their pet's face than they do their paws, so the nose print is much more familiar.

Simply take scrapbook paper, divide the sheet into quarters, and touch the inked nose to the paper. When done well, you will see the nose and the whiskers. Then, have someone with nice handwriting write the pet's name on the card with a calligraphy pen. The nose prints can be framed or placed in a scrapbook. In addition, we can clip a small lock of hair and place it into an empty, clear, and clean injectable drug or vaccine vial and reseal the top. Tie a ribbon around the top of the bottle and gift this, the nose print, a sympathy card from the team, and the pet's ashes, if they are returned through your practice. Place all this in a small, subdued-color gift bag. Another lovely touch is to place a packet of forget-me-not flower seeds in the bag to be planted in honor of the pet and a pack of small tissues for the tears that will certainly come when you present this package to the owner. If you have a relationship with a local grief counselor or veterinary social worker, you can add the contact information in the package or include an offer of links to books on grief. We kept these books in our library so clients could borrow them.

Sympathy cards are absolutely appropriate when a pet dies, but make sure the card goes out within one to two days. Waiting a week or more to get everyone to sign it only reopens old wounds when it is received. If you want to take it up a notch, arrange with a local florist to send a small floral arrangement to the pet owner's home. I think human doctors should certainly do this when one of their patients passes away.

Use Low-Stress Techniques. Functional MRIs have taught us the influence that fear has on our reactions. Medical visits are often painful, by no choice of the provider, but techniques have been developed to distract and redirect our brain from dwelling on the bad by reinforcing the good. My childhood dentist did this with the ice cream cone and being a wonderfully patient and kind person. Veterinarians do this with low-stress[22] and Fear

Free®[23] techniques. In researching how human doctors help their patients alleviate stress, it seems that the majority of the advice is to give drugs. Hopefully, with the lessons in hospitality discussed in this book, human medical care can learn from veterinarians trained in animal behavior about creating positive visits for people so they don't continue to create negative experiences that, over time, build into crippling phobias. After all, humans are just animals at the top of the food chain, and our limbic brain reactions are similar to our animal companions. Common human fears are fear of needles, fear of pain, fear of a poor diagnosis, fear of doctors, and fear of dental care. The Cleveland Clinic highlights some causes of the fear of doctors:[24]

> Children may develop a fear of doctors because they associate the doctor's office with getting shots for vaccinations. This fear may carry over into adulthood.

> You may be more likely to have a fear of doctors or medical tests if you:

- Had multiple doctor visits and tests as a child to manage a health condition.
- Received subpar medical care or had a bad experience with your doctor.
- Have a chronic condition, like diabetes, or a life-threatening disease, like cancer, that requires frequent, sometimes painful, tests or treatments.
- Received bad news from your doctor regarding your health or the health of a loved one.
- Served as a caregiver, accompanying a loved one to frequent doctor visits and tests.
- Lost a loved one to a medical condition or accident while the person was receiving care from a doctor.
- Have a family history of phobias or anxiety disorder.

Many of my veterinary communication class attendees tell me stories of children bursting into tears at the veterinary office because they think they are at the pediatrician. We can certainly do better!

Community Events. Practices should always remember that they are based in communities. Creating and participating in community events is a great way to bond with your clients. Fundraisers, open houses, school outreach, inviting school groups and Boy and Girl Scout troops for clinic tours and show-and-tell days are all good ways to connect with the people in your area. One of my students shared the story of their practice outreach. There was a very popular local farmers market that occurred during the spring and summer. Knowing that people would bring their pets to the market and that it was usually very warm, the student set up a shaded booth with a cooling station. They had pools of water, fans, and buckets for the dogs to drink from, and they passed out branded information on heat stroke and how to avoid it.

My first practice held a fundraiser event for the Friends of Animals Foundation. We collaborated with local artists and crafters and hung their work in our practice to temporarily replace our art. The artists agreed to donate a percentage of their sales to the cause. One of our doctors was a talented musician, and we had him play at the event, along with a few other client volunteers. We set up tours of the practice, with team members stationed at various points on the tour to explain the equipment and the work performed in each area. It was a fun day for all.

My practice owner helped create a coalition of business owners to transform an abandoned railroad track that was behind our office. The coalition created a walking and biking trail that eventually connected to span the city.

Our team took a vote and decided to participate in the Heart Walk for the American Heart Association. I designed team T-shirts with the slogan "Walk your dog. It's good for your heart." We dedicated our walk to one of my staff's dads who had heart issues and to a client who had a heart transplant. Our small team of 20 raised more than $2,000, coming in second place behind the local hospital, which had 2,000 employees. (We also won the T-shirt competition.)

Small businesses can have big impacts. As a bonus, we also took with us two greyhounds from the Oak Ridge Greyhound Rescue to publicize the availability of these wonderful dogs for adoption. A photo of our team at this event still sits proudly on my bookcase.

My next practice managed the animal shelter for the county, and it was in desperate need of expansion and upgrades. The team started a fundraising drive by selling paper paw prints for one dollar to clients as they checked out. We placed them all around the front desk and lobby and raised quite a bit of money. One of my doctors was very involved with the shelter, and, with his help, the county finally built a brand-new shelter with four times the existing capacity as the original. When I started there, the shelter didn't even have a phone number to call. I was very proud of what we accomplished.

Food Drives. In a 2021 United States Department of Agriculture (USDA) study[25], it was found that 33.8 million people in the United States lived in food-insecure households. Food insecurity is described as limited or uncertain access to adequate and affordable nutritious foods, and it is a major public health concern because it leads to other medical issues. Pets also live in many of these households. Practices can help! During times of disaster, we commonly see bins collecting food items, but this is a chronic need in most communities. Set up donation bins, offer to collect donations, or go work at a food bank or homeless shelter as a group. These events help teams bond and share the care that we bring to our patients with our communities.

Adopt a Soldier (or Two). Supporting our armed forces is a great way to show appreciation for the people who risk their lives so that we can be protected from harm. Perhaps you have a client who is in the military. There is no reason you can't pick them. You can allow clients and staff to donate items, send postcards with good wishes, and share your "adopted" soldier with your entire practice and client base on social media. Gather requested items and ship them out. Veterinarians can adopt canine officers, firehouse dogs, and so on. Be creative!

Team Training. The most important bonding idea is to train your team to "think hospitality" and constantly reinforce those skills. Reward team members who get compliments from clients as often as those who perform great medical skills.

EXERCISE: Brainstorm some unique bonding ideas with your team. What would you appreciate as a customer?

12

No Judgment Zone

You will find biases and norms in any society and in any country in the world. Often, our biases are minor, like preferring certain hair styles or clothing and expecting those around us to comply with those norms. But at other times, our biases cause us to lump a category of people into a stereotype and then treat them differently because of our misconceptions. As you read in my story about my tattooed waitperson, I immediately lumped her into a stereotype of youthful inefficiency, which turned out to be grossly incorrect.

In a 2021 article in *Medical News Today*, the author explains that implicit biases can often get in the way of specific groups of people being served by medical care providers.[26] Implicit biases often run under our personal radar because, by its very definition, we are unaware of the existence of these biases in our subconscious. In fact, they can even be in direct opposition to our conscious beliefs. Therefore, we form negative associations with certain groups of people. There has been a heightened awareness of these biases, thanks to recent events bringing them to the forefront and highlighting a much-needed dialogue about conscious awareness of implicit bias.

As a child raised in the South, it would follow that I would have an implicit bias against Black people. However, because I spent a great deal of time—from babyhood to college age—in the kitchen of a restaurant manned by people of color, the results from my Harvard Implicit Association Test

(IAT)[27] test for race shows that I have little implicit bias. But even with my background, it does exist. I would certainly not say that I did not encounter people in my daily life who were not only biased but also incredible bigots (some of them even were relatives), but because of my parents' attitudes towards and appreciation for people of all colors, I learned instead to see those bigots as unenlightened and to never model my behavior or thoughts after theirs. Because I also know that I do have some small implicit bias, I can catch and correct my brain when it tries to jump into stereotyping. I highly recommend that you explore taking the Harvard IAT, as it is quite illuminating. There are tests for race, gender, religion, sexual orientation, age, presidents, disabilities, weapons, and weight. The results are sometimes surprising, and I challenge you to learn about your implicit biases, just as I learned about mine. The results are given immediately, and you are anonymous as the tester.

When, as a speaker, I began to travel the country, I discovered different implicit biases based on geographic location. In some states, there were biases against Asian Americans, while in others, there were biases against Latinos, Native Americans, and Native Hawaiians or Pacific Islanders. All this made me scratch my head because, to me, they all looked like ... people.

Growing up during the Civil Rights Movement and knowing both white members of the National Guard and Black civil rights marchers have helped me better understand the social movement around race. I was very young, but I have always been a "buck-the-system" kind of girl, so I listened intently to Dr. King but more so to the Black people with whom I had grown up. They told me what it was like to be Black and live having to always watch your back. Tom Haith was the manager of our restaurant after my father died. He had come to work for my dad at the age of fifteen and never left until my mom closed the restaurant and retired some forty years later. Tom always called me "sis" because we really were raised in the same kitchen. He used to say, "Sis, a Black man has to be twice as good to get to the same place as a white man." We had this conversation in the 1970s. It seems irrational to think that we are still having it today, but we are.

> **People who think that they have no biases and "don't see color" are deluding themselves.**

Our senses are automatically registering information about others like skin and hair color, weight, height, and attire. Self-awareness is what is required to overcome the biases we really don't want ourselves to have. Most people want to be kind, good, and fair. Their brain and background are tripping them up. We have all heard the expression "you don't know what you don't know." **Unless you start to pay attention and learn about how your brain works and how your upbringing or social groups influence your unconscious reactions, you will never be the person you envision yourself to be.** Once you know, you can't unknow, and that is when the light comes in and you can catch and stop your unruly brain from running down an inaccurate path of prejudice.

Prejudice is not just about race, but it can also be about gender, weight, education levels, socioeconomic levels, sexual identity, age, and ableism. When you begin to think with a hospitality mindset, you acknowledge that you could have biases and work with intentionality to make ALL people feel welcome. A 2022 *New England Journal of Medicine* article states that "in medicine, bias-driven discriminatory practices and policies not only negatively affect patient care and the medical training environment but also limit the diversity of the healthcare workforce, lead to inequitable distribution of research funding, and can hinder career advancement."[28]

I'll share with you a story about socioeconomic bias in veterinary medicine.

One Saturday morning, a man came into our veterinary hospital wearing worn overalls and an equally tattered hat. He was carrying an injured chicken under his arm, and he was seeking medical care for the bird. The team took a brief history and discovered that the chicken had attempted to cross the road and had been hit by a car. It appeared as if it had a broken leg. We put the man and the chicken into the examination room and proceeded to diagnose the problem. The fracture was confirmed, our surgeon was consulted, and it was determined that the chicken would need an orthopedic pin placement in order to repair its leg. Even though this was many years ago, the surgery was considered expensive at around $700. Despite the appearance of this client, who looked as if he did not have a nickel in his pocket, our team shared the treatment plan and the estimate of cost. To our surprise, the treatment plan was approved, and the chicken received its needed surgery. Upon the patient's discharge, we discovered that the client had taken this chicken to two other veterinary practices that had discouraged him from having the animal treated, one even suggesting that he kill it and have it for dinner! We then discovered that this man was a physician who worked out of our local hospital. He was so impressed with the work that we did that he transferred all of his pets to our practice and referred many of his hospital associates. If we had judged him by his appearance, we would have not only not helped Henrietta the chicken, but we also would have lost what became an excellent client and innumerable new clients from his referrals to us.

> **EXERCISE:** Can you recall a time when you judged a person as unwilling or unable to afford the care you offered, and they ended up surprising you? What bias did you have towards that person? How can you work to avoid that going forward?

Because one of the legs of the hospitality stool is anticipation, we should understand our clients' implicit biases and work to overcome them. Thanks go to my friend, Elle, for this next enlightening story.

As a Black woman, Elle shared that her community can have a general mistrust of doctors, hearkening back to the infamous syphilis study at Tuskegee or the collection and use of a Black woman's, Henrietta Lacks, cells by a hospital without obtaining Lacks' consent in the 1950s. Additionally, oftentimes people of color have their problems dismissed or inadequately treated because doctors have implicit biases that assume that these patients won't listen or follow through with recommendations or aftercare.[29] Furthermore, the significantly higher maternal mortality rates among Black women in contrast to other women weighed heavily on her mind. But when Elle went into labor at the birth of her first child, the medical team in no way acted with any respect for or acknowledgment of these underlying concerns nor did they address her obvious anxiety. It was already emotionally taxing for her because, for a number of reasons, the only family that could be with her was her husband, but then she was informed they would have to perform an emergency C-section on her, further exacerbating how she was feeling. When her attending physician informed her that they were going to have a medical intern join them in the delivery room, she was unable to refuse. Recalling the moment, she said, "I was so afraid. I truly could not speak. I'm telling you—I opened my mouth, but the words absolutely would not come out!" Her fear was paralyzing. She felt even more vulnerable and exposed in front of this perfect stranger. In an already stressful situation, the fond memory of the birth of Elle's child is clouded by a lack of awareness by the doctor, a lack of awareness that also made the memory a traumatizing one.

What can we actively do to build our hospitality muscles towards **all** the humans that we serve? Here are some examples from an article by Janice A. Sabin, PhD, MSW: "Actions that clinicians can take immediately to manage the effects of implicit bias include practicing conscious, positive formal and informal role modeling; taking active-bystander training to learn how to address or interrupt microaggressions and other harmful incidents; and undergoing training aimed at eliminating negative patient descriptions and stigmatizing words in chart notes and direct patient communications. Teaching faculty at academic medical centers can develop curricular materials that contain inclusive, diverse imagery and examples and can strive to use inclusive language in all written and oral communications."[30]

Our job in medicine is to help and heal, not to judge. A recent meme thankfully got a lot of pushback from the veterinary community when it showed a veterinarian whispering to a pet, "I am sorry your owners are idiots." Certainly, it is frustrating when people don't follow our advice or take advice from sketchy sources, but people are usually trying to do the best that they can with the information they are given. Our goal is to be their trusted advisor so that the education they receive is accurate and up-to-date but also affordable and doable. We can only do that by being curious and actively listening. People can feel when they are being judged. That is poor hospitality.

13

Serving Your Teammates Like Your Best Client

I remember the day I first walked into a veterinary practice.

It was 1985, and I was a young woman in a new town. I had a new apartment, a new job, and a husband in the same boat. We knew no one. I had been hired by Jean, the current office manager. She said that she had remembered me when I came to interview because of my "red winter coat and my blue eyes," which is funny because my eyes are green. Then, she made the connection between me and my family's barbecue restaurant where she would periodically travel to for dinner. I'm guessing that she received good customer service because she gave me a job. But that first day at work was very intimidating, even for someone like me who had grown up working with the public and surrounded by a crowd. At this point in time, the practice did not take appointments, so it was a poorly controlled free-for-all. The training was limited with the majority of it being "follow them." (In the training industry, "them" is anyone nearby who has a clue!) It was kind of a sink-or-swim environment.

That first day, I was introduced to the majority of the staff and shown how to file records and answer the telephone. To say it was overwhelming is an understatement. I made it through the first day and went home still excited about the possibilities but feeling less than competent while sharing animal medical stories with my husband. I was working for minimum wage, and I took the job just to get my foot in the door of animal health. I don't know that I would have stayed at that practice as long as I did or even for the first week if it wasn't for a grilled cheese sandwich.

My second day at work involved coming in and working the morning shift. It was then that I met Clara. Clara had been working at the practice for several years as a part-time morning receptionist. Her husband was an FBI agent, and she was a former flight attendant. Clara raised Borzois and Chesapeake Bay Retrievers, and she was one of the best customer service people I have ever met. But Clara's customer service went beyond taking care of clients because, that day, she also took care of me. I think she remembered what it was like to be a new person in town and to be the new person at work.

So, at lunch on my second day, Clara asked me to come to her house so that she could make me a grilled cheese sandwich. She lived close by in a beautiful home surrounded by pastures with high-wire fences so the sight hounds could run. We sat on bar stools at the kitchen counter drinking Diet Coke, eating our sandwiches, and getting to know each other. I have often looked back on Clara's generosity and random act of kindness as a linchpin in my career. She made me feel welcome. She invited me into her home and made me feel like I was not an outsider. Because of her kindness, I had a mentor and a new friend. I stayed at that practice for nineteen years. Clara had retired a couple of years prior to my leaving the practice to live closer to her kids, but we stayed in touch on Facebook.

I tell this story because we work so hard to hire talent in our practices, but then we neglect to make them feel welcome.

We bring them in and have them fill out paperwork, we reiterate the job description, we hand them the employee manual and tell them the rules, and, if they're lucky, we show them where to put their things and where the bathroom is. Onboarding a new person should be so much more than this. It should be a celebration of a new team member. They should be introduced to the team, taken out to lunch, and assigned a mentor and a trainer, and we should touch base daily to see how they are fitting in and what concerns they have.

The stats on great onboarding are impressive. New hires get up to speed and are productive much faster. They bond to the business and become engaged with the work, and, because they feel a part of something bigger than themselves, they STAY. It is impossible to build the culture you want and the skills your team needs with a revolving door of employees.

Have a PLAN for your new hires.

Often when we hire new staff members, they come to us fresh out of school or from another city. They know nothing about the area, housing, schools, and so on. As a hospitable employer, we can help. (See Appendix B for a sample new employee onboarding plan.)

I recently saw a social media post in which a manager wanted to develop a list for new hires of their favorite coffee drinks, food likes and dislikes, and preferences in entertainment or places to dine. I loved the idea because she wanted to get them things they loved as shout-outs for good performance. What would be even better is to manage by walking around and talking to people about themselves, not just about the work. What do they dream? How can you help make it come true? Leaders, pay attention to your people! Notice if they are struggling and offer a hand. Be there when they need you and encourage them to be there for each other.

There is an old manager adage called storming, norming, and forming. It is often used as an excuse to understand why the existing team, even though they might be suffering because they are shorthanded, will not embrace a new person and willingly help them get up to speed. Instead, they gaslight, bully, ostracize, and judge until the new person either quits or starts to fight back and settles in by becoming just as jaded as the rest of the group. This is insanity. Great leaders don't allow this, and they work to build a psychologically safe workplace. This is another reason why a mentor is so important to a new person. It gives them an ally in the "norming" part of the process and protects them in the "storming" part.

Of course, not every hire is a great fit, but every hire is a human being who deserves respect, kindness, and a chance to prove their ability to do the job. A culture of hospitality does this.

Every hire is a human being who deserves respect, kindness, and a chance to prove their ability to do the job.

But what about the existing team? How can we improve the culture of our business when it seems overwhelming to change? How do we show hospitality to our coworkers?

In the current economy, there are more jobs than people to fill them.[31] Predictions show that all medical professions will be severely shorthanded in the very near future. By building a positive culture, we create a work environment of engaged staff that stay. Turnover has always been an issue in medicine, but there are practices that keep their team members for years. HOW? The answer is great culture and fair pay! You don't have to pay the top wages because people will willingly work for slightly less money as long as they enjoy coming to work and feel respected and valued there. But how do we know the truth about our culture and how our team perceives it?

To identify your culture, start with team surveys. Many practices find 360-degree reviews helpful to reveal problems. Reoccurring negative themes are signs that your team is feeling distressed by these issues. As a consultant, one of my first tasks is to perform one-on-one interviews with every staff member. I ask them how they feel about the practice, how they enjoy their coworkers and boss, and if they feel supported in their ambitions to grow in their career. We also do a "stop, start, and continue" exercise, which helps me find the operational processes that are working or lacking. I look for consistent themes from the group and usually find a few that everyone finds equally frustrating. There are many companies that offer 360-degree surveys; these surveys can be very helpful, but they must be used judiciously. If the team is not coached to be objective about the work performance they are reviewing, it can instead spiral into "mean girl"–type bashing and be more harmful than helpful, especially in a culture that needs improvement. Also, the person delivering the evaluations should review the content for biases and cliques and how they may negatively influence the feedback. If it is not going to be helpful and instead will cause emotional injury to the person being evaluated, then a judgment should be made about how to share feedback kindly, partially, or not at all.

> **As difficult as it is to hear negative feedback, it is vital to our personal growth and self-awareness.**

In her book *Insight*, author Dr. Tasha Eurich shares the value of being self-aware when it comes to being successful in all human interactions.[32] Repeatedly, leaders feel that they are doing a wonderful job. They are positive that they are admired and respected by their team, but when finding out that they are, instead, considered a person to be feared and avoided, they are shocked.

No one sets out with intention to be a bad boss, manager, or team member, but in some cases, our personality style and mistaken beliefs about how people should be treated and how work gets done create a monster. This ogre is causing a distinct lack of production by the team as they operate not to do great work but, instead, to not get raked over the coals for errors large or small, real, or perceived. On the opposite side of the coin is the boss who can't make a decision or confront a problematic employee who is undermining the success of the team because they fear and avoid conflict. Both leaders are equally unaware of how they are viewed by their subordinates and how much damage they are doing to the group.

Research shows that self-aware people are more successful, confident, and fulfilled.[31] They are more effective leaders. Yet most people don't truly know themselves or see themselves as others see them. In a presentation I attended by Dr. Eurich, she asked, "How many of you consider yourself a good driver?" Of course, most of the people in the room quickly raised their hands. Then, she asked, "How many of you think most people can't drive?" An equal number of audience members raised their hands. Laughingly, she said, "Do you see the problem here? Many of you are the bad drivers, yet all of you think you drive well. That is lack of self-awareness." If you are interested in learning more about your own self-awareness, Dr. Eurich offers a free quiz on her website at https://www.insight-book.com/Quiz.

Turnover is another sign of poor cultural health. How often are you placing ads for staff? I have known a practice that never removed their help-wanted ads from trade journals. Having visited the practice, I understood the reason for the need. The owner's wife was the manager and micromanaged everything and everyone. It was a stifling environment in which to work.

Other signs of poor culture are chronic absences by staff, unwillingness to step up to occasionally cover shifts for coworkers, and being locked into the letter of job descriptions. When I share that I used to allow my team to trade days off or arrange their own schedules without my approval, many managers are stunned. The rules were simple. You could trade with anyone who had equal skills and who, if you swapped, would not get overtime in that week. I did monitor the system for fairness because I didn't want people to be taken advantage of who were so kind that they never said "no." People appreciated my trust in them to make good decisions, and they liked the autonomy of making their own plans. I felt that I had hired responsible adults, and they were treated as such unless they proved otherwise. Granted, most of my team members were long-time employees, and their actions had earned them the privilege to trade with their coworkers.

We must certainly add gossip and drama to the bad-culture list. Good communication training solves many of these issues. In fact, learning about personality styles is one of the most drama-reducing skills I teach. But some people have developed a deeply ingrained habit of negativity, fault finding, and pot stirring and, even after appropriate coaching, do not work to change. In fact, they routinely blame everyone besides themselves for the problems. Remember the discussion about lack of self-awareness? These folks are the poster children. Sometimes removing these toxic staff members can be painful, especially if they are one of your most technically skilled people.

I remember well how difficult this was when I was a manager. I fired a very reliable, hardworking person for gossiping. She just couldn't break this bad habit and continually caused drama by pot stirring. I dismissed a tech with twenty years of experience because of her passive-aggressive actions. She would hide instruments, charts, and other items in what she deemed was "her" drawer. Everyone was afraid to go into the drawer because of her prickly demeanor. When I found out about this, I opened that drawer and found all our missing items. The wheels immediately went into motion to move her out. The day I released her was the best day ever. The entire team felt like a heavy burden had been lifted off their backs. The toxic tension in the treatment room dissipated. The remaining staff stepped up to cover the workload. It was amazing how the very air in the room seemed charged with positive energy after she was gone.

> **As hard as it is, you must release the people on your team that are undermining your success.**

How do you repair a broken culture?

First, define the culture that you desire. Create a set of core values for the whole team—including practice owners—to live by, as mentioned earlier. People who do not agree with or believe in the same core values as defined by the practice are not good fits and need to be released to grow elsewhere. As an example, if you have a high-end practice and one of your staff members does not support your fee structure because they feel that it is too expensive, then they are not advocating for the level of care that you provide. Their perception of value will also come across to your clients as they interact with them.

Second, purge toxic team members. Owners and managers are surprised at the stories shared after these people are fired. To start, determine if the toxic employee can be saved—because humans tend to avoid giving negative feedback until they are angry. Perhaps the employee has not had the opportunity to improve their behavior. Set deadlines for touching base. Have frequent feedback sessions. Find out if the employee's career goals are being met. If not, what can you do to help them accomplish their goals? Always try coaching for improvement first, and if that fails, release the employee. People who refuse to see themselves truthfully will not comply and will fire themselves with their refusal to change.

Third, train the staff to well-defined job descriptions. Frustration runs rampant in staff that is unsure of the job and how to perform it correctly. Phase training documents are essential for complete and thorough training of the staff. Basically, these checklists confirm that all the important skills of the job have been taught and both the trainee and trainer are comfortable with the knowledge that has been passed along. In addition, develop levels; as the trainee passes each level, they reach a new "status" and pay grade. Upward mobility can be achieved.

> **"The only thing worse than training employees and losing them is not training them and keeping them."**
> —Zig Ziglar

Fourth, choose wisely. "Hire slow and fire fast" is a time-worn adage, but it holds true. My audiences are often shocked when I share that I fired new hires after only two weeks once I realized that they were a poor fit for our work team. This accomplished several things. The new hire had the opportunity to accept other recent offers, which would have been filled if I had waited longer. My team was not wasting valuable time training a bad hire, and the culture was not disrupted by a person who would never fit in. In this decision, I was respectful of all the stakeholders needs and quickly corrected my mistake. Using better screening and behavior-based interview questions and calling references are all important parts of picking your next superstar employee. Don't go on gut—go on fact. Get other team members involved in the hiring process during work interviews. If they are engaged in picking the new person, there is greater chance that they will support and embrace them.

> **When hiring, don't go on gut—go on fact.**

Fifth, allow autonomy in your team. Personal growth and the practice's commitment to encourage career advancement improve culture. Multiple surveys support the importance of these features. People leave jobs when they feel stagnant. I recommend having job proficiency levels paired with pay grades. Level 1 includes new hires who still need to learn the basics. Level 2 employees have mastered the basics and move up to learning and mastering more complex responsibilities. Level 3 employees have achieved mastery of all the levels of skills and are qualified to train others. Level 4 is the master trainer who enjoys teaching and is highly proficient. By creating pay grades and levels based on skills, we allow people to move up, so they don't have to move out. Employees need to see a bright future with your business, especially if they have ambitions to achieve a higher rank. Another advancement opportunity is delegating specific functions to interested staff members. Delegating tasks to staff members not only gives them encouragement to grow but also takes a lot of the burden off of owners and managers, freeing them up for strategic planning and practice development. Delegating is a good way to reward your high-level staff when they have reached your highest pay grade. Owning and performing a new task well is another reason to bump pay. Don't dump tasks on people without first asking if they are interested in the project, and never assign someone more work without increasing their compensation. That is unfair and highly demotivating. Delegate, but always check back. Don't abandon people with a new task until you are sure that they are comfortable and doing it correctly. (See Appendix B for the steps of successful delegation.)

We discussed self-awareness and empowerment, but let's look at the hospitality factor of kindness. Are we being truly kind to one another as we work together to help our patients? In Christine Porath and Christine Pearson's *The Cost of Bad Behavior*, astonishing amounts of money were found to be lost each year from companies just because the staff was ill-treated by others—often management—who lead by fear rather than by positive reinforcement and kind corrections.[33] These "bad behaviors" may seem minor, as one of the listed problems was "coming in and not speaking to coworkers." Does a simple "good morning" require so much effort that you instead rudely ignore your teammates? There is truly no excuse unless you have laryngitis, and even then, you can wave! Manners are usually taught in childhood, but it is possible that some people have not had good training. If so, leaders should coach these team members on better behavior because their apparent rudeness is causing a rift and creating workplace stress. Leaders should also set the example. I remember walking down the hall one day, and as I passed my boss, he asked rather gruffly, "What are you smiling about?" I grinned and responded, "Lack of damn sense, I guess!" This made him laugh, shake his head, and walk on. I was smiling because I enjoyed my clients, my teammates, my work, and, of course, the animals. What was there not to smile about?

I can't stress the importance of how a lack of civility destroys culture and productivity in a business. Some of the actions that Porath and Pearson mention in *The Cost of Bad Behavior* are taking credit for others' work, texting or checking emails while in meetings, passing blame for personal mistakes on to others, belittling others' efforts, spreading rumors about teammates, failing to reply to calls or emails, not saying "please" or "thank you," leaving a mess for others to clean, not listening, talking down to others, making demeaning or derogatory remarks to others, and taking or hiding resources[34] (remember the story about the drawer). All these actions may seem minor but, added up, can rapidly eat holes in the fabric of a positive culture. Speaker Amy Newfield recently posted a video on Facebook called "Stop Throwing Instruments!" I have heard too many stories of doctors having meltdowns and, in a fit of temper, throwing surgical instruments either on the floor or at their attending nurse. This is, to me, a fireable offense. The problem comes when it is the practice owner who is the culprit. Once again, we need to step back to the self-awareness discussion and give feedback to the offender.

When I began my last position as the chief operating officer of a large veterinary practice, there was an assistant who was known to have temper tantrums and storm out of the building in a fit of rage. This happened around my fourth day at work. I called her into a private area and explained that her behavior was understandable because I was a new leader and everyone was a little tense, waiting to see how I would behave. I said, "Tiffany, I am going to give you this one because I know everyone is on edge, but in the future, please know that this behavior will not be tolerated." If you can't control your emotions, and if you pitch a fit and storm out the door, you will no longer be employed by this practice." I did not raise my voice or become angry. I just calmly stated the behavior that I expected from an adult. She never did it again.

When discussing this type of negative behavior, I sometimes have people push back with "sometimes you can't control it" to which I reply, "Nonsense! If you got angry at a stranger and began to verbally abuse them, and they pulled out a knife or a gun, I guarantee that you would immediately gain control of your mouth." You understand that it is in your best interest to shut up so that you don't die. Learning to control your behavior is one of the key elements of a successful career and an enjoyable life. People who fly off the handle do not get promoted, or at least they shouldn't be because they can't be trusted by their team. Words hurt us mentally and are remembered long after the memory of physical pain leaves us. Not only is incivility a productivity killer, but ninety-four percent of people treated this way work to get even with their offenders.[35] So if you are one of the people who feels that it is okay to treat others badly, watch your back, and if you are an employer who allows this behavior, eighty-eight percent of employees also work to get even with their company! Consider the number of mass shootings that occur in the workplace. Here are some eye-opening data from the FBI: "Of 160 active-shooter incidents in the

United States between 2000 and 2013, over 80 percent (132) occurred at work .... Of the 132 work-site shootings, seventy-three incidents (45.6 percent) took place at businesses. The seventy-three incidents that occurred in business environments resulted in 210 people killed (including twelve company owners, supervisors, or managers) and 272 people wounded (including six owners, supervisors or managers) .... Thirty-four shooters were employed or previously employed by the business, including twenty-two current employees, seven former employees, four terminated on the day of the shooting, and one suspended employee."[36] I certainly don't want to imply that if you don't behave kindly to your coworkers that they will intend to do you physical harm, but I do believe that treating people with respect and learning conflict resolution and communication skills could solve many of the problems we have with stress, burnout, poor productivity, and turnover.

To build a great team you must communicate well and often. Well-planned staff meetings are a bridge between the practice owner's goals and the team's understanding of them. They are also an opportunity to share information from different views. At a minimum, a practice should hold monthly team meetings, but quickly huddling every morning and afternoon is a great way to keep everyone in the loop. As the chief operating officer of a twenty-four-hour practice, it was challenging to have all-hands-on-deck meetings, but we made a point to hold them at least twice a year. Instead, every month we held department meetings, with the department heads of all departments attending each separate group's meeting. The idea was to ensure interdepartmental information flow. Then, the department leaders could be there to help find solutions to communication gaps and take the solutions back to their team. We don't need everyone at every meeting, but we do need everyone to stay informed about challenges and changes that affect them and their work. The meeting dates were posted in January for the entire year, and they rotated being held on Tuesday, Wednesday, or Thursday so that staff members who had regular days off did not have to always come in during their valuable downtime to attend. Minutes were also taken and posted so all could read and reference back to the discussions.

Meetings are frequently seen as a huge waste of time by employees. They are if not done correctly. Agendas should be posted at least a week in advance so that the staff can have time to contemplate the issues and consider ideas for solutions. The meetings should allow all attendees time to speak and avoid the "conversation hog" taking over the discussion. The facilitator has this duty. In addition to solving any problems the business has encountered, there should be a learning component where all are taught a new skill, share insights from a book, learn lessons from a podcast or a TED talk, receive training from an outside speaker on a new product, or are shown a new life skill.

Finally, the group needs to set goals for the month. These could be productivity goals, but even more important are communication goals and client service innovations that help bond clients to the team and the business. We should also review how the prior month's goals were met and diagnose failures and successes. The reason why people hate meetings is that they are poorly planned and like a dog chasing its tail: they often end in frustration rather than progress.

All agree that gaining client trust is a big part of successfully treating our patients and getting to "yes." But just as important is the trust our team has in their leadership and in each other.

We want to know that we have one another's backs—not that we are likely to stab one another in the back. When team members feel safe, they will self-monitor rather than bring every minor thing to the manager to solve.

I was in a recent practice visit working with the CSR team. These were some talented people. I could tell by their responses to my questions that they were great at problem-solving, bonding with clients, and building relationships. But their complaint was that "no one ever acknowledges our work or gives us a compliment on how we handle the front desk." So, I turned it back on them and asked, "When was the last time you gave a compliment to one another? Who said you can't give feedback and support to yourselves?" They seemed surprised and then delighted because they could see that they could be the change they wanted to see.

I wouldn't be surprised if, when they follow through on this support of one another, the other departments will start to observe and want what they have. They could be the model of a safe and kind culture to the rest of the team. The hospitality approach to work builds supportive and caring teams that stay.

A long time ago I learned about Maslow's hierarchy of human needs. It begins at the bottom—food, water, air—which is about as fundamental as you can get. Then, the next step is safety, which is embodied by security of body, employment, resources, morality, and health. You can easily see that when a business can't or won't meet the second, most basic need of a human—SAFETY—none of the other desires can happen.

You can't build belonging in a team when there is no trust. You can't gain the confidence and self-esteem needed to garner respect for yourself and for others if you are never safe. And you certainly can't grow to the transformative stage of self-actualization, where creativity and problem-solving flourish, when you are always afraid.

Great culture moves teams to the pinnacle of the hierarchy. Staff members are enveloped in such safety that they bond in friendships. Don't feel like coming to work? If I don't, I let my friends down ... so I will come. Want to feel a sense of belonging? Then I will pitch in and help when my work team is performing a task. Want to be respected by the people I work with? Then I will stretch myself to come up to their belief in me and meet their high expectations.

Great culture is not that hard—it is about choosing wisely the people who believe what you believe, who understand the why of our work. It is about hiring those who desire to be a part of something important in the world and then nurturing their core values with support, feedback, and kindness while protecting them from harm.

> **Great culture is about choosing wisely the people who believe what you believe, who understand the why of our work.**

I always believed that a significant part of my job as a manager was to protect my people. So, I took the heat from the difficult client. I was the go-between for my super-driver-personality boss and my staff. I found ways to teach them so that they would have confidence. I confessed my mistakes to them so that they felt free to come and confess theirs. I fired people who didn't perform. Leaders drive the culture, and great culture drives successful business, just as poor culture tears it down.

As we hire a young generation that does not believe in loyalty for the sake of loyalty, creating a positive culture that grows, supports, and engages staff members becomes essential for practice success. "My way or the highway" has never been a good management philosophy and becomes even more archaic in today's hiring environment. **Team members want to know that their leaders are working for a meaningful purpose and that these leaders are committed to guiding their team members to career success. Pick them well, train them hard, grow them fast, give them power—and love them lots.** You are going to like what happens.

The moral of the story is never waste a chance to share a grilled cheese. It set my career in motion, and thirty-five years later, I still smile about that lunch at Clara's.

EXERCISE: Consider the new employees on your team. What random act of kindness did you perform to make them feel welcome? What could you have done if you did nothing? What will you do to welcome the next new hire?

14

Conflict Happens: How to Successfully Navigate Difficult Encounters

As much as we would like to build a culture that never has drama, we are always working with humans who are imperfect and emotion-driven, so conflict will arise. The important and often missing piece of the puzzle is understanding the cause of conflict and teaching the team how to move into conflict correctly rather than avoiding it and allowing problems to fester until they explode.

Humans naturally avoid uncomfortable situations. They delay action until they are pressed to the point of extreme frustration and are forced to act. For some people, this point is much closer than for others who are more tolerant and laid back. For either, when that tipping point is reached, the "smart brain" that makes wise judgments has typically been hijacked by the "lizard brain" that reacts to fear. Let me share some brain science that will help clarify.

Our brain is typically broken down into three parts. The lizard brain, which is our brain stem, is the most primitive part of the brain; thus, it has the name "lizard brain" because we react like a reptile to stimuli. It controls most of the body's vital functions—like breathing, heart rate, sleeping, and waking—and it never rests (at least you hope it doesn't because you are going to die if it does). The lizard brain is also referred to as the limbic brain, and it is designed to keep us from harm and keep our body functioning at the most basic level. Neuroscientists say it controls the four Fs: fighting, feeding, fleeing, and *reproduction* (you can supply the fourth "F" on your own).

The paleomammalian brain is the part of the brain that sits on top of the brain stem. The amygdala is the part of this area of the brain that allows us to feel rage, pleasure, and fear and stores memories of those emotions. The hippocampus converts short-term memories to long-term memories, and the thalamus connects the senses, sending signals throughout the brain. The cortex is highly specialized, with sections for vision, speech, and memory.

The cerebrum is the third part and sits at the front part of the brain. It is the largest part of the brain and allows us to coordinate our movements, regulate our body temperature, speak, think, create art, reason, solve problems, develop emotions, and learn. Also associated with the cerebrum are vision, hearing, touch, taste, and smell.

Why does all this matter when discussing conflict?

Because when we were evolving, so were our brains. We learned that in order to survive around animals much larger and stronger than us, the best solution was teamwork. If you wanted to eat a wooly mammoth, you were going to starve or die if you tried killing it by yourself. Instead, you got together with others in your tribe and figured out a strategy. Humans are wired to collaborate. This is one of the reasons why we were so distressed in isolation during the COVID-19 pandemic. Our ability to be with others was severely curtailed, and it took an emotional toll on our collective mental health.

Humans have something that no other animal has; it is called "theory of mind." We attempt to see our world in terms of what motivates others' actions, and we try to predict another person's mental state. Are they happy, sad, angry, or calm? What were their intentions behind an action? Do they mean to help us or harm us? These judgments are an important part of our social structure. When we empathize with others, we are using theory of mind to "feel how they feel" by putting ourselves in their shoes. People who are good at reading the emotions of others and their own emotions are said to be emotionally intelligent. In the book *Emotional Intelligence 2.0* by Travis Bradberry and Jean Graves, the authors share a surprising finding. People with high IQs outperform people with average IQs only twenty percent of the time.[37] So being blessed with traditional intelligence is not a sure path to a successful life. However, people with high emotional intelligence and average IQs outperform high-IQ people **seventy percent of the time**. The conclusion is that emotional intelligence tops "book smarts" almost every time.

When we lack emotional intelligence, instead of working collaboratively with people, we cause them to mentally move from safety to fear, greatly reducing their performance. We also exacerbate situations with clients who are unhappy.

Why? Because in a fearful state, the paleomammalian brain is flooded with stress hormones. The hypothalamus signals the adrenals to dump adrenaline into your body to prepare to flee or fight. Our bodies evolved to react in seconds, so our hormones move fast. When the danger is perceived as over, cortisol shows up and calms us back down.[38]

This is truly oversimplified, but you get the picture. When you are frightened or angry, you can't learn, think, or perform to your best standards. Stress like this over time causes something called "learned helplessness." Social workers and psychologists see this behavior in an abused spouse or even in some staff members who are victimized by bullies on their team. This could certainly explain why these abused workers simply don't quit.

According to Dr. John Medina, author of *Brain Rules*, our brain at work and our brain at home can't be separated.[39] If we are living under a chronically stressed state, such as with an abusive spouse or parent, our brain becomes exhausted because it feels that it has no control over this terrible situation. Our hypothalamus dumps adrenaline into our system at the instant in which we perceive a threat to our life. During evolution, these threats were short-lived, like encountering a snake in the yard. Your brain signals danger, and you freeze in place with your heart pounding. The blood is pumping oxygen to all your limbs so you can flee the snake. Once it moves on, the human body responds by immediately calming down, and sometimes we can even feel slightly "deflated" as we relax, realizing the danger is over. Then, we go about our normal day.

When people are constantly subjected to abuse, the fear is never-ending, and the spikes of adrenaline happen multiple times a day, never giving the body a time to calm and rest. The spikes can even come *in anticipation* of abuse because of the memory of past incidents. Physically, this can lead to a heart attack or stroke because the heart-pumping reaction scars the blood vessels. Cortisol also damages the hippocampus, causing the victim of abuse to be unable to learn or remember. Keep in mind that this is not only limited to physical abuse but can also apply to verbal abuse. Memories of physical and emotional pain are stored in the same area of the brain.

In the book *The Cost of Bad Behavior*, the authors discuss how incivility at work harms employee health by sharing the Harvard University School of Public Health study information that concluded that stressful jobs were as detrimental to women's health as smoking and obesity.[40] A *Harvard Business Review* article notes the following: "The American Psychological Association estimates that more than $500 billion is siphoned off from the U.S. economy because of workplace stress, and 550 million workdays are lost each year due to stress on the job. Sixty percent to 80 percent of workplace accidents are attributed to stress, and it's estimated that more than 80 percent of doctor visits are due to stress."[41] The article additionally highlights the following: "In studies by the Queens School of Business and by the Gallup Organization, disengaged workers had 37 percent higher absenteeism, 49 percent more accidents, and 60 percent more errors and defects. In organizations with low employee engagement scores, they experienced 18 percent lower productivity, 16 percent lower profitability, 37 percent lower job growth, and 65 percent lower share price over time. Importantly, businesses with highly engaged employees enjoyed 100 percent more job applications."[41]

Consider how workplace stress can affect patient care if we are facing a sixty percent increase in errors and defects in organizations with negative workplace cultures. Over the years, I have listened to multiple stories of cultures so deep in conflict that team members will allow a doctor to make a mistake that harms a patient without intervening because they are afraid of the repercussions of speaking up or retaliation for perceived harms. It is inappropriate for us to fear our coworkers and superiors, and it is poor leadership that tolerates behavior that creates such fear.

The takeaway of this information is to keep your team "feeling safe" if you want them to learn, grow, and achieve high performance and have faith that calling out an error will be applauded rather than cursed.

Keep your team "feeling safe" if you want them to learn, grow, and achieve high performance.

How do you confront someone with necessary but negative feedback in a way that allows them to not only accept it but to also use it to make positive changes to avoid similar mistakes moving forward? The answer is to approach the problem with your "smart brain" and use curiosity rather than accusations.

When we approach someone with a statement like "You are always late to work," we are stating a false fact if that person is late only two days a week. They immediately become defensive and contradict your statement by saying, "That is not true. I am on-time almost every day." A better approach would be to say, "Toni, I see that you were late to work by twenty minutes on Tuesday and twenty-seven minutes on Friday. Can you share with me what is going on in your life that is causing you to be late to work?" The tone of the sentence has moved from an accusation of slack work habits to a concern something disruptive is happening to make this person late. The need for Toni to defend herself is gone, and an opening is given for a reasonable explanation.

For many years, I have sung the praises of the book *Crucial Conversations*,[42] touting it as my "bible for communication and conflict training." This book has more dog-eared pages and highlights than any other book on my shelves. The authors define these tough conversations as times when the participants have differing opinions, the outcome matters significantly to both parties, and highly emotional responses are manifesting on both sides. Many of our conflicts in the medical field are high-stakes discussions with the decision maker sitting on the fence between accepting the medical care we offer and understanding its value to their lives or accusing us of everything from price gouging to malpractice. The emotions in these types of conversations are powerful on both sides with the medical team feeling accused of horrible behavior far from their sworn oath and the client or patient feeling taken advantage of at a most vulnerable time when they or their beloved pet is ill. Learning how to navigate these conversations not only improves the outcome for the patient but also avoids the unnecessary stress of constant scolding by the public.

Remember that our limbic (lizard) brain is wired to react in milliseconds to threats of perceived danger. It moves through the freeze, flee, and fight response and quickly takes over our normal, cool intellect if we don't train ourselves to stop, breathe, and engage our higher-level thinking.

For me, visualization is helpful. I think of myself as a long camera lens. When engaged with a person in normal conversations, I am focused at a "close-up" level. If the conversation turns to conflict, I try to pull my "lens focus" back to a wide-angle view to take in the broader aspects of what is happening. I work to diagnose the situation, asking myself the following questions: "What is this person feeling? How did I miscommunicate to set this conflict in motion? Why do they feel like they need to defend themselves? Where did their fear or feeling of disrespect originate? What can I say to de-escalate this conversation?" I also give myself an internal pep talk, with language like, "This is not about you but rather something they perceive that you or the practice did to them. This is a challenge you enjoy. I can turn this conversation around with my skills. Just ride along and listen."

Notice that I removed my emotional response from the process, which allowed me to be objective about the situation. This does take practice and a lot of self-control, but it is a skill that should be honed. Not only does it work for difficult client or team member interactions, but the same skill can also be used at home with your family.

Another tool in these conversations is to find a common goal with your conversation partner. Why is this person in your office? Is it because they want to find a solution to a medical issue that is causing them distress or to help their pet who is ill? Because we are medical professionals, our goal is to heal and help; therefore, we are working towards the same objective as our client.

Human nature demands us to do the exact opposite of what I have described. Our limbic brain wants us to scamper away from these challenging conversations, avoiding confrontation at all costs, or wants us to attack our accuser, prove ourselves right, and WIN! If we can keep in mind that this is a negotiation and not a battle, we are more likely to come away with a compromise that both sides can live with.

Returning to a prior discussion of active listening, this is a vital tool in a difficult conversation, especially when the person you are speaking with seems to be pulling issues out of some make-believe universe visible only to them. In his book *Talking to Crazy: How to Deal with the Irrational and Impossible People in Your Life*, Dr. Mark Goulston gives us advice on managing those people who appear to be completely off the rails. He describes four irrational behaviors. First, they can't see the world clearly. Second, they make no sense in what they say or think. Third, they do things in opposition to their own best interest. Finally, they refuse to be guided to reason. For example, what rational person believes they will get better care by shouting at and disrespecting their medical caregiver? Or get better service from their waiter? Or have a loving relationship with their kids? None of these actions is logical, but the "lizard brain" defies logic.

Dr. Goulston's advice is to "lean in to crazy" to change the situation's dynamic. I used this tactic recently when attempting to buy a dog. I had searched for two years for a small fuzzy dog and, thanks to a friend, made a connection with a breeder who had a fourteen-month-old, retired champion Bichon Frise. In my estimation, this dog was old enough to not have to go through the up-every-two-hours puppy stage, had been well socialized because of the show ring and living at his handler's home with three kids and eight dogs, and came with three generations of health testing for genetic issues and proved sound. I began an email conversation with the breeder and, because of my long history in veterinary medicine, began to ask what I considered to be a lot of reasonable questions about behavior, health, medical care, and obedience training. Apparently, the breeder took these questions to be a personal affront to the quality of her dogs and her skill as a breeder. She was close to the point of refusing to sell me the dog. Finally, I texted her a message of apology, stating that the miscommunication was all my fault and that if I had started my dog project by first visiting her website, where many of my questions would have been answered, she would not believe that I questioned her commitment to her dogs. I explained that the only reason I shared my experience in veterinary medicine and animal behavior was to show her that the dog would have exceptional care at my home, which was our mutual goal. So, it all worked out, and I adore my new pup and frequently text his breeder pictures to keep her up to date. I simply realized that I was going to need to "lean in to crazy" to work through the communication with her.

Thinking back, I believe several things were going on. This lady really loves her dogs, and giving up a dog you raised and had for fourteen months would be difficult, especially to a stranger you had never met. Perhaps she had been bashed by someone in the veterinary community for breeding dogs, even though her regular veterinarian turned out to be a personal friend of mine and shared that she was an excellent owner. Quality preservationist breeders, who work to improve the genetic health of their breed, are often dumped in the same basket as the "backyard" breeder, who just wants to profit from the sale of animals. Having experienced both, I can assure you that there is a difference. So, giving her some grace and being willing to not have to prove myself right got me a wonderful pet.

Some people set out to make you crazy. They make snide remarks and little jabs about things that matter to you and hope to get a rise and negative reaction from you in return. Don't play their game. I used to have clients that made remarks about how expensive our care was for their pets. Rather than getting defensive, I just said, "In my experience, you get what you pay for, and quality care costs. But I really appreciate your business because, without you, I wouldn't have a job, and I really love my job! Besides, look how happy your pet looks. You are a great pet owner, and I wish everyone took as good of care of their pet as you do." Of course, this was not how they expected me to reply, and it completely threw them off their game. It was said in a playful manner and with a smile, but it was also said in seriousness and with a belief in our quality of care.

In all conflicts, assume positive intent. I found that my most helpful tools going into these challenging encounters were a pen, a pad of paper, and a few deep breaths. I would ask the client to start at the beginning and share their story while taking notes about *what they believed* had occurred. I never contradicted or corrected their story for accuracy. I continued to nod, take notes, and ask clarifying questions. I discovered that allowing the client to tell their story from their perspective without argument or interruption gave them the opportunity to get their frustrations and anger out and finally wind down to an emotional state that I could reason with. Before they got to that calmer state, there was no point in sharing my side because they were in amygdala hijack, and the logical part of their brain was not engaged, just the primitive limbic brain that believed it was fighting for its survival. Many people don't have the patience to wait until the end of the story; instead, they interrupt to attempt to tell their side. This only makes the client dig in harder because they don't believe that you are listening. I once had a disgruntled client tell me that he felt like he had to go to battle every time he came into the practice because of the poor customer service he encountered. I had been hired to change this issue a few weeks earlier and, thankfully, managed to do so in the months ahead. When I asked him why he kept returning, he replied, "Because these are the best veterinarians in the area, and I want them to care for my pets." Even then, the poor hospitality he was receiving could have eventually driven him away.

> **Once you get people to a calmer state, it is time to develop an allyship with them and help them fight for their cause.**

Thank people for complaining! Usually, there is a kernel of truth in even the most elaborate story. I always said to upset people, "Thank you for telling me about this because if I don't know, I can't fix it. I didn't want this to happen to you, and I really don't want to have it happen to others! I truly appreciate your feedback." It was typical for the complaining person to apologize for their behavior after we finished our conversation.

Never tell people to "calm down" or that they "can't seriously believe that is true" because you are not going to get through to them. You are only pouring fuel on the fire.

According to the book *Emotional Intelligence 2.0*, humans have five basic emotions: happy, sad, angry, afraid, and ashamed.[43] The Gottman Institute has six emotions: mad, scared, joyful, powerful, peaceful, and sad.[44] Both resources break down these basic emotions into more incremental intensity levels. For example, "mad" can be deconstructed into hurt, hostile, angry, rage, hateful, and critical at the medium-intensity level, but those then move into jealous, selfish, frustrated, furious, irritated, and skeptical at mild intensity. So, when my CSR used to come to me with a request to talk with Mrs. Smith who was MAD, I typically discovered that the client was in a milder state of frustration or irritation.

People are typically not very good at defining their emotions. I find that doctors in particular classify their reactions to an accuser as angry, when it is really about feeling disrespected about their skills and knowledge.

Sometimes they are also uneasy about the fact that there may be a word of truth in what they are being told. Imposter syndrome kicks in and confidence diminishes. We begin to tell ourselves a false story. Here is a very important brain fact that you need to keep at the forefront of your mind: THE BRAIN DOES NOT KNOW THE TRUTH FROM A LIE ... IT ONLY KNOWS WHAT YOU TELL IT.

When we feed our brain negativity, it seeks to find more of that to affirm our belief as a truth. For example, you believe that a fellow staff member doesn't care for you. You have never had a real conflict, but maybe one day in the treatment room, she gave you a sharp remark. Now your brain tries to mind read, and because you have told it that this girl doesn't like you, it looks for anything she does that confirms your belief. Even her most innocent remarks are perceived by your brain as hurtful. We allow this story to continue if we don't become the master of our emotions and talk to ourselves, saying, "Why would this person not like me? Perhaps that day she was very pushed and busy, and that is why she made that remark. Let me go and speak with her to clear this up." That is a grown-up thought process. Author and speaker Brené Brown has a great line for these situations: "The story I am telling myself about this situation is this … Now, can you please tell me how you see it?" This line should be in our employee manual!

The good news is that communication skills and emotional intelligence can be learned. As people age, they typically gain better emotional skills because they discover that what they did in the past didn't work effectively. Humans learn by failure. Fortunately, the books I have referenced, and many similar titles, can help you avoid the need to fail in order to improve because we can learn from others' mistakes by reading. I certainly wouldn't manage a difficult client interaction today the same way I did at age twenty-five. At the time, I was a new practice manager. I recall explaining an exam fee to a client, and when she complained about being charged the fee for her dog who had received a steroid injection, I said, "Lady, I won't kill your dog for twenty dollars, and, if you want me to, you need to go someplace else for vet care." Then, I copied her dog's one-page paper record and slid it across the counter. Please don't do that! Use your hospitality skills to do a much better job.

> **EXERCISE:** Think of a time when you told yourself a false story about a coworker or a friend. What effect did it have on your relationship? What happened when you discovered your mistake?

15

The Importance of Language in Discussing Money

Medical professionals and their team members are typically not trained in sales, so having to discuss financial matters with a client is considered to be the most uncomfortable conversation in practice. However, clients want us to be up-front about costs and to also have systems in place that aid them in affording care when necessary.

Our culture has trained us to be secretive about money. We are told not to discuss our salary and not to ask what an item costs or how much someone paid for their home. The downside of all this is that we can be taken advantage of by a boss who is underpaying us in comparison to another employee at the same level, or we go to buy the item that our friend has purchased only to find it unaffordable. We don't know how to negotiate for a home because we have no point of reference as to what someone else recently paid for a home of similar size and age in the same neighborhood on the same street. In recent years, technology has pulled back the curtain on many of these money secrets by posting salaries and home prices online.

Healthcare costs, however, are still held in mystery. Occasionally, a veterinary hospital will post fees for routine care like vaccinations, exams, or neutering, but by far, the majority of vet practices don't. In fact, they are so secretive about fees that they won't even answer these questions when clients call or email. All this cloak-and-dagger activity leads to a lack of trust and results in clients being surprised by costs once they're in the clinic.

Human patients with health insurance usually have an idea of their co-pays and deductibles, but because human health insurance pays the medical provider directly, the patient rarely has an idea of what the cost of care is for their own health services. As a cancer survivor, I used to review my explanation of benefits and be stunned at the cost of care compared to similar products or procedures in veterinary medicine. Even with insurance, the co-pays became significant, and I was thankful that my hospital had a system in place for payments. I also had the benefit of supplemental insurance.

Pet insurance is different than human health insurance. It works similar to property insurance. Clients must pay the provider out of pocket and then submit their claim to be reimbursed. Therefore, the challenge is how to help a client bridge the gap between the time of care and the time of reimbursement. Practices must have tools in place to be able to work with their clients on finances. Otherwise, pets who could be saved will be subject to economic euthanasia. Not only does the pet lose but so does the pet owner and the animal health team that came into the profession to heal animals, not euthanize them.

Veterinary staff members assume that pet owners don't want to pay for care. A provider may think they can make judgments about who can and will pay and who won't. In my experience, that is an impossible call.

> **We can never assume the extent to which people love their animals and neither can we X-ray their bank account to know if they can afford the care we offer.**

Doing so is arrogant. Some people can afford the gold-standard level of care yet still not be willing to pay for it, while others may struggle to pay yet desperately want the best for their pet. Having worked the front desk for many years, I saw this play out many times.

Practices must address costs and prepare clients for the expenses they will incur as responsible pet owners. In several recent studies, the lifetime cost of a pet was evaluated. The lifetime cost of caring for dogs ranges from $20,000 to $55,000 and $15,000 to $45,000 for cats, according to the Synchrony 2021 Pet Lifetime of Care study. The study found that seven out of ten pet owners said they consider their pets as members of the family, yet nearly half underestimated the lifetime cost of caring for pets. The Lifetime of Care research also revealed that dog owners can expect to spend between $1,300 and $2,800 and cat owners, approximately $960 to $2,500 in the first year alone. One out of four pet owners surveyed indicated an unexpected expense of only $250 would cause them stress.[45] Not only does this relatively small amount of money cause owners distress, but they also are woefully uninformed about the real costs involved in maintaining the health of their furry family members. In the Pet Owners Economic Value Study by the Veterinary Hospital Managers Association, when asked what a preferred cost of a pet's dental cleaning should be, the respondents shared a price of sixty-five to ninety dollars, which is much lower than the typical average anesthesia-based dentistry cost of $500 to $900.[46]

Education about care costs should start at the initial visit with information provided about what to do to keep pets healthy and the anticipated costs as the pet ages.

I used to give new pet owners a brochure that explained preventive care from puppyhood and the kitten stage to adulthood, then to the senior stage, and, finally, to the geriatric stage. The message was reinforced as the pet aged, and when the animal reached senior status, the extra diagnostics and exams were not a surprise. The one constant challenge that will certainly start conflict is blindsiding a client about costs. There are options for client financing, such as the CareCredit® health and pet care credit card—that I recommend practices should always accept—along with traditional credit cards, split billing, and auto drafting options. We can even provide piecemeal care over weeks and months, if the need is not urgent, to help clients afford services. Build out a tool kit in advance of need and advertise the availability of financing options to your clients. Veterinary practices should also recommend that owners get pet insurance and get it early in the pet's life before any preexisting conditions happen.

Still, another part of the money conversation is making sure we are using terminology that the client understands and showing the benefit to the pet. People buy on emotion. *Thinking Fast and Slow* is a best-selling book written in 2011 by Nobel Prize in Economic Sciences laureate Daniel Kahneman. In the book, he describes how humans make decisions. Before this book, it was believed that people created a logical thought path to make a wise choice, weighing the pros and cons carefully before taking the leap. In truth, that is far from how humans decide things. It was revealed that people make ninety percent of their decisions—big or small—based on gut![47]

How many people do you know who own an animal they got because someone else was going to not care for it or take it to the pound? Maybe this describes you. In that moment, your gut decided "I'll take it!" even if you already had five animals. Real estate agents know this, too. When you sell a house, you are told to make it look like you don't live there. Take down all your family photos, clean the closets, stage the furniture, fill the tub with water and floating candles and set a glass of wine on the edge, and bake bread or cookies. Now, you tell me, what does bread have to do with a real estate investment? Nothing! But when we do these things, our potential buyer's fast brain thinks, "Oh, if I live here, I will have no clutter, float in a tub with candles while drinking wine, and bake bread and cookies."

In the book *The Sandler Rules: 49 Timeless Selling Principles and How to Apply Them*, David Sandler is quoted as saying, "Every prospect or client is really three different people. The child, the parent, and the adult."[48]

Let me give you an example of how this works.

The Child sees an expensive purse. She loves the way it feels and looks when she holds it. She loves the color and even the smell of the leather. But the bag is $900. Still, the Child wants the bag. The Parent says, "You are a good Child. You work hard, you don't get many extravagant things, and you deserve a reward for how wonderful you are. You can buy the bag." The Adult justifies the purchase by thinking, "Well, the quality is excellent, the color is a good neutral and will go with all the things I wear, and they will repair it if it breaks, so I will keep it forever. If I buy fifteen $100 purses that don't last, this will really save me money over my lifetime, and, besides, IT IS ON SALE!" Sound familiar?

As medical care providers, we attempt to communicate first to the Adult. We give our medical reasoning, probable outcomes, and cost estimates set out in a logical sequence for the client. Then, we step back and ask them for a decision. This is fine for routine things that they came in for because they already wanted them but not for a new service or complex medical procedure. We must change our approach.

First, we need to recognize and reach the Child. An article I read years ago discussed a study of exam-room skills. The study discovered that doctors only listened to clients tell their story for about eleven to thirteen seconds before interrupting them and taking over the conversation. The client never got to finish what they planned to say or ask. However, when they did allow the client to go on with the full account, it only took 90 to 120 seconds, and the client left feeling better about the visit. They had accomplished everything they wanted to accomplish.

When we spend time listening—actively listening—we discover the needs of the Child because the Child says, "I WANT ..." whatever it is. If we have done a good job of listening, we know what the client is concerned about. We present our medicine in a way that supports the WANT. We need to discuss the service benefit in a more emotionally driven way.

To discover the emotional place that the pet holds in the family, we must ask our client open-ended questions. I am sure you know the definition of open-ended questions and close-ended questions, but, to me, an easy "test drive" for an open-ended question is asking myself "Does the question require that they tell me a story?"

This is our fact-finding phase. We tend to think that it is all about their medical history, but it is more. One of my favorite questions is "Where does Fluffy sleep?" This is an extremely telling question about the pet's place in the home. The answer may be "in a kennel in the laundry room." That tells me that the pet is loved, but that this may be a more practical-minded owner. The answer could also be "in his bed, which is at the foot of mine." Now we are moving up in status and sleeping in the same room. But when the answer is "he takes over my bed and sleeps between me and my wife," that pet is surely family, and the attachment is great.

I have often said that the only thing that can change the attitude of a pet owner about pets is to own a really great one—one that is so special that they change the Grinch's heart of stone to a heart the size of Texas.

> **Our job is to listen, listen, listen ... before we talk.**

We are gathering not just medical information but also emotional data. When psychiatrists begin medical school, they are trained with this lesson: the problem that the patient brings you is never the real problem. Why does this matter to us? Because clients don't like to show their vulnerability, and they want to save face. We often listen to a client's excuse and take it at face value. Delving into the situation a little deeper may reveal some other truths. Sometimes clients are unwilling to admit their lack of medical knowledge—or even basic anatomy. Some are embarrassed to reveal how much they really love the animal, so they present it as "my wife's dog."

> **The problem that the patient brings you is never the real problem.**

Have you ever had a client lie to you? Of course, you have! Physicians automatically increase the amount of alcohol their patients admit to drinking per week because they know they fudge the truth. Remember the story of the teenager and the stoned dog? Her body language was telling the story. I used to watch the TV show *House*. I loved it. House was a skeptic. He said, "It's a basic truth of the human condition that everybody lies. The only variable is about what." This is why it is important that we confirm the pieces of information our clients are feeding us. I remember well the client who told me he had only twenty dollars and then paid with a one-hundred-dollar bill.

When you don't listen to the client and you try to advance patient care for your reasons, you will not be as successful as when you approach the care from a client-benefit direction. We have to make a discovery. Why does the client care? Remember the lesson shared earlier about how people buy based on "what's in it for me?" This was recently brought home to me by my friend, Rachel. Rachel took her well-loved but elderly cat to her veterinarian to discuss end-of-life care. The vet discussed the cat's situation, which she had been treating for several months, and suggested running another diagnostic test. Rachel asked if it would change the outcome for the cat. The doctor answered, "No." "So, why would I put her through that if it will not make any difference in her life expectancy or quality of life?" she asked. The veterinarian apologized and confessed that her scientific need to know overcame her consideration for the cat and the situation and agreed that the test was not to benefit the cat, only her curiosity. Check your reasons, and make sure they are benefiting the patient ... not your desire for knowledge.

Sandler rule number twenty-seven states that "you can't sell anybody anything. They have to discover they want to buy it." What would buying or not buying this service mean to them? I often used the "many of our clients find ..." approach to service offerings in practice. "Mrs. Jones, I know you told me Spot has bad gas and is almost unbearable to live with. Many of our clients find that by switching to our sensitive-stomach diet, their pets are no longer having problems and life is a lot less smelly." People tend to be followers, and if it works for someone else, they are more comfortable agreeing to the purchase.

I also used this for collecting fees prior to euthanasia. CSRs in veterinary offices understand that this is an uncomfortable but necessary thing. It makes you feel like a vulture hanging over the body when you collect money after the fact. Since most people call ahead to make arrangements, we began to use the following approach on the phone. "Mrs. Smith, I know this is a difficult time, and we are here to support you. It has helped many of our clients in the past to go ahead and take care of the financials today on the phone so when you come in, you don't even have to consider this. It will just be about you and the time you have with Spot. Would you like to do that?"

> **When people are told what to do, they tend to rebel. When people discover they need what you have, they more readily accept what you offer.**

Doctors and techs worked long and hard to learn all the facts about medicine that they know and share. But any person at the front desk can tell you a story of the client who came to the front with a diagnosis of gastroenteritis and a dazed and confused look. They scratch their head and ask your receptionist to explain what that means, even though they nodded at the doctor during the entire explanation.

I have seen oversharing of information many times in my career. We love medicine and love discussing it. But our clients don't get it, and some don't really care. **Remember that the Child is the decision maker.**

When we dump complex information on a client, talking above their head, they tend to shut down because they don't want to appear ignorant to the doctor. This is more common in young associates, who tend to feel that their vast knowledge will impress the client enough to say "yes." Unfortunately, it more likely results in a "let me think about it" response, which, to the happy ears of the doctor, is a soon-to-be "yes," but in the mind of the client was a soft let-down "no." Don't dump more information than needed on a client. Keep it simple.

You can't overcome objections if you don't know what they are.

When you stay in a practice many years like I did, you develop good relationships with your clients. Most of the time, they would tell me if they had a concern. I was the No Judgement Zone. I had clients tell me that their hesitation was not the money but instead the fact that the pet was having to stay the night. Since the dog had never been away from home, the owner feared it would panic and die of a heart attack. Together, we found a solution that worked, but only because I discovered the real reason for the "no."

One year, I was asked to lecture to a group of veterinary technicians on the subject of pet dentistry. I am a big dental advocate, but I have never performed a dental procedure in my life, and I was a little nervous. I started doing some research and found an article in the *Journal of Dental Hygiene* website where, to my surprise, I found that up to eighty percent of Americans have an inordinate fear of the dentist—so much so that at least twenty percent don't go for regular visits and nine to fifteen percent avoid getting known and needed care and going altogether.[49] A light bulb went off because I know that clients transfer their fears and emotions onto their pets. If people are afraid of the dentist and they also fear anesthesia, veterinary teams have a lot to overcome to gain a "yes" for a dental cleaning.

We need to prepare a better story to overcome those intense objections. What would be powerful enough to move you to overcome your personal fear of the dentist?

Start by asking a good question. "Mrs. Smith, I understand that you are concerned about Fluffy's oral exam and cleaning. If I told you that we were looking for broken and damaged teeth, infection and pus in the gums, and cancer of the mouth, would you feel it important for us to do that?

I think it is important that we realize we need some reframing of our education to clients. People use stories to rationalize what they perceive to be going on. Our clients are sometimes deceiving themselves when they tell us false stories. They justify their poor decisions with an attack on our fees. They accuse us of only caring about money. Keep your cool ... it is only the Child fighting with the Parent.

Review what story you are telling yourself. Analyze your feelings. What story is the client telling themselves? Diagnose the situation and act accordingly. In the words of Steven Covey, "Seek first to understand, then to be understood."[50] We have two ears and one mouth for a reason. Listen more than you talk. Answer questions with simple answers then ask more questions to confirm understanding. **Lead your clients to discover why your patient care solves a problem.** Control your own negative emotions.

We must be better at this. Our patients' well-being depends on it.

EXERCISE: What reasons have clients given you to refuse your offered services? What language could you change to better overcome this objection?

16

Partnership and Collaboration: Meet Your Clients Where They Are

Hospitality requires that we shape our systems to accommodate the wishes and needs of our clients. When practices don't invest in modern technology tools that allow their clients to communicate easily with the practice, they are intentionally causing roadblocks to access to care.

As a frequent traveler, I can say that without my hotel, rental car, and airline apps, I would not only be inconvenienced but also aggravated if I had to attempt to book rooms, cars, or flights with a phone call. With a few clicks of a mouse, I can look at my accommodations, find a car that suits my needs, and compare flights. Recently, I visited a veterinary hospital with my new dog, Tucker. I called to make his appointment and had a nice customer service experience. I received an email notifying me to download the vet hospital's app, which I did. A few weeks later, I received a voicemail reminding me of Tucker's appointment and noting that, to confirm this event, I had to call the practice, which I did. Upon entering the clinic, I was given a clipboard with new patient and client paperwork to complete and then was called back to visit the doctor. Tucker had his visit, and there was some poor communication, so when I rated the practice, I gave it an average review. The practice manager called me to discuss my rating and my experience. I explained that I was a little irritated that I couldn't confirm my appointment online and that I didn't have the option of completing my new client paperwork digitally. I felt that this was an indication that the practice was behind the times. Of course, I eventually found out that I could have performed both functions in the app, but the person who called me never offered that option. She had been saying "call us to confirm" for so many years that she didn't change her spiel to include "or confirm in the app." The point of the story is that if you plan to offer the latest conveniences to your clients, make sure you tell clients that you have them.

> **If you plan to offer the latest conveniences to your clients, make sure you tell clients that you have them.**

Technology tools are a double-edged sword. In one aspect, they can save teams a lot of time by automating tasks and processes that humans used to do, freeing up many minutes or even hours in a day. On the opposite side, they can make communication impersonal. If we plan to take advantage of automation, we should use the valuable time we gain to connect on a human level with our clients. We should never lose sight of the importance of building relationships with others.

That being said, there are many studies that show that younger generations desire to use digital tools to make their own appointments, confirm those appointments, send text messages to the team or doctor, receive text messages on health status, fill out forms, view diagnostic results, share immunization history with other providers, request medication refills, and even use telehealth to triage health issues with themselves or their pet before heading to the ER. To serve this tech savvy generation well, we must embrace technology. However, we must never exclude older generations who do not live in a digital world. We must not ignore or discount them; rather, we should make sure our communication efforts cover all the avenues necessary to serve our clients well.

> **Practices cannot assume that everyone they care for is online.**

Seniors make up a large segment of our database. All must be considered when we are sending out important information such as reminders for services, medication and product recalls, and health alerts about contagious diseases.

Technology tools give practices the opportunity to educate people about health conditions so they can be informed about how to help themselves or their pets. Many studies share that when people receive written information in a language they can understand, which supports the instructions or education they receive from their provider, they are more likely to follow-through on care. People in exam rooms are often distracted and upset. Sharing information they can reference later helps them remember their instructions.

Many years ago, my practice took the time to create written take-home instructions for almost every procedure we performed. The documents were tied to service codes, and when the invoices were printed out for the client, the instructions were automatically printed, too. In today's world, we can attach web links to video instructions showing how to administer medications. This would certainly save time for the team because clients often go home and then call back to get the directions again because they either forgot or were not a hundred percent comfortable with what they remembered.

Successful providers are forward thinkers. Using tech to connect is a great way to save time while still providing personalized service.

EXERCISE: Consider the technology that you have in your practice. How can you improve service to your clients through this tool? What gaps in service need to be filled?

Conclusion

Proof That Hospitality Works in Healthcare

Let's face it—providing great hospitality to clients requires effort. The question is, is it worth it? A recent Harvard Business Review article titled "When Patient Experience and Employee Engagement Both Improve, Hospitals' Ratings and Profits Climb" found a distinct correlation between patient satisfaction scores and employee engagement, where high marks in both translated to a direct increase in profits.[51] In another article, "How U.S. Health Care Got Safer by Focusing on the Patient Experience," the authors shared the following: "My colleagues and I have analyzed data on patient experience as well as publicly reported data on patient safety and business performance. We have found that these performance 'outcomes' are correlated—that is, the organizations with better patient experience also have better safety records and report better financial margins."[52] These are just a couple of the many articles and data points that show that improving culture and creating a great patient experience in a medical facility can result in a happier team, happier consumers, and higher profits.

If we want to solve the many issues in medicine, we must move towards a hospitality mindset—not just for our patients but also with our coworkers. Collaboration, as humans evolved to do, is the path toward better job satisfaction. When teams work together with a common goal, in kindness and harmony, they can accomplish great feats of healing. Leaders must realize that dictatorial orders from above and driving medical professionals for profit alone only demotivates and causes anguish in their subordinates. Instead of working to create a positive culture and outstanding client experience, employees who have leaders that are harsh and uncaring have to mentally "gird their loins" just to walk in the door. They keep their heads down and hope for the best. It is no wonder that they are leaving the profession in droves.[53] However, if practices can embrace the rules of true hospitality and care for their clients and their team members as the valuable and important people that they are, they can see high employee retention, extraordinary client satisfaction, and a bottom line that is the envy of their competitors.

> **Great hospitality can create a practice that everyone wants to come to, everyone wants to work at, and everyone wants to buy.**

Humans are born to help each other. It is how we survived for eons and how we thrive today. Our brains are wired to experience joy when we give joy to others. I once listened to a keynote address by Michael J. Fox at a veterinary conference. It just so happened that because of his advanced Parkinson's disease, he had stumbled up the stage steps. He righted himself and made his way to the podium where I noticed his hands were scraped and bleeding. He never wavered but instead gave his speech. I will always remember when he said, "If you ever feel bad or sorry for yourself, go do something for someone else. I guarantee you will feel better!" He is right.

So, I challenge you to work to change the world around you for the better by using the lessons from this book. Each of us has the opportunity to share random acts of kindness many times a day. We need to make a point to do so. If we do, our work and homes will be more enjoyable places to be. Always assume positive intent and give grace to others. Then, watch the positive results roll in.

Appendices

Exam Room – Time and Motion Study

The idea behind the Time and Motion Study is to track, with accuracy, the actual time it takes to work with a client and patient, from the time they enter the practice until checkout. It is only when we measure that we truly know how to efficiently use our appointment schedule to its maximum benefit.

It will be easier to calculate the times if you use military hours, e.g., 2:00 p.m. is 14:00 hours. You may choose to highlight the species in different colors of highlighter to easily sort them at the end of the day.

This will be a team effort. Check after each other to confirm you have tracked the times. Do the calculations frequently and during downtime or it will be too overwhelming. Track for at least two weeks to give a good, well-rounded view of "normal" time frames. There will always be the surprise chatty client, but we are seeking averages.

> **TIP:** You may want to invest in some inexpensive clip-on timers for your rooms. These can act as a stopwatch in case you lose track of the time on the clock.

At the end of the testing and tracking period, sort the study cards into species and "type" of appointment. You may also sort them again by provider to see if certain doctors are faster or slower than others. The appointment book is a tool that can be sharply tuned with the right information.

EXAM ROOM – TIME AND MOTION STUDY

Date _____

Customer care representative _____

Species: CA   FE   Other _____

If sick, describe illness: _____

_____

_____

DVM _____ Tech _____

Appointment time _____

Arrival time _____ Time into room _____

DVM time into room _____ DVM time out _____

Tech time into room _____ Tech time out _____

CSR time of checkout

Type of visit (check one):

☐ Annual Vax

☐ Pup/Kit 1st

☐ Pup/Kit Series

☐ Senior Annual

☐ Sick Patient

☐ Behavior

☐ Derm

☐ Medical Discharge

☐ Oral Exam

☐ Nutrition

☐ Anal Exp

☐ Nail Trim (Normal)

☐ Nail Trim (Difficult)

Total wait time to get in room

Total time in room

Onboarding Plan

Here is a three-phase plan developed for onboarding new team members.

PHASE I

After Hiring and Before Start Date

1. If an employee has to relocate to your area, assist the new hire with information about the area. You might send articles of interest from the local newspaper—especially if clients are mentioned. This will give the new employee a grounding in the local market.

2. Refer the employee to a local real estate agent—preferably a client—to assist in housing procurement.

3. Provide a list of good schools, areas of town to avoid that have high crime rates, good restaurants for both dine-in and delivery, reputable auto repair shops, and the locations of local grocery stores.

4. Discover their hobbies and assist them in locating suppliers or locations to pursue them (for example, a runner needs a safe running track to use).

5. Find out if they have children. Can you recommend safe day-care centers or babysitters?

For Everyone Hired

6. Send a list of staff member names, staff positions and experience levels, and other relevant information on "day one" so that the new employee can recognize at least some of the names. This will make your new employee feel as if they know someone other than their interviewer and also shows your staff members that they are important as team members. Adding photographs is even better.

7. Have uniforms or lab coats ordered and ready for day one and have business cards and name tags ready if appropriate.

8. Mail a copy of the job description to allow it to be read thoroughly and learned before the first day on the job.

9. Mail a copy of the floor plan (especially if it's a larger facility) so the new team member may orient themselves to the building.

10. Have a workspace prepared. For example, if the new employee needs a desk, have it ready and in place before they come to work.

11. Choose a trainer and discuss with them their duties in training the new employee. Make sure that the trainer is a person you would like your new employee to emulate and that they have both the interest and the social skills to do the job.

12. Choose a mentor. The duty of the mentor is to help the new person understand the dynamics of the people in the practice. They are different from the trainer because they are the go-to person if there is a problem with the trainer or other staff members. They are there to help the person assimilate into the culture.

13. "Presell" your new employee to the clients and the staff. This is especially important for new veterinarians or physicians who often have problems getting established clients to work with them. Tout their skills, education, special interests, and experience to all that will listen.

PHASE II

First Day

1. Day one should be a celebration. Invite the family of the new employee to visit and meet coworkers.

2. Place a banner in the lobby introducing and welcoming your new hire.

3. Introduce them to their mentor and trainer.

4. Make sure the mentor is free to greet the new employee and introduce them to all the staff.

5. Give the employee an orientation tour of the hospital. Show them their work area, office, or desk.

6. Allow the employee time to fill out all standard tax forms, give them a copy of the employee manual, and have them sign that they received it. Have them sign all internal policies and store them in their employee file. Verify and record identification information. Complete all paperwork pertaining to benefits. Confirm with the employee their understanding of important policies: benefits, payroll information, vacation policy, etc.

7. Have the mentor explain the history of the practice, any partnerships or sister practices, if appropriate, and the dynamic of the group.

8. Give the employee the list of common questions (provided in the next section).

9. Explain the pattern of the flow of work.

10. Review goals for the day. For example, a new doctor will review all drugs in the pharmacy to familiarize herself with resources, or a new technician will shadow an experienced technician to learn exam-room procedures for a vaccination visit.

11. Show the location of safety equipment (e.g., fire extinguishers, eye-wash stations, protective clothing, etc.).

12. Set goals for the week. For example, a new office manager will interview all employees and discuss job descriptions.

13. Plan time for the end of week one to review the week, confirm that goals were met, and confirm with the employee that the trainer and mentor are providing them with education and feedback in a constructive manner.

PHASE III

1. Set longer-term goals, weekly and then monthly, for new employees.

2. Plan time to review goals and results with the employee, offering suggestions for improvement or encouragement for progress.

3. Create an action plan for advanced training, with timelines and reviews.

4. Reiterate the goals of the practice and confirm that the new hire understands the practice goals, mission, and core values.

5. Ask for feedback from the employee on company protocols. Remember that a fresh set of eyes often reveals areas needing improvement.

Common Questions We Should Answer for Our New Hires

- What is my schedule?
- Who is my supervisor?
- What do I wear?
- Where do I park?
- Where is the restroom?
- Where is the break room?
- Where are the office supplies? Who do I ask if I need something?
- Who orders medical supplies?

- Who orders office supplies?

- Where do soiled towels go?

- Where are fresh towels and blankets stored?

- What is the internet policy?

- What is my email address?

- What is the mailing address of the hospital?

- What are the telephone numbers?

- How does the intercom work?

- How does the phone system work?

- How do I retrieve voicemail messages?

- What diets do we recommend?

- What parasite preventatives do we recommend?

- What are our vaccination protocols?

- What are our requirements for pre-anesthetic lab work?

- Where do we send "outside" lab samples?

- What is our computer software system, and how can I learn the program?

- Who handles "upset" clients?

- When will I get my first paycheck?

- Who do I speak to if I have a problem with a fellow worker?

- How do I get continuing education?

- When do we have meetings, and are they mandatory?

- What is the procedure for bringing my pet to be treated?

- What is the payment policy for employees' animals?

- When am I allowed breaks?

- When am I allowed to make personal phone calls?

- What is the employee warning and discharge policy?

- Where are the required Department of Labor posters posted?

- How do I record my time?

- What do I do if I make a mistake on my timecard?

- What do I do if I break or spill a controlled drug?

- Where do I record controlled drugs?

- Who do I tell if equipment is broken?

- Who do I tell if I witness an employee stealing?

- What do I do if I see my supervisor or the owner make a mistake?

- What do I do if a patient "has an accident" on the floor?

- What do I do if I suspect that a patient is contagious?

- What do I do if there is an aggressive animal in the lobby?

- Who do I tell if there is a problem with the practice facility, e.g., a stopped-up toilet?

- What is the procedure for an emergency?

- What is the procedure for a fire in the building?

- What is the protocol for a sick animal whose owner has no funds?

- What is our credit card policy, and what types of payment to we accept?

- Who repairs computer problems?

- What is our procedure for patient euthanasia?

- What are our requirements for medication refills?

- Who will review my job performance, and when will my first review be given?

- What are common medical problems specific to our area?

- What unique services do we offer our patients?

- What unique services do our competitors offer their patients that we don't?

- What medical problems do we refer to specialty hospitals?

- Do any members of our staff have special skills that can be marketed to clients?

- What products do we sell for dental care?

- Who are our "frequent flyer" clients?

- What species of animals do we treat?

- How many times do we walk boarding dogs per day?

- What do we feed boarding animals?

- Do any employees have issues, medical challenges, allergies, or problems that I should be aware of? (Make sure to not disclose medical history, but you don't want the new hire to accidentally make an inappropriate remark because they don't know something that everyone else knows.)

This list is certainly not every question that a new team member will need to know, and, yes, some of them should be answered in the employee manual, provided that it is up to date. All practices are different, and you are advised to add questions to the list for future use. Still, this list will certainly help a new person orient themselves to the practice and help them avoid awkward and potentially embarrassing situations.

The Steps of Successful Delegation

1. Look at the task itself. Is it something that can be delegated?

2. Choose the staff member to perform the task, checking to see if they have the knowledge, skills, and interest in the task. Will they learn from the task? Will you gain from the delegation?

3. Will you give them, or do they have, the tools needed to perform the task? Do they understand what to do? Will you need to do some training?

4. Tell them why this task is important, necessary, and useful.

5. What is the desired end result? Don't assume that they know. How will you measure or determine completion?

6. Discuss what resources will be needed.

7. Both the manager and staff members must agree to the timeline. For ongoing tasks, when will management review progress? Deadlines are important.

8. Share the delegation with the rest of the team so they can support their coworker as well as understand why this person's job duties have changed.

9. Give feedback! Give credit! Don't abandon them if the task did not go as planned. Use the failure as a training lesson.

Finally, be kind. Team members have a great desire to feel SAFE in their work and home environments. When they are demeaned or threatened with job loss, they can't perform to the best of their abilities.

Core Values

Use this list as a foundation for creating your own facility's core values.

Performance – Our team will manifest outstanding performance by always following through on our work. When we see a job to be done, we will step up and complete it. To support great performance, we will work to show appreciation to one another for work well done.

Adaptable – Veterinary medicine is often unpredictable and ever changing. To serve our clients and patients, we will gladly learn new skills and share our skills with one another. We will help one another when faced with difficult patients or clients by offering to trade off. We will also agree to "laugh more and cry less" when our days throw us curveballs, always reacting with humor rather than drama.

Professional – We will work on self-mastery by controlling our minds and emotions and not allowing others to draw us to a negative place. We will always be willing to ask questions and disclose when we don't know an answer. We will maintain a professional image that is caring, nonjudgmental, and empathetic. We will act to read others' emotional states and communicate in an appropriate manner to help them.

Informative – We recognize that we are teachers and that our job is to educate our clients by meeting them at their knowledge level. We will also assume positive intent in our interactions with others.

Efficient – In order to maximize our efficiency, we recognize that our environment must remain neat, clean, and well organized, and we are committed to sustaining high standards in these areas. Standard operating procedures will be created and followed. Lists will be built to keep us from missing important duties, and labels will be used so that every item has its place. By doing so, we can serve our patients, their owners, and one another in the most timely manner.

Integrity – We agree that our greatest asset is our personal integrity. Because of this, we will always be open to giving and receiving feedback without taking offense. Our behavior will be respectful, honest, and ethical. We will only recommend care that is needed for our patients, and we will find a way to care for patients in crisis if at all possible. We will be on time for work and will make our best effort while working, as this shows respect for our employer and for one another.

By agreeing to live these core values, we will create and maintain a culture of joy, trust, and kindness. Our practice will be successful because of the exceptional care that we offer our clients and patients. Our team will enjoy a work environment that is the envy of other hospitals, and we will be known as a practice of excellence in our community.

Welcome Letter Example

Use this letter as a foundation for creating your own personalized letter that's sent from your practice to your new patients.

Dear [title] [first name] [last name],

The staff of The Animal Hospital would like to take a moment to thank you for choosing our hospital for your pet's care. We feel privileged to be able to provide veterinary and pet resort services for [animal's name]. Our goal is to offer superior medical care at a great value, an immaculate state-of-the-art facility for our patients' and clients' comfort, and exceptional customer service.

Our hours are Monday from 7:00 a.m. to 8:00 p.m.; Tuesday, Wednesday, and Thursday from 7:00 a.m. to 7:00 p.m.; Friday from 7:00 a.m. to 6:00 p.m.; and Saturday from 8:00 a.m. to 2:00 p.m. Please visit our website at [web address] to learn more about our team and visit our online pharmacy. We are happy to offer in-home delivery for all your pet's needs. Our Pet Resort & Spa also offers a medically supervised, full-service boarding facility with playtime, day care, and luxury suites furnished with webcams, TVs, and luxury bedding, along with spa services for the truly spoiled pet.

We have an outstanding and dedicated team of doctors, pet nurses, client care representatives, and resort staff to help partner with you to take the best possible care of your animal family member. We offer many advanced medical services, including an extensive array of surgical procedures, dentistry with digital radiology, hospitalization, and wellness care. Our facility is equipped with digital radiology, a complete in-house diagnostic laboratory, blood-pressure monitoring, ultrasound, a video otoscope, a laser surgery unit, and glaucoma screening. All this means that we can get results rapidly and treat patients without waiting when time is of the essence. We know that clients want to take great care of their pets, so client education and communication is a top priority.

Our doctors are focused on keeping your pet healthy. In keeping with the American Veterinary Medical Association and American Animal Hospital Association guidelines, we recommend a nose-to-tail physical examination twice a year. Pets age at a much faster rate than people, so a visit every six months is the equivalent of a child visiting their doctor every three years! Many times, with thorough physical exams and screening blood work, pets can be saved from months of unnecessary illness and suffering. Often, problems can be resolved with a simple change in diet.

We know that quality veterinary care is what our clients want for their pets, but costs can be challenging; so we offer multiple payment options which include all major credit cards (Visa, MasterCard, American Express, and Discover) and CareCredit®, a health and pet care credit card. Clients can apply for CareCredit® in our office, online at www.carecredit.com/apply, or by calling 1-866-893-7864. CareCredit® offers promotional financing options on purchases of $200 or more. We also strongly encourage you to investigate and purchase pet insurance as a safety net for the unexpected issues that often arise.

Once again, we thank you for allowing us to care for your pets. Please do not hesitate to call our office with questions or suggestions. We look forward to serving you and your animal family members for many years to come.

Sincerely,

The Doctors and Staff of The Animal Hospital

Notes

1 John Medina, "The Proust Effect" in *Brain Rules*, 212-214.

2 John Medina, "Principles for Surviving and Thriving at Work, Home, and School" in *Brain Rules,* 12, 84-87.

3 Daphne Maurer and Philip Salapatek, "Developmental Changes in the Scanning of Faces by Young Infants," *Child Development*, June 1976, vol. 47, no. 2, 523-527.

4 "Be Prepared for an Active Shooter," Federal Emergency Management Agency website, accessed May 2, 2023, https://community.fema.gov/ProtectiveActions/s/article/Active-Shooter.

5 Paul Ekman, "Facial Expressions" in Tim Dalgleish and Mick J. Power (eds.), *Handbook of Cognition and Emotion,* 301-320.

6 "Even Small Distractions Derail Productivity," Association for Psychological Science website, accessed May 2, 2023, https://www.psychologicalscience.org/news/minds-business/even-small-distractions-derail-productivity.html.

7 Veterinary Social Work Resource List, accessed May 2, 2023, http://vetsocialwork.utk.edu/wp-content/uploads/2018/04/Pet-Loss-Resource-Listupdated-April-2018-.pdf.

8 The Lifeline and 988, 988 Suicide & Crisis Hotline website, accessed May 2, 2023, https://988lifeline.org/current-events/the-lifeline-and-988.

9 Suicide Prevention and Mental Health seminar offering, American Veterinary Medical Association website, accessed May 2, 2023, https://axon.avma.org/local/catalog/view/product.php?productid=148.

10 Suicide Prevention Guide to Treat At-Risk Patients, American Medical Association website, accessed May 2, 2023, https://www.ama-assn.org/delivering-care/public-health/suicide-prevention-guide-treat-risk-patients.

11 Animal Charities & Helpful Financing Ideas for Pet Owners with Sick Pets, Debbie Boone website, accessed May 2, 2023, https://debbieboonecvpm.com/help-for-pet-owners.

12 Cynthia L. Ogden, Ph.D.; Cheryl D. Fryar, M.S.P.H.; Margaret D. Carroll, M.S.P.H.; and Katherine M. Flegal, Ph.D., "Mean Body Weight, Height, and Body Mass Index, United States 1960-2002," Division of Health and Nutrition Examination Surveys, U.S. Department of Health and Human Services, Centers for Disease Control and Prevention, accessed May 2, 2023, https://www.cdc.gov/nchs/data/ad/ad347.pdf.

13 Erik Lindecrantz, Madeleine Tjon, Pian Gi, and Stefano Zerbi, "Personalizing the Customer Experience: Driving Differentiation in Retail," McKinsey & Company website, accessed May 2, 2023, https://www.mckinsey.com/industries/retail/our-insights/personalizing-the-customer-experience-driving-differentiation-in-retail.

14 Will Guadara, "The Secret Ingredients of Great Hospitality," TED Talk, accessed May 2, 2023, https://www.ted.com/talks/will_guadara_the_secret_ingredients_of_great_hospitality.

15 Dealing With Difficult People. Pryor Training, accessed May 2, 2023, https://www.pryor.com/training-seminars/dealing-with-difficult-people.

16 Color Personality Test, accessed May 2, 2023, https://www.colorpersonalitytest.org.

17   The Myers-Briggs Foundation, accessed May 2, 2023, https://www.myersbriggs.org.

18   The Enneagram Institute, accessed May 2, 2023, https://www.enneagraminstitute.com.

19   Theodore B. Kinni, *Be Our Guest: Perfecting the Art of Customer Service,* (New York: Disney Editions, 2001).

20   Core Values List, James Clear website, accessed May 2, 2023, https://jamesclear.com/core-values.

21   Tom Wujec, "Got a Wicked Problem? First, Tell Me How You Make Toast," TED Talk, accessed June 2, 2023, https://www.ted.com/talks/tom_wujec_got_a_wicked_problem_first_tell_me_how_you_make_toast

22   Sophia Yin, *Low Stress Handling Restraint and Behavior Modification of Dogs & Cats: Techniques for Developing Patients Who Love Their Visits*, (Davis, CA, CattleDog Publishing, 2009).

23   Fear Free® website, accessed May 2, 2023, https://fearfreepets.com.

24   Iatrophobia (Fear of Doctors), Cleveland Clinic website, accessed May 2, 2023, https://my.clevelandclinic.org/health/diseases/22191-iatrophobia-fear-of-doctors.

25   Food Insecurity in the US, Key Statistics & Graphs, United States Department of Agriculture website, accessed May 2, 2023, https://www.ers.usda.gov/topics/food-nutrition-assistance/food-security-in-the-u-s/key-statistics-graphics/#insecure.

26   Biases in Healthcare: An Overview, *Medical News Today*, accessed May 2, 2023, https://www.medicalnewstoday.com/articles/biases-in-healthcare.

27   Project Implicit, accessed May 2, 2023, https://implicit.harvard.edu/implicit/education.html.

28   Janice A. Sabin, PhD, MSW, "Tackling Implicit Bias in Health Care" in *The New England Journal of Medicine,* July 14, 2022, vol. 387, 105-107, accessed May 2, 2023, https://www.nejm.org/doi/full/10.1056/NEJMp2201180.

29   FitzGerald, Chloë and Samia Hurst, "Implicit Bias in Healthcare Professionals: A Systematic Review," *BMC Medical Ethics,* March 1, 2017, vol. 18, no. 19, accessed May 2, 2023, https://bmcmedethics.biomedcentral.com/articles/10.1186/s12910-017-0179-8.

30   Janice A. Sabin, PhD, MSW, "Tackling Implicit Bias in Health Care" in *The New England Journal of Medicine,* July 14, 2022, vol. 387, 105-107, accessed May 2, 2023, https://www.nejm.org/doi/full/10.1056/NEJMp2201180.

31   Sai Balasubramaniam, MD, JD. August 26, 2022, "The Healthcare Industry is Crumbling Due to Staffing Shortages" in *Forbes*, accessed May 2, 2023, https://www.forbes.com/sites/saibala/2022/08/26/the-healthcare-industry-is-crumbling-due-to-staffing-shortages.

32   Tasha Eurich, *Insight: The Surprising Truth About How Others See Us, How We See Ourselves, and Why the Answers Matter More Than We Think*, (New York: Currency Penguin Random House, 2018).

33   Christine Pearson and Christine Porath, *The Cost of Bad Behavior: How Incivility Is Damaging Your Business and What to Do About It*, (New York: Portfolio Penguin Random House, 2009).

34   Pearson and Porath, *The Cost of Bad Behavior*, 1-2.

35   Pearson and Porath, *The Cost of Bad Behavior*.

36   Roy Mauer. March 3, 2015, "FBI: Over 80 Percent of Active Shooter Incidents Occur at Work,"
      Society for Human Resource Management website, accessed May 2, 2023, https://www.shrm.org/
      ResourcesAndTools/hr-topics/risk-management/Pages/FBI-Active-Shooter-Work.aspx.

37   Travis Bradberry and Jean Greaves, *Emotional Intelligence 2.0,* (San Diego, CA: TalentSmart, 2009).

38   John Medina, *Brain Rules: 12 Principles for Surviving and Thriving at Work, Home and School*, (Seattle:
      Pear Press, 2008), 40-42.

39   John Medina, *Brain Rules*, 183-188.

40   Christine Pearson and Christine Porath, 2009, *The Cost of Bad Behavior: How Incivility Is Damaging
      Your Business and What to Do About It*, New York: Portfolio (Penguin Random House), 73.

41   Emma Seppälä and Kim Cameron, December 1, 2015, "Proof That Positive Work Cultures are More
      Productive" in *Harvard Business Review,* accessed May 2, 2023, https://hbr.org/2015/12/proof-that-
      positive-work-cultures-are-more-productive.

42   Joseph Greeny, Ron McMillan, Al Switzler, Kerry Patterson, and Laura Roppe, *Crucial Conversations:
      Tools for Talking When Stakes Are High*, (New York: McGraw Hill, 2002).

43   Travis Bradberry and Jean Greaves, *Emotional Intelligence 2.0,* (San Diego, CA: TalentSmart, 2009).

44   The Gottman Institute, accessed May 2, 2023, https://www.gottman.com.

45   Lifetime of Care Study, Synchrony, accessed May 2, 2023, http://petlifetimeofcare.com.

46   VHMA Strategic Pricing Pet Owner Economic Value Study, Veterinary Hospital Managers Association
      website, accessed May 2, 2023, https://members.vhma.org/store/ViewProduct.aspx?id=14901966.

47   Daniel Kahneman, *Thinking Fast and Slow,* (New York: Farrar, Straus, and Giroux, 2013).

48   David Mattson, *The Sandler Rules: 49 Timeless Selling Principles and How to Apply Them,*
      (Beverly Hills, CA: Pegasus Media World, 2009).

49   Angela M. White, Lori Giblin, and Linda D. Boyd, February 2017, "The Prevalence of Dental Anxiety in
      Dental Practice Settings" in American Dental Hygienists' Association's *Journal of Dental Hygiene,* vol.
      91, no. 1, 30-34.

50   Stephen Covey, *The 7 Habits of Highly Effective People: Powerful Lessons in Personal Change*,
      (New York: Simon & Schuster, 1989).

51   Nell W. Buhlman and Thomas H. Lee, May 8, 2019, "When Patient Experience and Employee
      Engagement Both Improve, Hospitals' Ratings and Profits Climb" in *Harvard Business Review,* accessed
      May 2, 2023, https://hbr.org/2019/05/when-patient-experience-and-employee-engagement-both-
      improve-hospitals-ratings-and-profits-climb.

52   Thomas H. Lee, May 31, 2017, "How U.S. Health Care Got Safer by Focusing on the Patient Experience,"
      in *Harvard Business Review,* accessed May 2, 2023, https://hbr.org/2017/05/how-u-s-health-care-got-
      safer-by-focusing-on-the-patient-experience.

53   Ed Yong, November 16, 2021, "Why Health-Care Workers are Quitting in Droves," in *The Atlantic,*
      accessed May 2, 2023, https://www.theatlantic.com/health/archive/2021/11/the-mass-exodus-of-
      americas-health-care-workers/620713.

US Army Small Unit Tactics
Handbook

US Army Small Unit Tactics Handbook

Paul D. LeFavor

Blacksmith Publishing

Fayetteville, North Carolina

For our fallen comrades, you are not forgotten.

US Army Small Unit Tactics Handbook
2020 Revision

by Paul D. LeFavor

Copyright © 2015 by Blacksmith LLC

ISBN 978-0-9977434-1-8

Printed in the United States of America

Published by Blacksmith LLC
Fayetteville, North Carolina

www.BlacksmithPublishing.com

Direct inquiries and/or orders to the above web address.

Contents

Foreword

"We are opposed around the world by a monolithic and ruthless conspiracy that relies primarily on covert means for expanding its sphere of influence–on infiltration instead of invasion, on subversion–instead of elections, on intimidation instead of free choice, on guerrillas by night instead of armies by day–the dimensions of its threat have loomed large on the horizon for many years. Whatever our hopes may be for the future–for reducing this threat or living with it–there is no escaping either the gravity or the totality of its challenge to our survival and to our security–a challenge that confronts us in unaccustomed ways in every sphere of human activity."
– John F. Kennedy, 1961

President John F. Kennedy spoke these words six months before meeting with Brigadier General William P. Yarborough at Fort Bragg, North Carolina and tasking him and his Special Operators to meet this "old, but new form of operations" *on behalf of the United States and the free world.* This meeting was followed by an un-paralleled expansion of Special Forces that would see "Green Berets" deployed to an even greater number of countries and in greater strength across the globe–from Europe to Asia, throughout Central and South America and into the continent of Africa. Now, over half a century later, we find ourselves faced with the same historic recurrence. The need for an expanded, highly proficient, and keenly skilled Special Operations Force is again superseded by the "old, but new" threats that we face.

I've had the privilege of serving the Nation that I love for over three decades as a Soldier, Non-commissioned Officer, and Civil Servant–executing over twelve years of that service overseas. I've had the honor of leading men and women in military operations ranging from Peacetime Engagement to War in over thirty-seven countries, across five Continents, and six Geographic Combatant Commands. I've had the good fortune to serve alongside some truly phenomenal men of legend in two Ranger Battalions and four Special Forces Groups; culminating my career at the Joint Task Force, Sub-Unified Command, and Functional Combatant Command levels.

I've been blessed to live the history of US Special Operations in microcosm; from the Iranian Hostage Rescue Mission, to the DMZ in Korea, the Invasion of Panama, Task Force Ranger in Mogadishu, and operations in Haiti, Bosnia-Herzegovina and Iraq. I've seen the depths of man's inhumanity, the dire plight of the oppressed, and the exceptionalism of the indomitable American Spirit. I've learned and re-learned some hard lessons and lost some very good friends. I've seen our force become frayed at the edges, from over a decade of continuous combat.

But it is at this point in our history that we are required to re-double our efforts; to rise above a society possessed by individual comfort and fill the need for self-less service and sacrifice in what will prove to be a very long, generational struggle. We must seek God for guidance and solace; look to our families, leaders, and Team mates for strength; and study our legends and legacy to help us prepare for the struggle of our generation.

The legacy of the Special Forces is profound. It's filled with lessons where many stood against few and prevailed despite incredible odds; where an indomitable warrior spirit was combined with disciplined use of terrain, weapon and wit to carry the day. These lessons were recorded for us–and many apply to the "old, but new" threats we face today. For example, MAJ Robert Rogers "Standing Orders" are made more lethal by leveraging the advances in technology, firepower, kit, communications, and mobility to fit our current circumstances…but they still apply.

And that's why I like this book! This book provides not only a collective endowment of over sixty years of tactical lessons learned, but a further practical methodology in regards to the planning and execution of small unit tactics – the cornerstone of every successful Special Operation. This book is a timely whetstone, and warrants my strongest recommendation for your professional development. May you use it to hone your skills for the fight of our lives! If we fail–we may well doom parts of the world to generations of darkness and oppression.

Strength and Honor – CSM Richard "Rick" Lamb

Preface

"A mind without instruction can no more bear fruit than a field, however fertile, without cultivation." – Cicero

We tend to study all our disciplines in unrelated parallels. To alleviate this disparity, this handbook is intended as a conceptual overview of all relevant topics of small unit tactics every Special Forces soldier ought to be familiar with in order to be effective on today's battlefield. It seeks to define the course of study for the sound development of Special Forces soldiers so as to avoid the Scylla of mere academia and the Charybdis of pure pragmatism, and to preserve the heritage, lineage, and legacy of the United States of America's most often misunderstood and unsung heroes, the fighting men of Special Forces.

This handbook is categorized into five functional areas: history, doctrine, planning, operations, and common skills. In order to highlight the development of key doctrines, as well as mistakes to avoid, the object lesson throughout being both theoretical and practical; the handbook begins with history, thereby accentuating the why of planning and operations. "Fools say they learn by experience. I prefer to profit by others' experience." This expression attributed to Otto Von Bismarck, highlights an especially important truth in the study of war, namely, learning from history, especially the failures of others. Professional soldiers have always placed a high premium on it, for it yields the laurels of victory. In this respect, part one covers a short history of the development and implementation of Special Forces, from its historic progenitors: Rogers' Rangers, the First Special Service Force (FSSF), and the Office of Strategic Services (OSS), to the warfighting exploits of their progeny, the modern Special Forces Regiment.

Part Two, doctrine, begins with a theory of war and moving on to foundational principles, it seeks to cover in broad terms the levels of war from strategic to tactical with an emphasis on the tactical application of the principles. Building upon an introductory discussion on these ground floor principles, the chapter proceeds to introduce the nine principle tasks which Special Forces units perform: Unconventional Warfare, Foreign Internal Defense, Security Force Assistance, Counterinsurgency, Special Reconnaissance, Direct Action, Combating Terrorism, Counter-proliferation, and Information Operations.[1]

Parts three and four, covering planning and operations, seeks to bridge theory and practice by laying the foundational truths relevant for

---

[1] FM 3-18, 2-4. These missions make Special Forces unique in the U.S. military, because they are employed throughout the three stages of the operational continuum: peacetime, conflict, and war.

understanding the chasm between doctrine and execution. This section of the handbook seeks to provide the basics of small unit tactics (SUT), as everything from organizing a patrol to the execution of raids, ambushes, and reconnaissance patrols are discussed. This section along with part five, common tasks, will provide all pertinent information necessary to assist the Special Forces soldier as he navigates his way through all pertinent Army field manuals (FMs), graphic training aids (GTAs), including the Ranger Handbook. The desired end state is for this systematic arrangement of knowledge to serve as an institutional rudder for the Special Forces Community and the SUT Phase of the Special Forces Qualification Course.

According to visionaries like Aaron Bank, Russell Volckmann, and Robert McClure, Special Forces would carry on the legacy of the Office of Strategic Services (OSS) by conducting raids, sabotage, and guerilla warfare behind enemy lines. The "Quiet Professionals," Special Forces, are deployed worldwide displaying their dominance in full spectrum operations through their unconventional warfare expertise. From humanitarian assistance and training of indigenous forces, to direct action and special reconnaissance missions, Special Forces soldiers live up to the Special Forces motto: De Oppresso Liber, to Free the Oppressed.

In preparing this book I have been overwhelmed by the generous scale of assistance and inspiration I have received. My friends and fellow SUT instructors have graced me with sound advice and technical expertise which collectively amounts to hundreds of years of tactical experience, without which this book would amount to irrelevant drivel. I would like to take this opportunity to thank everyone who has been involved in the process, especially: Mike Blackburn, Steve Pumphrey, Ron Berryhill, Mark Ballas, JD Cobler, George Natvig, Dan Schewe, Jay Smith, Shane Ladd, John Butler, Troy Petersen, Steve Grewell, Tim Brown, George Marshall, Brandon Riel, Charles Tilton II, Tim Phelan, Tim Parker, Brad Ingram, Adam Watkins, Dustin Washam, Dave Stone, Joshua Bogart, Michael Hatfield, Kenny Young, Tim Kemp, Rick Lamb, Terry Peters, Jay Pope and Robert Webb. I am extremely grateful to all of the above for all their help.

Moreover, as any one who has ever taught knows, you learn a lot when you teach. I am therefore further indebted to my SUT students, both past and present, who not only gave this book its *raison d'etre*, but corporately served to shape its scope and sharpen its focus by providing me with invaluable insights, searching questions, and feedback. Thanks to all.

Paul D. LeFavor
Camp Mackall, NC
Christmas 2018

Special Forces Creed

I am an American Special Forces soldier. A professional! [3]

I will do all that my nation requires of me. I am a volunteer, knowing well the hazards of my profession.

I serve with the memory of those who have gone before me: Roger's Rangers, Francis Marion, Mosby's Rangers, the First Special Service Force and Ranger Battalions of World War II, The Airborne Ranger Companies of Korea. I pledge to uphold the honor and integrity of all I am - in all I do.

I am a professional soldier. I will teach and fight wherever my nation requires. I will strive always, to excel in every art and artifice of war.

I know that I will be called upon to perform tasks in isolation, far from familiar faces and voices, with the help and guidance of my God I will conquer my fears and succeed.

I will keep my mind and body clean, alert and strong, for this is my debt to those who depend upon me.

I will not fail those with whom I serve. I will not bring shame upon myself or the Forces.

I will maintain myself, my arms, and my equipment in an immaculate state as befits a Special Forces soldier.

My goal is to succeed in any mission - and live to succeed again.

I am a member of my nation's chosen soldiery. God grant that I may not be found wanting, that I will not fail this sacred trust.

De Oppresso Liber

---

[3] Special Forces Creed of 1961.

Ranger Creed

Recognizing that I volunteered as a Ranger, fully knowing the hazards of my chosen profession, I will always endeavor to uphold the prestige, honor, and high esprit de corps of the Rangers. [4]

Acknowledging the fact that a Ranger is a more elite soldier who arrives at the cutting edge of battle by land, sea, or air, I accept the fact that as a Ranger my country expects me to move further, faster and fight harder than any other soldier.

Never shall I fail my comrades. I will always keep myself mentally alert, physically strong and morally straight and I will shoulder more than my share of the task whatever it may be, one-hundred-percent and then some.

Gallantly will I show the world that I am a specially selected and well-trained soldier. My courtesy to superior officers, neatness of dress and care of equipment shall set the example for others to follow.

Energetically will I meet the enemies of my country. I shall defeat them on the field of battle for I am better trained and will fight with all my might. Surrender is not a Ranger word. I will never leave a fallen comrade to fall into the hands of the enemy and under no circumstances will I ever embarrass my country.

Readily will I display the intestinal fortitude required to fight on to the Ranger objective and complete the mission though I be the lone survivor.

Rangers Lead the Way!

---

[4] The Ranger Creed was authored by CSM Neal R. Gentry, the CSM of 1st Ranger Battalion when it was reactivated in 1974. He also developed the Ranger Battalion Coat of Arms and Distinguished Unit Insignia. The Creed was further edited by the 1st Ranger Battalion XO Major Hudson, and was adopted by the Ranger Regiment.

A Soldier's Promise

The people of the United States expect me to be an Elite Warrior, capable of doing things with my hands and weapons better than anyone else in the world; I will not violate that trust. I will live by the Special Forces and Ranger Creeds, committing their words to my memory. Wherever I go I will make it apparent that I am the best.

I will learn the lineage and honors of Special Forces and be a proud contributor to that heritage. I will show disdain for those who have no respect for themselves, their detachments or Special Forces; they are not worthy of my respect, trust or friendship.

I will study the art of war, learning the lessons of those who fought before me. Combat application will dictate everything that I do. I will possess and nurture the soul and mind of a Warrior. I will be a master of my profession, the Profession of Arms.

I understand that those who do not know history are doomed to repeat it. And those who do not revere the warriors who sacrificed before them are condemned to live a life with no heart, no soul, no conscience, no honor, and no purpose.

I am prepared to die for my teammates and my unit. I will become a rock when my mates are weak; no one will stumble because I failed to motivate. I will fill with rage at the sound of battle, knowing that the selfless act of the individual soldier will always carry the day. I understand that all men die, but few men really live. I choose to make my life the stuff of legend.

In the shadow of every teammate lies a family. I understand that the counsel of a loved one is an aspect of warfare older than time itself. I will take care of my teammates and their families because our collective lives depend on it. I realize that caring means making times tough, because tough times will ensure survival. A hardship borne by one will be borne by all; trust in me will be sacred.

If I am unwilling to sacrifice, unable to commit to the principles and lifestyle befitting a professional soldier; I understand that I must leave. In doing so, I will join the masses of citizenry that depend on others to keep them free.

All this I swear to that which I hold sacred.

Strength and Honor – CSM Richard "Rick" Lamb

The Special Forces Prayer

Almighty GOD, Who art the Author of liberty and the Champion of the oppressed, hear our prayer.[5]

We, the men of Special Forces, acknowledge our dependence upon Thee in the preservation of human freedom.

Go with us as we seek to defend the defenseless and to free the enslaved.

May we ever remember that our nation, whose motto is "In God We Trust," expects that we shall acquit ourselves with honor, that we may never bring shame upon our faith, our families, or our fellow men.

Grant us wisdom from Thy mind, courage from Thine heart, strength from Thine arm, and protection by Thine hand.

It is for Thee that we do battle, and to Thee belongs the victor's crown.

For Thine is the kingdom, and the power and the glory, forever. AMEN

---

[5] The Special Forces Prayer was written in 1961 at the request of Major General William P. "Bill" Yarborough by Chaplain John Stevey, the 7th Special Forces Group (A) Chaplain.

Part One:
Special Forces History

Chapter 1
A Concise History of the Special Forces

"To be ignorant of what occurred before you were born is to remain always a child. For what is the worth of human life, unless it is woven into the life of our ancestors by the records of history?" – Cicero

If there's one thing we don't learn from history, it's we don't learn from history. Therefore, if the study of history is to be meaningful then it must be interpreted. Moreover, because proud soldiers form the backbone of any successful military organization, a unit history is therefore invaluable to instilling a strong sense of pride.[1] Likewise, as the ancient historian Polybius observed, "the most instructive method of learning, is to recall the catastrophes of others." Thus, a unit armed with a knowledge of itself, untrammeled with hagiographic drivel, and a wantonness to cover over its faults, fosters esprit de corps, and may, as it were, enable its progeny to stand, in a sense, upon the storied shoulders of their forebears, to see further afield, and draw from the annals of time matchless lessons, purchased with skill, determination, and self-sacrifice.

With that in mind, the intent of this study is to cover in broad terms the history of Special Forces from its historic progenitors and official inception, to the Global War on Terrorism (GWOT). The reader should understand that this is not intended as a comprehensive account of such a glorious subject, nor is it meant to be an operational history. Nevertheless, as a thumbnail sketch, this chapter seeks to convey to the student of war a conceptual overview of SF's historical roots, major campaigns and engagements. It is hoped that this short study will provide the reader with an enlightened perspective from which to assess the development of the First Special Forces Regiment (Airborne).

Special Forces can trace its origins by way of a *heritage*, a *lineage*, and a *legacy*. To begin with, Special Forces share a historical heritage with the 75th Ranger Regiment through storied elite units such as Rogers' Rangers. Additionally, Special Forces derives its lineage from the First Special Service Force (FSSF), which was a joint US – Canadian commando unit otherwise known as the 'Devil's Brigade.' Finally, the Special Forces Regiment follows the legacy of the Office of Strategic Services (OSS). For a graphic depiction of this line of thought, see Figure 1-1.

---

[1] Jessup and Coakley, A Guide to the Study and Use of Military History, 349.

Chapter 1   A Concise History of the Special Forces

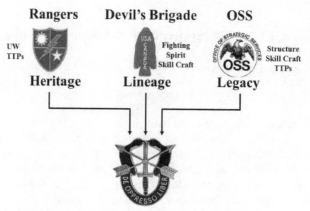

Figure 1-1. The Origins of the Special Forces Regiment.

Early Colonial Rangers

During the early Colonial days of America, the Colonists, without significant government support, successfully defended themselves against Indian attacks by organizing and employing Ranger companies. Benjamin Church (1639-1718), considered the father of American ranging, commanded the first Ranger force in America. Church was commissioned by Josiah Winslow, the Governor of Plymouth Colony, to organize, train, and lead the first Ranger Company during King Philip's War.[2]

Church sought men who were experienced in the woods and recruited both Native Americans and European settlers for his Ranger Company. Taking full advantage of the skills of both groups, Church prosecuted a successful war against King Philip (Metacomet) by conducting numerous ambushes and raids, culminating in Metacomet's death and an end of hostilities. Describing Church, Robert Black observes,

Benjamin Church was a towering figure on the early frontier. Like every other early American Ranger who wished to keep his hair, he learned to combine Indian tactics with European discipline and weaponry. Some eighty years before Robert Rogers wrote his ranging rules, Church was writing of the importance of not traveling the same route twice...he separated captives and questioned them individually...and attacked at night, with his men crawling on their bellies until close to the enemy. Church's lessons would serve the Rangers well in the years ahead.[3]

---

[2] King Philip's War (1675-1678) was an armed conflict between Native American inhabitants of present-day New England and English colonists and their Native American allies. The war was named after Metacomet, known to the English as "King Philip," the leader of the Native American belligerents.
[3] Black, Ranger Dawn, 21.

3

Church would later go on to lead his Rangers during the frontier wars which were fought between England and France. Church's Rangers became experts in reconnaissance and guerrilla warfare. Additionally, during King William's War (1688-1697), Church's Rangers developed a water-borne operations capability when John Gorham II of Massachusetts provided some fifty whaleboats which the Rangers used for infiltrations and coastal raids. The Gorham family had a long history of ranging with Benjamin Church. John Gorham I died while fighting alongside Church in the famous Great Swamp Fight of 1675. John Gorham II went on to range with Church during the expedition into Acadia (Canada), which involved the Raid on Chignecto in 1696 during King William's War, and in the summer of 1744, John Gorham III (1709-1751), took on the family mantle and began recruiting men for his own Ranger Company – Gorham's Rangers.

This company became one of the most famous and effective Ranger units raised in colonial North America. It served with distinction until it was disbanded in 1762. Like Church before him, Gorham recruited both Native American and European skilled frontiersmen. In the early days of Gorham's Rangers, the colonists learned guerrilla tactics from veteran Native American warriors, most of them being Wampanoag and Nauset Indians from Cape Cod. By acquiring these tactics, Gorham's Rangers could traverse great swaths of uncharted territory, strike deep into remote areas, and destroy the enemy with deadly ambushes and lightening raids.

When the French and Indian War erupted in 1754, Gorham's Rangers went on to play a prominent role under their new commander, Joseph Gorham (1725-1790), the brother of John Gorham III. Joseph had served as a lieutenant in his brother's company and was promoted to captain and took command after John's death in 1751. During the French and Indian War (1754-1763), Gorham's Rangers were highly prized guerrilla fighters who, in addition to their other exploits, prosecuted a successful counterinsurgency campaign against the Micmac Indians and rebel French Acadians. This led to the latter's expulsion from Nova Scotia. The success of Gorham's Rangers led to the creation of six additional ranger companies, one of which was Rogers' Rangers, led by Robert Rogers.

Rogers' Rangers

Of Scots-Irish descent, Robert Rogers (1731-1795) was born in the village of Methun in the Massachusetts Bay Colony. At the age of fourteen, he began to participate in scouting missions against the Indians, acquiring skills from experienced frontiersmen. In much the same way as Church and Gorham before him, Rogers took the initiative to organize, train and lead an elite guerrilla fighting force which became known as Rogers' Rangers.

Impressed with the Rangers' capabilities, Rogers' superiors authorized the augmentation of his company to include five more companies. Each Ranger company consisted of one captain, two lieutenants, one ensign, four sergeants, and one hundred privates. Rogers served as both the commandant and commander of his own company.

Rogers' patrols were not for the weak or fainthearted. On one such patrol, on 10 March, 1758, Rogers led a band of 184 Rangers and regulars out of Rogers' Island to scout French positions in the vicinity of Fort Carillon – Ticonderoga (Figure 1-2).

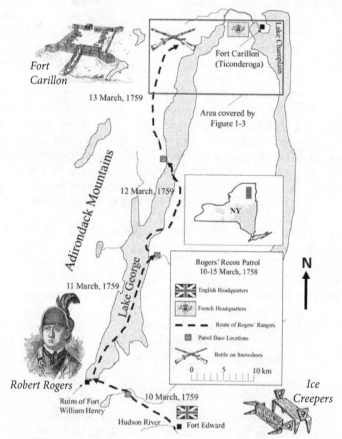

Figure 1-2. Rogers' Reconnaissance Patrol of 10-16 March, 1758

Rogers' force wore snow shoes and trudged through snow that at times was up to four feet deep. On the second day of the patrol, the Rangers marched passed the burnt out ruins of Fort William Henry, and then by wearing ice creepers on their feet, they proceeded north making their way across the frozen surface of the lake.

On the third day of the patrol (13 March), Rogers had his men don their snowshoes and proceed toward Fort Carillon along the west bank of Lake George. Early on 13 March, the French commander at Fort Carillon, Captain d'Hébécourt, having been alerted to the English movement, sent Ensign Durantaye with 100 men (a mixed force of Indians and Canadian marines) to intercept Rogers. Later, d'Hébécourt sent out a larger force of some 200-300 Indians under Ensign de Langy in support.[4] By 1500 hours on 13 March, Rogers' force had approached to within three miles of Fort Carillon when his scouts reported an enemy patrol of about 100 men (Durantaye's force) advancing up the frozen Trout Brook near his position (Figure 1-3).

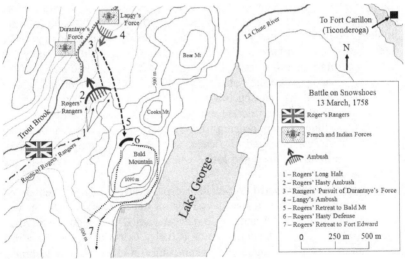

Figure 1-3. Battle on Snowshoes 13 March, 1758

Rogers immediately directed his men to drop packs, and taking up an ambush position, directed his men to stretch out their line along the high ground just opposite of the brook. Unbeknownst to Rogers, about 100 meters behind Durantaye was Langy's force in trail. Lying in wait, Rogers allowed the enemy force to advance until "their front was nearly opposite our left-wing," then, discharging his musket, he unleashed an eruption of murderous fire which, according to him, mowed down forty or so Indians.[5]

---

[4] According to Rogers this force was about 600 in strength.
[5] Rogers, Journals of Major Robert Rogers, 96.

Durantaye's force broke and retreated in disarray. Those who tried to escape were cut down with tomahawks and knives as Rogers and about half his men gave chase, scalping another forty. Rogers recounts, "I now imagined the enemy totally defeated and ordered a pursuit that none may escape, but we soon found our mistake."[6] And having failed to reload their muskets, Rogers' force ran straight into Langy's men, who alerted by the gunfire, set up their own ambush which produced equally devastating results; nearly decimating the Rangers.

Countering the French attack, Rogers ordered his remaining Rangers to fall back toward the high ground. There the remnants of his force fought on tenaciously as they continued to retreat up Bald Mountain. For over an hour the Rangers managed to keep themselves from being encircled. During this retreat, Rogers reportedly lost another 40 of his men. Describing the melee, Robert Black writes, "The Rangers fought a desperate delaying action, fighting from behind snow-covered rocks and trees. Clouds of powder smoke rolled over the battlefield as men screamed, cursed, and died. The fighting was hand-to-hand with the late afternoon sun glinting along the honed edge of tomahawks until the cold metal shine was dulled by blood."[7]

As the French pressed their attack, they drove the Rangers up the face of Bald Mountain. It was during this time, Rogers' tells us, that he lost an additional 108 men.[8] With darkness rapidly approaching, and his numbers quickly dwindling, Rogers ordered his Rangers to break contact in order to avoid capture. Few managed to escape, and when one group surrendered, they were promptly scalped and killed when a scalp was discovered in one of their pockets.

Undaunted, Rogers narrowly avoided capture and rallied his remaining men, reaching Fort Edward two days later on the night of 15 March with about twenty half-starved and frostbitten survivors. Although Rogers had critics, he had powerful supporters – namely, General Howe, who had recently replaced Lord Loudoun as commander-in-chief. Howe celebrated Rogers' courage, promoted him to major, and gave him funds and leave to recruit more Rangers.

St. Francis Raid

"Of all the episodes embraced within Rogers' checkered career," writes Stephen Brumwell, "none gained him greater fame than his 1759 raid upon the Abenaki village of St. Francis."[9] Following the capture of Fort Carillon,

---

[6] Rogers, Journals of Major Robert Rogers, 97.
[7] Black, Ranger Dawn, 66.
[8] Rogers, Journals of Major Robert Rogers, 98.
[9] Brumwell, White Devil, 14.

Rogers' was ordered to attack St. Francis in the fall of 1759. This attack was ordered for two main reasons: First, Amherst, the new commander-in-chief, had sent out an earlier patrol which was undertaken by Captain Kennedy, whose purpose it was to seduce the Abenaki away from the French. However, Kennedy, along with others, were taken prisoner and thought most likely to have been tortured. Second, the village of St. Francis had long been a known staging point for many of the war parties that had devastated the English Colonists. Rogers had been preaching this truth for years, and had petitioned for the destruction of St. Francis.[10]

Amherst's orders for Rogers' on 13 September, 1759 were as follows:

You are this night to join the detachment of two hundred men which was yesterday ordered out and proceeded to Missisquoi Bay. From thence you will proceed to attack the enemy's settlements on the south side of the St. Lawrence, in such a manner as shall effectually discharge and injure the enemy and redound to the success and honor of his majesty's arms. Remember the barbarities committed by the enemy's Indian scoundrels on every occasion where they have had opportunities of showing their infamous cruelties toward his majesty's subjects. Take your revenge, but remember that, although the villains have promiscuously murdered women and children of all ages, it is my order that no women or children are to be killed or hurt. When you have performed this service, you will again join the army wherever it may be.[11]

Rogers departed Crown Point on the night of 13 September with 200 men. The force consisted of 132 Rangers with the rest being made up of volunteers from line regiments. The raid patrol, occupying seventeen whaleboats, rowed north on Lake Champlain and reached Missisquoi Bay early on 23 September (See Figure 1-4). Enroute, Rogers had to send some 40 men back to Crown Point who became injured or sick. Once at Missisquoi Bay, Rogers concealed the boats, cached supplies for their return trip and left two Indian Rangers as guards.

Unfortunately for Rogers, the next day a large party of some 400 French, coincidentally led by Oliver de la Durantaye, who had battled Rogers in 1758, discovered the boats. Capturing some of the boats, Durantaye destroyed the rest and set up an ambush in the event Rogers would return the same route. Two days later, the Indian Rangers caught up with the force and brought Rogers the bad news, including the fact that an enemy force of about 200 men were now in pursuit.

---

[10] Loescher, The History of Rogers' Rangers, Vol 4, The St. Francis Raid, 3.
[11] Memoir and Official Correspondence of General John Stark, 448.

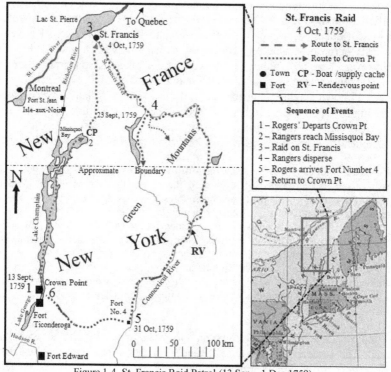

Figure 1-4. St. Francis Raid Patrol (13 Sep – 1 Dec 1759).

At this point, Rogers convened a council of war. His two main concerns were: first, the French would undoubtedly conclude that they were bound for St. Francis in response for Kennedy's capture; and second the French would most likely expect them to return the same route. Although behind enemy lines and far from any support, Rogers' decided to continue the mission. To make his new plan work, Rogers' sent a seven man team back to Crown Point, instructing them to cache supplies at the confluence of the Ammonoosuc and Connecticut rivers; about 100 kilometers north of Fort Number 4. Following the raid, Rogers would return to Crown Point via the Connecticut River and Fort Number 4 where he would utilize the cached stores.

After slogging through waterlogged forests for a week, Rogers' remaining 142 Rangers arrived in the vicinity of St. Francis on the twenty-second day of the patrol, with their rations completely exhausted. Earlier they had crossed their last obstacle, the St. Francis River, which was fast moving with a mean depth of five feet. That night, at 2000 hours (3 Oct, 1759), Rogers, accompanied by Lt Turner and Ensign Avery, conducted his leaders' reconnaissance of the town. Rogers' reconnaissance identified over sixty buildings, most of which were log cabins while a few were stone. The buildings were formed in an orderly square with the Jesuit mission in the center. The most telling detail of all was the 600 scalps, which were no doubt mainly English.[12] These hanging from various poles throughout the town, seemed to cry out for the coming vengeance.

Rogers returned around to the main body around 0200 on 4 October, brought his men forward to within 500 meters of the town, dropped packs and prepared for the assault.[13] At about 0500 hours the attack began. The raid achieved complete surprise as the Ranger force fell on the slumbering town. St. Francis scarcely put up a defense as Rogers' men shot, or tomahawked people where they lay. Amherst's order to avoid killing women and children was lost in the frenzy as Rogers was unable to restrain his men. Those who tried to escape were promptly shot down by sentries Rogers had posted outside the village.

As the sun was rising, Rogers consigned St. Francis to the flame, sparing only the storehouses for sustenance. As the houses burned, they became death traps for those who had attempted to escape the carnage by hiding in their attics. The church too was burned, but not before it was ransacked for its more valuable trappings and at least one priest refused quarter and perished in the flames.[14] By 0700 hours, the town of St. Francis was destroyed. The aftermath, according to Rogers, was 200 Indians were killed, twenty woman and children prisoners (fifteen were released), and five rescued English hostages. Rogers' force suffered only one killed and six wounded.[15] After gathering what corn from the storehouses they could carry, Rogers and his men began the 300 kilometer return trip through uncharted wilderness.

The journey to Crown Point soon turned into a nightmarish struggle for survival. The French were hot in pursuit and since Rogers had not originally planned to use this route, no caches had been emplaced along the way. Food supplies quickly ran out, and Rogers had to break up his starving force into foraging parties, which put them at risk of being overwhelmed by larger French forces. French pursuers eventually killed or captured more than 40 Rangers.

Most disconcerting of all was the fact that the man whom Amherst had dispatched to rendezvous (RV) with Rogers' force and deliver the needed supplies, Lt Stephens, departed the RV a scant two hours before Rogers

---

[12] Rogers, Journals of Major Robert Rogers, 147.
[13] Ibid, 141.
[14] Brumwell, White Devil, 198.
[15] Rogers, Journals of Major Robert Rogers, 141.

arrived; having waited only two days.[16] Undaunted, Rogers and three of his men, moved on ahead of their small party, and constructing a small raft out of trees and vines, reached Fort No. 4 on 31 October, and on 2 November started back with supplies to rescue the others. By 7 November, Rogers was able to send Amherst a report of the mission, and on 1 December, Rogers' exhausted raid patrol straggled back into Crown Point, bearing their prisoners, repatriated Colonists and loot.

Although the Rangers lost 45 men during the raid, Amherst and the colonial British population considered the attack a huge success, and Rogers' Rangers were celebrated as the heroes who struck an unprecedented blow against their French and Indians foes. Rogers' Rangers went on to serve with distinction until the end of the French and Indian war, at which time the unit was disbanded. At its peak of service, Rogers' Rangers swelled to a force of 1400 elite light infantry.

The Ranger Corps was the preeminent reconnaissance, ambush and raid asset to the British during the Colonial Era. Rogers' Rangers went on to serve with distinction until the end of the French and Indian war, at which time the unit was disbanded. At its peak of service, Rogers' Rangers swelled to a force of 1400 elite light infantry.

Perhaps most practical of all would be the codification of Major Rogers' patrolling experiences. His 28 Rules of Ranging and Standing Orders, encapsulate the essence of frontier unconventional warfare methodology and stand today as a practical guide for patrolling (See Annex B).

As we continue to review the salient points of our historical heritage, we would be remiss without surmising the major contributions the Ranger tradition has made upon the special operations community. Foremost is the tactical art of ranging that was devised by combining European light infantry skills and Native American unconventional warfare tactics.

Such skills include: scouting, long-range reconnaissance, tracking and counter-tracking, caching, camouflage, and foraging, not to mention the fighting skills of the tomahawk and knife, and of course the deadly ambush and the ability to strike distant targets of strategic value in lightning fast raids. These skillsets, along with the accompanying high esprit de corps and warrior spirit, constitute the shared inheritance of both the 75th Ranger Regiment and the 1st Special Forces Regiment.

---

[16] Rogers adds, "Finding a fresh fire burning in his camp, I fired guns to bring him back, which guns he heard, but would not turn back, supposing we were the enemy." Additionally, Rogers informs us that this Lt Stephens was later court marshalled for this act of negligence.

The Swamp Fox

As we shall discuss further, guerrilla warfare is a form of irregular warfare in which small groups of, predominately indigenous combatants, use military tactics, such as those we have described earlier, to harass larger and less-mobile traditional forces in enemy-held territory.[17] Francis Marion (1732-1795), one of the most distinguished patriots and heroes of the American Revolution, fought a successful guerrilla war or insurgency in South Carolina against the British.[18]

Disastrous American defeats at Charleston and Camden in the summer of 1780, led many to give up the fight for independence, but Marion kept the war alive by defeating Loyalist troops, and harassing the British with a measure of success that was disproportionate to the size of his partisan force.[19] Marion's elusive disappearances after surprise attacks earned for him the nom de guerre, "Swamp Fox."

Following the fall of Charleston to the British on 12 May, 1780, Marion became a fugitive, and upon hearing the news of a new American army gathering in North Carolina, he made his way there with about twenty men to offer his services. Major General Gates had recently assumed command of the remaining Continental forces in the South near Ramseur (North Carolina) on the Deep River. While at the camp of Gates, the residents of the Williamsburg District (Marion's home) rose against the British and sent Marion a message asking him to take command (See Figure 1-5). Marion who was renowned for his leadership capability, had earlier been commissioned a Lieutenant Colonel in the South Carolina Militia, and had extensive frontier fighting experience. He readily accepted.

Major General Gates was planning to move on Camden, the main inland British base, and with Marion's partisans he hoped to sever the British line of communications with Charleston. Gates' intent was for Marion to frustrate British efforts to reinforce Camden and likewise prevent a retreat once Gates defeated them. When Marion returned to the Williamsburg District of South Carolina he assumed command of four companies of partisans. Marion's militia consisted mainly of farmers and slaves from the surrounding countryside. For want of war supplies, Marion's men provided their own weapons, mounts and food. Additionally, because Marion

---

[17] For more on guerrilla warfare see chapter 4: Special Forces Doctrine.

[18] An Insurgency is an organized movement aimed at the overthrow of a constituted government or occupying power through the use of subversion and armed conflict. For more on insurgency see Chapter 4.

[19] A partisan is a member of an irregular military force which is formed to oppose, through insurgent activity, an army of occupation's control of an area.

couldn't pay his men, he allowed them to join the militia and leave freely at any time at their own discretion.

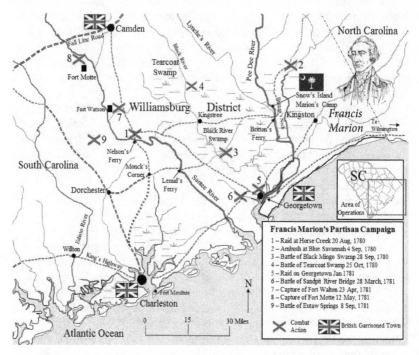

Figure 1-5. Francis Marion's Partisan Campaign.

Meeting Gates' intent, Marion moved at once to cut the British line of communications between Charleston and Camden. After moving a good ways inland along the upper Santee, on 16 August Marion received the shocking news that Gates had been annihilated by Lord Cornwallis near Camden. Half of Gates' 3,000 men were either killed, wounded or taken prisoner; the remainder fled to North Carolina. His confidence unshaken, Marion recognized that being astride the enemy's line of communications might still present an opportunity.

On his second day of command, Marion received word that 150 American prisoners were being held on a plantation near Horse Creek, just north of Nelson's Ferry. On the morning of 20 August, Marion's partisans surprised the detachment of British regulars guarding the Continentals. Surprise was complete as Marion's force of 52 men killed or captured 24 of the enemy while suffering only two casualties and liberating the prisoners. However, believing the war to be lost, only three of the repatriated soldiers joined Marion.

It was at this time that the Loyalists, also known as Tories (those who supported the British), began to move out in force to suppress the Patriots and attempt to establish a base in the Williamsburg District. Two weeks after his success at Horse Creek, Marion's force rode after a Tory militia under the command of Major Ganey on Britton's Neck. On the morning of 4 August, Marion set out for Ganey and met him head-on. Being outnumbered 50 to 250, Marion feigned retreat, and using himself as bait, lured the Tories after him into an ambush at a piece of ground known as the Blue Savannah. After being ambushed by Marion, and suffering an estimated 30-50 killed or wounded, Ganey's militia no longer existed as an effective fighting force.[20]

Bolstering the Patriot cause as well as raising the ire of the British, Marion's victory at Blue Savannah led to sixty plus volunteers, and prompted Lord Cornwallis to dispatch some 800 British and Loyalist troops to hunt him down. Although Marion was daring and aggressive, he was careful with the lives of men, and therefore wisely released them to return to their homes while he quietly slipped into North Carolina's Great White Marsh. British and Tory vengeance was served cold, but it served to solidify the Patriot cause. Then on 28 September, following the withdrawal of Cornwallis' force, Marion's partisans converged on and defeated another Tory militia at Black Mingo Creek. Following this engagement, Tory activity in the low-country fizzled, the Patriot cause rose, and Marion was promoted to brigadier general.

Making full use of his intimate knowledge of low-country riverine systems, for more than two years Marion's Militia attacked enemy columns, captured outposts, and even fought alongside Continentals in the pitched battle of Eutaw Springs. His resilience and efforts against British and Loyalist forces proved instrumental to Patriot morale. Using tactics honed while fighting the Cherokee, Marion combined Continental Army modes of fighting with Native American unconventional warfare tactics to lead a highly effective guerrilla war. According to Scott Aiken, Marion's standard tactic was: "swift movement to the objective area, an assault with more than one maneuver unit, and a rapid withdrawal."[21]

As one of the fathers of modern guerrilla warfare, along with Thomas Sumter and Andrew Pickens, Marion learned from the Native American to use the terrain to his advantage and repeatedly defeated larger and better-equipped forces with few losses. For nearly two years, General Marion proved himself a master at conducting partisan warfare. This was primarily

---

[20] Moore, The Life and Times of Gen. Francis Marion, 65.
[21] Aiken, The Swamp Fox: Lessons in Leadership from the Partisan Campaigns of Francis Marion, 118.

due to his ability to use tactics that suited the political situation, the terrain, the capabilities of his men, and the vulnerability of his enemies.[22]

General Nathaniel Greene, who replaced Gates, and witnessed the eventual collapse of the British strategy in the South, spoke of General Marion in glowing terms: "He lived without fear and died without reproach." And in a letter to Marion he wrote, "To fight the enemy bravely with the prospect of victory is nothing, but to fight with intrepidity under the constant impression of defeat, and to inspire irregular troops to do it, is a talent peculiar to yourself."

As far as a contribution to our historical heritage goes, what more could we want? As Marion, and those like him: Sumter and Pickens rightly deserve some credit for American independence. Due to guerrilla bands like Marion's partisans, not only were the British never able to secure South Carolina, but their entire Southern offensive was thwarted. And how significant was Marion's impact on the War of Independence? Well, if we bear in mind that it was due to setbacks in Carolina in the first place that led Cornwallis to attack Virginia, a decision which ended in his surrender at Yorktown, I'd say compelling. Additionally, Marion's courage, leadership and tactics offer us much to be studied and emulated.

Mosby's Rangers

During the Civil War (1861-1865), John Singleton Mosby and his regiment of partisans, known as Mosby's Rangers, were renowned as one of the most feared and successful guerrilla fighting units in the history of warfare. Mosby's Rangers regularly engaged much larger forces in ambushes and lightening raids deep behind enemy lines, and rode away victorious. Colonel John Singleton Mosby formed the 43[d] Battalion of Virginia Cavalry, a regimental-sized unit of partisan Rangers in January 1863.

Mosby was born in Powhatan County, Virginia, on December 6, 1833. Brought up near Charlottesville, Mosby entered the University of Virginia in 1849. While there he was charged with shooting another student and sentenced to prison. While in prison he befriended his prosecutor, began to study law, and became a lawyer in Bristol following his release. Like many idealists, at the outbreak of the Civil War, Mosby opposed succession (and slavery), but felt it was his patriotic duty to defend his home state of Virginia.

While serving in J.E.B. Stuart's cavalry, "Jeb" was keen to notice Mosby's talents as a leader, horsemen, and tactician. And in January 1863,

---

[22] Ibid, 28.

with the approval of General Lee, gave him a small command of nine men to "defend the good people of Virginia." When the Partisan Ranger Act of 1862 was repealed by the Confederate Congress, Lee had Mosby commissioned a captain. Before long, Mosby's small nucleus of men grew to eight companies, and at the height of Mosby's command, nearly 2000 men had rode with him at some point.

Lee and Stuart's intent for Mosby's partisan force was to keep Lee's Army of Northern Virginia informed of enemy movements, and harass the Federals as much as possible. Mosby was thus empowered to devastate the Union supply lines and depots – to wreak havoc. In his *War Reminiscences* Mosby recounts:

My purpose was to weaken the armies invading Virginia by harassing their rear. As a line is only as strong at its weakest point, it was necessary to be stronger than I was at every point in order to resist my attacks. To destroy supply trains, to break up the means of conveying intelligence, and thus isolating an army from its base, as well as its different corps from each other, to confuse their plans by capturing dispatches, are the objects of partisan war. It is just as legitimate to fight the enemy in the rear as in front. The only difference is the danger. Now, to prevent all these things from being done, heavy detachments must be made to guard against them. The military value of a partisan's work is not measured by the amount of property destroyed, or the number of men killed or captured, but by the number he keeps watching (on the defense). Every soldier withdrawn from the front to guard the rear of an army is so much taken from its fighting strength.[23]

Beginning in January, 1863, Stuart dispatched Mosby and 15 Rangers to conduct operations against the Union forces that were occupying Northern Virginia. On January 28, Mosby set off on his first raid against Federals in Chantilly. The following month, Mosby raided Fairfax County two more times, getting the better of larger Federal forces each time. In response to the raids, Colonel Wyndham dispatched 200 troopers of the 18th Pennsylvanian Cavalry under Major Joseph Gilmore to capture Mosby and his men. In the town of Middleburg, the Union force searched local residences, arrested citizens, and even threatened to burn the town in an attempt to smoke out Mosby's men. With no joy Gilmore departed for Fairfax, but no sooner had the Federals left the town did Mosby assemble his men and give chase. And they met up with the Union raiders at Aldie in Loudon County on March 2, 1863 (See Figure 1-6).

Almost without exception, the men who joined Mosby were exceptional horsemen and all became, or were already, deadly with the Colt .44 cal

---

[23] Mosby, War Reminiscences, 43-44.

pistol, the preferred weapon of the Rangers.[24] As the Rangers closed the distance, and finding the Federal cavalry dismounted and without security, with a bold curdling Rebel yell they charged. And in the sharp firefight that ensued, 19 Federal troopers and 28 horses were captured with only one Ranger casualty. This action demonstrated the fighting prowess of Mosby's Rangers in their ability to conduct surprise attacks against numerically superior forces sustaining few casualties while leaving the enemy with a good many empty saddles.

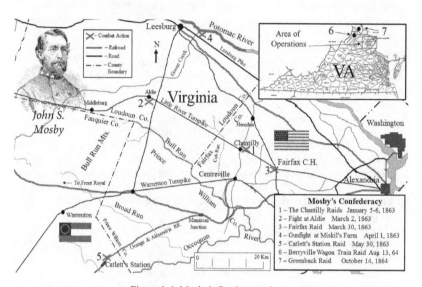

Figure 1-6. Mosby's Partisan Actions.

Mosby depended on surprise and knew how to make the most of foul weather. On one such night, Mosby embarked with 29 Rangers on his most daring and significant raid, the one on Fairfax Court House. Wyndham, a colonel of Vermont Cavalry, who had earlier dispatched the patrol to capture Mosby, had called Mosby nothing more than a horse thief. Mosby's plan was to teach Wyndham a lesson in proper etiquette.

Late on the afternoon of 8 March, 1863, Mosby led his 29 horsemen to Fairfax Court House; the objective – the capture of Colonel Wyndham. It was a daring feat. Mosby writes, "The safety of the enterprise lay in its novelty; nothing of the kind had been done before."[25] The Rangers departed

---

[24] The Federal cavalry fought with sabers until, as they quickly discovered, Mosby's Rangers didn't.
[25] Mosby, Memoirs, 172.

Dover, Virginia, two miles west of Aldie, and headed east down the Little River Turnpike toward Fairfax Court House. Mosby had ascertained where the gaps in the enemy picket lines were, and managed to slip into Fairfax County undetected, miles behind Union lines. Regarding the weather that night, Mosby recounts, "The weather conditions favored my success. There was a melting snow on the ground, a mist, and, about dark, a drizzling rain."

Arriving at Fairfax Court House just before midnight, Mosby designated the courthouse yard as the rendezvous point, cut the telegraph wires and dispatched Ames (who some time before had deserted the Union cavalry to join Mosby, and consequently knew where Wyndham was quartered) and a party to capture Wyndham. Fortune favored Wyndham that night as he was in Washington D.C. However, Ames was able to capture his old company commander Captain Barker. As squads were returning with prisoners and captured horses, one of them was discovered to be a guard at Brigadier General Stoughton's 2nd Vermont Brigade headquarters.

With about six men Mosby rode to the general's headquarters, dismounted and knocked loudly on the front door. Mosby recounts:

Soon a window above us opened, and someone asked who was there. I answered, "Fifth New York Cavalry with a dispatch for General Stoughton." The door opened and a staff officer, Lieutenant Prentiss, was before me. I took hold of his nightshirt, whispered my name in his ear, and told him to take me to General Stoughton's room. Resistance was useless, and he obeyed. A light was quickly struck, and on the bed we saw the general sleeping as soundly as the Turk when Marco Bozzaris woke him up. There was no time for ceremony, so I drew up the bedclothes, pulled up the general's shirt, and gave him a spank on his bare back side and told him to get up.[26]

Mosby then asked the general if he had ever heard of "Mosby." The general replied "yes, have you captured him?" And Mosby said, "I am Mosby." And desiring for Stoughton to give up quickly without trouble, Mosby said, "Stuart's cavalry has possession of the court house; be quick and dress." Mosby's men gathered at the RV with three times as many prisoners as Rangers. To deceive the enemy, Mosby led his cavalcade in several directions before making the risky trip back through the Union pickets. And without a shot fired, Mosby and his 29 Rangers had captured a Union general, two captains, along with 30 other prisoners (including an Austrian Baron), and 58 horses.

Mosby fought many such actions. He was especially adept at intelligence gathering, and causing a general state of mayhem for the Federals by attacking swiftly and disappearing into civilian crowds and evading capture by Union forces. Some of the key elements to Mosby's success were: (1) he

---

[26] Mosby, Memoirs, 175.

enjoyed the moral and logistical support of the populace (Northern Virginia); (2) his enemy was unable to guard everywhere; and (3) his speed and audacity with which he used his advanced tactics and weaponry. All of these key ingredients were later to be noted by T.E. Lawrence; one of Mosby's progeny.[27]

Known as the "Gray Ghost," Mosby had no camp, and used the friendly population of Virginia in a way that Mao would later describe as "a vast sea in which to drown the enemy."[28] Mosby's 'sea of Northern Virginia' allowed him to strike at the enemy and disappear like 'Children of the Mist.' His pursuers were striking at an invisible foe. Regarding the terrain of his operations, Mosby recounts:

While the country afforded an abundance of subsistence, it was open and scant of forests, with no natural defensive advantages for repelling hostile incursions. There was no such shelter there as Marion had in the swamps of the Pee Dee, to which he retreated. It was always my policy to avoid fighting at home as much as possible, for the plain reason that it would have encouraged an overwhelming force to come again, and that the services of my own command would have been neutralized by the force sent against it. On the contrary, it was safer for me, and greater results could be secured, by being the aggressor and striking the enemy at unguarded points. I could thus compel him to guard a hundred points, while I could select any one of them for attack.[29]

Thus, as one can readily observe, a study of Mosby's guerrilla tactics offers us much along the lines of a nineteenth century Virginian Swamp Fox. And by compelling his enemies to guard at ever point, he could attack the weakest point and be assured of relative superiority.[30] Mosby recounted, "I endeavored to compensate for my limited resources by stratagems, surprises, and night attacks, in which the advantage was generally on my side, notwithstanding the superior numbers we assailed."[31] Every day the newspapers spread the fame of Mosby's exploits. Trains were derailed, wagon trains ambushed, bridges were burned, camps were raided, and as John Munson writes, "Pickets disappeared as if swallowed by the earth, and stragglers from the Northern army were plucked from the landscape by invisible hands."[32]

---

[27] For more on T.E. Lawrence and his fundamentals of guerrilla warfare see chapter 4.
[28] Zhang, Mao's Military Romanticism, 13.
[29] Mosby, Mosby's War Reminiscences, 43.
[30] For more on *relative superiority* see Chapter 3: Mass.
[31] Mosby, Mosby's War Reminiscences, 79.
[32] Munson, Reminiscences of a Mosby Guerilla, 8.

Berryville and Greenback Raids

The largest group of Mosby's Rangers ever to operate together at one time were the 350 Rangers who took part in the Berryville Wagon Train raid on August 13, 1864. Just after dawn, Mosby and 350 Rangers attacked the rear column of Major General Sheridan's 600 vehicle wagon train at Berryville, Virginia. The wagon train, headed for Winchester, carried supplies for Sheridan's cavalry. At a halt for breakfast, Sheridan's troops were completely surprised by Mosby's Rangers who captured 200 soldiers, 200 beef cattle, 100 wagons, and around 600 horses. By sunrise, Mosby's Rangers rode off with the tremendous haul. With raids such as this, Mosby's Ranger partisans diverted thousands of Union troops, forcing the enemy to keep a large number on the defensive, materially reducing his offensive strength.

Arguably, Mosby's greatest piece of annoyance was the Greenback Raid, executed on October 14, 1864. Mosby's intent was to injure Sheridan by destroying a train and compelling him to divert more of his troops to guard the roads and RR line; thereby giving Lee less Federals to fight. On the evening of October 12, 1864, Mosby and 84 Rangers rode out from the vicinity of Middleburg, forded the Shenandoah River, and then headed west toward the Martinsburg-Winchester Turnpike.

After sundown, the Rangers rode toward the Baltimore & Ohio Railroad track. Sometime before midnight, they reached a patch of woods, left their horses with a few men, and walked about 300 meters to the tracks. The spot Mosby selected for the ambush was a deep cut about 300 meters west of Quincey Siding and a quarter of a mile from Duffield depot, so that the passengers might not sustain injury.[33] Here the Rangers set their typical ambush: with rear security, the main force overlooked the site while sentries were posted a few hundred meters on either side.

Just after midnight on 14 October, the westbound express locomotive pulling eight cars of assorted type approached. Just before it reached the ambush site, the Rangers displaced the rail and the engine ran off the track, the boiler burst, and the air was filled with red-hot steam and cinders. Pulling the passengers off the train, the Rangers discovered two payroll masters in Sheridan's army. The booty amounted to $173,000, with each raider receiving a $2000 share; though Mosby himself took nothing.

---

[33] Munson, Partisan Life with Colonel John S. Mosby, 335.

Chapter 1 A Concise History of the Special Forces

McNeil's Rangers

Contemporary to Mosby, yet less familiar, McNeil's Rangers conducted a remarkably similar and effective guerrilla war. With the permission of the Confederate Congress, Captain John McNeil formed E Company, 18th Virginia Cavalry (McNeil's Rangers) which ranged Northern Virginia and West Virginia from 1862 until the end of the war. Following numerous raids, ambushes, and skirmishes behind enemy lines, John McNeil was mortally wounded in action in October, 1864. His son Jesse assumed command, and in an action similar to Mosby's Fairfax raid, McNeill and 65 Rangers travelled 60 miles behind enemy lines to Cumberland, Maryland, and without detection, captured Generals George Crook and Benjamin Kelley from their beds on February 22, 1865. Returning to Virginia, they evaded pursuing Federal cavalry and delivered their precious cargo to the infamous Libby Prison in Richmond.

It is estimated that over 25,000 troops were diverted by Federal commanders to guard the B&O railroad against McNeill's Rangers. And just how effective was Mosby's Rangers to the overall Confederate war effort? It is difficult to evaluate. John Munson, one of Mosby's Rangers writes, "due to Mosby's comparatively tiny force it was necessary for the Federal troops to guard every wagon train, railroad bridge and camp with enough active and efficient men to prevent Mosby from using his three hundred raiders in one of his destructive rushes at any hour of the day or night. General Grant at one point reported that 17,000 of his men were engaged in keeping Mosby from attacking his weak points, and thus away from active service on the firing line. Finally it was not safe to send dispatches by a courier unless a regiment was sent along to guard him."[34]

Even if Mosby's operations made little effect on the outcome of the war, it made victory for the Union more costly. Mosby did more with less. In Lee's estimation, "Mosby was zealous, bold, and skillful, and with very small resources he had accomplished a great deal. By crippling Union movement and providing essential military intelligence, Mosby was therefore an indispensable asset to Lee's Army of Northern Virginia. Mosby endeavored "to diminish the aggressive power of the Army of the Potomac, by compelling it to keep a large force on the defensive."[35] Mosby wanted to use and consume the Northern cavalry in hard work. He adds, "For no human being knows how sweet sleep is but a soldier. I have often thought that their fierce hostility to me was more on account of the sleep I made them lose than the number we killed and captured."[36]

---

[34] Munson, Reminiscences of a Mosby Guerilla, 228.
[35] Mosby, War Reminiscences, 43.
[36] Ibid, 45.

Through the guerilla warfare expertise of leaders such as Marion and Mosby, the special operations community gains a rich heritage from which we may mine deeply, as they are significant to the study of modern special warfare. Having laid a foundational understanding of the shared inheritance of both the 75th Ranger Regiment and 1st Special Forces Regiment, we now move to discuss the further development of unconventional warfare fighting methods during the interval of time between the mid-19th century and the official inception of the 1st Special Forces Regiment. For that end, we now turn to consider the Filipino resistance movement against the Japanese during the Second World War.

Resistance Movement in the Philippines

The Philippine unconventional warfare (UW) campaign was one of the most successful of its kind in history. Following the Japanese invasion of the Philippines in December 1941, several Army officers, without orders or guidance, organized, trained, equipped, and commanded tens of thousands of guerrillas. Among these were Russell Volckmann, Donald Blackburn, and Wendell Fertig. Having this guerrilla capability, and countless contacts, together with an auxiliary force in place, General MacArthur and his staff, were able to galvanize a resistance movement among the Filipino people. The goal of this section of Special Forces history is to highlight several key leaders who were instrumental to the successful guerrilla war fought against the Japanese forces in the Philippines during WWII.

The Philippine archipelago, a chain of some 7,000 islands, sprawling across 1,000 miles of ocean, made it impossible for the Imperial Japanese forces to garrison any more than a few key towns and cities. This fact, together with the geography of the Philippines made it extremely difficult for the Japanese to interfere with the continued growth of the numerous, small guerrilla bands that sprung up on most of the main islands (Fig 1-7).

Likewise, for the resistance, though every island produced its own local forces, the topography presented a tremendous handicap to any effective unification of strength. Early on, lacking organization, these guerrilla bands exhausted themselves in uncoordinated actions. Summing up this situation, MacArthur's general staff writes:

These minor operations were generally fruitless and often did more harm than good since they brought swift and severe retaliatory measures by the Japanese. Even on the larger islands of Luzon, Mindanao, and Leyte, the terrain and poor communications caused a multiplicity of initially independent guerrilla commands to arise with intransigent leaders pursuing their own particular interests. A single driving force was badly needed to direct the guerrilla potential into channels which could produce maximum results. As soon as the facts concerning Filipino resistance became known in 1942, it was General MacArthur's purpose to provide this direction and to weld the scattered groups into unified and responsible forces through the designation and support of responsible local commanders.[37]

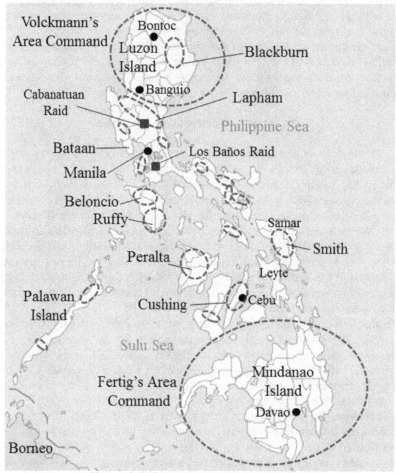

Figure 1-7. Resistance Movement in the Philippines.

While the guerrillas struggled to survive and build their organizations, their constant appeals for help had been reaching MacArthur's headquarters some 3,500 miles to the south in Australia. Before the war, as part of MacArthur's strategy for such a contingency, he established an underground

---

[37] The Campaigns of MacArthur in the Pacific, Volume 1, Chapter X, 298.

intelligence service among the numerous American businessmen, miners, and plantation owners on the islands and also contemplated the withdrawal of some Filipino reservists into the mountains to serve as guerrillas.[38] Beginning in July 1942, technicians began picking up radio transmissions from the islands of Luzon and Panay, confirming the existence of an incipient guerrilla movement. According to Colonel Whitney, "Probably no message ever gave MacArthur more of an uplift."[39]

Orchestrating the Philippine resistance movement from his headquarters in Australia, MacArthur's strategy was for the guerrilla forces to remain at a low level of harassment until they would be unleashed in support of his return. To organize the effective resistance potential of the Filipinos against Japan, General MacArthur created the Allied Intelligence Bureau (AIB), a joint US, British, Australian, and Dutch intelligence and special operations agency. It was formed in June 1942 to coordinate guerrilla, subversion, and propaganda organizations. The AIB conducted everything from coastal reconnaissance, and commando raids, to the smuggling of thousands of tons of weapons and supplies via submarine from remote bases in Australia.

Following the fall of Bataan, Army officers Russell Volckmann and Donald Blackburn, escaped to northern Luzon. Being greatly aided by Filipinos along the way, the two joined a guerrilla force under Army colonels Martin Moses and Arthur Noble. Like other early guerrilla commands, it spent itself in uncoordinated attacks on the Japanese, prompting swift retribution on both the guerrillas and local populace. After the capture and execution of Moses and Nobles, Volckmann assumed command and designated his Filipino-American guerrilla force the US Army Forces in the Philippines – Northern Luzon (USAFIP-NL). Its fighting strength in June 1943 was 2,000.

Volckmann, building up a strong intelligence network, funneled all information on Japanese movements to his headquarters in North Luzon, and conducted a remorseless counterespionage campaign, seeking collaborators and Japanese agents. Being conscious of public confidence and support, Volckmann brought rival tribes and factions together through personal diplomacy. Consolidating his forces, by the end of 1944, Volckmann's USAFIP-NL numbered some 10,000 men. It would encompass 22,000 Filipinos and Americans by the end of the war. Blackburn, later renowned for his significant role in Special Forces, was given command of the 11th Infantry Regiment under Volckmann. The 11th Regiment a.k.a. *Blackburn's Headhunters* numbered some 5,000 guerrillas by March of 1945. Also on the island of Luzon was Robert Lapham's force. Organized as the Luzon Guerrilla Armed Forces (LGAF), Lapham's

---

[38] Hogan, U.S. Army Special Operations in World War II, 65.
[39] Whitney, MacArthur: His Rendezvous with History, 128.

command consisted of some 13,000 guerrillas. It was Lapham, who, after the American liberation of the Philippines began, warned General Krueger of the impending massacre of prisoners at Cabanatuan POW camp.

From Australia, MacArthur and his staff organized some 270 guerrilla units under one command. No easy task. In preparation for America's return to the Philippines, MacArthur devised a UW strategy. MacArthur's general staff observes:

To guide the various guerrilla leaders in the prosecution of their operations and to make maximum use of their services in the war against Japan, General MacArthur directed that his agents follow a policy of general encouragement and careful instruction without direct command interference which might incur resentment. Guerrilla groups were advised to assist in maintaining civil order so that they might receive reciprocal popular support. They were also cautioned to refrain from open and aggressive warfare against Japanese troops lest they bring reprisals on the people out of all proportion to the results achieved. The collection, coordination, and transmission of useful intelligence were stressed as the most important, immediate contributions the guerrillas could make to the Allied cause until the actual invasion of the islands was begun. Before that time, all military operations were to be limited to strategic harassment, sabotage, and ambush.[40]

Hundreds of miles to the south, on Mindanao Island, Wendell Fertig, a reserve engineer officer, arrived as the Japanese were overrunning the island. Fertig was tasked with the demolition of main roads and bridges to prevent their use by the Japanese. Refusing to surrender, Fertig, along with others, such as, Charles Hedges, James Grinstead, and Frank McGhee, took to the hills of Mindanao. The collapse of the Philippine government created a vacuum which many of the emerging guerrilla forces at that time used as an opportunity to set themselves up as rulers of local areas. These rival guerrilla bands competed with each other for territory and authority. Some minority groups, such as the Hukbalahaps of central Luzon, in addition to ousting the Japanese, sought political reforms.[41] To meet this problem, MacArthur's staff reactivated the pre-war Philippine Military Districts. Based on population densities, these territorial entities had been used by the Philippine Army for administrative and mobilization purposes. This device had the advantage of being based on legal precedent and would probably be the most acceptable method of division to the majority of de facto guerrilla leaders.[42]

---

[40] The Campaigns of MacArthur in the Pacific, Volume 1, Chapter X, 304.
[41] Popularly known as *Huks*, the Communist Hukbalahaps began a rebellion against the Philippine Government in 1946. It was finally put down through a series of reforms and military victories.
[42] The Campaigns of MacArthur in the Pacific, Volume 1, Chapter X, 302.

In September of 1942, the leader of one strong group approached Fertig, hoping to use him as leverage to assume authority over the entire island of Mindanao. Fertig consented, but then used his knowledge of the Filipino people and the current situation to eventually take over the command of that group and then others.[43] In order to be taken seriously by potential recruits and rival guerrillas, Fertig promoted himself to brigadier general. This self-promotion did not endear him to General MacArthur. In fact, MacArthur made it a point to send Fertig full colonel rank insignia along with an accompanying commission.

One of Fertig's major hurdles, a critical shortage of supplies, was overcome by his engineering skills and the skills of other escaped Americans and resisting Filipinos. The Mindanao guerrillas created many supplies from scratch. For example, curtain rods were cut into pieces and shaped to provide ammunition for .30 caliber rifles, tuba (coconut palm sap) was brewed to provide alcohol to fuel gasoline vehicles, batteries were recharged by soaking them in tuba, and fencing wire was used to create a telegraph. Filipino fisherman, towing Japanese mines ashore, secured the explosive amatol to be used to make gunpowder.[44] Even money was printed (authorized by the government in exile) using wooden blocks.

Fertig, like many of his contemporary guerrilla commanders, depended highly on his American sergeants to train the guerrilla force. His force numbered some 33,000 men before war's end. With command of such a large force of guerrillas on Mindanao, Fertig consolidated his forces and wreaked havoc on the Japanese forces with raids and ambushes. At one point in the war, his operations were so successful, roughly 95 percent of the Island of Mindanao lay under guerrilla control. Whereas these operations sustained Fertig's force, it caused discord between him and MacArthur. In March 1943, an Allied submarine laden with much needed logistical and medical supplies, rendezvoused with Fertig's guerrillas. Meeting with Fertig, intelligence officers captains Charles Parsons and Charles Smith conveyed MacArthur's orders: Fertig was commanded not to engage in offensive activities against the Japanese but only to gather intelligence on Japanese activities. In return, the US Army would provide radios and other equipment for Fertig's command.

These directives presented Fertig with quite a conundrum. The Japanese occupation was severely oppressive. So much so, it's estimated that one in every twenty Filipinos died under the rising sun. David Hogan observes, "The brutality of the Japanese occupation policy also aided the growth of the Filipino resistance."[45] To retain the loyalty of his forces, as well as

---

[43] Keats, They Fought Alone, 101.
[44] Ibid, 209
[45] Hogan, U.S. Army Special Operations in World War II, 68.

disrupt such atrocities, Fertig was forced to wage an active campaign to kill Japanese along with their collaborators. Often these attacks reciprocated terrible Japanese reprisals against the local populace. Fertig stated that if he ordered his men to stop killing the Japanese, then his men would follow other leaders who would probably not be willing to cooperate with MacArthur's headquarters and its directives.[46] In acquiescence to MacArthur, Fertig issued orders for his guerrillas to avoid situations which would result in reprisals. However, as the Japanese occupation policy grew more vicious, retaliation escalated. Just managing to stay ahead of Japanese patrols, and facing extinction, Fertig's Gordian knot was at last unraveled with the coming of MacArthur's return at Leyte Gulf in October 1944.

Cabanatuan Raid

Following the fall of Bataan to the Japanese in early 1942, America suffered her largest surrender in US history with some 15,000 prisoners. These and 60,000 Filipinos were forced into the Bataan Death March, a 60 mile march which was characterized by severe physical abuse and murder.[47] Following the death march to Camp O'Donnell, many of these prisoners were then transferred to the camp at Pangatian (Cabanatuan), in early June of 1942 (see Figure 1-5). Facing brutal conditions including torture and disease, a plan was developed by Sixth Army leaders and Filipino guerrillas to send a small raiding force to rescue the prisoners. As noted earlier, it was here that Major Lapham's guerrillas of central Luzon played a prominent role.

This daring action, known as *the Great Raid*, was carried out some 30 miles behind Japanese lines by a mixed force of 286 guerrillas, 121 Rangers of the 6th Ranger Battalion, and 13 Alamo Scouts.[48] Lapham's guerrillas, acting as the eyes of the raiding force, guided the Rangers to the prison camp. Additionally, providing a cordon around the camp, the guerrillas constructed roadblocks along its approaches and cached food along the return route for the liberated prisoners.

The Rangers, commanded by Lieutenant Colonel Henry A. Mucci, choose Captain Robert Prince and First Lieutenant John Murphy to lead the operation.[49] The raid was launched on the night of 30 January 1945. In order to reach their assault positions, it was necessary for the Rangers to crawl across open fields. To distract the Japanese guards, the Rangers arranged for

---

[46] Keats, They Fought Alone, 101.
[47] It is estimated that 2,500 to 10,000 Filipino and 100 to 650 American prisoners of war died before they could reach their destination at Camp O'Donnell.
[48] The Campaigns of MacArthur in the Pacific, Volume 1, Chapter X, 321.
[49] McRaven, Spec Ops, 247.

a P-61 Black Widow to buzz the camp. During this ruse, the guerrillas accompanied by a small number of Rangers cut the camp's telephone lines, preventing communication with the large forces stationed in Cabanatuan.[50]

At 19:40, Lieutenant Murphy initiated the raid when he and his men fired on the guard towers and barracks. Within the first fifteen seconds, all of the camp's guard towers and pillboxes were targeted and destroyed.[51] Sergeant Ted Richardson rushed forward to shoot a padlock off of the main gate using his .45 pistol, and the Rangers flowed through the main gate, pouring fire into the officer quarters and guard barracks. Having received accurate intelligence from the Alamo Scouts, the Rangers eliminated the enemy positions while withholding fire to the prisoners' huts. And before some Japanese soldiers could escape in a couple of trucks, a bazooka team firing into a tin shack, destroyed the trucks and the shack, along with any hope of ever getting out of there alive.

Within thirty minutes the entire Japanese garrison had been wiped out and 522 prisoners were evacuated. The only substantial resistance to the Rangers consisted of a lone Japanese soldier who managed to fire off three mortar rounds. Although the Rangers quickly located and eliminated him, several Rangers, Scouts, and POWs were hit with shrapnel, including the Battalion surgeon Captain James Fisher, who was mortally wounded. Meanwhile, the litter patients from the camp were transported by guerrilla-organized carabao carts. Many were later evacuated to a hospital at Guimba. To cover the Rangers' withdrawal, a guerrilla delaying action successfully fought off Japanese counterattacks. What makes the raid at Cabanatuan so impressive is the overwhelming success despite the lack of rehearsals.[52]

Los Baños Raid

Following the success of Cabanatuan, on 23 February, another combined US Army and Filipino guerrilla task force liberated more than 2,100 prisoners from the Los Baños prison camp on the shores of Laguna de Bay. Prior to the attack, guerrilla units infiltrated through the Japanese lines and gathered intelligence on the internment camp. This intel, which came by way of an escaped prisoner, included sketches of the interior layout, as well as patterns of life. The actionable intel included the fascinating fact that the Japanese guards conducted physical training without equipment or weapons.

Apparently the enemy commander, being one more inclined for ceremony then readiness, directed the encumbrances to be neatly collected in one

---

[50] Breuer, The Great Raid on Cabanatuan, 165.
[51] Sides, Ghost Soldiers, 271.
[52] McRaven, Spec Ops, 280. For more on rehearsals, see Chapter 4, Principles of Special Operations.

location. On the morning of the 23rd, one element of the 11th Airborne (511 Parachute Infantry Regiment) crossed Laguna de Bay in amphibious craft while another element took off by plane for a daylight parachute drop. All forces converged in a swift and coordinated attack which caught the Japanese guards of the camp in the middle of their morning calisthenics. The entire garrison was annihilated with practically no loss to the Allies, and the Los Baños prisoners were evacuated across the Bay.

The Effectiveness of the Philippine UW Campaign

General MacArthur, as Hogan observes, was "emotional and romantic in temperament," viewing warfare "more in spiritual and moral terms than as a struggle of numbers and resources. A keen student of military history, he was well aware of numerous instances where small units had defeated larger ones and where guerrillas had eroded the ability of conventional forces to fight. His own father had experienced the frustrations of counterguerrilla warfare while leading American troops in the Philippines at the turn of the century."[53] In summing up the enormous contribution of the Philippine UW mission as it was presently enabling the US invasion, MacArthur said the following:

We are aided by the fact that for many months our plans of campaign have benefited from the hazardous labor of a vast network of agents numbering into the hundreds of thousands providing precise, accurate and detailed information on major enemy moves and installations throughout the Philippine Archipelago. We are aided by the fact that through a vast network of radio positions extending into every center of enemy activity and concentration throughout the islands, I have been kept in immediate and constant communication with such widespread sources of information.

We are aided by an air warning system affording visual observation of the air over nearly every square foot of Philippine soil established for the purpose of flashing immediate warning of enemy aircraft movement through that same vast network of radio communications. We are aided by provision of all inland waterways and coastal areas of complete observation over enemy naval movement to give immediate target information to our submarines on patrol in or near Philippine waters. This information has contributed to the sinking of enemy shipping of enormous tonnage, and through such same facilities was flashed the warning to our naval forces of the enemy naval concentration off the western Philippines during the Marianas operation.[54]

Finally we are aided by their interior vigilance that has secured for our military use countless enemy documents of great value, among which were the secret

---

[53] Hogan, U.S. Army Special Operations in World War II, 64.
[54] For example, Fertig's coastwatchers provided information leading to the great victories of the first Battle of the Philippine Sea and the Battle of Leyte Gulf.

defensive plans and instructions of the Commander-in-Chief of the combined Japanese areas and complete information on the strength and dispositions of enemy fleet and naval air units. That same Commander-in-Chief of the Combined Japanese Fleets was a prisoner of one of our guerrilla units prior to his death from injuries sustained in an air crash.[55]

As Commander-in-Chief of the forces of liberation I publicly acknowledge and pay tribute to the great spiritual power that has made possible these notable and glorious achievements, achievements which find few counterparts in military history....To those great patriots to whom I now pay public tribute I say stand to your battle stations and relax not your vigilance until our forces shall have swept forward to relieve you.[56]

In preparation, the insurgent forces identified key Japanese positions and strengths, as well as the most advantageous landing sites. Volckmann accomplished this in Luzon while Fertig undertook this in the south on Mindanao. It is estimated that the insurgent forces in the Philippines totaled some 182,000 prior to US invasion. By the time MacArthur returned three years later in 1945, the guerrilla forces conducting softening attacks against the Japanese were so effective, that US forces were able to bypass certain areas all together. Impressive, considering how General Charles Willoughby, MacArthur's domineering intelligence chief, had underrated the guerrillas to be mere information gatherers. The overall effectiveness of the Philippine UW campaign may be measured by the fact that it forced the Japanese to commit forces to counterinsurgency (COIN) rather than pushing on to Australia.[57]

Due to his wartime experiences and post-war work, Wendell Fertig is one of three men who used their wartime experience to formulate the doctrine of unconventional warfare that became the cornerstone of Special Forces. Along with Aaron Bank, and Russell Volckmann, he is considered one of the founding fathers of the US Army Special Forces.

Having traced the historical heritage of the Special Forces Regiment from its historical progenitors: Rogers' Rangers in the 17th Century to the guerrilla fighters of Volckmann, Fertig, and Blackburn of the Philippines Resistance movement in the 20th Century, we now move to consider the lineage which is derived from the First Special Service Force (FSSF) – the Devil's Brigade.

---

[55] MacArthur refers here to Yamamoto, a Japanese Marshal Admiral and the commander-in-chief of the Combined Fleet during World War II. He was killed when American codebreakers identified his flight plans and his plane was shot down.

[56] The Campaigns of MacArthur in the Pacific, Volume 1, Chapter X, 324-325.

[57] According to Russell Volckmann, the Imperial Japanese Army committed over 150,000 troops to Luzon Island alone. For a fuller treatment of: Volckmann's actions on Luzon, see *We Remained*; Fertig's actions on Mindanao, see *They Fought Alone*; and Blackburn, see *Blackburn's Headhunters* and *Shadow Commander*.

Chapter 1   A Concise History of the Special Forces

The First Special Service Force

The Devil's Brigade, officially the First Special Service Force (FSSF), was an elite, joint World War II American-Canadian commando unit organized in 1942 and trained at Fort William Henry Harrison near Helena, Montana. The brigade fought valiantly in the Aleutian Islands, Italy, and southern France before being disbanded in December 1944. The Special Forces Regiment traces its official lineage to the FSSF.

In the spring of 1942, British Chief of Combined Operations, Vice Admiral Lord Louis Mountbatten, introduced to US Army Chief of Staff General George C. Marshall a project conceived by an English civilian, Geoffrey N. Pyke. Pyke's plan, code named *Plough*, was devised to attack critical points in Nazi occupied Europe. Describing Pyke and his plan, David Hogan observes, he was "an eccentric British scientist who had developed a scheme to divert up to half-a-million German troops from the main fronts. Under Pyke's plan, commandos, using special vehicles, would conduct a series of winter raids against snowbound German garrisons of such vulnerable points as hydroelectric stations in Norway and oil refineries in Romania. Exactly how the raiding units would enter and leave the target areas remained hazy, but the concept fascinated Marshall."[58] Returning to the United States, Marshall concluded that an elite force recruited in Canada and the United States would be the best military organization for conducting the raids and strikes, and he selected US Army Lieutenant Colonel Robert T. Frederick, to assemble, organize, train, and command what would be called the First Special Service Force. Frederick gave the unit a service support sounding name in an apparent attempt to disguise its true purpose. The diagram below demonstrates the FSSF organizational structure (Figure 1-8).

To fill the ranks of the Force, Army recruiters combed the Pacific seaboard for hardened volunteers, especially those with a background as "lumberjacks, forest rangers, hunters, northwoodsmen, game wardens, prospectors, and explorers."[59] David Hogan observes, "Many post commanders used the recruiting drive to empty their stockades and rid themselves of malcontents, and some 'volunteer' contingents even arrived at Fort Harrison under armed guard."[60] On July 20, 1942 the Force was activated at Fort Harrison. Frederick wasted no time in weeded out the undesirables, putting the new unit through an extensive selection process.

In preparation for *Plough*, Force men were trained in demolitions, mountaineering, amphibious assault, and cross country and downhill skiing. Further, all Force men had to volunteer for basic airborne instruction.

---

[58] Hogan, U.S. Army Special Operations in World War II, 23.
[59] Ibid, 24.
[60] Ibid.

31

Initially, Colonel Frederick worried that the soldiers from both countries (US and Canada) would have trouble forming a cohesive unit. On a base level, the techniques and commands used by either army were confusing to the other. For example, commands had to be homogenized in order for the unit to operate in the field effectively. Thus, in order to satisfy the men from both countries, some compromises were made. As far as organization goes, the Force consisted of three regiments with two battalions each, and a service battalion. Under US command, the Force was outfitted entirely by the US, with uniforms, equipment and weapons.

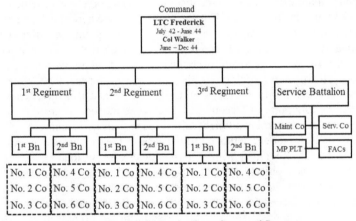

Figure 1-8. First Special Service Force Command Structure.

The original operation codenamed *Plough*, was abandoned. Frederick, seeking a mission for his unit, broadened its training to include more general infantry skills and amphibious operations. Finally in August 1943, the Force went into action for the first time, recapturing the island of Kiska, which had been occupied by Japanese forces since June, 1942. Following the successful completion of the campaign again left the Force without a mission. However, in October 1943, the commander of the Fifth United States Army, Lt. Gen. Mark W. Clark, brought the First Special Service Force to Italy.

The Winter Line Campaign

The Force was deployed to the Italian front near Naples on 19 November 1943 and immediately went into action. Attached to the 36th Infantry Division of Clark's Fifth Army, the Force was tasked with taking two heavily fortified Nazi positions; Monte La Difensa and Monte La Remetanea (See Figure 1-9). These mountain defenses consisted of Field

Marshal Kesselring's last entrenched positions buttressing the Winter Line; the German's last defense before Rome. These positions were held by the 104th Panzer Grenadier Division, some of the toughest fighting men in the Wehrmacht. In fact, General Clark had hurled his best troops in previous failed attacks resulting in heavy Allied casualties. When the Force arrived, an attack of 12 days had just failed. For the Army to advance on Rome, Monte la Difensa had to be taken.

Monte La Difensa, also known as Hill 960, was described as a "veritable fortress, a looming grey hulk crisscrossed by perilous trails leading to perpendicular cliffs at its snow-capped peak." The Force was ordered to take it and Monte la Remetanea, just beyond. Here is where the Force put its months of hard training to use. The paths leading up La Difensa were thoroughly scouted by the Force prior to their attack. A determination was made that the best way to approach the entrenched enemy was up an almost vertical escarpment. In doing this, the Force hoped to catch the Germans off guard, as previous allied attacks on the mountain had met the enemy head on. On the afternoon of December 1, the Force moved toward the German defenses; the heavy rain and night fall covering their movement.

While the 1st Regiment deployed to the base of the mountain and waited in reserve, the 2nd Regiment with 600 commandos began their stealthy climb up Difensa, their objective being a point about halfway to the crest where they would wait, under cover of darkness, to begin the attack.[61] On the morning of 3 December, 1944, the Forcemen had reached their forward positions. Then at dusk, all available air and artillery firepower was brought to bear on La Difensa. "It looked like the whole mountain was on fire."[62] By 10:30 pm the 2nd Regiment reached a point just below the crown of Difensa, poised for their ascent up a cliff face which jutted upwards at an angle of 65 degrees for 300 meters.

Using their mountaineering skills, the Forcemen, laden by their packs and weapons, climbed with knotted ropes, tied to one another in the freezing rain. "That night we just climbed," recounted a Forceman. And by midnight, with no sign of compromise, the majority of the 2nd Regiment collected itself, perched above the bowl-like rocky crown of Difensa. Beneath them lay hundreds of Germany's finest soldiers. Around 6:00 am, in the freezing rain, with all elements in position, Frederick gave the signal to advance, commando knives in hand, directing his men to hold their fire as they creped through the final yards up to the entrenched German position. *Good things of day begin to droop and drowse; whiles night's black agents to their prey do rouse.*[63]

---

[61] Aldeman, The Devil's Brigade, 124.
[62] Ibid.
[63] Shakespeare, Macbeth, Act III, Scene II.

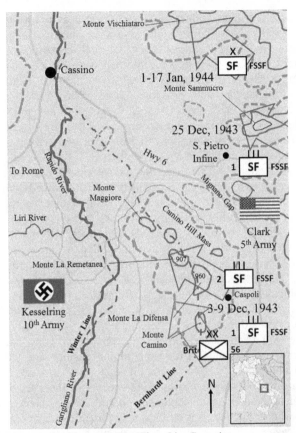

Figure 1-9. The Winter Line Campaign.

At this moment, Robert Adleman, observes, "The men of the Force slipped forward in the darkness, their blackened faces and dirt-stained uniforms making them almost invisible. Although in the distance, the rumble and cough of artillery could be heard, the only sound being made on the crest was the soft gurgle vented by German sentries who had their throats cut by the Forcemen gliding past them in the darkness"[64]

> *With Tarquin's ravishing strides, towards his design moves like a ghost.*
> *Thou sure and firm-set earth, hear not my steps, which way they walk,*
> *For fear thy very stones prate of my whereabout,*
> *And take the present horror from the time, which now suits with it.*[65]

---

[64] Aldeman, The Devil's Brigade, 127.
[65] Shakespeare, Macbeth, Act II, Scene I.

Nearly on top of the Germans, the Forcemen's stealthy forward trace was interrupted suddenly when rockfall gave their position away, followed immediately by German flares. Then all hell broke loose. With the advantage of the high ground, the battle began in earnest. The Forcemen, establishing a base of fire, rapidly swept down the face of the mountain, overwhelming the Germans positions in a series of shoot outs which involved close-quarter, grenade lobbing, trench line and pillbox clearing hand-to-hand combat. The assault was rapid and decisive, taking advantage of not only the cover of darkness and inclement weather but an approach from a seemingly impregnable cliff face obstacle.

The 5th Army Staff had predicted that the battle would last between 4 to 5 days, but within two hours, the Germans on La Difensa had giving up their mountain stronghold, and retreated across a connecting ridge to La Remetanea, the Brigade's next target. But as the smoke and fog cleared away, the Germans began to pound the Forcemen with artillery, driving them into their hard earned trench lines and pillboxes. From here the Force dug in awaiting badly needed reinforcements and supplies. Colonel Frederick, undaunted, prepared the Force for its next big assault on their primary objective, Hill 907, Monte La Remetanea. Regarding Frederick's coolness under fire, Robert Adleman observes, "His casual indifference to enemy fire was hard to explain, as there were times when a heavy barrage of mortar fire would send us scurrying for cover only to come back and find him smoking a cigarette – in the same sitting position and place we had vacated in a hurry."[66]

Leading directly to the overwhelming success of the operation was the strength, determination, and endurance of the 3rd Regiment and Service Battalion, who resupplied their brothers atop Difensa with an endless supply of rations, water, and ammunition. The resupply mission was extensive and due to the mountainous terrain, entirely on foot. Most men detailed to the resupply mission made two trips up the mountain each day.

After a few days on the summit, Frederick received news of the enemy situation: although massive allied artillery barrages and the flooding of both the Rapido and Garigliane rivers prevented the Germans from reinforcing from the west, the Germans had blunted a British attack on a nearby mountain. Frederick surmised the situation as dire, as the Germans could now isolate the Force on Difensa and pound them with artillery. With this information, Frederick now moved to take Monte La Remetanea with 1st Regiment in the lead.

The night before the assault on Monte La Remetanea was quite an uncomfortable one for the Forcemen. Howling winds, freezing rain, no

---

[66] Aldeman, The Devil's Brigade, 133.

shelter and little food made it pass slowly. Then at 11:00 pm the order was given to advance. Almost immediately, a German gunner opened up on the 1st Regiment with bursts from his MG42. Then German gunners unleashed a hail of *Nebelwerfer* rocket fire. Casualties forced Frederick to await daybreak before continuing the assault on Hill 907. It was at this time the British 46th and 56th Divisions broke through the German lines at Monte Camino. With the dawn came the 1st Regiment's assault. The Canadian Forceman, Don McKinnon recounts, "Our battle cries never ceased from the time of take-off until our final attack uphill to the enemy positions. I'm sure the howling and baying we did on that attack scared the hell out of the Kraut. The enemy was completely demoralized and withdrew under the overpowering wave coming at them. No prisoners were taken, as actually there was no chance for an enemy to give up and possibly if he had he would have been cut down by someone. His only chance was to run and that is finally what they did." Hill 907, Monte La Remetanea, fell to the Force on 9 December, 1944. And the 1st Regiment spent the night on the costly knob. The taking of Difensa and Remetanea were key to the Allied success in Southern Italy.

During the remainder of the campaign, the Force also captured Hill 720, starting from Monte Sammucro on 25 December, and after difficulties, assaulted Monte Majo and Monte Vischiataro almost simultaneously on 8 January 1944. It was at Monte Majo, where the 3rd Regiment, employing the lessons of Difensa and Remetanea, used surprise and an elevated positon to sweep down on German defenders twice their number. But the cost was high. On Christmas of 1943, the Force had 1,800 fighting men. By January 17, 1944, 1,400 of them had become casualties. During the Winter Line campaign, the Force suffered appalling casualties; roughly three-quarters: 511 total, 91 dead, 9 missing, 313 wounded with 116 exhaustion cases. The Force, then being relieved by the 142nd Infantry, was withdrawn in preparation for *Operation Shingle*, the Allied plan to outflank the German positions at Anzio.

Operation Shingle

Operation Shingle, commanded by American Major General John P. Lucas, was intended to outflank German forces of the Winter Line and facilitate an attack on Rome. Replacing the Ranger Battalions, which had suffered heavily at the Battle of Cisterna, the Force was tasked to hold the right flank of the beachhead. While the 1st and 3rd Regiments were to guard the Allied right flank, the 2nd Regiment, which had been badly mauled at La Difensa, was further tasked to conduct reconnaissance and raiding patrols into the German lines. In support of Shingle, the Force went into action on 1 February, 1944 (See Figure 1-10).

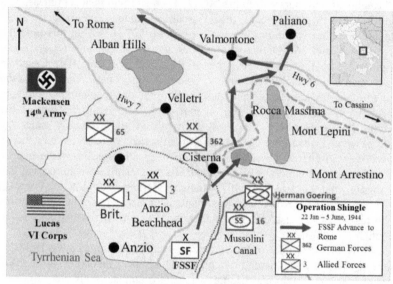

Figure 1-10. Operation Shingle.

While 1ˢᵗ and 3ʳᵈ Regiments fought to hold the Mussolini Canal, the flank of the Anzio beachhead, 2ⁿᵈ Regiment began aggressively patrolling deep behind German lines, often up to a quarter of mile. With their faces blackened with boot polish, it was at Anzio that the Force received its sobriquet the *Black Devils*. An order found on an enemy prisoner stated that the Germans in Anzio would be "fighting an elite Canadian-American Force. They are treacherous, unmerciful and clever. You cannot afford to relax. The first soldier or group of soldiers capturing one of these men will be given a 10 day furlough."[67]

Despite the successes of the Forcemen at Anzio, holding the canal and the aggressive active patrols were depleting their already limited manpower. Additionally, the Allied operation as a whole was encountering problems. The Allies achieved complete surprise by landing at Anzio and establishing a beachhead, they rapidly advanced 3 miles inland. However, General Lucas, while taking time to entrench against an expected German counterattack, failed to capitalize on the operational surprise achieved by the amphibious assault and delayed his advance to Rome until he judged his position was sufficiently consolidated and his troops ready.

---

[67] Horn, Of Courage and Determination, 222.

With the majority of their forces concentrated farther southeast around Cassino, the Germans couldn't possibly reinforce Anzio for another two or three days. If the Allies pressed their advantage, the road to Rome lay virtually undefended. The seizure of Rome would have had the effect of isolating the German defenders in the south and firmly establishing Allied control over Italy.[68] It was not until 29 January that Lucas felt strong enough to move on the offensive. However, by that time Kesselring had reinforced the beachhead and seizing the initiative, threatened to drive the Allies back into the sea. As a result, the Allied advance to Rome was stalled, and the purpose of Shingle forfeited.

Beginning on 25 May, 1944, the Force was sent into action against German defenses atop Monte Arrestino, and then Rocca Massima on 27 May. These actions were in support of Clark's Fifth Army breakout offensive. By 2 June, 1944, the Forcemen linked up with the advancing elements of Clark's Fifth Army, and following a short respite, went into action capturing several key bridges which prevented the Wehrmacht from retreating; the Black Devils had fought for 99 days without relief.

In August 1944, after being among the first to enter Rome, the Brigade came under the command of Colonel Edwin A. Walker following Frederick's promotion to Brigadier General. Under Walker's command, the Brigade repatriated the islands of Port Cros and Îles d'Hyères during Operation Dragoon, the invasion of southern France. During the Battle of Port Cros, the Brigade captured five island forts from the Wehrmacht. Toward the end of August the Force was attached to the 1st Airborne Task Force, Frederick's command. Along with the Task Force, it saw its final days entrenched in defensive positions on the Franco-Italian border.

All told, the FSSF accrued appalling casualties during the Italian campaign. Beginning with an operational strength of 1800 in December 1943, by January 17, 1944, 1400 men were either wounded or killed.[69] It has been estimated that the FSSF accounted for some 12,000 German casualties while capturing some 7,000 prisoners. Being critically understrengthed, the Force was disbanded in Southern France.

Following in the lineage of the First Special Service Force, the Special Forces Regiment received the Brigade's fighting spirit, branch of service insignia (the crossed arrows), along with specialized warfighting skills (amphibious and winter warfare). Today the spirit of the FSSF lives on in Special Forces of both Canada and the United States. Perhaps most of all, the Force demonstrated how incredible results can be achieved with a small determined elite force.

---

[68] MCDP 1-3 Tactics, 18.
[69] Aldeman, The Devil's Brigade, 148.

Chapter 1   A Concise History of the Special Forces

The Creation of the Office of Strategic Services

In 1941, concerned about American intelligence deficiencies, President Roosevelt appointed William Joseph "Wild Bill" Donovan (1883-1959), a retired Major General and Medal of Honor recipient, to draft a plan for an intelligence service. Donovan was sent to Britain in 1941 in order to meet with key officials in the war effort against Germany's aggression. Two of these organizations were the Special Operations Executive (SOE), formed in 1940 in order to organize local resistance forces to conduct espionage, sabotage, and reconnaissance in Nazi occupied Europe, and MI6 (Secret Intelligence Services), founded in 1909 to provide Britain with foreign intelligence. Donovan was greatly impressed with the SOE, and was determined to establish an American counterpart based upon this British model. In 1941, President Roosevelt founded the Office of the Coordinator of Information (COI), which was designed to coordinate information between the services; Donovan was named the coordinator.[70] Donovan's primary concern was military intelligence and covert operations in Nazi and Japanese occupied countries.

Six months after the Japanese bombing of Pearl Harbor, Roosevelt placed COI under the Joint Chiefs of Staff (JCS) and renamed it the Office of Strategic Services (OSS). Roosevelt tasked Donovan to collect and analyze strategic information to conduct special operations not assigned to other agencies. To this end Donovan would direct over 13,000 OSS personnel in Europe and Asia. During the War, the OSS supplied policy makers with facts and estimates, but the OSS never had jurisdiction over all foreign intelligence activities. For example, the FBI was responsible for intelligence work in Central and South America and the Army and Navy guarded their areas of responsibility.

Donovan divided his agency into two functional groups: intelligence and special operations (See Figure 1-11). Special Operations (SO), a branch of OSS, was tasked to organize and conduct sabotage operations behind enemy lines. It furnished agents, communications and supplies to underground and guerrilla groups in Norway, France, Denmark, northern Italy and China. SO also organized special teams sent behind enemy lines for destruction of specific targets, securing intelligence, waging guerrilla warfare, and included: maritime operations, special projects, research and development section, and morale operations, which was the deceptive title for psychological operations (PWO).

---

[70] Waller, Wild Bill Donovan, 75. The establishment of the Office of Coordinator of Information laid the foundation for what would become the Central Intelligence Agency by the National Security Act of 1947.

Broadening the capabilities of OSS, Donovan added the Maritime Operations. Organized to carry out sabotage against enemy shipping, this waterborne unit was responsible for waterborne infiltration and the development of the operational swimmer capability. Equipped with a rebreather, fins, compass and assorted demolitions, 15-32 man teams of OSS operational swimmers were fielded in the European, Pacific and Southeast Asia Theaters of operation; the heritage of the Special Operations Combat Diver. Later in 1943, Donovan added the Operational Groups (OG). These highly-trained foreign language speaking commandos, were organized to conduct guerrilla warfare. They were placed under PWO. [71]

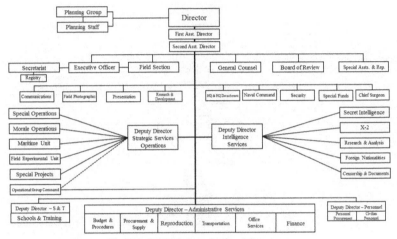

Figure 1-11. OSS Organizational Structure.

The Operational Groups (OG)

The OGs, consisting mainly of US Army officers and enlisted, were recruited chiefly from line units and service schools. The organizational structure of the OG units commanded by a captain, consisted of two OG sections, with one officer (1LT) and fifteen non-commissioned officers each. The function of the OGs was twofold: (1) to serve as the operational nuclei of guerrilla organizations which have been formed from resistance groups in enemy territory; and (2) to execute independent operations on enemy targets as directed by the theater commander (See Figure 1-12).[72] The NCOs of the team were equally trained in weapons and operational skills, with two being specialists - one a medical technician and the other a

---

[71] Paddock, Special Warfare, 25.
[72] Operational Group Field Manual, 3.

radio operator. With the exception of the radioman and the medic, every man had the same operational capabilities. This was a major factor which enabled flexibility of assignment and deployment to fit varied mission requirements.

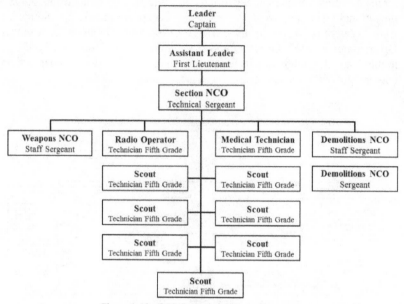

Figure 1-12. OSS Operational Group Structure.

A desirable OSS OG candidate was a basic training graduate and had a working knowledge of a foreign language, such as, German, French, Norwegian, Italian, and Greek. Perspective candidates were interviewed and given the opportunity to serve their country in a hazardous duty assignment behind enemy lines. OG training, based on the British commando model, was physically demanding and incorporated the field of special weapons, hand-to-hand combat, demolition, land navigation, parachuting and survival instruction.

Further, OSS personnel received extensive training in both conventional and guerrilla tactics. These skills were necessary for organizing resistance forces with limited external support for extended durations. OG units, organized by operational areas such as France, Norway, Italy, etc., received additional training pertaining to their OG's orientation. For example, some OGs received winter warfare, skiing, and amphibious training. While the OSS is generally regarded as the predecessor of the CIA, its Operational Groups, although largely undocumented, are the forerunners of the US Army Special Forces. The OSS established liaison at the theater level

41

through a Strategic Services officer. This officer coordinated the actions of indigenous forces which were influenced by OSS operational detachments and passed intelligence to and from assets in denied areas.

The purpose of OG activity was to aid actual and planned Allied military operations by harassing the enemy behind his lines, disrupting his lines of communications and supply, thereby forcing him to divert troops to protect himself from guerrilla attacks and wide-scale uprisings. The activities, mode of operation and personnel of OG differed from those of the Special Operations Branch. OG personnel activated guerrillas as military organizations to engage enemy forces (See Figure 1-13).

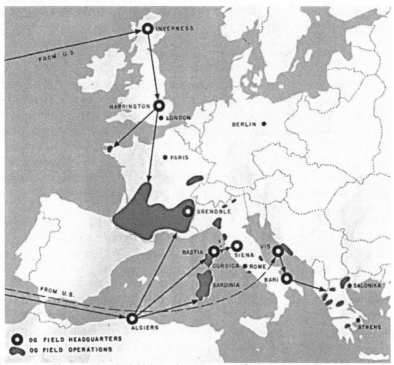

Figure 1-13. OG Field Operations. Courtesy of US National Archives.

The OGs always operated in uniform as military units and were not primarily concerned with individual acts of sabotage. OGs were active in Burma, China, France, Greece, Italy, Norway, and Yugoslavia. They presaged the basic organization, training, and military operational specialties of today's Special Forces Operational Detachment-Alpha.[73]

OG operations in France were based out of either England or Algeria. The former worked closely with the Maquis to harass the Nazis and protect American lines of communication. The latter coordinated the resistance movement in support of the invasions from England and North Africa. In cooperation with Maquis units, OGs killed 461, wounded 467, and captured 10,021 Germans; demolished 11 power lines and cables; mined 17 roads; shot down 3 aircraft and destroyed 2 trains and 3 locomotives. Additionally, they rescued downed Allied fliers, gathered intelligence, selected and prepared landing strips, and assisted the Free French Infantry (FFI). For security purposes, each team in the field had its own code name used in communications and command.[74]

Operation Jedburgh

In World War II, the OSS actively encouraged and supported resistance movements against the occupying Nazi and Japanese regimes. One of the greatest accomplishments of the OSS was the joint operation Jedburgh. It was conducted along-side British SOE and Free French, Belgian, and Dutch resistance forces. By the latter part of WWII British SOE forces were numerically inadequate to conduct the myriad of tasks; the OSS jumped at the opportunity. Operation Jedburgh consisted of dropping three-man teams into the Nazi-occupied Low Countries and France in support of the Allied invasion of Europe on D-Day (Fig. 1-14).

In May 1944, SOE and OSS established the Special Forces Headquarters SFHQ in London. SFHQ directed the resistance through personal messages tacked onto BBC broadcasts following the nine o'clock news. First, an alert message corresponding to a particular resistance group was sent, then an action message was sent directing the group to execute the assigned mission. Parachuting at night (through the belly of B-24 bombers) the Jedburgh teams linked up with groups of armed men and women such as the Resistance, called Maquis in rural areas. Many of these night airdrops were made by the *Carpetbaggers*, a U.S. Army Air Forces unit whose mission was to support covert operations in Europe. The mission for the Jedburgh teams was crucial to Allied success in the war against Germany in Europe.

Not only did the Jed teams function as the vital link between the Allied command and the resistance forces, but more importantly they slowed the Nazi response to Operation Overlord by sabotaging enemy supply lines, blowing bridges, and derailed trains. Operating hundreds of miles behind

---

[73] Paddock, Special Warfare, 35.
[74] OSS Operational Group Command pamphlet 1944.

enemy lines, the Jeds facilitated subversive action against the Nazis by providing not only leadership and logistics but a cohesive bond with the Allied command. Weapons carried by the Jed teams consisted of M1 .30 cal carbine and the 1911 Colt .45 cal pistol.

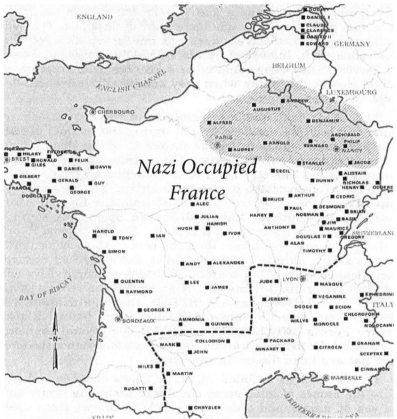

Figure 1-14. Jedburgh Team Disposition 1944. Courtesy of US National Archives.

Additionally, Jed teams, coordinating through SFHQ in London, dropped off tons of bombs, bazookas, rifles, Sten guns, and ammunition to outfit the Resistance. Jedburgh missions included: gaining vital intelligence on Nazi unit composition, disposition, and strength, organizing local resistance forces, boosting morale and effort of the resistance, severing enemy lines of communications, conducting ambushes on Nazi convoys, and attacking enemy installations. The first Jed team, code named 'Hugh' parachuted into Chateauroux the night before the Allied invasion of Normandy. Ninety-one Jedburgh teams were dropped into France and the Low Countries in support of Operation Overlord. Jed teams and Maquis greatly aided the Allied victory by sabotaging German communications and delaying enemy reinforcements to Normandy.

Regarding their menacing activities Eisenhower wrote, "They surrounded the Germans with a terrible atmosphere of danger and hatred which ate into the confidence of the leaders and the courage of the soldiers." Eisenhower's headquarters estimated that the value of the Resistance to Operation Overlord amounted to the equivalent of fifteen military divisions.[75] All told, the combined SOE / OSS effort in France from June to August 1944 had tallied the following: 885 rail lines cut, 140 telecommunications lines cut, 75 road ways and water ways cut, 44 factories sabotaged, 322 locomotives destroyed, 24 convoys attacked, and 7 aircraft shot down.[76]

One Jedburgh team, Ammonia, operating in Cahor with 75 Maquis, ambushed a 26 vehicle convoy producing over 2,000 German casualties.[77] Some of the American Jedburghs would later take prominent roles in the US Army and /or the CIA, viz., William Colby (1920-1996), who became the 10th Director of the CIA, and Colonel Aaron Bank, founder of the US Army Special Forces.

Following Operation Overlord six Jed teams were deployed in support of Operation Market Garden in September 1944, however poor intelligence due to *Das Englandspiel,* and a lack of understanding of Jedburgh capabilities on the part of division commanders and staffs stymied effectiveness.[78] Market Garden, the largest airborne operation in history, was an unsuccessful attempt at encircling the German industrial heartland and ending the war by Christmas of 1944.[79] Given one of the major setbacks in the operation, a general loss of communication, it is generally agreed that if the Jed teams had been deployed sooner, perhaps they would have, given their recent success in France, made a significant difference in the outcome of the battle.

---

[75] Beavin, Operation Jedburgh, 292. The OSS with only 423 Jedburghs and OG personnel trained and lead over 70,000 Maquis in France.
[76] Brown, The Secret War Report of the OSS, 460.
[77] Ibid, 414.
[78] Das Englandspiel, "The England Game" was the German name for the operation conducted by the Nazi counter intelligence agency, the Abwehr during WWII. By compromising the SOE's code system, Abwehr agents were able to fool them into sending more SOE agents and supplies into the waiting arms of the Gestapo. Over 50 Allied agents were caught and executed.
[79] Operation Market Garden, 17-25 September 1944, was the largest airborne operation up to that time. Operation Varsity, 24 March, 1945, involved more planes, gliders, and paratroopers in a single day and at a single location.

OG Operations in Southern France and Northern Italy

All OG operations in southern France and northern Italy were coordinated with Allied plans for the invasion (See Figure 1-15). Their purpose was to destroy the enemy's lines of supply and communication and force him to divert troops for their protection, to protect the flanks of the Allied forces driving in from the beaches, and to report on enemy strength and movements. To this end OGs were introduced throughout the area, organizing or equipping guerrilla forces and guiding them in operations. Operations in Italy were conducted from OG headquarters on Corsica and bases in Italy. Independently and in collaboration with Italian Partisans and British and French forces, OGs harassed the enemy by raids on military installations and lines of communication, as well as by occupying islands to establish observation posts.

1 OGs parachuted into Sardinia at the time of the German evacuation and operated throughout island.

2 Landed on Corsica, OGs fought with French troops through the entire campaign that drove Germans from the island. Established headquarters at Bastia.

3 OGs with British troops were landed by sea and dropped by air in the Chieti area to aid escaped American and British prisoners of war. They also killed Italian Fascist informers.

4 Occupied island of Capraia and established a permanent naval and air observation post with radio communication to headquarters on Corsica. Rescued downed American aviators.

5 Occupied island of Gorgona and established a permanent naval and air observation post with radio communication to headquarters on Corsica.

6 OGs landed with the Fifth Army in the invasion at Anzio and were used to gather intelligence.

7 Damaged a highway bridge just south of Leghorn and withdrew successfully.

8 OGs landed by sea to demolish tunnel entrances and the road fill of a railroad. An enemy convoy forced the withdrawal of OG boats and attempts at rescue proved unsuccessful. Enemy radio later announced a Commando-type unit had been wiped out.

9 Landed with a French force on Pianosa, surrounded barracks and isolated the local prison to seize 24 Italian guards for intelligence purposes.

10 Personnel and supplies flown from Brindisi were dropped by parachute to aid Italian Partisans. OGs were attached to the Third Garibaldi Brigade which controls the road from Torriglian to Bobbio and the surrounding country.

11 Four small teams were dropped in northern Italy to assist local Partisans and to transmit intelligence.

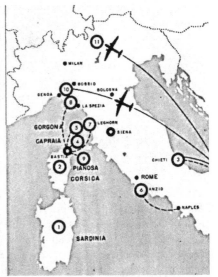

Figure 1-15. OSS operations in S. France and N. Italy 1944. National Archives.

The overall effectiveness of the resistance movement in Northern Italy is clearly demonstrated in a telegram from the southwest commander-in-chief Field Marshall Kesselring to commanders in Nazi occupied Italy:

Activity of partisan bands...has spread like lightening in the last ten days. The execution of partisan operations shows considerably more commanding leadership. Up to now it has been possible for us, with a few exceptions, to keep our vital rear lines of communication open by means of our slight protective forces, but this situation threatens to change considerably for the worse in the immediate future.

Speedy and radical countermeasures must anticipate this development. It is clear to me that the only remedy, and the one which is unavoidably necessary to meet the situation, is the concentration of all available forces, even if this means temporary weakening in other places. I request you therefore to combine with 14th Army and the Army of Liguria, in carrying out several large scale operations which will nip in the bud the increasing activity of the partisan bands in Northern Italy. Please let me have your proposals as to when these measures can be carried out, and with what forces.[80]

Figure 1-16. OSS Operations in Northern Italy.

As the Allied armies advanced, partisans, organized and equipped by the OSS, began operating in support of the Fifth US Army (Figure 1-16). By April 1945, when the Allies unleased their final offensive in Northern Italy, there were over 75 OSS teams active behind enemy lines. The partisan forces were so effective that they were able to independently clear large swaths of Northern Italy of the Germans. As German forces retreated from advancing Allied forces, partisans would block roads and call in air strikes on the floundering Nazis. Partisans even managed to capture the entire German 148th Infantry Division. OSS teams attached to Fifth Army were parachuted in as far north as Lake Garda on the Swiss border. These teams performed special reconnaissance (SR) along strategic enemy escape routes. Overall, the formidable OSS effort in Northern Italy is comparable with the extraordinary performance of the SOE and OSS teams of D-Day.

---

[80] Brown, The Secret War Report of the OSS, 243.

One the greatest OSS missions in history involved the surrender of all German forces in Northern Italy. Operation Crossword as it has come to be known was the secret negotiations that took place in Luzern between Waffen-SS General Karl Wolff and Allen Dulles on 8 March 1945. Later, OSS agents Jones and Daddario were sent to rescue Wolff who was now in danger of capture and execution at the hands of partisans. It was during this time that Mussolini and his mistress were captured and executed by an OG-trained group.[81] Finally, on May 2, 1945, under the protective custody of the OSS, General Wolff surrendered all German forces in Italy; roughly 120,000 troops.

OSS Operations in the Adriatic and Mediterranean

With Partisan and British troops, OGs engaged small German forces, ambushed naval convoys by shore fire, and rescued hundreds American aviators. Additionally, OGs penetrated Greece by sea and air to cooperate with guerrilla forces in attacking German supply lines and destroying enemy headquarters (Figure 1-17).

Figure 1-17. OSS OG Operations in the Adriatic and Mediterranean. National Archives.

---

[81] Brown, The Secret War Report of the OSS, 248.

Operations in Greece were based out of Cairo. OSS operations in Greece and Yugoslavia were both complicated by political problems. And in both regions, the Communists were the most numerous. Whereas British plans were laid with post war European politics in mind, the OSS supported whoever happened to be killing Germans. The SOE had been working with Greek partisan units since the beginning of 1942. In the later part of 1943, some 300 OSS teams (SI, OGs, MO, and SO) were inserted into Greece. These elements supplied the War Department with its only on-the-ground national intelligence. Intelligence included: German order of battle; shipping and rail tables; as well as industrial production in Greece.[82]

Major sabotage operations commenced in April 1944 when 190 OG teams entered Greece. These teams linked up with guerrilla bands at various strategic points. German forces began withdrawing from the Greek mainland in late 1944 as Soviet forces began advancing into Balkans threatening to cut them off. Similar to D-Day and operations in Northern Italy, this extensive operation, code named *Smashem*, detained and delayed vast amounts of retreating Germans. OSS operations in Greece between April and November 1944 amounted to the following: 14 trains ambushed; 15 bridges destroyed; 61 trucks destroyed; 6 miles of railroad lines cut; with an estimated 1,794 enemy dead and wounded.[83]

Korcula Island Ambush Patrol

OSS missions in the Adriatic were based out of the island of Vis. On 15 April 1944, an eight man OG element led by 1LT Dobrski left Lastovo Island for the Island of Korcula; the local Partisans furnished the boat. The mission was to interdict Nazi forces on the island. Previous attempts at infil had failed, but on the second attempt, the raiders landed successfully after an uneventful two hour trip in an open boat and were conveyed by the Partisans to their secret cave. It was decided to ambush the daily patrol operating between the towns of Blato and Smokivica (See Figure 1-18).

The party left the cave at 1800 hours, April 16, and marched through the countryside for almost two hours to the selected spot; two automatic rifle teams were picked up enroute; one was to aid in the ambush and the other was to cover the getaway. Shortly before 2000 hours the party arrived at the planned ambush site and was in the midst of the flurry that invariably attends the selection of a position from which one is to fight when the enemy appeared. The enemy was a party of five BMW R75 motorcycles, one with a sidecar attached. They proceeded west at a good clip toward Blato. The surprise was complete on both sides; they certainly didn't expect

---

[82] Brown, The Secret War Report of the OSS, 267.
[83] Ibid.

to see an ambush. The ambushing party in turn was caught standing straight up trying to decide which rock would offer best protection. Had they not been seen, they would have let them pass, for the real target was the foot patrol. Having been detected there was little to do but open fire.

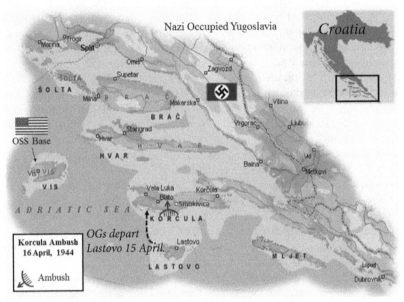

Figure 1-18. Korcula Island Ambush 16 April, 1944.

The Partisan's Commandant was the first to fire: his shots hit just before the first cycle and both bikes picked up speed and began to swerve from side to side. The lone occupant of the side car made himself as small as possible and ducked his head down next to the seat. The echo of the first shot was never heard, for hardly had the Commandant pressed the trigger, when the whole hillside seemed to leap into flame; automatic rifle, Tommy-guns, Garand, Sten guns, carbines, old rifles, and all opened fire. One Partisan nearest the road even threw rocks. The effect of the barrage was instantaneous; the two cycles careened to one side of the road just beyond the bend. One lay dead in the road and the other four scrambled for cover. The only available cover was a patch of brush just off the road. To get into the patch it was necessary to climb a four feet embankment; two of the enemy presented broad backs while climbing, were both hit, and both lay where they had fallen.

It was time to advance. Urged on by the Commandant's lusty "napried," and by Lt. Dobrski's corresponding "forward!" the men advanced. The

Commandant and two partisans charged directly across the road to open fire on the patch of brush. Under cover of this protective fire the other men moved off the hill across the ravine. The automatic rifle on the hill kept up a constant fire. Three OGs moved across the road in search of cover and a good field of fire. One of the Germans opened up with a light shoulder automatic weapon. The OGs hit the ground and returned fire. Lt. Dobrski kept advancing forward and was hit by a slug from the automatic weapon. Virtually all the enemy fire was directed directly upon the Commandant and the other partisan who had formed the SBF position. The Commandant, huddled down behind the rocks, raised his head and bellowed, "Napried!", a burst knocked up dust all across the field and he heard that ominous z-zing just to one side; he ducked his head down again and just as truculently bellowed again. One wild burst cut the limbs off a tree just behind Pekar and the twigs rained down upon his head.

In the meantime three other partisans advanced and poured a heavy fire into the brush, threw grenades and the enemy fire stopped. An OG applied a tourniquet to the lieutenant's thigh. All five of the Germans were killed. To insure their demise, an OG gave each one a burst from his Tommy gun. Quickly the bodies were searched, papers and weapons were removed, and the motorcycles were fired by a burst of incendiaries. Upon identification the men proved to be a first lieutenant, a lieutenant, two sergeants, and one private. The two officers wore Iron Crosses dated 1939. The Partisans systematically removed clothing and shoes such as could be salvaged. Time was short; the expected foot patrol was due any minute and the burning vehicles made such a tremendous pyre that it could have been seen for miles. A door was torn off a nearby shanty and utilized as a stretcher the lieutenant was loaded on, and the party made for the hills. With Sergeant Arsenault commanding, the party evaded Nazi patrols and exfiltrated the island by boat three days later.

Special Operations on Mainland Yugoslavia

On 6 April, 1941, the Nazis with 24 divisions and 1,200 tanks invaded Yugoslavia, overrunning it in twelve days. While the Allies contemplated an invasion of the Balkans, British SOE agents were sent into Yugoslavia. Initially, the British backed the Chetniks led by Mihailović. However, by mid-1943, British Prime Minister Winston Churchill decided to withdraw support from Mihailović and support the Communist Partisans led by Josip Broz Tito. This change was largely due to Ultra decryptions (Bletchley Park) which indicated that the Partisans were a more effective menace to the Germans. However, the US supported both the Partisans and Chetniks. One

51

of Donovan's principal objectives was to use the Balkans as a jumping off point for covert operations in greater Germany.[84]

For the Allies, UW operations in Yugoslavia were no doubt the most politically nebulous. Anthony Brown observes, "From the start, Yugoslavia was a highly-charged, most complicated affair that often seemed to defy definition."[85] The Partisan movement was not only a guerrilla army fighting against the Germans, it was also a Communist political movement. Making matters worse was the prevalence of savage ethnic and religious hatred, such as the traditional animosity between Serbs and Muslims. This was shrewdly agitated by the Axis. Reprisals were given full rein and were thoroughly vented. All told, it is estimated that 1.7 million Yugoslavs died in the war. Following the Allied switch to the Partisans, the Chetniks collaborated first with their Italian and later German occupiers, attacking the Partisans. Opportunistic, they played a dangerous game of collaboration with both the Axis and the Allies.

Similar to operations in France, OG teams organized and directed Yugoslav Partisans in combat actions aimed at disrupting enemy supply lines, derailing trains, ambushing patrols and forcing the Germans to divert combat units to rear area security missions. In this environment, SOE and OSS agents supplied tens of thousands of pounds worth of Allied air-dropped weapons, ammunition, explosives, and food, thereby keeping the Partisan forces alive. The overall effectiveness of the Yugoslav resistance movement may be demonstrated by the fact that during the height of the contest with the Partisans, the Germans were forced to divert 15 Wehrmacht divisions (roughly 250,000 men) to Yugoslavia to quell resistance activities. The Germans desperately needed these 15 divisions elsewhere in Europe. They might have made quite a difference in France or Northern Italy. By late 1944, Partisans forces swelled to roughly 650,000 men organized into 50 divisions and four field armies. These forces engaged the Germans in conventional battle. The point being made here is, the SOE and OSS were able to defeat the Germans in Yugoslavia without an Allied invasion force.[86]

As the Allied bombing intensified over German-held targets in Romania and Bulgaria; such as Ploesti. Bomber flight paths proceeded over Yugoslav airspace. Of downed pilots, a majority ended up in Yugoslavia; either Chetnik or Partisan-held territory. With the purpose of rescuing downed pilots, the OSS created the Air Crew Rescue Unit (ACRU). This OSS team, known as team Halyard, was led by Lieutenant George Muselin, and accompanied by Master Sergeant Michael Rajacich, and Specialist Arthur

---

[84] Lindsay, Beacons in the Night, 265. Before the end of the war some 100 teams had been infiltrated into Germany.

[85] Brown, The Secret War Report of the OSS, 270.

[86] For a thorough treatment of the OSS in Yugoslavia see Lindsay, Beacons in the Night.

Jibilian, the radio operator. Between 1 January and 15 October 1944, Team Halyard recovered a total of 1,152 American airmen. Of these, 795 airmen were recovered with the assistance of the Partisans while 356 were extracted with the help of the Chetniks. To the chagrin of the British, Donovan saw a necessity to back both sides (Chetnik and Partisan) as strategic factors useful against the Germans.

Later, a state of extreme tension developed between Tito (Partisan's leader), who was supported by the Red Army, and the Anglo-American military mission in Yugoslavia. The cause of the tension was Tito's claim on the port of Trieste, which happened to be occupied by the British as the custodians for the Italians.[87] At one point, Tito threatened war with the Western powers, and General Patton, backed by MI-6 and the OSS, made it seem that the Third US Army in Germany was preparing to move on Trieste in order to teach Tito good manners. Some historians believe this was the beginning of the Cold War. However, Tito backed off.

OSS Operations in Asia

OSS operations in Asia were quite a different matter. Apart from Detachment 101 in Burma, the OSS was unable to make a significant contribution to the struggle against Japan until 1945. For example, the OSS was blocked from operating in the Philippines due to General MacArthur's disdain for covert operations. Likewise, in the Pacific, Nimitz viewed the OSS in a similar vein. This forced Donovan to fight the Japanese in the only region left open to him, the distant China-Burma-India (CBI) Theater (See Figure 1-19).

In January 1942, the Japanese invaded Burma, captured Rangoon and quickly overwhelmed the combined British, Indian, and Burmese forces. The Allies had been supplying Chiang Kai-shek's Chinese Nationalist Army via the Burma Road (Lasho to Kunming). Following the collapse of Burma, the Japanese consolidated their forces along the Thai and Indian borders. Chiang Kai-shek's forces were now cut off by land and sea. The only way remaining to supply the Chinese was by air. Roger Hilsman observes, "Supplies went by sea to Calcutta, then by rail or river steamer to Ledo on the Brahmaputra River in upper Assam. A complex of American airstrips were built in the area from which a fleet of C-47s and C-46s flew the supplies five hundred miles over the Himalayas to Kunming. This last route was called the Hump."[88] Arriving in Burma as the Japanese invasion commenced, Lt. General Joseph Stilwell (1883-1946) assumed command of the politically nebulous CBI Theater. The Allied intent was to recover

---

[87] Brown, The Secret War Report of the OSS, 282.
[88] Hilsman, American Guerrilla: My War Behind Enemy Lines, 75.

Burma, reopen the land link with China in order to supply Chiang Kai-Shek's forces from India.

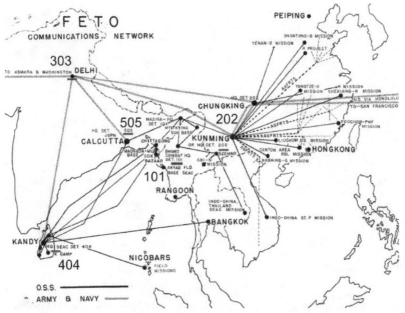

Figure 1-19. OSS Far East Theater of Operations. Courtesy of US National Archives.

Initially misunderstood and unwanted by everyone including Stilwell, Colonel Carl F. Eifler (1906-2002) and about twenty OSS men established a base camp at a tea plantation near Nazira in the northeastern Indian province of Assam (Figure 1-20). Lacking men, equipment, funds, a clear directive from Washington, and current intelligence on the situation in Burma, Eifler faced an immense task in building a clandestine organization.[89] From there, the Detachment's initial attempts at establishing a covert network in Burma proved untenable. David Hogan observes,

Frustrated in his attempts to infiltrate agents by foot, Eifler negotiated a deal with Brig. Gen. Edward H. Alexander, the chief of Air Transport Command. The general's planes were suffering heavily from Japanese fighters in their attempts to fly supplies over northern Burma and the Himalayas to China. Those crews that survived crashes in the primitive mountains of northern Burma faced little chance for survival in a region full of tigers, snakes, and Japanese. In a conference with the general, Eifler pointed out that if Detachment 101 personnel could reach the region and contact the friendly Kachin inhabitants, they could organize them into a network

---

[89] Hogan, US Army Special Operations in World War II, 102.

to help the airmen escape back to friendly lines. Alexander responded with enthusiasm, offering to provide planes and parachutes to the detachment immediately.[90]

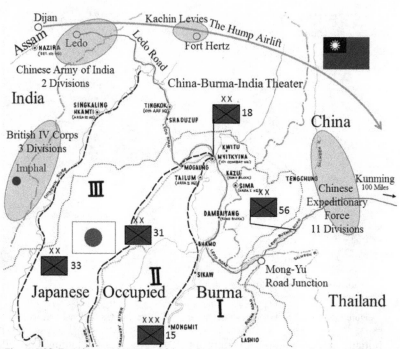

Figure 1-20. Detachment 101's Area of Operations. Note: Roman numerals indicate Det 101's three operating sectors.

In the summer of 1942, twenty OSS men of Detachment 101 parachuted into the Kaukkwe valley of Central Burma and organized Kachin tribesmen into a formidable guerrilla fighting force. With some initial setbacks, Eifler reoriented his unit's focus from sabotage to guerrilla warfare and was able to organize a formidable striking force consisting mostly of Kachin tribesmen. Impressed with Det 101's abilities, Stilwell authorized an expansion of the Detachment's strength and activities. With limited resources, Stilwell hoped that the Detachment could at a minimum frustrate the Japanese use of Myitkyina airfield, informing Eifler, "All I want to hear are booms from the jungle."

The OSS found the Kachins to be natural guerrilla fighters. David Hogan observes,

---

[90] Ibi Hogan, US Army Special Operations in World War II, 104-105.

They showed great care in the planning and preparation of an ambush, particularly in their use of the pungyi stick, a smoke-hardened bamboo stake of one to two feet in length. In preparing an ambush, the Kachins camouflaged the site to appear as natural as possible, placed their automatic weapons to rake the trail, and planted pungyis in the foliage alongside the path. Once the Japanese entered the area, the fire of the automatic weapons drove the surprised enemy troops into the undergrowth, where they impaled themselves on the pungyis.[91]

It has been estimated that 70 to 80 percent of all combat intelligence utilized by the CBI Theater headquarters originated from OSS Detachment 101. Additionally, the 10th Air Force reported that Detachment 101 furnished 70 percent of all its available intelligence and designated 90 percent of its targets. Det 101's efforts opened the way for Wingate's Raiders, Stilwell's Chinese forces and Merrill's Marauders (5307th Composite Unit), which was given the code name *Galahad*.

Myitkyina Airfield Seizure

Beginning in December 1942, under the direction of Stilwell, a new supply route to China was being built. With a jumping off point at Ledo railhead in Assam, India, the "Ledo Road" was to carve its way through the Kumon Mountain Range to Mong-Yu road junction where it joined the Burma Road (See Figure 1-21). Stilwell's staff estimated that the Ledo Road would be able to supply some 60,000 tons of material per month. This estimate greatly surpassing the tonnage airlifted over the Hump to China. Aware of Stilwell's intentions to reopen a supply link with China, the Japanese reinforced their forces in Burma bringing their strength to some 185,000 men. Japanese control of the north Burmese city of Myitkyina and the surrounding region blocked the completion of the new supply route. For this reason, and due to its strategic position at the terminus of the rail line from Rangoon and Mandalay, Stilwell's plan hinged upon taking Myitkyina. While British-led Kachin and Gurkha forces were fighting their way south, and Wingate's Chindits covering their flanks, Stilwell directed *Galahad* to take Myitkyina airfield. The Marauders had already fought their way through two arduous jungle campaigns. However, by this time, they had lost about 700 of their original 2,997 men to disease and wounds.

---

[91] Hogan, US Army Special Operations in World War II, 109.

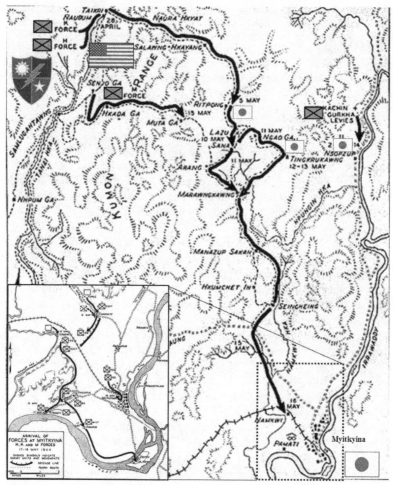

Figure 1-21. Myitkyina Raid 18 April, 1944.

OSS Det 101 veteran Roger Hilsman recounts, "Therefore a company of American-led OSS Kachin guerrillas was added to one of the Marauder columns and a whole Chinese regiment was attached to each of the two other columns (the 42nd and 150th Chinese Infantry Regiments), bringing the entire force to 7,000 men."[92]

Departing Nhpum Ga on April 21, 1944, hungry, tired and exhausted, with many weak from disease, the Marauders navigated their way through

---

[92] Hilsman, American Guerrilla: My War Behind Enemy Lines, 78.

100 kilometers of mountainous jungle. Traversing the 6,000 foot Kumon Range, the Marauders fought an action on the 6th of May, easily pushing the Japanese aside. Three weeks later, on 17 May 1944, Galahad attacked the unsuspecting Japanese garrison at the Myitkyina airfield (See Figure 1-20). With complete surprise, the airfield seizure was an unparalleled success. The Marauders sent the message "Merchant of Venice," the brevity code that airfield was secured; the resupply planes could now land.

As the Marauders secured the airfield perimeter, scores of gliders and C-47s landed on the bomb-pocked, shell ridden airfield. However, a sudden reversal of fortune threw the Marauders back on a defensive struggle. Due to faulty Allied intelligence, the town of Myitkyina had more Japanese than was expected, leaving Galahad with insufficient forces on hand to take the town. So instead of being relieved as promised, Galahad immediately went into the battle of Myitkyina. Making matters worse, the Japanese were able to quickly reinforce the town with some 4,000 more men, and repulsed an assault made by elements of two Chinese regiments. Further adding insult to injury, the Monsoon arrived, making a muddy soup of the airstrip. However, with the airfield secure, men and material began flowing into Myitkyina.

Undaunted by even dysentery, many of the Marauders resorted to cutting the seat of their trousers out in order to stay in the fight. Losses were heavy, but soon Allied reinforcements arrived to carry on the fight. When the town finally fell to the Allies on 3 August, only about 200 Marauders remained.[93] But the capture of the Myitkyina airstrip brought immediate results. It meant that as soon as the Ledo Road reached it, the Allies would have a great supply base within easy distance of China itself. Further, it enabled the Air Transport Command to not only shorten the *Hump* trip, it further doubled the monthly supply tonnage.[94]

By March 1944 the Burma (Ledo) Road was reopened and Detachment 101 moved farther north as the Japanese retreated. Operational until the end of the war, the OSS Detachment 101 organized 11,000 Kachin tribesmen into a force that eventually killed some 6,000 Japanese at a loss of only 206 of its own (22 were Americans).

In early 1945, the executive officer of Det 101, William Peers (1914-1984), was given the command of OSS Detachment 202. Detachment 202's mission was to build a Chinese commando unit of 3,000 to oust the Japanese

---

[93] Of the 1,300 Marauders that reached Myitkyina, some 600 were evacuated to rear hospitals between 18 May and 1 June. Of the remaining 700, before the fall of Myitkyina, 123 were killed, 293 wounded, 8 missing, 503 contracted amoebic dysentery, 149 scrub typhus, and 296 malaria. Following Myitkyina, the Marauders, nearly annihilated by disease, were reconstituted the 475th Infantry Regiment, and continued to fight the Japanese in Burma until the end of the war. On 21 June, 1954 the 475th was redesignated the 75th Infantry Regiment, which today is the 75th Ranger Regiment.

[94] Arquilla, From Troy to Entebbe, 287.

from China. Detachment 202 collected intelligence and supported Chinese forces in order to tie down as many Japanese troops as possible. However, working with Chiang Kai-shek's army proved to be a difficult assignment as few Chinese troops were of adequate physical condition to carry out commando type missions. In time, better food, physical training, and great instruction by the OGs produced seven Chinese commando units for combat. These SO guerrilla groups, some as large as 1,500 men, cut rails, blew up road and train bridges, rescued downed Allied pilots, and killed thousands of Japanese troops sometimes up to 500 miles behind enemy lines. The cessation of hostilities ended the Detachment's mission in China.

Within the CBI Theater, additional OSS Detachments conducted combat, intelligence, and sustainment operations. Detachment 303, a supplies and services unit, was based out of Delhi. In late 1943, Detachment 404 was established to help coordinate intelligence collection and operations between the OSS and SOE in the Far East. Based out of Sri Lanka, Detachment 404 worked closely with Admiral Lord Louis Mountbatten's British Southeast Asia Command (SEAC). Lastly Detachment 505 in Calcutta became the primary supply base for the OSS in China.

The fate of the OSS lay intertwined with President Roosevelt and so died along with him in April 1945. Roosevelt had been Donovan's most stalwart supporter but after his death many high ranking officers such as Nimitz and MacArthur viewed the OSS as unnecessary. Ultimately the combined jealous subterfuge of other agencies led to initial budget cuts and then disbandment in September of 1945. The functional areas of the OSS were absorbed back into the conventional military. The Special Operations branch died out but would be reborn with the efforts of BG Robert McClure, and Colonels Aaron Bank, Russell Volckmann, and Wendell Fertig. From its intelligence operations branch sprang the Central Intelligence Agency on Sept. 18, 1947.[95]

The Creation of Special Forces

The pathway to the creation of the Special Forces was through psychological warfare, the catalyst was the Korean War and the threat of the Soviet advance in Western Europe. Secretary of the Army Frank Pace created the Psychological Warfare department in 1951. Pace named Brigadier General Robert McClure, who served as Eisenhower's chief of psychological warfare in WWII, to head the revised department. McClure

---

[95] The US Security Act of 1947 signed by President Truman realigned and reorganized the US Armed Forces, foreign policy, and Intelligence community apparatus in the aftermath of WWII. This act of Congress created the Joint Chiefs of Staff, the National Security Council, the office of the Secretary of Defense, and the CIA. This act was later amended to create the Department of Defense in 1949.

envisioned special operations as a functional area of psychological warfare, and soon began to lobby for personnel to be assigned to his command for this endeavor. Seeking to create a "behind enemy lines" guerilla warfare capability, McClure created a Special Operations Division and gathered unto himself experienced officers with expertise in the field.

McClure brought in Colonel Melvin Blair and Lt Colonel Waters, who both had served in Merrill's Marauders; Colonel Aaron Bank, who fought alongside the Maquis in France as a Jedburgh; and Colonel Wendell Fertig, who had commanded guerilla forces in the Philippines; and Colonel Russell Volckmann, who organized and conducted guerrilla warfare against the Japanese in the Philippines as well as partisan warfare in North Korea.[96] Although McClure believed unconventional warfare (UW) and psychological warfare were inseparably joined, his vision of a Special Operations Division, eclectic sense to provide it with talented and experienced leadership, along with the vast experiences of these select men, effectively laid the foundation, as well as, the core doctrinal concepts, of what was to become the Special Forces.

As WWII ended, President Harry S. Truman began to dismantle the massive American war machine. Truman's administration drastically reduced the size and functional areas of the armed forces believing that nuclear weapons alone would be an effective deterrent to war, and that would render large scale conventional warfare obsolete. On June 25, 1950, the North Korean People's Army (NKPA) attacked South Korea. All of the specialized units of WWII such as the OSS, the Rangers, the First Special Service Force, and Merrill's Marauders had been disbanded. Thus at the outset of the Korean War the US Army had no organized UW organization. After the creation of 10th SF Group in 1952, and as the pool of SF personnel steadily grew at Fort Bragg, assignments were divided into three groups: the first would be bound for Bad Tölz, Germany with Colonel Bank, the second would remain at Fort Bragg and become the 77th SFG (A), and the third would be bound for Korea.

UW in the Korean War

The 8th Army, seizing the initiative, capitalized on the anti-Communist potential of North Korea by organizing some 25,000 guerrilla fighters into an effective UW campaign. This effort was consolidated under the United Nations Partisan Forces, Korea (UNPFK). Under the command of Colonel John H. McGee, the Attrition Section, later redesignated the Miscellaneous Division, conducted UW in concert with the Joint Advisory Commission,

---

[96] Paddock, US Army Unconventional Warfare, 119.

Korea (JACK), the CIA's UW arm in the Korean War. To conduct operations, McGhee created three operational areas: to the west Leopard, the east Kirkland, and along the 38th Parallel in the center, the Tactical Liaison Office or TLO (See Figure 1-22). McGhee's Miscellaneous Unit, known as the *White Tigers*, was later redesignated the 8086th and then the 8240th Army Units (AU). The White Tigers conducted guerrilla warfare consisting of: behind-the-lines tactical intelligence gathering, raids and sabotage, ambushes, rescued downed pilots and POWs, and provided bomb damage assessment (BDA) in North Korea from February 1951 to February 1954.

While the war in Korea had been raging, BG McClure had been urging the US Far East Command (FEC) to request SF soldiers to join the fight, however, the first school-trained SF soldiers would not be deployed to Korea until March 1953.[97] To complicate matters, FEC assigned the SF soldiers as individual replacements and not as members of operational teams. By the end of the war there were 200 SF troopers advising some 22,000 partisans.[98] Manned chiefly with anti-communist partisans originating from North Korea, the White Tigers were organized, trained and led by a select cadre of Army junior officers, mainly from the infantry branch, and operated from islands in the Yellow Sea.

In addition to the numerous raids, an ongoing attempt to establish base camps for guerrilla operations in the North was a perennial goal. McGhee's concept for developing the fighting potential of the anti-Communist forces was to accomplish the following three key tasks:

1. Establish a major base on Paengnyong-do, an island just off the western coast of North Korea's Hwanghae Peninsula.
2. Establish a mobile base in North Korea's eastern mountain range.
3. Establish a guerrilla training facility at Pusan in the south.

McGhee organized his forces along these conceptual lines. Its mission was: To conduct the guerrilla activities of intelligence, attrition, and haven (setting up a guerrilla base) in the enemy's rear as well as provide maximum tactical support to EUSA during its coming advance to liberate North Korea.[99]

---

[97] Finlayson, Guerrillas in Their Midst, Veritas, ARSOF in Korea: Part VI, 3.
[98] Malcom, White Tigers: My Secret War in Korea, 186. One such SF trooper, 2LT Joseph M. Castro, was the first Special Forces trained officer to die in combat. Castro volunteered for combat duty in Korea and was assigned to the 8240th AU. He was killed on a raid in North Korea on 17 May, 1953 while leading men of the 2nd Partisan Infantry Regiment, UNPIK, which was part of Wolfpack 8.
[99] Piasecki, Soldier, Leader, Trainer, Veritas, ARSOF in Korea: Part VI, 31.

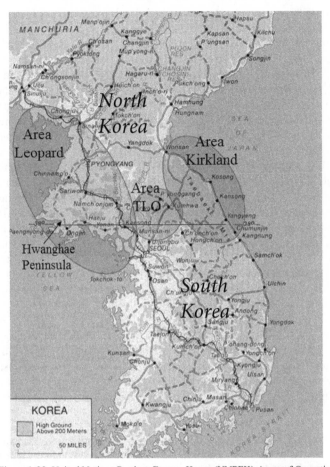

Figure 1-22. United Nations Partisan Forces, Korea (UNPFK) Areas of Operation.

One of the first covert missions, Operation Virginia I, a sabotage mission, was conducted on March 15, 1951, by twenty partisans of South Korea's officer candidate school and four advisors, three American, one Brit. The mission was to interdict an enemy rail line; all but five members of the raiding party were killed with no evidence of any significant damage to the enemy inflicted.[100]

---

[100] Malcom, White Tigers: My Secret War in Korea, 134. Malcom recounts that the majority of these air drop missions were virtually suicide, and one of the great failings of these missions was the fact that the agents were unfamiliar with the terrain. Additionally, he states, that the airborne operations in Baker Sector were an unqualified disaster. Available records indicate

Thousands of combat actions were planned and executed by the White Tigers from secure bases. One very successful sabotage operation was conducted in August 1952 by members of Miscellaneous AU based out of Area Leopard. The mission was to destroy a hydroelectric plant 40 miles north of Pyongyang. Earlier attempts at knocking out the plant had failed. Donkey-10 agents, based from Cho-do in the Yellow Sea, just off the coast of North Korea, infiltrated into North Korea, and emplaced flares around the plant. Guided by the light from the flares, the bombers destroyed the plant. Hundreds of similar small-scale raids and ambushes were launched from bases in the three operational areas.

By the summer of 1951, the front line had stabilized along the 38th Parallel making combat operations more static. This situation called for the need of more tactical and less strategic intelligence. To meet this need the Tactical Liaison Offices (TLO) was created. The TLO focused its efforts on behind-the-lines HUMINT. Line-Crossers, as they were known, were Korean men, women and teenagers who were led by US Army personnel. A typical TLO operation sent Line-Crossers behind-the-lines dressed in North Korean student clothes to gather intelligence on enemy troop concentrations, supply depots, and movements, which would serve as targets for American bombing missions.[101]

The White Tigers performed missions in Korea until it was disbanded in February 1954. Numbering over 20,000, some 10,000 were transferred to the ROK Army after the cease fire. All told, the partisan operations in Korea amounted to 69,000 enemy casualties, 950 prisoners, 5,000 weapons, 2,700 vehicles and 80 bridges destroyed, in 4,445 actions. The total cost to the US government: roughly $100 million.[102] Regarding the role of SF in the Korean War, Colonel Ben Malcom writes,

There was little question in my mind that the Special Forces were the appropriate way to deal with partisans, guerrillas, and indigenous paramilitary groups in a limited war. It was the logical extension of the OSS. It was the link necessary to carry unconventional warfare operations from what they had been in WWII into an era in which the superpowers fought limited wars by proxy.[103]

10th SFG (A)

Special Forces came into existence on May 19, 1952 with the establishment of HHC, 10th Special Forces Group with an authorization for

---

that 393 armed partisans and agents participated in 22 behind enemy line airdrops between December 1950 and April 1953.
[101] Piasecki, The Line-Crossers, Veritas, ARSOF in Korea: Part VI, 40
[102] Malcom, White Tigers: My Secret War in Korea, 192.
[103] Ibid, 199.

122 officers and NCOs. When Colonel Bank assumed command on June 19, 1952, he had a grand total of seven NCOs and one warrant officer present for duty. Earlier that year, Lt Colonel Blair and Colonel Volckmann had traveled extensively promoting the new unit. Volunteers had to be at least twenty-one years old, airborne qualified or willing to become so, as well as submit to physical and psychological testing. Additionally, as was hoped to bolster volunteers, the Lodge Act was passed which provided for the enlistment of up to 12,500 personnel. However, the actual recruitment fell quite short of expectations. By the end of 1952 only twenty-two Lodge Act personnel had been assigned to the 10th SFG. [104]

'Double volunteers' (for both Airborne and Special Forces training) reported to Smoke Bomb Hill and began their initial phase of SF training. By August of 1952, the strength of 10th SFG had grown to 259 personnel. Bank and his staff organized the force along the OSS Operational Group (OG) lines, which consisted of 15 personnel: a commander, an executive officer, and thirteen NCOs who specialized in weapons and tactics, engineering and explosives, radio communications, medical, and operations and intelligence functional areas.

The Group's mission concept was: "To infiltrate its component operational detachments, by air, sea, or land, to designated areas within the enemy's sphere of influence and organize the indigenous guerilla potential on a quasi-military basis for tactical and strategic exploitation in conjunction with our land, sea, and air forces."[105]

Camp Mackall

Small Unit Training and FTXs were conducted at Camp Mackall, NC, where Bank along with other experienced officers and NCOs drew upon their WWII and Korean War experiences to indoctrinate the new recruits. [106]

---

[104] The Lodge Act (Lodge-Philbin), a US law drafted pushed through Congress by Senator Henry C. Lodge Jr. of Massachusetts for the enlistment of foreign nationals into US military service. The Lodge Act was signed on June 30, 1950. Although the Act gained only a fraction of what was available, it did glean men like Captain Larry Thorne. Thorne, a legendary name in SF, was a Finnish Commando in the Winter War with Russia in the 1940s, joined the US Army by way of the Lodge Act, joined the 77th SFG (later the 7th SFG) in 1956, served as Team Leader of A-734 in the Mekong delta region, and finally as SOG's Ops Officer at Kham Duc in 1965. Thorne died 18 Oct, 1965 when the H-34 helicopter carrying him crashed in dense fog after ensuring his first cross border recon teams had infiltrated.

[105] Special Forces Training Circular, 13 May, 1952.

[106] UW training evolved into an exercise called Robin Sage, which was named after Major Jerry M. Sage's daughter. Major Sage was a COI / OSS agent who was wounded and captured in February 1943 while blowing bridges behind General Erwin Rommel's lines in North Africa. He posed successfully as a shot-down airman (and thus avoided being shot) and was brought into Stalag Luft III in April 1943. He was a great leader and was very active in organizing and

The emphasis of the training in the early 1950s was on supporting guerrilla operations because the mission that was envisioned was assisting anti-communist, anti-Soviet resistance groups operating in non-Russian territories of Eastern and Central Europe occupied by an invading Red Army; just as OSS groups had aided anti-fascist resistance groups behind German and Japanese lines in World War II. After individual and SF training were completed, personnel received additional training throughout the US such as: military mountaineering, pack mule transport, small boat operations, as well as additional radio and medical training. By April 1953, the Group had reached, largely through the recruiting efforts of 10th Group soldiers, its authorized strength of 1,700 officers and NCOs. The Joint Chiefs of Staff (JCS) had approved of the European war plans that incorporated the 10th SFG and Bank now readied his Group for deployment.

10th SFG (A) Moves to Bad Tölz

After less than a year and a half as a full SF Group, Bank's men proved to the Army's satisfaction that they had mastered the skills of their new trade. In the summer of 1953, Donovan visited Fort Bragg to inspect the troops of the new 10th Special Forces Group. Impressed after a day of briefing and demonstrations, Donovan recognized that they had adopted the legacy of OSS Special Operations. "You have revived precious memories," he said as he left. "You are the offspring of the OSS."[107] On November 11, 1953, half of the 10th SF Group was deployed to Bad Tölz, West Germany. There the Group prepared to support resistance movements and organize guerrilla forces inside the Soviet-Warsaw Pact nations of Eastern Europe. The other half remained at Fort Bragg, where it was redesignated as the 77th SF Group. The split of the 10th and the 77th was the first sign that SF had established itself as an integral part of the Army's basic structure. For the rest of the 1950s, SF would grow slowly but consistently.

By 1958, the basic operational unit of SF had evolved into a 12-man team known as the SF ODA. Each member of the team – two officers, two operations and intelligence sergeants, two weapons sergeants, two communications sergeants, two medics and two engineers – were trained in unconventional warfare, were cross-trained in each other's specialties, and spoke at least one foreign language. This composition allowed each detachment to operate if necessary in two six-man teams, or split-A teams.

---

executing escape attempts. After escaping from South Camp twice, the Germans got tired of his trouble-making and sent him to the U.S. Army officer's camp, Oflag 64. He again escaped when this camp was evacuated in January 1945 and got home early through the Russian lines. After WWII, COL Sage became the commander of the 10th SF Group.

[107] Bank, From OSS to Green Berets, 186.

On Oct. 30, 1960, all SF Groups were reorganized under the combat arms regimental system. 1st Special Forces Regiment was organized in recognition of its lineage with the First Special Service Force of World War II.

Vietnam War

The Vietnam War was the legacy of France's failure to suppress nationalist forces in Indochina as it struggled to restore its colonial dominion after World War II.[108] Vietnam, Laos, and Cambodia had been a part of the French colonial empire since the late 1800s. In 1940, Japanese Forces invaded Vietnam and left the French colonial administration intact. Vietnamese nationalists rallied to Japan, but Ho Chi Minh and his communist insurgents, the *Viet Minh* aligned themselves with the Allies. During World War II in Vietnam, the Viet Minh launched a low-level rural insurgency against the Vichy French authorities who were governing the colonies under Japanese supervision.

The U.S. Army's first encounters with Ho Chi Minh were brief and sympathetic. During World War II, Ho's anti-Japanese resistance fighters helped to rescue downed American pilots and furnished information on Japanese forces in Indochina.[109] In July 1945, an OSS team code-named Deer, parachuted into northern Vietnam to assist Ho's insurgents.[110] The Deer mission, consisting of three Americans, one Frenchman, and two Vietnamese trained the Viet Minh. After the defeat of Japan, the OSS left Vietnam. Ho Chi Minh, taking advantage of the political vacuum, hastily organized the Viet Minh as a nationalist front, masking its Communist leadership in order to appeal to broad patriotic sentiment.[111] Ho moved on Hanoi, which fell to him in September, 1945, while French and various factions in the south struggled for power in Saigon. Five years later, Army advisers of the newly formed U.S. Military Assistance Advisory Group (MAAG), Indochina, were aiding France against the Viet Minh.

Following the defeat of Japan in August 1945, and despite American disapproval, the French returned to stake their claim over Indochina, and began a protracted war with the Viet Minh for control of Vietnam. The revolution in Vietnam began in December 1946 after the Viet Minh

---

[108] CMH, The US Army in Vietnam, 619.

[109] Ibid.

[110] Additionally, seven OSS agents, commanded by LTC A. Peter Dewey, landed in Saigon in order to search for missing Americans and gather intelligence. Mistaking Dewey for a Frenchman, the Viet Minh killed him in an ambush while he was attempting to leave Saigon. He was the first of 60,000 Americans to die there.

[111] Karnow, Vietnam A History, 152.

Government and the French authorities failed to arrive at a mutually agreeable compromise concerning Vietnam's future.

The rebellion began with guerrilla warfare, but later developed into a combination of guerrilla and regular warfare.[112] However, after the Communist victory of 1949 in China, and with the outset of the war in Korea in 1950, President Truman amended America's approach to France's war in Indochina against Ho Chi Minh, by adding a new dimension to US foreign policy, the global containment of Communism. In 1950, Truman sent the Military Assistance Advisory Group (MAAG) to Vietnam to assist French forces and oversee the use of $10 million worth of US equipment. Aid to the French dramatically increased annually and would amount to over $2 billion by 1954.

American officials disagreed over the seriousness of the guerrilla threat, the priority to be accorded political or military measures, and the need for special counter guerrilla training for the South Vietnamese Army. Only a handful of the MAAG's advisers had personal experience in counterinsurgency warfare.

To compound matters, MAAG's attempts at forming a South Vietnamese Army was effectively resisted and stymied by the French arrogant colonial mentality. Provided with aircraft, artillery, tanks, vehicles, weapons, and other equipment and supplies the French did not fail for want of equipment. Instead, they put American aid at the service of a flawed strategy that sought to defeat the elusive Viet Minh in set-piece battles, but neglected to cultivate the loyalty and support of the Vietnamese people. Regarding the French forces in Vietnam, Robert Taber writes,

What they failed to realize initially was that, although they controlled the roads, they were fighting an enemy that had no need of roads, being without transport or heavy artillery to move. They seized strong points, but these strong points commanded nothing, since the enemy was not stationary but fluid and offered no contest for

---

[112] Casebook in Insurgency, 25.

strong points or for territory. For where the French were fighting to control the national territory – that meant to occupy it – the guerrillas were interested only in winning the population. Note: this is the essential contrast between conventional war and guerrilla war.[113]

Too few in number to provide more than a veneer of security in most rural areas, the French were unable to suppress the guerrillas or to prevent the underground Communist shadow government from reappearing whenever French forces left one area to fight elsewhere. In 1954, the commanding general of French forces in Indochina, General Henri Navarre, allowed the United States to send liaison officers to Vietnamese forces, but it was too late. The fall of Dien Bien Phu on 7 May, 1954, epitomized the shortcomings of French strategy. Following the French defeat, peace negotiations began in Geneva and hastened France's disengagement from Indochina. On 20 July, France and the Viet Minh agreed to end hostilities and to divide Vietnam temporarily into two zones at the 17th parallel (Figure 1-22 above). The Geneva Armistice Agreement separated Vietnam into the north under Ho Chi Minh, and the south under Bao Dai, the former emperor of Vietnam.[114]

In 1954, Eisenhower pledged economic aid to assist the government of South Vietnam in developing and maintaining a strong viable state which would be capable of resisting subversion and aggression through military means. With American economic aid, the South began to prosper. Defensive measures were enhanced in 1955 when the US along with several Asian nations signed a collective defense treaty and formed SEATO – South East Asia Treaty Organization. The North's response was to subvert the South's government through terrorism and insurgency. And by 1960, virtually all of South Vietnam had become a combat zone.

On January 6, 1961, Nikita Khrushchev, the Premier of the Soviet Union, made official what the world had known for some time. He announced that the Soviet Union stands behind and supports what he called, "wars of liberation." By this Khrushchev meant that insurgent action, consisting of subversion and covert aggression against the constituted governments of the free world, would bring in new territory under communist domination. The US, upholding its firm stance against Communism, continued to provide economic and military assistance to South Vietnam through the MAAG program. In the late 1950s, US policy-makers had an opportunity to observe the struggle of France with the insurgents and to become familiar with the

---

[113] Taber, War of the Flea: The Classic Study of Guerrilla Warfare, 61.
[114] The US refused to sign the Accord which stipulated, among other things, such as the withdrawal of the French Forces from Vietnam, that an overall (North and South) free election was to be held by 1956. President Diem refused to comply with this stipulation.

political and military situation in Vietnam. It was also during those years that the U.S. Army Special Forces came into existence.[115]

First in Asia

The 1st Special Forces Group (A) was activated at Camp Drake (near Tokyo), Japan, on 24 June, 1957.[116] Later that year, 1st SF Group sent Detachment A-14 to South Vietnam to begin the training of indigenous personnel at Nha Trang. In the summer and fall of that year, 58 indigenous personnel received commando training from A-14, and became the nucleus of the South Vietnamese 1st Observation Group. CPT Harry G. Cramer Jr., the Team Leader of A-14, died during a training exercise on the 21st of October, 1957, making him the first Green Beret to die in Vietnam. Later that year, following additional training, the 1st Observation Group reached a strength of 400 commandos. This new unit constituted South Vietnam's guerilla fighting capability. In November of 1961, the unit was redesignated the Vietnamese 77th Group.

Covert Operations in Vietnam

As part of the National Security Act of 1947, the CIA was created and later assigned responsibility for covert operations. The CIA became the sole proprietor of UW operations, and in 1956 began operating in Vietnam under the program entitled the First Observations Group. This program organized guerilla forces in Quang Tri province. Although the forces gathered under this program were considered for guerilla warfare in the North, for lack of interest it never got off the ground.

By the time Kennedy took office in 1960, the Cold War had shifted to the Third World. Communists sought to control independence movements and anti-colonial guerrilla wars through "wars of national liberation." President Kennedy saw the Special Forces as potentially effective agents of counter-insurgency. Kennedy provided the Special Forces with increased resources and status and allowed them to become the first American soldiers to wear berets, for which they became popularly known as "the Green Berets."

In the 1960s, Special Forces Groups, now emphasizing counter-insurgency tactics, and the multiplier effect of having 12-man A Teams,

---

[115] Vietnam Studies, 1961-1971, CMH Publication 93, 3.

[116] 1st SFG was inactivated 28 June, 1974, at Fort Bragg, North Carolina and spent ten years dormant until it was activated again 4 September, 1984, at Fort Lewis, Washington. 1st SFG holds the portentous distinction of having the first and last Special Forces men killed in Vietnam: CPT Harry Cramer killed 21 October 1957 and SGT Fred Mick killed 12 October 1972; as well as the first man, SFC Nathan Chapman killed 4 January, 2002, in Afghanistan.

which could assist or lead indigenous forces of up to 500 men, advised or actually fought against Communist-inspired guerrillas in Latin America and Southeast Asia. Witnessing this capability, the President demanded more action in Vietnam, and the CIA appeared to him as dragging their feet. Following the Bay of Pigs debacle of 17-19 April, 1961, Kennedy gave the CIA a vote of no confidence at planning and executing covert paramilitary operations.[117] Within two months, the President transferred executive branch responsibility for executing UW operations from the CIA to the Pentagon.[118] And within a year, the framework necessary for the military to take over operations in Vietnam would be established.

White Star

Project White Star began in 1959 as Operation Hotfoot with the deployment of 107 Green Berets of the 77th Special Forces Group (later designated the 7th SFG in May 1960). Under the command of LTC Arthur D. "Bull" Simons, additional SF A-Detachments from 1st SFG (A) were sent as White Star grew as a project operating under the guise of MAAG Laos. The purpose of the project was to train the Royal Laotian Army as well as indigenous Kha, Hmong, and Yao tribesmen to destroy the Pathet Lao communist insurgency.

Later, White Star's mission parameters expanded to include operations against the NVA, which was using Laos as a staging and resupply area for its operations in South Vietnam. At the project's height in early 1962, it had reached a total of 433 SF personnel. SF troopers used a variety of weapons in Laos, including the M1 and M2 carbines, along with the M3 .45 cal grease guns, and British Sten guns. Heavy weapons consisted of 81mm mortars (without sights) and 75 mm recoilless rifles.[119] White Star proved to be a training ground for what would lie ahead in Vietnam, namely Foreign Internal Defense (FID), and counterinsurgency (COIN).

Although, geopolitically White Star proved ineffectual, the experiences gained from it provided much wealth to the SF Teams involved. Overall, White Star was successful at clearing southern Laos, namely the Bolovens Plateau, from insurgent activity, and began to strike at the Ho Chi Minh Trail, the NVA center of gravity. However, the project met its untimely death at the hands of the Geneva Accords of 1962 which declared Laos a neutral state.

---

[117] It was the 77th Special Forces Group, who, in 1961, trained the infantryman and paratroopers of Brigade 2506, in Nicaragua and Guatamala, for the preparation of the invasion of Cuba at the Bay of Pigs.
[118] Shultz, The Secret War Against Hanoi, 18.
[119] Stanton, The Green Berets at War, 30.

Chapter 1   A Concise History of the Special Forces

The 6th and 8th SF Groups

The 6th Special Forces Group was activated in 1963 at Fort Bragg, North Carolina. Its area of operation was Southwest Asia, particularly Iraq and Iran. It also sent teams TDY to Southeast Asia. Many of the 103 original Son Tay raiders were volunteers from 6th SF Group. The 8th Special Forces Group was activated in 1963 at Fort Gulick, Panama Canal Zone. The primary mission of 8th Group was counterinsurgency training for the armies of Latin America. A mobile training team (MTT) from the 8th Special Forces Group trained and advised the Bolivian Ranger Battalion that captured and killed Che Guevara in the fall of 1967. Prior to that, MTTs from the 8th Group trained counterinsurgent units in Venezuela, Colombia and Ecuador that killed three of Che Guevara's lieutenants whom he had personally dispatched to those three nations to foment revolutions. The 6th SF Group was deactivated in 1971. A year later, the 8th SF Group was deactivated in 1972.

Viet Cong

The National Liberation Front for South Vietnam, also known as the Viet Cong, was a political and military organization based in South Vietnam (and Cambodia) that fought the Government of the Republic of Vietnam (South Vietnam) and its ally, the United States, in the Vietnam War from 1959 to 1975. The Viet Cong insurgency fought South Vietnamese and American forces on two fronts: an armed conflict and a political battle for the hearts and minds of villagers in rural South Vietnam. Initially, the insurgency used subversive and terrorist tactics to destabilize the South Vietnamese government, but began to use guerrilla warfare and eventually large conventional military units, following increased intervention by the United States.[120] The National Liberation Front (NLF) or Viet Cong was the North Vietnamese sponsored insurgency in South Vietnam. From a strength of approximately 5,000 at the start of 1959, the Viet Cong's ranks grew to about 100,000 at the end of 1964. The number of infiltrators alone during that period was estimated at 41,000.

The growth of the insurgency reflected not only North Vietnam's skill in infiltrating men and weapons, but South Vietnam's inability to control its porous borders, as well as Diem's failure to develop a credible pacification program to reduce Viet Cong influence in the countryside.[121] As Viet Cong military strength increased, attacks against the paramilitary forces, and

---

[120] Casebook in Insurgency and Revolutionary Warfare Volume II .
[121] CMH, The US Army in Vietnam, 627.

occasionally against the South Vietnamese Army, became more frequent. Many of these attacks were conducted to obtain equipment, arms, and ammunition, but all were hailed by the guerrillas as evidence of the government's inability to protect its citizens.

Regarding this central tenet of successful insurgency, Robert Taber observes,

Without the consent and active aid of the people, the guerrilla would be merely a bandit, and could not long survive. If, on the other hand, the counterinsurgent could claim this same support, the guerilla would not exist, because there would be no war, no revolution. The cause would have evaporated; the popular impulse toward radical change – cause or no cause – would be dead.[122]

The Viet Cong thrived on their access to and control of the people, who formed the most important part of their support base. The population provided both economic and manpower resources to sustain and expand the insurgency. Political agitation and military activity also quickened in the Central Highlands, where Viet Cong agents recruited among the Montagnard tribes.[123]

Viet Cong military forces varied from village guerrillas, who were farmers by day and fighters by night, to full-time professional soldiers. Organized into squads and platoons, part-time guerrillas had several military functions. They gathered intelligence, passing it on to district or provincial authorities; they proselytized, propagandized, recruited, and provided security for local cadres. They reconnoitered the battlefield, served as porters and guides, created diversions, evacuated wounded and retrieved weapons. Their very presence and watchfulness in a hamlet or village inhibited the population from aiding the government. Soon after John F. Kennedy became President in 1961, he sharply increased military and economic aid to South Vietnam to help Diem defeat the growing insurgency.

Strategic Hamlet and CIDG Programs

In order to eliminate the armed revolutionary movement of the Viet Cong, the US strategy in South Vietnam amounted to two initiatives: the Strategic Hamlet program and the Civilian Irregular Defense Group (CIDG). The first, planned by the CIA, and conducted largely by the Army of the Republic of Vietnam (ARVN), involved the forced removal of Vietnamese from their villages to reside in what amounted to armed defensive camps

---

[122] Taber, The War of the Flea: The Classic Study of Guerrilla Warfare, 12.
[123] Army Military History, The US Army in Vietnam,624.

called Strategic Hamlets. The program was a revision to Diem's rural community development program he began in 1959 in order to prevent the Viet Cong from assuming control of the peasant population.

The second, also developed by the CIA, was the CIDG program, which sought to counter the encroaching Viet Cong by developing South Vietnamese irregular military forces from minority populations. Due to the corruption in Diems' administration, the Strategic Hamlet program was, in short, an attempt to translate the newly articulated theory of counter-insurgency into operational reality, and as such fell far short of its goals.[124] However, the CIDG program was a great success. And following Operation Switchback in 1963, operational control of the program was transferred from the CIA to Military Assistance Command Vietnam (MACV).[125] MACV was created in February of 1962, and headquartered in Saigon in order to command and control the burgeoning advisory and assistance efforts.

Facing trouble spots in Latin America, Africa, and Southeast Asia, JFK took a keen interest in the US Army's Special Forces, believing that their skills in unconventional warfare were well suited to countering insurgency. During his first year in office, he increased the strength of the Special Forces from about 1,500 to 9,000 and authorized them to wear a distinctive green beret. In the same year he greatly enlarged their role in South Vietnam.[126] The CIDG program, the name given to the paramilitary counter-insurgency effort in Vietnam, began in Darlac province in late 1961. It proved to be one of the chief works of the Special Forces in Vietnam. There were two principal reasons for the creation of the CIDG program.

First, the US Mission in Saigon believed that a paramilitary force should be developed from the minority groups of South Vietnam in order to strengthen and broaden the counterinsurgency effort of the Vietnamese government. Second, the Montagnards and other minority groups were prime targets for Communist propaganda. This was partly because of their

---

[124] Pentagon Papers, IV, B 2. The Strategic Hamlet program which began in 1961 was exposed as nearly a complete failure following Diem's assassination in 1963. Several problems plagued the Strategic Hamlet program which consisted of at least the following: most peasants were Buddhists which practiced ancestor worship, and their relocation prevented this. This alone made it extremely unpopular with the people; displaced villagers lacked adequate security from the VC; Diem's administration was terribly corrupt, and was known to require the peasants to purchase the supplies necessary for building the hamlets which had already been provided by the US. It is estimated that fewer than 20% of the 8600 hamlets met defensive readiness and conditions worthy of such funding to the project. Overall it was the inability of the US to induce reform and ensure the correct execution of the program that led to failure.

[125] Operation Switchback was the operational name given to the transference of responsibility for overt UW paramilitary activities from the CIA to MACV, as specified by NSA Memorandum 57.

[126] Shultz, The Secret War Against Hanoi, 6.

dissatisfaction with the Vietnamese government, and it was important to prevent the Viet Cong from recruiting them and taking complete control of their large and strategic land holdings.[127]

The origins of the CIDG program (initially called the Village Defense Program VDP) began when the CIA Station Chief, William Colby, sent David Nuttles, Captain Pho (Diem's CIA), and an SF medical sergeant into one of the chief Rhade tribal villages, Buon Enao.[128] When they arrived they found that the VC had been extorting money and food from them, and the chieftain's daughter lay ill. Through Nuttle's fluent Rhade and the SF medic's expertise, the chieftain agreed to cooperate, and the program got off the ground. The first Green Berets to begin on the program were CPT Ronald A. Shackleton and half of A-113. The team had been diverted from their MTT mission in Laos, and flown up to Ban Me Thout from Saigon on an unmarked CIA C-46 with Chinese Nationalist pilots. They landed on 14 February, 1962, and got the program under way.

Unlike the Strategic Hamlet Program, the Montagnards would remain in their own villages and receive modern weaponry and defensive tactics to defend their homes and families – something Diem's program never did. Upon arrival, A-113 quickly set out to establish Buon Enao's defensive perimeter by constructing defensive works, including fences and shelters. A-113 further conducted security patrols and weapons training. Additional A-Teams were brought in: A-213 at Buon Ho; A-214 at Buon Mi Ga, and A-334 at Buon Don Bak from 1st SFG; with A-2 at Ban Don from 5th SFG.[129] The program's success was expanded to encompass the neighboring villages.

By August of 1962, these five SF A-Teams had organized 200 additional Montagnard villages which encompassed a population of 10,000 Rhade tribesmen. That same month, A-113 was replaced by CPT Terry D. Cordell's A-334 (1st SFG) from Okinawa. CPT Cordell, a Citadel graduate, quickly won the respect of the Rhade tribe. In October that year, the VC conducted an attack against Buon Enao's defenses. CPT Cordell, while directing fires from an Air Force T-38, was shot down in plain view of the defenders. The enraged Rhade quickly counterattacked and defeated the VC. Realizing the program's future potential to negate VC activity, it was expanded country-wide and its name changed from the Village Defense Program (VDP) to the Civilian Irregular Defense Group (CIDG) Program.[130]

---

[127] Vietnam Studies, 1961-1971, CMH Publication 93, 19.
[128] Prados, Lost Crusader: The Secret Wars of CIA Director William Colby, 85.
[129] Stanton, Green Berets at War, 46.
[130] Shackleton, Village Defense, 138.

Chapter 1   A Concise History of the Special Forces

CIDG Camps

The Special Forces teams seemed tailor-made for the CIDG program, and the South Vietnamese declared Darlac province secure.[131] Although, the program was a success, and greatly increased the presence of Special Forces in Vietnam, none the less it was opposed by the Diem government, particularly because the South Vietnamese government feared the training and arming of its indigenous population. In the early months of 1962, an additional eight A-Teams had been committed to Colby's project. Initially, all in-country SF teams were attached to MAAG. The 1st, 5th, and 7th Special Forces Groups had been providing teams on a six month TDY basis.

In February 1962, the Joint Chiefs of Staff established the United States Military Assistance Command, Vietnam (USMACV) in Saigon as the senior American military headquarters in South Vietnam. General Paul D. Harkins was appointed its first commander. By September 1962, in order to control all in-country US SF teams, MACV created the US Army Special Forces (Provisional) Vietnam. Colonel George Morton, the first commander of USASF(P)V, began to command and control all Special Forces personnel in Vietnam, and continued to rotate A-Teams from Okinawa and Fort Bragg into the camps. Operational control to include all CIDG camps was complete by January, 1963. To assist with the CIDG strike camps, Colonel Morton enlisted the engineering expertise of two US Navy Seabee Technical Assistance Teams. These teams, along with civil affairs advisors, provided invaluable services and resources, and greatly contributed to the success of the CIDG strike camps.

To detect and impede the Viet Cong, camps were established astride infiltration corridors and near enemy base areas, especially along the Cambodian and Laotian borders.[132] But the camps themselves were vulnerable to enemy attack and, despite their presence, infiltration continued. At times, border control diverted tribal units from village defense, the original heart of the CIDG program. The A-Teams also built border surveillance camps where no real local population existed for CIDG recruitment. One such camp was at Khe Sahn, which would eventually

---

[131] Stanton, Green Berets at War, 46.

[132] The Viet Cong was largely successful in its attempts to gain the trust and acceptance of the rural peasantry. This was done by providing civil services that the constrained and feeble Diem regime could not provide and by appealing to the villagers who became increasingly alienated by the corrupt, oligarchic, and repressive South Vietnamese government. Dich van (meaning "action among the enemy") was a propaganda effort to increase the legitimacy of North Vietnam (and Viet Cong cause) at the expense of South Vietnam, which was portrayed as a puppet government of the United States. Aimed at the South Vietnamese people, many methods and mediums were utilized, including plays, protests, rallies, leaflets, meetings, rumor campaigns, etc. Casebook on Insurgency, Vol II, 345.

become the home of the 26th Marine Regiment, as well as the scene of some of the most pivotal battles of the war.

All told by January 1963, there were 530 SF soldiers in 4 B-Teams, and 28 A-teams scattered throughout South Vietnam (See Figure 1-23). In all, the CIDG program made a significant contribution to the war effort in Vietnam. The SF Command in Nha Trang, with a collective strength of approximately 2,500 officers and NCOs from three SF Groups, essentially organized and led an army of over 50,000 hamlet militia, 10,000 strike forces soldiers, as well as thousands serving as medical and recon scouts.

Battle of Plei Mrong

In November 1962, CPT William Grace III and A-314, of 1st SFG(A) established a border surveillance camp among the Jarai in the vicinity of Plei Mrong, northwest of Pleiku. The defensive perimeter lay rectangular in shape on a plateau behind two double layers of barbed-wire. The outer perimeter was laced with glass and steel spikes, while the ground between the two layers of barbed-wire was ringed with M14AP mines and punji stakes. To round out the defenses, a line of trenches and fighting positions had been dug fifteen meters inside the fence line. Additionally, A-314 began a village defense program at Plei Mrong in December following a VC attack, which necessitated A-314 bringing the CIDG recruits inside the camp.

In pitch blackness, at 0130 hours, on 2 January, 1963, the camp came under a heavy barrage of small arms fire from a reinforced VC company. Earlier that night, CPT Grace and half the detachment had left on a reconnaissance mission. The VC raced through a twelve foot gap in the fence line that had been cut by pro-VC militia inside the camp. The battle was confused and ugly, as some of the militia camp recruits joined the attacking VC militia, while others manned the trenches and returned fire along with A-314. The team's 81mm was also sabotaged by the pro-VC militia and was out of commission. Small arms fire, 57mm recoilless rifle, and explosions rocked the camp for over two hours as executive officer, 1LT Leary, directed the counter attack and attempted to raise the B-Team, B-210, in Pleiku. The beleaguered camp defenders fought doggedly, and resisted four VC assaults. By 0600, the final VC assault was repulsed. They retreated carrying their dead and wounded. Shortly afterward, medical helicopters arrived from Kontum to evacuate the wounded (Figure 1-23).[133]

---

[133] Stanton, Green Berets at War, 60.

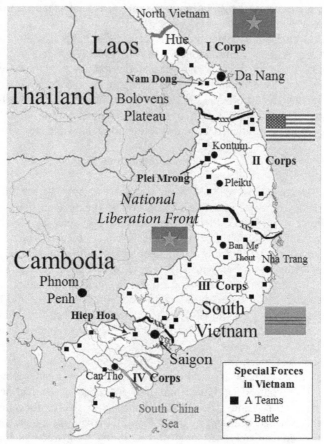

Figure 1-23. Special Forces in Vietnam.

At the Battle of Plei Mrong, the VC had nearly been successful at overrunning the SF camp. The casualties were grievous, with 29 camp defenders KIA, 38 WIA, and 73 MIA, including four wounded A-314 members. Later investigations revealed that the strike camp had been thoroughly infiltrated by VC agents. SF camps were deliberately placed in VC held territory and especially along VC infil routes. Along with the VC attack at Plei Mrong, additional camps had been probed, such as: A-729's camp at Gia Vuc in Quang Ngai province, A-734's camp at Chau Lang, and A-20's at Tan Phu in the Mekong Delta marshes. All told that year, there were over 400 engagements, including patrol contacts, and mortar attacks throughout South Vietnam, along with eleven known infiltrations of SF camps.

Battle of Hiep Hoa

The first SF camp overrun in the Vietnam War was A-21's camp at Hiep Hoa, west of Saigon in Hau Nghia Province. 5th SF Group's A-19 had established it in February 1963. The detachments assigned to Hiep Hoa were challenged with hostile locals, nearly 250 undisciplined CIDG soldiers, and shabby defenses. On the morning of 23 November, 1963, CPT Horne of A-21, led a 50 man force (36 CIDG, seven USSF, and three LLDBs – Luc Luong Dac Biet – South Vietnamese SF) on a recon patrol. This left 1LT Colby in command of four SF soldiers and some 200 CIDG soldiers in the camp.[134]

Just after midnight, an eruption of small arms and mortar fire was unleashed as a 500 man Viet Cong force attacked the camp. Like Plei Mrong, Hiep Hoa's camp defenders included many enemy agents. At the outset of the attack, VC sympathizers within the camp killed the CIDG guards and swung one of the captured machineguns around and mowed down the CIDG soldiers as they ran out of their bunkers.[135]

SF troopers began firing their 60 and 81mm mortars, and attempted to direct a counterattack against the Viet Cong who were pouring into the perimeter. SFC Camacho and another SF trooper managed to retake the machine gun position and held out for a while until they were wounded and captured. 1LT Colby was also wounded but managed to avoid capture by hiding in a sugar cane field. The VC had taken Hiep Hoa, and casualties were heavy. Four SF troopers had been captured. Among those captured, SFC Camacho, was the first POW to escape during the war, after being held by the VC for six months. In all, casualties were 41 KIA, over 100 WIA, and four MIA. Following the taking of Hiep Hoa, the other SF camps began taking more precautions and improving security. Additionally, Chinese Nungs were brought on to improve security. They proved to be very loyal to the SF A-Teams.

Battle of Nam Dong

In July of 1964, Viet Cong operations against SF border camps increased. It began on the 4th of July when a VC regiment overran A-122's camp at Polei Krong. They followed up their victory with an attack on A-726's camp at Nam Dong, which was situated west of Da Nang along the Laotian border. Commanded by CPT Roger H. Donlon, the Nam Dong camp included 381 CIDGs, 50 Nungs, 12 SF, and seven LLDBs. It was located in Thua Thien Province, and was scheduled to be closed. Achieving complete

---

[134] Stanton, Green Berets at War, 74.
[135] Ibid, 77.

surprise at 0230, the VC smothered the camp with a heavy mortar barrage. After overrunning the outer defenses, the VC were held back by the tenacious Nungs and LLDB machinegun fire and grenades.

After overrunning the outer perimeter, two VC assaults were repulsed. Running through a hail of rifle fire and exploding grenades, CPT Donlon killed a VC demolitions team who were preparing to blow open the inner gate. After being wounded in the stomach, CPT Donlon continued to direct the defense of the camp, and retrieve his wounded men back to cover who were in the line of fire. For his actions that day he would receive the Medal of Honor. Donlon's detachment was relieved in place by A-224, who destroyed the fort before returning to Da Nang.

Project Delta

Project Delta was a Special Forces reconnaissance project formed by MACV to collect operational intelligence. The project, code named Leaping Lena, began in May, 1964. The concept of Leaping Lena was to cross the border into Laos in order to provide direct observation of the North Vietnamese Army's (NVA) use of what became known as the Ho Chi Minh Trail. Due to Washington's fear of violating the Geneva Accords of 1962, the LLDB were tasked with the mission without the assistance of their USSF advisors.

Upon parachuting into Laos, the LLDB teams encountered scores of NVA troops and came under heavy fire. Leaping Lena became a debacle. Of the 40 LLDBs who had crossed into Laos, only five returned. Following the disaster, the project was redesignated Detachment B-52.[136] Throughout the war, B-52 deployed all over South Vietnam, and conducted a plethora of secret operations to include: long range recons into VC sanctuaries; air strikes on hard to reach targets; bomb damage assessments (BDA) in enemy-controlled territory; recovery of downed pilots and air crews; and wiretapping NVA/VC land lined communications. Another Greek letter project that was developed was Project Gamma. Gamma was the name given to Detachment B-57, Company E, 5th SF Group. It was tasked with covert intelligence collection operations in Cambodia.

5th Special Forces Group Comes to Vietnam

On 1 October, 1964, the Pentagon reassigned the newly activated 1,200-man 5th SFG (A) from Fort Bragg, NC to Nha Trang, South Vietnam in order to replace US Army Special Forces Provisional Command

---

[136] Colonel Charlie Beckwith, the founder of 1st SFOD-D was one of B-52's commanders.

USASF(P)V. The 5th SF Group had been activated at Fort Bragg, NC on 21 September, 1961, and had sent detachments TDY into Vietnam for the previous three years. 5th Group's overseas tour in Vietnam would now be a one year permanent change of station (PCS). The six-month temporary duty tours by SF ODAs would end by 1 May, 1965. During this time South Vietnam was organized into combat tactical zones (CTZ) – I – IV Corps. SF C-Teams, consisting of about 70 men, were commanded by a Lieutenant Colonel and were responsible for all the SF camps in their respective CTZ. Each C-Team commanded several B-Teams, approximately 30 men, which were headquartered in provincial capitals. The B-Teams were commanded by a Major and controlled several A-Teams which in turn controlled strike force camps. At all echelons, each team had an attached South Vietnamese SF team (LLDB).

MACV's mission statement approved for 5th Special Forces was: (1) exert constant, versatile, offensive pressure against the VC where the ARVN is not present in strength, (2) interdict VC movement across international boundary, (3) respond quickly to prevent a VC takeover of a critical area, and (4) assist in extending government of Vietnam (GVN) control.[137] Additionally, 5th Group sought to exercise less operational control of ODAs deployed with US senior advisers in each corps; advise MACV on opening and closing of CIDG camps; establish new CIDG camps; advise the Vietnamese Special Forces High Command; and when required, provide formal training for LLDB and CIDG units.

The Green Beret

The Green Beret was originally designed in 1953 by Major Herbert Brucker, a Special Forces officer and veteran of the OSS. Later that year, First Lieutenant Roger Pezelle adopted it as the unofficial headgear for his A-team, Operational Detachment FA32. They wore it whenever they went to the field for prolonged exercises. Soon it spread throughout all of SF, although the Army refused to authorize its official use. Finally, in 1961, President John F. Kennedy planned to visit Fort Bragg. He sent word to the Special Warfare Center commander, Brigadier General William P. Yarborough, for all SF soldiers to wear their berets for the event. President Kennedy felt that since they had a special mission, SF should have something to set them apart from the rest. Even before the presidential request, however, the Department of the Army had acquiesced and teletyped a message to the Center authorizing the beret as a part of the SF uniform.

---

[137] Stanton, Green Berets at War, 96.

Chapter 1   A Concise History of the Special Forces

When President Kennedy came to Fort Bragg Oct. 12, 1961, General Yarborough wore his Green Beret to greet the commander-in-chief. The president remarked, "Those are nice. How do you like the Green Beret?" General Yarborough replied, "They're fine, Sir. We've wanted them a long time." A message from President Kennedy to General Yarborough later that day stated, "My congratulations to you personally for your part in the presentation today ... The challenge of this old but new form of operations is a real one, and I know that you and the members of your command will carry on for us and the free world in a manner which is both worthy and inspiring. I am sure that the Green Beret will be a mark of distinction in the trying times ahead."

In an April 1962 White House memorandum for the U.S. Army, President Kennedy showed his continued support for SF, calling the Green Beret "a symbol of excellence, a badge of courage, a mark of distinction in the fight for freedom."

Studies and Observation Group (SOG)

"We gathered intelligence and killed human beings under extremely hazardous and adverse conditions." – SGM Franklin D. Miller

It was one thing to plan covert actions against North Vietnam, but quite another to establish a secret organization to carry it out. Established on 24 January 1964, Military Assistance Command Vietnam, Studies and Observation Group (MACV-SOG) or SOG was a joint service UW task force that conducted highly classified capture, search and rescue, personnel recovery operations; sabotage and psychological warfare; and strategic reconnaissance (SR) missions in South Vietnam, North Vietnam, Laos, and Cambodia (See Figure 1-24). According to Jack Singlaub, SOG was the Indochina equivalent of JACK in the Korean War.[138]

Organized by the JCS as a subordinate command of MACV, SOG operated under the guise of a staff agency, with personnel held officially under 5th SF Group's rosters. SOG included elements from the US Army Special Forces, the USMC's Force Recon, the Navy SEALs, and the US Air Force's 14th Special Operations Wing, not to mention the plethora of mercenary troops. SOG was in fact controlled by the Special Assistant for Counterinsurgency and Special Activities (SACSA) and his staff at the Pentagon. Its mission against Hanoi was divided into functional areas which were initiated by the CIA. It conducted four primary covert missions: agent

---

[138] Singlaub, Hazardous Duty, 292.

networks and deception; covert maritime raids; psychological operations; and cross-border operations against the *Ho Chi Minh Trail*. [139]

Organized by Colonel Clyde Russell, SOG had five numbered divisions: OP31 through OP35. OP31 was the maritime operations, OP32 was SOG's private air force, OP33 supervised psychological warfare, OP34 focused on sending agents into the North, and OP35, SOG's biggest and most interesting activity, conducted cross-border reconnaissance. OP35 was led by Colonel Arthur "Bull" Simons. His operational design of OPLAN35 was as follows: First, recon teams would be inserted into Laos and Cambodia to identify NVA headquarters, base camps, and supply caches. Once found, they would be attacked by air strikes that were called in by the recon teams (RTs. Next, a company sized "Hatchet Force" would raid the uncovered enemy sites, to capture personnel, conduct bomb-damage assessment (BDA, emplace wire taps and electronic sensors, and photograph. [140]

To facilitate operations, SOG created three command and control sections. Command and Control North (CCN, Command and Control Central (CCC, and Command and Control South (CCS. The first forward operating base (FOB was established in late 1965 at Kham Duc. A second FOB was added at Kontum. SOG's central focus was to take the fight directly to the enemy, where he operated virtually unscathed with sanctuaries in Laos and Cambodia. To this end, Donald Blackburn, SOG's first chief, began sending teams into Laos in 1966. Operation Prairie Fire, which began as Shining Brass, was initiated to learn precisely what the Ho Chi Minh Trail entailed, and to deny Hanoi easy access to Laos as a base from which to launch operations into South Vietnam (See Figure 1-24. [141]

Prairie Fire

SOG's Prairie Fire program, focused to conduct operations against the Ho Chi Minh Trail, got off the ground with sixteen volunteers from 1st Bn, 1st SF Group out of Okinawa. As Chief of SOG, Blackburn conceived that Recon Teams (RTs for the operation were organized as two or three USSF troopers with nine Yard or Nung fighters. This combination achieved a balanced complement of knowledge and experience. Arriving in Vietnam, the Green Berets linked up with their teams and went to work. The first cross-border operation, conducted by RT Iowa, was led by MSG Charles

---

[139] The Ho Chi Minh Trail was a logistical system that ran from North to South Vietnam through Laos and Cambodia. The trail network provided support, in the form of men and material, to the Viet Cong Insurgency in South Vietnam. It was first used during the First Indochina War 1946-1954. In 1964, the NVA managed to bring a regiment down it. By the end of 1968, over 300,000 enemy troops had used it to enter South Vietnam.

[140] Shultz, The Secret War Against Hanoi, 63.

[141] Ibid, 46.

Petry. His team consisted of seven Nungs and SFC Willie Card.[142] RT Iowa's objective *D-1* was 20 miles northwest of Kham Duc. It was the suspected point of origin (POO) that had been pounding Marine and USAF installations in Da Nang.

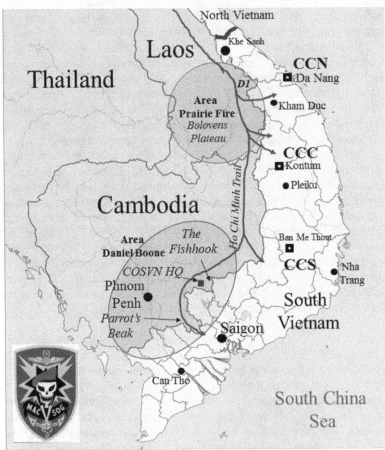

Figure 1-24. MACV SOG Operations in Vietnam 1964-1972.

The plan was for RT Iowa to be inserted at dusk by Sikorsky H-34 Kingbees, locate the enemy and blast them to kingdom come with airstrikes. On 18 October, 1965, with the weather turning sour, RT Iowa went in. CPT Larry Thorne, the operations officer for SOG actions at Kham Duc

---

[142] Plaster, SOG: The Secret Wars of America's Commandos in Vietnam, 18.

accompanied to oversee the team's insertion.[143] Thorne sent the two Kingbees who had inserted RT Iowa back to base while he loitered in case they got into trouble. When the team radioed they were safe, Thorne departed the area for Kham Duc. Larry Thorne was never seen again.[144]

RT Iowa found objective *D-1* to be heavily manned by NVA with many trails radiating out everywhere. On the third day, while maneuvering around to investigate the objective, RT Iowa was compromised and took a casualty in the firefight that followed. After being pursued for two days with a wounded Nung, the weather broke and Petry's force struck back by calling in thirty-seven sorties of F-105 Thunderchief fighter-bombers before the Kingbees lifted RT Iowa out. Additionally, Petry went back with a forward air controller (FAC and called in fifty-one more sorties on targets he'd discovered, touching off numerous secondary explosions as bombs hit munitions stockpiles.[145] By the end of 1965, seven more Shining Brass RT missions were launched, five more uncovering NVA base camps and munitions dumps.

The Prairie Fire RT missions gave the US a better understanding of what we were up against in Laos; the Ho Chi Minh Trail network. In 1966, 137 recon operations were executed, which included the taking of 15 enemy POWs.[146] However, due to political reasons, SOG was only authorized to move 10 kilometers inside Laos. Commenting on this restrictive policy, Jack Singlaub states:

Westmoreland continued to agitate for more freedom of operation in Cambodia, which had become the NVA's main staging area. But he was continually stymied by the State Department, which still hoped to somehow "woo" Prince Sihanouk to our side. It wasn't until the middle of the year that I received grudging authorization to employ cross-border Recon Teams in Cambodia. But by that time, my operations in Laos were continually running afoul of the American ambassador in Vientiane, Bill Sullivan. Good diplomat that he was, he believed in upholding the much-abused international agreements guaranteeing the "neutrality" of Laos, even though the embassy's own CIA station headed by my friend Ted Shackley actively conducted a guerrilla war against the NVA and its Pathet Lao allies. The core of the problem was

---

[143] Lauri Törni (1919-1965) was a Finnish Army captain who led an infantry company in the Winter War against the Russians during WWII. After the war, he joined the US Army in 1954 under the provisions of the Lodge-Philbin Act and adopted the name Larry Thorne. Known as the soldier who fought under three flags: Finnish, German (when he fought the Soviets in World War II) and American (where he was known as Larry Thorne) when he served in U.S. Army Special Forces in the Vietnam War.

[144] Plaster, SOG: The Secret Wars of America's Commandos in Vietnam, 20.

[145] Ibid, 20.

[146] Shultz, The Secret War Against Hanoi, 215. OP35 Prairie Fire mission metrics include: 1966 - 111 recon missions; 1967 - 275 missions (187 recons, 68 exploitation, 20 other); 1968 - 546 missions (310 in Laos, 236 in Vietnam); 1969 - 452 missions (404 recons, 48 exploitations); and 1970 - 441 missions; for a total of 1,825 missions of all types.

civilian-military turf jealousy. In reality, the Trail area of the lower Laotian panhandle was geographically separated from the rest of the country and contiguous to Vietnam. But – contrary to good security procedure – I had to submit detailed plans of all my Recon Team operations for approval by Sullivan's staff.[147]

Most recon missions were of a three to five day duration. When a team made contact or found a target, they'd direct airstrikes by communicating with their forward air controller (FAC) or *Covey Riders* as they became known in SOG. In all, 187 Prairie Fire missions were executed which seemed to put a dent logistically in Hanoi's operations against South Vietnam. According to Lt Colonel Carney, the deputy chief of OP35, "We hurt North Vietnam, killed a lot of people, and caused them to expend a lot of capabilities trying to prevent our operations. It hurt their logistic effort to an immeasurable degree."[148] In fact, Prairie Fire missions were so effective that the infiltration routes the NVA was using had to be moved further south, so as to enter South Vietnam from Cambodia. The NVA was also forced to commit an estimated 25,000 men to defend the Trail.

SOG Recon Teams

Each SOG recon team was assigned three Americans and nine native soldiers. However, the team leader could decide to take a smaller force of six or eight, depending upon the mission parameters (Fig. 1-25). Recon teams in CCN (Da Nang) were named after poisonous snakes, while those at CCC (Kontum) were named for states and CCS (Ban Me Thuot) for tools. The team leader was a One-Zero. On average he would have at least eight missions under his belt. John Plaster observes, "Each team's combat style reflected its One-Zero. RT California was bold and combative because Joe Walker was; RT Colorado's Ralph Rodd was quiet and intellectual and loved outfoxing the enemy to reach a heavily patrolled road; another team captured NVA prisoners because their One-Zero liked to get right in the enemy's face."[149]

Organizationally, each SOG command and control section, such as CCC, included 18 recon teams of three Green Berets each, with an indigenous complement to each team of either three to nine Nungs or Yards, plus three Hatchet Force companies, a dedicated air wing, security forces, and a command section. The 100-man Hatchet Force companies were organized much like the Mike Forces, with a nucleus of four Green Berets leading

---

[147] Singlaub, Hazardous Duty, 310.
[148] Ibid, 63.
[149] Plaster, Secret Commandos, 52.

each forty-man Nung or Montagnard platoon.[150] Further, each Hatchet Force company was led by a captain.

12-man Recon Team	6-man Recon Team
1-0 Team Leader	1-0 Team Leader
1-1 Assistant TL	1-1 Assistant TL
1-3 Radio Operator	1-3 Radio Operator
0-1 Indigenous TL	0-1 Indigenous TL
0-2 Interpreter	0-2 Interpreter
0-3 Grenadier	0-3 Grenadier
0-4 Grenadier	
0-5 Scout	
0-6 Scout	
0-7 Scout	
0-8 Scout	
0-9 Scout	

Note: Positions beginning with "1" were filled by Americans, "0" by indigenous.

Figure 1-25. SOG Recon Team Structure.

The most frequently conducted mission in SOG was cross-border reconnaissance. And because the US military wasn't officially operating in Laos or Cambodia, SOG weapons, kit, and uniforms had to be non-standard and sterile. Although some RTs wore NVA-style uniforms, most preferred jungle fatigues. All identifying articles, such as dog tags, ID cards, etc. were prohibited. Therefore, before a RT went out on a mission these items were collected and stored in a safe. Weapon types fell to shooter preference. Anything from the Sten gun, 9mm Swedish 'K,' the CAR-15 (XM-177), M14s, M16s, and AK-47s. Overall, SOG men were given a great degree of freedom regarding weapons and kit configuration. As SOG RT Vermont veteran SGM Frank Miller has observed, "I was never denied any type of weapon or ammunition."[151]

Web gear varied considerably. But, as always a high premium was placed on functionality and stealth. Regarding kit, SOG men were finicky and scientific. They were known to spend countless hours tailoring their gear

---

[150] Plaster, Secret Commandos, 33.
[151] Miller, Reflections of a Warrior, 92.

and often reconfiguring it, being judicially selective regarding weight and function of each piece of kit. A SOG man's web gear, or load-bearing equipment (LBE) would normally include: as many loaded magazines as he could feasibly carry (usually a double basic load – 410 rds. of 5.56mm), several grenades, a knife, a handgun, a smoke grenade, a CS grenade, gas mask, two canteens with iodine tabs, and an emergency radio, along with a couple of pressure dressings, as well as a few snap links, and a pair of gloves. All told about 60 lbs.

A SOG man's ruck on the other hand would generally be much lighter, carrying at most a couple of M18 claymore mines, some M112 C-4 plastic explosive, a firing system (made up of M700 time fuse and M60 fuse ignitors), some more smoke grenades, additional canteens of water, a few LRRP meals, a machete, and perhaps a small sleeping bag. Rounding out the SOG man's kit, he would carry essential items in his pockets. This way, even if he lost his web gear and ruck sack, he could still survive. These essential items normally included: a map and compass, a signal mirror, a small piece of VS-17 panel, a whistle, a small flashlight, some pen gun flares, a wrist watch, pocket knife, a notepad and pen, a camo stick, strobe light, and some anti-malaria tablets and morphine.

Whereas, there was no typical SOG man, usually they tended to be a bit more aggressive and sometimes a bit crazy, but at all times unapprehensive. Further, as Frank Miller recounts, they were killers. Miller observes, "Folks in MACV-SOG received privileges and freedom beyond most people's comprehension. That was because most of us had a talent, a very special talent. We gathered intelligence and killed human beings under the most extremely hazardous and adverse conditions. Killing someone is a unique ability all by itself. Not everyone can lay a weapon's sights on a fellow human being and crank off a round. Genuine killers are not to be confused with guys who simply spray an area and happen to hit and kill someone. But killing becomes a special talent when coupled with the ability to quietly invade an enemy's stronghold and deal with him in his own backyard. Just you and a handful of other people out there relying on your training and skills. No back up. No support other than a chopper to pull you out if you succeed."[152]

A typical cross-border recon mission entailed an infil via blacked-out helicopter at dusk as close to the "Trail" as possible. The RT would then find a suitable site, fishhook around to overwatch their trail and set up an ambush that night to hit any enemy troops attracted by the chopper. And at first light they would comb the area for suitable targets and then bomb them back to the Stone Age with air strikes. The duration of an RT mission could

---

last anywhere from two to three days or a week or two. It all depended on the particular mission and the team's success at evading enemy patrols. When it was time to exfil, teams were extracted via STABO harness, which enabled them to fire their weapons as they were lifted from the forest floor – a usual occurrence. There was always a high probability of being detected and ending up in a wicked firefight. A few RTs even disappeared, never having made radio contact after insertion. *These were the days of high adventure.*

In SOG, no two missions were quite the same. And often times, a 'dry hole' could be turned into a big payoff. This occurred in January 1966, while Dick Meadows' RT Ohio was inside Laos. RT Ohio had been on the ground several days without contact with the enemy, and according to Meadows nothing of any great importance to report. While near a recently discovered path which radiated off the Ho Chi Minh Trail, Meadows gave Ohio the hand and arm signal to take up a hasty ambush posture. Alan Hoe recounts what happened next:

As five NVA soldiers approached the team's position, Meadows was about to initiate the ambush by opening fire when, to his amazement, the soldiers halted, placed their rifles on the ground, and took off their packs. It soon became obvious that they were taking a lunch break. With a grin of utter delight on his face, Meadows told Ohio of his intentions by using hand signals. Taking great care, Meadows inched his way to within one pace of the five chattering men. Then in one flowing motion, he stood up and sidestepped onto the trail..."Good morning, gentlemen. Don't move. You are now my prisoners," he said. Three of the soldiers made a heroically fatal mistake and grabbed for their weapons. A burst from Meadows' submachine gun killed them instantly. The remaining two soldiers made no resistance as their hands were tied behind their backs. The dead bodies were searched, moved off the trail, and hastily covered with foliage. RT Ohio, having recovered from the 'dry hole,' was now happy to exfil back to Kontum.[153]

Daniel Boone

In 1967, under Colonel Jack Singlaub, SOG's second chief, operations in Vietnam were expanded to include covert operations in Cambodia. The new program, code-named Daniel Boone, was focused on intelligence collection in the tri-border area of Laos, Cambodia, and South Vietnam (See Figure 1-24.[154] As previously noted, SOG's primary mission was to infiltrate small teams into Laos and Cambodia to identify enemy troop concentrations, bases, supply depots, truck parks, weapons caches, command bunkers, and

---

[153] Hoe, The Quiet Professional, 86.
[154] OP35 Daniel Boone mission metrics include: 1967 – 99 missions; 1968 – 726 missions (287 cross-border, 439 in-country); 1969 – 454 missions.

all related targets for aerial bombardment. And SOG recon missions paid high dividends, providing intelligence that no one else could. However, as noted earlier, because of bureaucracy, SOG was tethered to restricted policies, which, if removed, would have allowed the organization to do much more damage to the enemy than what played out. And Hanoi took increasing steps to defend the Trail.

To counter SOG's dominance, Hanoi developed their own special operations forces. They evolved out of the NVA's first airborne unit, the 305th Airborne Brigade, which was formed in 1965.[155] These hunter-killer teams, also known as sappers, gave no quarter to SOG. One such attack was launched against CCN's compound at Dan Nang in 1969. At about 0230 hours, a 100-man sapper force approached CCN's compound from the sea. With a supporting mortar attack, the sappers entered the perimeter, and began throwing grenades and satchel charges into the buildings as they machine-gunned their way through the compound. Fighting their way through the attack, SOG men linked up and cleared the structures, eliminating the threats. In the confused three hour melee that followed, thirty-eight North Vietnamese commandos were killed and nine were captured, while eighty American and indigenous soldiers were killed or wounded.[156]

Besides identifying targets for air strikes, SOG teams executed other missions. These included the rescue of downed US pilots. Code named Bright Light, the first pilot recovery mission was led by MSG Dick Meadows. Inserted into North Vietnam from the USS Intrepid on October 12, 1966, Meadows' RT Ohio moved to recover Navy lieutenant Dean Woods. After just missing the pilot, Ohio got into a wicked firefight with the NVA and narrowly escaped. Overall, there was a total of four rescue missions in 1966. The last mission successfully recovered the pilot.

COSVN Raid

One of the most frustrating aspects of fighting Hanoi was its use of Laos and Cambodia as a logistical conduit. In 1969, SOG executed a covert raid against the Central Office for South Vietnam or COSVN, the almost mythical Viet Cong headquarters which claimed to run the whole war (See Figure 1-26). An NVA deserter had pinpointed the COSVN complex 14 miles southeast of Memot, Cambodia, in the Fishhook, just a mile beyond the South Vietnamese border.[157]

---

[155] Shultz, The Secret War Against Hanoi, 225.
[156] Plaster, Secret Commandos, 81.
[157] Plaster, SOG: The Secret Wars of America's Commandos in Vietnam, 236.

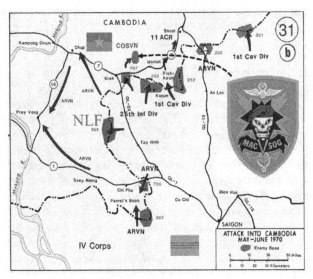

Figure 1-26. COSVN Vietcong Base in Cambodia. Courtesy US National Archives.

The raid was set for 24 April, 1969. The plan called for the insertion of a company-sized Hatchet Force that would capture enemy prisoners and report the effects of the B-52 air strikes. After receiving the mission several days before the Hatchet Force was to be inserted, LTC Trabue, commander of CCS, informed OPLAN35, MACV-SOG that he didn't believe the plan to attack the COSVN complex was viable.[158] LTC Trabue believed that the B-52s would fail to stun the enemy as anticipated. The size of the Hatchet Force was also limited as there weren't enough helicopters available at Quon Loi Airfield, CCS's launch site. There were only nine Huey helicopters from the 195th Assault Helicopter Company available; five to infil the Hatchet Force and four gunships for support.

The mission began with a massive airstrike that consisted of 98 B-52s from Okinawa and Guam.[159] CCS sent CPT O'Rourke's raider company consisting of three platoons of Green Berets, Nungs, and Yards. It would be a 10 minute flight into the VC secret lair. CPT O'Rourke was on the lead aircraft while SFC Jerry "Mad Dog" Shriver rode in trail. The plan was for the raiders to touch down on the objective as the dust from the B-52's was settling. As the Hueys lifted off, the aircraft carrying CPT O'Rourke and five other raiders, experienced malfunctions and had to return to base. Command passed to the S3, CPT Cahill, who just had come along for the

---

[158] Lindsey, Secret Green Beret Commandos in Cambodia, 312.
[159] B-52s carried a payload of 109 five hundred-pound bombs.

ride. Momentarily the raiders could see dirt geysers bounding skyward amid collapsing trees. Then as the dust settled a violin-shaped clearing took form and the Hueys descended in-trail, hovered for men to leap off, then climbed away.[160]

As the helicopters lifted away, a heavy barrage of interlocking machinegun and rocket fire erupted from concrete bunkers and entrenched positions. The only cover the raiders were afforded were the B-52 bomb craters. From his position in the western-most bomb crater, Mad Dog radioed other team members stating a machinegun bunker to his left front was pinning down his force, and asked if anyone could fire on it. CPT Cahill and others reported that they were pinned down and could not help. The medic, SGT Jamison, dashed out to retrieve a wounded man; heavy fire cut him down, killing him on the spot. CPT Cahill directed the gunships to suppress the enemy concrete bunkers who made multiple gun runs on the complex. About 10 to 15 minutes into the battle, CPT Cahill heard Shriver transmit a message that he and five Montagnards were going to flank the machinegun position. No one else could engage the machinegun that trapped Shriver's men - it was up to Mad Dog. Skittish Yards looked to Shriver and his half-grin restored a sense of confidence. Then they were on their feet, charging - Shriver was his old self, running to the sound of guns, a True Believer Yard on either side, all of them dashing through the flying bullets, into the woodline, into the very jaws of COSVN.[161] Shriver was never seen again.

The enemy fire was so intense that anyone trying to move out was cut down. A surviving raider related that it seemed like they had flown into an ambush. CPT Cahill lifted his head to evaluate the situation and an AK-47 round hit him in the jaw and exited his eye. For the next 45 minutes, 1LT Harrigan, 1st Platoon's PL, assumed command and continued to call for fire support. After the Huey gunships grew from four to eight, the enemy ground fire was suppressed. The gunships continued to refuel and discharge mini-gun and rocket fire. In order to bolster the ground force and flank the enemy bunker, a recon team of seven personnel was inserted onto the objective; however they were also pinned down. 1LT Marchantel assumed command when Harrigan was mortally wounded. Marchantel had to bring ordnance so close he wounded himself and his surviving nine Montagnards.

Later, two US Army Cobra helicopters from Quong Loi added their firepower to relieve the beleaguered raiders. Additionally, two USAF fighter jets made several attack runs, bringing machinegun fire, rockets, and bombs. The raiders reported that despite all of the fire support, there was still too much ground fire to attempt an evacuation. Weighing the remaining options,

---

[160] Plaster, SOG: The Secret Wars of America's Commandos in Vietnam, 236.
[161] Ibid, 237.

LTC Trabue decided on a napalm airstrike. After two napalm strikes, the raiders reported a sizable decrease in enemy activity, and that it was now safe for an evacuation. One medic ran to Harrigan's body and three Hueys raced in and picked up 15 wounded men. Thus ended the COSVN raid. Of the 54 raiders inserted into COSVN, only 25 came out alive.[162]

End Game in Vietnam

Many air strikes were conducted against the Fish Hook. By the time the air strikes ended in May of 1970, 3,857 B-52 sorties had been flown, dropping 108,823 tons of bombs.[163] The result was for the VC was to move their HQ and troop concentrations further into Cambodia. In early 1970, SOG had its revenge when the conventional Army went to work in Cambodia. Guided by SOG teams, hundreds of engagements followed as scores of enemy hamlets were destroyed. By the time the last American units left Cambodia in June 1970, some 11,000 Communist fighters had been killed, along with some 2,400 taken prisoner. What saved the NVA was the 30 kilometer operations limit, beyond which US forces were forbidden to penetrate.

Policy is supposed to set the goals for strategy. However, the US strategy for the Vietnam War was bereft of any such approach. For example, Westmoreland was the commander of forces inside Vietnam only; he had no authority outside its borders. Additionally, the JCS viewed SOG as peripheral and unrelated to the main war effort.[164] However, General Westmoreland credited SOG with having delivered over half of the available intelligence on enemy troop and logistical concentrations in theater, and 75 percent of the intelligence on the Ho Chi Minh Trail.[165]

Following the Tet Offensive, which jolted the American public, commitment for the war began to wane. The Pentagon began bringing scores of units home. Funds began to dry up. America's focus was now getting out. OP35's final months was becoming dangerous for recon teams. The Trail was becoming impenetrable. In June 1970, ground operations in

---

[162] Lindsey, Secret Green Beret Commandos in Cambodia, 316.

[163] Anderson, The Columbia History of the Vietnam War, 368. Hampering bombing runs against rebel bases like COSVN was the assistance provided by Soviet ships in the Pacific. Soviet ships in the South China Sea gave vital early warnings to Viet Cong forces in South Vietnam. The Soviet intelligence ships detected American B-52 bombers flying from Okinawa and Guam, and relayed their airspeed and direction to COSVN headquarters. COSVN used this data to determine probable targets, and directed assets along the flight path to move "perpendicularly to the attack trajectory." While the bombing runs still caused extensive damage, the early warnings from 1968-1970 prevented them from killing a single military or civilian leader in the headquarters complexes.

[164] Shultz, The Secret War Against Hanoi, 256.

[165] Rottman, US MACV-SOG Recon Teams, 62.

Cambodia were terminated and all US personnel were ordered out.[166] By the end of 1970, Colonel Skip Sadler, the last chief of SOG observed, "Only about forty percent of SOG teams were able to remain on the ground in Laos for anything over twenty-four hours. So strong had the NVA become...They were in position, they know you're coming, and that's a recipe for deadly results."[167] The NVA was developing a very good capability for reacting to SOG operations. Finally SOG, one of the world's foremost lethal covert organizations was deactivated on April 30, 1972.

Regarding SOG's lethality and patrolling expertise, what more shall I say? For time would fail me to tell of the exploits of Dick Meadows, Robert Howard, Fred Zabitosky, Frank Miller, John Kedenburg, Billy Waugh, John Plaster, Jerry Shriver, etc. How they killed thousands of NVA and Viet Cong in countless actions, annihilated hundreds of enemy vehicles, destroyed tens of thousands of pounds of enemy supplies, captured enemy POWs, and need I say kept well over 100,000 enemy troops stationed along the Trail to protect it from them. The number of SOG personnel killed in action from 1964-1972 was 407. A tremendous amount from a unit that size. It is observed that the kill ratio for SOG was one hundred and fifty enemy killed for each SOG man lost (150:1), much higher than the conventional unit kill ratio of 15:1. Probably the highest combat efficiency in US history.

Son Tay Raid (Operation Ivory Coast)

By the spring of 1970, there were 462 American POWs in SE Asia (80% in North Vietnam) and over 970 missing in action. The NVA did not adhere to Geneva Conventions, although North Vietnam signed them in 1959. Torture, stress positions, and malnutrition, all created horrendous conditions. In May 1970, reconnaissance photographs revealed the existence of two prison camps west of Hanoi. At Son Tay, one photograph identified a large "K" – a code for "come get us" – drawn in the dirt. Brigadier General Donald D. Blackburn, suggested a small group of SF volunteers rescue the prisoners of war. He chose Lieutenant Colonel Arthur D. "Bull" Simons to lead the group. Because the compound was more than 20 miles west of Hanoi, planners of the operation believed that Son Tay was isolated enough to enable a small group to land, rescue prisoners and withdraw. A full-scale replica of the compound was constructed at Eglin Air Force Base, Florida, where a select group of SF soldiers trained at night. The mock compound was dismantled during the day to elude detection by Soviet satellites. Despite security measures, time was running out. Evidence, although inconclusive, showed that perhaps Son Tay was being emptied.

---

[166] Shultz, The Secret War Against Hanoi, 240.
[167] Ibid, 241.

The leadership of the Son Tay raid proposed a simple yet bold, executable plan utilizing surprise, speed, and violence of action as the fundamentals. On Nov 18, 1970, fifty-nine Son Tay raiders moved to Takhli, Thailand. Only Simons and three others, including Captain Dick Meadows, knew what the mission was to be. Five hours before takeoff on Nov 20, Simons told his men: "We are going to rescue 70 American prisoners of war, maybe more, from a camp called Son Tay. This is something American prisoners have a right to expect from their fellow Soldiers. The target is 23 miles west of Hanoi" (See Figure 1-27.

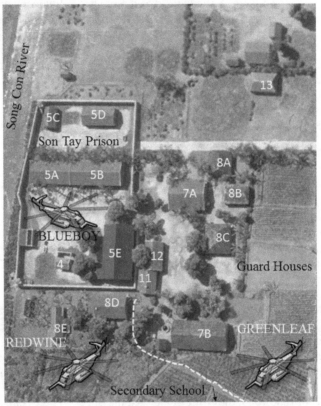

Figure 1-27. Operation Ivory Coast: Son Tay Raid.

The raiding force, consisting of five MH-53 helicopters and one HH-3E, code named *Blue Boy*, carrying Meadows' assault force, took off from Udorn, Thailand. The attack aircraft took off from Nakhon Phanom,

Thailand.[168] As a diversion, US Navy aircraft from the aircraft carriers USS Ranger, Hancock, and Oriskany in the Gulf of Tonkin dropped flares in Hanoi Harbor. The US Air Force also got onboard by having its F-4s and F-105s clear the raider's western approach to Hanoi of any surface-to-air missiles. The raiders had less than 30 minutes to complete their mission or face North Vietnamese reinforcements. Simons' aircraft, codenamed *Greenleaf* landed at a compound south of the prison referred to as the "Secondary School." It was occupied by some foreign soldiers.[169]

In five minutes, Simons' twenty-two raiders killed some 100 to 200 personnel located there. Meanwhile at Son Tay prison, following an MH-53 gun run destroying the camp's guard towers, *Blue Boy* conducted a planned/controlled crash landing inside the POW camp in its HH-3E Jolly Green Giant. A third helicopter, *Red wine* landed just outside the camp and cleared the outlying buildings. After Bull Simon's diversion to the secondary school, *Greenleaf* joined the fight at Son Tay.

At the prison, the raiders of aircrafts *Red Wine* and *Blue Boy* had eliminated most of the 60-plus guards at Son Tay, but there were no prisoners of war – they had been moved to another camp when the Song Con River threatened to flood. The Son Tay raid ended after 27 minutes. Simons hadn't lost a single man, and although there were no prisoners to rescue, the operation itself was nearly flawless. In the end, the raid on Son Tay was a historic anomaly and in the operational context, it remains a text book example of a raid. Additionally, the raid brought attention to US POW treatment in North Vietnam. This resulted in the consolidation of all POWs in Hanoi, which had the effect of improving matters for the POWs dramatically. Further, the raid had a long standing psychological impact as Communist forces were shocked by the capability and audacity of the US, wondering where we would strike next. This itself was an amazing confidence boost for the POWs.

On March 5, 1971, 5th Group returned to Fort Bragg. The role of Special Forces in Vietnam was over. However, some SF soldiers continued to serve in various covert missions as part of SOG. After Vietnam, the 1st, 3rd, 6th and 8th Special Forces Groups were all deactivated, and following the Desert One debacle, SOF was realigned under the Goldwater-Nichols Department of Defense Reorganization Act of 1986, and the Nunn-Cohen Amendment of 1987. In June 1983, the Army authorized the Special Forces tab, and later

---

[168] The total raider force included: 59 US Commandos (SF); 29 USAF aircraft 92 crew, and a total of 105 aircraft.
[169] Schemmer, The Raid, 171. Simons' men noted the soldiers were much taller, and better equipped than the NVA. Schemmer adds that in early November, photo reconnaissance revealed that the Secondary School began to be occupied by Russian and Chinese troops who were training the NVA on new surface to air missile defense systems.

established a separate career management field (CMF 18) for SF enlisted men on Oct. 1, 1984. The Special Forces Warrant Officer career field (180A) soon followed and, on April 9 1987, the Army Chief of Staff established a separate branch for SF officers (18A). Despite the numerous changes after Vietnam, the basic element of Special Forces, the Operational Detachment - Alpha (ODA), remained unchanged.[170]

Lebanese MTTs

From 1983 to 1985, the 10th Special Forces Group deployed 17 separate MTTs to support the Lebanese Army. Their mission was to advise and assist the Lebanese Army Training Centers. The 10th Special Forces Mobile Training Teams and the Lebanese Army developed a training program for over 5,000 officers, NCOs and soldiers. Training comprised of basic training, combined arms live fire, and urban live fire training. Despite the chaotic situation in Lebanon, the training programs conducted by 10th SF Group for the Lebanese Army were extremely successful; however, with the entry of the Syrian Army into Lebanon, the MTTs were brought to an end.

Central and South America

When President Reagan took office in 1980, communism was spreading rapidly throughout Latin America. Nicaragua was controlled by a communist regime, and with the support of Cuba, they were working hard to export their revolution to El Salvador and Honduras. The 3rd Bn, 7th SF Group drafted the initial plan for US Military trainers in El Salvador that was accepted by the Reagan Administration. Beginning in 1981, 7th SF Group began sending Green Berets into El Salvador to train the Salvadoran Army.

Throughout the decade of the 1980s, soldiers from the 7th SF Group played a critical role in helping the Salvadoran military grow from a constabulary force of 12,000 to a counterinsurgency force of 55,000. Additionally, the 7th Special Forces Group also played a very important role in preparing the Honduran military to resist and defeat any potential invasion from Nicaragua. The extensive 7th SF Group operations throughout Honduras in the 1980s not only prepared them for the threatened invasion, but also assisted the Honduran forces in conducting their own counter

---

[170] The only detachment position to change was that of the team executive officer, no longer filled by a lieutenant, but by an SF Warrant Officer with several years of detachment experience.

insurgency operations and ultimately defeating the Honduran communist-supported insurgency.

During the last half of the 1980s, the 7th Special Forces Group became involved in counter narcotics operations in the Andean Ridge countries of Venezuela, Colombia, Ecuador, Peru, and Bolivia. The purpose was not only to reduce the flow of drugs in the United States, but also to help control and reduce the violence that resulted from the flow of illegal and uncontrolled dollars into South America. In Colombia, SF teams conducted a long-term program of upgrading the capabilities of the Colombian military in its counterinsurgent fight against the insurgency and the drug cartels.

Operation Just Cause

The US invasion of Panama (OPLAN 90-2), code-named Operation Just Cause to oust Panamanian dictator Manuel Noriega, was executed between 21 December, 1989 and 31 January, 1990.[171] Immediately prior to the operation, American forces in Panama numbered some 13,000 troops including the 193[d] Infantry Brigade, a battalion each from the 7th and 5th Infantry Divisions, and two companies of US Marines. The newly formed US Army Special Operations Command, including a composite brigade of the 82[d] Airborne Division, brought in a further 7,000 troops, including the 75th Ranger Regiment and the equivalent of five battalions of other special operations forces. All told, there were five unconventional task forces involved in Just Cause: Green (1st SFOD-D), Black (Special Forces), Red (Rangers), and Blue (SEALs). Just Cause was to begin at 0100 hrs on the 20th of December, 1989 (See Figure 1-28). However, due to faulty operational security, the PDF had been alerted. The PDF prepared itself for the US invasion by establishing roadblocks along different routes leading to La Comandancia, their military headquarters in Panama City.

Shortly after midnight on Wednesday morning, the 21st of December, 1989, an unknown number of PDF personnel infiltrated Albrook Air Force Base and fired on a hangar where Army Special Forces personnel were assembling to board helicopters bound for the Pacora River Bridge. Two SF soldiers were wounded in the contact before the PDF withdrew. Twenty-four Green Berets from A Co, 3/7 SFG were tasked to established an ambush west of Fort Cimarron to block the advance of PDF Battalion 2000. Considered Noriega's best troops, Battalion 2000 was moving to rescue

---

[171] On 29 November the SICILY Drop Zone at Fort Bragg, North Carolina, was reconfigured to resemble a small international airport with a military airfield adjacent to it. In the scenario, a reinforced Ranger battalion parachuted onto the simulated airfields and secured them in advance of a brigade from the 82d Airborne Division parachuting onto the drop zone (DZ). CMH, Operation Just Cause, 14.

Noriega, who was being held captive in the Panamanian Comandancia. Led by Major Kevin Higgens, A 3/7 SFG departed Albrook in three Black Hawks to intercept Battalion 2000.

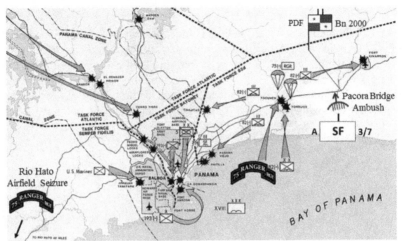

Figure 1-28. Operation Just Cause.

As Just Cause developed steam, Panama erupted into a series of cacophonous explosions. Rangers from 3/75 RGR were conducting an airfield seizure of the Rio Hato Airfield, 1/75 was jumping into Torrijos/Tocumen Airport, and Task Force Semper Fi, comprised of four companies of US Marines, eliminated PDF forces and secured the critical Bridge of the Americas which spans the Panama Canal. Also at Paitilla Airfield, a Navy SEAL task force of forty-eight men were tasked to destroy Noriega's personal jet. Just after H-hour the SEALs started clearing the airfield. In the firefights that followed, the jet was disabled and the Panamanians guarding the airfield were killed. But this task proved to be the most costly in Operation Just Cause. Four SEALs were killed in action, and eight were wounded.[172]

Simultaneously, 1st SFOD-D conducted a raid on Modelo Prison in Panama City to rescue Kurt Muse, thought to be a CIA operative. Landing on the roof, Unit snipers quickly dispersed, eliminating threats in nearby buildings. With this cover, the assault force effected entry and cleared down two flights of stairs to Muse's cell, eliminating numerous PDF along the way and securing their precious cargo. During the exfil, two MH-6 Little Birds crashed, wounding two operators. However, staying in the fight, Unit members fought their way to nearby

---

[172] CMH, Operation Just Cause, 23.

buildings and, while securing Muse, coordinated their return trip back to the US base via ground exfil.

Ambush at Pacora Bridge

As Task Force Black neared Pacora Bridge, the lead pilot spotted a convoy of six PDF vehicles approaching from the east. It was now a race to see who could take the bridge first. Judging the terrain just west of the bridge as the best place to ambush the PDF, Higgens' had his force dropped off, and the men of A 3/7 quickly dislodged the helicopters, deploying a hasty ambush at a point overlooking the key terrain on the Pan-American Highway (See Figure 1-29).

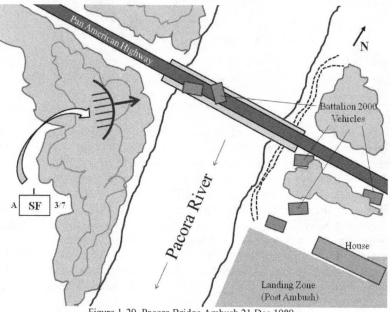

Figure 1-29. Pacora Bridge Ambush 21 Dec 1989.

The first Green Berets to arrive let loose a barrage of anti-tank rockets, grenades, and small arms fire onto the Battalion 2000 motorcade. As lead vehicle burst into flames, the motorcade screeched to a halt. In the ensuing chaos, Noriega's best abandoned their vehicles, and fired wildly at the US position. Higgens' Air Force Combat Controller then vectored in an AC-130 which unleashed a devastating salvo of fire at a mere hundred meters from the SF Company. Trapped PDF soldiers scrambled out of their vehicles to be waylaid by weathering fire. A second AC-130 was called in which

99

provided additional firepower and up to date enemy ground movement information. By daybreak, TF Black sent out a quick reaction force (QRF to reinforce Higgens' company. A 3/7 controlled the bridge while the QRF under Major Perez arrived and cleared the east side of the river. ODA 714 led the way and cleared a building near the bridge on the east side. The Battalion 2000 was destroyed with hundreds of PDF killed or wounded. A 3/7 was able to hold the bridge through the night, preventing the enemy elements from reinforcing PDF units in Panama City or interfering with the American assault on Torrijos and Tocumen Airports.[173]

Designated Task Force Black, soldiers from the 7th SF Group, many of whom were already stationed in Panama, supported the entire operation by conducting many reconnaissance and direct action missions as well as the "Ma Bell take downs" of numerous Panamanian Defense Force (PDF units throughout the country. Ever the resourceful warriors, the Green Berets of 7th Group came up with a plan they referred to as "Ma Bell take downs." A member of an ODA would find a working telephone outside a garrison and call the leader of the PDF unit inside while an AC-130 circled overhead.

As described by the commander of 7th SF Group, "we'd call them on the phone and say, look up. Do you see the C-130? You can surrender to us, or they can blow you away. What would you like to have happen? If the PDF commander declined the invitation, the gunship would fire some of its ordnance into a clearing or the nearby jungle or some helicopters would buzz by overhead at treetop level. If these "encouragements" failed, there was always a company on standby to be inserted into the operation. Usually the telephone call worked, and no force was necessary in these remote areas.[174] Other SF teams neutralized PDF units, raided enemy command and control facilities and later accepted the surrender of hundreds of enemy troops in distant provinces. After the end of Operation Just Cause, 7th Group played a key role in Operation Promote Liberty, which, over 6 months transformed Panama from a military dictatorship supported by a corrupt military, into a legitimate democratic government, protected by a police force.

Operation Desert Storm

During Operations Desert Shield and Desert Storm in 1990-91, elements of the 3rd, 5th and 10th SF Groups deployed in support of the coalition which moved to oust Saddam Hussein's forces from Kuwait. During the ground war, 109 SF ODAs accompanied virtually the entire range of forces into battle. The teams performed raids, special reconnaissance (SR, combat

---

[173] Ibid, 17.
[174] CMH, Operation Just Cause, 41.

search and rescue (CSAR), and trained the Kuwaiti resistance as well as coalition units. They were among the first US soldiers into Kuwait City. Additionally, SF teams performed important intelligence collection missions, such as conducting reconnaissance on the terrain the Coalition forces would use in the forthcoming ground attack.

Prior to the ground invasion, thirteen ODAs were infiltrated deep into Iraq, some up to 150 miles behind enemy lines. Colonel Jim Kraus's 5th SF Group was assigned the special reconnaissance (SR) mission. Three teams of three to six men each would be inserted north of the Euphrates to have eyes on the roads and ten teams would be positioned south of the river.[175] The teams would radio warnings if enemy reinforcements from Baghdad attempted to intercept the Coalition forces as they enveloped the Iraqi Army and liberated Kuwait (See Figure 1-29). The SR mission called for the teams to be inserted by Task Force 160 (TF160), the 160th Special Operations Aviation Regiment (SOAR), at off-set infil points approximately 5-10 kilometers away from their recce sites, walk for about five hours and spend some four hours digging their hide sites from where they would be the eyes and ears of the Coalition.[176]

One of the SR teams, ODA 525, led by CW2 Chad "Bull" Balwanz, was assigned Highway 7 (See Figure 1-30). They were to provide early warning in the event of an Iraqi counter-attack or additional forces moving south toward Kuwait and the Coalition forces. Early morning on the 24th of February, 1991, ODA 525 had just enough time to finish digging their hide sites. The team had infiltrated via two MH-60 Black Hawks, cached equipment, and walked for hours under rucksacks weighing in excess of 175 pounds.[177] About 300 meters east of Highway 7, Balwanz found ground suitable for the hide sites. The position was thought to be close enough to identify enemy vehicle types; detail was important. With the coming of morning, the team had just begun taking shifts when they were compromised by Bedouin children.[178] After initially thinking they might not be compromised, the area around ODA 525 came alive.

Battle of Suwayj Ghazi

After seeing some trucks pull up and unload about 150 Iraqi soldiers, Balwanz gave the command to detonate the gear and called in an air strike.

---

[175] Waller, The Commandos, 357.

[176] Ibid, 361.

[177] In order to survive up to 5 days on the ground, each man carried 20 quarts of water, rations, ammunition, radios, batteries, as well as hide site equipment. The hide sites took about 4 hours to dig and were about 5 feet by 3 feet and chest high.

[178] Waller, The Commandos, 9.

The Iraqi soldiers fired wildly as they closed in on the ODA, standing straight up and bunched together. DeGroff, a weapons sergeant, and another team mate, began dumping 40mm grenades from their M203s into the advancing Iraqis. In just ten minutes, the eight Green Berets of ODA 525 had killed about forty soldiers. When the F-16s arrived, the team used their emergency PRC-90 radio and signal mirror to direct a cluster bomb and 2,000-pound bombs to stop the Iraqi attack on the beleaguered team. Shortly before 8pm on 24 February, two TF160 MH-60 Black Hawks landed in Balwanz's perimeter and extracted the team back to King Fahd International Airport.

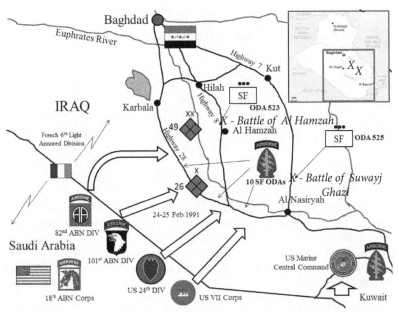

Figure 1-30. Operation Desert Storm. Special Forces SR Missions, February 1991.

Battle of Al Hamzah

On the night of 23 February, 1991, to the west of Balwanz's team, two MH-60s shuttled ODA 523 into a position to move into hide sites with eyes on Highway 8. Sims, the team sergeant of 523, and the team leader, CPT Conner, would command a split team, each at hide sites about 24 kilometers apart. Sims' team set up their hide site about a kilometer west of Highway 8. Similarly at daybreak, Sims' team was compromised by Bedouins, and within thirty minutes a reinforced Iraqi platoon arrived to attack the three-man element. Armed villagers and soldiers were gunned down by the Green Berets as they rushed their position.

Thirty minutes later another bus load of Iraqi soldiers arrived just in time for Sims' airstrike. An F-16 Eagle spotted the surrounded team's position, and with Sims' direction, dropped cluster bombs and 1000-pounders only 300 meters away.[179] The bombs held the Iraqis off. Soon afterward, a single TF160 MH-60 landed in between Sims' element and the attacking Iraqi platoon. With the miniguns mowing down advancing Iraqi soldiers, the three Green Berets threw themselves into the Black Hawk and under intense fire, the pilots made their way south, back to King Fahd International Airport.

The Scud Hunters

Another critical special operations mission that was conducted prior to the ground invasion was the one executed by elements of 1st SFOD-Delta along with Britain's 22nd SAS. The mission called for the Delta teams to patrol large open expanses of Iraq's western districts for Scud missile launch sites and then call in airstrikes to destroy the Scuds.[180] Saddam Hussein had called on the Arab world to destroy Israel and the western infidels. The Scuds targeted Israel's capital Tel Aviv, and would prove to be similar to Hitler's V-2s at the close of the Second World War. Destroying the Scuds on the ground proved to be quite a difficult mission as the Iraqi Scud crews remained constantly on the move and could drive to a coordinated launch site, fire their missiles, and drive away in less than ten minutes. To complicate the mission further, the Iraqis routinely deployed decoys. BG Downing, the JSOC commander, organized elements from two Delta squadrons, a company of Rangers, and some SEAL Team Six (ST-6) into a joint task force (JTF) based out of Ar Ar, Saudi Arabia.

After many days on the ground prior to the invasion some 40 Scuds were destroyed by Downing's JTF. With the average daily Scud launches dwindling from five to one, Downing's JTF undoubtedly saved countless lives, and effectively kept Israel out of the war, which had she joined would have collapsed the Arab contingent of the Coalition. Additionally, Downing's task force attacked a telephone station in western Iraq, severing the line of communication between Baghdad and Amman; crucial to

---

[179] Ibid, 369.

[180] The Scud, R-11 tactical ballistic missile, was Soviet made and widely exported. Scuds were responsible for most of the coalition deaths outside of Iraq and Kuwait. Throughout the war, Saddam's Scuds killed four Israelis, injured at least 289, and left some 4,000 homeless. Additionally, 128 Americans killed or wounded resulted from the Scud attack on Dhahran.

keeping Jordan out of the war which Saddam Hussein was attempting to bring to his side.

On the night of the 23rd of February, 1991, Allied armor and airborne forces, unleashed a massive enveloping attack, which by-passed the front line Iraqi forces and cut off their avenue of retreat. The result was a spectacular victory. Following the liberation of Kuwait and the cessation of hostilities, General Schwarzkopf commented that the special operations forces employed during Desert Shield and Storm were the glue that held the Coalition together and made it work. This was quite a concession as Schwarzkopf was not a big fan of special operations. In April 1991, Operation Provide Comfort and Provide Comfort II were conducted by the US and some of its Gulf War allies to defend Kurds fleeing their homes in northern Iraq in the aftermath of the Gulf War. Under Colonel Tangney, all three battalions of 10th SF Group were deployed in order to assist the Kurds and deliver humanitarian aid to them. 10th SF Group was credited by General Galvin, the commander of EUCOM as having saved half a million Kurds from extinction.

Operation Restore Hope

Operation Restore Hope was a US initiative conducted under the umbrella of the United Nations-sanctioned multinational force which operated in Somalia between December 1992 and March 1995. The operation was tasked with carrying out United Nations Security Council Resolution 794: to create a protected environment for conducting humanitarian operations in the southern half of Somalia. Throughout Operation Restore Hope, ODAs from 5th and 10th SF Groups conducted a multitude of stability operations.

During UNOSOM II, the second phase of the UN mission in Somalia, General Aidid, a renegade Somali warlord, had killed and injured several soldiers using improvised bombs. In response, President Clinton approved the proposal to deploy a special task force, TF Ranger, composed of 400 U.S. Army Rangers and 1st SFOD-Delta commandos. Operation Gothic Serpent, conducted from August to October 1993, was launched with the primary mission of capturing warlord Mohamed Farrah Aidid.

On the afternoon of 3 October 1993, informed that two leaders of Aidid's clan were at a residence in central Mogadishu, TF Ranger sent 19 aircraft, 12 vehicles, and 160 men to kill or capture them. The two Somali leaders were quickly captured, however armed militiamen and civilians converged on the target area from all over the city. When two MH-60 Black Hawk helicopters were shot down, ground forces converged to their locations to recover the personnel. The ensuing battle to get to the downed helicopters turned out to be the most intensive close combat that U.S. troops had engaged in since the Vietnam War.

During the raid, MSG Gary Gordon and SFC Randall Shughart, a sniper/observer team with Task Force Ranger, provided precision and suppressive fires from helicopters above the two helicopter crash sites. Learning that no ground forces were available to rescue one of the downed aircrews and aware that a growing number of enemy were closing in on the site, Gordon and Shughart volunteered to be inserted to protect their critically wounded comrades. After their third request they were inserted one hundred meters south of the downed chopper. Armed with only their personal weapons, the two commandos fought their way to the downed fliers through intense small arms fire, a maze of shanties and shacks, and the enemy converging on the site. After Gordon and Shughart pulled the wounded from the wreckage, they established a perimeter, put themselves in the most dangerous position, and fought off a series of attacks. The two commandos continued to protect their comrades until they had depleted their ammunition and were themselves fatally wounded. Their actions saved the life of CW3 Michael Durant. Gary Gordon and Randall Shughart, were posthumously awarded the Medal of Honor for their valiant efforts.

In the end, 18 U.S. troops on the rescue convoy were killed, while estimates of Somali fatalities are around 1,000 militiamen killed during the battle. Although the mission's objective of capturing Aidid's associates was accomplished, on October 7 in a nationwide television address, President Clinton effectively ended the US proactive policy in Somalia and called for the withdrawal of all US forces no later than March 31, 1994.

Operation Uphold Democracy

Operation Uphold Democracy was an intervention designed to remove the military regime installed by the 1991 Haitian coup d'état that overthrew the elected President Jean-Bertrand Aristide. The operation was effectively authorized by the 31 July 1994 United Nations Security Council Resolution 940. With an array of forces prepared to invade, including elements of the 82nd Division (Airborne) already in the air, a diplomatic element led by former President Jimmy Carter, U.S. Senator Sam Nunn and retired former Chairman of the Joint Chiefs of Staff, General Colin Powell persuaded the leaders of Haiti to step down and allow the elected officials to return to power. This effort was successful due in part because the U.S. delegation was able to point to the massed forces poised to enter the country. The military mission changed from a combat operation to a peace-keeping and nation-building operation at that point with the deployment of the U.S. led multinational force (MNF) in Haiti.

105

MNF-Haiti was made up primarily of 3rd SF Group along with the other active and reserve SF Groups in support, but also included the 10th Mountain Division. MNF-Haiti continued until June 1996. During stability operations in Haiti on 12 January, 1995, SFC Gregory Cardott of 1st Bn, 3rd SFG (A was shot and killed while detaining a local Haitian who had illegally crossed the Haitian-Dominican border. The assailant also shot his partner, SFC Tommy J. Davis. SFC Davis managed a difficult weak-handed rifle shot to the assailant, killing him.

Operation Enduring Freedom

When the U.S. was attacked on 9/11, SF played a major role in the U.S. response. The U.S. retaliated quickly against the Taliban, which supported the al-Qaeda terrorists who perpetrated the 9/11 attacks and sought protection in Afghanistan, by launching Operation Enduring Freedom (OEF. OEF officially began the evening of 7 October, 2001 with Operation Crescent Wind. This was the name given to the Coalition air campaign which targeted Taliban command and control as well as air defense sites.[181] The majority of the Taliban's antiquated air defense arsenal was destroyed the first night of airstrikes along with their aged MIG-21s and SU-22 aircraft. The first U.S. ground forces in Afghanistan after 9/11 were members of the CIA's Special Activities Division (SAD. Covert operations, under the name "Jawbreaker," brought real-time accuracy to the developing mission. The SAD teams facilitated the insertion and link-up of 5th SF Group's first teams on the ground with the Northern Alliance (NA.[182]

Al Qaeda

Al Qaeda was originally established to facilitate the integration of young Arabs into the anti-Soviet resistance in Afghanistan, but after the Soviet withdrawal in 1989, the organization evolved into the vanguard of a global fundamentalist insurgency seeking to unite the international Muslim community under a united political and religious authority. In 1985, Sheik Adallah Azam and Osama bin Laden created the Mekhtab al-Khidemat (MAK or "Services Bureau" to facilitate administrative problems for foreign Muslim fighters.[183]

---

[181] Neville, Special Operations Forces in Afghanistan, 6.
[182] The Northern Alliance, officially known as the United Islamic Front for the Salvation of Afghanistan, was organized to resist the Taliban in their attempt to control the whole of Afghanistan. The Northern Alliance fought a defensive war against the Taliban government from 1996-2001.
[183] Casebook in Insurgency and Revolutionary Warfare Volume II, 489.

Chapter 1   A Concise History of the Special Forces

At the most basic level of analysis, Al Qaeda represents the internationalization of Islamic militancy, facilitated by technological change, but ultimately driven by the failure of earlier Islamist movements to bring about serious political change in their own domestic environments. Notable incidents attributed to Al Qaeda include the 1992 bombings of two hotels in Yemen; the 1993 bombing of the World Trade Center in New York City; the 1998 bombings of two United States embassies in Tanzania and Kenya; the 2000 bombing of the USS Cole in Yemen, and the 2001 attacks that destroyed the World Trade Center in New York and damaged the headquarters of the U.S. Department of Defense in Washington DC.

Task Force Dagger

Led by COL John Mulholland, the 5th SF Group formed a joint special operations task force (JSOTF) known as Task Force Dagger to control special operations in northern Afghanistan (JSOTF-North). 5th Group teams based out of a former Soviet airbase in Karshi-Khandabad (K2), Uzbekistan, launched their first teams into Afghanistan, ODAs 555 and 595, on the night of 19 October, 2001. Mulholland decided that Dostum at Mazar-e Sharif would get ODA 595 and ODA 555 would go to Khan at Bagram, just 25 miles from Kabul, with a primary mission of destroying al Qaeda/Taliban forces (See Figure 1-31).

Early on the 20th of October, SOAR inserted ODA 595 into the Dari-a-Souf Valley some fifty miles south of Mazar-e-Sharif. Their mission was to coordinate the seizure of Mazar-e Sharif. The Green Berets linked-up with General Abdur Rashid Dostum, the commander of the largest NA faction. From there, ODA 595 advanced to clear the Dari-a-Souf river valley of the Taliban.

The terrain and weather in which ODA 595 and later ODA 523 worked in was quite incredible: at elevations exceeding 6,000 feet, movement was restricted to narrow winding mountain trails in which sheer rock face drop offs of thousands of feet were negotiated by mere foot-wide paths. Mounted on horseback, the men of ODA 595 took part in their first combat engagement when Dostum's force took the village of Bishqab from the Taliban on 21 October, 2001. The success was followed up by engagements at Cobaki on 22 October, Chapchal on October 23, and Oimentan on 25 October. Dostum's forces, along with ODA 595's coordinated airstrikes, pushed the Taliban out of the valleys.

Figure 1-31. Afghanistan.

Battle of Bai Beche

Fighting their way up the Dari-a-Souf with ODA 523 and General Atta's forces on their flank in the Balkh Valley, Dostum's horsemen and ODA 595 were wreaking havoc on the Taliban. On 2 November, ODA 523 linked-up with General Atta's forces to join the Allied push toward Mazar. The key battle came when the retreating Taliban brought all available forces forward and prepared defensive lines at Soviet-built defensive positions near the village of Bai Beche. On 5 November, 2001, ODA 595 coordinated a B-52 airstrike with a cavalry charge by Dostum's forces to overrun the Taliban defenses. With their center of gravity fractured, the routed Taliban retreated in disorder, unable to make any effective stand.[184] The victory at Bai Beche opened the way for Dostum and Atta's Northern Alliance forces to capture Mazar-e Sharif which fell to them on November 10. The fall of Mazar-e Sharif effectively ended any Taliban resistance in the north.

---

[184] Biddle, Afghanistan and the Future of Warfare, 18.

108

Chapter 1   A Concise History of the Special Forces

The Destruction of the Taliban in the North

To the east of ODA 595's operations, ODA 555 would be hundreds of miles from any Allied forces, and hours from any possible extraction in the event of a collapse of the NA. The MH-47 Chinooks shuttling ODA 555 were barely able to make it over the high mountain passes. The crew and passengers had to use oxygen. The round trip journey to deliver ODA 555 to Bagram took the 160th SOAR crew more than 11 hours, with three in-flight refuelings. ODA 555 linked up with the SAD team in the Panjshir Valley and were taken to a safe house to link-up with Fahim Khan's NA fighters. Operations began in earnest the following day. With Kahn's men as guides, ODA 555 arrived to a point overlooking Bagram airbase. Sprawling out in the Panjshir Valley floor were literally hundreds of Taliban and al Qaeda targets, all under camouflage for protection from aerial observation.

The Taliban defensive works, armored vehicles, guns and tanks were all densely clustered and could hardly be numbered. What followed was a systematic destruction of the Taliban. ODA 555 and their Air Force Combat Controller Sergeant Markham guided strike aircraft and heavy bombers in wave after wave of precision guided munitions (PGMs) onto targets around Bagram. Together with Khan's men, ODA 555 also planned and conducted a number of raids on Taliban and Al Qaeda targets.

For the next few weeks, ODA 555, assisted by ODA 586 who arrived later, and Khan's men annihilated Taliban forces in the Panjshir Valley taking Bagram and then after some resistance, Kabul on 13 November. There they cleared the U.S. embassy complex and set up the first American mission in Kabul since the Soviet invasion of 1979. To the west, Taliban forces near Bamian fell to ODA 553 and General Khalili's forces after a brief resistance before surrendering the city on November 11. The ten-man ODA 553 had been inserted into the Bamian Valley on 2 November. As the cities fell in rapid succession to the Allied forces, Mulholland focused his forces on the last Taliban stronghold of Konduz. ODA 586 deployed into Konduz to assist Khan's forces there. ODA 586 used 11 days of massive airstrikes to demoralize the Taliban in Konduz, which fell to Khan's men on 23 November.

Battle of Tarin Kowt

The Battle of Tarin Kowt took place November 13 and 14, 2001 during the War in Afghanistan. In early November, Hamid Karzai had entered Taliban-controlled eastern Afghanistan with a small force of guerrillas, led by CPT Amerine's ODA 574. In response to the approach of Karzai's force, the inhabitants of the town of Tarin Kowt revolted and expelled their

Taliban administrators. Karzai traveled to Tarin Kowt to meet with the town elders. While he was there, the Taliban marshaled a force of 500 men to retake Tarin Kowt. ODA 574 and Karzai's fighters deployed in front of the town to block their advance. At 0700, the Taliban with some 80 vehicles began their advance through the pass leading up to Tarin Kowt. The battle began as the team's USAF combat controller, SGT Yoshita, together with SFC Dan Petithory, 574's senior Communications sergeant, coordinated airstrikes on the advancing column of Taliban. All told, 27 enemy vehicles were destroyed with an approximate 150-200 enemy dead.

In the seven hour battle, using superior technology and guts, ODA 574 and their mujahadeen managed to halt the Taliban advance and drive them away from the town. The defeat of the Taliban at Tarin Kowt was an important victory for Karzai, who used the victory to recruit more men to his fledgling guerrilla band. His force would grow in size to a peak of around 800 men. On November 30, they left Tarin Kowt and began advancing on Kandahar.

The Siege of Qala-e-Gangi

Many of the Taliban and Al Qaeda fighters who surrendered in Mazar-e Sharif were detained as prisoners in the 19th century mud fortress of Qala-e-Gangi just west of the city. On 25 November, a revolt at the fortress led to the death of CIA officer Johnny Spann. The fortress had previously been used by Dostum's forces as a weapons and ammunition depot. The 300-500 prisoners at Qala-e-Gangi expected to be freed after surrendering, were improperly searched by the NA. Some carried weapons and grenades into the prison. The prisoners managed to break into the fort's armory and arm themselves with an array of small arms and RPGs.

Spann fought with his AK-47 until it ran out of ammunition, then drew his pistol and emptied it, then fought off his attackers until they overpowered and killed him. The surviving CIA officer and Dostum's men managed to contain the revolt until a 5th SF Group quick reaction force (QRF) arrived. The fighting continued for four days while 5th Group operators called in airstrikes. On 27 November the siege ended when the last remnants of resistance were crushed: all but 86 prisoners were killed in the siege. General Dostum later claimed responsibility for the security failure.

Tragedy at Kandahar

Following their victory at Tarin Kowt, Karzai and ODA 574 moved on Kandahar; Karzai gathering local Pashtun fighters as they drew nearer. For two days, ODA 574 called in precision airstrikes on dug-in Taliban positions on the approaches to the city. Tragedy struck on 5 December when a 2000-pound joint direct attack munition (JDAM) fell short of its intended target, killing three members of 574, some 20 members of Karzai's force, as well as wounding five ODA members along with Karzai.[185] "How the mighty have fallen" (2 Sam 1:19). ODB 570, ODA 524, along with a Marine casevac CH-53, were deployed to evacuate the wounded and replace the fallen members of 574. Five minutes after the blast, Hamid Karzai received a satellite phone call informing him that he'd been selected to lead Afghanistan's new interim government.

Battle of Tora Bora

Following the overwhelming success of the campaign in Afghanistan, Al Qaeda fighters and the remnants of Taliban fled east to a region known as Tora Bora in the White Mountains. Coalition human intelligence (HUMINT) suggested that significant numbers of enemy targets were congregating there. Tora Bora, south of Jalalabad, meaning "black cave," offered Al Qaeda a system of caves and defenses. The cave network had been developed by the Mujahadeen during the war against the Soviets. Beginning on 3 December, some 20 Jawbreaker operatives, along with ODAs 563 and 572, were inserted in Jalalabad to begin an operation against Al Qaeda forces in the Tora Bora caves.

This special operations task force would advise Mujahadeen under the control of two warlords; Hazrat Ali and Mohammed Zaman. Some 2,500 to 3,000 militiamen, paid for by the CIA, were recruited for the operation to isolate and destroy Al Qaeda forces in the Tora Bora caves. ODA 572 led the attack with precision-guided bombs, the militia, with varied success, pressed an attack on the Al Qaeda defensive positions.

With Jawbreaker and 5th SF Group stretched thin, operators from 1st SFOD-Delta were brought in to bolster the attack. Small teams attached themselves to the militia, taking over tactical command from the CIA. Continuing at a steady advance through the difficult terrain, and backed by air strikes, the combined force suffocated the entrapped Al Qaeda forces; however, on 12 December, Mohammed Zaman (incredibly) negotiated a truce with Al Qaeda, giving them time to surrender their weapons and escape over the mountains into Pakistan.[186] By conservative estimates, the amount of Al- Qaeda killed in the operation was around 300.

---

[185] Members of ODA 574 killed in the blast were MSG Jefferson Davis, SFC Dan H. Petithory, and SSG Brian C. Prosser.

[186] Berntsen, Jawbreaker: The attack on bin Laden and al Qaeda, 123. Berntsen adds that two large groups of al Qaeda escaped: one 135-man headed east into Pakistan, while bin Laden together with some 200 jihadists entered Pakistan through the Peiwar pass.

Operation Anaconda

Operation Anaconda, which took place in early March 2002, utilized the combined resources of the U.S. military and CIA. Working with allied Afghan military forces, and North Atlantic Treaty Organization (NATO) forces, the operation attempted to destroy the remnants of Al Qaeda and Taliban forces. SF intelligence sources believed surviving Al Qaeda forces, upwards of 4,000 in size, to be gathering in the Shahi-Kot Valley, some 60 miles south of Gardez. Anaconda was to be the first large-scale battle in the U.S. invasion of Afghanistan. Additionally, it was the first operation in the Afghanistan Theater to involve a large number of U.S. conventional forces participating in direct combat activities.

Similar to Tora Bora, the Shahi Kot area was an Afghan guerrilla enclave, which enjoyed significant success against the Soviets in the 1980s. The defensive works included caves, bunkers and entrenchments. TF Dagger developed a plan that involved Zia Lodin's Afghan fighters as the main offensive punch (TF Hammer) driving into the valley supported by precision airstrikes and close air support (CAS) orchestrated by ODAs 594 and 372. The attack would force the enemy forces to squirt into the valley while an additional Afghan force (TF Anvil), led by Kamal Khan and Zakin Khan, supported by the 101st Division (Airborne) and the 10th Division (Mountain), would hold key blocking positions.

The operation began on 2 March 2002, and immediately ran into problems primarily with driving trucks over difficult terrain and in blackout conditions. Additionally, it was learned, through late-breaking information, that enemy forces were massed on the peaks rather than in the villages as earlier believed. To complicate matters, the usual large-scale ordinance involved in the airstrikes that had achieved overwhelming superiority for the Coalition up to this point was not fully used to its potential. The infantry forces of the 101st Airborne and 10th Mountain Divisions mistakenly landed in the middle of the valley, instead of the outside and immediately came under heavy Taliban fire from the peaks. In the intense fighting that followed, two Chinooks were shot down and a number of others were severely damaged. Allied forces eventually gained the upper hand, inflicting heavy casualties on the Taliban forces and pushing them out of the valley.

Following six hard days of combat, the majority of Al-Qaeda and Taliban presence was removed from the Shahi-Kot Valley. U.S. forces suffered 80 casualties in the operation, with eight killed and 72 wounded. Estimates of Al Qaeda and Taliban casualties range from 100 to 1,000.[187]

---

[187] CW2 Stanley L. Harriman was killed when a Spectre AC-130 misidentified his convoy. Two other ODA members were injured along with NA fighters.

Chapter 1   A Concise History of the Special Forces

Beginning in October 2001, 5th Group operational detachments supported the tribal coalitions known as the Northern Alliance, and by December, the Taliban had been routed from the cities, and the campaign transitioned to hunting the insurgents in the mountain valleys of eastern Afghanistan. The key to success in the early combat operations in Afghanistan was due to the by-with-through operational philosophy of the SF ODAs on the ground. Working with their Afghan allies, using precision airstrikes, the Special Forces soldiers brought the Taliban to their knees. In only 49 days from infil, the ODAs drove the Taliban out of its strongholds in the north, retook the capitol city of Kabul (14 November), and seized the strategic city of Kandahar (7 December). The initial campaign ended with the establishment of Combined Joint Special Operations Task Force-Afghanistan (CJSOTF-A) and the formation of a duly elected Afghan government.

Operation Enduring Freedom continued with subsequent rotations from all the SF Groups with the 3rd and 7th Groups forming the core element of the CJSOTF-A. Training and fighting with the Afghan National Army, the Afghan police and security forces and continuing the search for high-value targets were the primary missions of the SF teams. In October 2006, the U.S. led coalition turned over operations in Afghanistan to NATO-ISAF (International Security Assistance Force), with SF Groups continuing to form the core of the CJSOTF.

Coinciding with OEF and OIF has been Operation Enduring Freedom-Philippines, a campaign targeted at the Communist insurgency in the Philippines and various Islamic terrorist groups. 1st Group ODAs, rotating in and out of the Southern Philippines have trained and advised Philippine army units to combat Al-Qaeda groups like Abu Sayyaf. With the establishment of CJSOTF-Philippines, 1st Group ODAs work at the request of the Philippine government and continue the support the GWOT in the Philippines.

Operation Iraqi Freedom

March 19, 2003 signaled the start of the second major campaign in the United States' Global War on Terror (GWOT), Operation Iraqi Freedom, or OIF. The U.S. led coalition that invaded Iraq to overthrow the government of Saddam Hussein included elements from three SF Groups. In the west, 5th SF Group (CJSOTF-West), was tasked to seize airbases and conduct "Scud-hunting" to prevent the launch of Iraqi missiles against coalition forces and Israel. On the night of 19 March 2003, ODA 574 infiltrated via MH-53 helicopters into Iraq in order to capture Wadi Al Khirr airbase. The airbase would be used to bring in Coalition forces. The invasion of Iraq was scheduled to begin within hours.

113

The team was tasked to ensure the suitability of the air strip. They would radio back to 5th Group headquarters when their hasty assessment was completed. With the positive assessment of the team, the airbase was used hours later to infiltrate Coalition forces into Iraq on 20 March. To the west, on the border of Iraq, fifteen 1st Bn 5th SF Group ODAs under the command of LTC Chris Haas infiltrated after ODA 531 breached the 12-foot high berm that lay on the border. The ODAs of TF Dagger ranged far and wide in the trackless desert, seizing numerous airfields, preventing the deployment of scud missiles and halting the reinforcement of Saddam's forces. From the north, 10th SF Group, along with a battalion from 3rd SF Group, would thrust southward with their Peshmerga allies (See Figure 1-32).

On March 20, 2003, CJSOTF-N, Task Force Viking, comprised of members of the 3rd and 10th Special Forces Groups (Airborne), flew from their base in Romania to link-up with Kurdish resistance fighters, the Peshmerga. 10th SF Group, with members from 3rd SF Group, along with officers of the CIA's Special Activities Division (SAD), were the first to enter Iraq prior to the invasion.

The 10th SF Group, augmented with one Battalion from the 3rd SF Group, comprised 20 ODAs and along with the Kurdish militias fixed the Iraqi divisions stationed along the political boundary known as the Green Line and prevented them from reinforcing Saddam's army in Baghdad. Executing a classic SF mission, TF Viking trained and supplied the Kurdish forces that subsequently drove the Iraqi army out of the towns of Mosul and Irbil and secured the northern flank of the U.S. coalition. OIF rotations continued with the 5th and 10th SF Groups training the rebuilt Iraqi army and police forces, as well as conducting operations to capture high-value targets.

10th SF Group organized the Kurdish Peshmerga to attack and defeat the Ansar al-Islam, a terrorist organization allied with al-Qaeda. This battle was fought in critical terrain controlled by Ansar al-Islam in northeastern Iraq. Kurdish forces and their 10th SF Group advisors soundly defeated the terrorists and uncovered a chemical weapons production plant at Sargat, the only facility of its type discovered in the Iraq war. Three Silver Stars and six Bronze Stars for Valor were awarded in this engagement. 10th Group then organized and led the Peshmerga against Saddam's Army in the north. In a series of battles along the Green Line, the U.S.-led Kurdish forces prevented Saddam's divisions, to include thirteen armored divisions, from redeploying to Baghdad to contest the Allied invasion force coming from the south. The 10th Group teams assisted their Kurdish allies in recapturing and controlling the key cities of Mosul, Kirkuk and Tikrit.

Figure 1-32. The Invasion of Iraq 2003.

Operation Viking Hammer

On March 28, 2003, fifty Green Berets from 3rd Bn, 10th SFG(A) and some 7,000 Peshmerga fighters conducted an operation, known as Viking Hammer, to eliminate the Ansar al-Islam (AI) terrorist as they had occupied parts of Kurdistan (See Figure 1-33). Their objective was AI's base near Halabja. AI had taken over Halabja along with several other surrounding villages to create a terrorist salient along the border with Iran. The raid force consisted of ODAs 091, 094, 095, and 081 along with the Peshmerga militiamen. The Kurds were armed with AK-47s with some 200 rounds and no helmet or body armor. The battle began just after sunrise in a downpour of rain as the ODAs drew closer to the edge of the AI mountain lair. The AI terrorists opened up on the raiding force with 23mm ZSU fire.

The raiding force jumped out of their Land Rovers and began assaulting uphill in the mud toward the first enemy position. The raider force support position opened up with its own ZSU, MK-19, and .50 caliber machine gun

115

fire.[188] Subsequent enemy positions fell as the raid force advanced; the enemy then retreated up into the mountains raining down fire on the advancing Allied force. At this point the ODAs and the Peshmerga were pinned down but called in an airstrike of two Navy F-18 Hornets. On command the pilot loosed two 500 pound JDAM bombs and racked the terrorists with 25mm cannon fire. With that, the battle was virtually over, and the raid force swept through and cleared the enemy held structures.

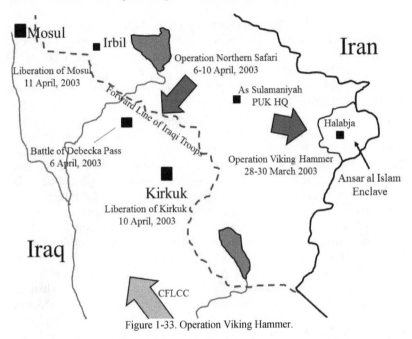

Figure 1-33. Operation Viking Hammer.

Many AI fighters fled to Iran, some were returned by Iranian border police who were taken prisoner by Kurdish forces, others were believed to be harbored by Iran. With minimal casualties, three killed and 23 wounded (all Peshmerga), Operation Viking Hammer was a major victory. It had eliminated Ansar al-Islam's presence in northern Iraq, and allowed Kurdish units to join the fight against Iraqi troops in northern Iraq.[189] Additionally, American intelligence personnel inspected the suspected chemical weapons site in the former AI held village of Sargat and discovered traces of Ricin in

---

[188] Moore, Hunting Down Saddam, 32.
[189] Ansar-al-Islam casualties are estimated at being 150-200 KIA out of a total force of 800; the remaining AI fighters fled into Iran. AI would later re-emerge as a group in the Iraqi insurgency.

the ruins, as well as potassium chloride. They also discovered chemical weapons suits, atropine nerve gas antidotes, and manuals on manufacturing chemical weapons, lending credence to the idea that the site was related to the manufacture of chemical weapons and poisons.[190] Three Green Berets were awarded the Silver Star for their actions around Sargat.

Battle of Debecka Pass

On April 6, 2003, the eighteenth day of the U.S.-led invasion of Iraq, Coalition Forces continued to move southward toward Iraqi battle lines consisting of two divisions of Iraqi Republican Guard, two mechanized infantry divisions, one armored division, eight infantry divisions and Fedayeen Saddam militia.[191] The Iraqi forces, in the face of the air strikes, withdrew to Kirkuk. The TF Viking objective was to capture a strategically important junction between Mosul and Kirkuk, near the village of Debecka. The battle began with an aerial bombardment from B-52 bombers. TF Viking and the Peshmerga resistance reached the base of the ridge. Peshmerga troops then proceeded to clear a minefield before them. Iraqi troops attacked and stopped the coalition force from destroying a large dirt berm. The coalition force made their way over the top of the ridgeline, and engaged the Iraqis in bunkers, capturing about twenty of them.

TF Viking then mounted a small hill, obscuring an approach to the crossroads from the south (See Figure 1-34). The US force consisted of: 26 Green Berets, three USAF Combat Controllers, and two Military Intelligence soldiers; totaling 31 Americans and 80 Peshmerga militiamen. As an Iraqi mechanized company with hundreds of troops approached, the four hour battle began. The initial Iraqi assault began with four T-55 main battle tanks, eight MTLB APCs, three 2-1/2 ton trucks, plus additional small jeeps and SUVs. All told, approximately 150-200 men. Of the 19 Javelin missiles fired, 16 hit enemy vehicles; two actually hit other structures (mud hut and a monument) as a result of gunner error, (accidentally locking on the wrong target) and one missile actually missed.[192]

On the next day, April 7, the Iraqi forces counter attacked with a larger force of six T-55 main battle tanks and sixteen MTLBs. Initially, the Iraqis approached the ODAs with headlights flashing. This was likely an attempt to fool the Green Berets into believing that it might be a surrender, however, Green Berets of ODA 391 took out the lead tank with a Javelin and dropped bombs on the rest. This action caused the Iraqi counter attack to stall and

---

[190] Antenori and Halberstadt, Roughneck Nine-One, 96.

[191] Robinson, Masters of Chaos, 299.

[192] Antenori and Halberstadt, Roughneck Nine-One, 137-194. So technically the missiles were 18 for 19 for hitting what they locked on.

eventually withdraw, abandoning their vehicles. The battle of Debecka pass was an overwhelming victory despite the friendly fire incident that occurred during the fighting.[193]

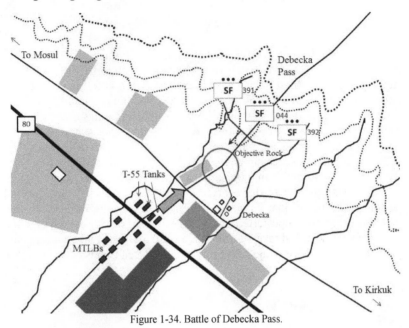

Figure 1-34. Battle of Debecka Pass.

Overall, the performance of the Special Forces Regiment in Afghanistan and Iraq have been and continue to be *sine pare*. This is evident from the fact that in one month, fewer than 100 soldiers toppled the Taliban and witnessed a democratic form of government take root; the accomplishments in Iraq are no less impressive. The war in Iraq and Afghanistan are indicative of the types of war the United States will continue to face in the future, because what began as a conventional conflict has since evolved into a counterinsurgency. And this environment, along with foreign internal defense (FID), is the primary mission of Special Forces.

Today, the Special Forces Regiment continues to play a key role in the US campaign against terrorism worldwide. On point for America, all seven Special Forces groups regularly rotate through Afghanistan, Iraq, and the

---

[193] This incident occurred near Pir Daoud on Sunday, 6 April 2003, when 18 members of TF Viking were killed and 45 were injured. An F-15 mistakenly dropped a bomb on the US Special Forces and Peshmerga troops instead of on the Iraqi tanks the ODAs were engaged with 1 mile away. One of the injured was Wajih Barzani, the brother of Masoud Barzani, leader of the Kurdistan Democratic Party (KDP).

Philippines, as well as Africa and South America. Committed to upholding their motto, Special Forces ODAs deploy world-wide to execute any number of critical tasks, destroying the enemies of liberty.[194]

Conclusion

In regards to the history of the Special Forces Regiment, this chapter has merely scratched the surface. There yet remains much to be chronicled and studied. A smorgasbord of rich theoretical experience is waiting to yield its bounty. For as Cicero has observed, "History illuminates reality, vitalizes memory, provides guidance in daily life and brings us tidings of antiquities." Thus, the student of war need only appreciate its dividends and mine deeply.

Perhaps the myriad accounts of undaunted courage, self-sacrifice and determination will go unsung and unheard. Yet, for the really good history, the kind you can't get from a book, a man must pay the price of admission. And for those of us who have made history, having seen it upclose and personal, understand that its actual process is often quite different to that which is presented to posterity. Only let us be honest with ourselves, learn from our mistakes, and take a healthy interest in passing on the vast amount of experience we have to the next generation of Green Berets.

---

[194] For the nine Special Forces critical tasks, see chapter 4.

Chapter 2   A Legacy of Honor

"Battle is the most magnificent competition in which a human being can indulge. It brings out all that is best; it removes all that is base. All men are afraid in battle. The coward is the one who lets his fear overcome his sense of duty. Duty is the essence of manhood." – Patton

As we've seen, the Special Forces Regiment is as rich in heritage as it is in honor. This chapter, presents us with a forum of heroes by setting before us first, the Regimental medal of honor recipients and secondly, some of the great leaders of the past who have made the Regiment what it is today.

Special Forces Medal of Honor Recipients

"They fought for freedom, a possession of inestimable value."

The Medal of Honor is the highest military decoration awarded by the United States government. It is bestowed by the president, in the name of Congress, upon members of the United States Armed Forces who distinguish themselves through "conspicuous gallantry and intrepidity at the risk of his or her life above and beyond the call of duty while engaged in an action against an enemy of the United States."[1] Due to the nature of its criteria, it is often awarded posthumously (more than half have been since 1941). There have been twenty-six Special Forces Medal of Honor recipients – *Strength and honor!* Here is the Regiment's finest:

CSM Bennie G. Adkins	SFC Eugene R. Ashley
SFC Gary B. Beikirch	MSG Roy P. Benavidez
SFC William M. Bryant	SGT Brian L. Buker
SGM Jon R. Cavaiani	MAJ Drew D. Dix
COL Roger H. Donlon	MSG Gary I. Gordon
1LT Loren D. Hagen	MSG Charles E. Hosking
COL Robert L. Howard	SP5 John J. Kedenburg
SGM Frank D. Miller	SSG Robert J. Miller
SFC Melvin Morris	MSG Jose Rodela
CPT Gary M. Rose	SFC Randall D. Shughart
SSG Ronald J. Shurer	1LT George K. Sisler
CPT Humbert R. Versace	MAJ Charles Q. Williams
SGT Gordon D. Yntema	MSG Fred W. Zabitosky

---

[1] Department of the Army (July 1, 2002), Section 578.4 Medal of Honor, Code of Federal Regulations Title 32, Volume 2.

CSM Bennie G. Adkins   1 Feb 1934 –
Detachment A-102, 5th Special Forces Group (A)
Place and Date: Camp A Shau, Republic of Vietnam,
9th to 12th of March, 1966
Place of Birth: Opelika, Alabama

For conspicuous gallantry and intrepidity at the risk of his life above and beyond the call of duty: Sergeant First Class Bennie G. Adkins distinguished himself by acts of gallantry and intrepidity at the risk of his life above and beyond the call of duty while serving as an Intelligence Sergeant with Detachment A-102, 5th Special Forces Group, 1st Special Forces, during combat operations against an armed enemy at Camp A Shau, Republic of Vietnam from March 9 to 12, 1966. When the camp was attacked by a large North Vietnamese and Viet Cong force in the early morning hours, Sergeant First Class Adkins rushed through intense enemy fire and manned a mortar position continually adjusting fire for the camp, despite incurring wounds as the mortar pit received several direct hits from enemy mortars. Upon learning that several soldiers were wounded near the center of camp, he temporarily turned the mortar over to another soldier, ran through exploding mortar rounds and dragged several comrades to safety. As the hostile fire subsided, Sergeant First Class Adkins exposed himself to sporadic sniper fire while carrying his wounded comrades to the camp dispensary. When Sergeant First Class Adkins and his group of defenders came under heavy small arms fire from members of the Civilian Irregular Defense Group that had defected to fight with the North Vietnamese, he maneuvered outside the camp to evacuate a seriously wounded American and draw fire all the while successfully covering the rescue. When a resupply air drop landed outside of the camp perimeter, Sergeant First Class Adkins, again, moved outside of the camp walls to retrieve the much needed supplies. During the early morning hours of March 10, 1966 enemy forces launched their main attack and within two hours, Sergeant First Class Adkins was the only man firing a mortar weapon. When all mortar rounds were expended, Sergeant First Class Adkins began placing effective recoilless rifle fire upon enemy positions. Despite receiving additional wounds from enemy rounds exploding on his position, Sergeant First Class Adkins fought off intense waves of attacking Viet Cong. Sergeant First Class Adkins eliminated numerous insurgents with small arms fire after withdrawing to a communications bunker with several soldiers. Running extremely low on ammunition, he returned to the mortar pit, gathered vital ammunition and ran through intense fire back to the bunker. After being ordered to evacuate the camp, Sergeant First Class Adkins and a small group of soldiers destroyed all signal equipment and classified documents, dug their way out of the rear of the bunker and fought their way out of the camp. While carrying a wounded soldier to the extraction point he learned that the last helicopter had already departed. Sergeant First Class Adkins led the group while evading the enemy until they were rescued by helicopter on March 12, 1966. During the thirty eight hour battle and forty eight hours of escape and evasion, fighting with mortars, machine guns, recoilless rifles, small arms, and hand grenades, it was estimated that Sergeant First Class Adkins killed between one hundred thirty five and one hundred seventy five of the enemy while sustaining eighteen different wounds to his body. Sergeant First Class Adkins' extraordinary heroism and selflessness above and beyond the call of duty are in keeping with the highest traditions of the military service and reflect great credit upon himself, Detachment A-102, 5th Special Forces Group, 1st Special Forces and the United States Army.

During his career that spanned twenty-two years, Adkins attained the rank of Command Sergeant Major, earned his bachelor's degree from Troy State University, in 1979, and his Master's Degree in Education, in 1982, and then, a second Master's Degree in Management, in 1988.

Chapter 2   A Legacy of Honor

SFC Eugene Ashley Jr.   12 Oct 1931 – 7 Feb 1968
C Company, 5th Special Forces Group (A)
Place and Date: Near Lang Vei, Republic of Vietnam, 6th and 7th February 1968
Place of Birth: Wilmington, North Carolina

For conspicuous gallantry and intrepidity at the risk of his life above and beyond the call of duty: SFC Ashley, distinguished himself by conspicuous gallantry and intrepidity while serving with Detachment A-101, Company C. SFC Ashley was the senior Special Forces Advisor of a hastily organized assault force whose mission was to rescue entrapped U.S. Special Forces Advisors at Camp Lang Vei. During the initial attack on the Special Forces camp by North Vietnamese army forces, SFC Ashley supported the camp with high explosive and illumination mortar rounds. When communications were lost with the main camp, he assumed the additional responsibility of directing air strikes and artillery support. SFC Ashley organized and equipped a small assault force composed of local friendly personnel. During the ensuing battle, SFC Ashley led a total of five vigorous assaults against the enemy, continuously exposing himself to a voluminous hail of enemy grenades, machinegun and automatic weapons fire. Throughout these assaults, he was plagued by numerous booby-trapped satchel charges in all bunkers on his avenue of approach. During his fifth and final assault, he adjusted air strikes nearly on top of his assault element, forcing the enemy to withdraw and resulting in friendly control of the summit of the hill. While exposing himself to intense enemy fire, he was seriously wounded by machinegun fire but continued his mission without regard for his personal safety. After the fifth assault he lost consciousness and was carried from the summit by his comrades only to suffer a fatal wound when an enemy artillery round landed in the area. SFC Ashley displayed extraordinary heroism in risking his life in an attempt to save the lives of his entrapped comrades and commanding officer. His total disregard for his personal safety while exposed to enemy observation and automatic weapons fire was an inspiration to all men committed to the assault. The resolute valor with which he led 5 gallant charges placed critical diversionary pressure on the attacking enemy and his valiant efforts carved a channel in the overpowering enemy forces and weapons positions through which the survivors of Camp Lang Vei eventually escaped to freedom. SFC Ashley's bravery at the cost of his life was in the highest traditions of the military service, and reflects great credit upon himself, his unit, and the U.S. Army.

SGT Gary B. Beikirch August 29, 1947 –
B Company, 5th Special Forces Group (A)
Place and Date: Kontum Province, Republic of Vietnam, 1 April 1970
Place of Birth: Buffalo, New York

For conspicuous gallantry and intrepidity at the risk of his life above and beyond the call of duty: SGT Beikirch, medical aidman, Detachment B-24, Company B, distinguished himself during the defense of Camp Dak Seang. The allied defenders suffered a number of casualties as a result of an intense, devastating attack launched by the enemy from well-concealed positions surrounding the camp. SGT Beikirch, with complete disregard for his personal safety, moved unhesitatingly through the withering enemy fire to his fallen comrades, applied first aid to their wounds and assisted them to the medical aid station. When informed that a seriously injured American officer was lying in an exposed position, SGT Beikirch ran immediately through the hail of fire. Although he was wounded seriously by fragments from an exploding enemy mortar shell, SGT Beikirch carried the officer to a medical aid station. Ignoring his own serious injuries, SGT Beikirch left the relative safety of the medical bunker to search for and evacuate other men who had been injured. He was again wounded as he dragged a critically injured Vietnamese soldier to the medical bunker while simultaneously applying mouth-to-mouth resuscitation to sustain his life. SGT Beikirch again refused treatment and continued his search for other casualties until he collapsed. Only then did he permit himself to be treated. SGT Beikirch's complete devotion to the welfare of his comrades, at the risk of his life are in keeping with the highest traditions of the military service and reflect great credit on him, his unit, and the U.S. Army.

After his military service, Gary Beikirch attended White Mountain Seminary in New Hampshire, graduating in 1975. He had planned to go back and serve as a missionary to the Vietnamese people but the country fell to North Vietnamese forces before he could return. Since then Gary received a master's degree in counseling and has invested into the lives of middle school students for 33 years.

MSG Roy P. Benavidez   Aug 5, 1935 – Nov 29, 1998
MACV-SOG
Place and Date: West of Loc Ninh, Republic of Vietnam, 2 May 1968
Place of Birth: Cuero, Texas

For conspicuous gallantry and intrepidity at the risk of his life above and beyond the call of duty: Master Sergeant (then Staff Sergeant) Roy P. Benavidez United States Army, who distinguished himself by a series of daring and extremely valorous actions on 2 May 1968 while assigned to Detachment B56, 5th Special Forces Group (Airborne), 1st Special Forces, Republic of Vietnam. On the morning of 2 May 1968, a 12-man Special Forces Reconnaissance Team was inserted by helicopters in a dense jungle area west of Loc Ninh, Vietnam to gather intelligence information about confirmed large-scale enemy activity. This area was controlled and routinely patrolled by the North Vietnamese Army. After a short period of time on the ground, the team met heavy enemy resistance, and requested emergency extraction. Three helicopters attempted extraction, but were unable to land due to intense enemy small arms and anti-aircraft fire. Sergeant Benavidez

125

was at the Forward Operating Base in Loc Ninh monitoring the operation by radio when these helicopters returned to off-load wounded crewmembers and to assess aircraft damage. Sergeant Benavidez voluntarily boarded a returning aircraft to assist in another extraction attempt. Realizing that all the team members were either dead or wounded and unable to move to the pickup zone, he directed the aircraft to a nearby clearing where he jumped from the hovering helicopter, and ran approximately 75 meters under withering small arms fire to the crippled team. Prior to reaching the team's position he was wounded in his right leg, face, and head. Despite these painful injuries, he took charge, repositioning the team members and directing their fire to facilitate the landing of an extraction aircraft, and the loading of wounded and dead team members. He then threw smoke canisters to direct the aircraft to the team's position. Despite his severe wounds and under intense enemy fire, he carried and dragged half of the wounded team members to the awaiting aircraft. He then provided protective fire by running alongside the aircraft as it moved to pick up the remaining team members. As the enemy's fire intensified, he hurried to recover the body and classified documents on the dead team leader. When he reached the leader's body, Sergeant Benavidez was severely wounded by small arms fire in the abdomen and grenade fragments in his back. At nearly the same moment, the aircraft pilot was mortally wounded, and his helicopter crashed. Although in extremely critical condition due to his multiple wounds, Sergeant Benavidez secured the classified documents and made his way back to the wreckage, where he aided the wounded out of the overturned aircraft, and gathered the stunned survivors into a defensive perimeter. Under increasing enemy automatic weapons and grenade fire, he moved around the perimeter distributing water and ammunition to his weary men, reinstilling in them a will to live and fight. Facing a buildup of enemy opposition with a beleaguered team, Sergeant Benavidez mustered his strength, began calling in tactical air strikes and directed the fire from supporting gunships to suppress the enemy's fire and so permit another extraction attempt. He was wounded again in his thigh by small arms fire while administering first aid to a wounded team member just before another extraction helicopter was able to land. His indomitable spirit kept him going as he began to ferry his comrades to the craft. On his second trip with the wounded, he was clubbed and suffered additional wounds to his head and arms before killing his adversary. He then continued under devastating fire to carry the wounded to the helicopter. Upon reaching the aircraft, he spotted and killed two enemy soldiers who were rushing the craft from an angle that prevented the aircraft door gunner from firing upon them. With little strength remaining, he made one last trip to the perimeter to ensure that all classified material had been collected or destroyed, and to bring in the remaining wounded. Only then, in extremely serious condition from numerous wounds and loss of blood, did he allow himself to be pulled into the extraction aircraft. Sergeant Benavidez' gallant choice to join voluntarily his comrades who were in critical straits, to expose himself constantly to withering enemy fire, and his refusal to be stopped despite numerous severe wounds, saved the lives of at least eight men. His fearless personal leadership, tenacious devotion to duty, and extremely valorous actions in the face of overwhelming odds were in keeping with the highest traditions of the military service, and reflect the utmost credit on him and the United States Army.[1]

SFC William M. Bryant   Feb 16, 1933 – Mar 24, 1969
A Company, 5th Special Forces Group (A)
Place and date: Long Khanh Province, Republic of Vietnam, 24 March 1969
Place of Birth: Cochran, Georgia

For conspicuous gallantry and intrepidity at the risk of his life above and beyond the call of duty: SFC Bryant, assigned to Company A, distinguished himself while serving as commanding officer of Civilian Irregular Defense Group Company 321, 2d Battalion, 3d Mobile Strike Force Command, during combat operations. The battalion came under heavy fire and became surrounded by the elements of 3 enemy regiments. SFC Bryant displayed extraordinary heroism throughout the succeeding 34 hours of incessant attack as he moved throughout the company position heedless of the intense hostile fire while establishing and improving the defensive perimeter, directing fire during critical phases of the battle, distributing ammunition, assisting the wounded, and providing the leadership and inspirational

---

[1] For more on Roy Benavidez see *Medal of Honor: One Man's Journey from Poverty and Prejudice.*

example of courage to his men. When a helicopter drop of ammunition was made to re-supply the beleaguered force, SFC Bryant with complete disregard for his safety ran through the heavy enemy fire to retrieve the scattered ammunition boxes and distributed needed ammunition to his men. During a lull in the intense fighting, SFC Bryant led a patrol outside the perimeter to obtain information of the enemy. The patrol came under intense automatic weapons fire and was pinned down. SFC Bryant single-handedly repulsed 1 enemy attack on his small force and by his heroic action inspired his men to fight off other assaults. Seeing a wounded enemy soldier some distance from the patrol location, SFC Bryant crawled forward alone under heavy fire to retrieve the soldier for intelligence purposes. Finding that the enemy soldier had expired, SFC Bryant crawled back to his patrol and led his men back to the company position where he again took command of the defense. As the siege continued, SFC Bryant organized and led a patrol in a daring attempt to break through the enemy encirclement. The patrol had advanced some 200 meters by heavy fighting when it was pinned down by the intense automatic weapons fire from heavily fortified bunkers and SFC Bryant was severely wounded. Despite his wounds he rallied his men, called for helicopter gunship support, and directed heavy suppressive fire upon the enemy positions. Following the last gunship attack, SFC Bryant fearlessly charged an enemy automatic weapons position, overrunning it, and single-handedly destroying its 3 defenders. Inspired by his heroic example, his men renewed their attack on the entrenched enemy. While regrouping his small force for the final assault against the enemy, SFC Bryant fell mortally wounded by an enemy rocket. SFC Bryant's selfless concern for his comrades, at the cost of his life above and beyond the call of duty are in keeping with the highest traditions of the military service and reflect great credit upon himself, his unit, and the U.S. Army.

Chapter 2   A Legacy of Honor

SGT Brian L. Buker   Nov 3, 1949 – Apr 5, 1970
Detachment B-55, 5th Special Forces Group (A)
Place and date: Chau Doc Province, Republic of Vietnam, 5 April 1970
Place of Birth: Benton, Maine

For conspicuous gallantry and intrepidity at the risk of his life above and beyond the call of duty: SGT Buker, Detachment B-55, distinguished himself while serving as a platoon adviser of a Vietnamese mobile strike force company during an offensive mission. SGT Buker personally led the platoon, cleared a strategically located well-guarded pass, and established the first foothold at the top of what had been an impenetrable mountain fortress. When the platoon came under the intense fire from a determined enemy located in 2 heavily fortified bunkers, and realizing that withdrawal would result in heavy casualties, SGT Buker unhesitatingly, and with complete disregard for his personal safety, charged through the hail of enemy fire and destroyed the first bunker with hand grenades. While reorganizing his men for the attack on the second bunker, SGT Buker was seriously wounded. Despite his wounds and the deadly enemy fire, he crawled forward and destroyed the second bunker. SGT Buker refused medical attention and was reorganizing his men to continue the attack when he was mortally wounded. As a direct result of his heroic actions, many casualties were averted, and the assault of the enemy position was successful. SGT Buker's extraordinary heroism at the cost of his life are in the highest traditions of the military service and reflect great credit on him, his unit, and the U.S. Army.

SGM Jon R. Cavaiani   Aug 2, 1943 – Jul 29, 2014
MACV-SOG
Place and date: Republic of Vietnam, 4 and 5 June 1971
Place of Birth: Royston, United Kingdom

For conspicuous gallantry and intrepidity at the risk of his life above and beyond the call of duty: SSG Cavaiani distinguished himself by conspicuous gallantry and intrepidity at the risk of life above and beyond the call of duty in action in the Republic of Vietnam on 4 and 5 June 1971 while serving as a platoon leader to a security platoon providing security for an isolated radio relay site located within enemy-held territory. On the morning of 4 June 1971, the entire camp came under an intense barrage of enemy small arms, automatic weapons, rocket-propelled grenade and mortar fire from a superior size enemy force. SSG Cavaiani acted with complete disregard for his personal safety as he repeatedly exposed himself to heavy enemy fire in order to move about the camp's perimeter directing the platoon's fire and rallying the platoon in a desperate fight for survival. SSG Cavaiani also returned heavy suppressive fire upon the assaulting enemy force during this period with a variety of weapons. When the entire platoon was to be evacuated, SSG Cavaiani unhesitatingly volunteered to remain on the ground and direct the helicopters into the landing zone. SSG Cavaiani was able to direct the first 3 helicopters in evacuating a major portion of the platoon. Due to intense increase in enemy fire, SSG Cavaiani was forced to remain at the camp overnight where he calmly directed the remaining platoon members in strengthening their defenses. On the morning of 5 June, a heavy ground fog restricted visibility. The superior size enemy force launched a major ground attack in an attempt to completely annihilate the remaining small force. The enemy force advanced in 2 ranks, first firing a heavy volume of small arms automatic weapons and rocket-propelled grenade fire while the second rank continuously threw a steady barrage of hand grenades at the beleaguered force. SSG Cavaiani returned a heavy barrage of small arms and hand grenade fire on the assaulting enemy force but was unable to slow them down. He ordered the remaining platoon members to attempt to escape while he provided them with cover fire. With 1 last courageous exertion, SSG Cavaiani recovered a machinegun, stood up, completely exposing himself to the heavy enemy fire directed at him, and began firing the machinegun in a sweeping motion along the 2 ranks of advancing enemy soldiers. Through SSG Cavaiani's valiant efforts with complete disregard for his safety, the majority of the remaining platoon members were able to escape. While inflicting severe losses on the advancing enemy force, SSG Cavaiani was wounded numerous times. SSG Cavaiani's conspicuous gallantry, extraordinary heroism and intrepidity at the risk of his life, above and beyond the call of duty, were in keeping with the highest traditions of the military service and reflect great credit upon himself and the U.S. Army.

MAJ Drew D. Dix   Dec 14, 1944 –
U.S. Senior Advisor Group, IV Corps, Military Assistance Command
Place and Date: Chau Doc Province, Republic of Vietnam, 31 January and 1 February 1968
Place of Birth: West Point, New York

For conspicuous gallantry and intrepidity at the risk of his life above and beyond the call of duty: SSG Dix distinguished himself by exceptional heroism while serving as a unit adviser. Two heavily armed Viet Cong battalions attacked the Province capital city of Chau Phu resulting in the complete breakdown and fragmentation of the defenses of the city. SSG Dix, with a patrol of Vietnamese soldiers, was recalled to assist in the defense of Chau Phu. Learning that a nurse was trapped in a house near the center of the city, SSG Dix organized a relief force, successfully rescued the nurse, and returned her to the safety of the Tactical Operations Center. Being informed of other trapped civilians within the city, SSG Dix voluntarily led another force to rescue 8 civilian employees located in a building which was under heavy mortar and small-arms fire. SSG Dix then returned to the center of the city. Upon approaching a building, he was subjected to intense automatic rifle and machinegun fire from an unknown number of Viet Cong. He personally assaulted the building, killing 6 Viet Cong, and rescuing 2 Filipinos. The following day SSG Dix, still on his own volition, assembled a 20-man force and though under intense enemy fire cleared the Viet Cong out of the hotel, theater, and other adjacent buildings within the city. During this portion of the attack, Army Republic of Vietnam soldiers inspired by the heroism and success of SSG Dix, rallied and commenced firing upon the Viet Cong. SSG Dix captured 20 prisoners, including a high ranking Viet Cong official. He then attacked enemy troops who had entered the residence of the Deputy Province Chief and was successful in rescuing the official's wife and children. SSG Dix's personal heroic actions resulted in 14 confirmed Viet Cong killed in action and possibly 25 more, the capture of 20 prisoners, 15 weapons, and the rescue of the 14 United States and free world civilians. The heroism of SSG Dix was in the highest tradition and reflects great credit upon the U.S. Army.

Drew Dix later received a direct commission to First Lieutenant and retired as a Major after 20 years of service.

COL Roger H. C. Donlon   Jan 30, 1934 -
Detachment A-726, 1st Bn, 7th Special Forces Group (A)
Place and date: Near Nam Dong, Republic of Vietnam, 6 July 1964
Place of Birth: Saugerties, New York

For conspicuous gallantry and intrepidity at the risk of his life above and beyond the call of duty: while defending a U.S. military installation against a fierce attack by hostile forces. Capt. Donlon was serving as the commanding officer of the U.S. Army Special Forces Detachment A-726 at Camp Nam Dong when a reinforced Viet Cong battalion suddenly launched a full-scale, predawn attack on the camp. During the violent battle that ensued, lasting 5 hours and resulting in heavy casualties on both sides, Capt. Donlon directed the defense operations in the midst of an enemy barrage of mortar shells, falling grenades, and extremely heavy gunfire. Upon the initial onslaught, he swiftly marshaled his forces and ordered the removal of the needed ammunition from a blazing building. He then dashed through a hail of small arms and exploding hand grenades to abort a breach of the main gate. En route to this position he detected an enemy demolition team of 3 in the proximity of the main gate and quickly annihilated them. Although exposed to the intense grenade attack, he then succeeded in reaching a 60mm mortar position despite sustaining a severe stomach wound as he was within 5 yards of the gun pit. When he discovered that most of the men in this gunpit were also wounded, he completely disregarded his own injury, directed their withdrawal to a location 30 meters away, and again risked his life by remaining behind and covering the movement with the utmost effectiveness. Noticing that his team sergeant was unable to evacuate the gun pit he crawled toward him and, while dragging the fallen soldier out of the gunpit, an enemy mortar exploded and inflicted a wound in Capt. Donlon's left shoulder. Although suffering from multiple wounds, he carried the abandoned 60mm mortar weapon to a new location 30 meters away where he found 3 wounded defenders. After administering first aid and encouragement to these men, he left the weapon with them, headed toward another position, and retrieved a 57mm recoilless rifle. Then with great courage and coolness under fire, he returned to the abandoned gun pit, evacuated ammunition for the 2 weapons, and while crawling and dragging the urgently needed ammunition, received a third wound on his leg by an enemy hand grenade. Despite his critical physical condition, he again crawled 175 meters to an 81mm mortar position and directed firing operations which protected the seriously threatened east sector of the camp. He then moved to an eastern 60mm mortar position and upon determining that the vicious enemy assault had weakened, crawled back to the gun pit with the 60mm mortar, set it up for defensive operations, and turned it over to 2 defenders with minor wounds. Without hesitation, he left this sheltered position, and moved from position to position around the beleaguered perimeter while hurling hand grenades at the enemy and inspiring his men to superhuman effort. As he bravely continued to move around the perimeter, a mortar shell exploded, wounding him in the face and body. As the long awaited daylight brought defeat to the enemy forces and their retreat back to the jungle leaving behind 54 of their dead, many weapons, and grenades, Capt. Donlon immediately reorganized his defenses and administered first aid to the wounded. His dynamic leadership, fortitude, and valiant efforts inspired not only the American personnel but the friendly Vietnamese defenders as well and resulted in the successful defense of the camp. Capt.

Donlon's extraordinary heroism, at the risk of his life above and beyond the call of duty are in the highest traditions of the U.S. Army and reflect great credit upon himself and the Armed Forces of his country.

In his career of over thirty years, Roger Donlon attained the rank of full Colonel, and retired after commanding the 3rd Battalion, 7th Special Forces Group (A) in Panama. Colonel Donlon is the current Honorary Colonel of the Special Forces Regiment.[2]

MSG Gary I. Gordon   Aug 30, 1960 – Oct 3, 1993
1st Special Forces Operational Detachment (Delta)
Place and Date: 3 October 1993, Mogadishu, Somalia
Place of Birth: Lincoln, Maine

For conspicuous gallantry and intrepidity at the risk of his life above and beyond the call of duty: Master Sergeant Gordon, United States Army, distinguished himself by actions above and beyond the call of duty on 3 October 1993, while serving as Sniper Team Leader, United States Army Special Operations Command with Task Force Ranger in Mogadishu, Somalia. Master Sergeant Gordon's sniper team provided precision fires from the lead helicopter during an assault and at two helicopter crash sites, while subjected to intense automatic weapons and rocket propelled grenade fires. When Master Sergeant Gordon learned that ground forces were not immediately available to secure the second crash site, he and another sniper unhesitatingly volunteered to be inserted to protect the four critically wounded personnel, despite being well aware of the growing number of enemy personnel closing in on the site. After his third request to be inserted, Master Sergeant Gordon received permission to perform his volunteer mission. When debris and enemy ground fires at the site caused them to

---

[2] For more on Roger Donlon see *Outpost of Freedom*.

abort the first attempt, Master Sergeant Gordon was inserted one hundred meters south of the crash site. Equipped with only his sniper rifle and a pistol, Master Sergeant Gordon and his fellow sniper, while under intense small arms fire from the enemy, fought their way through a dense maze of shanties and shacks to reach the critically injured crew members. Master Sergeant Gordon immediately pulled the pilot and the other crew members from the aircraft, establishing a perimeter which placed him and his fellow sniper in the most vulnerable position. Master Sergeant Gordon used his long range rifle and side arm to kill an undetermined number of attackers until he depleted his ammunition. Master Sergeant Gordon then went back to the wreckage, recovering some of the crew's weapons and ammunition. Despite the fact that he was critically low on ammunition, he provided some of it to the dazed pilot and then radioed for help. Master Sergeant Gordon continued to travel the perimeter, protecting the downed crew. After his team member was fatally wounded and his own rifle ammunition exhausted, Master Sergeant Gordon returned to the wreckage, recovering a rifle with the last five rounds of ammunition and gave it to the pilot with the words, "good luck." Then, armed only with his pistol, Master Sergeant Gordon continued to fight until he was fatally wounded. His actions saved the pilot's life. Master Sergeant Gordon's extraordinary heroism and devotion to duty were in keeping with the highest standards of military service and reflect great credit upon him, his unit and the United States Army.

1LT Loren D. Hagen   Feb 25, 1946 – Aug 7, 1971
MACV-SOG, CCN
Place and date: Republic of Vietnam, 7 August 1971
Place of Birth: Fargo, North Dakota

For conspicuous gallantry and intrepidity at the risk of his life above and beyond the call of duty: 1st Lt. Hagen distinguished himself in action while serving as the team leader of a small reconnaissance team operating deep within enemy-held territory. At approximately 0630 hours on the morning of 7 August 1971 the small team came under a fierce assault by a superior-sized enemy force using heavy small arms, automatic weapons, mortar, and rocket fire. 1st Lt. Hagen immediately began returning small-arms fire upon the attackers and successfully led his team in repelling the first enemy onslaught. He then quickly deployed his men into more strategic defense locations before the enemy struck again in an attempt to overrun and annihilate the beleaguered team's members. 1st Lt. Hagen repeatedly exposed himself to the enemy fire directed at him as he constantly moved about the team's perimeter, directing fire, rallying the members, and resupplying the team with ammunition, while courageously returning small arms and hand grenade fire in a valorous attempt to repel the advancing enemy force. The courageous actions and expert leadership abilities of 1st Lt. Hagen were a great source of inspiration and instilled confidence in the team members. After observing an enemy rocket make a direct hit on and destroy 1 of the team's bunkers, 1st Lt. Hagen moved toward the wrecked bunker in search for team members despite the fact that the enemy force now controlled the bunker area. With total disregard for his own personal safety, he crawled through the enemy fire while returning small-arms fire upon the enemy force. Undaunted by the enemy rockets and grenades impacting all around him, 1st Lt. Hagen desperately advanced upon the destroyed bunker until he was fatally wounded by enemy small arms and automatic weapons fire. With complete disregard for his personal safety, 1st Lt. Hagen's courageous gallantry, extraordinary heroism, and intrepidity above and beyond the call of duty, at the cost of his own life, were in keeping with the highest traditions of the military service and reflect great credit upon him and the U.S. Army.

Chapter 2   A Legacy of Honor

MSG Charles E. Hosking   May 12, 1924 – Mar 21, 1967
A Company, 5th Special Forces Group (A)
Place and Date: Phuoc Long Province, Republic of Vietnam, 21 March 1967
Place of Birth: Ramsey, New Jersey

For conspicuous gallantry and intrepidity at the risk of his life above and beyond the call of duty: MSG Hosking (then SFC), Detachment A-302, Company A, greatly distinguished himself while serving as company advisor in the III Corps Civilian Irregular Defense Group Reaction Battalion during combat operations in Don Luan District. A Viet Cong suspect was apprehended and subsequently identified as a Viet Cong sniper. While MSG Hosking was preparing the enemy for movement back to the base camp, the prisoner suddenly grabbed a hand grenade from MSG Hosking's belt, armed the grenade, and started running towards the company command group which consisted of 2 Americans and 2 Vietnamese who were standing a few feet away. Instantly realizing that the enemy intended to kill the other men, MSG Hosking immediately leaped upon the Viet Cong's back. With utter disregard for his personal safety, he grasped the Viet Cong in a "Bear Hug" forcing the grenade against the enemy soldier's chest. He then wrestled the Viet Cong to the ground and covered the enemy's body with his body until the grenade detonated. The blast instantly killed both MSG Hosking and the Viet Cong. By absorbing the full force of the exploding grenade with his body and that of the enemy, he saved the other members of his command group from death or serious injury. MSG Hosking's risk of his life above and beyond the call of duty are in the highest tradition of the U.S. Army and reflect great credit upon himself and the Armed Forces of his country.

COL Robert L. Howard   Jul 11, 1939 – Dec 23, 2009
MACV-SOG
Place and Date: Republic of Vietnam, 30 December 1968
Place of Birth: Opelika, Alabama

For conspicuous gallantry and intrepidity at the risk of his life above and beyond the call of duty: 1LT Howard (then SFC), distinguished himself while serving as platoon sergeant of an American-Vietnamese platoon which was on a mission to rescue a missing American soldier in enemy controlled territory in the Republic of Vietnam. The platoon had left its helicopter landing zone and was moving out on its mission when it was attacked by an estimated 2-company force. During the initial engagement, 1LT Howard was wounded and his weapon destroyed by a grenade explosion. 1LT Howard saw his platoon leader had been wounded seriously and was exposed to fire. Although unable to walk, and weaponless, 1LT Howard unhesitatingly crawled through a hail of fire to retrieve his wounded leader. As 1LT Howard was administering first aid and removing the officer's equipment, an enemy bullet struck 1 of the ammunition pouches on the lieutenant's belt, detonating several magazines of ammunition. 1LT Howard momentarily sought cover and then realizing that he must rejoin the platoon, which had been disorganized by the enemy attack, he again began dragging the seriously wounded officer toward the platoon area. Through his outstanding example of indomitable courage and bravery, 1LT Howard was able to rally the platoon into an organized defense force. With complete disregard for his safety, 1LT Howard crawled from position to position, administering first aid to the wounded, giving encouragement to the defenders and directing their fire on the encircling enemy. For 3 1/2 hours 1LT Howard's small force and supporting aircraft successfully repulsed enemy attacks and finally were in sufficient control to permit the landing of rescue helicopters. 1LT Howard personally supervised the loading of his men and did not leave the bullet-swept landing zone until all were aboard

138

safely. 1LT Howard's gallantry in action, his complete devotion to the welfare of his men at the risk of his life were in keeping with the highest traditions of the military service and reflect great credit on himself, his unit, and the U.S. Army.

After 54 months of combat, Robert Howard was wounded 14 times, and was awarded 8 Purple Hearts, 4 Bronze Stars, and was nominated for the Medal of Honor on three separate occasions. Additionally, Howard received two Masters Degrees during his career which spanned nearly 50 years (1956-1992), and retired as a full Colonel in 1992. He died of pancreatic cancer in Waco, Texas on December 23, 2009 and was laid to rest at Arlington National Cemetery on February 22, 2010. In 2014, Howard was announced as the recipient of United States Special Operations Command's Bull Simons award for his lifetime achievements in Special Operations.[3]

SP5 John J. Kedenburg   Jul 31, 1946 – Jun 13, 1968
MACV-SOG
Place and Date: Republic of Vietnam, 13 June 1968
Place of Birth: Brooklyn, New York

For conspicuous gallantry and intrepidity in action at the risk of his life above and beyond the call of duty: Sp5c. Kedenburg, U.S. Army, Command and Control Detachment North, Forward Operating Base 2, 5th Special Forces Group (Airborne), distinguished himself while serving as advisor to a long-range reconnaissance team of South Vietnamese irregular troops. The team's mission was to conduct counter-guerrilla operations deep within enemy-held territory. Prior to reaching the day's objective, the team was attacked and encircled by a battalion-size North Vietnamese Army force. Sp5c. Kedenburg assumed immediate command of the team which succeeded, after a fierce fight, in breaking out of the encirclement. As the

---

[3] For more on Robert Howard see *Reflections of a Warrior.*

team moved through thick jungle to a position from which it could be extracted by helicopter, Sp5c. Kedenburg conducted a gallant rear guard fight against the pursuing enemy and called for tactical air support and rescue helicopters. His withering fire against the enemy permitted the team to reach a preselected landing zone with the loss of only 1 man, who was unaccounted for. Once in the landing zone, Sp5c. Kedenburg deployed the team into a perimeter defense against the numerically superior enemy force. When tactical air support arrived, he skillfully directed air strikes against the enemy, suppressing their fire so that helicopters could hover over the area and drop slings to be used in the extraction of the team. After half of the team was extracted by helicopter, Sp5c. Kedenburg and the remaining 3 members of the team harnessed themselves to the sling on a second hovering helicopter. Just as the helicopter was to lift them out of the area, the South Vietnamese team member who had been unaccounted for after the initial encounter with the enemy appeared in the landing zone. Sp5c. Kedenburg unhesitatingly gave up his place in the sling to the man and directed the helicopter pilot to leave the area. He then continued to engage the enemy who were swarming into the landing zone, killing 6 enemy soldiers before he was overpowered. Sp5c. Kedenburg's inspiring leadership, consummate courage and willing self-sacrifice permitted his small team to inflict heavy casualties on the enemy and escape almost certain annihilation. His actions reflect great credit upon himself and the U.S. Army.

SGM Franklin D. Miller   Jan 27, 1945–Jun 30, 2000
MACV-SOG, CCN
Place and date: Kontum province, Republic of Vietnam, 5 January 1970
Place of Birth: Elizabeth City, North Carolina

For conspicuous gallantry and intrepidity at the risk of his life above and beyond the call of duty: SSG Miller, 5th Special Forces Group, distinguished himself while serving as team leader of an American-Vietnamese long-range reconnaissance patrol operating deep within enemy controlled territory. Leaving the helicopter insertion point, the patrol moved forward on its mission. Suddenly, 1 of the team members tripped a hostile booby trap which wounded 4 soldiers. SSG Miller, knowing that the explosion would alert the enemy, quickly administered first aid to the wounded and directed the team into positions across a small stream bed at the base of a steep hill. Within a few minutes, SSG Miller saw the lead element of what he estimated to be a platoon-size enemy force moving toward his location. Concerned for the safety of his men, he directed the small team to move up the hill to a more secure position. He remained alone, separated from the patrol, to meet the attack. SSG Miller single-handedly repulsed 2 determined attacks by the numerically superior enemy force and caused them to withdraw in disorder. He rejoined his team, established contact with a forward air controller and arranged the evacuation of his patrol. However, the only suitable extraction location in the heavy jungle was a bomb crater some 150 meters from the team location. SSG Miller reconnoitered the route to the crater and led his men through the enemy controlled jungle to the extraction site. As the evacuation helicopter hovered over the crater to pick up the patrol, the enemy launched a savage automatic weapon and rocket-propelled grenade attack against the beleaguered team, driving off the rescue helicopter. SSG Miller led the team in a valiant defense which drove back the enemy in its attempt to overrun the small patrol. Although seriously wounded and with every man in his patrol a casualty, SSG Miller moved forward to again single-handedly meet the hostile attackers. From his forward exposed position, SSG Miller gallantly repelled 2 attacks by the enemy before a friendly relief force reached the patrol location. SSG Miller's gallantry, intrepidity in action, and selfless devotion to the welfare of his comrades are in keeping with the highest traditions of the military service and reflect great credit on him, his unit, and the U.S. Army.[4]

---

[4] For more on Frank Miller see *Reflections of a Warrior*.

SSG Robert J. Miller   14 Oct 1983 - 25 Jan 2008
A Company, 3rd BN, 3rd Special Forces Group (A)
Place and Date: Afghanistan, January 25, 2008
Place of Birth: Harrisburg, Pennsylvania

For conspicuous gallantry and intrepidity at the risk of his life above and beyond the call of duty: Staff Sergeant Miller distinguished himself by extraordinary acts of heroism while serving as the Weapons Sergeant in Special Forces Operational Detachment Alpha 3312, Special Operations Task Force-33, Combined Joint Special Operations Task Force-Afghanistan during combat operations against an armed enemy in Konar Province, Afghanistan on January 25, 2008. While conducting a combat reconnaissance patrol through the Gowardesh Valley, Staff Sergeant Miller and his small element of U.S. and Afghan National Army soldiers engaged a force of 15 to 20 insurgents occupying prepared fighting positions. Staff Sergeant Miller initiated the assault by engaging the enemy positions with his vehicle's turret-mounted Mark-19 40 millimeter automatic grenade launcher while simultaneously providing detailed descriptions of the enemy positions to his command, enabling effective, accurate close air support. Following the engagement, Staff Sergeant Miller led a small squad forward to conduct a battle damage assessment. As the group neared the small, steep, narrow valley that the enemy had inhabited, a large, well-coordinated insurgent force initiated a near ambush, assaulting from elevated positions with ample cover. Exposed and with little available cover, the patrol was totally vulnerable to enemy rocket propelled grenades and automatic weapon fire. As point man, Staff Sergeant Miller was at the front of the patrol, cut off from supporting elements, and less than 20 meters from enemy forces. Nonetheless, with total disregard for his own safety, he called for his men to quickly move back to covered positions as he charged the enemy over exposed ground and under overwhelming enemy fire in order to provide protective fire for his team. While maneuvering to engage the enemy, Staff Sergeant Miller was shot in his upper torso. Ignoring the wound, he continued to push the fight, moving to draw fire from over one hundred enemy fighters upon himself. He then again charged forward through an open area in order to allow his teammates to safely reach cover. After killing at least 10 insurgents, wounding dozens more, and repeatedly exposing himself to withering enemy fire while moving from position to position, Staff Sergeant Miller was mortally wounded by enemy fire. His extraordinary valor ultimately saved the lives of seven members of his own team and 15 Afghanistan National Army soldiers. Staff Sergeant Miller's heroism and selflessness above and beyond the call of duty, and at the cost of his own life, are in keeping with the highest traditions of military service and reflect great credit upon himself and the United States Army.

SFC Melvin Morris   7 June 1942 –
Company D, 5th Special Forces Group (A).
Place and Date: Chi Lang, Vietnam, 17 September 1969
Place of Birth: Okmulgee, Oklahoma

For conspicuous gallantry and intrepidity at the risk of his life above and beyond the call of duty: Staff Sergeant Melvin Morris distinguished himself by acts of gallantry and intrepidity above and beyond the call of duty while serving as Commander of a Strike Force drawn from Company D, 5th Special Forces Group (Airborne), 1st Special Forces, during combat operations against an armed enemy in the vicinity of Chi Lang, Republic of Vietnam on September 17, 1969. On that afternoon, Staff Sergeant Morris' affiliated companies encountered an extensive enemy mine field and were subsequently engaged by a hostile force. Staff Sergeant Morris learned by radio that a fellow team commander had been killed near an enemy bunker and he immediately reorganized his men into an effective assault posture before advancing forward and splitting off with two men to recover the team commander's body. Observing the maneuver, the hostile force concentrated its fire on Staff Sergeant Morris' three-man element and successfully wounded both men accompanying him. After assisting the two wounded men back to his forces' lines, Staff Sergeant Morris charged forward into withering enemy fire with only his men's suppressive fire as cover. While enemy machine gun emplacements continuously directed strafing fusillades against him, Staff Sergeant Morris destroyed the positions with hand grenades and continued his assault, ultimately eliminating four bunkers. Upon reaching the bunker nearest the fallen team commander, Staff Sergeant Morris repulsed the enemy, retrieved his comrade and began the arduous trek back to friendly lines. He was wounded three times as he struggled forward, but ultimately succeeded in returning his fallen comrade to a friendly position. Staff Sergeant Morris' extraordinary heroism and selflessness above and beyond the call of duty are in keeping with the highest traditions of military service and reflect great credit upon himself, his unit, and the United States Army.

SFC Jose Rodela   15 June 1937 –
Detachment B-36, Company A, 5th Special Forces Group (A)
Place and Date: Phuoc Long, Vietnam, 1 September 1969
Place of Birth: Corpus Christi, Texas

For conspicuous gallantry and intrepidity at the risk of his life above and beyond the call of duty: Sergeant First Class Rodela distinguished himself by exceptionally valorous actions on 1 September 1969 while serving as the company commander of a mobile strike force unit on an operation in Phuoc Long Province. When the battalion came under an intense barrage of mortar, rocket, and machine gun fire, Sergeant Rodela, ignoring the withering enemy fire, immediately began placing his men into defensive positions to prevent an enemy assault which might overrun the entire battalion. Repeatedly exposing himself to enemy fire, he began to move from position to position, suppressing fire and assisting wounded men, and was himself wounded in the back and head by rocket shrapnel while recovering a wounded comrade. Alone, Sergeant Rodela assaulted and knocked out the rocket position. Successfully returning to the battalion's perimeter, Sergeant Rodela continued in command of his company, despite his painful wounds, throughout eighteen hours of continuous contact until he was evacuated. Sergeant First Class Rodela's extraordinary heroism and devotion to duty were in keeping with the highest traditions of the military service and reflect great credit upon himself, his unit, and the United States Army.

CPT Gary M. Rose   Oct 17, 1947 -
5th Special Forces Group (Airborne)
Place and Date: 12 Sept, 1970, Loas
Place of Birth: Watertown, New York

For conspicuous gallantry and intrepidity at the risk of his life above and beyond the call of duty: Sergeant Gary M. Rose distinguished himself by acts of gallantry and intrepidity while serving as a Special Forces Medic with a company-sized exploitation force, Special Operations Augmentation, Command and Control Central, 5th Special Forces Group (Airborne), 1st Special Forces, Republic of Vietnam. Between 11 and 14 September 1970, Sergeant Rose's company was continuously engaged by a well-armed and numerically superior hostile force deep in enemy-controlled territory. Enemy B-40 rockets and mortar rounds rained down while the adversary sprayed the area with small arms and machine gun fire, wounding many and forcing everyone to seek cover.Sergeant Rose, braving the hail of bullets, sprinted fifty meters to a wounded soldier's side. He then used his own body to protect the casualty from further injury while treating his wounds. After stabilizing the casualty, Sergeant Rose carried him through the bullet-ridden combat zone to protective cover. As the enemy accelerated the attack, Sergeant Rose continuously exposed himself to intense fire as he fearlessly to position, suppressing fire and assisting wounded men, and was himself wounded in the back and head by rocket shrapnel while recovering a wounded comrade. Alone, Sergeant Rodela assaulted and knocked out the rocket position. Successfully returning to the battalion's perimeter, Sergeant Rodela continued in command of his company, despite his painful wounds, throughout eighteen hours of continuous contact until he was evacuated. Sergeant First Class Rodela's extraordinary heroism and devotion to duty were in keeping with the highest traditions of the military service and reflect great credit upon himself, his unit, and the United States Army.

SFC Randall D. Shughart   Aug 13, 1958 - Oct 3, 1993
1st Special Forces Operational Detachment (Delta)
Place and Date: 3 October 1993, Mogadishu, Somalia
Place of Birth: Newville, Pennsylvania

For conspicuous gallantry and intrepidity at the risk of his life above and beyond the call of duty: Sergeant First Class Shughart, United States Army, distinguished himself by actions above and beyond the call of duty on 3 October 1993, while serving as a Sniper Team Member, United States Army Special Operations Command with Task Force Ranger in Mogadishu, Somalia. Sergeant First Class Shughart provided precision sniper fires from the lead helicopter during an assault on a building and at two helicopter crash sites, while subjected to intense automatic weapons and rocket propelled grenade fires. While providing critical suppressive fires at the second crash site, Sergeant First Class Shughart and his team leader learned that ground forces were not immediately available to secure the site. Sergeant First Class Shughart and his team leader unhesitatingly volunteered to be inserted to protect the four critically wounded personnel, despite being well aware of the growing number of enemy personnel closing in on the site. After their third request to be inserted, Sergeant First Class Shughart and his team leader received permission to perform this volunteer mission. When debris and enemy ground fires at the site caused them to abort the first attempt, Sergeant First Class Shughart and his team leader were inserted one hundred meters south of the crash site. Equipped with only his sniper rifle and a pistol, Sergeant First Class Shughart and his team leader, while under intense small arms fire from the enemy, fought their way through a dense maze of shanties and shacks to reach the critically injured crew members. Sergeant First Class Shughart pulled the pilot and the other crew members from the aircraft, establishing a perimeter which placed him and his fellow sniper in the most vulnerable position. Sergeant First Class Shughart used his long range rifle and side arm to kill an undetermined number of attackers while traveling the perimeter, protecting the downed crew. Sergeant First Class Shughart continued his protective fire until he depleted his ammunition and was fatally wounded. His actions saved the pilot's life. Sergeant First Class Shughart's extraordinary heroism and devotion to duty were in keeping with the highest standards of military service and reflect great credit upon him, his unit and the United States Army.

SSG Ronald J. Shurer   Dec 7, 1978 -
ODA-3336, 3rd Special Forces Group (Airborne)
Place and Date: 8 April, 2008, Shok Valley, Afghanistan
Place of Birth: Fairbanks, Alaska

For conspicuous gallantry and intrepidity at the risk of his life above and beyond the call of duty: On 6 April 2008, Staff Sergeant Ronald J. Shurer, as Medical Sergeant for Operational Detachment Alpha 3336 (ODA-3336), 3d Special Forces Group (Airborne), heroically and with complete disregard for his own safety fought his way up a mountain in order to render aid and evacuate casualties from his ODA and Afghan Commandos. Sergeant Shurer was initially pinned at the base of a wadi by accurate Insurgent sniper, Rocket Propelled Grenade (RPG), small arms, and machine gun fire when he received communications that the forward assault element could not move due to a high volume of Insurgent fire and sustained multiple casualties. With disregard for his own safety, Sergeant Shurer took off through a hail of bullets and began scaling the rock face to get to the casualties. During initial movement to the base of the mountain he treated a teammate wounded by shrapnel to his neck from an RPG blast that blew him off his feet. Once his teammate received aid, he then fought several hundred meters under fire, for over an hour, killing multiple Insurgents, as he made his way to the besieged location. Under intense Insurgent fire, Sergeant Shurer reached the pinned down element of his ODA and immediately rendered aid to four critically wounded US and ten injured Commandos.

He treated multiple life-threatening gunshot wounds until additional teammates arrived. Sergeant Shurer courageously exposed himself by running 15 meters through heavy Insurgent fire to render aid to his seriously wounded Team Sergeant. Despite being hit in the helmet and wounded in the arm by Insurgent sniper fire, he immediately pulled his Team Sergeant to a covered position, and rendered aid as Insurgent rounds impacted inches from their location. Without hesitation, he moved back through heavy Insurgent fire to treat another teammate that suffered a traumatic amputation of his right leg from Insurgent sniper fire. Sergeant Shurer rendered lifesaving aid to four critically wounded casualties for more than five and a half hours. As the lone medic at the besieged location, and almost overrun and fighting against nearly 200 Insurgent fighters, Sergeant Shurer's bravery and poise under fire saved the lives of all wounded casualties under his care. He evacuated three critically wounded, non-ambulatory, teammates down a near vertical 60-foot cliff, despite being under heavy Insurgent fire, and falling debris from numerous danger-close air strikes. Sergeant Shurer ingeniously used a six-foot length of nylon webbing to lower casualties, and physically shielded them from falling debris to ensure their safety.

His actions are in keeping with the finest traditions of military heroism and reflect distinct credit upon himself, Special Operations Task Force – 33, the Combined Joint Special Operations Task Force – Afghanistan, Special Operations Command Central, and the United States Army.

1LT George K. Sisler   Sep 19, 1937 - Feb 7, 1967
MACV-SOG, CCN
Place and Date: Republic of Vietnam. 7 February 1967
Place of Birth: Dexter, Missouri

For conspicuous gallantry and intrepidity at the risk of his life above and beyond the call of duty: 1LT Sisler was the platoon leader/adviser to a Special United States/Vietnam exploitation force. While on patrol deep within enemy dominated territory, 1LT Sisler's platoon was attacked from 3 sides by a company sized enemy force. 1LT Sisler quickly rallied his men, deployed them to a better defensive position, called for air strikes, and moved among his men to encourage and direct their efforts. Learning that 2 men had been wounded and were unable to pull back to the perimeter, 1LT Sisler charged from the position through intense enemy fire to assist them. He reached the men and began carrying 1 of them back to the perimeter, when he was taken under more intensive weapons fire by the enemy. Laying down his wounded comrade, he killed 3 onrushing enemy soldiers by firing his rifle and silenced the enemy machinegun with a grenade. As he returned the wounded man to the perimeter, the left flank of the position came under extremely heavy attack by the superior enemy force and several additional men of his platoon were quickly wounded. Realizing the need for instant action to prevent his position from being overrun, 1LT Sisler picked up some grenades and charged single-handedly into the enemy onslaught, firing his weapon and throwing grenades. This singularly heroic action broke up the vicious assault and forced the enemy to begin withdrawing. Despite the continuing enemy fire, 1LT Sisler was moving about the battlefield directing air strikes when he fell mortally wounded. His extraordinary leadership, infinite courage, and selfless concern for his men saved the lives of a number of his comrades. His actions reflect great credit upon himself and uphold the highest traditions of the military service.

CPT Humbert R. Versace   Jul 2, 1937 - Sep 26, 1965
U.S. Military Assistance Advisory Group
Place and Date: Republic of Vietnam, 29 October 1963 to 26 September 1965
Place of Birth: Honolulu, Hawaii

For conspicuous gallantry and intrepidity at the risk of his life above and beyond the call of duty: Captain Humbert R. Versace distinguished himself by extraordinary heroism during the period of 29 October 1963 to 26 September 1965, while serving as S2 Advisor, Military Assistance Advisory Group, Detachment 52, Ca Mau, Republic of Vietnam. While accompanying a Civilian Irregular Defense Group patrol engaged in combat operations in Thoi Binh District, An Xuyen Province, Captain Versace and the patrol came under sudden and intense mortar, automatic weapons, and small arms fire from elements of a heavily armed enemy battalion. As the battle raged, Captain Versace, although severely wounded in the knee and back by hostile fire, fought valiantly and continued to engage enemy targets. Weakened by his wounds and fatigued by the fierce firefight, Captain Versace stubbornly resisted capture by the over-powering Viet Cong force with the last full measure of his strength and ammunition. Taken prisoner by the Viet Cong, he exemplified the tenets of the Code of Conduct from the time he entered into Prisoner of War status. Captain Versace assumed command of his fellow American soldiers, scorned the enemy's exhaustive interrogation and indoctrination efforts, and made three unsuccessful attempts to escape, despite his weakened condition which was brought about by his wounds and the extreme privation and hardships he was forced to endure. During his captivity, Captain Versace was segregated in an isolated prisoner of war cage, manacled in irons for prolonged periods of time, and placed on extremely reduced ration. The enemy was unable to break his indomitable will, his faith in God, and his trust in the United States of America. Captain

Versace, an American fighting man who epitomized the principles of his country and the Code of Conduct, was executed by the Viet Cong on 26 September 1965. Captain Versace's gallant actions in close contact with an enemy force and unyielding courage and bravery while a prisoner of war are in the highest traditions of the military service and reflect the utmost credit upon himself and the United States Army.

Captain Versace was captured by the Viet Cong in 1963 and executed in 1965. Versace was captured and taken to a prison deep in the jungle along with Lieutenant Nick Rowe. He tried to escape four times, insulted the Viet Cong during the indoctrination sessions and cited the Geneva Convention treaty time after time. The Viet Cong separated Versace from the other prisoners. The last time the prisoners heard his voice, he was singing "God Bless America" at the top of his lungs.[5]

MAJ Charles Q. Williams   Sep 17, 1933 – Oct 15, 1982
5th Special Forces Group (A)
Place and Date: Dong Xoai, Republic of Vietnam, 9 to 10 June 1965
Place of Birth: Charleston, South Carolina

For conspicuous gallantry and intrepidity at the risk of his life above and beyond the call of duty: 1LT Williams distinguished himself by conspicuous gallantry and intrepidity at the risk of his life above and beyond the call of duty while defending the Special Forces Camp against a violent attack by hostile forces that lasted for 14 hours. 1LT Williams was serving as executive officer of a Special Forces Detachment when an estimated Vietcong reinforced regiment struck the camp and threatened to overrun it and the adjacent district headquarters. He awoke personnel, organized them,

---

[5] For more on Humbert 'Rocky' Versace see *Five Years to Freedom*.

determined the source of the insurgents' main effort and led the troops to their defensive positions on the south and west walls. Then, after running to the district headquarters to establish communications, he found that there was no radio operational with which to communicate with his commanding officer in another compound. To reach the other compound, he traveled through darkness but was halted in this effort by a combination of shrapnel in his right leg and the increase of the Vietcong gunfire. Ignoring his wound, he returned to the district headquarters and directed the defense against the first assault. As the insurgents attempted to scale the walls and as some of the Vietnamese defenders began to retreat, he dashed through a barrage of gunfire, succeeded in rallying these defenders, and led them back to their positions. Although wounded in the thigh and left leg during this gallant action, he returned to his position and, upon being told that communications were reestablished and that his commanding officer was seriously wounded, 1LT Williams took charge of actions in both compounds. Then, in an attempt to reach the communications bunker, he sustained wounds in the stomach and right arm from grenade fragments. As the defensive positions on the walls had been held for hours and casualties were mounting, he ordered the consolidation of the American personnel from both compounds to establish a defense in the district building. After radio contact was made with a friendly air controller, he disregarded his wounds and directed the defense from the District building, using descending flares as reference points to adjust air strikes. By his courage, he inspired his team to hold out against the insurgent force that was closing in on them and throwing grenades into the windows of the building. As daylight arrived and the Vietcong continued to besiege the stronghold, firing a machinegun directly south of the district building, he was determined to eliminate this menace that threatened the lives of his men. Taking a 3.5 rocket launcher and a volunteer to load it, he worked his way across open terrain, reached the berm south of the district headquarters, and took aim at the Vietcong machinegun 150 meters away. Although the sight was faulty, he succeeded in hitting the machinegun. While he and the loader were trying to return to the district headquarters, they were both wounded. With a fourth wound, this time in the right arm and leg, and realizing he was unable to carry his wounded comrade back to the district building, 1LT Williams pulled him to a covered position and then made his way back to the district building where he sought the help of others who went out and evacuated the injured soldier. Although seriously wounded and tired, he continued to direct the air strikes closer to the defensive position. As morning turned to afternoon and the Vietcong pressed their effort with direct recoilless rifle fire into the building, he ordered the evacuation of the seriously wounded to the safety of the communications bunker. When informed that helicopters would attempt to land as the hostile gunfire had abated, he led his team from the building to the artillery position, making certain of the timely evacuation of the wounded from the communications area, and then on to the pickup point. Despite resurgent Vietcong gunfire, he directed the rapid evacuation of all personnel. Throughout the long battle, he was undaunted by the vicious Vietcong assault and inspired the defenders in decimating the determined insurgents. 1LT Williams' extraordinary heroism, are in the highest traditions of the U.S. Army and reflect great credit upon himself and the Armed Forces of his country.

SGT Gordon D. Yntema   Jun 26, 1945 - Jan 18, 1968
D Company, 5th Special Forces Group (A)
Place and Date: Near Thong Binh, Republic of Vietnam, 16-18 January 1968
Place of Birth: Bethesda, Maryland

For conspicuous gallantry and intrepidity at the risk of his life above and beyond the call of duty: SGT Yntema, U.S. Army, distinguished himself while assigned to Detachment A-431, Company D. As part of a larger force of civilian irregulars from Camp Cai Cai, he accompanied 2 platoons to a blocking position east of the village of Thong Binh, where they became heavily engaged in a small-arms fire fight with the Viet Cong. Assuming control of the force when the Vietnamese commander was seriously wounded, he advanced his troops to within 50 meters of the enemy bunkers. After a fierce 30 minute fire fight, the enemy forced SGT Yntema to withdraw his men to a trench in order to afford them protection and still perform their assigned blocking mission. Under cover of machinegun fire, approximately 1 company of Viet Cong maneuvered into a position which pinned down the friendly platoons from 3 sides. A dwindling ammunition supply, coupled with a Viet Cong mortar barrage which inflicted heavy losses

153

on the exposed friendly troops, caused many of the irregulars to withdraw. Seriously wounded and ordered to withdraw himself, SGT Yntema refused to leave his fallen comrades. Under withering small arms and machinegun fire, he carried the wounded Vietnamese commander and a mortally wounded American Special Forces advisor to a small gully 50 meters away in order to shield them from the enemy fire. SGT Yntema then continued to repulse the attacking Viet Cong attempting to overrun his position until, out of ammunition and surrounded, he was offered the opportunity to surrender. Refusing, SGT Yntema stood his ground, using his rifle as a club to fight the approximately 15 Viet Cong attempting his capture. His resistance was so fierce that the Viet Cong were forced to shoot in order to overcome him. SGT Yntema's personal bravery in the face of insurmountable odds and supreme self-sacrifice were in keeping with the highest traditions of the military service and reflect the utmost credit upon himself, the 1st Special Forces, and the U.S. Army.

SGM Fred W. Zabitosky   October 27, 1942 – January 18, 1996
MACV-SOG
Place and Date: Republic of Vietnam, 19 February 1968
Place of Birth: Trenton, New Jersey

For conspicuous gallantry and intrepidity at the risk of his life above and beyond the call of duty: SFC Zabitosky, U.S. Army, distinguished himself while serving as an assistant team leader of a 9-man Special Forces long-range reconnaissance patrol. SFC Zabitosky's patrol was operating deep within enemy-controlled territory when they were attacked by a numerically superior North Vietnamese Army unit. SFC Zabitosky rallied his team members, deployed them into defensive positions, and, exposing himself to concentrated enemy automatic weapons fire, directed their return fire.

154

Realizing the gravity of the situation, SFC Zabitosky ordered his patrol to move to a landing zone for helicopter extraction while he covered their withdrawal with rifle fire and grenades. Rejoining the patrol under increasing enemy pressure, he positioned each man in a tight perimeter defense and continually moved from man to man, encouraging them and controlling their defensive fire. Mainly due to his example, the outnumbered patrol maintained its precarious position until the arrival of tactical air support and a helicopter extraction team. As the rescue helicopters arrived, the determined North Vietnamese pressed their attack. SFC Zabitosky repeatedly exposed himself to their fire to adjust suppressive helicopter gunship fire around the landing zone. After boarding 1 of the rescue helicopters, he positioned himself in the door delivering fire on the enemy as the ship took off. The helicopter was engulfed in a hail of bullets and SFC Zabitosky was thrown from the craft as it spun out of control and crashed. Recovering consciousness, he ignored his extremely painful injuries and moved to the flaming wreckage. Heedless of the danger of exploding ordnance and fuel, he pulled the severely wounded pilot from the searing blaze and made repeated attempts to rescue his patrol members but was driven back by the intense heat. Despite his serious burns and crushed ribs, he carried and dragged the unconscious pilot through a curtain of enemy fire to within 10 feet of a hovering rescue helicopter before collapsing. SFC Zabitosky's extraordinary heroism and devotion to duty were in keeping with the highest traditions of the military service and reflect great credit upon himself, his unit, and the U.S. Army.

Great Leaders of Special Forces History

Colonel Aaron Bank (1902-2004)

Colonel Aaron Bank was born on November 23, 1902 in New York City. Entering the US Army in 1939, he graduated Officer Candidate School and proceeded to Fort Polk, Louisiana as a transportation officer. In 1941, he volunteered for OSS service, and after completing training in England was assigned to command the Jedburgh team "Packard" with the mission of conducting UW operations with the Maquis in southern France. Bank's team managed to tie up German forces thereby allowing the 7th Infantry Division to advance from the coast of Southern France up through the Rhone River Valley. Bank was later transferred to the work in French Indo-China to repatriot prisoners of war as a part of an Operational Group (OG) with OSS Detachment 202.

After WWII, Colonel Bank commanded the Regional Counter-Intelligence Corps in Bavaria, Germany. He then served as the executive officer of the 187th Airborne Regimental Combat Team in the Korean War. In 1951, Major General Robert McClure recruited Bank as the Chief of Psychological Warfare. Working with McClure and Colonel Russell Volckmann, the three men recommended the establishment of a special warfare capability within the US Army based on the successes of previous UW operations. n 1952, Colonel Bank became the commander of 10th Special Forces Group (Airborne). In September of that year, the 10th was split in half and took up station in Bad Tölz, Germany as a counter to the growing Soviet threat in Europe; while the other half, reconstituted as the 77th SF Group, remained at Fort Bragg. In 1955, Bank assumed duties as the G3 of 7th US Army Europe. Following that assignment, he served at the Pentagon until he retired in 1958. Colonel Bank was buried in 2004 in Riverside National Cemetery in Riverside, California.

Brigadier General Donald D. Blackburn (1916 – 2008)

Donald Blackburn was born on 14 September, 1916 in McLean, Virginia. He was commissioned a second lieutenant in the Infantry Reserve on May 30, 1938, and entered into active duty with the Army September 22, 1940, assigned to the 24th Infantry at Fort Benning, Georgia. At the outbreak of World War II, he was serving as an advisor to a battalion of the 12th Infantry Regiment, Philippine Commonwealth Army. Upon the fall of Bataan in April 1942, he evaded capture with his friend Captain Russell W. Volckmann, and until October 1945 conducted guerrilla warfare on the island of Luzon. During this latter period, he reorganized and commanded the 11th Infantry, Philippine Commonwealth Army, which was integrated in October 1945 as a regular unit in the Philippine military establishment.

Following World War II Blackburn served in various command and staff assignments. He was assigned to the Department of Military Psychology and Leadership, Tactical Department, United States Military Academy, in 1950. He was then assigned to NATO's Allied Forces Northern Europe, Oslo, Norway. On return to the United States in 1956, he was assigned as commanding officer, 3rd Training Regiment, Fort Jackson, S.C. In 1957, he was assigned to MAAG, Vietnam, and served as the senior advisor to the commanding general, 5th Military Region (Mekong Delta). In October 1958, he was assigned as commanding officer, 77th Special Forces Group where he was instrumental in initiating Special Forces operations in Southeast Asia. He served as deputy director of developments for Special Warfare, Office of the Chief of Research and Development from 1961 to 1964, and then was reassigned to the office, Deputy Chief of Staff for Operations as Director of Special Warfare. Blackburn was SOG Commander from May 1965 to May 1966. He served as assistant deputy director, Defense Communications Planning Group from August 1966 to August 1967. He was the assistant division commander, 82nd Airborne Division from September 1967 to October 1968. He was the Director of Plans and Programs, office of the Chief of Research and Development from October 1968 until his retirement in 1971.

Brigadier General Blackburn was instrumental to the development of Special Forces doctrine and was a highly decorated and distinguished commander in SOG.

157

Major General William J. Donovan
(1883 – 1959)

William Joseph "Wild Bill" Donovan was born in Buffalo, New York to Irish immigrants. He graduated from Columbia University and Law School and practiced law on Wall Street. Before America's involvement in WWI, Donovan organized and led a cavalry troop in the New York State Militia during the campaign against Pancho Villa. After America entered World War I, Major Donovan organized and led the 1st Battalion of the 165th Regiment of the 42nd Infantry Division. His unit distinguished itself in the fighting near Landres-et-St. Georges, France, on 14 and 15 October 1918. For his service, Donovan would receive the Medal of Honor.

After the First World War, Donovan was elected as the US Attorney for the Western District of New York. Later, he ran unsuccessfully as a Republican for Lieutenant Governor of New York in 1922, and for Governor of New York in 1932. On July 11, 1941, President Franklin D. Roosevelt named Donovan the Coordinator of Information (COI). From this post, conceived by Donovan himself, the Office of Strategic Services (OSS) was created in 1942. As head of the OSS, Donovan returned to active service in the U.S. Army, restored to his World War I rank of colonel. Attaining the rank of major general, Donovan lead the OSS to conduct successful espionage and sabotage operations in Europe and Asia. After Truman disbanded the OSS in September 1945, Donovan returned to civilian life. However, less than two years later the Central Intelligence Agency was founded; a realization of Donovan's dream for a centralized intelligence agency. Donovan died on February 8, 1959 from complications of vascular dementia.

Colonel Wendell Fertig (1900 – 1975)

Wendell Fertig had been a United States Army Reserve officer and mining engineer before the WWII. When the Japanese invaded the Philippines on December 8, 1941, he found himself in a position to lead a guerrilla resistance on the island of Mindanao in the Southern Philippines. Fertig came to the Philippines five years before the invasion during the mining boom of the 1930s with many other American engineers who had heard of great untapped gold and coal resources.

Tall with an athletic build, Fertig was born in the small town of La Junta, Colorado, which in 1900 was every bit a frontier western town. Attending the University of Colorado, majoring in chemistry, he transferred to the Colorado School of Mines in Golden, Colorado to be a mining engineer. While there, he enrolled in the US Army Reserve Officer Corps. After graduating in 1924, he was commissioned a reserve lieutenant and married his wife Mary. Then, in 1936, he moved his family to the Philippines where he pursued a career as a civil engineer. His first job was an on-site supervisor of a start-up mine in the Province of Batangas, south of Manila. Later, Fertig moved to Manila to take on a consulting position.

Along with other "unsurrendered" Army officers and NCOs, Fertig consolidated bands of guerrillas into what became arguably the most successful US-led resistance in history. Fertig's guerrilla war against Japanese occupation was successful for several reasons. Foremost was the ability of Fertig and his subordinate leaders to unify disparate groups under one unified command and give the movement vision and direction. With a guerrilla force of some 36,000, Fertig's resistance movement was able to tie up a Japanese occupation force of up to 150,000, keep freedom alive on the Island of Mindanao, and greatly assist the US invasion in 1945.

Due to his wartime experiences and post-war work, Fertig is one of three men who used their wartime experience to formulate the doctrine of unconventional warfare (UW) that became the cornerstone of Special Forces. Moreover, along with Aaron Bank, and Russell Volckmann, he is considered one of the founding fathers of the US Army Special Forces.

Major Richard J. Meadows (1931 – 1995)

Richard "Dick" Meadows was born in Richmond Virginia on 16 June, 1931. He enlisted in the Army at age 15, and first saw combat in Korea. By age 20, he was promoted to Master Sergeant; the youngest in the Army at that time. In 1953, he entered the U.S. Army Special Forces. In 1960, Meadows was one of the first U.S. Army officers to participate in an exchange program with the British Special Air Service (SAS). Meadows completed SAS training and was an acting troop leader for 12 months, and participated in a field combat operation with the SAS in the Middle East. Meadows' SAS experience helped form the basis for future US Army Special Forces selection, training, and organizational structures.

While assigned to the 8th Special Forces Group in Panama, Master Sergeant Meadows volunteered for a tour in Vietnam. At the end of his first tour, serving in the MACV-SOG, Meadows received a direct commission as a captain on April 14, 1967. On Nov 21, 1970 CPT Meadows was the team leader for the initial assault team in the Son Tay prison camp raid. In the mid-1970s, Meadows was a key figure in the founding of 1ˢᵗ Special Forces Operational Detachment – Delta.

Major Meadows retired in 1977. In 1980, Major Meadows returned to service as a special consultant and performed a covert reconnaissance of the U.S. Embassy in Tehran prior to and during Operation Eagle Claw, better known as the Iran Hostage Rescue mission. That mission ended in a major accident at a ground refueling point in the Iran desert, and was aborted. Documents found at the crash site compromised both the mission and Meadows' cover in Iran. Under cover as a foreign businessman, Meadows escaped Iran aboard a commercial flight. In 1995, Meadows was diagnosed with and subsequently died of leukemia.

Colonel James N. Rowe (1938 – 1989)

James N. Rowe was born in McAllen, Texas on February 8, 1938. In 1960, Rowe graduated from the United States Military Academy at West Point, New York, and was commissioned as an artillery officer. In 1963, First Lieutenant Rowe was sent to the Republic of Vietnam (South Vietnam) and assigned as Executive Officer of Detachment A-23, 5th SF Group. Located at Tan Phu in An Xuyen Province, A-23 organized and advised a CIDG camp in the Mekong Delta. On October 29, 1963, after only three months in country, Rowe was captured by VC elements along with Captain Humbert "Rocky" R. Versace and Sergeant Daniel L. Pitzer. Separated from his comrades, Rowe spent 62 months in captivity with only brief encounters with fellow American POWs. Rowe was held in the U Minh Forest, better known as the "Forest of Darkness," in extreme southern Vietnam. During most of his five years in captivity Rowe was held in a cage. He managed to escape on December 31, 1968, after overpowering his guard, he was picked up by a UH-1 helicopter.

In 1971, he authored the book, *Five Years to Freedom*, an account of his years as a prisoner of war. In 1974, he retired from the Army. In 1981, Rowe was recalled to active duty as a lieutenant colonel to design and build a course based upon his experience as a POW, Survival, Evasion, Resistance, and Escape (SERE). In 1987, Colonel Rowe was assigned as the chief of the Army division of the Joint U.S. Military Advisory Group (JUSMAG), providing counter-insurgency training for the Armed Forces of the Philippines.

Working closely with the Central Intelligence Agency and intelligence organizations of the Republic of the Philippines, he was involved in its nearly decade-long program to penetrate the New People's Army (NPA), the communist insurgency that threatened to overthrow the Philippines' government. On April 21, 1989, as he was being driven to work at the JUSMAG headquarters in an armored limousine, Rowe's vehicle was hit by small arms in Quezon City. Twenty-one shots hit the vehicle; one round entered through an unarmored portion of the vehicle frame and struck Colonel Rowe in the head, killing him instantly. Years later, the New

161

People's Army eventually claimed responsibility for his assassination. Rowe was buried May 2, 1989 in Section 48 of Arlington National Cemetery.[10]

Colonel Arthur D. Simons (1918 – 1979)

Arthur D. Simons was born 28 June, 1918 in New York City. He attended the University of Missouri-Columbia and majored in journalism, entering the ROTC program there in 1937. In 1941, Simons was commissioned as an artillery officer, and was initially assigned to the 98th Field Artillery Battalion, a part of one of the Army's pack mule units. This unit was later redesignated as the 6th Ranger Battalion. On Luzon in the Philippines, he participated in the Raid at Cabanatuan that rescued approximately 500 POWs who were mostly survivors of the Bataan Death March.

At the conclusion of the Second World War, Major Simons left the active Army for five years. In 1951, he was recalled to active duty to serve as an infantry instructor and Ranger trainer in the Amphibious and Jungle Training camp at Eglin AFB, Florida. Simons also completed tours with the Military Assistance Advisory Group, Turkey and XVIII Airborne Corps before joining the 77th Special Forces Group in 1958. In 1960 he served as Deputy Commander/Chief of Staff of the U.S. Army Special Warfare Center. Promoted to Lieutenant Colonel in 1961, he commanded the 107-man Operation White Star Mobile Training Team in Laos from 1961 to 1962 and was the first commander of the 8th Special Forces Group, Panama from 1962 to 1964. From Panama, he was assigned to the Military Assistance Command, Vietnam Studies and Observations Group (MACV-SOG), which conducted numerous behind-the-line missions in Southeast Asia.

In 1970, Simons was hand-picked to be the ground commander of Operation Ivory Coast, a joint special operations effort to rescue American prisoners of war from the Son Tay prison in North Vietnam. While the mission rescued no prisoners, it did force North Vietnam to consolidate all of the prisoners into a few central compounds in Hanoi, resulting in a boost in the prisoners' morale and improved treatment. In 1971, Simons retired from the US Army. In late 1978, Simons was contacted by Texas businessman Ross Perot, who requested his direction and leadership to help

---

[10] For more on Nick Rowe see *Five Years to Freedom*.

free two employees of Electronic Data Systems who were arrested shortly before the Iranian Revolution. Simons organized a rescue mission and ultimately freed the two men from the Iranian prison. All involved returned safely to the United States. Three months later, while on vacation in Vail, Colorado, COL Simons died of heart complications at the age of 60. He is buried in the Barrancas National Cemetery in Pensacola, Florida.[11]

Colonel Russell Volckmann (1911 – 1982)

Russell Volckmann was born 23 October 1911, in Clinton, Iowa. In 1934, graduated from the United States Military Academy at West Point, New York, and was commissioned a second lieutenant in the infantry. In 1940, Volckmann was assigned to the Philippines. Upon arrival in the Philippines, he became the commander of Company H, 31st Infantry Regiment. In July 1941, he was transferred to the 11th Infantry Regiment, 11th Infantry Division (Philippine Army) as the regimental executive officer.

In August 1941, Volckmann's wife and son, along with all other U.S. military dependents, were sent back to the United States due to war concerns. On 8 December 1941, the Japanese attacked the Philippines. At the fall of Bataan in 1942, Volckmann refused to surrender and accompanied by Donald Blackburn, another American officer also serving in the Philippine Army left Bataan and began a trek to northern Luzon.[12] Volckmann organized a resistance force among the Ifugao's 11th Infantry Battalion. His forces operated in the western and northern coasts of Luzon, launching attacks against the Japanese occupiers. During the U.S. and Filipino invasion of the Philippines in January 1945, Volckmann's guerrillas cut key communication lines and bridges and isolated enemy forces. Once the invasion had landed, he led attacks against the retreating Japanese forces far behind the lines, capturing bases and air fields, thereby allowing the American advance to proceed at a much quicker pace.

After the war, he remained in the U.S. Army and together with Colonels Aaron Bank and Wendell Fertig helped create the U.S. Army Special Forces. He eventually retired as a brigadier general. BG Volckmann was buried in Springfield Cemetery, Clinton, Iowa.

---

[11] For more on Arthur 'Bull' Simons see *The Raid*.
[12] Volckmann, We Remained: Three Years Behind Enemy Lines in the Philippines, 54.

Major General William P. Yarborough
(1912 – 2006)

William P. Yarborough was born 12 May, 1912 in Seattle, Washington. A 1936 graduate of the United States Military Academy with a Bachelor of Science in Engineering, Yarborough's first assignment was with the 57th Infantry Regiment in the Philippines. Upon returning to the US, he was then a company commander with the 501st Parachute Infantry at Fort Benning, and worked on the early development of airborne operational doctrine. While at Fort Benning, Yarborough designed the US Parachutist Badge, for which he received a patent, as well as the jump boot and the parachutist uniform. His service in World War II started as the primary advisor for airborne operations on the staff of Gen. Mark Clark. He was instrumental in the planning for Operation Torch, America's first airborne combat operation into North Africa. Yarborough served as the executive officer for the Airborne Task Force prior to taking command of the 509th Parachute Infantry Battalion. As a member of the 509th, he participated in Operation Torch and detailed the story in his book *Bail Out Over North Africa*. He subsequently commanded parachute battalions that jumped in Sicily and Southern France.

From 1956 to 1957, he was assigned as Deputy Commander of the US Military Assistance Command - Cambodia. He then became the Commanding Officer for the 1st Battle Group, 7th Infantry where he moved the entire unit from Fort Benning to Germany. In January 1961, Yarborough was appointed commander/commandant of the US Army Special Warfare Center/School for Special Warfare at Fort Bragg, North Carolina. Remaining until 1965, he was instrumental in the build-up of Special Forces, overseeing the activation of four new groups. He initiated an exhaustive review of training programs and doctrine, and wrote numerous monographs on subjects pertaining to Special Operations, which are still relevant today.

It was also under his direction that foreign students were fully integrated into training and language instruction was expanded. He established five new courses including the Military Assistance Training Advisor School, the Unconventional Warfare course and the Counter-Terrorism course.

He also initiated a staff study that later resulted in the movement of the US Army Civil Affairs School from Fort Gordon, Georgia to Fort Bragg. During his tenure as Commander of the Special Warfare Center in 1961, Yarborough arranged for President John F. Kennedy to visit Fort Bragg. This resulted in the authorization of the Green Beret for wear as the official headgear of Special Forces, and the general became known as the father of the modern Green Berets. He retired from the Army in 1971 and died on December 6, 2006.[13]

Conclusion

Looking back at the lives of these great warriors, who earned their nation's highest honor, we are left with both inspiration and a summons. As great leaders do, these men inspire us to see there's something greater than ourselves, to go the distance and not quit, no matter how tough going the task. And as a great cloud of witnesses clad in the unfading splendor of their gallantry, they summon us to quietly bear up arms for truth and freedom. As a collective symbol, they represent to us the man in the arena. Immortalizing their heroism, President Theodore Roosevelt observes:

It's not the critic who counts. It's not the man who points out how the strong man stumbled. Credit belongs to the man who really was in the arena, his face marred by dust, sweat, and blood, who strives valiantly, who errs to come short and short again, because there is no effort without error and shortcoming. It is the man who actually strives to do the deeds, who knows the great enthusiasm and knows the great devotion, who spends himself on a worthy cause, who at best, knows in the end the triumph of great achievement. And, who at worst, if he fails, at least fails while daring greatly, so that his place shall never be with those cold and cruel souls who know neither victory nor defeat.

---

[13] For more on William Yarborough see *Bail Out Over North Africa*.

Part Two: Doctrine

Chapter 3 Doctrinal Concepts and Principles

"Principles provide the thinking man with a frame of reference." – Clausewitz

Practice without theory and reflection, like 'the unexamined life,' dwindles into unsatisfactory routine. With that in mind, the goal of this chapter is to lay a foundational understanding of the doctrinal concepts and principles that are pertinent to small unit tactics (SUT). Such an understanding will provide us, the thinking man, with a frame of reference so as to assist us in our successful planning and execution of missions.

Army doctrine establishes a particular way of thinking about war and a way of fighting. It's the foundation for all planning and execution. As a body of thought, it consists of fundamental principles, tactics, techniques, and procedures (TTPs), as well as terms and symbols. *Army doctrine focuses on how to think – not what to think.*[1] Therefore, doctrine is a guide to action, and not a fixed set of rules. We will find that doctrine suggests, but does not dictate our tactical employment. This chapter will cover the following topics:

1. The Theory of War.
2. The Levels of War.
3. The Principles of War.

The Theory of War

"To move swiftly, strike vigorously, and secure all the fruits of victory is the secret of successful war." – Stonewall Jackson

Our mission is to deploy, engage, and destroy, the enemies of the United States of America in close combat. As we prepare for that end, an understanding of the fundamental nature of war, along with a foundation of Army doctrine and its principles, will prove beneficial. To begin, we need to define war. The Army defines war as armed conflict between major powers in which the total resources of the belligerents are employed, and the national survival of a major belligerent is in jeopardy.[2] War is "a violent clash of interests between or among organized groups characterized by the use of military force."[3] In the simplest terms, war may be compared to a

---

[1] FM 3-0 Operations, D-1.
[2] Ibid, 2-2.
[3] Warfighting, (MCDP 1), 3.

duel on a larger scale. However, war is also a complex endeavor, and "a matter of vital importance to the State."[4]

The nature of war may be best understood by three propositions: (1) war is an instrument of policy; (2) war is an act of violence to compel our opponent to fulfill our will; and (3) war is the province of danger, the realm of uncertainty, the domain of physical exertion, and the sphere of chance.

War is an instrument of policy – War is a political instrument that is controlled and shaped by policy. The political object is the goal for which war is the means. Critical to us, if we are to prosecute a war that serves political ends, we must understand how politics and war interact. As Clausewitz observed, the endstate in war is defined in three ways: first, the destruction of the enemy's armed forces; second, the occupation of the enemy's country; and third, the destruction of the enemies will to resist.[5]

War must serve policy. And at the highest level, war involves the use of all the assets that one political entity can bring against another. These are referred to as our instruments of national power, which include; diplomatic, information/intelligence (including psyops), military, and economic force – these may be remembered by the acronym DIME (JP-1).

War is an act of violence to compel our opponent to fulfill our will – The object in war is to impose our will on our enemy. Essentially there are two strategies to this aim: annihilation/incapacitation and erosion. The first strategy calls for the elimination of the enemy's capacity to fight, but not necessarily the physical annihilation of the enemy's military forces. The second, convinces the enemy that our terms will be less painful than if he resists. The means to both of these approaches is the organized application or threat of violence by military force. War is therefore an act of violence; of sheer brutality. This assertion is over against the kind-hearted quaint belief of some people who might think there is some ingenious way of disarming or defeating their enemy without too much bloodshed.

War is the province of danger, the realm of uncertainty, the domain of physical exertion, and the sphere of chance – these four intangibles make up

---

[4] Sun Tzu, The Art of War, Samuel Griffith Translation, 63.
[5] Clausewitz, On War, Howard and Paret Translation (Everyman's Library Edition), I, 2, 102.
Carl Philip Gottfried von Clausewitz (1780-1831) was a Prussian general and military theorist. As a career infantry officer, Clausewitz entered Prussian army service in 1792, and saw his first action in 1793. He was admitted to the Kriegsakademie in 1801 and graduated first in his class in 1804. Being influenced heavily by Kantian and Hegelian thought, Clausewitz's treatise On War follows the dialectical structure of thesis, antithesis, and synthesis; a paradoxical trinity.

the Clausewitzian climate of war.[6] War is an organized form of violence, and its immediate result is bloodshed, suffering, and death. And since war is a human phenomenon, "fear, the human reaction to danger, has a significant impact on the conduct of war. Everybody feels fear. Courage is not the absence of fear; rather, it is the strength to overcome fear."[7] As leaders, we must understand fear and overcome it to succeed.

War is the province of danger, the realm of uncertainty, the domain of physical exertion, and the sphere of chance. The manner in which war is governed by these intangible forces, led Napoleon to say, "The battlefield is a scene of constant chaos. The winner will be the one who controls that chaos, both his own and the enemies." Within this chaotic climate of war, the two factors of friction and fog together bring chance and uncertainty to play. Friction is the disparity between the ideal performance of units, organization or systems and their actual performance in real world scenarios. According to Clausewitz, "The conduct of war resembles the workings of an intricate machine with tremendous friction, *so that combinations which are easily planned on paper can only be executed with great effort.*"[8]

Friction is the force that makes the apparently easy so difficult and the difficult seemingly impossible. Friction may be mental, as a leader's indecision over a course of action. It may be physical, such as actions imposed by an enemy force. It may be self-induced, such as the lack of a clearly defined goal, lack of coordination, or complicated plans and command and support relationships. Combat experience is the only true remedy to friction. And its Siamese twin, the fog of war, is whatever is hidden from full view, creating uncertainty. Describing this phenomenon of war Clausewitz states:

War is the realm of uncertainty; three quarters of everything on which all action in war is based are wrapped in a fog of greater or lesser uncertainty. War is the realm of chance. No other human activity gives it greater scope: no other has such incessant and varied dealings. Chance makes everything more uncertain and interferes with the whole course of events.[9]

The point in this discussion is that these intangible (moral) factors exert a great influence upon both the nature and the outcome of war. Fog and friction create opportunities for exploitation. As leaders, we must understand them, come to grips with them, and as Clausewitz put it, "follow that inner

---

[6] Regarding Clausewitz's climate of war, I have added the synonyms *domain, province* and *sphere* for clarity, as he simply used the noun realm for each element.
[7] Warfighting (MCDP 1-3), 9.
[8] Clausewitz, Principles of War, 61.
[9] Clausewitz, On War, I, 3, 117.

light so he may see through the fog and friction of war, and navigate the way to victory."

The Art and Science of War

As we continue to lay a foundational understanding of Army doctrine and its principles, it's important to note that war is both art and science. This is important because some have tried to make war one or the other, either art or science, leading to either national embarrassment or great carnage. War is art because creative skill, judgment, and discipline are required to apply its empirical laws. Thus, "in war the will is directed against an animate object that reacts." Similarly, Sun Tzu identified the human dimension to be essential for victory.

Antoine Henri Jomini, a contemporary of Clausewitz, was a proponent of war being both a science and an art.[10] He sought to take the complexities of war and boil it down to simple, practical application. In pursuit of the essence of war, Jomini became convinced that the fundamentals of war were objective, unchanging, and independent of either weapons or time. As such, in his *The Art of War,* he offers us concrete tactical solutions by way of fixed formations and methods.

However, in order to extricate Jomini from the charge of being concerned only with the geometry of war, as is often the case, it is important to point out that while he viewed war as governed by timeless and well-developed principles, he also believed that "war is a great drama, in which a thousand physical or moral causes operate more or less powerfully, and which cannot be reduced to mathematical calculations."[11] Jomini saw war as an art governed by scientific principles. And Clausewitz, although he believed that war was more art than science, he also said that it is neither because he felt its outcomes are too unpredictable to consider it a science. Like forces that react when acted upon, so it cannot be an art, like a painting. According to Clausewitz, it's impossible to separate art and knowledge altogether.[12]

War is thus both art and science. It's art because creative skill and intuitive ability are necessary to assess a situation and decide upon a course of action. War is science because various aspects of it fall principally in the

---

[10] Baron Antoine Henri Jomini (1779-1869), Swiss-French, was a general in the French and later in the Russian service. Jomini's writings were the principle means by which Napoleonic technique was transfused into the military thought of those who had attended West Point. It has been said with good reason that many a Civil War general went into battle with a sword in one hand and Jomini's *Summary of the Art of War* in the other.

[11] Jomini, Preface to the Summary of the Art of War, 14.

[12] This statement is more impressive when we recall that science, the English word for *scientia,* means knowledge.

realm of science, such as the laws of ballistics and the effects of weapons, surface danger zones (SDZs), rates of fire, maximum effective ranges, etc. Therefore, war is both science and art. Is this a contradiction? No. The science of war depends upon art for its application; weaponry and the men who wield them must be maneuvered and employed on the field of battle. This concept was poignantly summed up by Captain Francis Greene who observed, "War is, above all things, an art, employing science in all its branches as its servant, but depending first and chiefly upon the skill of the artisan." Thus, no degree of technological development or scientific calculation will diminish the human dimension in war. For according to B.H. Liddell Hart, "No man can exactly calculate the capacity of human genius or stupidity."[13] War is thus an intensely violent human endeavor which calls upon both art and science in order to serve political ends. This is one of the fundamental dynamics in war.

Methods of Warfare

To add a further dimension to our discussion, an understanding of the methods of warfare will prove beneficial. Methods in warfare can be described by the two book ends of attrition and maneuver. Regarding attrition warfare, the USMC doctrinal publication *Warfighting* poignantly states:

Warfare by attrition pursues victory through the cumulative destruction of the enemy's material assets by superior firepower. It is a direct approach to the conduct of war that sees war as a straightforward test of strength and a matter principally of force ratios. An enemy is seen as a collection of targets to be engaged and destroyed systematically. Enemy concentrations are sought out as the most worthwhile targets. The logical conclusion of attrition warfare is the eventual physical destruction of the enemy's entire arsenal, although the expectation is that the enemy will surrender or disengage before this happens out of unwillingness to bear the rising cost. The focus is on the efficient application of fires, leading to a highly proceduralized approach to war. Technical proficiency – especially in weapons employment – matters more than cunning or creativity.[14]

On the other end of the spectrum lies maneuver warfare which may be defined as a thought process which seeks to pit strength against weakness to break the enemy's will. Maneuver warfare stems from a desire to take on an opponent indirectly and attack him from a position of advantage rather than head on. In B.H. Liddell Hart's estimation, "throughout the ages, effective

---

[13] Hart, Strategy, 323.
[14] Warfighting (MCDP 1), 36.

results in war have rarely been attained unless the approach has had such indirectness as to ensure the opponent's unreadiness to meet it."[15]

Maneuver is movement supported by fire to gain a position of advantage over the enemy. Thus, rather than being viewed as desirable targets, enemy concentrations are generally avoided as enemy strengths. In maneuver warfare, the goal in each situation is to attain a decisive result. Thus, instead of attacking enemy strength, the goal is the application of our strength against selected enemy weakness – a gap in the surface – in order to maximize advantage, so that we "push our adversary beyond his ability to adapt."[16]

These concepts of maneuver warfare will be developed further, for now it's important to note that all warfare incorporates both maneuver and attrition in some manner. Further, "at least empirically," writes Richard Hooker, "there is much to suggest that the physical destruction of the enemy by massed fire systems remains central to our (Army) view."[17] The point being made here is doctrine may be observed as refined theory and requires human judgment when applied to specific situations.

The Levels of War

Actions in war take place on three related levels: *strategic, operational,* and *tactical* (See figure 3-1). These levels of war are doctrinal perspectives that clarify the links between strategic objectives and tactical actions.[18] The highest level of war is the *strategic* level. Strategy is the calculated application of ways and means to achieve a political objective. Strategy is 'the use of time and space,' and deals with the application of armed force in order to attain national objectives.

The strategic level involves national and military strategy. Whereas, national strategy coordinates and focuses all the elements of national power to achieve policy objectives, military strategy applies military force to gain policy objectives. The *operational* level of war begins with strategic goals. It is the link which translates strategic objectives into tactical employment. At the operational level, campaigns and major operations are undertaken by

---

[15] Hart, Strategy, 5. Sir Basil Henry Liddell Hart (1895-1970), was a Captain in the British Army, a poignant military historian, and one of the foremost military thinkers of the twentieth century. As a military theorist, he is perhaps best known for his theory of the indirect approach which posits three fundamental principles: (1) avoid enemy strength; (2) deceive the enemy and refuse him the ability to bring his strength to bear; and (3) create and attack enemy vulnerabilities.

[16] Boyd, Patterns of Conflict, 129.

[17] Hooker, Maneuver Warfare: An Anthology, 77.

[18] FM 5-0 The Operations Process, 2-1.

corps and echelons above corps in order to accomplish the theater goals which are articulated at the strategic level.

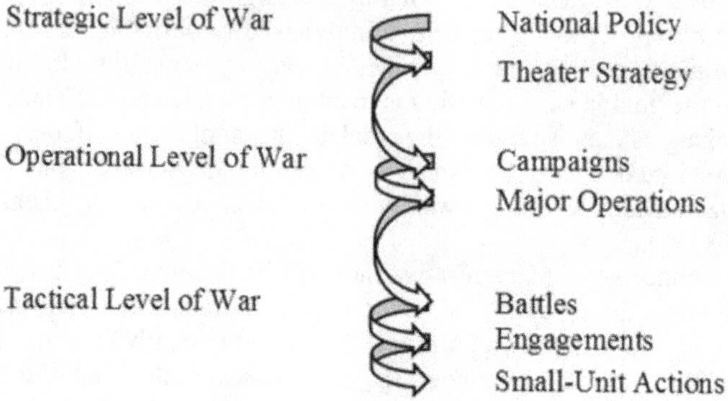

Strategic Level of War   National Policy

                                               Theater Strategy

Operational Level of War   Campaigns

                                               Major Operations

Tactical Level of War   Battles

                                               Engagements

                                               Small-Unit Actions

Figure 3-1. The Three Levels of War.

At the *tactical* level of war, battles, engagements, and small-unit actions are conducted; normally at brigade and below. The tactical level of war is concerned with the planning and conduct of battle and is characterized by the application of concentrated force and offensive action to gain objectives. Tactics are therefore the art of using troops in battle, whereas strategy is the art of using battles to win the war. Or, as Jomini states, "tactics executes movements – strategy directs them."[19]

This is an important matter, because as we've stated, if war is to be prosecuted in a manner that serves political ends, then we must understand how the two, war and politics, interact. As Clausewitz observed:

War, therefore, is an act of policy. Were it a complete, untrammeled, absolute manifestation of violence (as the pure concept would require), war would of its own independent will usurp the place of policy the moment policy had brought it into being; it would then drive policy out of office and rule by the laws of its own nature, very much like a mine that can explode only in the manner or direction predetermined by the setting.[20]

The Principles of War

The principles of war are an attempt to bridge the gap between war as an art and war as a science.[21] They represent the most important intangible

---

[19] Jomini, The Art of War, 159.

[20] Clausewitz, On War, I, 1, 98.

[21] The first American use of the principles of war can be traced to the US Army's Field Service Regulations first published in 1921.

factors that affect the conduct of operations at the strategic, operational, and tactical levels. Regarding these principles, a glance back to the views of the historic progenitors of our modern warfighting doctrine will again prove beneficial. For example, Jomini believed there could be fundamental, almost mathematical principles of war which, stemming from the study and observation of Napoleonic warfare and strategy, could stand for all time.[22] Thus, he writes, "There have existed in all times fundamental principles on which depend good results in warfare. These principles are unchanging, independent of the kind of weapons, of historical time and of place."[23] And although Clausewitz regarded war as the realm where a genius and chance could joust creatively, he did agree that "the study of the history of war has given us principles."[24] Albeit, in Clausewitz's view, the principles of war are theory, and thus are a means of study, rather than 'a sort of manual for action.'[25]

What is important for the tactician to realize is: the principles of war are not a checklist, they are tools for understanding the dynamics of war that cannot be indiscriminately applied. While they are considered in all operations, they do not apply in the same way to every situation. Rather, they summarize characteristics of successful operations. The greatest value of the principles of war lies in the education of the military professional. Applied to the study of past campaigns, major operations, battles, and engagements, the principles of war are powerful analysis tools, and lend rigor and focus to the purely creative aspects of tactics and provide a crucial link between pure theory and actual application.

As we examine the principles of war, we must bear in mind that Special Forces adapts the principles of war differently than do conventional forces. For example, Special Forces must influence, rather than dominate their operational environment, and create favorable political and military conditions to promote U.S. goals. Moreover, Special Forces must routinely apply military power indirectly through foreign military and paramilitary forces. Special Forces missions may require unorthodox approaches, but these approaches do not negate the principles of war.[26]

The Special Forces Regiment uses the principles of war and Army doctrine as the basis for mission planning and execution. No priority exists among the principles, and they should be viewed as a collective whole, not

---

[22] As John Alger tells us, these principles have their distant roots in Baron Jomini's *The Art of War*, and their immediate roots in the work of Major General J.F.C. Fuller as he attempted to distill lessons from the failed British campaigns of 1914-1915.

[23] Jomini, Traité des Grandes Opérations Militaires, III, 333.

[24] Clausewitz, Principles of War, 19.

[25] Clausewitz, On War, II, 2, 162.

[26] ADRP 3-05 Special Operations, 1-6.

independently. For the tactician, these principles provide an operational framework for the military actions he has been trained to carry out. They are neither intended nor designed to be prescriptive; the principles of war, if understood and applied properly, should *stimulate thought and enhance flexibility of action.* [27]

The principles of war may be memorized using the acronym:
MOOSE MUSS

Maneuver
Place the enemy in a disadvantageous position through the flexible application of combat power.

Maneuver is the movement of forces supported by fire to gain a position of advantage from which to destroy or threaten the destruction of the enemy. Maneuver concentrates and disperses combat power to keep the enemy at a disadvantage. It achieves results that would otherwise be more costly. Crucial to the principle of maneuver is speed and flexibility which keeps enemy forces off balance by making them confront new problems and new dangers faster than they can counter them; so that we "push our adversary beyond his ability to adapt." According to Jomini, success depends upon the skillful maneuver of one's forces upon the decisive point. [28]

Maneuver orients on the enemy force, avoids his strength, finds a weak point or gap and exploits it with the maximum amount of combat power available. As Sun Tzu observes, "In all fighting, the direct method may be used for joining battle, but indirect methods will be needed in order to secure victory." This principle requires the tactician to possess a flexibility of mind to deal with fluid and disorderly situations, and a willingness to act with initiative and boldness, to exploit the full advantage of every opportunity.

Although Special Forces can't always maneuver against an enemy in the conventional sense, SFODAs apply combat power indirectly – by, with, and through indigenous or surrogate forces. These forces expand the flexibility and impact of operations far beyond the numbers that an SFODA can field.

Objective
Direct every military operation toward a clearly defined, decisive, and attainable objective.

---

[27] Summers, On Strategy, 197.
[28] Jomini, The Art of War, 326.

The principle of objective drives all military activity. At the operational and tactical levels, the principle of objective ensures all actions contribute to the higher commander's intent. Clearly stated objectives promote individual initiative. These objectives clarify what subordinates need to accomplish by emphasizing the outcome rather than the method. Tacticians should avoid actions that do not contribute directly to achieving the objectives. As Clausewitz has stated, "we should not take the first step without considering the last."[29]

The purpose of military operations is to accomplish the military objectives that support achieving the conflict's overall political goals. Tactical operations must contribute to achieving operational and strategic objectives. Just as the strategic military objective focuses on the political ends, so must tactical military operations be directed toward clearly defined, decisive, and attainable tactical objectives that ultimately assist in achieving the strategic aims.

Tacticians must clearly understand the overall mission of the higher command, his own mission, and the tasks he must perform and the reasons thereof; he must consider each contemplated action in light of his mission, and he must communicate clearly to his subordinate commanders the intent of the operation upon which the command as a whole is about to embark.[30]

Additionally, military leaders cannot dissociate objective from the related joint principles of restraint and legitimacy, particularly in stability operations. The amount of force used to obtain the objective must be prudent and appropriate to strategic aims. Means used to accomplish the military objective must not undermine the local population's willing acceptance of a lawfully constituted government. Without restraint or legitimacy, support for military action deteriorates, and the objective becomes unobtainable.

With this principle of war in mind, objectives assigned to Special Forces may often be as political, economic, or psychological as they are military. SF objectives can lead directly to accomplishing national or theater political, economic, or psychological objectives. In summary, the principle of objective tells us we must "pursue one great decisive aim with force and determination."[31]

Offensive
Seize, retain, and exploit the initiative. Pressure, pursue, and punish.

---

[29] Clausewitz, On War, VIII, 3, 706.
[30] Summers, On Strategy, 198.
[31] Clausewitz, Principles of War, 19.

As a principle of war, offensive is synonymous with initiative. The surest way to achieve decisive results is to seize, retain, and exploit the initiative. Seizing the initiative dictates the nature, scope, and tempo of an operation. *Seizing the initiative compels an enemy to react to friendly action.* Combat leaders use initiative to impose their will on the enemy force or situation. War is the realm of uncertainty in which changes occur rapidly. And in order to shape and adapt to change one cannot be passive; instead one must take the initiative.[32]

Initiative is categorized as operational and individual. Operational initiative is the setting or dictating the terms of action throughout the operation. Operational initiative is the essence of the principle of offensive, and relies heavily on the collective individual initiative. *Individual initiative is the willingness to act in the absence of orders.* It is the quality most praised of the military virtues.[33] Initiative is key when existing orders no longer fit the situation, or when unforeseen opportunities or threats arise. A subordinate leader's initiative realizes his superior intent. It is a key element in mission command.[34]

In the spirit of the principle of offense, John Boyd prescribes,

Give lower-level commanders wide freedom, within an overall mind-time-space scheme, to shape/direct their own activities so that they can exploit faster tempo/rhythm at tactical levels yet be in harmony with the larger pattern/slower rhythm associated with the more general aim and larger effort at the strategic level.[35]

In combat operations, offensive action is the most effective and decisive way to achieve a clearly defined objective. Offensive operations are the means by which a military force seizes and holds the initiative while maintaining freedom of action and achieving decisive results. Offensive action takes the fight to the enemy and never allows him to recover from the initial shock of the attack.

Shock results from applying overwhelming violence and swiftness of action to throw an enemy off his *center of gravity* (COG) from which, the enemy will merely react to.[36] The importance of offensive action is

---

[32] Boyd, Patterns of Conflict, 12.

[33] Marshall, Men Against Fire, 22.

[34] For mission command see Chapter 6, the Operations Process.

[35] Boyd, Patterns of Conflict, 72. Colonel John Richard Boyd (1927-1997) was a US Air Force fighter pilot and strategist whose theories have been highly influential in the military. Boyd's key concept was the decision cycle or OODA loop, which will be discussed in Chapter 5, Tactical Decision Making.

[36] Center of gravity (COG) is the source of power that provides moral or physical strength, freedom of action, or will to act (ADRP 1-02, Terms and Military Symbols 1-8).

fundamentally true across all levels of war. For example, while economizing forces in the defense, Special Forces create conditions suitable for counterattacks.

Further, while the principle of objective requires that all efforts be directed toward a clearly defined 'common goal,' the principle of offense suggests that offensive action, or *maintenance of the initiative*, is the most effective and decisive way to pursue and attain that 'common goal.' This is fundamentally true in both the strategic and tactical sense.

While it may sometimes be necessary to adopt a defensive posture, this should be only a temporary condition until the necessary means are available to resume offensive operations. An offensive spirit must be inherent in the conduct of all defensive operations. It must be an *active* defense, not a *passive* one. No matter what the level, strategic or tactical, the side that retains the initiative through offensive action forces the foe to *react* rather than *act*.[37]

Surprise

Strike the enemy at a time or place or in a manner for which he is unprepared.

Surprise is the reciprocal of security. It becomes the means to gain superiority. It is primarily a tactical device because at the tactical level time and space are limited. It is a major contributor to achieving shock. According to Clausewitz, the two factors that produce surprise are secrecy and speed.[38] It results from taking actions for which the enemy is unprepared. Surprise is a powerful but temporary combat multiplier. It is not essential to take enemy forces completely unaware; it is only necessary that they become aware too late to react effectively. Factors contributing to surprise include speed, operations security, and asymmetric capabilities. [39]

As originality and novelty play an important part in the application of the principle of surprise, Special Forces achieves surprise by exploiting indirect approaches. SF operations often require bold, imaginative, and audacious action, especially when SF units are tasked to apply combat power directly and with surgical precision. SF soldiers often conceal not only their

---

[37] Summers, On Strategy, 199.

[38] Clausewitz, On War, III, 9, 233.

[39] Clausewitz states, "Surprise is, therefore, the medium to numerical superiority; but it is besides that also to be regarded as a substantive principle in itself, on account of its moral effect. When it is successful in a high degree, confusion and broken courage in the enemy's ranks are the consequences; and of the degree to which these multiply a success, there are examples enough, great and small. With effeminacy and loose principles it is in vain to calculate upon a surprise" (On War, I, 4).

capabilities and intentions but also their activities. Indirect SF operations exploit the enemy's misunderstanding of the operational environment. These operations can create unsettling conditions within a hostile power's environment without revealing the source. The effects of surprise are maximized when the hostile power cannot define the means of the disruption and, therefore, cannot implement effective countermeasures.

Economy of Force
Allocate minimum essential combat power to secondary efforts.

Economy of force is the reciprocal principle of mass. Tacticians allocate only the minimum combat power necessary to shaping and sustaining operations so they can mass combat power for the decisive operation. As H. Liddell Hart put it, "Economy of force is a method that seeks to achieve a greater force behind the blow at a reduced cost in personnel." At the strategic level, in the absence of unlimited resources, a nation may have to accept some risk in areas where vital interests are not immediately threatened. Hence, the Prussian maxim, "to defend everywhere is to defend nowhere." This requires accepting prudent risk.

At the tactical level, the principle of economy of force requires that minimum means be employed in areas other than where the main effort is intended to be employed. When the time comes to execute, all units should have tasks to perform. It requires, as at the strategic level, the acceptance of prudent risks in selected areas in order to achieve superiority in the area where the decision is sought. This principle may require the forces employed to attack, defend, delay, or conduct deception operations. [40]

The employment of SF is often as a strategic economy-of-force measure to allow the concentration of other forces elsewhere. Specifically designed, SF can divert hostile forces into secondary theaters. This tactic prevents hostile concentration against the friendly main effort. SF is particularly effective when employed in combination with indigenous or surrogate forces as a force multiplier.

Mass
Concentrate the effects of combat power at the decisive place and time.

Mass is concentrated combat power to exploit an enemy weakness. Combat leaders mass the effects of power in time and space to achieve victory. Massing in time applies the elements of combat power against

---

[40] Summers, *On Strategy*, 200.

multiple decisive points simultaneously. Massing in space concentrates the effects of combat power against a single decisive point.

Jomini's essential thought was to win a favorable result through the concentration of strength against weakness. He would say that one should hurl mass along a line of operation toward an object which the enemy holds dear.[41] This he would call the *decisive point*. Jomini defined a decisive point as anything "whose attack or capture would imperil or seriously weaken the enemy."[42]

In the tactical dimension, this principle suggests that superior combat power must be concentrated at the decisive place and time in order to achieve decisive results. This does not imply that massed fires alone bring victory. Rather, rapid and fluid maneuver complements the effects of fire. The massing of forces, together with the proper application of the other principles of war, may enable numerically inferior forces to achieve decisive battle outcomes. [43]

In contrast to conventional forces, Special Forces normally do not seek dominance in the size of the force or in firepower. SFODAs compensate for their lack of combat power through the use of such combat multipliers as surprise, advanced training, and unconventional tactics. Special Forces employ indigenous or surrogate forces to magnify the effect of these multipliers. This use of combat multipliers may equate to relative superiority.[44]

SFODAs concentrate their combat power indirectly so the effects of their actions impact at decisive times and places. SFODAs must not be at the margin of their operational capabilities during mission execution. Care must be taken not to fragment the efforts of SFODAs by committing them against targets that are tactically attractive but operationally or strategically irrelevant.

Unity of Command
For every objective, ensure unity of effort under one responsible commander.

---

[41] Jomini, The Art of War, 63.

[42] John Shy, "Jomini," in The Makers of Modern Strategy: From Machiavelli to the Nuclear Age, ed. Peter Paret (Princeton Univ. Press, 1986), pp. 152–4. Decisive point or schwerpunkt was applied to war by Clausewitz to refer to the 'point of main effort,' or 'focus of energy.' It is based on Clausewitz's maxim, "The forces available must be employed with such skill that even in the absence of absolute superiority, relative superiority is attained at the decisive point." Army doctrine defines a decisive point as a geographic place, specific key event, critical factor, or function that, when acted upon, allows commanders to gain a marked advantage over an adversary or contribute materially to achieving success (ADRP 1-02, 1-17).

[43] Summers, On Strategy, 200.

[44] For more on relative superiority see chapter 4.

Applying a unit's full combat power requires unity of command. Unity of command means that a single commander directs and coordinates the actions of all forces toward a common objective. As Machiavelli put it, "Let only one command in war: several minds weaken an army."[45] Cooperation may produce coordination, but giving a single commander the required authority is the most effective way to achieve unity of effort.

The joint, interagency, intergovernmental, and multinational nature of unified action creates situations where the commander does not directly control all organizations in the operational area. In the absence of command authority, commanders cooperate, negotiate, and build consensus to achieve unity of effort. In the tactical dimension, it is axiomatic that the employment of military forces in a manner that develops their full combat power requires unity of command.

To achieve unity of effort, SF soldiers organize with clear, uncluttered chains of command. In this manner, a single commander has the requisite authority to direct and coordinate all forces employed in pursuit of a common goal. SF personnel, however, often conduct operations with multiple U.S. Government agencies. In such cases, the Department of Defense (DOD) plays a supporting role and requires cooperation rather than command of other agencies.

As a result, coordination and cooperation replace unity of command. During combined operations with indigenous military forces, SF tacticians must stress the requirement for cooperation between indigenous military and civilian organizations. SF soldiers also assist in synchronizing indigenous objectives with those of the United States.

Security
Never permit the enemy to acquire an unexpected advantage. Preserve your force as a whole.

Security protects and preserves combat power. Security results from measures a command takes to protect itself from surprise, interference, sabotage, annoyance, and threat surveillance and reconnaissance. Military deception greatly enhances security. Risk is an inherent condition in war; application of the principle of security does not suggest over-cautiousness or the avoidance of calculated risk. [46]

In Special Forces, security often dominates rather than supports operations. Because of the nature of special operations, a breach in security

---

[45] Fuller, The Generalship of Ulysses S. Grant, 6.
[46] Summers, On Strategy, 202.

can affect mission success, as well as national credibility and legitimacy. SF must emphasize security throughout mission planning and execution and after the mission is completed. As a result, SF may require compartmentation and deception measures. Active and passive counterintelligence (CI) efforts must minimize the potential for hostile penetration or accidental disclosure of sensitive information.

Simplicity
Prepare clear, uncomplicated plans and clear, concise orders to ensure thorough understanding.

Plans and orders should be simple and direct. Simple plans and clear, concise orders reduce misunderstanding and confusion. Regarding this principle, JFC Fuller states, "An original plan should aim at simplicity, and novel action should not demand movements the troops do not understand."[47] The situation determines the degree of simplicity required.

Simple plans executed on time are better than detailed plans executed late, or in the words of Patton, "a simple plan violently executed now, is better than a perfect plan executed next week." Thus, tacticians at all levels weigh potential benefits of a complex concept of operations against the risk that subordinates will fail to understand or follow it. Orders should use clearly defined terms and graphics. Doing this conveys specific instructions to subordinates with reduced chances for misinterpretation and confusion.

Further, multinational operations put a premium on simplicity. Differences in language, doctrine, and culture complicate them. In this complex environment, Special Forces uses simple plans and orders to minimize confusion and marginalize the moral factors of fog and friction. The same should be applied to operations involving interagency and nongovernmental organizations. Moreover, although Special Forces often use sophisticated and unorthodox methods and equipment, their plans and procedures must be simple and direct. A complex, inflexible plan that relies on precise timing is likely to be destroyed by chance events, as Operation Market Garden demonstrated.

Additional Principles of Special Operations

Army special operations follow the nine principles of war and always consider the principles of operations that add value to activities and operations that are population or threat focused. The three additional principles of operations that Army SOF consider are *restraint, perseverance,*

---

[47] Fuller, The Foundations of the Science of War, 217.

and *legitimacy*. Together with the principles of war, these twelve make up the principles of joint operations.

Restraint
Limit collateral damage and prevent the unnecessary use of force.

Restraint requires careful and disciplined balancing of security, the conduct of military operations, and the desired strategic end state. Clausewitz states that civilized nations do not put their prisoners to death, and do not devastate towns and countries because their intelligence exercises great influence on their mode of carrying on war, and has taught them more effectual means of applying force than these rude acts of mere instinct.

Excessive force antagonizes those friendly and neutral parties involved. Hence, it damages the legitimacy of the organization that uses it while potentially enhancing the legitimacy of any opposing party.[48] The rules of engagement must be carefully matched to the strategic end state and the situation. Leaders at all levels ensure their personnel are properly trained in rules of engagement and quickly informed of any changes. Rules of engagement may vary according to national policy concerns but should always be consistent with the inherent right of self-defense.

Restraint is best achieved when rules of engagement issued at the beginning of an operation address a range of plausible situations. Commanders should consistently review and revise rules of engagement as necessary. Additionally, commanders should carefully examine them to ensure that the lives and health of soldiers are not needlessly endangered. National concerns may lead to different rules of engagement for multinational participants; commanders must be aware of national restrictions imposed on force participants.

Perseverance
Ensure the commitment necessary to attain the national strategic end state.

SOF commanders prepare for measured, protracted military operations in pursuit of the desired national strategic end state. Some joint operations may require years to reach the desired end state. Resolving the underlying causes of the crisis may be elusive, making it difficult to achieve conditions supporting the end state. The patient, resolute, and persistent pursuit of

---

[48] Regarding this point, J F C Fuller writes, 'Though in wars of all types there is no belt which may not be hit below, nevertheless a wise fighter will think twice before hitting below a certain moral line, because the material advantage accruing may be cancelled out by the ethical loss resulting." The Foundations of the Science of War, 71.

national goals and objectives often is a requirement for success. This will frequently involve diplomatic, informational, and economic measures to supplement military efforts. In the end, the will of the American public, as expressed through their elected officials and advised by expert military judgment, determines the duration and size of any military commitment.

Endurance and perseverance are necessary to accomplish long-term missions. A decisive offensive operation may swiftly create conditions for short-term success. However, protracted stability operations, executed simultaneously with defensive and offensive tasks, may be needed to achieve the strategic end state. Commanders balance their desire to enter the operational area, accomplish the mission quickly, and depart against broader requirements. These include the long-term commitment needed to achieve national goals and objectives.

Legitimacy
Develop and maintain the will necessary to attain the national strategic end state.

For Army forces, legitimacy comes from three important factors. First, the operation or campaign must be conducted under US law. Second, the operation must be conducted according to international laws and treaties recognized by the United States, particularly the law of war. Third, the campaign or operation should develop or reinforce the authority and acceptance for the host-nation government by both the governed and the international community. This last factor is frequently the decisive element.

Conclusion

In this chapter we have attempted to lay a doctrinal foundation for the remainder of this book. As has been said, doctrine may be observed as refined theory and requires judgment to be applied to specific situations. Toward this end our focus has been on how to think – not what to think. And our goal is to make sound and timely decisions based on Army doctrine and the factors of mission, enemy, terrain and weather, troops and support available, time available, and civil considerations (METT-TC).[49] Additionally, the uncertainties of war require a correct application of fundamentals and guts, albeit we must always tether audacity with prudence.

---

[49] For more on METT-TC, see chapter 7.

Chapter 4   Special Forces Doctrine

"There is another type of warfare, new in its intensity, ancient in its origin, war by guerrillas, subversives, insurgents, assassins; war by ambush instead of by combat, by infiltration instead of aggression, seeking victory by eroding and exhausting the enemy instead of engaging him. It preys on unrest." – President John F. Kennedy

The two primary missions of Special Forces are unconventional warfare (UW) and foreign internal defense (FID).[1] These may be considered conceptually antithetical. UW is designed to overthrow unfriendly governments (or occupying powers) through a combination of direct and indirect activities, often in denied areas. The FID mission employs Special Forces to enable foreign governments to combat insurgency, terrorism, or transnational criminality. In both missions, Special Forces focus on interacting with and empowering indigenous partners to act. Thus, both UW and FID are population oriented, austere and asymmetric requiring a high degree of versatility, skill, and determination – hallmarks of Special Forces.

The purpose of this chapter is to provide a conceptual overview of Special Forces doctrine as well as outline the principle Special Forces tasks. This chapter will discuss the following:

1. Special Forces Imperatives.
2. SOF Truths.
3. The Principles of Special Operations.
4. Special Forces Principle Tasks.

Special Operations Imperatives

SF tacticians must incorporate the 12 SOF imperatives into their mission planning and execution to use their forces effectively.[2] SOF imperatives are the foundation for planning   and executing SO in concert with other forces, interagency partners, and foreign organizations. Although the imperatives may not apply to all SOF operations, SF tacticians must include the applicable imperatives in their mission planning and execution.

1. Understand the operational environment.

SF soldiers do not dominate their environment, they influence it. They must assess and understand all its aspects (political, economic, sociological,

---

[1] FM 3-18 Special Forces Operations, vi.
[2] FM 3-05.201, 1-21.

psychological, geographic, and military) before acting to influence it. Special operations cannot shape the operational environment without first gaining a clear understanding of the theater of operations, to include civilian influence and enemy and friendly capabilities.[3] The conditions of conflict can change based on a variety of military, friendly, and enemy factors. SF personnel must identify friendly and hostile decision makers, the objectives and strategies of those decision makers, and their means of interacting. They must influence friendly decision makers to make sure they understand the implications and consequences of SO mission requirements. SF tacticians must remain flexible and adapt their operations to changing situations. They must anticipate changes in their environment to exploit fleeting opportunities.

The civilian population is the critical factor. SFOD members must understand the demography, culture, taboos, beliefs, customs, history, goals, ethnic composition, and expectations of the civilian population. Most important, they must be aware of the dynamics of the many correlations among these various aspects of a society. SFOD members must be aware of who can influence whom, and how that influence is achieved and exercised. They must also be aware of any incidental effect the actions with any one factor have on another.[4]

2. Recognize political implications.

SF must not expect a conventional battlefield environment where military concerns dominate. The role of SF is frequently a supporting one that creates the conditions for decisive military and nonmilitary activities to occur. Whether conducting military operations independently or in conjunction with conventional forces, SF must consider both the short and long-term political implications of their actions.[5]

Additionally, many special operations are conducted to advance critical political objectives. Whether conducting operations independently or in coordination with partners, SOF must consider the political effects of their actions. SOF must anticipate ambiguous strategic and operational environments where military factors are not the only concern. SO frequently create conditions for nonmilitary activities to occur within indigenous populations and for civil institutions to achieve U.S. and HN objectives. The

---

[3] ADRP 3-05, 1-13.
[4] FM 3-05.201, 1-21.
[5] The ramification of failing to consider this principle is evidenced by the execution of SOF personnel under Hitler's 1942 Commando Order.

advancement of the political objective may take precedence over the military disadvantages.[6]

3. Facilitate interagency activities.

SF soldiers often participate in interagency activities. SF tacticians must strive for unity of effort (synchronization), yet recognize the difficulty of achieving such unity. They must expect ambiguous missions, conflicting interests and objectives, compartmentation of activity, and disunity of command. When unity of command is lacking, SF tacticians must promote unity of effort by requesting clear mission statements and intent. SF must actively and continually coordinate its activities with all relevant parties.

4. Engage the threat discriminately.

Special Operations missions often have sensitive political implications. Therefore, commanders must carefully select when, where, and how to employ SOF. SO may be applied with precision to minimize collateral effects and in a concealed or clandestine manner (or through the actions of indigenous military or other security forces) so that only the effects are detectable.[7]

5. Anticipate long-term effects.

SFODAs must look at each problem in its broader political, military, and psychological context. They must then develop a long-term approach to solving the problem. They must accept legal and political constraints, such as restrictive rules of engagement (ROE), to avoid strategic failure while achieving tactical success. Commanders must not jeopardize the success of national and theater long-term objectives by their desire for immediate or short-term effects. SO policies, plans, and operations must be consistent with the national and theater priorities and objectives they support. Inconsistency can lead to a loss of legitimacy and credibility at the national and international levels.

Additionally, SO policies, plans, and operations must be consistent with the national and theater of operations priorities and objectives they support.

---

[6] ADRP 3-05, 1-13.
[7] Ibid.

Inconsistency can lead to a loss of legitimacy and credibility at the national level.[8]

6. Ensure legitimacy and credibility.

Significant legal and policy considerations exist with SO, particularly in peacetime operations. In modern conflict, legitimacy is the most crucial factor in developing and maintaining domestic and international support. Without this support, the United States cannot sustain its assistance to a foreign power. The concept of legitimacy is broader than the strict international legal definition. It also includes the moral and political legitimacy of a government or resistance organization. The people of the nation and the international community determine credibility. Credibility is based on the collective perception of the reliability of the cause and methods.

Without legitimacy and credibility, SO will not receive the support of indigenous elements, the U.S. population, or the international community. SFODAs must make sure their legal advisors review all aspects of their mission. SF soldiers must understand the laws of armed conflict and the ROE as they apply to their mission. They must be alert to human rights violations possibly committed by their foreign counterparts. SF soldiers must know what procedures to follow should such violations occur. Finally, they must understand that their behavior, both on duty and off, may have profound effects on their mission accomplishment

7. Anticipate and control psychological effects.

All SO have significant psychological effects, regardless of the overall objective. In some SO missions, however, the specific objective itself is to produce a desired psychological effect. To control psychological effects, SF soldiers must blend PSYOP TTPs into their activities.

8. Apply capabilities indirectly.

When participating in combined operations, the primary role of SF is to advise, train, and assist indigenous military and paramilitary forces. The supported indigenous forces then serve as force multipliers in the pursuit of U.S. national security objectives with minimum U.S. visibility, risk, and cost. SF must avoid taking charge when supporting a foreign government or group. The foreign government or group must assume authority and

---

[8] ADRP 3-05, 1-14.

responsibility for the success or failure of the combined effort. All U.S. efforts must reinforce and enhance the legitimacy and credibility of the supported government.

9. Develop multiple options.

SF must maintain its operational flexibility by developing a broad range of options and contingency plans. It must be able to shift from one option to another before and during mission execution.

10. Ensure long-term sustainment.

SF soldiers conduct peacetime operations around the world and must prepare to continue this effort in the future. The U.S. response to conflict varies from case to case. SF leaders must recognize the need for persistence, patience, and continuity of effort. They should not begin programs that are beyond the economic or technological capacity of the HN to maintain without U.S. assistance. U.S.-funded programs can be counterproductive if the population becomes dependent upon them. SO policy, strategy, and programs must, therefore, be durable, consistent, and sustainable.

11. Provide sufficient intelligence.

SFODs normally cannot infiltrate denied territory and develop an ambiguous situation. They do not have the combat power or the reinforcement and support capabilities to deal with unanticipated hostile reactions. The success of SO missions often depends on detailed, near-real-time, all-source intelligence products. SF priority intelligence requirements (PIR) and information requirements (IRs) impose great demands on supporting intelligence capabilities. SFODs must identify their IRs in priority and distinguish mission-essential requirements from nonessential requirements. Without realistic priorities, the intelligence community can quickly become overly committed in attempting to satisfy SF PIR and IRs.

12. Balance security and synchronization.

Security concerns often dominate SO. Too much compartmentalizing, however, can exclude key personnel from participating in the planning cycle. SF tacticians must resolve these conflicting demands on mission planning and execution. Insufficient security may compromise a mission. Excessive security, however, can cause the mission to fail because of inadequate coordination.

189

SOF Truths

The Special Operations Forces (SOF) Truths are the five governing principles that have been the foundation for all special operations forces since the establishment of the United States Special Operations Command. These principles guide the acquisition, training, employment and sustainment of all SOF.

1. Humans are more important than Hardware.
People—not equipment—make the critical difference. The right people, highly trained and working as a team, will accomplish the mission with the equipment available. Yet the best equipment in the world cannot compensate for a lack of the right people.

2. **Quality is better than Quantity**. A small number of people, carefully selected, well-trained, and well-led are preferable to larger numbers of troops, some of whom may not be fully capable.

3. **Special Operations Forces cannot be mass produced**. It takes years to train operational units to the level of proficiency needed to accomplish difficult and specialized SOF missions. Integration of mature, competent individuals into fully capable units requires intense training, both in the SOF schools and units. Hastening this process only degrades the ultimate capability.

4. **Competent Special Operations Forces cannot be created after emergencies occur**. Creation of competent, fully mission-capable units takes time. Employment of fully capable SOF elements on short notice requires highly trained and constantly available SOF units in peacetime.

5. **Most Special Operations require non-SOF assistance**. Conducting special operations by, with, and through host nation forces, as well as indigenous and surrogate forces, is a crucial capability in accomplishing the United States' national interests.

Special Forces Principle Tasks

Special Forces are organized, manned, trained, and equipped to execute nine principle tasks. Special Forces conduct these tasks using specialized techniques, tactics, and procedures (TTPs) in a manner that complement conventional force capabilities.[9] The following diagram outlines these nine principle tasks (See Figure 4-1):

Figure 4-1. Special Forces Principle Tasks.

Unconventional Warfare

"The guerrilla fights the war of the flea, and his military enemy suffers the dog's disadvantages: too much to defend, too small, ubiquitous, and agile an enemy to come to grips with." – Robert Taber

Unconventional warfare (UW) is the core activity and organizing principle for Army Special Forces and the nine principle Special Forces tasks.[10] UW is defined as "activities conducted to enable a resistance movement or insurgency to coerce, disrupt, or overthrow a government or occupying power by operating through or with an underground, auxiliary, and guerilla force in a denied area."[11]

UW as a formal mission can trace its roots to the opening days of World War II, especially in the Philippines, and the establishment of the Office of

---

[9] FM 3-18 Special Forces Operations, 2-4.
[10] Ibid.
[11] Ibid.

Strategic Services (OSS). As noted earlier, the Philippine UW campaign was one of the most successful of its kind in history, in that it tied up hundreds of thousands of Japanese forces who were forced to commit to counterinsurgency rather than continue their advance to Australia. Similarly, in the European theater, Allied SOF personnel, such as the SOE and OSS organized, trained, equipped, and led menacing resistance movements. For example, the Maquis in France which totaled some 100,000 resistance fighters, contributed directly to the success of Operation Overlord, the Allied invasion of France. As has been said, according to Eisenhower, the value of the Maquis to Operation Overlord amounted to the equivalent of fifteen military divisions.

At the end of World War II, the Army developed its UW concept based largely on the experiences of men like Bank and Volckmann who had worked with resistance movements during the war. The concept was formally introduced into doctrine in 1955, specifically to convey a wider responsibility than simply working alongside guerrilla forces. President John F. Kennedy's interest in UW and his understanding of the threat posed by Communist-inspired "wars of national liberation" led to increased emphasis on UW capabilities which resulted in the development of national policy, doctrine, and force structures to respond to the increasing threat. The Army responded to the President's concern, reorienting SF to include support to indigenous forces fighting against Communist-inspired insurgencies.

The goal of UW is a change in political control and/or perceived legitimacy of regimes.[12] To that end, the United States may undertake long-term operations in support of selected resistance organizations. When directed, Special Forces advises, trains, and assists indigenous resistance organizations. A US sponsored insurgency involves long-term campaigns. An insurgency is an organized movement aimed at the overthrow of a constituted government or occupying power through the use of subversion and armed conflict. For example, in late 2001, the 5th Special Forces Group joined forces with Afghanistan's Northern Alliance to defeat the country's ruling Taliban. And within two months, some 350 Special Forces soldiers, 100 CIA operatives along with about 15,000 Northern Alliance fighters routed a Taliban army of 50,000 strong, and overthrow the Taliban government.

UW will vary in its application as each environment is unique but will generally pass through seven distinct phases. The Seven Phases of a US sponsored insurgency are:

---

[12] FM 3-18 Special Forces Operations, 2-5.

- Phase I <u>Preparation</u> – intelligence preparation, planning, and shaping activities.
- Phase II <u>Initial Contact</u> – USG agencies coordinate with resistance or government in exile.
- Phase III <u>Infiltration</u> – SF unit infiltrate and establish communications with resistance movement.
- Phase IV <u>Organization</u> – SF unit organize, train, and equip resistance cadre into three basic components: guerillas, underground, and auxiliary.
- Phase V <u>Build Up</u> – Development of infrastructure: SF unit assists cadre with expansion into effective organization.
- Phase VI <u>Employment</u> – Resistance forces conduct combat operations.
- Phase VII <u>Transition</u> – UW forces revert to national control.

As we've said, UW is activities conducted to enable a resistance movement or insurgency to coerce, disrupt or overthrow an occupying power or government by operating through or with an underground, auxiliary and guerrilla force in a denied area. In order for a resistance movement to be successful there are three necessary components. These are the: the Underground, the Auxiliary, and the Guerrillas (See Figure 4-2). These three elements by design are to be self-sufficient and self-contained. Further, they should be capable of centralized command, but decentralized execution.

1. *The Guerrilla force* – is the overt military aspect of an insurgency or other armed resistance. They conduct military and paramilitary operations by irregular, predominately indigenous forces in enemy-held or hostile territory. It is often rurally based, with full-time and part-time membership.

2. *The Underground* – supports the area command, auxiliary, and guerrilla force. These personnel commit sabotage, intelligence gathering, and acts of deception through the action arm, intelligence, supply, and personnel sections.

3. *The Auxiliary* – is the internal support element of the resistance movement whose organization and operation are both covert and clandestine in nature; they normally do not openly indicate their sympathy or involvement with the resistance movement. Their primary mission is to provide logistical support, security, and intelligence for the guerrilla force by organizing civilian supporters of the resistance movement.

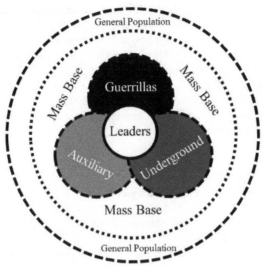

Figure 4-2. Elements of a Resistance Movement.

Guerrilla warfare has a heritage as old as war itself. It has so often brought to a halt some of the most powerful military machines. Russell Volckmann describes one such guerrilla campaign:

Napoleon sent a powerful military force of 670,000 men and 520 guns across the Pyrenees between 1807 and 1813 to conquer Spain. This unprovoked French invasion aroused a uniform uprising, and the Spaniards by conducting guerrilla warfare prevented the French from concentrating their forces against Wellington, causing French effort instead to be frittered away against the guerrillas. Napoleon finally withdrew the remnants of his forces from Spain without achieving his military and political objectives, and only 250,000 men and 250 guns returned to France.[13]

The point being made here is, a guerrilla campaign can make an enormous impact, often incommensurately disproportionate to the amount of forces employed. After Napoleon's war with the flea in Spain, a man named Thomas Lawrence similarly demonstrated the effectiveness of guerrilla warfare in Arabia.

Thomas Edward Lawrence, (1888-1935), known as Lawrence of Arabia, was a self-taught master of guerrilla warfare. His leadership skills, creativity, cultural competence, idealism, diplomacy and courage allowed the British and the Arabs to drive the Turks out of the Middle East. Son of

---

[13] Volckmann, We Remained, 221.

an aristocrat and educated in Oxford, Lawrence spent some five years before WWI in the Middle East at archaeological digs.[14] At the outbreak of World War I, Lawrence was commissioned a lieutenant of British Army Intelligence, and until late in 1916, he manned a desk in Cairo.

When opportunity knocked, Lawrence was discovered and sent to liaise with Arab forces, who, believing the promise of the British Government, begin an insurrection with the prospects of nationhood.

To this purpose, Lawrence was especially adept, and demonstrating the importance of military theory in warfare, he formulated the following *six principles of UW*:

1. A successful guerrilla movement must have an unassailable base.
2. The guerrilla must have a technologically sophisticated enemy.
3. The enemy army of occupation must be sufficiently weak in numbers so as to be unable to occupy the disputed territory in depth with a system of interlocking fortified posts.
4. The guerrilla must have at least the passive support of the populace, if not its full involvement.
5. The irregular force must have the fundamental qualities of speed, endurance, presence and logistical independence.
6. The guerrilla must be sufficiently advanced in weaponry to strike at the enemy's logistics and signals vulnerabilities.[15]

As we've discussed this complex topic, we might ask: What's the difference between a resistance movement and an insurgency? A resistance is an organized effort by some portion of the civil population to *resist* the government or an occupying power and to disrupt civil order and stability. An example being the French Maquis and the Filipino resistance movements of WW II. And an insurgency is an organized movement aimed at the *overthrow* of a constituted government or occupying power through the use of subversion and armed conflict. An example being the US overthrow of the Taliban government in 2001.

Since World War II, insurgency and terrorism have become the dominant forms of conflict.[16] And according to Max Boot, it's not hard to see why. Because, He writes, this mode of warfare is "cheap and easy: waging guerrilla warfare does not require procuring expensive weapon systems or

---

[14] Wilson, Lawrence of Arabia, 29-30.

[15] These principles are found in Lawrence's *Seven Pillars of Wisdom*, 196.

[16] Boot, Invisible Armies: An Epic History of Guerrilla Warfare from Ancient Times to the Present, xx. This is a valuable account of some of the challenges our military faces in confronting terrorist and guerrilla insurgencies.

building an elaborate bureaucracy. And it works. At least sometimes."[17]
Here is a short list of some successful guerrilla campaigns since Francis
Marion's guerrilla war in South Carolina:

- Francis Marion's UW Campaign (1781–1783).
- Haitian Revolution (1791 – 1804).
- Peninsular War in Spain (1808 – 1814).
- Greek War of Independence (1821 – 1830).
- First Boer War (1880 – 1881).
- Lawrence's Arab Revolt (1916 – 1918).
- Irish War of Independence (1919 – 1921).
- The Partisans of Yugoslavia during WWII (1941 – 1945).
- Burma Campaign (1942 – 1945).
- MacArthur's Philippine UW Campaign (1942 – 1945).
- Indonesia (1945 – 1949).
- Mao's Communist Revolution in China (1946 – 1949).
- First Indochina War (1946 – 1954).
- Algerian War (1954 – 1962).
- Castro's Cuban Revolution (1956 – 1959).
- Vietnam War (1959 – 1975).
- Eritrean War of Independence (1961 – 1991).
- Cambodian Civil War (1967 – 1975).
- Bangladesh Liberation War (1971).
- Rhodesian Bush War (1972 – 1980).
- Nicaragua (1977 – 1979).
- Afghanistan Mujahidin against the USSR (1978 – 1989).
- Kosovo Liberation Army (1992 – 1999).
- People's War in Nepal (1996 – 2006).
- East Timor (1975 – 1999).

Here is a short list of some unsuccessful guerrilla campaigns:

- Irish Guerrilla campaign (1799 – 1803).
- Caucasian War (1817 – 1864).
- Abd al-Qadir in Algeria (1830 – 1847).
- Taiping Rebellion in Qing China (1850 – 1864).
- Mosby's Confederacy (1863 – 1865).
- Polish uprising (1863 – 1865).
- Second Boer War (1899 – 1902).

---

[17] Boot, Invisible Armies: An Epic History of Guerrilla Warfare from Ancient Times to the
Present, xx.

- Philippine–American War (1899 – 1902).
- Basmachi rebels in Soviet Central Asia (1916 – 1931).
- Ukrainian nationalist partisans and guerrillas during and after the Russian Civil War (1917).
- Tambov Rebellion in Soviet Russia (1919 – 1921).
- Irish Civil War (1922 – 1923).
- IRA S-Plan campaign (1939 – 1941).
- Spanish Maquis (1939 – 1965).
- Italian guerrilla war in Ethiopia (1941 – 1943).
- IRA Northern Campaign (1942 – 1944).
- (UPA) Ukrainian Insurgent Army (1944 – 1949).
- Nazi German Werwolf movement (1945).
- Greek Civil War (1945 – 1949).
- Malayan Emergency (1948 – 1960).
- Mau Mau Uprising in Kenya (1952 – 1960).
- IRA Border Campaign (1956 – 1962).
- Tibet (1958 – 1974).[18]
- Parrari in Pakistan (1962 – 1969).
- Dhofar Rebellion in Oman (1962 – 1976).
- Communist Party of Thailand (1964 – 1982).
- Dominican Republic (1965 – 1966).
- Uruguay (1965 – 1973).
- Argentina (1969 – 1981).
- El Salvador (1980 – 1992).
- Contras – Nicaragua (1981 – 1990).
- Second Sudanese Civil War (1983 – 2005).
- Sri Lankan Civil War (1983 – 2009).

As stated earlier, UW is activities conducted to enable a resistance movement or insurgency to coerce, disrupt, or overthrow a government or occupying power by operating through or with an underground, auxiliary, and guerilla force in a denied area. As guerrilla warfare will not only continue but will play an increasingly important role in modern warfare, Special Forces will continue to play a vital role as SF was specifically designed to conduct these missions (Figure 4-3).

---

[18] Tibetan resistance against Chinese occupation ultimately failed when the CIA withdrew its support in light of President Nixon's diplomatic overtures to the People's Republic of China.

Unconventional Warfare	Foreign Internal Defense
Coerce, disrupt, or overthrow a government or occupying power through: policy, indigenous force, or subversion/sabotage.	Improve a nation-state's security apparatus by: training, advising, and assisting primarily through COIN.
Degrade legitimacy and destabilize.	Reinforce legitimacy and stabilize.

Figure 4-3. Role of Special Forces in UW and FID.

Foreign Internal Defense

"Let every nation know, whether it wishes us well or ill, that we shall pay any price, bear any burden, meet any hardship, support any friend, [and] oppose any foe to assure the survival and the success of liberty." – President John F. Kennedy

Foreign Internal Defense (FID) is defined as "participation by civilian and military agencies of a government in any of the action programs taken by another government or other designated organization to free and protect its society from subversion, lawlessness, and insurgency, terrorism, and other threats to its security."[19] FID is characterized as an overt, direct method of assistance to free and protect a host nation (HN) government from insurgency or lawlessness.

While FID is characterized as overt and direct assistance to a host nation (HN) government to free and protect it from insurgency or lawlessness, UW is clandestine or covert application of the military by using an irregular force to extend operational reach in an indirect manner.

Like UW, FID is an umbrella concept that covers a broad range of activities, for example, counterinsurgency (COIN) is one such aspect of FID. SF may conduct FID to enable a nation to combat insurgency, terrorism, or transnational criminality. In the past, the objective of most SF FID missions was to support an ally or a friendly government against an insurgency or a similar internal threat.

The objective may be to establish or strengthen an alliance between the United States and a host nation (HN) facing an internal threat. Regardless of

---

[19] JP 3-22 Foreign Internal Defense, ix.

the threat, the primary FID mission for SF during conflict is to train, advise, and assist the HN military and paramilitary forces and, when required, accompany them on operations. Additionally, FID is not restricted to times of conflict and may take place in the form of training exercises.

When we look at the two primary missions of Special Forces, UW and FID, we may note that while UW seeks to coerce, disrupt or overthrow a government or occupying power, FID seeks to improve a nation state's security, primarily through COIN, by training, advising, and assisting HN forces.

Security Force Assistance

The third principle SF task we are considering is Security Force Assistance (SFA). SFA and FID overlap without being subsets of each other. At the strategic and operational levels, both SFA and FID focus on developing the Foreign Security Forces' (FSF) capacity and capability.[20] SFA differs from FID only with respect that SFA prepares Foreign Security Forces to defend against external threats and to perform as part of an international coalition.

Counterinsurgency

"This is a game of wits and will. You've got to be learning and adapting constantly to survive." – General Peter J. Schoomaker

Insurgency and counterinsurgency (COIN) are complex subsets of warfare. As we've seen, an insurgency is a civil war. Yet there is a difference in the form the war takes in each case.[21] Insurgency, is the agency of radical social pursuit or political change. Joint doctrine defines an insurgency as an organized movement aimed at the overthrow of a constituted government through the use of subversion and armed conflict (JP 1-02). Its counterpart, COIN is a form of counter-revolution. COIN is the war for men's minds. It is the process by which the revolution is resisted. COIN is a competition with the insurgent for the right to win the hearts, minds, and acquiescence of the population.[22] COIN is defined as comprehensive civilian and military efforts taken to defeat an insurgency and to address any core grievances.[23]

---

[20] FM 3-18 Special Forces Operations, 2-9.
[21] Galula, Counterinsurgency Warfare: Theory and Practice, 2.
[22] FM 3-24.2 Tactics in Counterinsurgency, C-1.
[23] FM 3-18 Special Forces Operations, 2-11.

An insurgency must be understood before it can be defeated. An understanding of the *five elements of an insurgency*, the *eight dynamics of an insurgency*, and the *six insurgent strategies*, will provide leaders at all levels a means to comprehend and defeat the insurgent.

Five Elements of an Insurgency

Though insurgencies take many forms, most share some common attributes. An insurgent organization normally consists of five elements:
- Movement leaders.
- Combatants.
- Political cadre.
- Auxiliaries.
- Mass base – the bulk of the membership (FM 3-24.2, 2-1).

The proportion of each element relative to the larger movement depends on the strategic approach the insurgency adopts. According to Robert Taber, "the ultimate goals or end states desired by insurgents vary significantly and may include creating new independent countries."[24] Insurgents attempt to obtain political goals with an organized and primarily indigenous group or groups using protracted, irregular warfare and coordinated political techniques.[25]

Insurgency is a form of conflict that denotes the use of organized violence to effect change within a state.[26] Insurgencies may arise when the populace perceives that the government is unable or unwilling to redress their issues or the demands of important social groups. These groups band together and begin to use violence to change the government's position. As this occurs, there are normally *eight dynamics common to most insurgencies*. These are:

- Leadership – An insurgency requires leadership to provide direction, guidance, coordination, and organizational cohesiveness. The goal of insurgent leadership is to replace the government's legitimacy with that of their own.
- Ideology – To win, the insurgency must have a program that explains what is wrong with society and justifies its own actions. An insurgency's ideology must promise great improvements after the government is overthrown.
- Objectives – (strategic-operational-tactical) such as, the replacement of the government in power.

---

[24] Taber, The War of the Flea, viii.
[25] Williams, Insurgency Terrorism: Attitudes, Behavior and Response, 14.
[26] Ibid, 14.

- <u>Environment and geography</u> – these are the cultural and demographic factors which influence insurgent doctrine, decisions, and TTPs.
- <u>Internal support</u> – Without the consent and active aid of the people, the guerrilla would be merely a bandit and couldn't hope to survive very long. The population, therefore, is the key to the struggle.[27]
- <u>External support</u> – examples, such as Vietnam, Nicaragua, Afghanistan, and Iraq show that external support can accelerate events and influence the outcome.
- <u>Phasing and timing</u>. Insurgencies often progress through three phases in their efforts: *latent or incipient, guerrilla warfare,* and *war of movement*. While the use of these three phases is common in most writings concerning insurgencies, the titles used for these three phases vary considerably.[28]
- <u>Organizational and operational patterns</u>. Insurgent organizational and operational patterns vary widely between one province or urban area and another. Different insurgent groups using different methods may form loose coalitions when it serves their interests.

The following depicts the components of the Malayan Insurgency circa 1950 (See Figure 4-4).

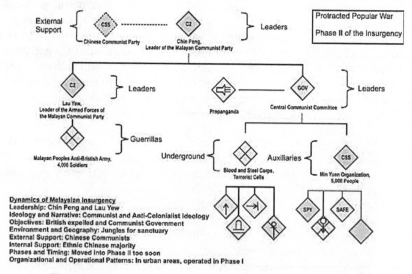

Figure 4-4. The Components of the Malayan Insurgency (FM 3-24.2, 2-2).

---

[27] Taber, The War of the Flea, 12.
[28] FM 3-24.2 Tactics in Counterinsurgency, 2-15.

Insurgent Strategies

"The strategy of guerilla warfare is to put one man against ten, but the tactic is to pit ten men against one." – Mao Zedong

Insurgencies are often a coalition of disparate forces united by their common enmity for the government. Central to any insurgency is the gaining of political power through the galvanizing of the people's dissatisfaction, in order to overthrow the constituted government. To be successful, an insurgency must develop unifying leadership, doctrine, organization, and strategy. The six common insurgent strategies are *urban, military-focused, protracted popular war, identity-focused, conspiratorial,* and *composite and coalition.*[29]

1. *Urban Strategy* – the insurgents attack government targets with the intention of causing government forces to overreact against the population. This approach was employed by the National Liberation Front in Algeria when they launched a series of bombings and attacks, causing significant civilian casualties, in order to shock the French into negotiations.

2. *Military-Focused Strategy* – believes that military action can create the conditions needed for success. Che Guevara and Fidel Castro both used this approach.

3. *Protracted Popular War Strategy* – is based on Mao Zedong's theory of protracted popular war. This strategy is broken down into three distinct phases—*latent or incipient, guerrilla warfare,* and *war of movement.* Each phase builds upon the previous phase, and continues activities from the previous phases. Jeffery Record tells us, "In Vietnam, the Communists waged a classic, peasant-based, centrally directed, three-stage, Maoist model insurgency, culminating in a conventional military victory. The Communists also had a clear and well-publicized political, economic, and social agenda."[30] The protracted popular war strategy has both a political wing and a military wing. This strategy requires a high level of organization and indoctrination, actions along multiple lines of effort, and leadership to direct the shifting of phases according to circumstances.[31]

4. *Identity-Focused Strategy* – mobilizes support based on the common identity of religious affiliation, clan, tribe, or ethnic group. This was the

---

[29] FM 3-24.2 Tactics in Counterinsurgency, 2-16.
[30] Record, Iraq and Vietnam: Differences, Similarities and Insights, 2.
[31] FM 3-24.2 Tactics in Counterinsurgency, 2-17.

strategy employed unsuccessfully by the Tamil Tigers against the constituted government of Sri Lanka.

5. *Conspiratorial Strategy* – attempts to subvert the government from within and often involves a few leaders and a militant cadre. This was the successful approach used by the Bolshevik Party in 1917.

6. *Composite and Coalition* – applies when different insurgent groups using different strategies combine to form loose coalitions that serve the purposes of the different groups. This approach has been used by Al Qaeda in Iraq and is currently being used by ISIS.

Insurgent Tactics

"If the enemy advances, we retreat. If he halts, we harass. If he tires, we attack"
– Mao Zedong

Insurgency is the traditional strategy of the weak resisting the strong. They will often employ both violent and nonviolent tactics to achieve their objectives. As FM 3-24.2 states, "Violent insurgent tactics are normally characterized by elusiveness, surprise, and brief, violent action. These tactics are often divided between terrorism and guerrilla warfare early in the insurgency."[32] Insurgents use military tactics, such as ambushes, sabotage, and raids to harass larger and less-mobile traditional forces in enemy-held territory, or strike a vulnerable target and withdraw almost immediately. Additionally, successful insurgents may often use nonviolent tactics in conjunction with violent tactics, such as subversion and propaganda; the two most prevalent forms of nonviolent warfare.

According to FM 3-24.2, guerrilla operations are generally offensive, not defensive, and are often harassing in nature. Guerrillas seldom attempt to seize and defend physical objectives and, in general, avoid decisive engagement. Their overall aim is often to cause confusion, to destroy infrastructure or security forces, and to lower public morale. Guerrilla harassment attempts to keep government forces on the defensive and weaken the Host Nation, which can include destroying resources and disrupting lines of communication.[33]

What counterinsurgents have to keep in mind is the insurgent's mere survival is a political victory; it encourages and raises the popular opposition to the incumbent regime. Thus he can afford to run and hide. On the other

---

[32] FM 3-24.2 Tactics in Counterinsurgency, 2-20.
[33] Ibid, 2-22.

hand, the counterinsurgent gains nothing by running and hiding. He surrenders everything.[34]

Additionally, it should be noted that in order for a COIN operation to be successful, it must include a program of civic action. As has been said, in order for the insurgent to win, he must have a good degree of support from the people. To counter this, civic action will enable the people to identify themselves with their government, who should be seen as the people's defenders and caretakers. This is a positive step toward breaking the physical and psychological connection the insurgent may have on the populace. This leads us to discuss Village Stability Operations (VSO).

Village Stability Operations (VSO)

"Essential though it is, the military action is secondary to the political one, it's primary purpose being to afford the political power enough freedom to work safely with the population." – David Galula

VSO are a range of planned activities designed to stabilize a village and connect it to formal governance at the district and provincial levels by facilitating infrastructure development. It is an effective counter measure to rural insurgent movements. In VSO, stability comes from a bottom-up, grass-roots mobilization of locals that establish and maintain security, development, and governance in a rural environment. The VSO concept is rooted in SF doctrine and has been successfully conducted throughout history, the Civilian Irregular Defense Groups (CIDGs) in Vietnam being a prime example.

In August 2010, President Karzai authorized the establishment of the Afghan Local Police (ALP) program. The program aims to train local Afghans in rural areas to defend their communities against insurgents and other illegally-armed groups. The program was designed, and is currently funded and supported by, US SOF in a broader initiative to enhance security and stability at the village level through the VSO program.

The VSO concept encompasses SF, Civil Affairs (CA) and MISO (Psyops) in the capacity for which they were designed — to conduct operations at the grassroots level in villages in towns where the contest between the people and the insurgents is an everyday reality. VSO teams focus first on bringing security to usher in development and a connection of local traditional governance to the formal governance at the district level and above. The goal of VSO is to work in the area between the district and

---

[34] Taber, The War of the Flea, 13.

the village and connect the villagers back to their district and provincial government.

A central component to VSO is the Village Stability Platform (VSP). The key to a VSP's success is US SOF living among the people in rural villages. SFOD-As engage with the surrounding community and provide the link with district and provincial levels of governance. Building relationships and assisting the populace to stand up against insurgents, VSPs re-empowering the traditional local governance structures within the village through a decision making council to establish a militia to enable a local security bubble around the village. When this localized stability is achieved and subsequently expanded to other villages, the VSP then facilitates the delivery of goods and services to facilitate infrastructure development, and connect the village leadership to the centralized government.

Principles of VSO

Several principles are common to VSO in any environment. The three pillars are *security*, *development*, and *governance*. The following acronym will facilitate VSO operations: **S T A B L E**

S – *Separate but Mutual*

- VSO and other programs are separate but mutually supporting programs. According to FM 3-18, "This bottom-up approach provides stability for rural villages within key districts and empowers the local government structure."[35]
- VSO should be used as an enabler for reintegration but not as an incentive for it.
- A reward for successful operations and repelling insurgent influence should be developmental projects that will allow the villages to flourish and create unity of the populace.

T – *Tribal and Ethnic Dynamics*

- Engagement of the community is paramount with respect to the tribes in the area. For example, Major Jim Gant writes, "We must support the tribal system because it is the single, unchanging political, social and cultural reality in Afghan society and the one system that all Afghans

---

[35] FM 3-18 Special Forces Operations, 2-12.

understand, even if we don't. We must also remember that the Pashtun tribes are fighting to preserve a centuries old way of life."[36]

- Care needs to be taken to avoid empowering one tribe over another.
- Understanding tribal and ethnic dynamics is vital.
- Empower traditional structures within the local culture, making sure elders or others are accountable to the villages and districts they represent. Gant writes, "The key to a successful tribal engagement strategy is the ability to identify men (Tribal Engagement Team members) who have a special gift for cross-cultural competency and building rapport—that is, they must become educated in the ways of the tribes and build strong relationships with them based on mutual trust and objectives."[37] Thus, support for the tribal systems already in place is key.

A – *Acceptance*

- VSO success depends profoundly on the local populations' acceptance. Without the support of the people, VSO are doomed before they start.
- The goal of VSO is to empower and galvanize villagers to stand up for themselves against insurgents and to generate solutions for their problems.

B – *Build*

- Central government sponsored small-scale development projects led by the community act as a medium for effective governance.
- More often than not, VSOs are about community action and confidence-building.
- The key to VSO is face-to-face relationships based upon mutual respect.
- An effective operation diminishes insurgent influence in the village and provides security to the area.
- Improvements in security, local governance and development will bring increasing opportunities for reintegrating former insurgents into the community.

L – *Local Governance*

---

[36] Gant, One Tribe at a Time: A Strategy for Success in Afghanistan, 14.
[37] Ibid, 31.

- Villagers are easily persuaded by insurgent propaganda when there are no representatives of the central government in the area with a constant presence.
- VSO empowers local representative governance through the decision making council utilizing the most locally-appropriate form of representatives; these may be village elders, political leaders or members of community-development councils.
- As security and development increases, the local council can offer the populace a better alternative to the totalitarian rule that the insurgents are attempting to impose.

E – *Endstate*

- The goal of VSO is to work in the area between the district and the village and connect the villagers back to their district and provincial government.
- The ultimate end state of VSO is a population inhospitable to the insurgents and a village where legitimate local leaders can provide security and public services with an enduring connection to the central government. Good governance is the follow-on to reliable security. Tribal Security Forces can facilitate both.

Justin Kelly offers this thought, "Whatever government is in power and whatever your political leanings, unless you are confident in the ability of your government to enforce its peace then the man with a gun at your door at midnight is your master. It doesn't matter if you are happy with your electricity, content with your children's educational arrangements and satisfied with the government's agenda—you are in thrall to the threat posed to you and your family by that man with the gun. His removal resolves the competition for control and is the first step towards establishing the coercive authority of the state in that place."[38]

Principles of COIN

As we've seen, COIN is a competition with the insurgent for the right to win the hearts, minds, and acquiescence of the population. According to David Galula, "the support of the people is the primary objective of a counterinsurgency campaign. Without the support of the population, it is impossible to root out all the insurgents and stop further recruitment."[39]

---

[38] Kelly, How to win in Afghanistan, Quadrant on-line, 5.
[39] Galula, Counterinsurgency Warfare: Theory and Practice, 86.

Conducting successful COIN requires an adaptive force led by agile leaders. While every insurgency is different because of distinct environments, root causes, and cultures, all successful COIN campaigns are based on common principles. The following principles reflect the concept of counterinsurgency and should be kept in mind while conducting operations.

1. *Ensure legitimacy in all operations.* Not only must tacticians consider all actions in light of ROE but also the perception of the manner in which actions are carried out. Actions must be perceived to be in the best interest of the local governance.[40] The people must perceive that the legally constituted government of their country is working in their best interest. Regarding this principle, Galula writes, "Having attained the support of the population it is imperative to remember that this support is conditional. What you do matters, and support can be lost if your actions are unfavorable to the population.[41]

2. *Unity of effort is essential.* Connecting with joint, interagency, coalition, and indigenous organizations is important to ensuring that objectives are shared and that actions and messages are synchronized. Jeffery Record writes, "A key principle of classical counterinsurgency is unity of effort — unified control of all elements of power, vertically from local to national level, and horizontally between districts."[42]

3. *Political factors are key.* In counterinsurgencies, military actions conducted without proper analysis of their political effects will at best be ineffective and at worst aid the enemy.[43]

4. *Intelligence drives operations* (as it should all operations). Without understanding the environment, one cannot understand and properly apply intelligence. Without good intelligence, a counterinsurgent is like a blind boxer wasting energy flailing at an unseen opponent. With good intelligence, a counterinsurgent is like a surgeon cutting out the cancers while keeping the vital organs intact. All operations must be shaped by carefully considered actionable intelligence gathered and analyzed at the lowest possible levels and disseminated and distributed throughout the force.[44]

---

[40] Kilcullen, Counterinsurgency, 160.
[41] Galula, Counterinsurgency Warfare: Theory and Practice, 86.
[42] Record, Iraq and Vietnam: Differences, Similarities and Insights, 10.
[43] Military Review: March-April 2006, Principles, Paradoxes, and Imperatives of Counterinsurgency, 49.
[44] Ibid, 50.

5. *Counterinsurgents must understand the environment* (First Special Operations Imperative). Analyzing the effect of any operation is impossible without understanding the society and culture within which the COIN operation occurs.[45]

6. *Insurgents must be isolated from their cause and support*. Regarding this principle, Galula writes, "Those willing to actively support a counterinsurgency operation should be supported in their efforts to rally the relatively neutral majority and neutralize the hostile minority."[46]

7. *Security under the rule of law is essential*. The cornerstone of any COIN effort is security for the populace. Without security, no permanent reforms can be implemented, and disorder will spread. To establish legitimacy, security activities must move from the realm of major combat operations into the realm of law enforcement. Insurgents seen as criminals will lose public support. If they are dealt with by an established legal system in line with local culture and practices, the legitimacy of the host government will be enhanced. This process will take time, but soldiers must be aware of the legal procedures applicable to their conduct and support them.[47]

8. *Counterinsurgents should prepare for a long term commitment.* "Because COIN requires a large concentration of effort, resources, and personnel," writes Galula, "it is unlikely that it can be pursued effectively everywhere at once. Rather, action should be taken in select areas, and resources moved as needed."[48] Additionally, Jim Gant offers, "Time is on their side. In an insurgency, all the insurgents have to do is not lose."[49]

As we've stated, COIN is the war for men's minds. And even with superior equipment, this is a difficult war to prosecute. There are no front lines and the war is everywhere against an enemy that is seldom clearly seen. It's a competition with the insurgent for the right to win the hearts, minds, and acquiescence of the population. According to David Kilcullen, to succeed, the West needs to remain agile, and to protect the people who support the government, with what he calls "population-centric security." Effective COIN, writes Kilcullen, "provides human security to the population, where they live, 24 hours a day. This, not destroying the enemy,

---

[45] Ibid.
[46] Galula, Counterinsurgency Warfare: Theory and Practice, 104.
[47] Military Review: March-April 2006, Principles, Paradoxes, and Imperatives of Counterinsurgency, 50.
[48] Galula, Counterinsurgency Warfare: Theory and Practice, 104.
[49] Gant, One Tribe at a Time: A Strategy for Success in Afghanistan, 11.

is the central task."[50] COIN is graduate level warfare. Just what type of leader is required in counterinsurgency? According to General Petraeus, "Counterinsurgency of course requires more in the realm of stability and support, although you literally do go back and forth. So you need a leader who is capable in those different types of operations, who is adaptive, who learns and makes adjustments, who can lead in the toughest of combat and yet also succeed in the toughest of stability and support operations."[51]

Here is a short list of some active insurgencies in the world as of 2014:
- Karen National Union (KNU) vs. Burma (1949 –).[52]
- Revolutionary Armed Forces of Colombia (FARC) vs. Columbia (1963 –).
- Palestinian Liberation Organization (PLO) vs. Israel (1965 –).
- Shining Path vs. Peru (1980 –).
- Lord's Resistance Army vs. the governments of Uganda, DRC, and Sudan (1986 –).
- Hamas vs. Israel (1987 –).
- Al Qaeda vs. USA and Allies (1988 –).
- Kashmiri Separatists vs. India (1989 –).
- Abu Sayyaf vs. Philippines (1991 –).
- Zapatistas (EZLN) vs. Mexico (1994 –).
- Chechnya Republic vs. Russia (1999 –?).
- Ansar al-Islam vs. Iraq (2001 –).
- Forces Nouvelles vs. Ivory Coast (2002 –).
- Islamic State (ISIS) vs. the free world (2014 –).

These movements are animated by a sinister dream. In the sweep of their tortuous vision, defeats are temporary. Ahead lies another day, another opportunity for subversion; another poor and struggling nation to be raped by the sword of revolution. To defeat them is quite a challenge. To crush the hope of victory of men who grind their heels on mankind's face. In lands bleeding now, and yet to bleed in the torment of insurgency. To banish their dark dream to the shadows of history as it is written by free men – *De Oppresso Liber*.

Direct Action

Direct action (DA) is a principle task of Special Forces and is defined as "short-duration strikes and other small-scale offensive actions conducted as

---

[50] Kilcullen, The Accidental Guerrilla, 266.

[51] Moyar, A Question of Command: Counterinsurgency from the Civil War to Iraq, 242.

[52] The Karen conflict is the longest internal war in the world, having been waged since 31 January 1949.

a special operation in hostile, denied, or politically sensitive environments."[53] DA employs specialized military capabilities to seize, destroy, capture, exploit, recover, or damage designated targets. DA differs from conventional offensive operations either by the level of physical or political risk involved; the operational techniques employed; or the degree of discrimination and precision use of surgical force required.

In the conduct of DA operations, Special Forces may employ raids, ambushes, or direct assault tactics (including close-quarters battle) – unilaterally or combined; sniper-observer operations; emplace mines or other munitions; conduct standoff attacks by fire from air, ground, or maritime platforms; provide terminal guidance for precision-guided munitions (TGO); conduct independent sabotage; or anti-ship operations.[54]

Throughout the history of Special Forces, successful DA operations have been characterized by surgical precision. And due to the small size and limited firepower of SFODs, DA mission success depends on the synergistic effect of speed, stealth, surprise, violence of action, and oftentimes the cover of darkness.

Special Reconnaissance

SR is defined as "reconnaissance and surveillance actions conducted as a special operation in hostile, denied, or politically sensitive environments to collect or verify information of strategic or operational significance, employing military capabilities not normally found in conventional forces."[55] SR provides "eyes on target" in a hostile, denied, or diplomatically sensitive area; such as those missions conducted by SOG in North Vietnam, Laos, and Cambodia. These SR missions located enemy concentrations and disrupted lines of communications with devastating B-52 airstrikes.[56]

Moreover, SR missions may be performed before open hostilities so as to provide essential information and situational awareness for a command decision, such as the SR missions 5th SFG and Task Force 160 executed during Operation Desert Storm in 1991. Prior to the ground invasion, thirteen ODAs were infiltrated deep into Iraq, some up to 150 miles behind enemy lines. These SR teams were the eyes and ears of the Allied Coalition. Additionally, SR operations may include: information on activities of an actual or potential enemy or secure data on the meteorological, hydrographic, or geographic characteristics of a particular area. Also, SR

---

[53] FM 3-18 Special Forces Operations, 2-14.
[54] Ibid.
[55] Ibid.
[56] For more on SOG, see Chapter 1.

may involve the assessment of chemical, biological, residual nuclear, radiological, or environmental hazards in a denied area, as well as target acquisition, area assessment, and poststrike reconnaissance.

Counterterrorism

Counterterrorism (CT) is defined as "actions taken directly against terrorist networks and indirectly to influence and render global and regional environments inhospitable to terrorist networks."[57] Like DA and SR, Special Forces units possess the capability to conduct CT in environments that may be hostile, denied, or politically sensitive. As most CT activities are classified and therefore beyond the scope of this discussion, however, it may be said that the primary mission of Special Forces in CT is to apply specialized capabilities to preclude, preempt, and resolve terrorist incidents abroad.

When directed by the NCA or the appropriate theater CINC, designated SFODAs conduct or support CT missions, including hostage rescue, recovery of sensitive material from terrorist organizations, and attacks on the terrorist infrastructure. Additionally, CT may include nonlethal activities to defeat the ideologies or motivations that spawn terrorism. These activities may include, but are not limited to, Military Information Support Operations (MISO) – Psyops, intelligence operations (IO), civil affairs operations (CAO), UW, and FID.

Counter Proliferation (CP) of Weapons of Mass Destruction (WMD)

Counterproliferation (CP) is defined as "those actions taken to defeat the threat and/or use of weapons of mass destruction against the United States, our forces, allies, and partners."[58] Further a WMD is defined as "chemical, biological, radiological, or nuclear weapons capable of a high order of destruction or causing mass casualties."[59] CP is a specialized mission assigned to designated SOF. And like CT, most CP activities are classified and therefore beyond the scope of this discussion. However, it may be said that SF participation in CP is through the conduct of UW, SR, and DA.

---

[57] FM 3-18 Special Forces Operations, 2-15.
[58] Ibid.
[59] Ibid.

212

Information Operations

Information operations (IO) is defined as "the integrated employment, during military operations, of information-related capabilities in concert with other lines of operation to influence, disrupt, corrupt, or usurp the decision-making of adversaries and potential adversaries while protecting our own."[60]

The Army's contribution to the joint information operations effort is inform and influence activities (IIA). The IIA capabilities are integrated into the planning and execution of operations in the information environment. ARSOF commanders and staff develop information themes and messages to inform domestic audiences and influence the foreign friendly, neutral, adversary, and enemy populations. They do this through IIA—the integration of designated information-related capabilities in order to synchronize themes, messages, and actions with operations to inform U.S. and global audiences, influence foreign audiences, and affect adversary and enemy decisionmaking.[61]

As the definition states, IO involves actions taken to affect adversary information and information systems, while defending one's own information and information systems to achieve information superiority in support of national military strategy, i.e. MISO (psyops) on one end of the spectrum with operational security on the other (See Figure 4-5).

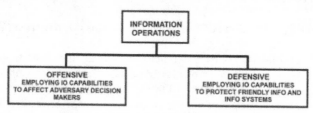

Figure 4-5. Information Operations Paradigm.

Information superiority is the capability to collect, process, and disseminate an uninterrupted flow of information while exploiting or denying an adversary's ability to do the same. SF may apply IO across all phases of an operation. The ultimate targets of offensive IO are the human decision-making processes; to get inside your opponents OODA loop and manipulate the *what* and the *way* they are observing.[62]

---

[60] FM 3-18 Special Forces Operations, 2-15.
[61] ADRP 3-05, 4-4.
[62] For more on OODA Loop, see Chapter 5.

The Principles of Special Operations

Vice Admiral William McRaven's seminal book *Spec Ops* is a case study of nearly forty years of Direct Action missions. McRaven's thesis develops a theory that explains why special operations succeed; they achieve *relative superiority* by adhering to the six principles of special operations. Special operations forces (SOF) are able to achieve relative superiority over the enemy by preparing a simple plan, which is carefully concealed, repeatedly and realistically rehearsed, and executed with surprise, speed, and purpose.[63] The following diagram presents the six principles of Special Operations:

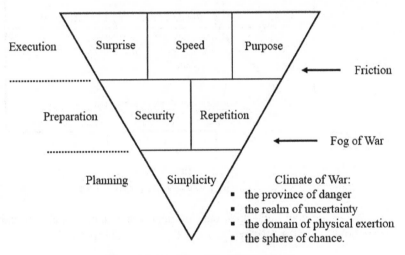

Figure 4-6. Principles of Special Operations.

This theory is important because successful special operations defy conventional wisdom. Central to the theory of special operations is the Clausewitzian concept of *relative superiority*. Admiral McRaven writes,

Relative superiority is a concept crucial to special operations; it is a condition that exists when an attacking force, generally smaller, gains a decisive advantage over a larger or well-defended enemy. Relative superiority is achieved at the pivotal moment in an engagement. If relative superiority is lost, it is difficult to regain. To achieve relative superiority, the practitioner of special operations must take account of the principles in the three phases of an operation; planning, preparation, and execution.[64]

---

[63] McRaven, Spec Ops, 4-7.
[64] Ibid.

Once relative superiority is gained, it must be sustained in order to guarantee victory. The following diagram provides a visual demonstration of relative superiority (Figure 4-7).

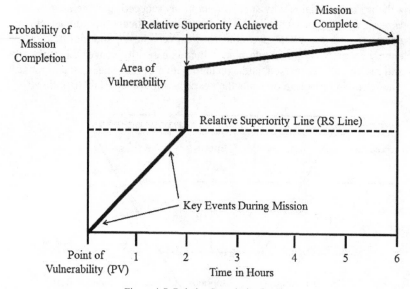

Figure 4-7. Relative Superiority Graph.

As we continue to build upon our doctrinal foundation, a brief look into the six principles of special operations will prove most beneficial.

Simplicity – a principle of war and of planning, simplicity is the most crucial and yet often the most underrated principle with which Special Operations Forces should comply.[65] Simplicity buttresses the other five principles. Often, plans that are too rigid run the risk of being destroyed by chance events. For example, Operation Eagle Claw, the failed hostage rescue mission in Iran, was one of the most difficult operations of its size ever planned and undertaken. There was simply no margin for error. How does one make a plan simple? McRaven gives us three elements of simplicity which are critical to success: (1) limiting the number of objectives; (2) good intelligence; and (3) innovation.[66]

---

[65] See Chapter 7 for the principles of planning.
[66] McRaven, Spec Ops, 12.

Security – also a principle of war, prevents the enemy from gaining an advantage through foreknowledge of a planned attack. However, McRaven writes, "the nature of special operations is to attack a fortified position. It naturally follows, whether in war time or peace, that the enemy is 'prepared' for an attack. Therefore it is not so much the impending mission that must be concealed, but the timing and to a lesser degree the means of insertion."[67] Regarding the correlation between simplicity, security, and repetition, McRaven writes: "if a plan is complex it will require extraordinary security, and an overabundance of security hinders effective preparation."[68]

Repetition – McRaven tells us, "In the preparation phase, repetition, like routine, is indispensable in eliminating the barriers to success."[69] When the Air Force Task Group, involved in the Son Tay Raid, first attempted to fly the UH-1H in formation with the C-130, they found flying in such a tight formation so difficult that it was not within the capability of the average Army aviator. After hundreds of hours of flying the same profile, however, the tactics of drafting with the UH-1 were proven and could be applied in future plans. Further, McRaven writes, "Constant repetition, as manifested in training and rehearsals, is the link between the principle of simplicity in the planning phase and the principles of surprise and speed in the execution phase."[70]

Surprise – In addition to being a principle of war, surprise is a tactical tool. As Sun Tzu tells us, it's the ability to strike the enemy at a time or place, or in a manner, for which he is unprepared. Tactical surprise can cause the enemy to hesitate or misjudge a situation. But tactical surprise is fleeting. Leaders must exploit it before the enemy realizes what is happening.

Regarding surprise McRaven writes, "At the Belgian fortress of Eben Emael antiaircraft guns were positioned on top of the fort to prevent an airborne assault; North Vietnam had one of the densest air defense systems in the world; Benito Mussolini was guarded by 250 Italian soldiers, the POWs in Cabanatuan held by 225 Japanese; and the airport at Entebbe, Uganda was surrounded by 100 Ugandan soldiers with two battalions close by. The enemy, in each of these cases, was prepared to prevent an assault on their position and yet, surprise was achieved in all instances."[71] According to Clausewitz, the two factors that produce surprise are secrecy and speed.[72]

---

[67] McRaven, Spec Ops, 21.
[68] Ibid, 13.
[69] Ibid, 23.
[70] Ibid, 10.
[71] Ibid, 26.
[72] Clausewitz, On War, III, 9, 233.

Speed – In a manner of speaking, speed is security. And in special operations the concept of speed is simple: get to your objective as fast as possible. Any delay will expand your area of vulnerability and decrease your opportunity to achieve relative superiority. As Sir William Slim put it, "There is only one principle of war and that's this. Hit the other fellow, as quick as you can, and as hard as you can, where it hurts him the most, when he ain't looking."[73]

Purpose – Purpose is understanding and then executing the prime objective of the mission regardless of emerging obstacles or opportunities. First, the purpose must be clearly defined by the mission statement rescue the POWs, destroy the dry dock, sink the battleship, etc. This mission statement should be crafted to ensure that in the heat of battle (the execution phase), no matter what else happens, the individual soldier understands the primary objective.

Conclusion

Special Forces operations are unique in the US military, because they are employed throughout the three stages of the operational continuum; peacetime, conflict, and war. The goal of this chapter was to introduce the reader to the nine principle tasks that the Special Forces Regiment executes. Additionally, a situational awareness should have been gained to such complex subsets of warfare as UW, FID and COIN. Further, it is hoped that the student of war gain a working knowledge of the relevant theory of special operations together with its six principles. With this doctrinal foundation, the Special Forces tactician will be better prepared to lead in the planning and execution of any number of tasks which he may be privileged to be called on to perform.

---

[73] Slim, Defeat into Victory, 550-551.

Chapter 5 Leadership

"Wars may be fought with weapons, but they are won by men. It is the spirit of men who follow and of the man who leads that gains the victory." – Patton

According to Herodotus, the most hateful misfortune is for a wise man to have no influence. If leadership is to be defined in one word, then that word is "influence." Leaders inspire others to succeed. However, as Christopher Kolenda observes, "This concept hinges on the notion of influence. If by influence we mean to get someone to do what we want them to do, then we are left with the very significant problem of legitimizing coercion as an appropriate method of leadership."[1] So we must qualify our definition of leadership to be one that views influence as inspirational and not coercive. The US Army defines leadership as "the process of influencing people by providing *purpose*, *direction*, and *motivation* while operating to accomplish the mission and improving the organization."[2]

This is the definition of leadership. However, no book can reduce leadership to a set of learnable skills. In spite of the volumes written on the subject of leadership, precision in this field of study remains elusive. Nevertheless, we will attempt to frame a workable outline of what a leader is, and what a leader does. The focus of this chapter is leadership – the warrior's art. It will discuss the following:

- What Makes a Successful Special Forces Soldier? The Three Imperatives.
- The Twelve Leadership Traits.
- Situational Leadership.
- Officer / NCO Professional Relationship.
- The Eleven Principles of Leadership.

What Makes a Successful Special Forces Soldier?

"A man must be big enough to admit his mistakes, smart enough to profit from them, and strong enough to correct them." – John Maxwell

Leadership begins with character. So before we move to discuss leadership any further, we pause to look at what makes a successful SF soldier; the foundational characteristics of every leader in the Regiment. To begin with, the desired character attributes of every Special Forces soldier include: professionalism, personal responsibility, adaptability, courage, team

---

[1] Kolenda, Leadership: The Warrior's Art, xviii.
[2] FM 6-22 Leadership, 1-2.

player, integrity, capability, and perseverance. Collectively these are referred to as the SOF attributes. What every Special Forces soldier should ask himself is: Am I living up to these attributes? So what exactly makes a successful SF soldier? I believe at least the following three imperatives:

1. He is Smart.
2. He is Strong.
3. He is Socially Astute.

In light of the Special Forces attributes, we now move to discuss these three imperatives.

1. A successful SF soldier is smart – that is, he understands basic Army doctrine (tactics, techniques, and procedures), all pertinent aspects of his own military occupational specialty (MOS), as well as the standard operating procedures (SOPs) of his Group, Company, and ODA. The point here is, a successful SF soldier places a high premium on the technical and tactical aspects of his job.

Additionally, there is a long-standing tradition of cross-training on an ODA. For example, the Weapons Sergeant trains the rest of the team on the recoiless rifle, while the Intelligence Sergeant instructs others on finger printing, etc. In short, the guys who succeed in Group know their jobs and want to grow intellectually. The following three SF attributes seem best to fall within this imperative: *professionalism, personal responsibility* and *adaptability* –

Professionalism – means behaving as a standard-bearer for the Regiment. It means having a professional image, to include a level of maturity and judgment mixed with confidence and humility. Professionalism means, not only forming sound opinions, and making one's own decisions, but standing behind those decisions, and following through with tasks with the best of our ability.

Additionally, professionalism means being reliable and consistent with good performance. One of the prevailing woes of late is a marked decrease in work ethics. It seems hard to find a good work ethic these days. Americans seemed to be infected with an entitlement attitude. However, professionalism is still placed at a high premium in any vocation.

Personal Responsibility – Being self-motivated and an autonomous self-starter; anticipates tasks and acts accordingly; takes accountability not only for his actions but for the actions of those under his charge.

Adaptability – arguably the most critical attribute after integrity, adaptability reflects a quality that a man exhibits through critical thinking, a comfort with ambiguity and uncertainty, and a willingness to accept prudent risk, while rapidly adjusting and continuously assessing a situation. According to John Boyd, "Adaptability is the power to adjust or change in order to cope with new or unforeseen circumstances."[3] Being adaptable means accepting the fact that there are no prefabricated solutions for each and every problem. SF leaders adapt their thinking, their formations, and their employment techniques to the specific situations they face.[4]

To add a further dimension to this discussion, successful SF soldiers are smart because they have 'growth' mindsets over against 'fixed' mindsets. With the right mindset, we can stretch ourselves and benefit more from our mistakes (as well as the mistakes of others which we may readily use more as a means to grow rather than a way to jeopardize our reputation (See Figure 5-1.

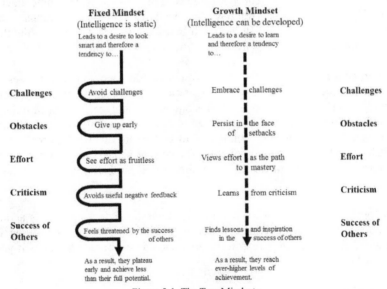

Figure 5-1. The Two Mindsets.

Just what are the two mindsets? A fixed mindset avoids challenges and obstacles because they call for a man to prove himself. A fixed mindset sees one's intelligence as something that can't change. That is, a man with a fixed mindset believes he can learn new things, but he does't believe he can

---

[3] Boyd, Patterns of Conflict, 125.
[4] ADRP 3-0, 2-13.

change how smart he is. Fixed mindsets see a challenge as a way that might make them look bad. For the fixed mindset person, "Every situation is evaluated: Will I succeed or fail? Will I look smart or dumb? Will I be accepted or rejected? Will I feel like a winner or loser?[5]

However, as Dweck observes, "The growth mindset is based on the belief that your basic qualities are things you can cultivate through your efforts. Although people may differ in every which way – in their initial talents and aptitudes, interests, or temperaments – everyone can change and grow through application and experience."[6] In other words, growth mindset people embrace a challenge as a way to grow as a man, because as our society teaches us, if mediocrity is your goal, you'll reach it every time.

2. *A successful SF soldier is strong* – apart from the obvious, that is, physical strength, he is morally strong, meaning he does the hard right over the easy wrong. Successful SF soldiers have character. Character is the real man underneath all the veneer. Character is made up of one's temperament, upbringing, education, training, as well as beliefs, traditions, and motivations. The following four attributes seem best to fall within this imperative: *courage, integrity, capability,* and *perseverance* –

Courage – means acting on your own convictions despite consequences. It is a willingness to sacrifice for a larger cause. And because courage is both physical and moral in scope, it means one is not paralyzed by fear of failure. In Sherman's estimation, true courage is a perfect sensibility of the measure of danger, and a mental willingness to endure it. Likewise, according to Patton, "All men are afraid in battle. The coward is the one who lets his fear overcome his sense of duty."[7] Therefore, there can be no courage without fear.

Integrity – means being trustworthy and honest. Having integrity is acting with honor and unwavering adherence to ethical standards. According to Sam Storms, "The only reason integrity should be a burden to you is if you enjoy being dishonest."[8]

Capability – means maintaining physical fitness, to include strength and agility, as well as having an operational knowledge which enables one to plan and communicate effectively.

---

[5] Dweck, Mindset: The New Psychology of Success, 6-7.
[6] Ibid, 6.
[7] Connelly, On War and Leadership, 126.
[8] Storms, Pleasures Evermore, 236.

Perseverance – means working toward an end, having commitment to a purpose. Further, perseverance involves having a physical and mental resolve – a motivation which doesn't quit despite obstacles and failure (See the Two Mindsets.

The overwhelming majority of guys that have trouble in Group, have gotten into trouble morally. The successful SF soldier loves his God, his family, his Team, and his Country. And all of his actions are executed in light of truth. He lives out his life in duteous selfless service, with no thought of personal advancement or applause.

3. A successful SF soldier is socially astute – another pertinent field of discussion for us is that of social navigation, namely a man's temperament. Temperament is the combination of inherited traits which subconsciously affect our behavior. What's the purpose of understanding temperament types you might ask? To begin with, a basic knowledge of temperaments helps us better understand ourselves and others. As far as temperament goes, there are simply different types of people out there, and an understanding of these types will assist us to not only navigate socially but will make us a more effective leader. For as S.L.A. Marshall observed, "The art of leading, is the art of dealing with humanity" (See Figure 5-2.

Choleric	Sanguine
(Task-oriented extrovert)	(People-oriented extrovert)
Ambitious leader-like. Passionate. Task Driven. Strong-willed. Can be dictatorial or tyrannical. Can be "my way or the highway" type person.	*Socialable pleasure seeker.* Charismatic. Creative-Daydreamer. Prefer to do things as a group. Flighty: may have trouble following through on tasks.
Melancholic	**Phlegmatic**
(Task-oriented introvert)	(People-oriented introvert)
Deep thinker. Cautious Independent Prefer to do things alone. Prefer to Avoid attention. Tend to procrastinate and plan in excess.	*Relaxed and quiet.* Diplomatic. Steady and faithful. Passive-aggressive. Fear change. May appear to be lazy.

Figure 5-2. Four Traditional Temperaments.

The point of defining temperaments is not only informative but I believe an understanding of them helps to explain the why we do what we do. These four temperaments or 'humors' are rather ancient. They were first devised by Hippocrates of Greece (460-370 BC).[9] The Hippocratic Oath guy. I should also state that there are other behavior theories out there; anything from Freud to Myers-Briggs. However, I consider the traditional theory the best and easiest to understand. It also lends itself well for self-improvement.

Generally speaking, the top two types (looking at the diagram) are the Type As, or the 'extraverts' as Jung would have it. And the Type Bs at the bottom are the introverts. What I've learned is that it takes all types on the ODA. Generally speaking, you have a good mix of types on any Team, some outgoing and more talkative, and some more quiet and reserved. Generally speaking the quieter and reserved guys, that is the melancholies and phlegmatics, are generally perceived to be not team players. This is because they don't speak their minds as much, whereas the choleric or sanguine guy can rarely shut up.

Having said that, some melancholies (task oriented introverts) and phlegmatics (people oriented introverts) are more of the Type B minus guys. That is, they are simply too quiet and too reserved and have to be brought out of their shell a bit. Many of these Type B guys are thinking, "Well, everything is getting done as it's supposed to, I don't want to seem pushy. I'll just wait until someone calls on me to do something. Until then I'll support what's going on." And that's just it. This is the guy who does everything in his mind. He just appears to be lazy, when in reality he is mentally active. Often these are the more intelligent guys on the Team.

On the other hand, there are Type A plus guys. Normally, they have problems fitting in as well. These are the know-it-alls. These are the guys who not only get ulcers but give them to others. They are impatient with others who fail to share their drive and energy. They are the guys that are too outgoing. They pride themselves on being brutally and sarcastically frank. For example, a man who is choleric would be advised to remind himself of regularly getting feedback, if time and the situation permits. This may mitigate any dictatorial leanings on the choleric leader's part.

The SF attribute which falls within this imperative best is *team player.*

Team Player – means possessing the ability to work on a team for a greater purpose than oneself. The attribute of team player means being dependable

---

[9] What is most interesting is that Hippocrates, the father of Western medicine, believed that bodily fluids regulated a person's temperament. He postulated that an excess or deficiency of any of four distinct bodily fluids in a person - known as humors - directly influences their temperament and health.

and loyal. It means being a man who works selflessly with a sense of duty, and respects others and recognizes diversity.

The point being made here is, I find that a good understanding of temperaments brings out your own best performance. Besides, successful SF soldiers are what we call 'plug and plays,' that is, they can fit in all environments and make things work. A good introspective question to ask yourself is: The longer I am at a job, do things improve or get worse? If they get worse, why? Further, when we look back at these attributes as a whole, we are reminded of the fact that without this foundation, one may never hope to be an effective leader in any unit let alone the Special Forces Regiment.

The Twelve Leadership Traits

"Build me a son, O Lord, who will be strong enough to know when he is weak, and brave enough to face himself when he is afraid, one who be proud and unbending in honest defeat, and humble and gentle in victory." – MacArthur.

Having discussed the common attributes each Special Forces soldier is to possess, we move on to consider what a leader is. A leader is any one who by virtue of assumed role or assigned responsibility inspires and influences people to accomplish goals. SF Leaders motivate people both inside and outside the chain of command to pursue actions, focus thinking, and shape decisions for the greater good of the Regiment, the Army, and the Nation. In this sense, everyman in Special Forces is a leader – from the junior Engineer Sergeant on an ODA to the commanding general of the Regiment.

General Patton once observed, "Leadership is the thing that wins battles. I have it, but I can't define it." As we seek to define leadership, we move to discuss the particulars of a leader's constitution – his mental, volitional, and emotional foundation. What follows is a consideration of what amounts to be widely held as the chief virtues or traits of a leader, irrespective of nation or time period. Further, these traits have been subdivided into the three categories of purpose, direction, and motivation – the leader's *raison d'etre*.

Mind (Purpose) *Smart* – regarding the mind, we mean the seat of cognition, from which the following six intellectual traits are considered to be foremost: *intellect, imagination, judgment, initiative, decisiveness,* and *flexibility.*

1. Intellect (Capability – This is the defining trait of a successful leader. A man may make up for what he lacks in intellectual capacity by strength and courage, but not if he's to be an effective leader. A good leader must possess domain knowledge, that is, thoroughly grasp all the aspects of his profession. A high level of competency commands respect. He must understand what must be done, and how it is to be done. Leaders give us purpose. Purpose gives subordinates the reason to act in order to achieve a desired outcome. Leaders get us pointed in the right direction and get us moving. Further, a leader is a planner. When a leader plans, he must have a definite purpose in view and be readily able to communicate it to others. Further, a leader must understand his followers: their capabilities, strengths, weaknesses, and needs.

For instance, MacArthur was a brilliant strategist, whose commanding intellect and foresight arguably remain unparalleled. What made MacArthur a superb leader was his ability to think critically, take in the big picture, intellectualize an operational design, anticipate potential contingencies, and then direct his approach to a decisive result. Additionally, a leader doesn't have to know everything. In fact, it's especially commendable when a leader admits he doesn't. For example, the visionary OSS leader Wlliam Donovan, had the wisdom to surround himself with excellent subordinate leaders.

2. *Imagination* – While knowledge and good character are imperative, by themselves they are not enough without application. Imagination may be defined as applicatory knowledge. It is fleshing out an idea, while understanding the ramifications, as well as foreseeing the potential affects involved to the action that will follow. A leader is not effective unless he can apply knowledge. Additionally, what a leader does is directly related to the influence he has on his men and what must be accomplished. Innovative leaders prevent complacency by finding new ways to challenge subordinates with forward-looking approaches and ideas.

For example, Dick Meadows, one of the greatest warriors in Special Forces was an exceptional leader who had a mind for actively finding new ways to improve old tactics. Further, to be innovators, leaders learn to rely on intuition, experience, knowledge, and input from subordinates. Innovative leaders reinforce team building by making everybody responsible for, and stakeholders in, the innovation process.

3. *Judgment* – Judgment is complementary to decisiveness. As John Gardner observes,"Judgment is the ability to combine hard data, questionable data and intuitive guesses to arrive at a conclusion that events prove to be correct."[10] That is, a leader considers potential second and third order of effects. Judgment is a critical part of problem solving and decision making.[11] Additionally, good judgment includes the ability to size up subordinates, peers, and the enemy for strengths, weaknesses, and to create

---

[10] Gardner, On Leadership, 49.
[11] A further dimension to decision making (analytical and intuitive) will be discussed in chapter 6.

appropriate solutions and action. Judgment involves having skills with people (socially astute. Leaders acquire sound judgment skills through trial and error and by watching the experiences of others.

A method of expanding experience is self-development through reading biographies and autobiographies of the notable warriors of history; to learn from their successes and failures. As noted earlier, the most instructive method of learning, is to recall the catastrophes of others. Thus, the histories of successful people offer ageless insights, wisdom, and methods that might be adaptable to the current environment or situation.

4. Initiative – This quality of a leader demonstrates a willingness to get things done. It is taking ownership for a situation, and often, making decisions in the absence of direction from superiors. Initiative requires confidence in one's abilities, and is reciprocal to intellect and imagination. If a leader cannot mentally grasp a situation and consider its potential outcomes, he won't look for or figure out a better or more efficient way to do something. Further, confident and initiative based leaders inspire confidence in others and encourage them to take initiative.

Charles Martin observes, "A man who lacks initiative and the sense of responsibility can plod along in the beaten path marked out for him by others, and keep in the ruts of time-warn customs. He hesitates to understand anything which involves new and untold issues. He is unwilling to assume responsibility."[12] Martin goes on to relate, "A man with initiative who has been told to take a message to the opposite bank of a river, and who finds a bridge over which he expected to cross to be missing, will find some other means of getting across; but he will deliver the message."[13]

5. Decisiveness – All leaders have to be able to make decisions. This trait requires that one know when to make a decision and when to wait for a situation to develop further. Decisiveness requires judgment and initiative. Decisiveness is one's ability to make a decision within a reasonable amount of time. Indecisive leaders are the scourge of any unit.

An exceptional example for both initiative and decisiveness may be witnessed by the actions of Major General Warren at Little Round Top at the Battle of Gettysburg. On the second day of the Battle of Gettysburg, July 2, 1863, as Longstreet's attack developed, Warren, reaching Little Round Top and finding it unoccupied, recognized the immense tactical importance of the undefended position (the left flank of the Union Army, and directed, on his own initiative, the brigade of Colonel Strong Vincent to occupy it just minutes before it was attacked.

---

[12] Martin, Winning and Wearing Shoulder Straps, 29.
[13] Ibid, 29.

6. *Flexibility* (Adaptability) – This trait tends to highlight the leader's constitution, in that its presence will not only display the maintenance of one's composure in an ambiguous and austere environment but will result in an adjustment of one's thoughts and actions to meet developing situations as well. Donald Vandergriff observes, decision-making is central to the United States Army leader. An Army leader who is incapable of making a timely decision or uses poor judgment in his choices is a leader who puts his mission and soldiers in jeopardy.[14]

Looking at another example from the Battle of Gettysburg, a great example of a leader's flexibility may be seen in Colonel Chamberlain's decision on 3 July, 1863. Defending the Union left flank, out of ammunition, and facing another enemy advance, Chamberlain gave the order for the 20th Maine to conduct a bayonet charge against Hood's Alabama and Texas Regiments. The charge was successful and prevented the left flank of the Union Army from being overrun and the Battle of Gettysburg to be lost.

Will (Direction) *Strong* – a man's will directs his activity and motivation supplies the will to do what is necessary to accomplish a mission.[15] It is arguably a leader's center of gravity. "Will is the chemistry of battle."[16] Further, the will of the leader takes on a collective identity and becomes the will of the unit. In this regard, when Clausewitz states, "War is an act of violence to compel our opponent to fulfill our will," he means the will of the leader; for it's against the will of the enemy commander, that we as leaders pit our will. Regarding the will, the following three traits are deemed foremost: *determination, courage* and *perseverance.*

7. *Determination* – A leader provides direction, prioritizes tasks, assigns responsibility and ensures subordinates understand the standard. A leader must be fully committed to his mission and unit goals despite obstacles. Determination relies upon patience and perseverance. It enables leaders to navigate a pathway to success through the wreckage of failed plans and unforeseen catastrophes.

One famous example of how a leader's will saved an entire unit is the Lost Battalion of World War I. A battalion of the 77th Infantry Division consisting of nine companies commanded by Major Charles Whittlesey became encircled by German forces. Having one day's ration per man, the Lost Battalion with 700 men, doggedly held their ground for six days, dispite relentless artillery, grenade and machinegun barrages, appalling

---

[14] Vandergriff, How to Create Adaptive Leaders Handbook, 7.
[15] FM 6-22 Leadership, 1-2.
[16] Malone, Small Unit Leadership: A Commonsense Approach, 29.

casualties, lack of water, and finally no ammunition. Called upon to surrender on numerous occasions, the indomitable Major Whittlesey refused, and on October 7, 1918, an Allied relief force broke through.[17]

8. Courage – As we have seen, courage is acting on one's own convictions despite the consequences, and involves both a physical and moral dimension. Physical courage requires overcoming fears of bodily harm and doing one's duty. Courage involves taking risks in combat in spite of the fear of wounds or even death. According to Marshal de Saxe, courage is the first of all qualities in a leader, and in Clausewitz's estimation, because war is the province of danger, "Courage above all things is the first quality of a warrior."

Famous examples of exemporary courage abound. One is that of Sergeant York. In France during World War I, York defended his squad against overwhelming German machinegun fire. Undaunted, with expert marksmanship, York calmly and systematically eliminated twenty-five enemy threats, putting thirty-five German machineguns out of action. He then proceeded with his seven men, to march 132 German prisoners back to the American lines. Who can match an inspired marksman who believes that God is with him?

Courage also involves risk taking. Regarding the lives of one's men, courage and audacity should be tempered with prudence. Dave Grossman observes, "The responsibilities of a combat leader represent a remarkable paradox. To be truly good at what he does, he must love his men and be bonded to them with powerful links of mutual responsibility and affection. And then he must ultimately be willing to give the orders that may kill them."[18]

Additionally, courage involves taking responsibility, not only for your own mistakes, but also for the failures of the unit you lead. Courage is being straight with people and ascertive when necessary, especially your boss. Every leader wants to please his commanding officer, but courage means disagreeing with him when he is wrong. To add a further dimension, moral courage is the willingness to stand firm on values, principles, and convictions. It enables all leaders to stand up for what they believe is right, regardless of the consequences. Leaders, who take full responsibility for their decisions and actions, even when things go wrong, display moral courage.

---

[17] Infantry in Battle, 407-411. Seven men, including Major Whittlesey, were awarded the Congressional Medal of Honor for their actions.
[18] Dave Grossman, On Killing, 89.

*9. **Perseverance (Energy)*** – As we've said, perseverance may best be understood as a physical and mental resolve – a motivation which doesn't quit despite obstacles and failure. A leader's energy is his drive that sustains him as he executes his duty. Because perseverance preserves the other traits by sustaining emotional health and conceptual abilities under prolonged stress, not to mention the fact that leaders represent their unit as well as the Army and Nation, a high level of physical fitness should always be maintained.

A great example of perseverance is the leadership of Field Marshal Arthur Wellesley, the Duke of Wellington. His distinguished career of leading men in combat transversed thirty battlefields, culminating in his defeat of who was arguably history's ablest general – Napoleon. John Keegan observes, Wellington "risked indeed a mental and emotional overload which commonly brought lesser commanders to breakdown."[19]

Emotion (Motivation) *Socially Astute* – That aspect of a leader which inspires others to follow him is the emotive faculty. Regarding a leader's emotional foundation, the following three traits are deemed foremost: *tenacity, self-control, and presence.*

*10. **Tenacity (Resilience)*** – Tenacity is communicable perseverance. This positive emotional attribute shows a leader's tendency to recover quickly from operational setbacks and failures, as well as personal injury and stress, while remaining mission focused. Tenacity is not having the strength to go on; it's going on when you don't have the strength. It is going on because of the mission and your men. What has made the great leaders of the past 'great' was what Pete Blaber referred to as the *mission, men, and me* concept. A historical caricature of this attribute can be seen by B Company, 24th Regiment of Foot's stalwart defense of Roark's Drift on 19 January, 1879. Following the destruction of the bulk of the British 24th Regiment of Foot at Isandlwana a day prior, Lieutenants Chard and Bromhead with 120 men faced a force of some 10,000 Zulus and using superior tactics, weaponry, but above all tenacity, successfully avoided annihilation.

A more recent example is that of Master Sergeant Roy Benavidez, whose tenacious action in the face of insurmountable odds at Loc Ninh saved the lives of eight of his comrades. And who could forget the indomitable spirit of 7th Group's ODA-726 at Nam Dong, who, together with a CIDG force of some 400 indigenous soldiers, doggedly defended their border camp against a motivated and determined battalion of Viet Cong, and likewise avoided annihilation.

---

[19] Keegan, The Mask of Command, 162.

11. Self-Control – is essential in exercising leadership. Self-control is the power of self-restraint. Its corollaries are military bearing, tact and especially humility and selfless service. Self-control may be understood as a leader's center of gravity (COG. A man who would wisely govern others must be able to govern himself. Charles Martin observes, a leader "who cannot control his emotions of anger, excitement, etc., or who is swayed by his impulses of vanity, egotism, ambition, or personal prejudices, cannot obtain the best results from others, nor give his own best service to the cause."[20] In short, a leader without self-control loses the confidence of those he leads.

Self-control is not mere Stoic behavioral maintenance which is apathetic, it's the avoidance of emotional excess. Leadership is all about balance. In a practical sense, self-control is controlling your voice and gestures so that extremes of emotion don't show in your actions, except at times you carefully choose.[21] Something every successful leader comes to understand is, you don't get worked up about what you can't control. An enduring insight regarding this comes to us from Viktor Frankl: forces beyond our control can take everything away from us accept our freedom to choose the manner in which we will respond to the situation.[22]

12. Presence – Presence is not just a matter of the leader showing up, it involves the image that the leader projects. Its essence is projecting a commanding presence and a professional image of authority. In short, presence is the manner in which a leader carries himself. For example, it was said that the commanding presence of Napoleon on the field of battle was worth 40,000 men. More than any other trait, the capacity to motivate people to action, is the essence of leadership. And for a leader to be effective, he must be self-motivated, as all Special Forces soldiers should be. And communication is the primary instrument.

Inspiring others requires effectively communicating with them. It means being out front and leading by example. It also involves moving to where duties are performed so the leader may have firsthand knowledge of the real conditions his men are facing. A good leader never asks his subordinates to do anything they wouldn't do themselves. Besides, there is no greater inspiration than leaders who routinely share in team hardships and dangers. Describing the manner in which a leader's presence inspires his men, Erwin Rommel observes, "All the young faces radiated joy, animation, and anticipation. Is there anything finer than marching against an enemy at the

---

[20] Martin, Winning and Wearing Shoulder Straps, 57.
[21] Malone, Small Unit Leadership: A Commonsense Approach, 37.
[22] See Viktor Frankl, Man's Search for Meaning.

head of such soldiers?"[23]

And when one thinks of presence as a leader's ability to rally a cause, one immediately thinks of Civil War General Jackson at the First Battle of Bull Run in 1861. As the thinning Confederate line collapsed, General Barnard Bee used Jackson's newly arrived brigade as an anchor. Pointing to Jackson, Bee shouted, "There stands Jackson like a stone wall! Rally behind the Virginians!" Jackson's presence rallied an entire army, which led to a Confederate victory.

Another critical component of presence is composure, that is, a leader's command over his own emotions. In Liddell Hart's estimation,

The moral equilibrium of the man is tremendously affected by an outward calmness on the part of the leader. The soldier's nerves, taut from anxiety of what lies ahead, will be soothed and healed if the leader sets an example of coolness. Bewildered by the noise and confusion of battle, the man feels instinctively that the situation cannot be so dangerous as it appears if he sees that his leader remains unaffected, that his orders are given clearly and deliberately, and that his tactics show decision and judgment...But if the leader reveals himself irresolute and confused, then, more even than if he shows personal fear, the infection spreads instantly to his men.[24]

Presence is a critical attribute that leaders need to understand, for it's the manner in which a leader projects self-confidence and certainty in the unit's ability to succeed in whatever it does. Part of Patton's instructions for his commanders included: "Your primary mission as a leader is to see with your own eyes and be seen by your troops while engaged in personal reconnaissance." Further, he stated, issuing an order is worth only about 10 percent. The remaining 90 percent consists in assuring proper and vigorous execution.[25]

Situational Leadership

The traits necessary in a leader are directly proportionate to the situation and the nature of those being led. Situational Leadership is based on the premise that there is not just one style of leadership. Traditionally, there are five styles: *directing, participating, delegating, transformational,* and *transactional.*[26]

The *directing style* is leader-centered. Leaders use this style to give detailed instructions to subordinates, without input, and then closely supervise its execution. how, when, and where they want a task performed.

---

[23] Rommel, Infantry Attacks, 4.
[24] Infantry in Battle: From Somalia to the Global War on Terrorism, 1.
[25] Connelly, On War and Leadership, 127.
[26] FM 22-100, 3-16.

This style is appropriate when there is inadequate time to explain everything, that is, in particular combat situations, or when working with inexperienced soldiers. The *participating style* centers on both the leader and the subordinates. Leaders actively ask for input, information, and recommendations, but make the final decision. This style is especially appropriate for leaders who have time for such consultations or who are dealing with experienced subordinates.

The *delegating style* involves giving subordinates the authority to solve problems on their own. This approach is used when leading mature and experienced subordinates. Leaders must still provide clear guidance and purpose. As always, the leader is ultimately responsible for what does or does not happen, but in the delegating leadership style, the leader holds subordinate leaders accountable for their actions. The following two leadership styles are developmental in nature: *transformational* and *transactional* styles.

The *transformational style* emphasizes individual growth (both professional and personal. For it to work, the leader must empower and motivate his subordinate(s. The transformational style allows you to take advantage of the skills and knowledge of experienced subordinates who may have better ideas on how to accomplish a mission. The last style, *Transactional*, is an effective way to motivate soldiers to work by offering rewards or threatening punishments. This approach is used in most service schools, and is only useful in attaining short-term goals. It should be used sparingly, as it has a tendency of creating an adverse leader-follower environment. In short, competent leaders assess the situation, task, and assess the people involved in order to arrive at a particular style to employ to meet the goal. The most effective leaders combine techniques from all of the five leadership styles to fit the situation.

Officer / NCO Professional Relationship

For an organization to excel, officers and non-commissioned officers (NCOs must understand the proper professional relationship. Commissioned officers are the only persons able to act as a commanding officer of a military unit. This is because officers derive their authority from the President of the United States. Under US law, officers are responsible for all of the men, equipment, and missions assigned to them. NCOs are placed in positions of authority, and have control or charge rather than command. In short, officers are in command and NCOs are in charge.

Officers give orders and NCOs enforce those orders, implementing them among the enlisted ranks, and carrying them out to the best of their ability. Additionally, NCOs are responsible for advising the officer on making the best decisions. NCOs must never loose sight of who is in command and never confuse being in charge with being in command. Similarly, officers must accept and respect the fact that NCOs are in charge of implementing orders and intent. NCOs who fail to understand this paradigm resist an officer trying to take command, interpreting it as trying to be in charge. Conversely, some officers try to take charge instead of commanding. Exceptional units are the ones who are lead by officers and NCOs who understand this professional relationship and work together to achieve decisive action. Finally, all leaders, both officers and NCOs would do well to remember Patton's leadership axiom: "Tell people what to do but not how to do it."

Principles of Leadership

"We herd sheep, drive cattle, we lead people. Lead me, follow me, or get out of my way." – Patton

The following eleven principles of leadership are basic guidelines for what a leader must do. They apply at all levels and epitomize the successful Special Forces leader:

1. Be technically and tactically proficient – Effective SF leaders are smart. They not only possess domain knowledge of their field of expertise and their own duties and responsibilities but they know those of their team as well. Your proficiency will earn the respect of your team. Additionally, SF leaders must understand how best to employ the equipment and weaponry of their team in order to achieve success.

2. Know yourself and seek self-improvement – An effective SF leader is strong. He evaluates his strengths and weaknesses in light of the Special Forces attributes. An accurate and clear understanding of yourself and a comprehension of group behavior will help you determine the best way to deal with any given situation. What you value exerts influence on your behavior so that it becomes your character.

3. Seek responsibility and take responsibility for your actions and decisions – Actively seek out challenging assignments for your professional development. Seeking responsibilities also means taking responsibility for your actions. You are responsible for all your unit does or fails to do. Be willing to accept justified and constructive criticism. As iron sharpens iron, so does a man sharpen the countenance of his friend.

4. Know your men and look out for their well-being – Leaders must know and understand those being led. When your men trust you, they will

233

willingly work to accomplish any mission. Successful SF leaders know their team and how they react to different situations. This knowledge can save lives. Knowledge of your team's personalities will enable you, as the leader, to decide how best to employ each man.

5. *Keep your men informed* – The members of your team expect to be kept informed, and when possible have the reasons behind the requirements and decisions explained to them. Your team will perform better and, if knowledgeable of the situation, can carry on without your personal supervision. Providing information inspires initiative.

6. *Set the example* – No aspect of leadership is more powerful. Set the standards for your team by personal example. The men of your team all watch your appearance, attitude, physical fitness and personal example. If your personal standards are high, then you can rightfully demand the same of your team. Your personal example affects the team more than any amount of instruction or form of discipline.

7. *Make sound and timely decisions* – Leaders must be able to reason under the most critical conditions. Rapidly estimate a situation and make a sound decision based on that estimation. There's no room for reluctance to make a decision. And MacArthur reminds us to "never give an order that can't be obeyed." Likewise, a team respects the leader who corrects mistakes immediately.

8. *Build a team* – An effective SF leader is socially astute, and understands that one must train your team with a purpose and emphasize the essential elements of teamwork and realism. SF leaders foster a team spirit that motivates team members to work with confidence and competence. Ensure your team members know their positions and responsibilities within the team framework.

9. *Ensure each task is understood, supervised, and accomplished* – Team members must know the standard. Communicate your instructions in a clear, concise manner, and allow your men a chance to ask questions. Check progress periodically to confirm the assigned task is properly accomplished. This allows your team to know you are concerned about mission accomplishment as well as them.

10. *Develop a sense of responsibility in your subordinates* – Show your team you are interested in their welfare by giving them the opportunity for professional development. Assigning tasks and delegating authority promotes mutual confidence and respect between the leader and the team. The key element of trust, the fundamental bedrock in the relationship between the leader and the led, is fostered in this way.[27]

11. Employ your team in accordance with its capabilities – Successful completion of a task depends upon how well you know your team's capabilities. Seek out challenging tasks for your team that they are not only prepared for, but have the ability to successfully complete the mission as well.

One of the strongest attributes of an effective leader is his ability to assess the circumstances correctly and then act appropriately, in any given situation. Memorizing templates and reciting doctrine cannot take the place of the individual's ability to think clearly, act decisively, and influence the fight at the decisive point. This ability is critical in accomplishing the mission, while taking care of our most precious resource: the soldier.[28]

Conclusion

The fundamental element of combat power is leadership. In Patton's estimation, "It may well be that the greatest leaders have possessed superior intellects, may have been thinkers; but this was not their dominant characteristic. They owed their success to indomitable wills and tremendous energy in execution and achieved their initial hold upon the hearts of their troops by acts of demonstrated valor."[29] Looking back at this chapter and evaluating our own leadership, how well do we stand up? Here are some investigative questions we may use to evaluate our own leadership:

1. Are you able to use the ideas of others?
2. Can you accept criticism of your decision(s) without taking offense?
3. Do you depend on the praise of others to keep you going?
4. Can you hold steady in the face of disapproval and even temporary loss of confidence?
5. The longer you lead, do things improve or get worse?
6. Can you anticipate how your words will be received?
7. Can you forgive? Do you nurse resentments?
8. Do you criticize or encourage?
9. Can you admit it when someone else's view is better?
10. Do you make excuses for your failures?

---

[27] Kolenda, Leadership: The Warrior's Art, xxii.
[28] Infantry in Battle 2005, 21.
[29] Blumenson, The Patton Papers. Vol. I, 817-818.

Chapter 6 Tactics

"In tactics, the most important thing is not whether you go left or right, but why you go left or right." – A. M. Gray

All Special Forces soldiers are tacticians. As tacticians our goal is to think and act faster than our opponent in order to achieve a decisive result. To begin we need to define tactics. This is one of the most used yet least understood words in our Army vocabulary. Tactics range from the methods we use to win engagements and battles to the approaches we use to sustain troops, control crowds, conduct stability operations or provide humanitarian aid.

Tactics are: (1) the employment of units in combat; and (2) the ordered arrangement and maneuver of units in relation to each other or to the enemy to utilize their full potential (FM 1-02). The purpose of this chapter is to lay a foundational understanding of tactics, and introduce several key tactical concepts and ideas, with a goal of achieving decisive results in battle. This chapter will discuss the following:

1. The Tactical Level of War.
2. The Art and Science of Tactics.
3. Mission Command.
4. Tactical Decision Making.
5. Tactical Success.
6. Decisive Action.
7. Offensive Operations.
8. Defensive Operations.

The Tactical Level of War – Tactics is the employment and ordered arrangement of maneuver units in relation to each other, which includes the use of firepower and maneuver. In this sense, tactics is the orchestration of men and weaponry in order to conduct a direct exchange of violence at the decisive moment and at the decisive point on the field of battle. Tactics answers the question of how best to employ men and weaponry. Further, tactics is the integration of different arms and the immediate exploitation of success to defeat the enemy, as well as the sustainment of forces during combat.

The tactical level of war is the level at which battles and engagements are planned and executed. A *battle* consists of a set of related engagements that last longer and involves larger forces than an engagement. And an *engagement* is a small, tactical conflict between opposing maneuver forces, which are usually conducted by lower echelon forces, i.e. at the brigade level and below. Engagements are typically short, and are executed in terms of minutes, hours, or days.[1] The strategic and operational levels provide the context for tactical operations. Without this context, tactical operations are reduced to a series of disconnected and unfocused actions. Combat at the tactical level of war is characterized by tough, brutal, and desperate engagements.

The Science and Art of Tactics – A leader cannot rely on a book to solve tactical problems. As tacticians, we must understand and master the art and science of tactics. This is imperative if we are ever going to attain our stated goal – *to think and act faster than our opponent in order to achieve decisive results.* As we delve into this subject, we first move to discuss the science of tactics, followed by the relationship between techniques and procedures, then the art of tactics.

The Science of Tactics – As we've observed, war is both an art and science. So is tactics. The science of tactics lies in the technical application of combat power. It comprises the sum total of all relevant tactical employments, techniques, and procedures (TTPs) that can be systematized. In order for the tactician to master the science of tactics, he must understand how *terrain, time, space, and weather* affect the fire and maneuver of his force.[2]

Without mastery of basic warfighting skills, artistry and creativity in their application are impossible.[3] However, as we've observed, war is an intensely human activity, therefore the solution to tactical problems cannot be reduced to a mere formula. While tactical doctrine may be derived by scientific methods, it should never become dogma, and its application should never be automatic but should always require careful adaptation and consideration.[4] Likewise, in tactics, lack of science, leads to chaos in art.[5]

Techniques and Procedures – The tactical formations we use today are less defined as distances between elements have increased, complicating command and control. War is more fluid as a result of technology. Increased weapons lethality, communications range, and tactical mobility cause us to disperse forces over greater distances.

---

[1] FM 3-0, 6-14.

[2] These physical and spatial constraints must be considered in order to maximize the effectiveness of the weapon systems that are being employed. Hence, the effects of fire must be exploited by maneuver.

[3] MCDP 1-3, Tactics, 4.

[4] MAJ Doughty, The Art and Science of Tactics, Parameters, Journal of the US Army War College, Vol VII, No 3, 43.

[5] Fuller, The Foundations of the Science of War, 32.

The ever improving capabilities of modern weaponry aside, the success of a tactician remains dependent upon a variety of factors which cannot be ordered or approached strictly as if war were a technical trade. Recalling that doctrine consists of fundamental principles, TTPs provide additional detail, and more specific guidance based on collective experience. *Techniques are flexible methods that suggest a way, not the only way to perform tasks, functions, or missions.* The success of any given technique will vary by situation. Thus it's incumbent upon tacticians to be judicial in their selection of techniques to employ.

On the other hand, procedures are standardized, detailed steps which prescribe how a given task is to be performed. For example, the 9-line medical evacuation (MEDEVAC is a procedure that is used to call for medical assistance. Likewise, the call for fire radio procedure is used for fire support. Procedures are usually based on specific types of equipment, and normally require a set procedural order of execution for success regardless of the situation. The point being made here is, as tactics includes the technical application of combat power, which consists of techniques and procedures for accomplishing specific tasks, we should however, avoid the oft repeated mistake of confusing a technique for a procedure or vice-versa.

The Art of Tactics – The art of tactics relies upon intuition, ability, and skill. Beyond mere knowledge of doctrine, the skill of the tactician is tempered through experience. The word 'tactic' comes to us from the Greek *taktike* – meaning 'art of arrangement.' The art of tactics lies in *how* we creatively apply military force in a given situation.

Tactics answers the question of how best to deploy and employ men and weaponry. Questions such as: When should we attack the enemy, and which form of maneuver should we use? Where should we ambush him? Or, how may we use speed and momentum to achieve a decisive advantage? Are answered by the art of tactics. There are three aspects to the art of tactics that define a competent tactician:

- Creative and flexible application of doctrine, principles, and tactics – each tactical problem is unique.
- Decision making under conditions of danger, uncertainty, physical exertion, and chance (climate of war) in a time-constrained environment; where time and space are the dominant factors.
- An understanding of the human dimension. Success depends as much on the human dimension of combat as it does numerical and technological superiority.

The tactician's experience, gained through various circumstances, serves as a type of matrix for his mastery of the art of tactics. The tactician relies on his decision making capability and knowledge of doctrine (Figure 6-1).

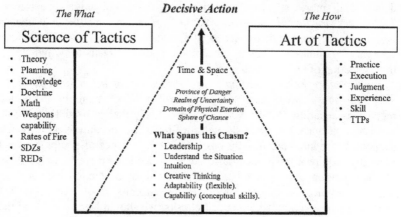

Figure 6-1. The Science and Art of Tactics.

As we've seen, doctrine is a codification of principles which guides the tactician in his tactical employment, giving him a frame of reference. However, because tactics are also an art, intuition, innovation, agility (both mental and physical), and initiative is required to achieve decisive results. These concepts we will have to develop further. At this point we move to discuss the Army's preferred command and control philosophy – mission command.

Mission Command – Mission command, is the warfighting function that supports commanders as they exercise authority and direction.[6] It's essential to the effective conduct of operations. Commanders use mission orders to assign tasks, allocate resources, and issue broad guidance.[7] *Mission orders are directives that emphasize to subordinates the results to be attained, not how they are to achieve them* (ADP 6-0). Mission command traces its roots back to the German concept of *Auftragstaktik*, which translates roughly to mission-type tactics.[8]

---

[6] For more on the warfighting functions (WFF) see Chapter 7.
[7] Mission command replaces the Army doctrinal term command and control. The former command and control warfighting function is now called the mission command WFF.
[8] Auftragstaktik held all German commissioned and noncommissioned officers duty-bound to do whatever the situation required, as they personally saw it. Understanding and achieving the

Mission orders seek to maximize individual initiative, while relying on lateral coordination between units and vertical coordination up and down the chain of command. Mission orders provide subordinates the maximum freedom of action in determining how to best accomplish their assigned missions.

The mission command philosophy helps commanders counter the uncertainty of operations by reducing the amount of certainty needed to act. This philosophy enables the rapid building of momentum by allowing the commander to see and understand the situation so quickly that subordinates can act before the enemy forces can react to the initial situation.[9] Commanders understand that some decisions must be made quickly and are better made at the point of action.

Mission command is based on mutual trust and a shared understanding and purpose between commanders and subordinates. It requires every soldier to be prepared to assume responsibility, maintain unity of effort, take prudent action, and act resourcefully within the commander's intent.[10] Mission command consists of:

- Commander's intent.
- Subordinate's initiative.
- Mission orders.
- Resource allocation.

The commander's intent provides the direction and guidance required to focus the activities on the achievement of the main objective. Commanders further set priorities, allocate resources, and influence the situation. In order for mission type orders to work, subordinates must have initiative. For a simple, workable plan, a clear, understandable order is important; but supervision to see that the will of the commander is executed is all-important.[11] Initiative is also the willingness to act in the absence of orders, when existing orders no longer fit the situation, or when unforeseen opportunities or threats arise.

The mission orders technique does not mean commanders do not supervise subordinates in execution. It means leaders should intervene during execution only to direct changes as necessary to the concept of operations. Leaders tell subordinates what to do, but not how to do it. The following discussion examines some of the variables a leader faces in

---

broader purpose of a task was the central idea behind this style of command. Commanders expected subordinates to act when opportunities arose.

[9] ADRP 3-90 Offense and Defense, 1-7.

[10] ADRP 6-0, 2-1.

[11] Infantry in Battle, 204.

expected and unexpected contact situations and discusses the actions-on-contact sequence.

Tactical Decision Making – To demonstrate how these concepts are worked out on the ground, we now move to discuss actions on enemy contact. As we do, these actions may be thought of in the broadest terms possible, so as to include the actions of a squad in contact to a brigade in battle. Actions on contact involve a series of combat actions, often conducted simultaneously. Leaders use the actions-on-contact process as a decision making technique when in contact with the enemy.

The four-step actions-on-contact process is not intended to generate a rigid, lockstep response to the enemy. Rather, the goal is to provide an orderly framework that enables the unit to survive the initial contact and then to apply sound decision-making and timely actions to complete the operation. Ideally, the unit will acquire the enemy before being sighted by him. It then can initiate physical contact on its own terms by executing a designated COA. [12]

If contact is expected, leaders should transition to the bounding overwatch movement technique. In a worst-case scenario, the unit may be engaged by a previously undetected (but expected) enemy element. If so, the element in contact conducts a *battle drill* for its own survival and then initiates actions on contact.[13] Unlike battle drills which are executed without a deliberate decision making process, action-on-contact is a tactical tool for leaders to use when making decisions in contact. Actions-on-contact is used when there is at least some time available to make a decision.

The logic of *assess, decide,* and *direct* underlies this decision making process. As the leader evaluates and develops the situation, he assesses what is currently happening and its relation to what should be happening. The actions-on-contact sequence has four steps:

1. Deploy and Report.
2. Evaluate and Develop the Situation.
3. Choose a Course of Action (COA).
4. Execute the COA.

Within this sequence, four critical actions are conducted. These are: *find, fix, finish,* and *follow-through.*

---

[12] There are eight forms of contact: visual, direct fire, indirect fire, obstacle, air, CBRN (chemical, biological, radiological, and nuclear), signal EW (electronic warfare), and civil/non-lethal.

[13] A battle drill is a collective action, rapidly executed, without applying a deliberate decision making process.

- *Find* – the unit must *find* the enemy and make contact.
- *Fix* – the unit *fixes* the enemy with direct and indirect fires.
- *Finish* – the unit must *finish* the enemy with fire and movement directed towards a vulnerable point in order to fight through to defeat, destroy, or capture the enemy.
- *Follow-through* – the unit must *follow-through* with consolidation, reorganization, and prepare to continue the mission or receive a new mission.[14]

1. Deploy and Report – This step begins with enemy contact. This contact may be expected or unexpected. During this step, subordinates fight through the contact with the appropriate battle drill. While this is occurring, leadership has the following primary tasks:

- Fix the enemy with direct and indirect fires.
- Isolate the enemy.
- Achieve fire superiority.
- Report to higher.
- Begin "fighting" for information—actively pursue and gather it.

First, the unit must *find* the enemy and make contact. The leader *finds* the enemy force and *fixes* it with direct and indirect fires. Then the leader must consider the factors of METT-TC, visualize a mental map which consists of where he is in relation to his enemy, and form a mental image of how he may proceed to employ his force.[15] He should ask, "What efforts will be decisive?" As the situation unfolds, multiple solutions to his tactical problem will present themselves. The leader sorts through potential solutions, and based on what he determines the enemy is trying to do, decides on a particular course of action.

Thus, after seeing only a few pieces of the puzzle, skilled tacticians have the ability to fill in the rest of the picture correctly. This skill, often called 'pattern recognition,' is the ability to understand the true significance and dynamics of a situation with limited information. During the troop leading procedure (TLP), leaders develop a vision of how their operation will unfold.[16] Part of this process involves the leader anticipating where he expects the unit to make contact. This enables him to think through possible decisions in advance.

If the leader expects contact, he will have already deployed his unit by transitioning from tactical movement to maneuver. Ideally, the

---

[14] FM 3-21.8, 1-35 – 1-36.
[15] For METT-TC see Chapter 6 – The Operations Process.
[16] For TLP see Chapter 8 – The Principles of Planning.

overwatching element will make visual contact first. Because the unit is deployed, it will likely be able to establish contact on its own terms. If the contact occurs as expected, the leader goes through the procedure making decisions as anticipated and minor adjustments as required.

Regardless of how thorough the leader's visualization, there will always be cases in which the unit makes unexpected contact with the enemy. In this case, it is essential that the unit and its leader take actions to quickly and decisively take back the initiative.

2. Evaluate and Develop the Situation – This step begins with the leader evaluating and developing the situation. The leader quickly gathers the information he needs to make a decision on his course of action. He does this through either personal reconnaissance or reports from subordinates. At a minimum, the leader needs to confirm the friendly situation and determine the enemy situation using the SALUTE format (size, activity, location, unit, time, and equipment), and enemy capabilities (defend, reinforce, attack, withdraw, and delay). During this analysis, the leader should look for an enemy vulnerability to exploit.

Achieve a decision – The objective of tactics is to achieve decisive results in battle. Indecisive leaders waste lives and effort. To be decisive, battles and engagements must lead to measurable results. They should lead to achieving operational and strategic goals. The leader's first step toward achieving a decision in battle begins with the estimate process. This process entails fighting to gain a clear understanding of the tactical situation one has just encountered. In a meeting engagement – the sudden collision of opposing forces (planned or unplanned) – the leader must develop in his mind a clear picture of what is happening, how it got that way, and how it might further develop. This is why maintaining situational awareness (SA) is imperative.

Regarding decisions in battle, there may be time to analyze situations deliberately to consider multiple options. Comparing several options and selecting the best one is known as analytical decision making. *Analytical decision making* is an approach used to analyze a dilemma and determine the best course of action to implement. Analytical decision making is time intensive and is therefore less effective for time sensitive decisions.

Additionally, it requires complete information to produce best results.[17] Thus, when time permits, a leader should make the most of every opportunity to use this approach. However, once the battle has been joined, the leader finds time is short, and the need for speed paramount. In some cases, speeding up the analytical decision making process may be sufficient.

---

[17] Analytical decision making is normally the approach taken in operational planning like the military deliberate decision making process (MDMP).

However, in most cases intuitive decision making is needed to generate and maintain tempo.[18] *Intuitive decision making* is a decision making process which relies on intuition, judgment, and experience to recognize the key elements of a particular problem in order to arrive at an appropriate timely decision. Tactics is not a thing, but a mental process, and the goal is to determine and implement the first solution that could result in success. Often, these are called 70 percent solutions. This type of decision making relies on a leader's intuitive ability to recognize the key elements of a particular problem and arrive at the proper decision without having to compare multiple options.

Intuition is not some mysterious quality. It's a developed skill, firmly grounded in experience, and one that can be further developed through education and practice. The true test of the solution to any military problem is not whether it uses the specific tactics, techniques, or procedures contained in manuals but whether the tactics, techniques, and procedures used were appropriate to the situation (See Figure 6-2.[19]

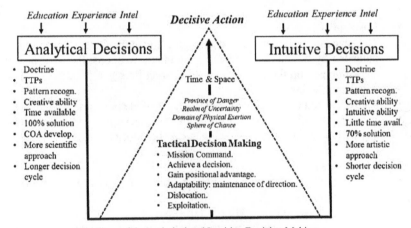

Figure 6-2. Analytical and Intuitive Decision Making.

Gain positional advantage – Once the enemy force is fixed in place, the leader must decide on a particular enemy vulnerability to target, and maneuver available forces to gain a position of advantage.[20] Maneuver is the employment of forces in the operational area through movement in

---

[18] MCDP 1-3 Tactics, 26.
[19] ADRP 3-90 Offense and Defense, 1-8.
[20] The enemy is fixed when his movement is stopped, his weapons are suppressed, and his ability to effectively respond is disrupted.

combination with fires to achieve a position of advantage in respect to the enemy (JP 3-0).

To gain positional advantage, where the enemy is in a position of disadvantage, the leader maneuvers onto the enemy force, generating the effects of overwhelming combat power against the enemy at the decisive point using the characteristics of the offense: surprise, concentration, audacity, and tempo. Liddell Hart observes, "Maneuver is a *collective tactical ju-jitsu* which is essentially based on the indirect approach."[21] It is characterized by moving faster than the enemy to defeat him through superior tempo. Thus, in maneuver, speed is a weapon. We employ speed and use time to create tempo. Tempo is not merely a matter of acting fastest or at the earliest opportunity. It is also a matter of timing – acting at the right time.[22]

As part of developing the situation, the leader seeks a *position of advantage* to maneuver his force. During this process, the leader considers the following:

- Mutually supporting enemy positions.
- Obstacles.
- The size of the enemy force engaging the unit. (Enemy strength is indicated by the number of enemy automatic weapons, the presence of any vehicles, and the employment of indirect fires.)
- A vulnerable flank to the position.
- A covered and concealed route to the flank of the position.
- If after his initial evaluation the leader still lacks information, he may attempt one or all of the following to get the information he needs:
- Reposition subordinate(s) or a subordinate unit.
- Reconnaissance by fire.
- Request information from adjacent units or from the controlling headquarters.

For tactical success, leaders must generate combat power and concentrate its destructive power at enemy critical vulnerabilities. This means striking against the enemy's weakness (rather than his strength) and at a time when the enemy is not prepared. The Expanding Torrent theory of Liddell Hart draws an analogy between maneuver and flowing water. He observes:

If we watch a torrent bearing down on each successive bank or earthen dam in its path, we see that it first beats against the obstacle, feeling and testing it on all its points. Eventually it finds a small crack at some point. Through this crack pour the

---

[21] Hart, *Strategy*, 29.
[22] MCDP 1-3 *Tactics*, 64.

first driblets of water and rush straight on…Thus nature's forces carry out the ideal attack, automatically maintaining the speed, the breadth, and the continuity of the attack.[23]

Seeking the enemy's vulnerabilities means striking with our strength against his weakness. This is where we can often cause the greatest damage at the lowest cost to ourselves. This often means avoiding his front, where his attention is focused, and striking his flanks and rear, where he does not expect us. This concept, known as the indirect approach, may entail using fire and maneuver to exploit a vulnerable flank, or a gap in the enemy's field of fire so we can cut off his line of communications (LOC and route of escape.[24]

To enable us to gain positional advantage, we use our forward elements to pull us through the gaps, while avoiding the surfaces. This concept, known as reconnaissance pull, enables us to avoid the enemy strength (surfaces while exploiting his vulnerabilities (gaps. Once we have developed an understanding of the situation and have determined enemy critical vulnerabilities to attack, we try to shape the situation to our advantage.

Leaders look for an enemy's vulnerable flank, a gap in his line, or lulls in his fire. When leaders cannot find a weakness, they create one with suppressive fire and the shock effect by suddenly coming from an unexpected direction.

Before attempting to maneuver, leaders must establish a base of fire. A base of fire is placed on an enemy force or position to reduce or eliminate the enemy's ability to interfere with friendly maneuver elements. And in this way, fires are used to create the conditions which support maneuver. Our goal in this stage of the combat sequence is to *isolate* the enemy force. According to FM 3-21.8, "Isolate" means cutting the adversary off from the functions necessary to be effective. Isolation has both an external aspect of cutting off outside support and information, and an internal aspect of cutting off mutual support. Isolating the adversary also includes precluding any break in contact.[25]

3. Choose a Course of Action (COA) – After developing the situation, the leader determines what action his unit must take to successfully conclude

---

[23] Lind, Maneuver Warfare, 9.

[24] *Manoeuvre sur les derrière* (move onto the rear) was a Napoleonic tactic employed to cut off the enemy's lines of communication (LOC) and escape route. This was executed when Napoleon's advance guard would first fix the enemy's position. Next, a maneuver element would rapidly gain positional advantage astride the enemy's LOC. This maneuver was then finished with a bold strike to the enemy's flank and rear. This maneuver won Napoleon countless victories.

[25] FM 3-21.8, 1-37.

the engagement. The leader then determines if the chosen task is consistent with the original COA. If it still applies, he continues the mission. If it is not consistent, he issues a FRAGO modifying the original COA. If the leader is unsure, he continues to develop the situation and seeks guidance from higher.

The key to reaching a decisive result in battle is the identification of enemy critical vulnerabilities. The leader, based on his initial estimate and his situational awareness, visualizes how to focus his unit's combat power and overwhelm the enemy at a decisive point. Thus, the objective for maneuver is usually aimed at a center of gravity (COG) or decisive point.

A *decisive point* is a geographic place, specific key event, critical factor, or function that, when acted upon, allows leaders to gain a marked advantage over an enemy or contribute materially to achieving success. The decisive point might orient on terrain, enemy, time, or a combination of these. It might be where or how, or from where, the unit will mass the effects of combat power against the enemy. Or it might be the event or action that will ultimately and irreversibly lead to the unit achieving its purpose.[26]

For example, during an ambush the decisive point may occur at initiation of the ambush when overwhelming coordinated firepower is achieved. Another example could be when a unit conducting a raid achieves relative superiority at a critical place and time. And the center of gravity (COG) is the source of power that provides moral or physical strength, freedom of action, or will to act (ADRP 1-02). As William Lind observes, a center of gravity is "a hinge in the enemy's system which, if shattered, will bring it down"[27] The enemy's COG may also be our chosen decisive point. The topographical key of a battlefield is not always the tactical key.

The decisive point of a battlefield is a point in time and space which combines strategic with topographical advantages. "It is almost always easy to determine the decisive point on the field of battle, but not so with the decisive moment; and it is precisely here that genius and experience are everything, and mere theory of little value."[28]

The leader develops his entire COA from the decisive point. Designating a decisive point is critical to the leader's vision of how he will use combat power to achieve the purpose, how he will task organize his unit and how his shaping operations will support the decisive operation, and how the decisive operation will accomplish the unit's purpose. The leader anticipates any requirements to shift the decisive operation or main effort during the offense to press the fight and keep the enemy off balance.

---

[26] FM 3-21.10, 2-41.
[27] As quoted in Maneuver Warfare: An Anthology, 9.
[28] Jomini, The Art of War, 304.

While the unit deploys, the leader evaluates and develops the situation. The goal of these actions is to create conditions, which provide for the successful execution of the decisive action. The leader gathers as much information as possible, either visually or, more often, through reports from elements in contact. In general, the following options are open to the leader:

- Achieve fire superiority by battle drills.[29]
- Support by fire for another unit.
- Break contact.
- Defend.
- Bypass enemy position.

The order of COAs listed above is relative to the effectiveness of fire and strength of the enemy position. If the enemy is an inferior force, the unit in contact should be able to achieve fire superiority and still have enough elements to maneuver onto the enemy force. If the entire unit is needed to gain and maintain fire superiority, the next feasible COA is to establish a base of fire so another element can conduct maneuver to attack the enemy.

If the unit cannot achieve fire superiority, or there is no other element to conduct an assault, the unit breaks contact. If the unit is decisively engaged and cannot break contact, it establishes a defense until assistance from another unit arrives. A decisive engagement is one in which a unit is considered fully committed and cannot maneuver or extricate itself. In the absence of outside assistance, the action must be fought to a conclusion and either won or lost with the forces at hand.[30] Additionally, in some instances, based on METT-TC, the unit may bypass the enemy position.

When designating a decisive point, Liddell Hart offers us eight timeless tactical principles, which have an application to all three levels of war.[31] Six are positive and two are negative. They are:

1. Adjust your end to your means.
2. Keep your object always in mind, while adapting your plan to circumstances.
3. Choose the line (or course) of least expectation.
4. Exploit the line of least resistance.
5. Take a line of operation which offers alternative objectives.
6. Ensure that both plan and dispositions are flexible – adaptable to circumstances.
7. Do not throw your weight into a stroke while your opponent is on guard.

---

[29] See Chapter 11 for Battle Drills.
[30] ADRP 3-90 Offense and Defense, 2-10.
[31] Hart, Strategy, 335-336.

8. Do not renew an attack along the same line (or in the same form) after it has once failed.

3. Execute the COA – Following his decision, the leader gives the order. When describing his visualization, he uses doctrinal terms and concepts, and if time permitting, the five-paragraph field order format. The leader only needs to state those directions and orders that have changed from the original order and emphasizes other items he deems essential. During this step, the leader must direct the engagement. There are three key things that the leader needs to control: *movement, fires,* and *unit purpose.* These controls may be standard procedures or hands-on positive controls.

Adaptability: maintenance of direction – Our goal is to achieve decisive results in battle. One of the ways we do this is to think and act faster than our opponent. In the meeting engagement, leaders shape the action by orienting on the enemy force, by finding, fixing, and finishing them, providing direction and tempo. Decisive results will usually be rewarded to the leader who can quickly take advantage of his opponent's mistakes.

John Boyd, a military philosopher and former US Air Force colonel, studied a wide range of historic battles. From his research, he concluded that where numerically inferior forces had defeated their opponents, they often did so by presenting the other side with a sudden, unexpected change or a series of changes.

According to Boyd, these superior forces fell victim because they could not adjust to the changes in a timely manner. Generally, defeat came at relatively small cost to the victor. This research led to the Boyd theory, which states that conflict may be viewed as time-competitive cycles of observation, orientating, deciding, and acting (OODA) – (See Figure 6-3).

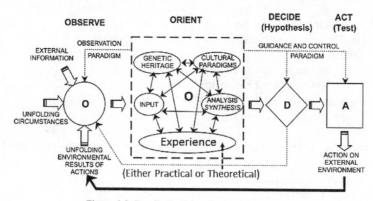

Figure 6-3. Boyd's Decision Cycle (OODA Loop).

As we've said, pattern recognition is key. At the commencement of a meeting engagement, we begin by *observing* ourselves, our surroundings, and our enemy. We begin fighting for information: seeking out the enemy and seeing what he is doing or is about to do. Next, we *orient* to the situation, and use our situational awareness as the foundation of a plan. The better our appreciation of the situation, the better the plan. Then, we *decide* upon a course of action. The decision becomes our plan and is communicated through orders. Finally, we *act*, and the plan is executed. Since this action has changed the situation, the cycle begins anew.

Regarding the OODA Loop, Robert Coram tells us, "Becoming oriented to a competitive situation means bringing to bear the cultural traditions, genetic heritage, new information, previous experiences, and analysis / synthesis process of the person doing the orienting; a complex integration that each person does differently."[32]

Colonel Boyd explained as we move through our decision or time-competitive cycle, we're to travel through the Loop faster than our opponent. We're to present confusing and ambiguous information to our opponent so that he has difficulty orienting himself and thus is slower to decide and act. The goal at this point of the decision cycle is for our opponent to start falling behind, paralyzed by their inability to analyze the situation. As is apparent, time is the key factor in the decision cycle.

A modern example of the time-competitive cycle comes to us from aerial combat during the Korean War:

Aviators achieved a high kill ratio of about 10:1 over their North Korean and Chinese opponents. At first glance, this is somewhat surprising. The main enemy fighter, the MiG-15, was superior to the American F-86 in a number of key respects. It could climb and accelerate faster, and it had a better sustained turn rate. The F-86, however, was superior to the MiG in two critical, though less obvious, respects. First, because it had high-powered hydraulic controls, the F-86 could shift from one maneuver to another faster than the MiG. Second, because of its bubble canopy, the F-86 pilot had better visibility. The F-86's better field of view provided better situational awareness and also contributed to fast transitions because it allowed its pilot to understand changing situations more quickly.

American pilots developed new tactics based on these two advantages. When they engaged the MiGs, they sought to put them through a series of maneuvers. The F-86's faster transitions between maneuvers gave it a time advantage that the pilot transformed into a position advantage. Often, when the MiG pilots realized what was happening, they panicked—and thereby made the American pilot's job all the easier.[33]

---

[32] Coram, Boyd: The Fighter Pilot Who Changed the Art of War, 335.
[33] MCDP 1-3 Tactics, 68.

Crucial to the time-competitive cycle is once the process begins it mustn't slow down. It must continue and must accelerate. Robert Coram tells us, "Success is the greatest trap for the novice who properly implements the OODA Loop. He is so amazed at what he has done that he pauses and looks around and waits for reinforcements. But this is the time to exploit the confusion and to press on."[34] Thus, as we've seen, the art of making decisions rapidly, depends upon our ability to recognize patterns of tactical problems, and intuitively and aggressively apply doctrine. As combat leaders, we must be capable of adapting to rapidly changing situations.

As Boyd would tell us, it is often the ability to make quality decisions quickly and execute them *within the enemy's decision cycle* that determines who wins a sudden engagement or battle. When we make decisions rapidly, we can enter our opponent's decision cycle as he is merely reacting to conditions as they occur. Then, recognizing a fleeting opportunity, we prevent the enemy from reorganizing, and pushing him to make more mistakes, we achieve decisive results.

A further critical component to the time-competitive cycle is friction. Friction, as we have discussed, is the only concept which, in a general way, corresponds to that which distinguishes real war from war on paper. Clausewitz succinctly states, "Everything is very simple in war, but the simplest thing is difficult. These difficulties accumulate and produce a friction, which no man can imagine exactly who has not seen war." John Antal tells us, "Speed of decision making and speed in execution can be critical to reducing friction."[35]

Thus, the successful tactician recognizes the friction of war and understands that the tactical concepts he learns in the classroom may be applied in a dramatically different fashion when he faces the same problem on the battlefield. When he is faced with a different situation, he is able to create new techniques which are derived from the existing tactical concept. The leader must possess a flexible mind, a creative intellect, and the ability and willingness to make independent, time-critical decisions in a changing tactical environment.

Combat experience is the only mitigating element to friction and fog. The intuitive tactician must recognize friction in order to overcome it whenever possible. A leader must anticipate friction points and position himself nearby to mitigate their effects. This concept is called a 'fingertip feeling.' And it's practiced when a leader has a 'pulse' on the fluid motions of his unit's tactical employment. Further, the leader mustn't expect such a standard of achievement in his operations which friction and the fog of war

---

[34] Coram, Boyd: The Fighter Pilot Who Changed the Art of War, 338.
[35] As quoted in Hooker, Maneuver Warfare, 71.

make impossible. A tendency we are trying to avoid is well said by Liddell Hart:

The training of armies is primarily devoted to developing efficiency in the detailed execution of the attack. This concentration on tactical technique tends to obscure the psychological element. It fosters a cult of soundness rather than of surprise. It breeds commanders who are so intent not to do anything wrong, according to 'the book,' that they forget the necessity of making the enemy do something wrong.[36]

Having fixed the enemy force, the leader must decide if he has sufficient forces to finish the engagement with either an assault (in the offense or a counterattack (in the defense. We are now considering how best to finish the enemy force. As we do this, we do not want a pushing match with the enemy. We want to dislocate his balance (COG. Jomini observes, "An enemy is dislodged either by overthrowing him at some point in his line, or by outflanking him so as to take him in flank and rear, or by using both these methods at once; that is, attacking him in front while at the same time one wing is enveloped and his line turned."[37]

If we push him off of a piece of terrain, he can withdraw, regroup, and return to fight the next day. Mass overwhelming combat power at the decisive point to trap the enemy, leading to decisive victory.

Finish – the unit must finish the enemy with fire and movement directed towards a vulnerable point in order to fight through to defeat, destroy, or capture the enemy. According to Jomini, the fundamental principle of war is:

To throw by strategic movements the mass of an army, successively, upon the decisive points of a theater of war, and also upon the communications of the enemy as much as possible without compromising one's own. To throw the mass of one's forces upon the decisive point, or upon that portion of the hostile line which it is of the first importance to overthrow.[38]

In other words, one should hurl mass along a line of operations toward an object that the enemy holds dear. Jomini would call this object the COG or decisive point. As Jomini observed, "The decisive point of a battlefield will be determined by – (1 the features of the ground; (2 the relation of the local features to the ultimate strategic aim; and (3 the positions occupied by the respective forces."[39] If available, a reserve is used at this point. A

---

[36] Hart, Strategy, 336-337.
[37] Jomini, The Art of War, 171.
[38] Ibid, 63.
[39] Ibid, 80.

reserve is that portion of a body of troops which is withheld from action at the beginning of an engagement, in order to be available for a decisive movement. The reserve is not a committed force and thus does not normally have a full suite of combat multipliers available to it until its commitment. It is normally the echelon's *main effort* once committed.

Tactical victory occurs when the opposing enemy force can no longer achieve its tactical objectives or prevent friendly forces from accomplishing their mission. That is the end goal of all offensive and defensive tasks. Decisive tactical victory occurs when the enemy no longer has the means to oppose the friendly force. It also occurs when the enemy admits defeat and agrees to a negotiated end of hostilities.[40] Once we have gained an advantage, we exploit it. We use it to create new opportunities.[41] "When we have incurred the risk of a battle," de Saxe tells us, "we should know how to profit by the victory, and not merely content ourselves, according to custom, with possession of the field." And like the chess grandmaster, we must think ahead to our next move and the one beyond it: How am I going to use this advantage to create another one?[42]

Follow-through – the unit must *follow-through* with consolidation, reorganization, and preparing to continue the mission or receive a new mission.[43] In summary, our ability to understand the situation is useless if we are not prepared to act decisively. For, "It is more valuable to be able to analyze one battle situation correctly, recognize its decisive elements and devise a simple, workable solution for it, than to memorize all the erudition ever written on war."[44] And I would add, we must do this quickly, as we exploit fleeting opportunities. Further, tacticians can have the greatest probability of success in achieving decisive results in battle when they Orient-Observe-Decide-Act faster than their opponent, and hit him strenuously, but indirectly, with maneuver aimed at his vulnerabilities.

Tactical success requires a scientific understanding of one's profession and a mental flexibility for adapting doctrinal concepts to the reality of the moment. Tactical success will come to the tactician who displays the greatest resourcefulness, initiative, and creativity when he carries out a combat mission, not to the tactician who slavishly applies rigid theories and rules memorized in some classroom.

---

[40] ADRP 3-90 Offense and Defense, 1-8.
[41] MCDP 1-3, 101.
[42] Ibid.
[43] FM 3-21.8, 1-35 – 1-36.
[44] Infantry in Battle, 14.

The seminal book, *Infantry in Battle* encapsulates these truths:

It follows, then, that the leader who would become a competent tactician must first close his mind to the alluring formulae that well-meaning people offer in the name of victory. To master his difficult art he must learn to cut to the heart of a situation, recognize its decisive elements and base his course of action on these.[45]

The mature tactician knows he must understand current tactical techniques and procedures of combining and employing personnel and equipment on the battlefield, but he does not search for fixed rules or inflexible formulas. He understands that tactical problems must be approached in a rational manner. He uses a systematic method to collect, order, and analyze evidence, but his final decision will be affected by non-quantifiable factors which will be weighed as much by artistic or intuitive judgment as by scientific methods. This insight has often been called *coup d'oeil*, a French term meaning literally "stroke of the eye." It has also been called "tactical sense."

Offering us timeless insight into tactical decision making, General Pershing writes,

Whatever your previous instruction may have been, you must learn in the actual experience of war, the practical application of the tactical principles that you have been taught during your preliminary training. As we have seen, fog of war is whatever is hidden from full view and creates uncertainty. When confronted with a new situation, do not try to recall examples given in any particular book on the subject; do not try to remember what your instructor has said in discussing some special problem; do not try to carry in your minds patterns of particular exercises or battles, thinking they will fit new cases, because no two sets of circumstances are alike. The main reliance after all must be upon your determination, upon the aggressiveness of your men, upon their stamina, upon their character, and upon their will to win.[46]

The challenge is to recognize opportunity when it occurs in the midst of chaos and uncertainty and seize it to obtain a clear, unambiguous victory. The emphasis is on pattern recognition; even the most chaotic of situations can reveal recurring patterns, so that the successful tactician may "follow that inner light so he may see through the fog and friction of war, and navigate the way to victory."

Decisive Action – We now move to provide an overarching framework for the many tactical tasks which we may be called upon to perform. This

---

[45] Infantry in Battle, 1.
[46] Pershing, My Experiences in the World War, 393.

framework in the Army is referred to as *unified land operations*, which is based on the central idea that Army units seize, retain, and exploit the initiative to gain a position of relative advantage over the enemy. The Army executes unified land operations through an operational concept referred to as *Decisive action*. This process is the continuous, simultaneous combinations of offensive, defensive, and stability or defense support of civil authority's tasks (See Figure 6-4).

Offensive Operations	**Defensive Operations**
Task: • Movement to Contact • Attack • Exploitation • Pursuit. **Purpose:** • Dislocate, isolate, disrupt, and destroy enemy forces • Seize key terrain • Deprive the enemy of resources • Develop intelligence • Deceive and divert the enemy • Create a secure environment for stability tasks.	**Task:** • Mobile defense • Area defense • Retrograde. **Purpose:** • Deter or defeat enemy offense • Gain time • Achieve economy of force • Retain key terrain • Protect the populace, critical assets, and infrastructure • Develop intelligence.
Stability Operations	**Defense Support of Civil Authorities**
Task: • Establish civil security (including security force assistance) • Establish civil control • Restore essential services • Support to governance • Support to economic and infra-structure development (VSO). **Purpose:** • Provide a secure environment • Secure land areas • Meet the critical needs of the populace • Gain support for host-nation government • Shape the environment for inter-agency and host-nation success.	**Task:** • Provide support for domestic disasters • Provide support for radiological / NBC incidents • Provide support for domestic civil law enforcement agencies • Provide other designated support (Disaster relief). **Purpose:** • Save lives • Restore essential services • Maintain or restore law and order • Protect infrastructure and property • Maintain or restore local government • Shape the environment for interagency success.

Figure 6-4. Decisive Action Operational Concept.

Offensive Operations – Offensive operations are conducted to defeat and destroy enemy forces and seize terrain, resources, and population centers. Offensive operations are characterized by *surprise, concentration, audacity, and tempo.* For each mission, the leader decides how to apply these characteristics to focus the effects of his combat power against enemy weakness.[47] Focus should be on fighting the enemy, not the plan.[48]

---

[47] FM 3-21.10, 4-1.

[48] You can be sure of succeeding in your attacks if you only attack places which are undefended. You can ensure the safety of your defense if you only hold positions that cannot be attacked. Hence that general is skillful in attack whose opponent does not know what to defend; and he is skillful in defense whose opponent does not know what to attack. Sun Tzu, Art of War, VI.7, 8.

There are four general purposes for the offense:
- Throw the enemy off balance.
- Overwhelm the enemy's capabilities.
- Disrupt the enemy's defense.
- Ensure the enemy's defeat or destruction.

In practice, each of these purposes has orientation on both the enemy force and the terrain. Leaders employ enemy-oriented attacks to destroy enemy formations and their capabilities, and employ terrain-oriented attacks to seize control of terrain or facilities.

Offensive Tasks – An offensive task is a task conducted to defeat and destroy enemy forces and seize terrain, resources, and population centers (ADRP 3-0). The four primary offensive tasks are:

1. Movement to contact (MTC).
2. Attack.
3. Exploitation.
4. Pursuit.

Operations should be fluid, as these four types flow readily from one to another. An attack may lead to an exploitation, which can lead to pursuit. There are also occasions when pursuit may be followed by attack. The ebb and flow of battle opens up many avenues for the attack; *audaces fortuna iuvat* – fortune favors the bold.

1. Movement to Contact (MTC) - Movement to contact is an offensive task that is designed to develop the situation or regain contact (ADRP 3-90). Platoons and squads participate in a movement to contact as part of a company. A MTC is normally used when the tactical or enemy situation is vague, when the enemy has broken contact, or there is no time to reconnoiter extensively to locate the enemy. Contact results in initiation of another offensive task such as attack, defense, delay, or withdrawal.

There are two techniques used: approach march and search and attack. The first technique, approach march, is used when the enemy's location is relatively certain, and they are a considerable distance away. The second, search and attack is shares many of the same characteristics as an area security mission. A leader employs this form of MTC when the enemy is operating as small, dispersed elements, or when the task is to deny the enemy the ability to move within a given area (See Figure 6-5).

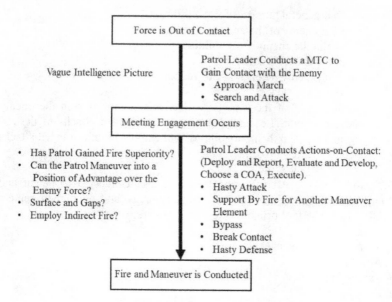

Figure 6-5. Movement to Contact.

2. Attack – The second offensive task is an attack. Attack is an offensive task that destroys or defeats enemy forces, seizes and secures terrain, or both (ADRP 3-90). Attacks are characterized by maneuver supported by fire. The attack should always try to strike the enemy where he is weakest. The platoon can attack independently or as part of a company, battalion or larger element. The two basic types of attack are the *hasty attack* and the *deliberate attack.*

The differences between types of attacks lie in the amount of planning, coordination, and preparation before execution. Additionally, attacks fall into the two objective categories of force-oriented objectives, and terrain-oriented objectives. Force-oriented objectives allow greater freedom of action than terrain-oriented objectives and are therefore the preferred option.

As we've stated, the leader may conduct a hasty attack during MTC, as part of a defense, or whenever he determines that the enemy is in a vulnerable position and can be quickly defeated by immediate offensive action. A hasty attack is used to:

■ Exploit a tactical opportunity.
■ Maintain the momentum.
■ Regain the initiative.
■ Prevent the enemy from regaining organization or balance.
■ Gain a favorable position that might be lost with time.

Because its primary purpose is to maintain momentum or take advantage of the enemy situation, the hasty attack is normally conducted with available resources. Maintaining unrelenting pressure through hasty attacks keeps the enemy off balance and makes it difficult for him to react effectively. Attacking before the enemy can act often results in success even when the combat power ratio is not as favorable as desired. With its emphasis on agility and surprise, however, this type of attack may cause the attacking force to lose a degree of synchronization. To minimize this risk, the leader should maximize use of standard formations; well-rehearsed, thoroughly understood battle drills and SOPs; and digital tools that facilitate rapid planning and preparation.[49]

Execution begins with establishment of a base of fire, which then suppresses the enemy force. The maneuver force uses a combination of techniques to maintain its security while making contact in order to achieve a position of advantage. These techniques include, among others, the following:

- Use of internal base of fire and bounding elements.
- Use of covered and concealed routes.
- Use of indirect fires to suppress or obscure the enemy or to screen friendly movement.
- Execution of bold maneuver that initially takes the maneuver force out of enemy direct fire range.
- Once the maneuver force has gained the positional advantage, it can execute a tactical task to destroy the remaining enemy.

Forms of Maneuver – are distinct tactical combinations of fire and movement with a unique set of doctrinal characteristics that differ primarily in the relationship between the maneuvering force and the enemy.[50] Each form of maneuver attacks the enemy differently. Each poses different challenges for attackers and different dangers for defenders. Maneuver places the enemy at a disadvantage through the application of friendly fires and movement. The six forms of maneuver are *envelopment, turning movement, infiltration, penetration, frontal attack, and flank attack.* Leaders

---

[49] The control of a large force is the same principle as the control of a few men: it is merely a question of dividing up their numbers. Fighting with a large army under your command is nowise different from fighting with a small one: it is merely a question of instituting signs and signals. To ensure that your whole host may withstand the brunt of the enemy's attack and remain unshaken - this is effected by maneuvers direct and indirect. That the impact of your army may be like a grindstone dashed against an egg--this is effected by the science of weak points and strong. In all fighting, the direct method may be used for joining battle, but indirect methods will be needed in order to secure victory. Sun Tzu, Art of War, V.1-5.

[50] FM 3-90-1 Offense and Defense, 1-2.

use these forms of maneuver to orient on the enemy, not the terrain. The forms of maneuver and types of offensive operations complement each other and may apply to linear or nonlinear battlefields. A single operation may contain several forms of maneuver, such as a frontal attack to clear a security area followed by a penetration to create a gap in enemy defenses. Then, the commander might use an envelopment to destroy the enemy's first line of defense.[51]

Envelopment – is a form of maneuver in which an attacking force seeks to avoid the principal enemy's defenses by seizing objectives to the enemy rear or flank in order to destroy him in his current positions. A successful envelopment requires discovery or creation of an assailable flank.[52] The envelopment is the preferred form of maneuver because the enemy must fight in at least two directions and the attacking force tends to suffer fewer casualties while having the most opportunities to destroy the enemy. Envelopments focus on *seizing terrain, destroying specific enemy forces,* and *interdicting enemy withdrawal routes* (See Figure 6-6).

Figure 6-6. Envelopment.

---

[51] FM 3-90-1 Offense and Defense, 1-3.

[52] Envelopments are flanking maneuvers which successful commanders have used throughout history. Some excellent examples include: Miltiades' double envelopment of Darius I's Persians at Marathon, 490 BC; Hannibal's double envelopment of the Roman legions under Paulus and Varro at Cannae, 216 BC; Julius Caesar's envelopment of Pompey's forces at Pharsalus, 48 BC; Napoleon's envelopment of Mack's Austrian forces at Ulm, 1805; the Wehrmacht's envelopment of the French and BEF during Fall Gelb (Battle of France), 10 May – 25 June, 1940, etc.

Adding a further dimension, vertical envelopments are tactical maneuvers in which troops, either air-dropped or airlanded, attack the rear and flanks of a force, in effect cutting off or encircling the force (JP 3-18).

Turning Movement – is a form of maneuver in which the attacking force avoids the enemy's principal defensive positions by seizing objectives to the enemy's rear and causing the enemy to move out of his current positions, or to divert major forces to meet the threat (See Figure 6-7). For a successful turning movement, the unit trying to turn the enemy must attack something that the enemy will fight to save. This might be a supply route, artillery emplacement, or headquarters. In addition to attacking a target the enemy will fight to save, the attacking unit should be strong enough to pose a real threat to the enemy. The attacker seeks to secure key terrain deep in the enemy's rear and along his lines of communication. Faced with a major threat to his rear, the enemy is turned out of his defensive positions and forced to fight to the rear or his flanks.

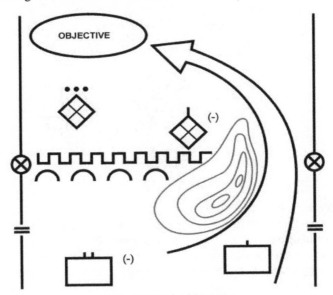

Figure 6-7. Turning Movement.

Infiltration – is a form of maneuver in which combat elements conduct undetected movement through or into an area occupied by enemy forces to occupy a position of advantage in the enemy's rear.[53] The purpose of an

---

[53] FM 3-21.20 The Infantry Battalion, 4-12.

infiltration is to occupy a position of advantage in the enemy rear area to concentrate combat power against enemy weak points (See Figure 6-8).

Infiltration occurs by land, water, air, or a combination of means. SOF and light infantry units up to brigade size are best suited to conduct an infiltration. Moving and assembling forces covertly through enemy positions takes a considerable amount of time. To successfully infiltrate, the force must avoid detection and engagement. Since this requirement limits the size and strength of the infiltrating force, and infiltrated forces alone can rarely defeat an enemy force, infiltration is normally used in conjunction with and in support of the other forms of offensive maneuver.[54]

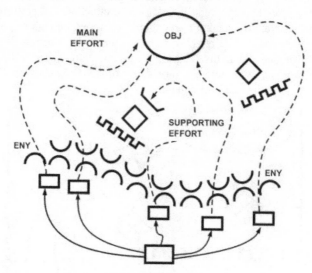

Figure 6-8. Infiltration.

A leader can infiltrate in order to:

- Reconnoiter known or templated enemy positions and conduct surveillance of named areas of interest and targeted areas of interest.
- Attack enemy-held positions from an unexpected direction.
- Occupy a support by fire position to support the decisive operation.
- Secure key terrain.
- Conduct ambushes and raids to destroy vital facilities and disrupt the enemy's defensive structure by attacking enemy reserves, fire support and air defense systems, communication nodes, and sustainment.
- Conduct a covert breach of an obstacle or obstacle complex.

---

[54] FM 3-90-1 Offense and Defense, 1-10.

Penetration – is a form of maneuver in which an attacking force seeks to rupture enemy defenses on a narrow front to disrupt the defensive system. A penetration creates an assailable flank and access to the enemy's rear. Penetration is used when enemy flanks are not assailable, when enemy defenses are overextended, when weak spots in the enemy defense are identified, and when time does not permit some other form of maneuver (See Figure 6-9).

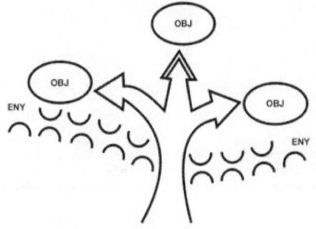

Figure 6-9. Penetration.

A penetration normally consists of three steps:
- Breach the enemy's main defense positions.
- Widen the gap created to secure flanks by enveloping one or both of the newly exposed flanks.
- Seize the objective. As part of a larger force penetration, the company will normally isolate, suppress, fix, or destroy enemy forces; breach tactical or protective obstacles in the enemy's main defense (secure the shoulders of the penetration); or seize key terrain. A battalion may also use penetration to secure a foothold within a large built-up area.

Frontal attack – is a form of maneuver in which an attacking force seeks to destroy a weaker enemy force or fix a larger enemy force along a broad front. It is the least desirable form of maneuver, because it exposes the attacker to the concentrated fire of the defender and limits the effectiveness of the attacker's own fires. However, the frontal attack is often the best form of maneuver for an attack in which speed and simplicity are key; it helps overwhelm weak defenses, security outposts, or disorganized enemy forces (See Figure 6-10).

Figure 6-10. Frontal Attack.

Flank Attack – the sixth form of maneuver – flank attack, is directed at the flank of an enemy. A flank is the right or left side of a military formation and is not oriented toward the enemy. It is usually not as strong in terms of forces or fires as is the front of a military formation. (See Figure 6-11).

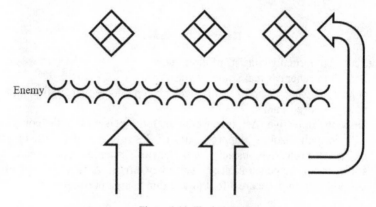

Figure 6-11. Flank Attack.

A flank may be created by the attacker through the use of fires or by a successful penetration. A flanking attack is similar to an envelopment but generally conducted on a shallower axis. The primary difference between a flank attack and an envelopment is one of depth. A flank attack is an envelopment delivered squarely on the enemy's flank. Conversely, an envelopment is an attack delivered beyond the enemy's flank and into the

263

enemy's support areas, but short of the depth associated with a turning movement.[55]

3. Exploitation – The third offensive task is exploitation. Exploitation is an offensive task that usually follows the conduct of a successful attack and is designed to disorganize the enemy in depth (ADRP 3-90). They are conducted at the battalion level and higher. Exploitations seek to disintegrate enemy forces to where they have no alternative but to surrender or fight. Companies and platoons may conduct movements to contact or attack as part of a higher unit's exploitation.[56]

4. Pursuit – The fourth and last offensive task is pursuit. Pursuit is an offensive task designed to catch or cut of a hostile force attempting to escape, with the aim of destroying it (ADRP 3-90). Pursuits are normally conducted at the brigade or higher level. A pursuit typically follows a successful exploitation.

Confederate Army Lieutenant General Thomas J. "Stonewall" Jackson summed up pursuit when he said, "Strike the enemy and overcome him, never give up the pursuit as long as your men have strength to follow; for an enemy routed, if hotly pursued, becomes panic-stricken, and can be destroyed by half their number."[57] Companies and platoons will participate in a larger unit's exploitation and may conduct attacks as part of the higher unit's operation.[58]

Special Purpose Attacks – are subordinate forms of an attack. The commander's intent and METT-TC determine which of these forms of attack are employed. The commander can conduct each of these forms of attack, except for a raid, as either a hasty or a deliberate operation.[59] As forms of attack, these share many planning, preparing, and executing considerations of the offense and they include the following:

- Spoiling Attack.
- Counter Attack.
- Ambush.
- Raid.
- Feint.
- Demonstration.

---

[55] FM 3-90-1 Offense and Defense, 1-22.
[56] FM 3-21.10, 4-3.
[57] Heinl, Dictionary of Military and Naval Quotations, 259.
[58] Ibid.
[59] FM 3-90-1, Offense and Defense, 1-2.

Spoiling Attack – Leaders mount spoiling attacks from a defensive posture to disrupt an expected enemy attack. A spoiling attack attempts to strike the enemy while he is vulnerable during his preparations for attack in assembly areas and attack positions or while he is on the move prior to crossing his line of departure (LD). When the situation permits, commanders exploit a spoiling attack like any other attack.

Counter Attack – A counterattack is an attack by defensive forces to exploit the success of a defense, regain the initiative, or to deny the enemy success with his attack. Commanders conduct counterattacks either with a reserve or with lightly committed forward elements. They counterattack after the enemy launches his attack, reveals his decisive operation, or creates an assailable flank. Infantry commanders conduct counterattacks much like other attacks. However, synchronizing counterattacks within the overall defensive effort requires careful timing. Remember that timing is critical. To be decisive, the counterattack must occur when the enemy is overextended, dispersed, and disorganized during his attack. All counterattacks should be rehearsed in the same conditions that they would be conducted. Careful consideration must be given to the event that will trigger the counterattack. Once committed, the counterattack force conducts the decisive operation.

As in spoiling attacks, commanders prepare to seize the opportunity to exploit success by the entire force. However, counterattacks might be limited to movement to better terrain in order to bring fires on the enemy. Given the same forces on both sides, counterattacks can achieve greater effects than other attacks because the defender can create better conditions by rehearsing and by controlling timing.

Ambush - An ambush is a form of attack by fire or other destructive means from a concealed position that relies on surprise and speed, coordinated firepower, and violence of action in order to destroy a moving or temporarily halted target. It is one of the oldest and most effective types of guerilla tactics. An ambush is conducted in order to reduce the enemy's overall combat effectiveness and destroy his *center of gravity*.[60]

Raid – A raid is a surprise attack which involves a swift entry into hostile territory to destroy installations, gather intelligence, liberate captured personnel, and to kill or capture personnel.[61] The raid force retains terrain just long enough to accomplish the intent, and unless it is a stay-behind unit, recovers to friendly lines. Raids are governed by four fundamentals: surprise

---

[60] Ambushes will be discussed more in depth in Chapter 12 – Combat Patrols.
[61] Raids will be discussed more in depth in Chapter 12 – Combat Patrols.

and speed, coordinated fires, violence of action, and a planned withdrawal. The target type, terrain, and enemy forces will greatly influence the raiding force composition.

When possible, the leader should maintain squad and fire team integrity. The task organization of a raid is determined by the purpose of the operation; however the raiding force normally consists of the following elements:

- Headquarters – command and control: PL, PSG, RTO, medic, etc.
- Security – provides early warning, isolates OBJ, and covers withdrawal.
- Support – provides direct fires IOT suppress and neutralize.
- Assault – seize and secure the objective.
- Breach – execute breach to allow entry onto objective.

The main differences between a raid and other attack forms are the limited objectives of the raid and the associated withdrawal following completion. Raids might be conducted in daylight or darkness, within or beyond supporting distance of the parent unit. When the area to be raided is beyond supporting distance of friendly lines, the raiding party operates as a separate force. A specific objective is normally assigned to orient the raiding unit. During the withdrawal, the attacking force should use a route or axis different from that used to conduct the raid itself.

The following are some notable raids in SOF history:

Raid on Eben Emael	10 May 1940	German Fallschirmjäger raid.
Operation Archery	27 Dec 1941	British Commando destruction raid.
Operation Chariot	28 Mar1942	British Commando destruction raid.
Operation Jubilee	19 Aug 1942	British-Canadian destruction raid.
Operation Gunnerside	27 Feb 1943	SOE sabotage raid.
Operation Eichte	12 Sept1943	Waffen-SS Kommando rescue raid.
Raid on Cabanatuan	30 Jan 1945	Ranger prisoner liberation raid.
Raid on Los Baños	23 Feb 1945	Airborne prisoner liberation raid.
Operation Ivory Coast	21 Nov 1970	USSF prisoner liberation raid.
Operation Thunderbolt	4 July 1976	Sayeret Matkal hostage rescue raid.
Operation Acid Gambit	20 Dec 1989	JSOC hostage rescue raid.
Battle of Mogadishu	2-3 Oct 1993	JSOC capture/kill raids.
Operation Neptune Spear	2 May 2011	JSOC capture/kill raid.

Feint – A feint is a form of attack used to deceive the enemy of the location or time of the actual decisive operation or main attack. Its purpose is to deceive the enemy and cause him to react in a particular way; such as by repositioning forces, committing its reserve, or shifting fires. The feint seeks direct fire contact with the enemy but avoids decisive engagement.

The feint, in many ways, is identical to other attack forms. The feint is much more limited in scope than other attack forms, in part due to its extremely specific objective. The scale of the operation, however, is usually apparent only to the controlling headquarters. For the element actually conducting the feint, such as an infantry company or battalion, execution is just as rapid and violent as in a full-scale attack.[62]

Demonstration – A demonstration is a form of attack used for deception.[63] It is made with the intention of deceiving the enemy; however contact with enemy forces is not sought. Feints and demonstrations deceive the enemy as to the true intentions of the attacking force. They pin the enemy in place, divert his attention, and allow the decisive action elsewhere. If they unveil weaknesses in the enemy, they are followed up with a hasty or deliberate attack. Demonstrations must be clearly visible to the enemy without being transparently deceptive in nature.[64]

Defensive Operations – A defensive task is a task conducted to defeat an attacking enemy force, retain key terrain, gain time, economize forces, and develop conditions favorable for offensive or stability tasks (ADRP 3-0). In Clausewitz's estimation, "the defensive form of warfare is intrinsically stronger than the offense."[65] As part of defensive operations, the company may *defend, delay, withdraw, or counterattack*, along with additional security tasks. The three defensive tasks are:

1. Area Defense.
2. Mobile Defense.
3. Retrograde Operations.

1. Area Defense – The area defense is a defensive task that concentrates on denying enemy forces access to designated terrain for a specific time rather than destroying the enemy outright (ADRP 3-90). The focus of the area defense is on retaining terrain where the bulk of the defending force positions itself in mutually supporting, prepared positions (See Figure 6-12).

---

[62] A feint is designed to divert the enemy's attention from the decisive operation. During Operation Desert Storm, elements of the 1st Cavalry Division of VII Corps, conducted feints in the Rugi pocket, aside the Wadi al-Batin prior to the ground assault on 24 February, 1991. This action fixed Iraqi frontline units and deceived Iraqi commanders that the coalition main attack was going to be in the Wadi al-Batin.
[63] FM 3-21.20 The Infantry Battalion, 4-58.
[64] Ibid.
[65] Clausewitz, On War, VI, 1, 428.

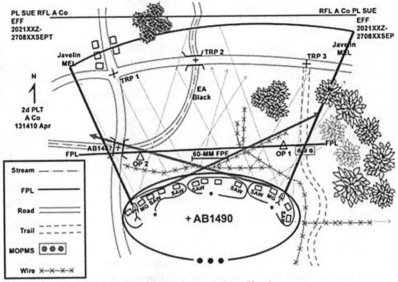

Figure 6-12. Platoon Defense Sketch.

Units maintain their positions and control the terrain between these positions. The commander can use his reserve to reinforce fires; add depth, block, or restore the position by counterattack; seize the initiative; and destroy enemy forces. Units at all echelons can conduct an area defense.

Defensive Techniques – The company normally defends using one of these basic defensive techniques:
- Defend in sector.
- Defend from a battle position (BP).
- Defend a strongpoint.
- Defend a perimeter.
- Defend in a linear defense.
- Defend in a nonlinear defense.
- Defend on a reverse slope.

Sector Defense – A sector is the company control measure that provides the most freedom of action to a platoon. It gives the platoon the flexibility to operate decentralized, while ensuring sufficient control to avoid confusion and synchronize the company's operation. In restricted terrain, where dismounted Infantry forces prefer to work, mutual support between the company's platoon battle positions is difficult to achieve. Seeing and

268

controlling the fight throughout the company sector are also very difficult for the commander.

Battle Positions – A battle position is a general location orientation of forces on the ground where units defend. The platoon is located within the general area of the BP. When fighting a company defense in sector from platoon battle positions, the concept is to defeat the attacker through the depth of his formation by confronting him with effective fires from mutually supporting BPs as he tries to maneuver around them.

One technique is to allow the enemy to move into the engagement area (EA) and destroy him with massed fires. Another technique is to engage the attacker at maximum range with fires from field artillery, (and mortars) and then engage with organic antiarmor weapons positioned to deliver fires at maximum effective ranges from the flanks and rear. As the enemy closes, antiarmor weapons may move to alternate or supplementary firing positions within the BP to continue firing and avoid being bypassed.

A platoon moves from its primary, alternate, supplementary, or subsequent position only with the commander's approval, or when the commander has prescribed a particular condition as a reason to move. The four types of battle positions are: primary, alternate, supplementary, and subsequent. The three levels of preparedness are: occupied, prepared but not occupied, planned.

Strongpoint Defense – A company might be directed to construct a strongpoint as part of an Infantry battalion defense. In order to do so, it is augmented with engineer support, more weapons, and sustainment resources. A strongpoint is defended until the commander directing the defense formally orders the unit out of it. The specific positioning of units in the strongpoint depends on the company commander's mission analysis. Additionally, the strongpoint must be divided into several independent, but mutually supporting, positions or sectors. If one of the positions or sectors must be evacuated or is overrun, limit the enemy penetration with obstacles and fires, and support a counterattack.

Construct obstacles and minefields to disrupt and canalize enemy formations, to reinforce fires, and to protect the strongpoint from the assault. Place the obstacles and mines out as far as friendly units can observe them, within the strongpoint, and at points in between where they will be useful. Prepare range cards for each position and confirm them by fires. Plan indirect fires in detail and register them. Plan and test several means of communication within the strongpoint and to higher headquarters; possibilities include radio, wire, messenger, pyrotechnics, and other signals. Improve or repair the strongpoint until the unit is relieved or withdrawn.

More positions can be built, tunnels and trenches dug, existing positions improved or repaired, and barriers built or fixed.[66]

The defending leader exploits the defending force's advantages of occupying the terrain where the fight will occur. The defending force engages the attacker from locations that give the defending force an advantage over the attacking enemy. These locations include defilades, rivers, thick woods, swamps, cliffs, canals, built-up areas, and reverse slopes. Defensive positions in the MBA should make use of existing and reinforcing obstacles. The commander may choose to shape the battlefield by defending one area to deny terrain to the enemy while delaying in another area to deceive the enemy commander into believing he has achieved success.

The defending commander plans how to use *key terrain* to impede the enemy's movement. He seeks out terrain that allows him to mass the effects of his fires but forces the enemy to commit his force piecemeal into friendly EAs. This exposes portions of the enemy force for destruction without giving up the advantages of fighting from protected positions. Examples of key terrain include terrain that permits the defending force to cover a major obstacle system by fire, and important road junctions and choke points that impact troop movements, such as the movement of reserves and LOCs.

2. Mobile Defense – The mobile defense is a defensive task that concentrates on the destruction or defeat of the enemy through a decisive attack by a striking force (ADRP 3-90). The focus of this form of defense is to allow the enemy to advance to a point where he is exposed to a decisive counterattack by the striking force.

The striking force is a dedicated counterattack force constituting the bulk of available combat power. A fixing force supplements the striking force. The commander uses his fixing force to hold attacking enemy forces in position, to help channel attacking enemy forces into ambush areas, and to retain areas from which to launch the striking force. The commander must be able to shape the battlefield, causing the enemy to overextend his lines of communication (LOCs), expose his flanks, and dissipate his combat power. Likewise, the commander must be able to move around and behind the enemy force he intends to cut off and destroy.

3. Retrograde Operations – The retrograde is a defensive task that involves organized movement away from the enemy (ADRP 3- 90). The enemy may force these operations, or a commander may execute them voluntarily. The

---

[66] Additional terms not discussed here, such as: perimeter defense, linear defense, nonlinear defense, reverse slope defense, and exploiting the advantages of terrain are covered in depth in FM 3-21.10.

retrograde is a transitional operation; it is not conducted in isolation. It is part of a larger scheme of maneuver designed to regain the initiative and defeat the enemy. A defending commander transitions from the defense to the retrograde. A retrograde usually involves a combination of *delay, withdrawal, and retirement* operations.

Delay – A delay is a form of retrograde in which a force under pressure trades space for time by slowing down the enemy's momentum and inflicting maximum damage on the enemy without, in principle, becoming decisively engaged. The delay is one of the most demanding of all ground combat operations. A delay wears down the enemy so that friendly forces can regain the initiative through offensive action, buy time to establish an effective defense, or determine enemy intentions as part of a security operation.

Normally in a delay, inflicting casualties on the enemy is secondary to gaining time. For example, a flank security force conducts a delay operation to provide time for the protected force to establish a viable defense along its threatened flank. Except when directed to prevent enemy penetration of a phase line (PL) for a specific duration, a force conducting a delay normally does not become decisively engaged.

Withdrawal – A withdrawal, a form of retrograde, is a planned operation in which a force in contact disengages from an enemy force (FM 3-0). The leader may or may not conduct a withdrawal under enemy pressure. Subordinate units may withdraw without the entire force withdrawing. Withdrawals are inherently dangerous because they involve moving units to the rear and away from what is usually a stronger enemy force.

In the below example (Figure 6-13), a platoon conducts a withdrawal under pressure from a superior enemy force. 1st Squad reacts to contact and creates a base-of-fire (1) while 2nd Squad displaces to create a second base-of-fire position (2) to the left or right METT-TC dependent. When 2nd Squad is set, 3rd Squad establishes their base-of-fire position (3). By this action the platoon forms an inverted wedge, maximizing firepower. On order from the PL, 1st Squad (or initial base-of-fire element) displaces toward the left or right, to the flank of another squad's base-of-fire (4). This action frees up the neighboring squad to bound back (by squad or fire team) to a position which will again establish an inverted wedge (5). This action continues until the unit can either regain the offense or establish itself in a more tenable defensive position.

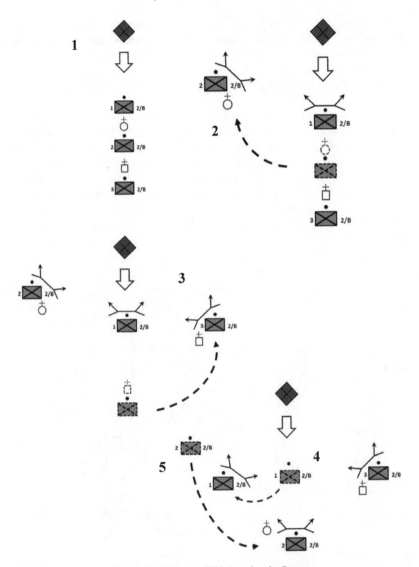

Figure 6-13. Platoon Withdrawal under Pressure.

Retirement – A retirement is a form of retrograde in which a force out of contact with the enemy moves away from the enemy (JP 1-02). A retiring unit organizes for combat but does not anticipate interference by enemy ground forces. Typically, another unit's security force covers the movement of one formation as the unit conducts a retirement. However, mobile enemy

272

forces, unconventional forces, air strikes, air assaults, or long-range fires may attempt to interdict the retiring unit. The commander must plan for enemy actions and organize the unit to fight in self-defense. The commander usually conducts retirement operations to reposition his forces for future operations or to accommodate the current concept of the operation.

Wire Obstacles – The three types of wire obstacles are *protective, tactical, and supplementary* (See Figure 6-14). For best effect, protective obstacles are tied into existing or tactical reinforcing obstacles along with mines and wire. In planning protective obstacles, the commander evaluates the potential threat to the company's position. Then, he employs the best system for that threat. Protective obstacles are usually located beyond hand grenade distance (40 to 100 meters) from the soldier's fighting position, and may extend out 300 to 500 meters to tie into tactical obstacles and existing restricted terrain.

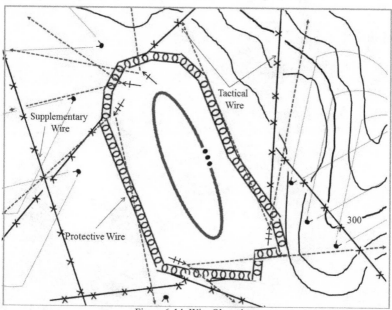

Figure 6-14. Wire Obstacles.

Protective wire can be a complex obstacle providing all-round protection of a platoon perimeter. It might also be a simple wire obstacle on the likely dismounted avenue of approach into a squad ambush position. Command-detonated M18 Claymore mines can be integrated into the protective wire or used separately. Tactical wire is positioned to increase the effectiveness of the company's fires. Usually, it is positioned along the friendly side of the machine gun final protective lines (FPLs). Tactical minefields may also be integrated into these wire obstacles or used separately. Supplementary wire obstacles can break up the line of tactical wire. This helps prevent the enemy from locating friendly weapons (particularly the machine guns) by following the tactical wire.

Tactical Enabling Operations – support the larger unit's effort to accomplish its mission. They always play a supporting role in decisive action. There are six types of tactical enabling operations: reconnaissance; security; troop movement; relief in place; passage of lines; and combined arms breach.

Conclusion

Historical volumes will never furnish a model that need only be reproduced in order to defeat the enemy. As we've said, tactical success will come to the tactician who displays the greatest resourcefulness, initiative, and creativity, not to the one who slavishly applies rigid theories and rules memorized in the classroom. In this chapter we have explored the doctrinal concepts and principles that will enable us to master the art and science of tactics. Our goal is to be decisive in battle. To that end we must clearly visualize the battlespace through situational awareness, a recognition of patterns and indicators along with an ability to make sound decisions intuitively.

Part Three: Planning

Chapter 7 The Operations Process

"Visualize a desired outcome, proactively shape circumstances to meet it, while adaptively accounting for chance and friction."

The purpose of this chapter is to gain an understanding for the operations process and how the warfighting functions (WFF), operational and mission variables, as well as certain aspects inherent to SOF operations work together. This chapter consists of the following:

1. The Operations Process.
2. Operational and Mission Variables.
3. Warfighting Functions.
4. SOF Operational Methodology.
5. SOF Mission Criteria.
6. Target Analysis.

The Operations Process – while simple in concept (plan, prepare, execute, and assess), is dynamic in execution (See Figure 7-1). The operations process is the exercise of command and control (C2) throughout the conduct of operations. It is the Army's method of planning, preparing, executing, and assessing operations. Throughout the operations process, leaders seek to build and maintain their situational awareness.

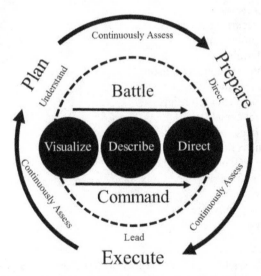

Figure 7-1. The Operations Process.

276

Leaders continuously update their understanding as the operation progresses. As the operations process begins, leaders provide visualization—the mental process of developing situational understanding, determining a desired end state, and envisioning a broad concept on how the force may achieve the end state. This provides the basis for developing plans and orders, and during execution, it helps leaders determine if, when, and what to decide as they adapt to changing conditions. Throughout the operations process, leaders exercise C2 to integrate the other warfighting functions (WFF) to synchronize the activities of forces in time, space, and purpose.[1]

The operations process consists of four major activities – plan, prepare, execute, and assess:

Plan – A plan is the art and science of understanding a situation, envisioning a desired future, and laying out effective ways of bringing that future about. The Army's three planning methodologies are:
- TLP (Troop Leading Procedure).
- MDMP (Military Decision Making Process).
- Design.

Prepare – These are the activities performed by a unit to improve their ability to execute an operation. To help ensure the force is protected and prepared for execution, units conduct the following activities:
- Conduct ISR.
- Conduct security operations.
- Conduct protection.
- Manage terrain.
- Coordinate and conduct liaison.
- Continue to build partnerships and teams.
- Conduct confirmation briefs.
- Conduct rehearsals.
- Conduct plans-to-operations transitions.
- Revise and refine the plan.
- Complete task organization.
- Integrate new soldiers and units.
- Train.
- Initiate troop movements.
- Prepare terrain.

---

[1] Command and control is the exercise of authority and direction by a properly designated commander over assigned and attached forces in the accomplishment of a mission. The Army's means of command and control is mission command.

- Conduct sustainment preparation.
- Initiate deception operations.
- Conduct pre-combat checks and inspections (PCC/PCI).

Execute – Putting a plan into action by applying combat power to accomplish the mission. The three fundamentals of execution are:
- Seize and retain the initiative.
- Build and maintain momentum.
- Exploit success.

Assess – The continuous determination of the progress toward accomplishing a task, creating an effect, or achieving an objective. Assessment consists of the following activities:
- Monitoring the current situation to collect relevant information.
- Evaluating progress toward attaining end state conditions, achieving objectives, and performing tasks.
- Recommending or directing action for improvement.

The guiding principles in the operations process are (1) commanders drive the process; (2) apply critical and creative thinking; (3) build and maintain situational awareness; and (4) encourage collaboration and dialogue. The following diagram visually demonstrates how the operations process fits within the context of unified land operations (See Figure 7-2).

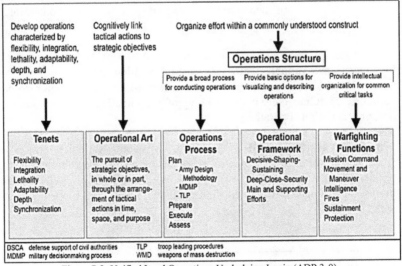

Figure 7-2. Unified Land Operations Underlying Logic (ADP 3-0).

Operational and Mission Variables – Commanders and staffs use the operational and mission variables to help build their situational understanding. They analyze and describe an operational environment in terms of eight interrelated operational variables.[2] They consist of:

- Political – describes the distribution of responsibility and power at all levels of governance—formally constituted authorities, as well as informal or covert political powers.
- Military – explores the military and paramilitary capabilities of all relevant actors (enemy, friendly, and neutral) in a given operational environment.
- Economic – encompasses individual and group behaviors related to producing, distributing, and consuming resources.
- Social – describes the cultural, religious, and ethnic makeup within an operational environment and the beliefs, values, customs, and behaviors of society members.
- Information – describes the nature, scope, characteristics, and effects of individuals, organizations, and systems that collect, process, disseminate, or act on information.
- Infrastructure - is composed of the basic facilities, services, and installations needed for the functioning of a community or society.
- Physical environment – includes the geography and manmade structures, as well as the climate and weather in the area of operations.
- Time – describes the timing and duration of activities, events, or conditions within an operational environment, as well as how the timing and duration are perceived by various actors in the operational environment.

Upon receipt of a mission, the leader filters information categorized by the operational variables into relevant information with respect to the mission. They use the mission variables, in combination with the operational variables, to refine their understanding of the situation and to visualize, describe, and direct operations.

Mission Variables (METT-TC) – Mission variables describe characteristics of the area of operations, focusing on how they might affect a mission. The mission variables are mission, enemy, terrain and weather, troops and support available, time available, and civil considerations (METT-TC).[3]

---

[2] ADRP 5-0, 1-7.
[3] Ibid, 1-8.

Mission – The mission is the task, together with the purpose, that clearly indicates the action to be taken and the reason therefore. It is always the first variable leaders consider during decision making. A mission statement contains the "who, what, when, where, and why" of the operation.

Enemy – The second variable to consider is the enemy dispositions (including organization, strength, location, and tactical mobility), doctrine, equipment, capabilities, vulnerabilities, and probable courses of action.

Terrain and weather – Leaders analyze terrain using the five military aspects of terrain expressed in the memory aid **OAKOC**: observation and fields of fire, avenues of approach, key and decisive terrain, obstacles, cover and concealment. The military aspects of weather include visibility, wind, precipitation, cloud cover, temperature, and humidity.

Troops and support available –This variable includes the number, type, capabilities, and condition of available friendly troops and support.

Time available – Leaders assess the time available for planning, preparing, and executing tasks and operations. This includes the time required to assemble, deploy, and maneuver units in relationship to the enemy and conditions.

Civil Considerations – These are the influence of manmade infrastructure, civilian institutions, and activities of the civilian leaders, populations, and organizations within an area of operations on the conduct of military operations. Civil considerations comprise six characteristics, expressed in the memory aid ASCOPE: areas, structures, capabilities, organizations, people, and events

The Warfighting Functions – As we continue to lay a firm foundation for everything we may be called upon to perform as a tactical leader, we are now moving from theory to practice, which brings us to the Army's six warfighting functions. These warfighting functions enable the leader to conceptualize all aspects of the battlespace, plan and execute missions, while leaving as little as possible to chance. By synchronizing these warfighting functions, the leader can maximize his unit's combat power. Combat power is the total means of destructive, constructive, and information capabilities that a military unit or formation can apply at a given time. Combat power has eight elements: leadership, information, mission command, movement and maneuver, intelligence, fires, sustainment, and protection.

The Army collectively describes the last six elements as the warfighting functions. The following is a short overview of the six war fighting functions (See Figure 7-3):

Figure 7-3. The Warfighting Functions.

Intelligence. The intelligence warfighting function involves the related tasks and systems that facilitate understanding of the enemy, terrain, weather, and civil considerations. It includes those tasks associated with intelligence, surveillance, and reconnaissance. The intelligence warfighting function combines a flexible and adjustable architecture of procedures, personnel, organizations, and equipment to provide commanders with relevant information and products relating to an area's threat, civil populace, and environment.[4]

The intelligence warfighting function includes the following tasks:
- Support force generation.
- Support situational understanding.
- Provide intelligence support to targeting and information capabilities.

---

[4] FM 3-21.10, 1-19.

- Collect information.[5]

Movement and maneuver. The movement and maneuver warfighting function is the related tasks and systems that move forces to achieve a position of advantage in relation to the enemy. It includes those tasks associated with employing forces in combination with direct fire or fire potential (maneuver), force projection (movement), and mobility and countermobility. Movement and maneuver are the means by which commanders concentrate combat power to achieve surprise, shock, momentum, and dominance.[6]

Fire support. The fire support warfighting function is the related tasks and systems that provide collective and coordinated use of Army indirect fires, joint fires, and offensive information operations. It includes those tasks associated with integrating and synchronizing the effects of these types of fires with the other warfighting functions to accomplish operational and tactical objectives.[7]

Protection. The protection warfighting function is the related tasks and systems that preserve the force so the commander can apply maximum combat power. The protection warfighting function includes the following tasks:
- Conduct operational area security.
- Employ safety techniques (including fratricide avoidance).
- Implement operations security.
- Implement physical security procedures.
- Provide intelligence support to protection.
- Implement information protection.
- Apply antiterrorism measures.
- Conduct law and order.
- Conduct survivability operations.
- Provide force health protection.
- Conduct chemical, biological, radiological, and nuclear operations.
- Provide explosive ordnance disposal and protection support. Coordinate air and missile defense.
- Conduct personnel recovery operations.
- Conduct internment and resettlement.[8]

---

[5] ADRP 3-0, 3-4.
[6] FM 3-21.10, 1-19.
[7] Ibid.
[8] ADRP 3-0, 3-4.

Sustainment. The sustainment warfighting function is the related tasks and systems that provide support and services to ensure freedom of action, extend operational reach, and prolong endurance. It includes those tasks associated with:

- Conduct logistics.
- Provide personnel services.
- Provide health service support.[9]

Sustainment allows uninterrupted operations through adequate and continuous logistical support such as supply systems, maintenance, and other services.[10]

Command and control. The command and control warfighting function includes the related tasks and systems that support commanders in exercising authority and direction. It includes the tasks of acquiring friendly information, managing relevant information, and directing and leading subordinates. Command and control has two parts: the commander and the command and control (C2) system. Through command and control, the commander initiates and integrates all warfighting functions.

SOF Operational Methodology – Another concept we need to introduce is the SOF operational methodology. Special warfare uses the SOF operational methodology to identify gaps, and builds and strengthens friendly networks in the execution of UW and FID. There are a few differences between *the operations process* and the *SOF operational methodology*. First, the SOF operational methodology is normally dependent on non-SOF assistance (Fifth SOF Truth). Second, it requires operational intelligence, and third, the level of participation by mission personnel is greatly increased.

The SOF operational methodology includes find, fix, finish, exploit, and analyze (F3EA). This methodology—F3EA—is inherent in the execution of all special operations. A surgical strike uses F3EA to satisfy the requirement of reliable, actionable intelligence for targeting purposes.[11]

The following diagram visually demonstrates – the SOF operation methodology (F3EA).

---

[9] ADRP 3-0, 3-4.
[10] FM 3-21.10, 1-19.
[11] ADRP 3-05, 3-10.

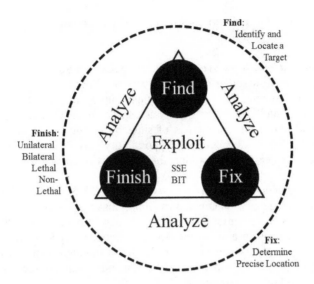

Figure 7-4. SOF Operational Methodology (F3EA).

SOF Mission Criteria – As we continue to discuss the planning particulars of SOF operations, a look at the five basic operational mission criteria will prove beneficial. These five criteria support the employment of SOF in support of the joint force campaign or operation plan (OPLAN). Additionally, these criteria provide guidelines for conventional and SOF commanders and planners to use when considering the employment of SOF. As these questions are applied to planning, an affirmative response is optimal. The five basic operational mission criteria include:

1. Is the mission appropriate? SOF should be used to achieve effects that require SOF's unique skills and capabilities. If the effects do not require those skills and capabilities, SOF should not be assigned. SOF should not be used as a substitute for other forces.

2. Does the mission support the campaign plan? If the mission does not support the JFC's campaign or major OPLAN, more appropriate missions available for SOF should be considered instead.

3. Is the mission operationally feasible? SOF are not structured for attrition or force-on-force warfare and should not be assigned missions beyond their capabilities. SOF commanders and their staffs must consider the

284

vulnerability of SOF units to larger, more heavily armed or mobile forces, particularly in hostile territory.

4. Are required resources available for the mission? Some SOF missions require support from other forces for success. Support involves aiding, protecting, complementing, and sustaining employed SOF. Support can include airlift, intelligence, communications, IO, medical, logistics, space, weather, and numerous other types of support. Although a target may be vulnerable to SOF, deficiencies in supportability may affect the likelihood for success or may entirely invalidate the feasibility of employing SOF.

5. Will the outcome of the mission justify the risk? SOF have high-value and limited resources. Commanders must make sure the benefits of successful mission execution are measurable and in balance with the risks inherent in the mission assessment. Some operations that SOF can execute make only a marginal contribution to the JFC campaign plan and present great risk to personnel and materiel. Commanders should recognize the high-value and limited resources of SOF.

A consideration of these risk managing criteria may not only prevent the potential loss of SOF units and equipment, but also the risk of adverse effects on US diplomatic and political interests if the mission fails.

Target Analysis – One of the targeting tools of SOF methodology is the CARVER matrix. The criticality, accessibility, recuperability, vulnerability, effect, and recognizability (CARVER) method was developed by the OSS during WWII and is used to prioritize targets. CARVER can be used from an offensive or defensive perspective. When using this tactical metric tool, the planner enumerates critical vulnerabilities (CVs) according to their analyzed rank-order, thereby prioritizing the targeting process. The six criteria listed below are applied against each CV to determine the impact on the threat organization: **CARVER**[12]

Criticality—Criticality or target value is the primary consideration in targeting. Criticality is related to how much a target's destruction, denial, disruption, influencing, and damage will impair the adversary's political, economic, or military operations, or how much a target component will disrupt the function of a target complex. In determining criticality, individual targets within a target system must be analyzed with relation to the other elements critical to the function of the target system or complex. Critical targets may also be selected for SR missions.

---

[12] ADRP 3-05, 4-6.

Accessibility—In order to damage, destroy, disrupt, deny, influence, or collect data on a target, SOF must be able to reach it with the necessary equipment, either physically or via indirect means. During SR missions, SOF not only must observe the target, but also must remain in the area undetected for extended periods of time. The SOF unit also must be able to safely exfiltrate once the mission is complete. Weather, light data, physical security measures, and the adversary's disposition at the target area are all considered. Sometimes, accessibility is judged as either feasible or infeasible.

Recuperability—In the case of DA missions, it is important to estimate how long it will take the adversary to repair, replace, or bypass the damage inflicted on a target. Primary considerations are spare parts availability and the ability to reroute production. A target is not a valid SOF target if it can be repaired or bypassed in a short amount of time or with minimal resources.

Vulnerability—A target is vulnerable if SOF have the means and expertise to attack it. At the strategic level, a much broader range of resources and technology is available to conduct the target attack. At the tactical level, resources may be limited to organic personnel, weapons, and munitions or assets that can be attached, borrowed, or improvised.

Effect—The target should be attacked only if the desired effects can be created to achieve the objective. These effects may be of a military, political, economic, informational, or psychological nature. The effect on the populace is viewed in terms of alienating the local inhabitants, strengthening the resistance movement, or triggering reprisals against the indigenous people in the immediate target area. The effect on the populace may also impact on the detachment's infiltration, exfiltration, and evasion and recovery routes. Collateral damage must also be calculated and weighed against the expected military benefit to determine if an attack would be advisable under the concept of proportionality. Collateral damage includes, but is not limited to, civilian injuries, deaths, and adverse economic impacts of the proposed attack.

Recognizability—The target must be identifiable under various weather, light, and seasonal conditions without being confused with other targets or target components. Sufficient data must also be available for SOF to find the target on the ground and to differentiate the target from similar objects in the target area. The same requirement exists to distinguish target critical damage points and target stress points from similar components and their parent structures and surroundings. With appropriate training or augmentation, SOF also should be able to recognize appropriate computer programs, communications circuits, or similar targets of cyber/electromagnetic activities.

The purpose of strategic target analysis (CARVER) is to determine the critical systems or subsystems that must be attacked to progressively destroy or degrade the adversary's warfighting capacity and will to fight. The following diagram visually demonstrates the CARVER matrix (Figure 7-5).

SAMPLE STRATEGIC CARVER MATRIX APPLICATION							
TARGET SYSTEMS	C	A	R	V	E	R	TOTAL
Bulk Electric Power	5	3	3	5	5	5	26*
Bulk Petroleum	5	3	5	4	3	5	25*
Water Supply	3	5	3	5	5	3	24*
Communication Systems	3	4	5	2	2	2	18
Air Transport	1	1	3	1	2	2	10
Ports and Waterways	1	1	3	1	1	1	8
Rail Transport	2	4	4	1	4	3	18
Road Networks	1	5	3	5	2	5	21
*Indicates target systems suitable for attack. In this example, the Bulk Electric Power target system has been selected.							

Figure 7-5. CARVER Matrix.

Looking at the table, the target with the highest score is the bulk electric power plant which has a score total of 26. Thus, using the system, more resources should be assigned to hit the bulk electric power plant.

Conclusion

The purpose of this chapter was to gain an understanding of the operations process, warfighting functions (WFF), and certain aspects inherent to SOF operations. Success in operations demands timely and effective decisions based on applying judgment to available information and knowledge. It requires knowing both when and what to decide.[13]

---

[13] FM 5-0 The Operations Process, 1-5.

Chapter 8 Principles of Planning

"We should never take the first step without considering the last."
- Clausewitz

Planning is the art and science of understanding a situation, envisioning a desired future, and laying out an operational approach to achieve that future (FM 5-0). It is both a continuous and a cyclical activity of the operations process. *A plan is meant to be a framework from which to adapt, not a script to be followed to the letter.* The purpose of this chapter is for the student of war to gain an understanding of the principles of planning along with the elements that make up a good plan and consists of the following:

1. Principles of Planning.
2. Key Planning Concepts.
3. Troop Leading Procedure (TLP).
4. Assumption of Command.

Principles of Planning – A plan is a continuous, evolving framework of anticipated actions that maximizes opportunities. It guides subordinates as they progress through each phase of the operation. Planners must be technically and tactically competent, be disciplined to use doctrinally correct terms and symbols, and understand the fundamental principles of planning.

There are seven principles of planning:
- Visualize a desired end-state.
- Adapt the plan as necessary.
- Planning is continuous.
- Time is the dominant factor.
- Emphasize simplicity and flexibility.
- Planning should be decisive.
- Avoid planning pitfalls.

Visualize a desired end-state – As we've said, when planning is at its best, it involves the correct understanding of a situation, an envisioning of a desired future (imagination/innovation), and a laying out of an operational approach to achieve that future (foresight).

Adapt the plan as necessary – A plan is a framework from which to adapt, not a script to be followed to the letter (FM 5-0). It has been said, "No plan of battle survives the first contact." Although this is true to an extent, we should rather make flexible plans that will survive the first contact. Further, any operation may outrun the initial plan, as fleeting opportunities or unexpected enemy action may require a quick decision to implement a new or modified plan.

Planning is continuous – Plans are revised as time allows and variations (options or branches) continue to be developed.

Time is the dominant factor – Effective planners skillfully use available time to optimize planning and preparation throughout the unit. Effective planners remember not to violate the 1/3 2/3 Rule. This rule reminds planners to use no more than 1/3 of the time available to plan and issue the order so that subordinates have 2/3 of available time to prepare for the mission.

Emphasize simplicity and flexibility –The focus of any planning process should aim to quickly develop a flexible, sound, and fully integrated and synchronized plan (FM 5-0).

Planning should be decisive – Plans should be directed to achieve a clearly defined and obtainable goal within the capabilities of the unit.

Avoid planning pitfalls – Decisive planners recognize the value of planning and avoid common planning pitfalls. These pitfalls generally stem from a common cause; failure to appreciate the unpredictability and uncertainty of military operations. The four common pitfalls consist of:
- Attempting to forecast and dictate events too far into the future.
- Trying to plan in too much detail.
- Using planning as a scripting process.
- Institutionalizing rigid planning methods.

Key Components of a Plan

"It is always well to keep in mind that one fights to gain a definite end – not simply to fight." – Infantry in Battle

While each plan is unique, all plans seek a balance for combining ends, ways, and means against risk. Ends are the desired conditions of a given operation. Ways are actions to achieve the end state. Means are the resources required to execute the way. The key components of a plan are:
- Mission statement.
- Commander's intent.
- Concept of the operation.

- Nested concepts.
- Decisive points and objectives.
- Lines of operations.
- Lines of effort.
- Coordinated instructions.
- Tasks to subordinate units.
- Control measures.

Mission statement – The mission is the task, together with the purpose, that clearly indicates the action to be taken and the reason therefore (JP 1-02). Commanders analyze a mission in terms of the commander's intent two echelons up, specified tasks, and implied tasks. The mission statement contains the elements of who, what, when, where, and why, but seldom specifies how.[1]

Commander's intent – The commander's intent is a clear, concise statement of what the force must do and the conditions the force must establish with respect to the enemy, terrain, and civil considerations that represent the desired end state (FM 3-0). The commander's intent succinctly describes what constitutes success for the operation. It includes the operation's purpose and the conditions that define the end state. It links the mission, concept of operations, and tasks to subordinate units.[2]

Concept of the operation – The concept of operations is a statement that directs the manner in which subordinate units cooperate to accomplish the mission and establishes the sequence of actions the force will use to achieve the end state. It is normally expressed in terms of decisive, shaping, and sustaining operations (See Figure 8-1). Additionally, when writing the concept of operations, leaders consider *nested concepts*, the *sequence of actions and phasing*, *decisive points* and *objectives*, and *lines of operations* and *lines of effort*.

Operation – An operation is a military action or the carrying out of a strategic, tactical, service, training, or administrative military mission.

Decisive operations (DO) – The decisive operation is the operation that directly accomplishes the mission (ADRP 3-0). There is only one decisive operation for any major operation, battle, or engagement for any given echelon (FM 3-21.10).

---

[1] FM 5-0, 2-15.
[2] Ibid.

Shaping operations (SO) - A shaping operation is an operation at any echelon that creates and preserves conditions for the success of the decisive operation through effects on the enemy, other actors, and the terrain (ADRP 3-0). Shaping operations include lethal and nonlethal activities conducted throughout the AO. They support the decisive operation by affecting the enemy capabilities and forces, or by influencing enemy decisions.

Sustaining operation – A sustaining operation is an operation at any echelon that enables the decisive operation or shaping operation by generating or maintaining combat power (ADRP 3-0).

Offensive Operations	Defensive Operations	Tactical Enabling Ops
Movement to Contact	Area Defense	Reconnaissance Ops
Attack	Mobile Defense	Security Operations
Exploitation	Retrograde	Troop Movement
Pursuit	Relief in Place	Passage of Lines
		Combined Arms Breach
Special Purpose Attacks	Forms of Retrograde	Forms of Recon Ops
Spoiling Attack	Delay	Zone Recon
Counterattack	Withdrawal	Area Recon
Ambush	Retirement	Route Recon
Raid		Recon in Force (RIF)
Feint		
Demonstration		
Forms of Maneuver	Forms of Security Ops	
Turning Movement	Screen	
Frontal Attack	Cover	
Infiltration	Local Security	
Envelopment	Area Security (Route/convoy)	
Penetration		

Figure 8-1. Doctrinal Hierarchy of Operations.

Nested concepts - Nested concepts is a planning technique to achieve unity of purpose whereby each succeeding echelon's concept of operations is aligned by purpose with the higher echelons' concept of operations. Commanders ensure the primary tasks for each subordinate unit include a purpose that links the completion of that task to achievement of another task, an objective, or an end state condition.

Area of operations – An area of operations is an operational area defined by the joint force commander for land and maritime forces that should be large enough to accomplish their missions and protect their forces (JP 3-0).

Decisive point – A decisive point is a geographic place, specific key event, critical factor, or function that, when acted upon, allows commanders to gain a marked advantage over an adversary or contribute materially to achieving success (JP 3-0).

Objective – An objective can be physical (an enemy force or terrain feature) or conceptual in the form of a goal (rule of law established). As a graphic control measure, an objective is a location on the ground used to orient operations, phase operations, facilitate changes of direction, and provide for unity of effort (FM 3-90).

Task – A task is a clearly defined and measurable activity accomplished by individuals and organizations (FM 7-0). Tasks are specific activities that contribute to accomplishing missions or other requirements. Tasks direct friendly action. The purpose of each task should nest with completing another task, achieving an objective, or attaining an end state condition (See Figure 8-2).

Tactical Tasks

Enemy Oriented		Terrain Oriented	Friendly Oriented
Ambush	Exploit	Clear	Breach
Attack by Fire	Feint	Control	Cover
Block	Fix	Occupy	Disengage
Breach	Interdict	Recon	Displace
Bypass	Neutralize	Retain	Exfiltrate
Canalize	Penetrate	Secure	Follow
Contain Defeat	Recon	Seize	Guard
Destroy	Rupture		Protect
Disrupt	Support by Fire		Screen
Suppress			

Environmental Oriented	Purpose		
Assess the Population	Allow	Find	Support
Build/Restore Infrastructure	Cause	Identify	Surprise
Coordinate with Civil Authorities	Create	Isolate	
Enable/Engage Civil Authority	Deceive	Influence	
Influence Population	Delay	Locate	
Liaison with Civil Authority	Deny	Observe	
Transfer to Civil Control	Divert	Open	
	Enable	Preserve	
	Envelope	Prevent	
	Expel	Protect	
	Facilitate	Provide Early Warning	

Figure 8-2. Doctrinal Tasks and Purposes (FM 3-21.10)

Purpose – The desired or intended result of the tactical operation stated in terms relating to the enemy or to the desired situation.

Endstate – End state is what the leader wants the situation to be when operations conclude—both military operations, as well as those where the military is in support of other instruments of national power.

Control measure – Control measures are directives communicated graphically or orally by leaders to their subordinates. Leaders use them to assign responsibilities, coordinate fires and maneuver, and control operations.

Further, as we look at the major components of a plan, the following introspective questions will assist us:

- What is the force trying to accomplish and why (ends)? This is articulated in the unit's mission statement and the commander's intent.
- What conditions, when established, constitute the desired end state (ends)? The desired conditions are described as part of the commander's intent.
- How will the force achieve these desired conditions (ways)? The way the force will accomplish the mission is described in the concept of operations.
- What sequence of actions is most likely to attain these conditions (ways)? The sequence of actions, to include phasing, is described in the concept of operations.
- What resources are required, and how can they be applied to accomplish that sequence of actions (means)? The application of resources throughout the operation is addressed in the concept of operations, the warfighting function schemes of support (for example, the scheme of protection and scheme of sustainment), tasks to subordinate units, and task organization.
- What risks are associated with that sequence of actions, and how can they be mitigated (risks)? The concept of operations incorporates risk mitigation as does coordinating instructions.

Reverse and forward planning – Additional planning concepts include reverse and forward planning. Reverse planning involves starting with the operation's end state and working backward in time. Leaders begin by identifying the last step, the next-to-last step, and so on. They continue until they reach the step that begins the operation. It answers the question: Where do we eventually want to be? And forward planning involves starting with the present conditions and laying out potential decisions and actions forward in time, identifying the next feasible step, the next after that, and so on. In forward planning, the envisioned end state serves as a distant and general aiming point rather than as a specific objective. Forward planning answers the question: Where can we go next?[3]

The climate of war – As has been said, intangible factors such as, chance and friction contribute to the uncertain nature of operations. Chance is the lack of order or clear predictability of operations, while friction is the combination of countless factors that impinge on the conduct of operations. During operations, leaders make decisions, develop plans, and direct actions under varying degrees of uncertainty. Each operation is rich in unique episodes. Clausewitz writes,

Each is an uncharted sea, full of reefs. The commander may suspect the reefs' existence without ever having seen them; now he has to steer past them in the dark. If a contrary wind springs up, if some major mischance appears, he will need the greatest skill and personal exertion, and the utmost presence of mind, though from a distance everything may seem to be proceeding automatically.[4]

Leaders contend with thinking, adaptive enemies in areas of operations where many events occur simultaneously. A difficulty is accurately predicting how enemies will act and react, how populations will perceive or react to friendly actions, or how events will develop. Within these complex, ever-changing, and uncertain environments, leaders conduct planning.

Conclusion

While planning may start an iteration of the operations process, planning does not stop with production of an order. During preparation and execution, the plan is continuously refined as situational understanding improves. Subordinates and others provide feedback as to what is working, what is not working, and how the force can do things better. In some circumstances, leaders may determine that the current order is no longer relevant to the situation. In these instances, leaders reframe the problem and initiate planning activities to develop a new plan. The measure of a good plan is not whether execution transpires as planned, but whether the plan facilitates effective action in the face of unforeseen events. Good plans and orders foster initiative.

---

[3] FM 3-21.10, 2-8.
[4] Clausewitz, On War, I, 7, 140.

Chapter 9 Combat Orders

"We consider it axiomatic that in war there will always be a plan. But history is replete with instances where organizations have drifted into battle for no particular reason and with no particular plan. Simple and direct plans and methods make for foolproof performance." –Infantry in Battle

Effective leaders recognize the value of planning, avoid common planning pitfalls, and mitigate friction as much as possible by forethought, careful planning, and good troop leading while ever conscious of the fact that time is the dominant factor. This chapter outlines the two most prominent forms of combat orders used in small units: the Warning Order (WARNO), and Operations Order (OPORD).

Warning Order

Roll call, pencil/pen/paper, SUT handbook, map, protractor, leaders monitor, hold all questions till the end.
References: Refer to higher headquarters' OPORD, and identify map sheet for operation.
Time Zone Used throughout the Order: Task Organization:

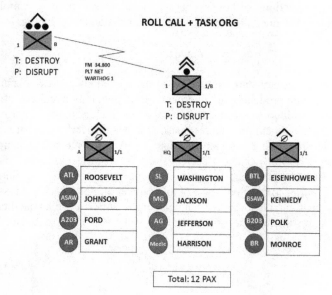

Figure 9-1. Task Organization

1. SITUATION. Find this in higher's OPORD para 1a(1-3).
a. **Area of Interest.** Outline the area of interest on the map.

295

(1) Orient relative to each point on the compass (N, S, E, W)
(2) Box in the entire AO with grid lines (See Figure 9-2).

b. **Area of Operations.** Outline the area of operation on the map. Point out the objective and current location of your unit.
(1) Trace your Zone using boundaries
(2) Familiarize by identifying natural (terrain) and man-made features in the zone your unit is operating (See Figure 9-2).

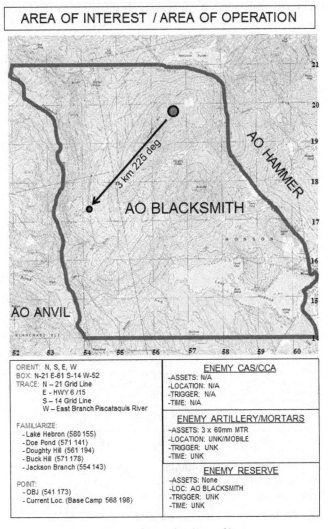

Figure 9-2. Area of Operations/Area of Interest.

296

c. **Enemy Forces**. Include significant changes in enemy composition, disposition, and courses of action. Information not available for inclusion in the initial WARNO can be included in subsequent warning orders (WHO, WHAT, WHERE).

d. **Friendly Forces**. Optional; address only if essential to the WARNO.
(1) Give higher commander's mission and 5 Ws (See Figure 9-3).
(2) State higher commander's intent. (Higher's [go to mapboard] OPORD para 1b[2]), give task and purpose.
(3) Point out friendly locations on the map board.

FRIENDLY FORCES	
HIGHER'S MISSION (2 LEVELS UP)	B CO, 1/1 conducts area ambushes NLT 030300RNOV2013 IVO AO BLACKSMITH to destroy enemy personnel and equipment, gather PIR and disrupt the establishment of enemy FOBs in Sector.
HIGHER'S INTENT (2 LEVELS UP)	Deny enemy freedom of movement in AO BLACKSMITH by destroying enemy personnel and equipment through conduct of multiple ambushes on enemy patrols maneuvering through the area. End State: When enemy is destroyed and Command and Control is non-functional.
HIGHER'S MISSION (1 LEVEL UP)	2nd PLT, B CO conducts area ambush NLT 030300RNOV2013 IVO AO BLACKSMITH to destroy enemy personnel and equipment, gather PIR, and disrupt the establishment of enemy FOBs in AO YUKON.
HIGHER'S INTENT (1 LEVEL UP)	Destroy Enemy personnel and equipment, gather PIR, disrupt Enemy LOC and movement. End State: When enemy forces are unable to utilize high speed AoA within AO BLACKSMITH, thereby isolating current enemy FOBs and denying the construction of new ones.
ADJACENT UNITS	2ND SQD: **19T DL 542 180** T: Destroy P: Disrupt 3rd SQD: **19T DL 543 164** T: Destroy P: Disrupt

Figure 9-3. Friendly Forces Mission.

e. **Attachments and Detachments.** Give initial task organization, only address major unit changes, and then go to the map board.

2. MISSION. State mission twice (Who, What, Where, When, and Why):

ODA 9311 conducts point ambush to destroy enemy personnel & equipment IVO 19TDL 541 173 NLT 022300ROCT2014 IOT disrupt enemy movement throughout AO BLACKSMITH, and gather PIR for future operations. (x 2)

3. EXECUTION.

a. **Concept of Operations.** This includes a brief overview of the entire mission from start to finish to include all movement; air, vehicular, foot, etc. It should specify general direction, distance, time of travel, mode of travel, and major tasks to be conducted.

b. **Tasks to Subordinate Units.** Provide specified tasks to subordinate units. Focus on non-tactical instructions for planning and preparation of the operations order. Leaders should also include tactical instructions for executing the mission using control, movement, AOO for each element in task organization. Planning guidance consists of tasks assigned to elements in the form and order of teams, special teams, and key individuals (See Figure 9-4).

TASKS TO SUBORDINATE UNITS	TASKS TO SUBORDINATE UNITS
HQ: -2nd in OOM -MG TM will provide supporting fires into the kill zone during AOO -AB is primary recorder & Alternate Demo -SL will be primary DEMO **A TM:** -1st in OOM -ATL is responsible for Land Navigation & Designation of ERRP (200-300m) -Provide a 2 x Man EPW TM (PRI) -Provide a 2 x Man Aid & Litter TM -Provide a 2 x Man RECON TM (APT & ASAW) -Provide AT4 & M203 for Security during AOO -1 x Compass-man & 1 x Pace-man **B TM** -3rd in OOM -1 x AT4 & 1 x 203 for Security during AOO -1 x SAW Gunner & 3 x RM to Assault Element during AOO -1 x Compass-man & 1 x Pace-man -Provide a 2 x Man EPW TM (ALT) -Provide a 2 x Man Aid & Litter TM **Squad Leader** -Responsible for writing Para. 2,3 & 5 of the OPORD -All reporting to Higher HQ **Gun Team** -Construction of AOO Terrain Model (ORP, RP, & OBJ) -Ensure all Radios are in working order -Test Fire of MGs	**ATL:** -3rd in COC -Write Paragraph 1 of the OPORD & Trucking Annex -Develop Primary & Alternate, Mounted & Dismounted Routes to our OBJ and from the OBJ to the PB -Construct Routes & AOO Terrain Models -ATL is Assault team Leader -ATL controls the Assault during AOO **BTL:** - 2nd in COC / In charge at all times in my absence - BTL is Security TL for AOO - Write Paragraph 4 of the OPORD & Patrol Base Annex - Draw & Issue all Items - Conduct WPNs Test Fire - Ensure accountability of patrol at all times - Set up MWE Poncho & be prepared to brief during the OPORD - Ensure all EQUIP is tied down IAW SOP - Develop & Coordinate for all HLZs & AXPs - Prepare & Brief Scheme of Medical Support during OPORD - Develop & Brief LOAD/BUMP PLAN during OPORD **PACE:** Pass Pace Count every 300 meters **DEMO:** 3 Charges – 1 block of C4 each dual primed, 2 min firing system **EPW:** 2 x Sand Bags, 2 x Gags, 2 pair of Hand Restraints each **MEDIC:** 1 x Poleless Litter, 1 x M-3 Bag **ALL:** Memorize all Distances, Directions, & Grids; Ensure NVGs are working & have fresh Batteries; Test Fire Weapon(s) and Oil

Figure 9-4. Tasks to Subordinate Units.

c. **Coordinating Instructions.** Include any information available at that time. If you know it, then at least cover the following items:
• Uniform and equipment common to all.
• Consider the factors of METT-TC and tailor the load for each soldier.

• Timeline. (State when, what, where, who and all specified times. Reverse plan. Use 1/3 - 2/3 rule).
• Give specific priorities in order of completion.
• Give information about coordination meetings.
• Time of OPORD.
• Rehearsals / Inspections by priority.
• Earliest movement time.

4. SUSTAINMENT. Include any known logistics preparation for the operation (See Figure 9-5).

a. **Logistics.**
(1) Maintenance. Include weapons and equipment DX time and location.
(2) Transportation. State method and mode of transportation for infil/exfil. Identify any coordination needed for external assets. Task subordinate leader (if needed) to generate load plan, number of lifts/serials, and bump plan.
(3) Supply. Only include classes of supply that require coordination or special instructions (rations, fuel, ammo etc).

SUSTAINMENT		
MAINT		•LEVEL 1 MAINTENANCE ON M240, M249, AT4, M4, CLAYMORES, RADIOS, AND SQUAD EQUIPMENT •DX EQUIPMENT REQUEST RESUPPLY
TRANSPO		•MOUNTED MOVEMENT WILL BE CONDUCTED ON 20 PAX TROOP CARRIER •MOVEMENT AFTER VDO WILL BE DISMOUNTED SQD MOVEMENT •RECOVERY: SECURE VEHICLE, REQUEST RECOVERY ASSETTS.
SUPPLY	I	•EACH MAN WILL HAVE 7x MREs AND 6x QUARTS OF WATER PRIOR TO INFIL •WATER RESUPPLY IS THROUGH LOCAL SOURCES AND IODINE TABLETS
	III	•1 BOTTLE OF CLP PER PERSON AND 1 LARGE CLP BOTTLE FOR M240B
	V	•BTL WILL ENSURE EACH MAN HAS 2x UBL •SPEEDBALL WILL BE LOADED WITH 1x UBL AND KEPT AT BASECAMP
	VIII	•SQD WILL HAVE 1x M3 MEDIC BAG AND 2x POLELESS LITTERS •EACH MAN WILL HAVE 1x ISRAELI DRESSING AND 1x TOURNIQUET IN IFAC
RESUPPLY		•AT RESUPPLY POINT •SPEEDBALLS AND OTHER ITEMS AVAILABLE UPON COORDINATION (BASECAMP)
EPW (Personnel Services Support)		•EPW COLLECTION POINT IS AT AXP 2 FOR RANK OF MAJOR AND ABOVE •OTHERS WILL BE RELEASED AFTER PHASE IV OF THE OPERATION •EPWs WILL BE MARKED WITH SANDBAG OVER HEAD AND ZIP TIES AROUND THEIR HANDS.
MEDICAL		•TREATMENT: SELF AID, BUDDY AID, MEDIC, REQUESTED MEDEVAC PERSONNEL •EVACUATION: UH-60, AMBULANCE, POLELESS LITTER, BUDDY CARRY •PRIORITY OF TREATMENT: FRIENDLY WIA, ENEMY WIA, CIVILIAN WIA, FRIENDLY KIA. CO CMD NET IS PRI MEDEVAC NET •PREVENTATIVE MEDICINE: 2x BOTTLES IODINE TABLETS, CONDUCT PERSONAL •HYGIENE (BRUSH TEETH, WASH GROIN/ARM PITS/FRICTION POINTS, CHANGE SOCKS, AND BOOTS)

Figure 9-5. Sustainment.

b. **Personnel Services Support.** State any pertinent services for soldiers (religious services etc).

c. **Army Health System Support.** Identify any medical equipment, support, or preventative medicine that needs to be coordinated.

5. COMMAND AND CONTROL.

a. **Command.** Succession of Command. State the succession of command if not covered in the unit's SOP.

SL followed by; BTL, ATL, AG, and then service members by date of rank.

b. **Control.**
(1) Command Posts. Describe the employment of command posts (CPs), including the location of each CP and its time of opening and closing, as appropriate. Typically at platoon level the only reference to command posts will be the company CP.

PL located at Company TOC at FOB Howard through the duration of the operation. SL located by phase as follows: Phase I – Planning: ODA 9311 Bay; Phase II – Infiltration: w/ HQ; Phase III – Occupation: CP @ Halts; LDRs RECON; MG Position during AOO; Phase IV – Execution: IVO Center of Kill Zone; Phase V – Withdraw: w/ HQ Element; Phase VI – Recovery: CP.

(2) Reports. List reports not covered in SOPs.

SL – responsible for submitting daily SITREP and a 100% Sensitive Items (SI) report to PL NLT 0700.
SL – responsible for submitting SITREP to Company TOC following all engagements of enemy contact.
ATL and BTL – submit SI to SL NLT 0645 daily.
Follow-on FRAGOs: Medic responsible for monitoring SCORPION NET 30.000 from 0700-1000 daily.

c. **Signal.** Describe the concept of signal support, including current SOI edition or refer to higher OPORD.

Give subordinates guidance on tasks to complete for preparation of the OPORD and the mission. Give time, place, and uniform for the OPORD. Give a time hack and ask for questions.

Patrol Operation Order [1]

Time zone used throughout the order: If the operation will take place in one time zone, use that time zone throughout the order (including annexes and appendixes). If the operation spans several time zones, use Zulu time.

Task organization: Describe the allocation of forces to support the commander's concept. You may show task organization in one of two places: just above paragraph 1, or in an annex, if the task organization is long or complex.

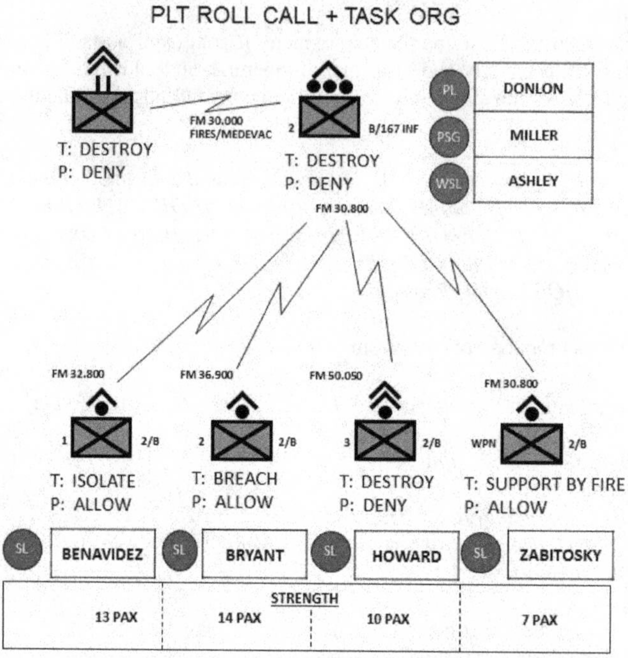

PLT ROLL CALL + TASK ORG

Figure 9-6. Example Task Organization for a Platoon Raid.

1. SITUATION.

a. **Area of Interest.** Describe the area of interest or areas outside of your area of operation that can influence your area of operation.

b. **Area of Operations.** Describe the area of operations. Refer to the appropriate map and use overlays as needed.

•Go to the map.

---

[1] The five-paragraph field order was introduced into the Army at Fort Leavenworth in 1894-95 by Captain Eben Swift, who was seeking a more systematic method to examine tactical problems.

•Apply the Orient, Box, Trace, and Familiarize technique only to the area the unit is moving through. (Get this info from the platoon OPORD.)

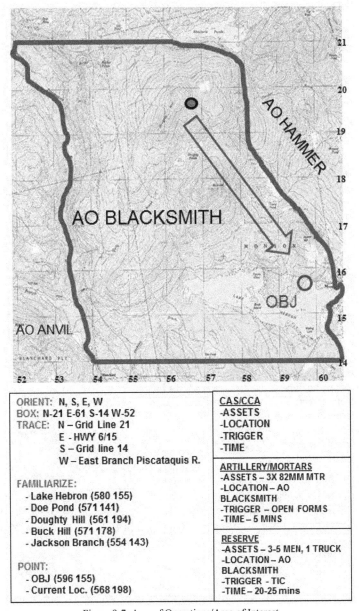

ORIENT: N, S, E, W
BOX: N-21 E-61 S-14 W-52
TRACE: N – Grid Line 21
  E - HWY 6/15
  S – Grid line 14
  W – East Branch Piscataquis R.

FAMILIARIZE:
 - Lake Hebron (580 155)
 - Doe Pond (571 141)
 - Doughty Hill (561 194)
 - Buck Hill (571 178)
 - Jackson Branch (554 143)

POINT:
 - OBJ (596 155)
 - Current Loc. (568 198)

CAS/CCA
-ASSETS
-LOCATION
-TRIGGER
-TIME

ARTILLERY/MORTARS
-ASSETS – 3X 82MM MTR
-LOCATION – AO BLACKSMITH
-TRIGGER – OPEN FORMS
-TIME – 5 MINS

RESERVE
-ASSETS – 3-5 MEN, 1 TRUCK
-LOCATION – AO BLACKSMITH
-TRIGGER - TIC
-TIME – 20-25 mins

Figure 9-7. Area of Operations/Area of Interest.

302

(1) Terrain: Using the OAKOC format, state how the terrain will affect both friendly and enemy forces in the AO. Use the OAKOC from higher's OPORD. Refine it based on your analysis of the terrain in the AO. Follow these steps to brief terrain.

Obstacles: Natural Obstacles: Creeks, draws, and large clearing areas.
-Friendly Effect: Slow movement by canalizing forces into restricted terrain, mounted movement susceptible to IEDs.
-Enemy Effect: Enjoys freedom of maneuver on higher ground and less restricted terrain.
Avenues of Approach: 3 Major: HWY 6-15, Blanchard Road, and Jackson Brook Trail.
-Friendly Effect: Primary and Secondary Roads present multiple danger areas which must be deliberately crossed.
-Enemy Effect: Use of roads will increase mobility and reduce response time of reserve
Key Terrain: K1 – Buck Hill, K2 – Blanchard Road, K3 – Jackson Brook Trail.
-Friendly Effect: K1 provides excellent observation of the area, K2 and K3 must be controlled to reduce enemy Freedom of Movement.
-Enemy Effect: Favors mobility and observation of indirect fires throughout area.
Observation/Field of Fire: In restricted terrain = 50m max, on higher ground = 300m max
-Friendly effect: Favors friendly movement through low ground, will be difficult to observe. Limit range of large weapon systems.
-Enemy effect: To observe possible friendly AoA Enemy forces will have to abandon positions of strength on higher ground. Will be able to observe IDF from large open areas on high ground.
Cover and Concealment: In lower areas both will be excellent, on higher ground concealment will be sparse and cover will be thin.
-Friendly effect: Favors movement through low ground with greater degrees of concealment.
-Enemy effect: Unlikely to use low ground which will make observation of their movements easier.

Figure 9-8. Terrain Analysis.

(2) Weather. Describe the aspects of weather that impact operations. Consider the five military aspects of weather to drive your analysis (V,W,T,C,P- Visibility, Winds, Temperature/Humidity, Cloud Cover, Precipitation)

Temp High	Temp Low	Sunrise	Sunset
Moonrise	Moonset	Moon phase	% Illum
BMNT	EENT	Wind Direction	& Speed

Weather Analysis

	EFFECTS ON FRIENDLY	EFFECTS ON ENEMY
	1 mile visibility	
VISIBILITY	Low ceiling and visibility will limit use of rotary assets and reduce effectiveness of NODs	Reduce the effectiveness of NVGs
	6 knots from NE; highest winds during afternoon	
WINDS	Smoke will need to be thrown further NE of intended target to obscure. Enemy elements will be easier to detect to NE during SLLS (sound & smell) and while waiting to initiate the ambush.	Friendly elements will be easier to detect during movement from enemy OPs and base camps.
	Rain from approx. 140600ROCT14 to 161600ROCT14	
PRECIPITATION	Draws and creeks will rise and limit ability to traverse during exfil. No rain expected during infil. Rain will begin after the ambush is set. Advantage to friendly forces due to the enemies degraded ability to detect the ambush.	Friendly forces will be more difficult to detect during the rain, degrade ability to detect ambush prior to initiation.
	Cloudy from 030100ROCT14 through 06OCT14 **BMNT: 0611 EENT: 1845** **SR: 0707 SS: 1749** **MR: 1246 MS: 0120** **Illum.: 52%**	
CLOUD COVER & ILLUMINATION	**This will benefit friendly forces since limited illumination decreases chances of detection during movement. No illum. during AOO will decrease chances of enemy early detection.**	No illumination during ambush limits enemy ability to detect friendly element during movement and AOO.
	Low: 58 degrees High: 78 degrees (06OCT14)	
TEMPERATURE & HUMIDITY	Lower temperature after movement, friendly forces will need to utilize snivel gear at ORP to maintain operation tempo and morale	Limited impact on enemy since they are likely to stay relatively dry on roads, and the temperature will not have a significant impact on movement since the enemy generally carries lighter loads.

Figure 9.9 Example Weather Analysis.

c. **Enemy Forces.** The enemy situation in higher headquarters' OPORD (paragraph 1c) forms the basis for this. Refine it by adding the detail your subordinates require. • Point out on the map the location of recent enemy activity known and suspected.
(1) State the enemy's composition, disposition, and strength.

(a) <u>Enemy Composition</u>:

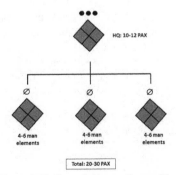

Figure 9-10. Example Enemy Composition.

(b) <u>Enemy Disposition</u>:
-Force is arrayed in AO BLACKSMITH with a HQ element controlling 3-4x team-size elements.

(c) <u>Enemy Strength</u>:
-Insurgent force in AO BLACKSMITH total of 20-30 PAX
-PLT HQ of 10-12 PAX
-3-4x cells, of 4-6x PAX
-Estimated to be at 100% strength

<u>Capability by Warfighting Function</u>:

Intelligence
-Limited ground based intel, relies on HUMINT
Fire Support
-May possess 60mm Mortars, unconfirmed
Protection
-No special protection methods
Sustainment
-Reliant on the local economy and pilfering of UN relief efforts
Command and Control
-Cellphone and Messenger are primary communication means
-Cell leaders meet directly with group leader periodically
Movement and Maneuver
-Insurgents are highly mobile (more in recent activities)

(2) Describe recent enemy activities.

Recent activities:
Insurgent elements are mobile, driving military-style vehicles, carrying small arms and dressed in military clothing when targeting UN convoys, distribution centers and warehouses.

(3) Describe his known or suspected locations and capabilities.
(4) Describe the enemy's most likely and most dangerous course of action.

MLCOA: *Insurgent elements will continue operating in 4-6x PAX TMs, targeting soft targets, such as unsecured UN warehouses, UN convoys, and UN relief workers operating in AO BLACKSMITH.*

MDCOA: *Insurgent smaller operational cells unite and form larger force (SQD-sized and above) IOT attack larger UN convoys, guarded UN warehouses, FOB Howard.*

d. Friendly Forces. Get this information from paragraphs 1d, 2, and 3 of the higher headquarters' OPORD.
(1) Higher Headquarters' Mission and Intent
(a) State mission and intent two levels up.
(b) State mission and intent one level up.
(2) Mission of Adjacent Units. State locations of units to the left, right, front, and rear. State those units' tasks and purposes; and say how those units will influence yours, particularly adjacent unit patrols.
(a) Show other units' locations on map board.
(b) Include statements about the influence each of the above patrols will have on your mission, if any.
(c) Obtain this information from higher's OPORD. It gives each leader an idea of what other units are doing and where they are going. This information is in paragraph 3b(1) (Execution, Concept of the Operation, Scheme of Movement and Maneuver).
(d) Also include any information obtained when the leader conducts adjacent unit coordination.

FRIENDLY – GENERAL SITUATION

HIGHER'S MISSION	B CO conducts unilateral offensive operations in AO BLACKSMITH NET 28 0700 NOV 14 IOT destroy enemy personnel and equipment, gather PIR, and to deny enemy elements refuge or freedom of movement within AO.
HIGHER'S INTENT	US forces must unilaterally clear insurgent cells and facilities within AO BLACKSMITH IOT begin building ROM forces capabilities.
ADJACENT UNITS	2ND PLT – 19T DL 5521 1510, 3rd PLT 19T DL 5430 1987
ATTACHMENTS/ DETACHMENTS	None
HIGHER'S CONCEPT	PLTs will SP from FOB HOWARD and conduct separate PLT raids, then conduct PB operations and follow on operations.

Figure 9-11. Example Friendly Situation.

e. Attachments and Detachments. State when attachment or detachment will be in effect, if that differs from when the OPORD is in effect such as on order or on commitment of the reserve. Use the term "remains attached" when units will be or have been attached for some time.

2. MISSION. State the mission derived during the planning process. A mission statement has no subparagraphs. Answer the 5 W's: Who? What (task)? Where? When? And Why (purpose)?
• State the mission clearly and concisely. Read it twice.

1st Platoon conducts a raid to destroy enemy logistical storage area and training camp located VIC 19T DL 5960 1551, NLT 29 0600R NOV 2014 IOT attrite enemy forces. (x 2)

3. EXECUTION

a. **Commander's Intent**. State the commander's intent which is his clear, concise statement of what the force must do and the conditions the force must establish with respect to the enemy, terrain, and civil considerations that represent the desired end state.

b. **Concept of Operations**. Describe how the unit will accomplish its mission from start to finish. The following subparagraphs from FM 5-0 show what might be required within the concept of the operation. Ensure that you state the purpose of the war fighting functions within the concept of the operation: Fire support, Movement and Maneuver, Protection Command and Control Intelligence Sustainment (formerly called "CSS").

COMMANDER'S INTENT	
PURPOSE	My intent for this operation is to destroy all enemy and equipment on the OBJ, and gather PIR IOT develop future targets in AO BLACKSMITH.
KEY TASKS	-Emplace raid NLT 29 0600 NOV 13 -Move undetected to OBJ -Postured for future operations
END STATE	**ENEMY:** Destroyed and unable further utilize AO to mount attacks **TERRAIN:** Enemy denied further usage of AO BLACKSMITH **CIVILIAN:** Civilian casualties minimized, see superior capabilities of US forces **FRIENDLY:** PLTs consolidated at PB postured for follow on missions.
CONCEPT STATEMENT	
PURPOSE OF OPN	Attrite the enemy forces in the AO, negatively impact the enemy's moral and confidence in moving through their AO.
DECISIVE TO THIS OPN IS:	One team from ASLT 1 crossing PL Red
THIS IS DECISIVE BECAUSE:	We will have an established foothold with numerical superiority in the OBJ while providing overwhelming firepower.
DO THIS BY:	Conducting an infiltration
DO T/P	3rd SQD T: Destroy P: Prevent enemy from attaining control in AO BLACKSMITH
SO1 T/P	2nd SQD T: Breach P: Facilitate FOM of Assault element
SO2 T/P	WPNs SQD T: Support by Fire P: Enable FOM of Assault element
SO3 T/P	1st SQD T: Isolate P: Allow FOM of Assault element
END STATE	**ENEMY:** Destroyed and unable further utilize camp and storage area **TERRAIN:** Enemy denied further usage of area **CIVILIAN:** Civilian casualties minimized, see superior capabilities of US forces **FRIENDLY:** PLT consolidated at PB postured for follow on missions.

Figure 9-12. Example Intent and Concept Statement.

307

Task to Maneuver Units: (See Figure 9-12).

3rd Squad – You are the DO. Your task is to destroy all enemy personnel on the objective. Your purpose is to prevent enemy from attaining control in AO BLACKSMITH and collect all available PIR in support of future follow-on missions.

2nd Squad – You are SO1. Your task is breach. Your purpose is to enable the DO's assault process.

Security – You are SO2. Your task is to isolate the enemy in the kill zone thereby allowing no one in or out. Your purpose is to protect our flanks as well as provide early warning IOT prevent compromise and block any enemy QRF.

This operation will be conducting in 5 phases:
1. Planning and preparation. Receipt of order to SP.
2. Infiltration. SP to the security halt for the ORP.
3. Establishment. Sec halt for the ORP to raid established.
4. Execution. Raid initiation to dissemination of info.
5. Reconsolidation. Security halt to disseminate info to PB.

c. **Scheme of Movement and Maneuver**. Describe the employment of maneuver units in accordance with the concept of operations. Address subordinate units and attachments by name. State each one's mission as a task and purpose. Ensure that the subordinate units' missions support that of the main effort. Focus on actions on the objective. Include a detailed plan and criteria for engagement / disengagement, an alternate plan in case of compromise or unplanned enemy force movement, and a withdrawal plan. The brief is to be sequential, taking you from start to finish, covering all aspects of the operation.
- Brief from the start of your operation, to mission complete.
- Break operation into phases for simplicity and coherency.
- Cover all routes, primary and alternate, from insertion, through AOO, to link-up, until mission complete.
- Brief your plan for crossing known danger areas.
- Brief your plan for reacting to enemy contact.
- Brief PACE plan for initiation and cease fire.
- Brief contingencies.

d. **Scheme of Fires**. State scheme of fires to support the overall concept and state who (which maneuver unit) has priority of fire. You can use the PLOT-CR format (purpose, location, observer, trigger, communication method, resources) to plan fires. Refer to the target list worksheet and overlay here, if applicable. Discuss specific targets and point them out on the terrain model.

e. **Casualty Evacuation**. Provide a detailed CASEVAC plan during each phase of the operation. Include CCP locations, tentative extraction points, and methods of extraction.

f. **Tasks to Subordinate Units**. Clearly state the missions or tasks for each subordinate unit that reports directly to the headquarters issuing the order. List the units in the task organization, including reserves. Use a separate subparagraph for each subordinate unit. State only the tasks needed for comprehension, clarity, and emphasis. Place tactical tasks that affect two or more units in Coordinating Instructions (subparagraph 3h). Platoon leaders may task their subordinate squads to provide any of the following special teams: reconnaissance and security, assault, support, aid and litter, EPW and search, clearing, and demolitions. You may also include detailed instructions for the platoon sergeant, RTO, compass-man, and pace-man.

g. **Coordinating Instructions**. This is always the last subparagraph under paragraph 3. List only the instructions that apply to two or more units, and which are seldom covered in unit SOPs. Refer the user to an annex for more complex instructions. The information listed below is required.
(1) Time Schedule. State time, place, uniform, and priority of rehearsals, backbriefs, inspections, and movement.
(2) Commander's Critical Information Requirements. Include PIR and FFIR.
(a) Priority intelligence requirements. PIR includes all intelligence that the commander must have for planning and decision making.
(b) Friendly force information requirements. FFIR includes what the commander needs to know about friendly forces available for the operation. It can include personnel status, ammunition status, and leadership capabilities.
(3) Essential Elements of Friendly Information. EEFI are critical aspects of friendly operations that, if known by the enemy, would compromise, lead to failure, or limit success of the operation.
(4) Risk-Reduction Control Measures. These are measures unique to the operation. They supplement the unit SOP and can include mission-oriented protective posture, operational exposure guidance, vehicle recognition signals, and fratricide prevention measures.
(5) Rules of Engagement (ROE).
(6) Environmental Considerations.
(7) Force Protection.

4. SUSTAINMENT. Describe the concept of sustainment to include logistics, personnel, and medical.

a. **Logistics.**
(1) Sustainment Overlay. Include current and proposed company trains locations, CCPs (include marking method), equipment collection points, HLZs, AXPs, and any friendly sustainment locations (FOBs, COPs etc).
(2) Maintenance. Include weapons and equipment DX time and location.
(3) Transportation. State method and mode of transportation for infil/exfil, load plan, number of lifts/serials, bump plan, recovery assets, recovery plan.
(4) Supply.
Class I--Rations plan.
Class III--Petroleum.
Class V--Ammunition.
Class VII--Major end items.
Class VIII--Medical.
Class IX--Repair parts.
Distribution Methods.
(5) Field Services. Include any services provided or required (laundry, showers, etc).

b. **Personnel Services Support.**
(1) Method of marking and handling EPWs.
(2) Religious Services.

c. **Army Health System Support.**
(1) Medical Command and Control. Include location of medics, identify medical leadership, personnel controlling medics, and method of marking patients.
(2) Medical Treatment. State how wounded or injured soldiers will be treated (self aid, buddy aid, CLS, EMT, etc).
(3) Medical Evacuation. Describe how dead or wounded, friendly and enemy personnel will be evacuated and identify aid and litter teams. Include special equipment needed for evacuation.
(4) Preventive Medicine. Identify any preventive medicine soldiers may need for the mission (sun block, chap stick, insect repellant, in-country specific medicine).

5. COMMAND AND CONTROL. State where command and control facilities and key leaders are located during the operation.

a. **Command.**

(1) Location of Commander/Patrol Leader. State where the commander intends to be during the operation, by phase if the operation is phased.

(2) Succession of Command. State the succession of command if not covered in the unit's SOP.

b. **Control.**

(1) Command Posts. Describe the employment of command posts (CPs), including the location of each CP and its time of opening and closing, as appropriate. Typically at platoon level the only reference to command posts will be the company CP.

(2) Reports. List reports not covered in SOPs.

c. **Signal.** Describe the concept of signal support, including current SOI edition or refer to higher OPORD.

(1) Identify the SOI index that is in effect.

(2) Identify methods of communication by priority.

(3) Describe pyrotechnics and signals, to include arm and hand signals (demonstrate).

(4) Give code words such as OPSKEDs.

(5) Give challenge and password (use behind friendly lines).

(6) Give number combination (use forward of friendly lines).

(7) Give running password.

(8) Give recognition signals (near/ far and day/ night).

*Actions after Issuance of OPORD: Issue annexes, highlight next hard time, give time hack, and ASK for questions.

Conclusion

As we've said, a good plan facilitates effective action in the face of unforeseen events. Good plans and orders foster initiative, mitigate friction and instill confidence. A good WARNO and OPORD should be clear and concise enough so any member of the patrol can execute, and apply initiative in carrying out the intent.

Chapter 10   Prepare a Patrol

"The Patrol Leader is responsible for whatever the patrol does or fails to do."

For a patrol to succeed, all its members must be well trained and briefed with actions rehearsed. Further, "successful patrolling demands the highest of soldierly virtues. Therefore, the selection of personnel for an important patrol must not be perfunctory affair. The men should be carefully selected and only the intelligent, the physically fit and the stout of heart should be considered. One careless or stupid individual may bring about the death or capture of the entire patrol or cause it to fail in its mission. The moron, the weakling and the timid have no place in this hazardous and exacting duty."[1]

The purpose of this chapter is to discuss the preparation of a patrol from notification until the time of departure. This will be accomplished by an elaboration of Troop Leading Procedures (TLP) – the framework for the planning and preparation of small unit missions (See Figure 10-1).

Figure 10-1. Troop Leading Procedures.

Troop Leading Procedures

Troop Leading Procedures (TLP) consist of eight steps which are not necessarily sequential. However, steps 1-3 of the TLP usually do not change,

---

[1] Infantry in Battle, 324.

steps 4-7 are interchangeable, and step 8 occurs throughout the process. Patrol leaders modify the sequence to meet the mission, situation, and available time. Some steps are done concurrently while others may go on continuously throughout the operation. The TLP consists of the following steps:

1. Receive the mission – The mission assigned to a patrol must be clear and concise, oriented toward one objective with a specific task and purpose. The patrol leader must have a clear understanding of his mission, the commander's intent, and the enemy and friendly situations. At this initial step in the TLP, the patrol leader reviews the mission and decides what efforts must begin immediately. He makes a tentative time schedule to resource available time (1/3 2/3 rule).[1] A proper use of subordinates to manage these initial tasks reduces preparation time and frees up the patrol leader for proper planning and reconnaissance. Some of these tasks may include:[2]

- How should I task organize my element for this patrol?
- When will the patrol depart and return? How many days rations will the patrol require? How much ammunition will be required?
- Is fire support (artillery, mortars) available? If so, what type?
- Is close air support (CAS) available?
- What MEDEVAC assets are available?
- Is a quick reaction force (QRF) available?
- What type of infil/exfil platforms are available?
- What is the enemy composition, disposition, and strength? Recent activities?
- What are the locations and activities of friendly troops?
- Will the patrol have to pass through outposts or other security elements (passage of forward friendly lines)?
- What are the rules of engagement (ROE) for this patrol?
- What are the missions and routes of other patrols?
- What are some suitable routes going into and out of the objective? By air movement? By vehicle movement? By foot movement?

During this step, and prior to the warning order (WARNO), the patrol leader must ensure:
- Each member of the patrol has an assigned position and weapon.
- Specialty teams have been assigned and equipment issued.

---

[1] This rule reminds planners to use no more than 1/3 of the time available to plan and issue the order so that subordinates have 2/3 of available time to prepare for the mission.
[2] The majority of this information will normally be listed in higher's operations order.

- Rucksacks are packed according to the packing list with equipment tied down.
- A tentative time schedule is posted.

2. Issue a warning order – A warning order (WARNO) is a preliminary notice of an order or action that is to follow (FM 1-02). At this step, the patrol leader issues a WARNO as outlined in Chapter 9.

3. Make a tentative plan – Once the WARNO is given and initial preparations are set in motion, the patrol leader begins analyzing the mission. Instead of a leader trying to come up with the whole plan himself, he should delegate as many planning tasks as possible. To organize thinking, the patrol leader uses METT-TC:

Mission – the mission assigned to the patrol and how it relates to the mission of the commander who is sending the patrol. As the patrol leader analyzes the mission he considers various courses of action (COA). Principal variables between COAs normally consist in the following:
- Patrol task organization.
- Form of maneuver employed.
- Type of ambush to be used (area or point).
- Formation of ambush to be used (linear, L-shaped, etc.).
- Routes to be used.

Type of Terrain	Distance Covered in Meters Per Hour
Trail	1,500
Temperate Forest	1,000
Tropical Rain Forest	500
Swamp	300

Enemy – what is known or suspected of enemy presence and capabilities, habits and characteristics, and fighting techniques? The leader considers all available information of known or suspected enemy positions and previous ambush sites.

Terrain and weather – including ground, vegetation, drainage, weather, and visibility (weather and light data). In studying maps of the terrain over which the leader will move his unit, the leader first checks the map's marginal data to determine reliability at the time the map was made. If reliability is not good, or if the map is old, he evaluates its reliability in light of all other information he can obtain.

For example, a 20-year-old map may not show several nearby roads and trails; more recent building development in the area will not be shown. The patrol leader considers the factors of OACOK (observation/fields of fire, avenues of approach, cover and concealment, obstacles, and key terrain). For example, he considers how the terrain will influence his movement, particular formations, the rate of movement, and methods of control. His map study includes evaluation of the terrain from the enemy's viewpoint: How would the enemy use this terrain? Where could the enemy position troops, installations, and ambushes?

Additionally, the patrol leader considers reports of units or patrols that have recently operated in the area. All available information is considered.

Troops and support available – friendly situation and support available. The leader plans artillery and mortar fires so they will deceive, harass, or destroy the enemy. They may be planned as scheduled or on-call fires. Fires are planned:
- On key terrain features along the route. These can serve as navigational aids or to deceive, harass, or destroy the enemy.
- On known enemy positions.
- On known or suspected ambush sites.
- On the flanks of identified danger areas.
- Wherever a diversion appears desirable. For example, if the unit must pass near an identified enemy position, artillery or mortar fires on the position may distract the enemy and permit the unit to pass undetected.
- At intervals along the route, every 500 to 1000 meters for example. With fires so planned, the unit is never far from a plotted concentration from which a shift can be quickly made.

Coordination with the supporting unit includes:
- Route to be followed.
- Scheduled and on-call fires.
- Call signs and frequencies.
- Checkpoints, phase lines, and other control measures.
- Times of departure and return.

Time available – the constraints and impact of time on preparation and mission accomplishment (planning 1/3 2/3 rule).

Civil considerations – the patrol leader considers ASCOPE (areas, structures, capabilities, organizations, people, and events).[3] He considers the

---

[3] See Chapter 7 – METT-TC.

attitude of the civilian population and the extent to which they can be expected to cooperate or interfere. He considers the specified and implied tasks of his mission in light of this information.

The patrol leader uses the following checklists to ensure nothing is missed:

Intelligence Checklist –
1. Identification of enemy unit.
2. Weather and light data.
3. Terrain update.
a. Aerial photos.
b. Trails and obstacles not on map.
4. Known or suspected enemy locations.
5. Weapons.
6. Probable course of action.
7. Recent enemy activities.
8. Reaction time of reaction forces.
9. Civilians on the battlefield.
10. Update to CCIR.

Operations Checklist –
1. Mission backbrief.
2. Identification of friendly units.
3. Changes in the friendly situation.
4. Route selection, LZ/ PZ/ DZ selection.
5. Linkup procedures.
a. Contingencies
b. QRF
c. QRF Frequency
6. Transportation/movement plan.
7. Resupply (with S4).
8. Signal plan.
9. Departure and reentry of forward units.
10. Special equipment requirements.
11. Adjacent units in the area of operations.
12. Rehearsal areas.
13. Method of insertion/extraction.

Fire Support Checklist –
1. Mission backbrief.
2. Identification of supporting unit.
3. Mission and objective.
4. Route to and from the objective (include alternate routes).
5. Time of departure and expected time of return.
6. Unit target list (from fire plan).

7. Type of available support (artillery, mortar, naval gunfire and aerial support, to include Army, Navy and Air Force) and their locations.
8. Ammunition available (to include different fuses).
9. Priority of fires.
10. Control measures.
  a. Checkpoints.
  b. Boundaries.
  c. Phase lines.
  d. Fire support coordination measures.
  e. Priority targets (target list).
  f. RFA (restrictive fire area).
  g. RFL (restrictive fire line).
  h. NFA (no-fire area).
  i. Precoordinated authentication.
11. Communication (include primary and alternate means, emergency signals and code words).

Vehicular Movement Coordination Checklist –
1. Identification of the unit.
2. Supporting unit identification.
3. Number and type of vehicles and tactical preparation.
4. Entrucking point.
5. Departure time.
6. Preparation of vehicles for movement.
  a. Driver responsibilities.
  b. Platoon/ squad responsibilities.
  c. Special supplies/ equipment required.
7. Availability of vehicles for preparation/ rehearsals/ inspection (times and locations).
8. Routes.
  a. Primary.
  b. Alternate.
  c. Checkpoints.
9. Detrucking points.
  a. Primary.
  b. Alternate.
10. Order of march.
11. Speed.
11. Communications (frequencies, call signs, codes).
12. Emergency procedures and signals.[4]

4. *Initiate movement* – the patrol leader initiates any movement necessary to continue mission preparation or to posture his element for the start of the mission. This step can be executed at any time throughout the sequence of

---

[4] Checklists provided from the SH 21-76 Ranger Handbook 2011, 2-24 – 2-25.

the TLP.[5] For example, a PL for a raid patrol may assign one of his elements the mission to conduct a reconnaissance on the unit's objective. Based on backwards planning, he may have to do this early on, even before he issues the WARNO.

5. Conduct reconnaissance – Often the patrol must provide its own intelligence support. Members must be alert to report information and leaders must be able to evaluate the significance of this information in relation to the situation. Whenever time and circumstances allow, patrol leaders personally conduct reconnaissance (aerial if possible) of critical mission aspects. No amount of planning can substitute for firsthand assessment of the situation. At a minimum, a thorough map study of the area is made. If possible, leaders should include their subordinate leaders in their reconnaissance efforts. This allows the subordinates to see as much of the terrain and enemy as possible. The reconnaissance also helps subordinate leaders gain insight into the leaders' visions of the operation.[6]

When conducting a reconnaissance for a larger unit, it's not only imperative that a good line of communication be left open (for updating existing information) but to have covered certain critical particulars such as link-up and ORP locations.

Counterintelligence (CI) plan – a unit is especially vulnerable to ambush if the enemy knows the unit is to move, what time it is to move, where it is to go, the route it is to follow, and the weapons and equipment it is to carry. The efforts made to deny or delay enemy acquisition of this information comprise the CI plan. As a minimum, the plan restricts dissemination of information. The patrol leader gives out mission information only on a need-to-know basis. This procedure is especially important when the indigenous personnel operating with the unit might possibly be planted informers. Once critical information is given, personnel are isolated so that nothing can be passed out. If it is likely that the enemy or enemy informers will observe the departure of a unit, deception plans should be used.

Aerial Reconnaissance – If possible, the leader makes an aerial reconnaissance. The information gained from the aerial reconnaissance enables him to compare the map and terrain. He also obtains current and more complete information on roads, trails, man-made objects, type and density of vegetation, and seasonal condition of streams. An aerial reconnaissance reveals:

- Movement or lack of movement in an area (friendly, enemy, civilian).

---

[5] It can include movement to an assembly area, battle position (BP), or new AO, or the movement of guides or quartering parties (FM 3-21.10).
[6] FM 3-21.10, 2-51.

- Indications of enemy activity. Smoke may indicate locations of campsites, patrols, or patrol bases. Freshly dug soil may indicate positions or ambush sites. Shadows may aid in identifying objects. Unusual shapes, sizes, shadows, shades, or colors may indicate faulty camouflage.

Despite its many advantages, aerial reconnaissance has limitations. Some examples include the following:
- Strength of bridges cannot be determined.
- Terrain surface may be misinterpreted.
- Mines and booby traps cannot be seen.
- Presence of aircraft may warn enemy.

6. Complete the plan – During this step, leaders expand their selected (or refined) COAs into a complete OPORDs. They prepare overlays, refine the indirect fire list, complete sustainment and C2 requirements and update the tentative plan based on the latest reconnaissance or information. If time allows, the patrol leader makes final coordination with adjacent units and higher headquarters before issuing the order.

During this step and prior to the operations order (OPORD), the patrol leader must ensure:
- Missions and routes of other patrols in the area are known and deconflicted if necessary.
- Infil/Exfil transportation is coordinated.
- Resupply is coordinated.

7. Issue the order – The OPORD precisely and concisely explains both the leader's intent and concept of how he envisions the unit accomplishing the mission. The order does not contain unnecessary information. The OPORD is delivered quickly and in a manner that allows subordinates to concentrate on understanding the leader's vision and not just copying what he says verbatim.

8. Supervise and refine – This final step of the TLP is crucial. After issuing the OPORD, the leader and his subordinate leaders must ensure that the required activities and tasks are completed in a timely manner prior to mission execution. *Supervision is the primary responsibility of all leadership.* Both officers and NCOs must check everything that is important for successful mission accomplishment. This includes, but is not limited to:
- Conducting numerous backbriefs on all aspects of the unit and subordinate unit operations.

- Ensuring the second in command in each element is prepared to execute in his leader's absence.
- Listening to subordinate's operation order.
- Observing rehearsals of subordinate units.
- Checking load plans to ensure they are carrying only what is necessary for the mission or what the OPORD specified.
- Checking the status and serviceability of weapons.[7]
- Checking on maintenance activities of subordinate units. Ensuring local security is maintained.

Rehearsals are practice sessions conducted to prepare units for an upcoming operation or event. They are essential in ensuring thorough preparation, coordination, and understanding of the commander's plan and intent. Rehearsals should follow the crawl-walk-run methodology. Platoons and squads use five types of rehearsals:
- Confirmation brief.
- Backbrief.
- Combined arms rehearsal.
- Support rehearsal.
- Battle drill or SOP rehearsal.

Assumption of Command – Any member of the patrol might have to take command of his element in an emergency, so each man must be prepared to do so. During an assumption of command, time and situation permitting, the leader assuming command accomplishes the tasks (not necessarily in order) based on METT-TC listed below:
1. Inform higher of the change.
2. Establish / maintain security.
3. Identify chain of command and inform all personnel.
4. Check personnel status and location of crew-served weapons and re-man if necessary. Maintain unit integrity if possible.
5. Correct unsatisfactory actions, i.e., security, noise and light discipline violations.
6. Determine location within 200 meters.
7. Exchange necessary information and equipment with previous leader.
8. Obtain accurate status report from subordinate leaders within 10 minutes.
9. Delegate authority to accomplish tasks.
10. Establish a priority for tasks.
11. Issue FRAGO if necessary.

---

[7] Before departing on any mission a good leader will always conduct precombat checks (PCCs) and precombat inspections (PCIs). These are critical to the success of any combat patrol.

Pre-combat inspection – Pre-combat inspections (PCIs) are critical to the success of any combat patrol. The patrol leader inspects before rehearsals to ensure completeness and correctness of uniform and equip ment. The following areas are checked; prescribed weapons, equipment and ammunition are available and serviceable; individual and equipment are camouflaged, personnel have identification tags, and ID cards, tape and other items are used to silence equipment to prevent noise produced during movement; OPSEC – items that could provide information to the enemy: letters and papers, remain behind; and unnecessary equipment and excess weight remain behind. Additionally, the patrol leader questions each patrol member to ensure the following is known: mission, planned routes (primary and alternate), fire support plan, MEDEVAC plan, and the man's role on the patrol.

Conclusion

The purpose of this chapter was to understand Troop Leading Procedures (TLP) so as to assist leaders in the planning and preparation of patrols. As we've said, the traits necessary in a leader are directly proportionate to the situation and the nature of those being led. Leaders must supervise in the planning and execution of their orders. A superficial reading of military text books is likely to convey the idea that duties of a leader consist only of estimating the situation, reaching a decision, and issuing an order. It is evident, however, that unless the orders of the commander are executed, even a perfect plan will fail. On the other hand, a poor plan, if loyally and energetically carried out, will often succeed.[8]

---

[8] Infantry in Battle, 195.

Part Four: Operations

Chapter 11 Patrolling

"When the enemy is at ease, be able to weary him; when well fed, starve him; when at rest, to make him move. Appear at places at which he must hasten; move swiftly where he does not expect you." – Sun Tzu

Patrols act as both the eyes and ears of a larger elements and are sent out to conduct a specific combat, reconnaissance, or security mission. Patrols operate semi-independently and return to the main body upon completion of their mission.[1] When a unit is not actively fighting the enemy, it should be actively searching for the enemy; this is the primary purpose of patrolling. A commander sends a patrol out from the main body to conduct a specific tactical task with an associated purpose.

If a patrol is made up of an organic unit, such as a rifle squad, the squad leader is responsible. If a patrol is made up of mixed elements from several units, an officer or NCO is designated as the patrol leader. This temporary title defines his role and responsibilities for that mission.[2] Additionally, patrol missions can range from security patrols in close proximity to the main body, or to perform raids deep into enemy territory. The planned action determines the type of patrol. *The two categories of patrols are reconnaissance and combat.* This chapter will serve as an introduction to patrolling and will focus on the following:

1. Principles of Patrolling.
2. Principles of Tactical Movement.
3. Movement Formations
4. Movement Techniques.
5. Actions at Halts.
6. Actions at Danger Areas.
7. Battle Drills.

Principles of Patrolling

The lives of an entire unit may depend upon the success or failure of a patrol. All patrols are governed by five principles:
- Planning
- Reconnaissance
- Security
- Control
- Common Sense

---

[1] FM 3-21.8, 9-1.
[2] Ibid.

Planning – *Make a simple plan and effectively communicate it to all.* General Patton's axiom encapsulates this principle by saying, "A good plan violently executed now is better than a perfect plan executed next week." Plan and prepare to a realistic standard and rehearse everything. Planning, an essential element of command and control, is a continuous process by which a commander's visualization is translated in a specific course of action. Planning is the art and science of envisioning a desired end state. Rules that govern its process make it a science, while required skill, make it an art. A plan is a continuous, evolving framework of anticipated actions that maximizes opportunities.[3]

Reconnaissance – *As a leader, your responsibility is to confirm what you know, and learn what you do not already know.* Reconnaissance is a focused collection effort that leaders use in order to gain the most accurate picture of an objective possible by filling information gaps. Leaders ensure they perform recons prior to movement and occupation of areas in order to preserve their force as well as combat power.[4]

Security – *Preserve your force as a whole.* All forces, regardless of size, are inherently responsible to provide their own local security. Successful security provides early and accurate warning, reaction time, and maneuver space, while remaining vigilant and oriented toward the main body. Also a principle of war, security considers the protection of the force, and involves the use of dispersion, cover and concealment, while remaining undetected.[5]

Control – *Clear understanding of the concept of the operation and commander's intent along with discipline.* Leaders use control measures in order to clarify intent and synchronize effort in such a manner as to avoid restricting initiative. Another of Patton's axiomatic expressions encapsulates this principle: "Tell people what to do, not how to do it."

Common Sense – *Use all available information and good judgment to make sound, timely decisions.* Common sense is the basic level of practical knowledge and prudent judgment based on a simple perception of a given situation or facts. Common sense equates to knowledge or experience and should always govern the other principles.

---

[3] For more on planning, see chapters 8 and 9.
[4] For more on reconnaissance, see chapter 12.
[5] For more on security, see chapter 3, principles of war.

Tactical Movement

"When you're on the march, act the way you would if you was sneaking up on a deer. See the enemy first." – Rogers' Standing Orders #3

Tactical movement is based on the anticipation of enemy ground contact. Movement is not maneuver. Movement ends when ground contact is made or the unit reaches its destination. Tactical movement is movement in preparation for contact. Maneuver is movement supported by fire to gain a position of advantage over the enemy.[6]

The patrol leader selects the best combination of movement formations and techniques for each situation while considering the factors of METT-TC. The patrol leader selects the appropriate formation and technique using the nine principles of tactical movement: **M O V E   S E C U R E**

Maintain all around security.
Observe unit cohesion – team, squad, and platoon integrity.
Visual contact / communication maintained.
Enforce proper speed and maintain momentum.

Screen movement with covered and concealed routes.
Enforce noise and light discipline.
Contact made with smallest element forward.
Use appropriate movement formation and technique based on METT-TC.
Route selection (avoid suspected enemy concentrations).
Enforce proper dispersion (don't bunch up).

Movement Formations

Movement formations include elements and individuals arranged in relation to each other. Fire teams, squads, and platoons use several formations. Formations give the patrol leader control. Thus, leaders should position themselves where they can best control the formations. Formations allow the fire team leader to lead by example, "Follow me and do as I do." All members in the team must be able to see their leader.

Each formation aids control, security, and firepower to varying degrees. Leaders use formations for control, flexibility, and security. Leaders select formations based on their analysis of METT-TC. This section will discuss team, squad, and platoon movement formations.

---

[6] FM 3-21.10, 3-1.

Fire Team Wedge – The wedge is the basic formation for the fire team. The interval between soldiers is normally 10 meters; however this distance is dependent upon terrain. The team leader modifies the wedge when terrain or poor visibility makes control difficult (See Figure 11-1).

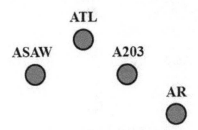

Figure 11-1. Fire Team Wedge.

Fire Team File – Team leaders (TL) employ the file when the wedge is impractical due to restrictive terrain or limited visibility. Like the wedge, the interval between soldiers is normally 10 meters; however this distance is dependent upon terrain. The file is easy to control, affords fast movement, and while allowing excellent security to the flanks, affords little to the front and rear (See Figure 11-2).

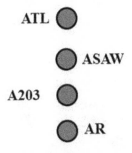

Figure 11-2. Fire Team File.

Fire Team Line – The line is more difficult to control, affords slower movement, allows little security to the flanks, but offers maximum security and potential fire power to the front and rear (See Figure 11-3).

Figure 11-3. Fire Team Line.

326

Diamond – The diamond formation is used to maximize control and security. Distance between men is 5 to 10 meters. The example below is generally used during a leader's reconnaissance (See Figure 11-4).

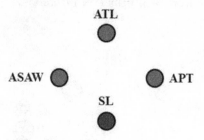

Figure 11-4. Diamond Formation.

Squad Column – The squad column is the squad's primary movement formation unless preparing for an assault. It provides good control and dispersion both laterally and in depth. Distance between men is 5 to 10 meters (See Figure 11-5).[7]

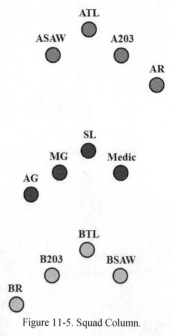

Figure 11-5. Squad Column.

---

[7] The illustrations depict a 'heavy' squad with attached gun team and medic for detached/independent operations.

327

Squad File – The squad file has the same characteristics as the fire team file. Like the wedge, the interval between soldiers is normally 10 meters. However, this distance is dependent upon terrain (See Figure 11-6). At halts, members of the squad take a knee and face out two to three steps of the line of march to allow movement at the halt (See 11-7).

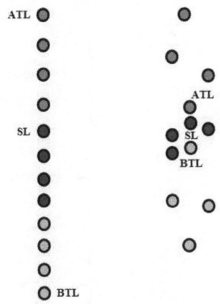

Figure 11-6. Squad File.   Figure 11-7. Squad File at halt.

Squad Line – The Squad line provides maximum firepower to the front and is used to assault or as a pre-assault formation. The squad leader designates one of the teams as the base team. From this formation, the squad leader may employ any of the three movement techniques or conduct fire and maneuver. Fire team wedges are shallow to provide maximum coverage to the front (See Figure 11-8).

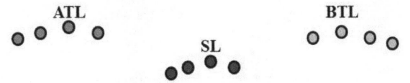

Figure 11-8 Squad Line.

328

Platoon Column, Squads in Column – The column formation allows the platoon to make contact with one squad and maneuver with the two trail squads. It is a flexible formation, allowing easy transition to other formations, while providing good all-round security. The platoon can deliver a limited volume of fire to the front and to the rear, but a high volume to the flanks (See Figure 11-9).

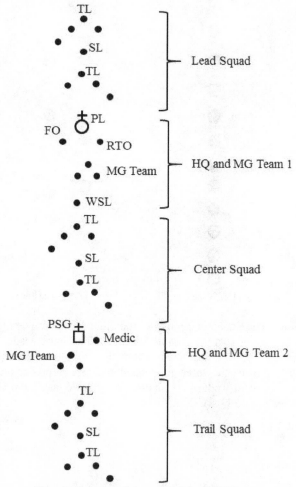

Figure 11-9. Platoon Column with Squads in Column.

Platoon Line, Squads on Line – This formation puts all squads forward along the same direction of movement, and it provides for the delivery of maximum fire to the front, but less to the flanks. It is the most difficult formation to control. The platoon leader designates a base squad, normally the center one, for the others to guide on. Flank and rear security is generally poor but is improved when the flank squads use echelon formations (See Figure 11-10)

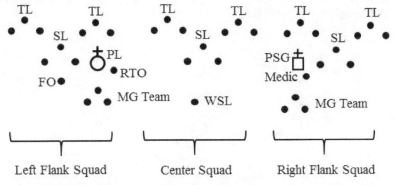

Note: PL, PSG, and SLs position themselves where they can best provide control.

Figure 11-10. Platoon Line, Squads on Line.

Platoon Line, Squads in Column – When two or more squads are moving, the platoon leader chooses one of them as the base squad. The base squad's center fire team is its base fire team. When the squad is not the base squad, its base fire team is its flank fire team nearest the base squad. The platoon line with squads in column formation is difficult to transition to other formations (Figure 11-11).

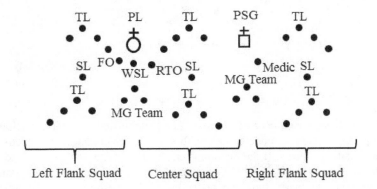

Figure 11-11. Platoon Line, Squads in Column.

330

Platoon Vee, Squads in Column – The platoon vee formation has two squads forward to provide immediate fire on contact or to flank the enemy. It also has one squad centered trailing the two forward squads. If the platoon is engaged from either flank, two squads can provide fire, and at least one squad is free to maneuver. This formation is hard to control and slows movement. The platoon leader designates one of the forward squads as the base squad (See Figure 11-12).

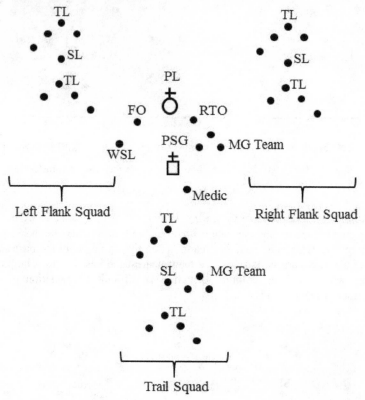

Figure 11-12. Platoon Vee, Squads in Column.

Platoon Wedge, Squads in Column – The platoon wedge formation allows the platoon leader to make contact with a small element and still maneuver the remaining squads. If the platoon is engaged from the flank, one squad is free to maneuver. This formation is hard to control, but it allows faster movement than the platoon vee, as well as rapid transition to the bounding overwatch (See Figure 11-13).

331

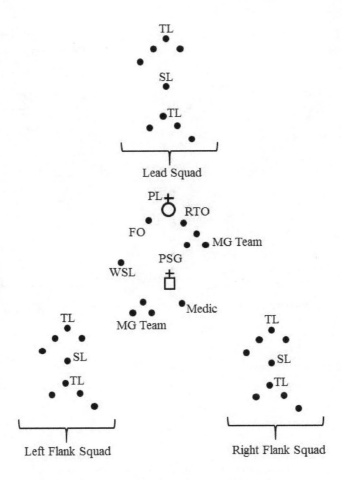

Figure 11-13. Platoon Wedge, Squads in Column.

Platoon File – The platoon file formation is the easiest formation to control. It allows rapid movement in restricted terrain and in limited visibility, and it enhances control and concealment. Light forces use a file predominantly as its movement formation during times of limited visibility. It is, however, the least secure formation and the hardest from which to maneuver.

This formation may be set up in several methods. One method is to have three-squad files follow one another using one of the movement techniques. Another method is to have a single platoon file with a front security element (point) and flank security elements (See Figure 11-14).

332

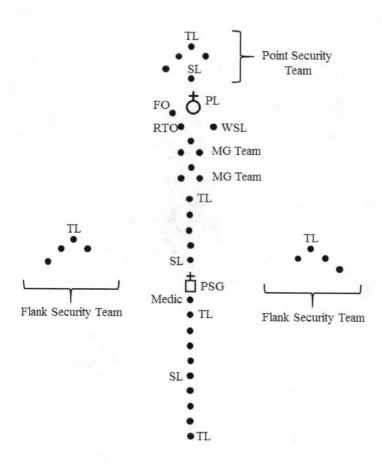

Figure 11-14. Platoon File with Point and Flank Security.

Movement Techniques

Selecting a movement technique is based on the likelihood of enemy contact and the relative need for speed. Specifically, factors to consider include *control, dispersion, speed, and security*. Movement techniques are neither fixed nor are they rigid inflexible formations. Instead, movement techniques are distinguished by a set of criteria such as distance between individuals and between teams or squads. Movement techniques vary depending on METT-TC.

The patrol leader selects from the three movement techniques (traveling, traveling overwatch, and bounding overwatch) based on several battlefield factors:

- The likelihood of enemy contact.
- The type of contact expected.
- The availability of an overwatch element.
- The terrain over which the moving element will pass.
- The balance of speed and security required during movement.

Traveling – Continuous movement characterizes the traveling technique by all elements. It is best suited for situations in which enemy contact is unlikely and speed is important. This technique calls for 10 meters between men, and 20 meters between squads (See Figure 11-15). This technique allows for:

- More control than traveling overwatch but less than bounding overwatch.
- Minimum dispersion.
- Maximum speed.
- Minimum security.

Traveling Overwatch – Traveling overwatch is an extended form of traveling that provides additional security when speed is desirable but *contact is possible*. Dispersion between the two elements must be based on the trail element's ability to see the lead element and to provide immediate suppressive fires in case the lead element is engaged. The intent is to maintain depth, provide flexibility, and maintain the ability to maneuver even if contact occurs, although a unit should ideally make contact while moving in bounding overwatch rather than traveling overwatch.

Traveling overwatch offers good control, dispersion, speed, and security forward. The lead squad must be far enough ahead of the rest of the platoon to detect or engage any enemy before the enemy observes or fires on the main body. However, the lead squad must stay between 50 and 100 meters in front of the platoon so the platoon can support them with small arms fires. This is normally between 50 to 100 meters, depending on terrain, vegetation, and light and weather conditions (See Figure 11-15).

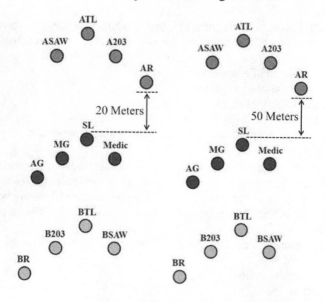

Figure 11-15. Traveling (Left) and Traveling Overwatch (Right).

Bounding Overwatch – Bounding overwatch is used when *contact is expected* (Figure 11-16). It is the most secure, but slowest, movement technique. The purpose of bounding overwatch is to deploy prior to contact, giving the unit the ability to protect a bounding element by immediately suppressing an enemy force. The patrol leader can employ either of two bounding methods: alternate or successive.

Leader tasks during successive bounding method:

ATL halts the patrol and passes back the appropriate hand & arm signal for danger area. SL passes back the hand & arm signal and moves forward to assess the danger area and determine the best course of action to take. SL determines which method (successive or alternating) and designates overwatch and bounding elements. For example, B team plus HQ overwatch as A team bounds. SL stays with the overwatch team and emplaces gun team. SL designates where lead team should bound and directs lead TL to make his initial bound.

335

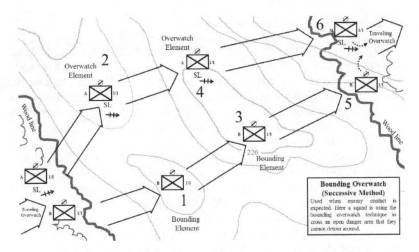

Figure 11-16. Bounding Overwatch, Successive Method.

(1, 3, 5) The bounding element avoids masking the fires of the overwatch element; it never bounds beyond the range at which the overwatch element can effectively suppress likely or suspected enemy positions. In the successive method, the SL and gun team remain attached to the overwatch element as they cover the bounding elements progress (2); taking the terrain the bounding element has gained (4, 6).

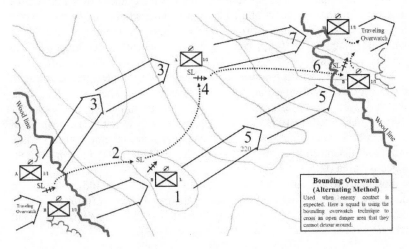

Figure 11-17. Bounding Overwatch, Alternating Method.

336

Leader tasks during alternate bounding method:

ATL halts the patrol and passes back the appropriate hand & arm signal for danger area. SL passes back the hand & arm signal and moves forward to assess the danger area and determine the best course of action to take. SL determines which method (successive or alternating) and designates overwatch and bounding elements. For example, A team plus HQ overwatch as B team bounds. SL designates where lead team should bound and directs lead TL to make his initial bound.

When teams bound, they avoid masking the fires of the overwatch element; it never bounds beyond the range at which the overwatch element can effectively suppress likely or suspected enemy positions. In the alternating (leap frog) method, HQ (SL and gun team) will alternate positions as they, overwatch the bounding team. After the lead team has bound forward and established overwatch (1), HQ moves to their position in order to provide overwatch (2), covering the next bounding team as they move (3). This action is repeated, as the teams bound past (leap frog) each other, allowing HQ to position itself with the overwatching team prior to their movement forward.

Actions at Halts

There are planned and unplanned halts which are either short or long in duration. In a halt, the patrol leader gives the hand and arm signal, patrol members find nearest cover and concealment, take a knee and face out while leaders give hasty sectors of fire (10 to 2 o'clock, interlocking 35 meters out with the man on their left and right). The patrol leader emplaces the machinegun team.

In a short halt, which is normally used up to two minutes, the patrol, with the exception of the machinegun team, remains on a knee. In a long halt, which is normally used for planned halts, such as: Initial RP, Security Halt for the ORP, ORP, and PB, the whole patrol moves to the prone position in a controlled manner. As a general rule, halts are planned with certain minimum distances from either the next planned halt (ORP, PB), or from an objective area (OBJ).

For tactical reasons, halts are normally planned 200-400 meters from danger ares during daylight hours and half that distance (100-200 meters) during hours at night. The following diagrams graphically represent squad (Figure 11-18) and platoon halts (See Figure 11-19).

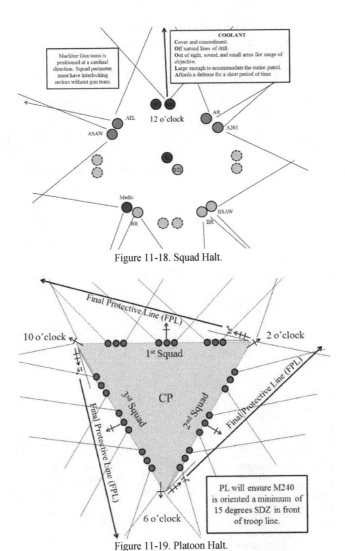

Figure 11-18. Squad Halt.

Figure 11-19. Platoon Halt.

Actions at Danger Areas

A danger area is any place on a unit's route where the leader determines his unit may be exposed to enemy observation or fire. Some examples of danger areas are open areas, roads and trails, urban terrain, enemy positions, and natural and manmade obstacles. Bypass danger areas whenever possible. The following techniques will be discussed:

338

- Deliberate Linear Danger Area Crossing.
- Small Open Areas.

Deliberate Linear Danger Area (LDA) Crossing

Road/Trail Crossing 1
Squad approaches a linear danger area (LDA) which calls for a deliberate crossing technique (Steps 1 and 2).

Far-side RP

Road/Trail Crossing 2
A Team provides near-side security and early warning (Step 3). Note: one team member from each side faces center IOT pass appropriate hand & arm signals.

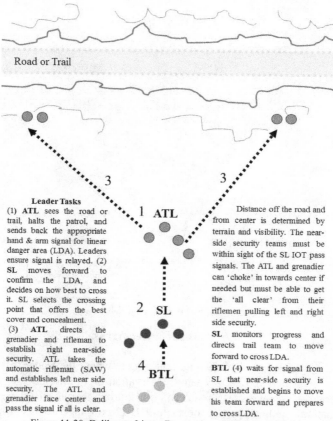

Road or Trail

Leader Tasks
(1) **ATL** sees the road or trail, halts the patrol, and sends back the appropriate hand & arm signal for linear danger area (LDA). Leaders ensure signal is relayed. (2) **SL** moves forward to confirm the LDA, and decides on how best to cross it. SL selects the crossing point that offers the best cover and concealment.
(3) **ATL** directs the grenadier and rifleman to establish right near-side security. ATL takes the automatic rifleman (SAW) and establishes left near side security. The ATL and grenadier face center and pass the signal if all is clear.

Distance off the road and from center is determined by terrain and visibility. The near-side security teams must be within sight of the SL IOT pass signals. The ATL and grenadier can 'choke' in towards center if needed but must be able to get the 'all clear' from their riflemen pulling left and right side security.

SL monitors progress and directs trail team to move forward to cross LDA.

BTL (4) waits for signal from SL that near-side security is established and begins to move his team forward and prepares to cross LDA.

Figure 11-20. Deliberate Linear Danger Area (LDA) Crossing 1.

339

Road/Trail Crossing 3
BTL gets his team on line and crosses LDA (Steps 3).

Far-side RP

Road/Trail Crossing 4
B Team clears far-side deep enough to accommodate entire squad (Step 4). HQ moves forward and prepares to cross.

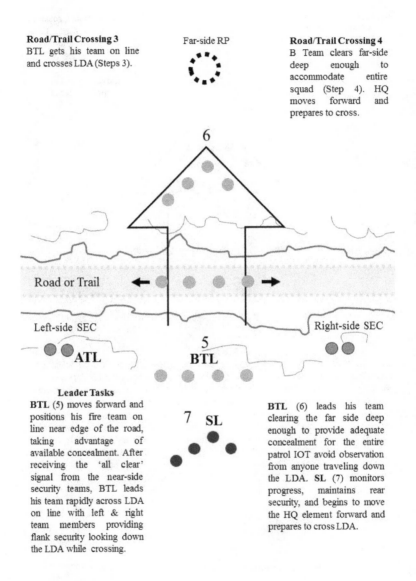

Road or Trail

Left-side SEC

ATL

5

BTL

Right-side SEC

7 **SL**

Leader Tasks
BTL (5) moves forward and positions his fire team on line near edge of the road, taking advantage of available concealment. After receiving the 'all clear' signal from the near-side security teams, BTL leads his team rapidly across LDA on line with left & right team members providing flank security looking down the LDA while crossing.

BTL (6) leads his team clearing the far side deep enough to provide adequate concealment for the entire patrol IOT avoid observation from anyone traveling down the LDA. SL (7) monitors progress, maintains rear security, and begins to move the HQ element forward and prepares to cross LDA.

Figure 11-21. Deliberate Linear Danger Area (LDA) Crossing 2.

340

Road/Trail Crossing 4
BTL establishes choke point on far-side (Steps 4). HQ moves forward to cross LDA.

Road/Trail Crossing 5
B Team clears far-side deep enough to accommodate entire squad (Step 5). HQ moves forward and prepares to cross.

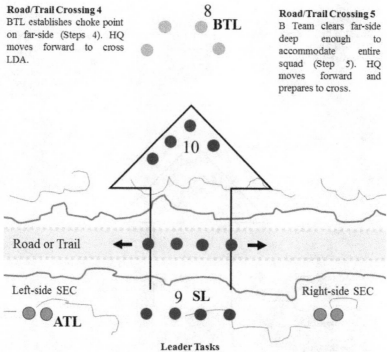

Leader Tasks

BTL (8) after clearing far side, puts his team in wedge, signals far side 'clear', and establishes a choke point for accountability of entire patrol once crossing is complete.

SL (9) positions HQ element on line and within sight of the road, taking advantage of available concealment. After receiving the 'all clear' signal, moves forward, conducts check of the LDA and receives 'clear' from far side security. Once satisfied, he directs his element to rapidly cross the LDA. SL (10) quickly crosses the LDA on line with left & right element members providing flank security looking down the LDA while crossing. The HQ element moves forward on line and deep enough to avoid observation from anyone traveling on the LDA, but will not pass thru the far side security team until after the near side security teams have been accounted for by the BTL.

Figure 11-21. Deliberate Linear Danger Area (LDA) Crossing 3.

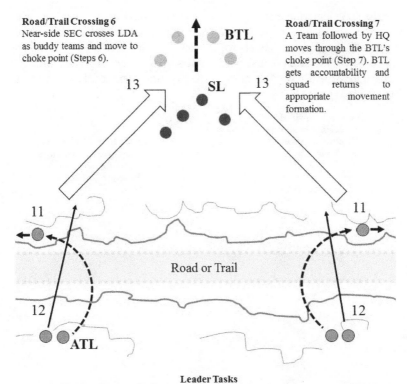

Road/Trail Crossing 6
Near-side SEC crosses LDA as buddy teams and move to choke point (Steps 6).

Road/Trail Crossing 7
A Team followed by HQ moves through the BTL's choke point (Step 7). BTL gets accountability and squad returns to appropriate movement formation.

Road or Trail

Leader Tasks

ATL (11) after observing the HQ element crossing, signals his team to cross the LDA with each element providing their own local security during their crossing (12) and move in buddy teams towards the BTL's chokepoint (13). ATL links up with right side security element and passes thru the BTL's chokepoint with his entire team and flows into designated movement formation. SL passes thru the BTL's chokepoint and flows into designated movement formation. BTL gets accountability of his fire team, passes up 'headcount good' and flows into designated movement formation. SL receives 'headcount good' from BTL, continues mission.

Figure 11-22. Deliberate Linear Danger Area (LDA) Crossing 4.

342

Small Open Danger Areas

When encountering a small open danger area, the patrol leader bypasses it by either the detour bypass or contour method. When using the bypass method, the paceman suspends the current pace and initiates an interim pace count. Alternate pace/compass man offsets compass 90 degrees left or right as designated and navigates in that direction until clear of danger area (See Figure 11-23).

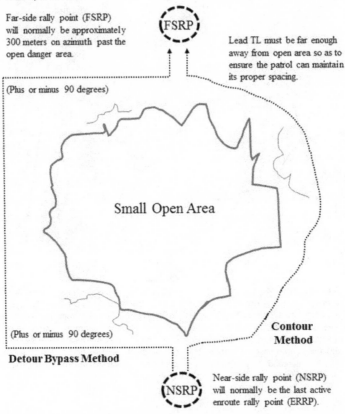

Far-side rally point (FSRP) will normally be approximately 300 meters on azimuth past the open danger area.

FSRP

Lead TL must be far enough away from open area so as to ensure the patrol can maintain its proper spacing.

(Plus or minus 90 degrees)

Small Open Area

(Plus or minus 90 degrees)

Contour Method

Detour Bypass Method

NSRP

Near-side rally point (NSRP) will normally be the last active enroute rally point (ERRP).

Figure 11-23. Actions at Small Open Danger Areas.

After moving set distance as designated, the lead element assumes original azimuth, and primary pace man resumes original pace. After the open area, the alternate pace/compass man offsets his compass 90 degrees left or right, and leads the squad/platoon the same distance back to the original azimuth.

343

Battle Drills

"Fire without movement is indecisive. Exposed movement without fire is disastrous. There must be effective fire combined with skillful movement." – Infantry in Battle

A battle drill is a collective action rapidly executed without a deliberate decision making process. Battle drills provide automatic responses to contact situations where immediate, often violent execution is critical, both to initial survival and to ultimate success in combat. Rather than being a substitute for carefully planned COAs, drills buy time for the unit in contact, and frame the development of the situation. When enemy contact occurs, the platoon or squad deploys immediately, executing the appropriate battle drills under the direction of the leader. The following battle drills are covered in this section:

- React to Contact.
- Squad Attack.
- Knock Out a Bunker.
- React to Near Ambush.
- Break Contact.
- (For Enter and Clear a Room see Chapter 14).

Fundamentals of Tactical Movement – The following are the basic fundamentals common to all tactical movement:

- Make enemy contact with smallest element possible.
- Rapidly develop combat power upon enemy contact.
- Provide all around security for the unit.
- Support higher unit's concept.
- Report all information rapidly and accurately and strive to gain and maintain contact with the enemy.
- Requires decentralized execution.
- PL selects the appropriate movement formation based on likelihood of enemy contact.
- Maintains contact, once contact is made, until ordered to do otherwise.[8]

---

[8] For more on maneuver, see chapter 6.

React to Contact

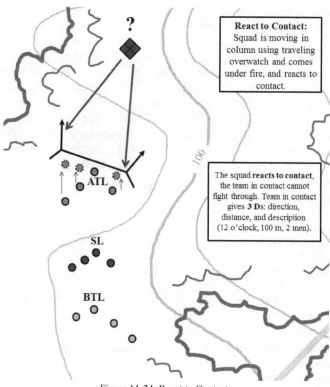

React to Contact:
Squad is moving in column using traveling overwatch and comes under fire, and reacts to contact.

The squad **reacts to contact**, the team in contact cannot fight through. Team in contact gives **3 Ds**: direction, distance, and description (12 o'clock, 100 m, 2 men).

Figure 11-24. React to Contact.

All – hit the prone, return fire (if possible), take nearest covered and concealed position.

Team leader in contact – directs his team into covered and concealed positions from which they can return well aimed fire. Gives 3 Ds: direction, distance, description (1).

Squad leader – maintains positive control of his squad, completes the assessment of the 3 Ds, and determines if his squad can; (a) achieve fire superiority, and (b) maneuver on the enemy's position. If the answer is 'yes' to both questions, then the squad conducts attack. If 'no,' the squad breaks contact (2).

Team leader not in contact – directs his team into covered and concealed positions and observe the flanks and the rear of patrol (3).

Squad Attack

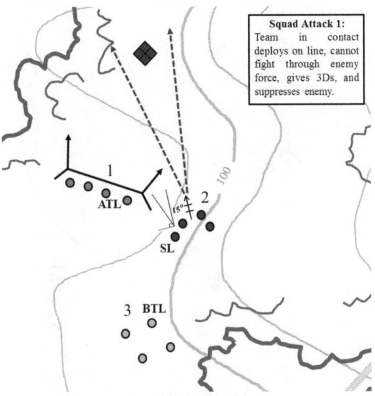

Figure 11-25. Squad Attack 1.

Team leader in contact – directs his team into covered and concealed positions from which they can return well aimed fire. Gives point/area fire commands, employs organic weapon systems (M203/249), and maintains control (1).

Squad leader – maintains positive control of his squad, and assesses terrain to determine how best to maneuver onto the enemy position (frontal attack or envelopment, etc). SL gives the brevity code which is echoed. SL employs his key weapons (M240) to suppress enemy position and passes control to the TL in contact (2).

Team leader not in contact – directs his team into covered and concealed positions and observe the flanks and the rear of patrol (3).

346

Squad Attack

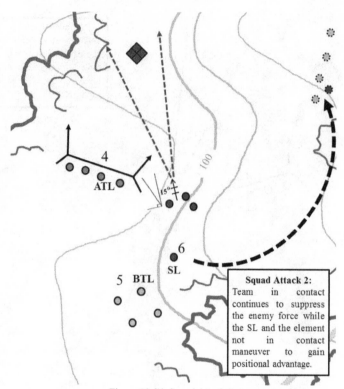

Figure 11-26. Squad Attack 2.

Inside figure:

Squad Attack 2:
Team in contact continues to suppress the enemy force while the SL and the element not in contact maneuver to gain positional advantage.

Team leader in contact – assumes control of the M240, and directs the base of fire element as a whole, controlling rates of fire and maintains suppressive fire on the enemy (4).

Team leader not in contact – upon hearing the brevity code, directs his team to drop rucksacks and prepares his team for maneuver (5).

Squad leader – leads the team not in contact along a covered and concealed route and conducts a bold flanking maneuver IOT gain positional advantage (6).

Squad Attack

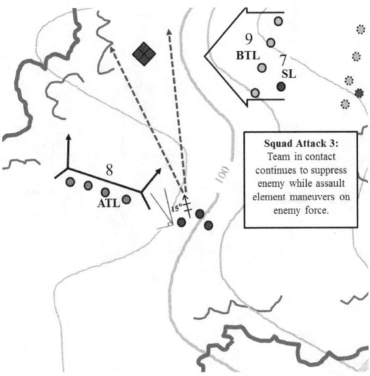

Figure 11-27. Squad Attack 3.

Squad leader – maintains control of the maneuver element as well as communication with the support element. SL maneuvers the flanking element into a position IOT assault through the enemy. In order to prevent fratricide, SL will control the maneuver element and give the command of "shift fire" to the support TL. SL halts the advance until he receives confirmation (7).

Assault team leader – will control his team and bring them on line. Assault team will move at a careful hurry closing with the enemy force (8).

Base of fire team leader – will monitor the progress of the assault and position himself to best control the base of fire element (to include the M240). Base of fire TL will be prepared to "shift fire" and communicate confirmation of shift fire to SL (9).

348

Squad Attack

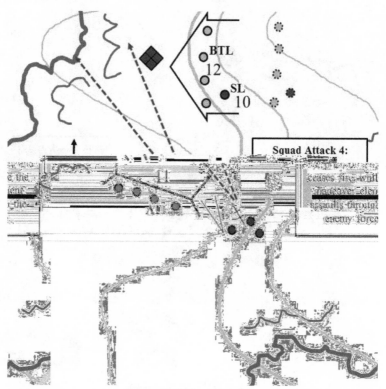

Figure 11-28. Squad Attack 4.

Squad leader – in order to prevent fratricide, controls maneuver element and gives command, "cease fire" to the base of fire TL. He is prepared to halt the advance if he doesn't receive confirmation (10).

Assault team leader – controls his team and bounds the team if receiving effective fire (11).

Base of fire team leader – monitors the progress of the assault element and ensures the entire base of fire element, to include the M240, ceases fire as well as communicates confirmation to the SL. TL ensures the M240 is oriented in a position that mitigates fratricide in the event of a cook off. TL then repositions himself to best control the team, monitor flank and rear security and prepares his team to move/tie-in with the assault element and establish his team's LOA (12).

Squad Attack

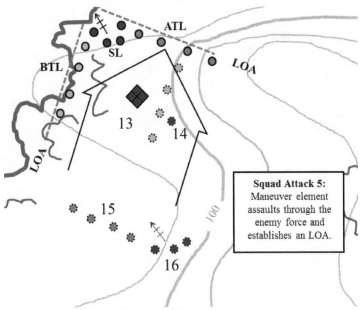

Figure 11-29. Squad Attack 5.

Assault team leader – controls his team: on line and in their lanes as the team assaults through the enemy force and ensures all enemy personnel have been neutralized with their weapons swept away. TL halts the team at a limit of advance (LOA) approximately 35 meters from engaged enemy position. TL provides ACE report to the SL (13).

Squad leader – monitors the progress of the assault and makes corrections as necessary (14).

Base of fire team leader – on order, assaults his team through the enemy force, duplicating the actions of the assault TL (15).

Machinegun team – picks up and follows at a safe distance behind the base of fire element, making their way to the apex of the squad formation and is emplaced by the SL (16).

Squad Attack

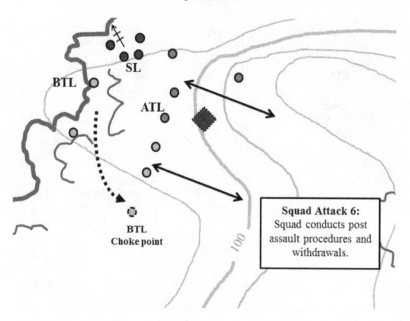

Figure 11-30. Squad Attack 6.

Squad leader – receives consolidated ACE reports from the TLs and AG, calls EPW & search teams to his location and gives task and time limit. SL ensures enemy personnel are cleared and searched, prepares explosive charge to destroy captured equipment (or battlefield recovers equipment).

ATL - controls EPW & search teams and ensures they move quickly IOT systematically clear out and search back all enemy personnel, gathering all equipment and PIR, bringing it back to the SL's position within the time standard.

BTL – on order, positions himself to form a choke point in order to get accountability of all squad members leaving the objective.

Squad leader – gives withdrawal sequence beginning with B team, followed by gun, with A team in trail. ATL accompanies SL off objective.

Knock Out Bunker

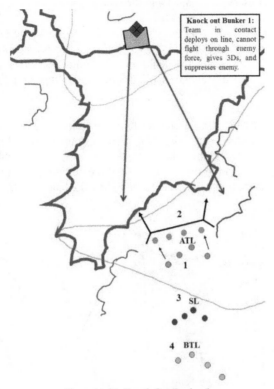

Figure 11-31. Knock Out Bunker 1.

Ideally the team is able to destroy the bunker with standoff weapons and HE munitions. However, when required, the fire team can assault the bunker with small arms and grenades.

All – React to Contact Battle Drill (1).

Team leader in contact – directs his team into covered and concealed positions from which they can return well aimed fire. Gives point/area fire commands, employs organic weapon systems (M203/249) to destroy or suppress enemy crew-served weapons, and maintains control (2).

Squad leader – if the team in contact has achieved fire superiority, SL assesses terrain to determine how best to maneuver onto at least one enemy bunker (3).

Team leader not in contact – directs his team into covered and concealed positions and observe the flanks and the rear of patrol (4).

Squad leader – SL gives the brevity code which is echoed. SL employs his key weapons (M240) to suppress enemy bunker and passes control to the TL in contact (5). SL leads the team not in contact along a covered and concealed route to the bunker's blind side, remaining alert for additional bunkers (6, 7).

Assault team riflemen and grenadier bound to blind side of bunker. On the SL's signal, the squad shifts fire. One man takes up a covered position near the bunker's exit while the other man cook's off (two seconds) a grenade, shoots "frag out!" and throws it into one of the bunker's openings. After the grenade detonates, the two men enter and clear the bunker (8).

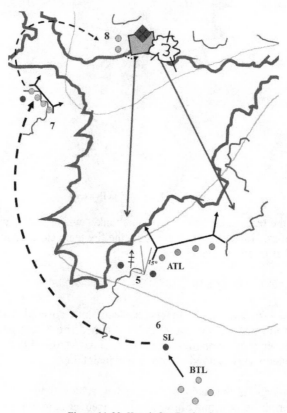

Figure 11-32. Knock Out Bunker 2.

React to Near Ambush

If the patrol enters a kill zone (KZ) and the enemy initiates an ambush that is within 35 meters, the patrol take sthe following actions:

- Soldiers in the KZ immediately return fire, take up covered positions, and throw grenades (fragmentation, concussion, smoke).
- Immediately after grenades detonate, soldiers in the KZ assault through the ambush using fire and maneuver.
- Those not in the KZ, establish a support-by-fire position, suppress the enemy position(s), and shift fires as those in the KZ assault through (See Figure 11-33).

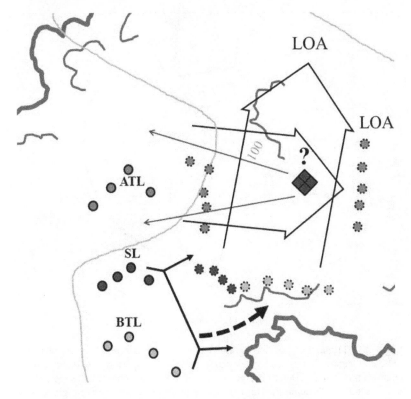

Figure 11-33. React to Near Ambush.

For a far ambush (> 35 meters), patrol conducts either a squad/platoon attack (patrol can achieve fire superiority and can maneuver) or break contact (patrol cannot achieve fire superiority and cannot maneuver).

354

Break Contact

A break contact battle drill is used when a patrol cannot gain fire superiority over the enemy.

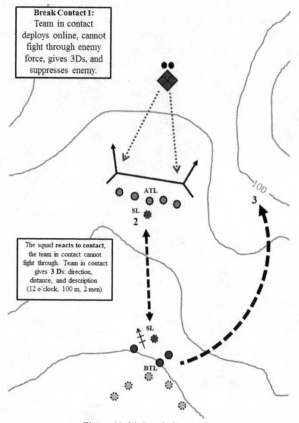

Figure 11-34. Break Contact 1.

Sqd Ldr- (1) maintains positive control of his squad, completes assessment of the 3Ds, and determines if his squad can achieve fire superiority and maneuver on enemy's position. (2) Determines team in contact cannot achieve fire superiority and assesses terrain to determine how best to maneuver out of the area, gives brevity code for break contact which is echoed by all. (3) Leads or directs the team not in contact and his most casualty producing weapon (M240) to a position that will provide a SBF position IOT allow the team in contact to withdraw under fire.

Tm Ldrs- (1) react to contact.

355

Break Contact

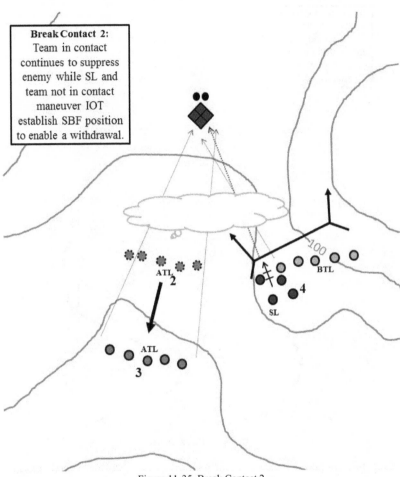

Break Contact 2:
Team in contact continues to suppress enemy while SL and team not in contact maneuver IOT establish SBF position to enable a withdrawal.

Figure 11-35. Break Contact 2.

Tm Ldr in contact- (2) maintains control of his team and deploys smoke grenades. (3) On order, bounds back to next position IOT establish a new SFB position to support the withdrawal of the other element providing the current SBF position.

Sqd Ldr- (4) controls the withdrawal with simple commands to bound back (successive or alternating bounds) while controlling fires. Calls for indirect fire (IDF) when possible.

Break Contact

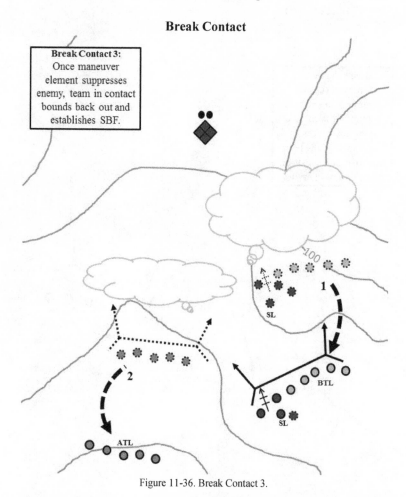

Break Contact 3:
Once maneuver element suppresses enemy, team in contact bounds back out and establishes SBF.

Figure 11-36. Break Contact 3.

Tm Ldrs- control their team's rate of fire by increasing it while the other team is bounding back, and control movement by bounding back either by teams or by twos. Tm Ldrs maintain accountability of personnel and distribute ammunition and re-man weapons as needed.

Sqd Ldr- directs Tm Ldrs when to bound back with their teams once conditions are set to include proper placement of the M240. Teams will make alternating bounds to the rear until the entire squad is beyond effective enemy small arms range. SL implements indirect fires when REDS are safe.

357

Countertracking

"If the enemy pursue your rear, take a circle till you come to your own tracks, and there form an ambush to receive them, and give them the first fire."
– Rogers' 28 Rules of Ranging #21

Knowledge of countertracking enables a patrol to survive by remaining undetected. Although the following discussion on countertracking techniques is focused more toward evasion, the techniques are applicable for a patrol of any size. If the person tracking the patrol is not an experienced tracker, some of the following deception techniques may throw him off.

Leaving Footprints - Soldiers walk backward over soft ground to leave reasonably clear footprints. They try not to leave every footprint clear and do not leave an impression of more than 1/4 inch deep. Soldiers continue this deception until they are on hard ground. They select the ground carefully to ensure that they have at least 20 to 30 meters of this deception. This technique should always be used when exiting a river or stream and can be used in conjunction with all other techniques as well.

Backward Walking – One of the basic techniques used is that of walking backward in tracks already made, and then stepping off the trail onto terrain or objects that leave little sign. Skillful use of this maneuver causes the tracker to look in the wrong direction once he has lost the trail.[1]

Large Tree – A good deception tactic is to change directions at large trees. To do this, move in any given direction past a large tree (12 inches wide or larger) from 5 to 10 paces, then carefully walk backwards to the forward side of the tree and makes a 90-degree change in the direction of travel, passing the tree on its forward side. This technique uses the tree as a screen to hide the new trail from the pursuing tracker.[2]

Cut the Corner – This technique is used when approaching a known road or trail. About 100 meters from the road, change direction of movement, either 45 degrees left or right. Once the road is reached, leave a visible trail in the same direction of the deception for a short distance on the road. The tracker should believe you "cut the corner" to save time. Next, backtrack on the trail to the point where you entered the road, and then carefully move on the road without leaving a good trail. Once the desired distance is achieved, change directions and continue movement.

---

[1] FM 23-10 Sniper Training, 8-12.
[2] Ibid, 8-13.

Crossing a Stream - Approach a stream at an angle in the same manner as a road. Move downstream for about 30 meters, backtrack, and move off into the intended direction. To delay the trackers, set up false tracks leaving footprints as described above. Additional tactics include:

- Stay in the stream for 100 to 200 meters.
- Keep in the center of the stream and in deep water.
- Watch (near the banks) for rocks or roots that are not covered with moss or vegetation, and leave the stream at this point.
- Walk out backward on soft ground.
- Walk up small, vegetation-covered tributaries and replace the vegetation, in its natural position.
- Walk downstream until coming to the main river, and then depart on a log or pre-positioned boat.

Techniques Used to Confuse Dogs – Enemy tracking teams may use dogs. The focus of all your effort must be on defeating or delaying the handler(s) rather than the dog(s). The goal is to break the trust and confidence the handler has in the information being provided by the tracking dog. Dogs track scent from either a disturbed trail or an actual individual. The scent travels with the direction of the wind forcing the handler downwind from your actual route. You may confuse or delay dogs by scattering black or red pepper or, if authorized, a riot control agent (such as CS powder) along the route.

Fishhook Technique – When you are unable to lose trained, persistent enemy trackers, the best COA is to outrun or outdistance the trackers or double back and ambush them. The fishhook technique involves a double back on your own trail ending up in an overwatch position. You may then observe the back trail for trackers or ambush pursuers. If the pursuing force is too large to be destroyed, strive to eliminate the tracker.

Conclusion

The purpose of a patrol is to act as both the eyes and ears of a larger unit. Patrols actively search for the enemy. From information gained, a commander learns that an enemy is withdrawing, or advancing, constructing a defensive position, or that an attack is eminent. Further, patrols normally seek to avoid becoming decisively engaged with enemy forces. Effective employment of patrols gain vital information regarding enemy intentions and are decisive to tactical success.

Chapter 12 Reconnaissance Patrols

"Agitate the enemy and ascertain the pattern of his movement. Determine his dispositions and so ascertain the field of battle. Probe him and learn where his strength is abundant and where deficient." – Sun Tzu

Reconnaissance is any mission undertaken to get information about the activities and resources of enemy forces or the physical characteristics of a particular area, using visual observation or other methods. Recons are also used to secure data on the meteorological, hydrographic, or geographic characteristics of a particular area, and also includes target acquisition, area assessment, and post-strike reconnaissance (BDA).

This chapter will discuss reconnaissance patrols and will cover the following:

1. The Three Types of Reconnaissance.
2. The Fundamentals of Reconnaissance.
3. Organization of a Recon Patrol.
4. Execution of a Recon Patrol.
5. Recon Products.

As previously stated, as a leader, your responsibility is to confirm what you know, and learn what you do not already know. The purpose of a reconnaissance patrol is to collect information in order to confirm or disprove the accuracy of information previously gained. The intent for this type of patrol is to move stealthily, avoid enemy contact, and accomplish its tactical task without engaging in close combat. There are three types of reconnaissance: *route, zone,* and *area.*[1]

Route Reconnaissance – A route reconnaissance is a focused collection effort to get detailed information on a specific route as well as on all terrain where the enemy could influence movement along that route (See Figure 12-1). Route reconnaissance might be oriented on a specific area of movement, such as a road or trail, or on a more general area, like an axis of advance.

Critical tasks of a zone recon may include:

---

[1] Regarding forms of reconnaissance, there are four: *route, zone, area* and *reconnaissance in force*. A *reconnaissance in Force* is a reconnaissance squadron-level mission. The investigating platoon conducts area, zone, and route reconnaissance in support of the unit conducting the mission (See FM 3-20.96 for more information).

- The available space in which a force can maneuver without being forced to bunch up due to obstacles (reported in meters).
- The size of trees and the density of forests are reported due to the effect on vehicle movement.

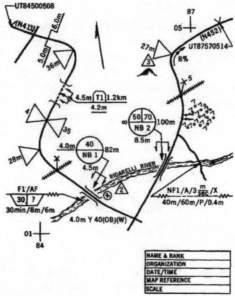

Figure 12-1. Example Route Reconnaissance Overlay (ATP 3-21.98).

- The location and types of all obstacles and the location of any available bypass. Obstacles can consist of minefields, barriers, steep ravines, marshy areas, or NBC contamination.
- The enemy forces that can influence movement along the route.
- The observation and fields of fire along the route and adjacent terrain.
- The locations along the route that provide good cover and concealment.
- The trafficability for the type of forces using the route.
- The bridges by construction type, dimensions, and classification.
- The landing zones and pickup zones.

Further information on route reconnaissance is beyond the scope of this book (See ATP 3-21.98, Chapter 3).

Zone Reconnaissance – A zone reconnaissance is a focused collection effort to get detailed information about all routes, terrain, enemy forces, and obstacles, including areas of chemical and radiological contamination, within specified boundaries. A company normally conducts a zone

361

reconnaissance when the enemy situation is vague, or when the company needs information about cross-country trafficability.

The three basic zone reconnaissance methods are: the fan, successive sectors, and box techniques (See diagrams below).

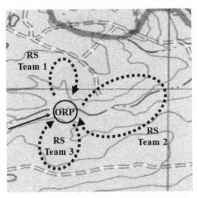

Figure 12-1. Fan Technique.

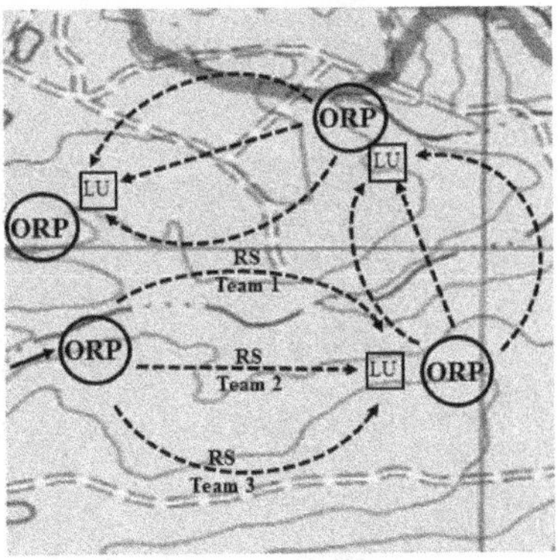

Figure 12-2. Successive Sectors Technique.

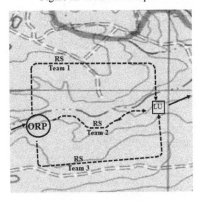

Figure 12-3. Box Technique.

Critical tasks of a zone recon may include:
- Find and report all enemy forces within the zone.
- Reconnoiter specific terrain within the zone.
- Inspect and classify all bridges.
- Locate fords or crossing sites.
- Locate and clear all mines, obstacles, and barriers.

Area Reconnaissance – An area reconnaissance is a focused collection effort to get detailed information about a specific location and the area immediately around it. This includes the terrain or enemy activity within the prescribed area. The area can be any location that is critical to the unit's operations.

Examples include easily identifiable areas covering fairly large spaces such as towns or military installations; terrain features such as ridge lines, wood lines, or choke points; or single points such as bridges or buildings

362

(See Figure 12-4). The critical tasks of an area reconnaissance may be the same as those for a zone reconnaissance.

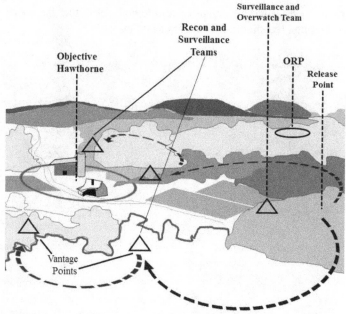

Figure 12-4. Area Reconnaissance.

Before an operation, a unit focuses its reconnaissance effort to confirm or deny a possible course of action. For example, in the diagram above, a platoon ordered to raid Objective Hawthorne sends out a squad area recon patrol to: confirm or deny the enemy situation, and select tentative security, support, and assault positions for the follow-on platoon raid.

Fundamentals of a Reconnaissance

As has been said, successful reconnaissance is a focused collection effort, aimed at gathering timely and accurate information about the enemy and the terrain in the area of operations. In planning a recon patrol, leaders determine the objective of the mission, and identify whether the reconnaissance will orient on the terrain or on the enemy force. The leader provides subordinate units with clear guidance on the objective of the reconnaissance. For example, in an enemy force-oriented recon patrol, the critical task is to find the enemy and gather information on him, whereas the terrain considerations are a secondary concern. In order to conduct a

363

successful recon, the patrol leader applies the four fundamentals of reconnaissance: **G A T E**

Gain required information – The parent unit tells the patrol leader what information is required. This is in the form of the information requirement (IR) and priority intelligence requirements (PIR). The patrol's mission is then tailored to what information is required. During the entire patrol, members must continuously gain and exchange all information gathered, but cannot consider the mission accomplished unless all PIR has been gathered.

Avoid detection by the enemy – A patrol avoids letting the enemy know it is operating in the objective area. If the enemy knows he is being observed, he may move, change his plans, or increase his security measures. Methods of avoiding detection are:

- Minimize movement in the objective area.
- Move slow and low – stealth.
- Move no closer to the objective than necessary.
- Maximize the use of long range surveillance and night vision devices.
- Minimize radio traffic.
- Use camouflage, and noise and light discipline.

Task Organize – When the PL receives the order, he analyzes his mission to ensure he understands what must be done. Then he task organizes his element to best accomplish the mission in accordance with METT-TC. Recons are typically squad sized missions. Figure 12-4 depicts a task organization for a squad size recon patrol. The squad in the diagram has five available radios.

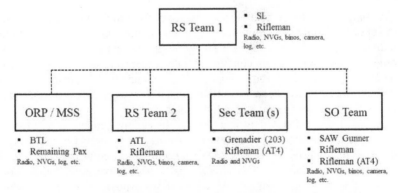

Figure 12-4. Organization of a Squad Size Recon Patrol.

Regardless of how the recon and security elements are organized, each element always maintains responsibility for its own local security. In a small recon patrol, the patrol headquarters may form a part of one of the subordinate elements rather than being a separate element. The number and size of the various teams and elements must be determined through the leader's METT-TC analysis. Regarding task organization, the determining factor is normally the amount of radios available.

Employ security measures – A patrol must be able to return to the friendly unit with the information it has gathered. Leaders emplace security elements where they can best overwatch the reconnaissance elements. In the event of compromise, they suppress the enemy so the reconnaissance elements can break contact.

Execution of a Reconnaissance

The following sequence of events describe a typical area recon patrol:

1. The patrol occupies an ORP and reports to higher. The patrol leader (PL) confirms his location on a map while subordinate leaders make necessary perimeter adjustments. The PL organizes the patrol in one of two ways: separate recon and security elements, or combined recon and security elements (See Figure 12-4).

2. The BTL preps men, weapons, and equipment (MWE) for actions on the OBJ. The example in Figure 12-4 depicts 9 personnel going out on the mission in four elements: RS Team 1 (PL and a riflemen); RS Team 2 (ATL and a riflemen); SO Team (3 pax); and a two man security team.

Camouflage – The principal purpose of camouflage in the field is to prevent direct observation and recognition – to break up the outline. When applying individual camouflage, one must recognize the terrain's dominant color in order to blend in and avoid contrasting with the terrain. When applying face paint, shiny areas (forehead, cheekbones, nose, and chin) are painted with a dark color, whereas shadow areas (around the eyes, under the nose, and under the chin) are painted with a light color.

Exposed skin reflects light and attracts the enemy's attention. Even very dark skin will reflect light because of its natural oil. Skin that is exposed on the back of the neck and hands is painted with a two-color combination in an irregular pattern. When issue face paint is not available, burnt cork, charcoal or lamp black can be used to tone down exposed areas of skin. Mud is used only in an emergency because it changes color as it dries and may peel off, leaving the skin exposed. Since mud may contain harmful bacteria, mud should be washed off as soon as possible.

When applying camouflage to individual equipment and weapons, ensure the function of the weapon is not impaired. Any equipment that reflects light should be covered with a non-reflective material (such as burlap). Additionally, straight lines are very conspicuous to an enemy observer. The barrel and hand guard should be wrapped with strips of contrasting colored cloth or tape to break the regular outline. Additionally, all loose clothing must be secured (string or tape can be used) to prevent snagging on barbed wire, brambles, and brush. Rifle slings should be taped to prevent rattling. All weapons parts should be checked for glare elimination measures.

3. The PL issues a 5 point contingency plan to the assistant patrol leader (APL) before departing.

4. The PL establishes a suitable release point (RP) that out of sight and sound of the objective if possible, but that is definitely out of sight (See Figure 12-5). The RP should also have good rally point characteristics (see ORP acronym in Annex A). The RS teams remain in the RP while the PL is pinpointing the objective and emplacing the SO team.

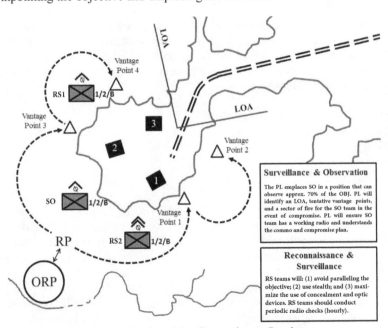

Surveillance & Observation

The PL emplaces SO in a position that can observe approx. 70% of the OBJ. PL will identify an LOA, tentative vantage points, and a sector of fire for the SO team in the event of compromise. PL will ensure SO team has a working radio and understands the commo and compromise plan.

Reconnaissance & Surveillance

RS teams will: (1) avoid paralleling the objective; (2) use stealth; and (3) maximize the use of concealment and optic devices. RS teams should conduct periodic radio checks (hourly).

Figure 12-5. Squad Area Reconnaissance Patrol.

Observation Plan – Once the patrol leader understands the IR, he then determines how best to obtain it by developing an observation plan. The leader's observation plan asks two basic questions: (1) What is the best location(s) to obtain the information required? (2) How can I best obtain the information without compromising the patrol?

The answer to the first question is; all vantage points (VP) and observation posts (OP) from which the patrol can best obtain the IR. A VP is a temporary position that enables observation of the OBJ. It is meant to be occupied only until the IR is confirmed or denied. The answer to the second question is; use routes and number of teams necessary to occupy the required VPs. A PL should use as many RS teams as necessary so as to avoid extraneous noise.

An OP is a position from where observations can be made and fire can be directed and adjusted. OPs must possess appropriate communications. Unlike a VP, the OP is normally occupied and surveillance is conducted for a specified period of time. The SO team is emplaced at an OP which can either be short term (12 hours or less) or long term, depending on guidance from higher. The patrol views the reconnaissance objective from as many perspectives as possible, using whatever combinations of OPs and VPs are necessary.

5. The PL pinpoints the OBJ and selects an OP where he will emplace the SO team. OPs should be the least prominent positions in an objective area (See Figure 12-5). A selected OP should be observed for 10 to 15 minutes to ensure it is not occupied. Keep the following acronym in mind when selecting an OP: **BLISS**

B - Blends in with the surroundings.
L - Low in silhouette.
I - Irregular in shape.
S - Small in size.
S - Secluded.

Further, if possible, avoid the use of existing buildings or shelters. Construction of OP hide sites should only be made in cold weather and desert environments. When leaving the OP, use a different route from the one used during the appraoch. The PL selects an OP which:

▪ Affords good observation - approximately 70 percent visibility of the objective (If possible, and if observation is optimum, PL may opt to conduct long-range reconnaissance from the SO team's location).

- Provides good cover and concealment, as well as cover and concealment to and from the location.
- Is large enough for the SO team.
- Has clear a field of fire onto the objective (if compromised).
- OPs should not be manned for more than 24 hours.

If possible a three-man SO should be used. This allows for shifts on optics and recon logs. For example an SO team might consist of the ASAW, alpha point man (APT) and a third man for rear security. SO team equipment should include a radio, optic(s), M249, AT4, and recon log.

7. Before departing the SO team's position, the PL identifies a limit of advance (LOA), tentative vantage points, gives the SO team a definitive sector of fire, and identifies targets for suppression in the event of compromise. Normally, AOO will terminate when one of the following occurs: RS teams have reached the LOA; observation window (eyes-on time) has elapsed; PL has determined that all available intel has been obtained; or patrol has been compromised.

8. During the reconnaissance, the APL maintains security and communications with higher HQ, and supervises priorities of work in the ORP.

9. PL moves back to the RP and briefs Security Team and RS teams regarding the OBJ particulars. Additionally, the PL ensures all recon elements understand any/all NLT times or communication windows, then releases his RS teams. PL has an option of either emplacing security or giving the senior man an azimuth, distance and grid to their primary position.

10. Throughout the patrol, the PL maintains communications with all recon elements, security, and the ORP. Radio checks should be made periodically. For example, radio checks may be made every hour on the hour. RS teams manage their time and move away from the OBJ for radio checks.

11. RS teams move stealthily to vantage points and avoid paralleling the OBJ by using the cloverleaf technique (See Figure 12-5). Recon teams should plan every movement and move in segments of the route at a time.

Target Indicators – To gain information while avoiding detection, recon teams must understand target indicators. Target indicators are anything a soldier does or fails to do that could result in detection. A recon team must know and understand target indication not only to move undetected, but also to detect enemy movement. Target indicators are sound, movement, improper camouflage, disturbance of wildlife, and odors.[2]

Consider the following target indicators:

- Sound – Most noticeable during hours of darkness. Caused by movement, equipment rattling, or talking. Small noises may be dismissed as natural, but talking will not. Recon teams should move stealthily, stopping frequently to listen as this gains information about the enemy and by exercising care, keeps information from the enemy.
- Movement – Most noticeable during hours of daylight. The human eye is attracted to movement. Quick or jerky movement will be detected faster than slow movement.
- Improper camouflage, shine, outline; contrast with the background.
- Disturbance of wildlife. Birds suddenly flying away. Sudden stop of animal noises. Animals being frightened.
- Odors, smoking, soap, lotions and insect repellents.

Recon teams should consider the following seven principles of stealth movement:

(1) Avoid unnecessary movement. Remain still—movement attracts attention. When the team must change positions, it moves carefully over a concealed route to a new position, preferably during limited visibility. Before moving, recon teams should assess the terrain for potential cover and concealment.

(2) Use all available cover and concealment. Cover is protection from hostile weapons fire. Concealment is protection from observation from both air and ground observation, but not from hostile fire. Although total darkness provides concealment, recon teams must observe the same principles of concealment during moonlight conditions as in the daytime.

The team selects trees or bushes to blend with the uniform and to absorb the figure outline.[3] Recon teams should always assume they are under observation, both day and night, and should likewise assume enemy employment of night observation devices. While moving to different vantage points, avoid walking laterally within sight of the OBJ, as the enemy will most likely pick out this movement. Instead use the 'clover leaf technique,' that is, do your lateral movement out of sight of the objective

---

[2] FM 23-10 Sniper Training, 4-1.
[3] Ibid, 4-7.

area in order present less of a signature. Further, while moving forward to a vantage point, to aid in concealment, use the 'staking trees' method of approach. This is accomplished by putting one tree, two if possible, between you and the objective area. Similarly, at night, the same method is used to avoid casting shadows.

(3) Stay low to observe. A low silhouette makes it difficult for the enemy to see a recon team. Therefore, the team observes from a crouch, a squat, or a prone position.

(4) Avoid shiny reflections. Reflection of light on a shiny surface instantly attracts attention and can be seen from great distances. Optics should be covered with netting or hose and used cautiously in bright sunshine because of the reflections they cause.

(5) Avoid skylining. Figures on the skyline can be seen from a great distance, even at night, because a dark outline stands out against the lighter sky. The silhouette formed by the body makes a good target.

(6) Alter familiar outlines. Military equipment and the human body are familiar outlines to the enemy. Recon teams alter or disguise these revealing shapes by using ghillie suits or outer smocks (*Mossy Oak*) that is covered with irregular patterns of garnish. The team must alter its outline from the head to the soles of the boots.

(7) Observe noise discipline. Noise, such as talking, can be picked up by enemy patrols or observation posts. Sounds are transmitted a greater distance in wet weather and at night than in dry weather and in the daytime. Sound travels approximately 370 meters a second.[4]

Movement Imperatives – Stop, look, and listen often. The RS team's movement to a VP should include a series of listening halts, as this acclimates them to the sights, sounds, and smells of the objective area. Avoid causing the overhead movement of trees, bushes, or tall grasses by rubbing against them. Move during disturbances such as gunfire, explosions, aircraft noise, wind, or anything that will distract the enemy's attention or conceal the team's movement.

---

[4] For example, when a flash from a fired weapon is observed, the range to the weapons can be easily estimated by counting the time interval between the flash and hearing the report. For example, counting to three (one thousand one, one thousand two, one thousand three), indicates the distance is 1,110 meters.

Walking is used when there is good concealment, it is not likely the enemy is close, and speed is required.[5] When walking, place the heel down first, balancing the weight of the body on the rear foot until a secure spot is found, then lower the sole of the forward foot slowly; gradually transferring body weight to that foot. Step over fallen logs and branches, not on them. As R/S teams near the OBJ, movement should be slow, deliberate, and with as small a silhouette as possible.

Movement is slow and tedious, since it must be done silently. Therefore, the low crawl and high crawl are not suitable as shuffling noises result. Creeping (hand-and-knees crawl) is the recommended method of movement.

This is done using your hands to feel for twigs, leaves or other substances that might make a noise. Clear a spot to place your knee. Keeping your hand at that spot, bring your knee forward until it meets your hand. Then place your knee on the ground and repeat the action with the other hand and knee.

Vantage points (VPs) should provide adequate observation as well as cover and concealment. If VPs must be occupied for longer periods, wilted foliage should be replaced during periods of reduced visibility. Above all, avoid using too much material for camouflage, as it may stand out from its surroundings, thus attracting the attention of a hostile observer.

R/S Team Observation Plan – While observing, RS teams avoid all unnecessary movement. Using all senses available, one man observes and records while the other maintains security. At night, RS teams should move away from the objective area prior to recording information.

12. During the conduct of the recon, each RS team returns to the RP when any of the following occurs:
- They have gathered all their PIR.
- They have reached the LOA.
- The allocated time to conduct the recon has elapsed.
- Contact has been made.

13. At the RP the PL analyzes what information has been gathered and determines if he has met the IR. If the PL determines that he has not gathered sufficient information or if the information he and the subordinate leader gathered differs drastically, he may have to send RS teams back to the OBJ. In this case, RS teams alternate areas of responsibilities. For example, if one team reconnoitered from the 6 – 3 – 1 o'clock, then that team will now recon from the 6 – 9 – 11 o'clock.

---

[5] FM 23-10 Sniper Training, 4-10.

If the IR has been met, the PL ensures that all available IR is disseminated to the patrol at the ORP, or moves to a position at least one major terrain feature or one kilometer away to disseminate if compromised. To disseminate, the leader has the RTO prepare three sketches of the objective site based on the leader's sketch and provides the copies to the subordinate leaders to assist in dissemination.

Reporting – Verbal and written reports must be accurately and completely conveyed. Messages should be brief, accurate, and clear (facts and opinions are distinguished). If secondhand information is reported, its source is included. Information about the enemy should be annotated within a **SALUTE** report format (See Figure 12-6).

SALUTE Report	
Size	What is the size of the unit (number of personnel, vehicles [highway, rail, etc.], and equipment [tents, weapons, etc.])?
Activity	What are they doing (moving in column/mass, or setting up a defensive position or deploying, redeploying, sustainment activities, or training)?
Location	Where are they located? Use a map, if available. If no map is available, describe their position as accurately as possible (grid coordinates or airfield, military base, and/or terrain association).
Unit/Uniform	What unit do they belong to (company, battalion, brigade, division, and/or country)? What type of uniform are the soldiers wearing?
Time	What time of day/night unit was observed (DTG, Zulu, or local)?
Equipment	What type of equipment was observed (types of weapons, vehicles, aircraft, and/or other gear)?

Figure 12-6. SALUTE Report.

Range Estimation – accuracy is essential to reconnaissance. Lasers are the preferred means of determining distance. However, in the absence of a more accurate method, the observer must still estimate distance to capture the most accurate depiction of the objective possible. Here are some methods of estimating distance:

(1) Assisted Method – uses binoculars and mil relation to determine range. To use this method, the width or height of the target must be known. To determine the range (R), identify the target width (height or length) on the mil scale in the binoculars. When looking through the M22 binoculars, each

larger increment is equal to 10 mils while the smaller is equal to 5 mils (See Figure 12-7).[6]

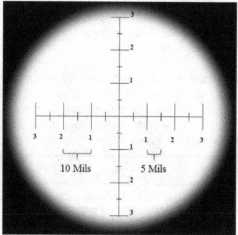

Figure 12-7. M22 Binoculars Mil Relation.

The known target width (W) in either meters or inches is then divided by the mil (m) width; this equals the range (R) factor. Multiply R by 1,000 to determine the target's range. This is known as the WoRM formula: W (width/length/height) divided by M (mils) = R (range). See Figure 12-7.

$$\frac{W \text{ (target size in meters)} \times 1000}{M \text{ (target size in mils)}} = \text{Range to target in meters}$$

$$\frac{W \text{ (target size in inches)} \times 25.4}{M \text{ (target size in mils)}} = \text{Range to target in meters}$$

Figure 12-8. WoRM Formula.

Note: The observer should mask binocular lenses with cloth or panty hose as direct sunlight can reflect off of them; potentionally giving away his position.

(2) Mental Estimation – distance may be estimated to the nearest 100 meters by determining the number of known units of measure, such as a football field (100 yards), between the observer's position and a target.

---

[6] A mil is a unit of angular measurement equal to 1/6400 of a circle. There are 18 mils in one degree. One mil equals the width (or height) of 1 meter at a range of 1,000 meters.

(3) Flash-to-Bang – Sound travels at a speed of approximately 350 meters per second. An observer can estimate range from his location to the objective by estimating the elapsed time between a sound on the objective and his position. Use the following equation: elapsed time (in seconds) between impact and sound x 350 = distance. Multiply the number of seconds between sound impact (flash) and when the sound reaches the observer (bang) by 350 meters. The answer is the approximate number of meters between the observer and the round. (This procedure can also be used to determine the distance to enemy weapon muzzle flashes).[7]

Reconnaissance Products – Information gathered by the recon team is reported, analyzed, and processed into intelligence reports. Information difficult to describe may be given accurately on a simple sketch. The sketch may give all the necessary information or it may be used to supplement a written message. Generally, there are two basic types of sketches a recon element may use: a *topographic* (overhead) sketch and a *military* (panoramic) sketch.

(1) Topographic Sketch. A topographic sketch (Figure 12-9) is a graphic representation of an area drawn to scale as seen from above. This type of sketch is useful in describing road systems, flow of streams/rivers, or locations of natural and man-made obstacles. The most prominent building is always building #1.

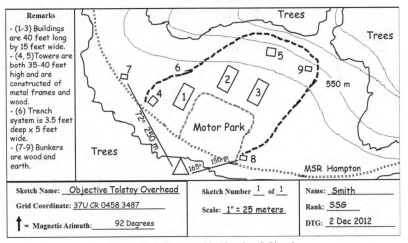

Figure 12-9. Topographic (Overhead) Sketch.

---

[7] FM 3-60, 3-6.

(2) <u>Military Sketch</u>. A military or panoramic sketch is used to record information about a general area, terrain features, or man-made structures that are not shown on a map. Military sketches provide an on-the-ground view of an area or object that is otherwise unobtainable (Figure 12-10).

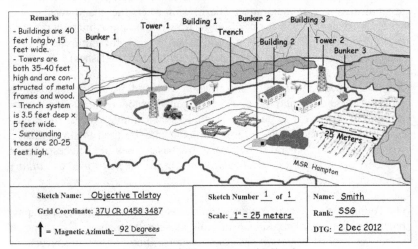

Figure 12-10. Military (Panoramic) Sketch.

Guidelines for Drawing Sketches – Military drawing focuses on accuracy, not so much artistic skill. The following are guidelines when drawing sketches: First, work from the whole to the part. First determine the boundaries of the sketch. In the diagram below (Figure 12-11), an 8 ½ x 11 sheet of paper is first folded (landscape) into three equal parts. This will facilitate correct dimensions. Next fold the paper in half. This will indicate the horizontal plane. Then sketch the larger objects such as hills, mountains, or outlines of large buildings.

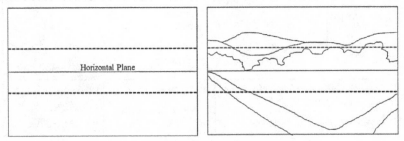

Figure 12-11. Preparing a Sketch.

375

After drawing the large objects in the sketch, start drawing the smaller details. Second, use common shapes to show common objects. Do not sketch each individual tree, hedgerow, or wood line exactly. Use common shapes to show these types of objects. Do not concentrate on the fine details unless they are of tactical importance.

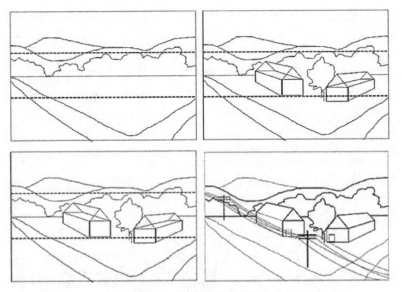

Figure 12-12. Preparing a Sketch.

Third, draw in perspective; use vanishing points. Try to draw sketches in perspective. To do this, recognize the vanishing points of the area to be sketched. Parallel lines on the ground that are horizontal vanish at a point on the horizon (Figure 12-11).

(3) <u>Reconnaissance Log</u>. A reconnaissance log is a written, chronological record of all activities and events that take place during recon actions on the objective. It is used in combination with other recon products and provides commanders and intelligence personnel with information and an accurate record of the activity in the area. A recon log should include all pertinent details.

(4) <u>Grid Reference Graphic (GRG).</u> Similar to the overhead sketch, the GRG should include all structures within an established target area. The target building is always building number 1. Normal numbering convention is to number buildings in a clockwise method from building 1 (See Figure 12-12). Additionally, the GRG should include a north-seeking arrow. GRGs

are used to coordinate all forces (ground and air) in an operation. The focus should be on ease of reference and usefulness. For example, to direct close air support to the northeast corner of building 1, you would send J11. Or, if you needed to consolidate all personnel post assault at the southern side of building 8, you would call it C7.

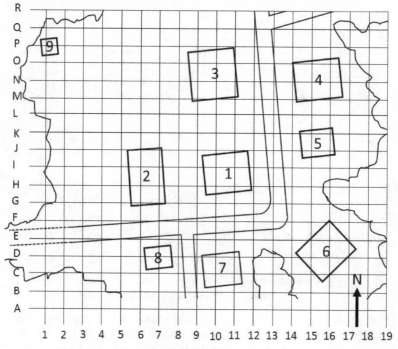

Figure 12-12. Grid Reference Graphic.

(5) <u>Grid Structure Sketch (GSS)</u>. An additional product which a recon team may be directed to provide is a Grid Structure Sketch (GSS). Similar to a panoramic sketch, the GSS is used to provide specific details on a particular building. For example, roof type, type of doors (steel, wood), window type (including height from ground floor), lighting, etc (See Figure 12-13). Data may be included on an accompanying document. Numbering convention for a GSS is as follows: top left opening (window or anything that can be used to shoot through) is always A1. From that point, number from left to right. The next opening down from A1 is B1, etc. When including questionable data you are not completely sure about, a good rule is to append information with 'appears to be' (ATB).

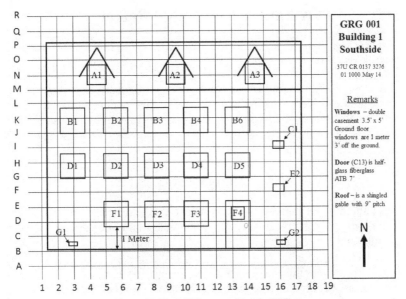

Figure 12-13. Grid Structure Sketch (GSS).

Actions on Compromise – If contact is made, the RS element moves to the release point (conducting buddy team fire and maneuver if necessary); the SO team will cover their withdrawal with a high volume of small arms fire, AT4s, 40mm on preplanned targets within the sector of fire given by the PL. This action will enable the RS teams to break contact. The recon element will break contact and return to the ORP, secure rucksacks, and quickly move out of the area. Once they have moved a safe distance away, the PL informs higher HQ of the situation and gets further instructions.

Conclusion

The most vital of all combat commodities, according to S.L.A. Marshall, is information. The moral is to the material three to one, and information is the soul of morale in combat and the balancing force in successful tactics.[8] Reconnaissance is confirming what we know, and learning what we don't already know; to gain information. The goal of this chapter was to understand that reconnaissance is vital to decisive action. Moreover, there is no substitute for personal reconnaissance.

---

[8] Marshall, Men Against Fire, 92.

Chapter 13 Combat Patrols

"Let the enemy come till he's almost close enough to touch, then let him have it and jump out and finish him up with your hatchet." – Rogers' Standing Orders #19

A combat patrol provides security and either harasses, destroys, or captures enemy troops, equipment, or installations. The intent of the combat patrol is to make contact with the enemy and engage him in close combat. This chapter will discuss the three types of combat patrols: *ambush, raid, and security.*

Ambush Patrols

An ambush is a surprise attack from a concealed location on a moving or temporarily halted target.[1] It is one of the oldest and most effective type of guerilla tactics. An ambush is conducted in order to reduce the enemy's overall combat effectiveness and destroy his *center of gravity.* An ambush lowers troop morale and harasses the enemy force as a whole. It may include an assault to close with and destroy the engaged enemy force. However, the ground objective does not have to be seized and held. Destruction is the primary purpose of an ambush because loss of men (killed or captured), and loss of equipment and supplies (destroyed or captured), reduces the overall combat effectiveness of the enemy.[2]

Ambush Fundamentals – Surprise and speed, coordinated fires and violence of action are the three fundamentals of a successful ambush.
Surprise and speed – Surprise must be achieved or the attack will not be an ambush. Surprise allows the ambush force to retain control of the situation. The enemy force is attacked when and where and in a manner they least expect, with explosive, aggressive force. *Coordinated Firepower* – All weapons, direct and indirect, including mines and demolitions, are positioned and coordinated to achieve:
1. Isolation of the kill zone in order to prevent escape and/or reinforcement.
2. Surprise delivery of a murderous volume of concentrated firepower into the kill zone in order to inflict the maximum amount of damage so that the target may be assaulted and destroyed.
Violence of action – Violence of action is explosive force directed against the enemy. It is both mental and physical.
Control – An additional consideration for a successful ambush is control. Control is maintained by personnel within the ambush force while in

---

[1] FM 3-90, 5-122.
[2] MCWP 3-11.3 Scouting and Patrolling, 13-3.

ambush posture. Self-discipline is required to endure unfavorable weather conditions, insect bites, and fatigue in order to maintain the required level of alertness. Control is maintained during the occupation and withdrawal from the ambush site. Control of all ambush elements during the approach of the enemy force is critical for mission success. Control measures for an ambush include:

1. Early warning of target approach.
2. Withholding of fire until the ambush commander initiates.[3]
3. Ceasing supporting fires when the ambush includes an assault.
4. Rapid withdrawal to a Release Point (RP).

Categories and Types of Ambushes

Ambushes are categorized as hasty or deliberate, typified as point or area, and executed from an array of formations, such as: linear, L-shaped, V-shaped, etc. A point ambush, whether independent or part of an area ambush, is positioned along the target's expected route of approach. A point ambush attacks a single kill zone. An area ambush uses multiple point ambushes around a central kill zone.

A deliberate ambush is one in which prior information about the enemy permits detailed planning before the patrol departs for the ambush site. A hasty ambush is an immediate reaction that is conducted to exploit an unexpected opportunity. Hasty ambushes rely on the same principles as the deliberate but require battle drill precision in the form of SOPs.

The patrol leader considers the factors of METT-TC, such as, expected enemy size, terrain, and troops available in order to determine the appropriate category, type, and formation of ambush to employ. Normally, the desired goal of the ambush is a large scale expenditure of enemy personnel in the kill zone (KZ).[4] Additional goals may include the destruction of designated enemy vehicles or the capture of high value individuals (HVI).

Ambush Site Selection – The patrol leader uses maps and aerial photographs to select the ideal ambush site. When selecting an ambush site, the patrol leader considers terrain that will provide the following:

- Fields of fire.
- Canalizing terrain.
- Covered routes of withdrawal for the ambush force.

---

[3] Weapons should remain on safe until initiation. This avoids breaking noise discipline prior to initiation. The ambush leader should initiate when the target is center of the kill zone, or to have the target come to a halt in the center if accounting for forward momentum.
[4] A kill zone (KZ) is the linear and vertical box on the OBJ where fires are concentrated in order to isolate, fix, and destroy the enemy force.

Squad Linear Ambush

The Linear formation ambush is used on roads, trails, and streams to place a volume of fire from the assault and support which parallel a kill zone road 35 to 50 meters in length. The Linear ambush is easy to establish and control. This formation positions the attack element parallel to the long axis of the killing zone and subjects the target to heavy flanking fire.

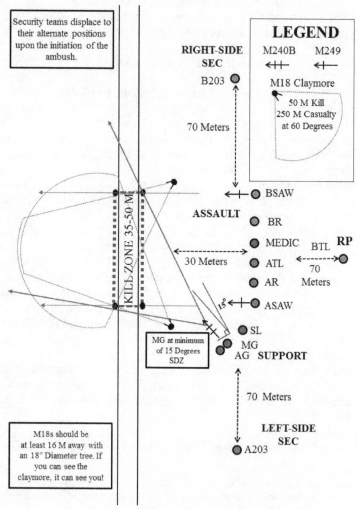

Figure 13-1. Squad Linear Ambush.

381

Squad L-Shaped Ambush

The L-Shaped formation is a variation of the Linear that subjects the enemy force to enfilading and interlocking fire. In the L-Shaped, the assault element is placed parallel to the kill zone (interlocking fire) while the support element is placed at the end and at a right angle (enfilading fire).

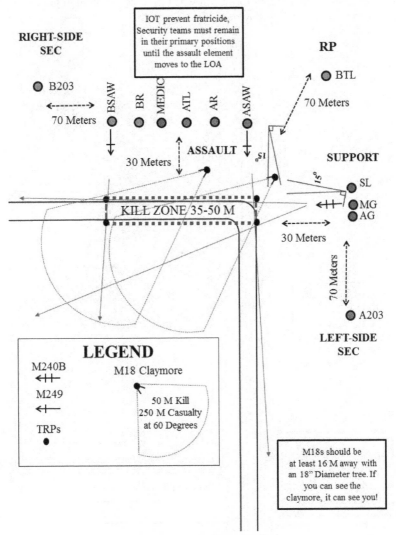

Figure 13-2. Squad L-Shaped Ambush.

382

Squad V-Shaped Ambush

The V-Shaped formation is a variation of the Linear that subjects the enemy force to enfilading and interlocking fire. In the V-Shaped, fires are carefully coordinated to prevent fratricide. Its main advantage is that it is difficult for the target to detect the ambush until it has moved well into the kill zone, and is an optimal formation when established on high ground with the enemy travelling uphill towards the formation.

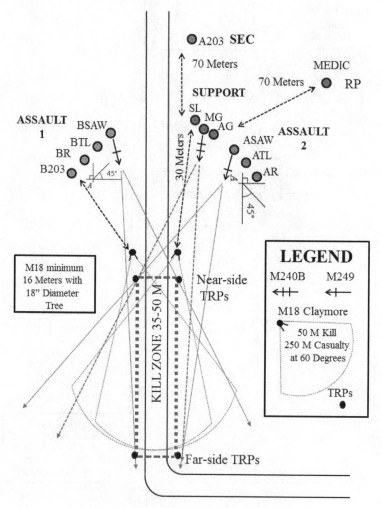

Figure 13-3. Squad V-Shaped Ambush.

Squad V-Shaped Ambush Post Assault

Following initiation of the ambush, Assault 1 assaults through the kill zone and establishes an LOA, followed by Assault 2 which does the same. The gun team moves behind Assault 2, similar to their actions during a squad attack and is emplaced at the apex by the squad leader. AOO proceed as usual with the specialty teams clearing, searching, etc..

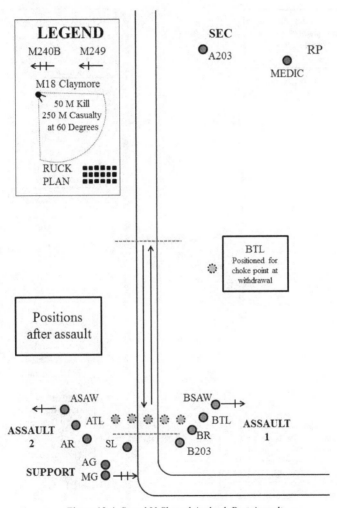

Figure 13-4. Squad V-Shaped Ambush Post Assault.

Platoon Linear (Trifecta) Ambush

The Platoon Linear formation point ambush is used on roads, trails, and streams to place a volume of fire from the assault and support which parallel a kill zone road 50 to 100 meters in length. The Linear ambush allows enfilading fire from the support position and interlocking fire from the assault position. The linear is easy to establish and control.

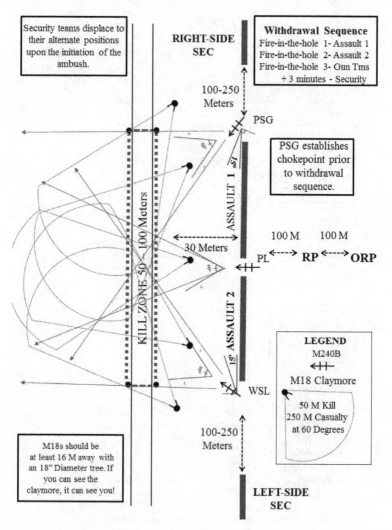

Figure 13-5. Platoon Linear (Trifecta Technique) Ambush.

385

Platoon L-Shaped Ambush

The L-Shaped formation is a variation of the Linear that subjects the enemy force to enfilading and interlocking fire. In the L-Shaped, the assault element is placed parallel to the kill zone (interlocking fire) while the support element is placed at the end and at a right angle (enfilading fire). Fires are carefully coordinated to prevent fratricide.

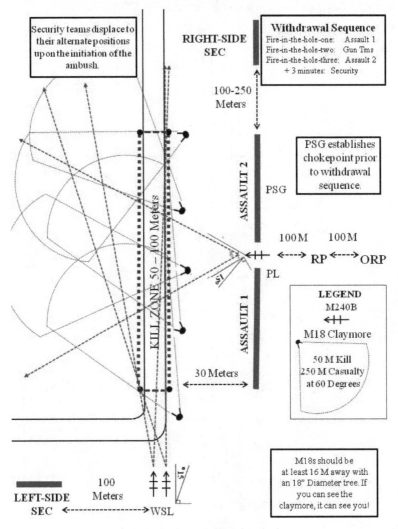

Figure 13-6. Platoon L-Shaped Ambush.

386

Platoon X-Shaped Ambush

The X-Shaped formation is a platoon level ambush that facilitates enfilading and interlocking fire to be placed on the enemy in either direction. The PL's position should enable him to 'flex' to the ambush element that initiates first, while the senior leader for the ambush element that does not initiate assumes control of the element and provides rear security. Distance between ambush elements METT-TC dependent.

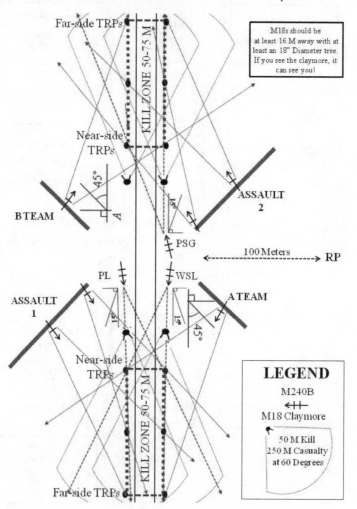

Figure 13-7. Platoon X-Shaped Ambush.

387

Platoon X-Shaped Ambush Post Assault

Following initiation of the Assault 1 ambush, Assault 1 assaults through the kill zone and establishes an LOA, followed by A Team which does the same. The gun teams are then emplaced at the apex by the platoon leader. Another technique is to have the WSL move the far side gun team to the rear security ambush (not shown). AOO proceed as usual with the specialty teams clearing, searching, etc.

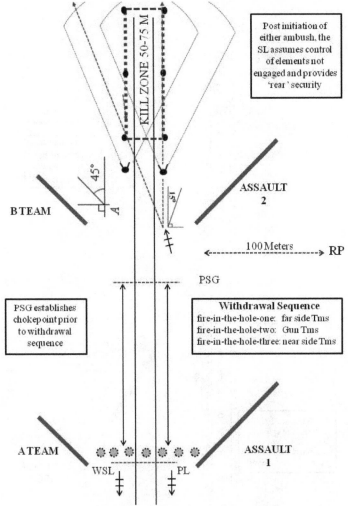

Figure 13-8. Platoon X-Shaped Ambush Post Assault.

388

Platoon K-Shaped Ambush

The K-Shaped formation is a platoon level ambush variation of the Linear that subjects the enemy force to enfilading and interlocking fire. The K-Shaped allows for ambiguity in the enemy situation by being prepared for the enemy's advance in either direction. Additionally, the K-Shaped allows for the benefits of the X-Shaped without having to cross the kill zone road, and/or when terrain dictates, i.e., on a spur running perpendicular to the kill zone road.

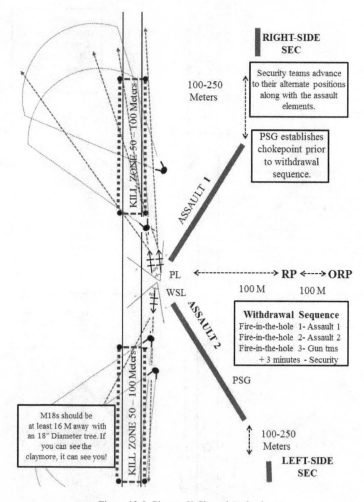

Figure 13-9. Platoon K-Shaped Ambush.

389

Platoon Z-Shaped Ambush

The Z-Shaped formation is a platoon level ambush variation of the Linear that is used on roads, trails, and streams with multiple bends which afford enfilading as well as flanking fire. In the Z-Shaped ambush, fires are carefully coordinated to prevent fratricide.

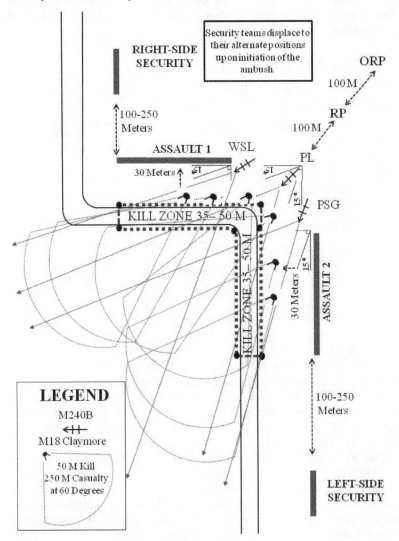

Figure 13-10. Platoon Z-Shaped Ambush.

390

Area Ambush

In the area ambush, squads deploy in two or more related point ambushes as part of a platoon or higher. The platoon may conduct an area ambush as part of a company offensive or defensive plan, or it may conduct a point ambush as part of a company area ambush (See Figure 13-11). The platoon is the smallest level to conduct an area ambush. Point ambushes are established along the trails or other escape routes leading away from the central kill zone.

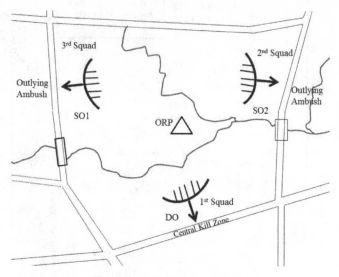

Figure 13-11. Platoon Area Ambush.

The target, whether a single group or several groups approaching from different directions, is permitted to move to the central kill zone. Outlying ambushes do not attack unless discovered. The ambush is initiated when the target moves into the central kill zone. When the target breaks contact and attempts to disperse, escaping portions are intercepted and destroyed by the outlying ambushes. The multiple contacts achieve increased casualties, harassment, and confusion.

The PL considers the factors of METT-TC to determine the best employment of the weapons squad. He normally locates the medium machine guns with the support element in the principal ambush site. Squads responsible for outlying ambushes do not initiate their ambushes until the central ambush has been initiated. They then engage to prevent enemy forces from escaping the principal ambush or reinforcing the ambushed force.

391

Anti-armor Ambush

Patrols conduct anti-armor ambushes to destroy armored vehicles. The patrol leader considers the following when planning an anti-armor ambush. Decisive to this type of ambush is the positioning of the armor-killer team, which is built around the man portable antitank weapon (MAW) system (Carl Gustav, Dragon, AT4, etc). The patrol leader carefully positions all anti-armor weapons to ensure the best shot (rear, flank, or top). The remainder of the squad or platoon must function as support and security elements in the same way that they do for other combat patrols.

The patrol leader selects a site for the ambush that restricts the movement of armored vehicles out of the kill zone (for example, a bridge or canalized part of a road). The leader should attempt to place his elements so that an obstacle is between them and the kill zone (See Figure 13-12).

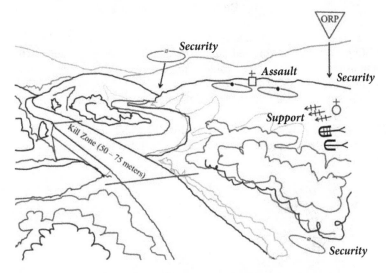

Figure 13-12. Platoon Anti-armor Ambush.

The patrol leader should consider the method for initiating the anti-armor ambush. The preferred method is to use a command-detonated anti-armor mine placed in the kill zone. The MAW can be used to initiate the ambush, but its signature and slow rate of fire make it less desirable. Additionally, security elements must consider dismounted avenues of approach into the ambush site.

Initiation – The armor-killer team attempts to kill the first and last vehicles in the column, if possible. All other weapons open fire once the ambush has begun. If the kill zone is within range of light anti-armor weapons, each soldier fires one during the ambush. The patrol leader must consider how the presence of dismounted enemy forces with armored vehicles will affect the success of his ambush. The leader's choices include:

- Initiate the ambush as planned.
- Withdraw without initiating the ambush.
- Initiate the ambush using only automatic weapons without firing anti-armor weapons.

Because of the speed with which other armored forces can reinforce the enemy in the ambush site, the leader should plan to keep the engagement short, and the withdrawal rapid. As in other ambushes, the patrol may or may not clear through the kill zone.

Baited-Trap Ambush

A variation of the area ambush is the baited trap version where a central killing zone is established along the target's route of approach. Point ambushes are established along the routes over which relieving or reinforcing units will have to approach. The target in the central kill zone serves as bait to lure relieving or reinforcing units into the killing zones of the outlying ambushes. The outlying point ambushes need not be strong enough to destroy their targets. They may be small, harassing ambushes that delay, disorganize, and eat away the target by successive contacts (See Figure 13-13).

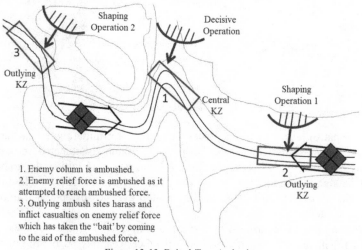

1. Enemy column is ambushed.
2. Enemy relief force is ambushed as it attempted to reach ambushed force.
3. Outlying ambush sites harass and inflict casualties on enemy relief force which has taken the "bait' by coming to the aid of the ambushed force.

Figure 13-13. Baited-Trap Ambush.

393

Ambush Sequence of Events

The following sequence of events chronologically outline a typical ambush patrol. The patrol occupies an objective rally point (ORP) and calls higher passing the brevity code for ORP occupied. The patrol leader (PL) then prepares for the conduct of his leader's reconnaissance by first checking men, weapons, and equipment (MWE). Once MWE is complete, the PL issues a 5 point contingency plan to the assistant patrol leader (APL). Using the acronym **GOTWA**, the 5 point contingency plan is given as follows:

G – Where the leader is GOING.
O – OTHERS he is taking with him.
T – TIME he plans to be gone.
W – WHAT to do if the leader is not back in time.
A – The unit's and the leader's ACTIONS on chance contact while the leader is gone. Additionally, the PL gives specific guidance stating what tasks are to be accomplished in the ORP in his absence, such as: disseminate the 5 point, monitor the radio at all times, and keep everyone awake.

Leader's Reconnaissance for an Ambush Objective – The PL conducts a reconnaissance of the tentative ambush site with the minimum amount of personnel while using stealth. After emplacing the surveillance overwatch (SO) team, the PL moves forward to pinpoint the objective. The acronym **PINPOINT** assists in remembering critical steps.

P – Pinpointing the OBJ and verifying its overall suitability, i.e. analyzing the terrain to ensure its acceptability. The ambush site should be generally a flat table-top like surface of 35 to 50 meters of usable kill zone (KZ).
I – Identify left, center, and right target reference points (TRP) for the KZ to enable coordinated fires.
N – No obstacles should be present from the tentative assault line to the limit of advance (LOA). An obstacle, such as a fallen tree, would impede the progress of the assault.
P – Point out two claymore trees which optimally should be 18" in diameter and at least 16 meters from the tentative assault line to prevent any potential fratricide resulting from the back-blast of the claymore. In the event suitable claymore trees are unavailable, the claymores must be emplaced at the fullest extent possible that the wire will allow, i.e. 30 meters.
O – Overall, the potential KZ terrain should offer a clear field of fire to maximize the effects of claymore and small arms fire (SAF).
I – Identify suitable support and assault positions. Based on intelligence and /or probability, the PL should identify a support position that will effect

enfilading fire and cover the entirety of the KZ. Additionally, the support position should be placed at least a meter in front of the assault line in order to achieve the desired effects of fire as well as a 15 degree surface danger zone – SDZ (see page 459). After identifying the support position, the PL should ensure that his assault element will have suitable cover and concealment, and enough room to accommodate the entire assault element. Optimally, there should be 3 to 5 meters between each assaulter.

N – No deadspace present. The PL should ensure that his KZ is void of deadspace, i.e. terrain that obscures direct fire. This could be ditches alongside the KZ, or dense vegetation, like a draw.

T – Travel to recce left and right side security. After verifying the suitability of the potential KZ, the PL checks in with the SO element and travels to recce suitable security positions to the left and right of the KZ. Security positions should take into account two factors; early warning and adequate back-blast area for the AT-4. Additionally, during the process of the leader's recon of the OBJ, the PL should: maintain security, noise and light discipline, and avoid paralleling the KZ road.

Overall, during the leaders' recon of the objective, the PL:

1. Ensures the leader's recon party moves undetected.
2. Confirms suitability of assault and support positions, and routes to and from the ORP/RP.
3. Selects position of each weapon system in support by fire position, then designates sectors of fire.
4. Adjusts his plan based on info from the reconnaissance and confirms the ambush formation to be employed, i.e., Linear, L-Shaped, etc.

Assistant Patrol Leader (APL) Actions – During the leaders' recon for the objective, the APL has the following critical tasks:

1. The APL maintains security and supervises priorities of work in the ORP.
2. Reestablishes security at the ORP.
3. Disseminates the PLs contingency plan.
4. Conducts/oversees the preparation of men, weapons, and equipment (MWE) in the following order: security, support, and assault.

Emplacement of Ambush – The PL returns with his recon party to the ORP, confirms the plan or issues a FRAGO, and allows subordinate leaders time to disseminate the plan, then leads the patrol to occupy the realease point (RP).

Ambush Objective Occupation – At the RP, the PL halts the patrol and ensures both security teams (left and right side) have radio equipment and issues them a **EWAC** brief:

Engagement criteria. The security team is reminded of the engagement criteria in order to ensure the patrol doesn't fire upon a force too large. The standard is normally a 1 to 3 ratio. For example, the engagement criteria for an ambush patrol consisting of 12 men would consist of four personnel and a light-skinned vehicle.

Withdrawal. Security teams move back to the release point (RP) after the blast of the demolition charge or after waiting three minutes following the "fire-in-the-hole three" call.

Abort criteria. This is met by an arrival of an enemy quick reaction force (QRF) or the receipt of indirect fire (IDF).

Compromise. If the security team is detected it conducts fire and maneuver back to the RP.

Additionally, during the OPORD, security teams should be given reporting instructions: upon visual, security teams positively identify approaching element as threat, and give the PL an alert brief consisting of the size and speed of the approaching force. For example: "PL, this is right-side security, we have one vehicle with two personnel moving at 5 mph, over."

Actions on the Objective – From the RP, the PL emplaces the security team(s) first, securing the flanks of the ambush site, and providing early warning. The security element must be in position before the support and assault elements move forward of the release point. An additional security team remains in the ORP if the patrol plans to return to the ORP after actions on the objective. If the ORP is abandoned, a rear security team should be emplaced. Next, the PL emplaces the support element and assigns sectors of fire. The PL and team leader(s) emplaces the assault element and assigns sectors of fire for each man using the acronym **SPARC**:

  S – Sector of fire.
  P – Priority of targets.
  A – Assault lane.
  R – Rate of fire.
  C – Conceal position.

The PL and team leader(s) emplace claymores and obstacles as designated.

Initiation of Ambush – The security element spots the enemy and notifies the PL, and reports the direction of movement, size of the target, and any special weapons or equipment carried. The security element also keeps the patrol leader informed if any enemy forces are following the lead force.

1. The PL then alerts other elements, and determines if the enemy force is too large, or if the ambush can engage the enemy successfully.

396

2. The PL initiates the ambush using the highest casualty producing weapon once he determines the enemy to be in the center of the kill zone (KZ).
For example, the PL's PACE plan for initiation could be:

      P – Primary: M18 Claymore mine.

      A – Alternate: M240B machinegun.

      C – Contingency: PL's weapon firing.

      E - Emergency: PL yells "fire"!

3. The PL ensures that the assault and support elements deliver fire with the heaviest, most accurate volume possible on the enemy in the KZ. In limited visibility, the PL may use infrared lasers to further define specific targets in the KZ.

4. Prior to assaulting the target, the PL gives the signal to shift or cease fires, and conducts an abbreviated SLLS.

5. The assault element:

- If needed, reestablishes the chain of command, re-mans key weapon systems.
- Loads fresh magazines or drums using the buddy system.
- Assaults before the remaining enemy can react.
- Uses individual movement techniques or bounds by fire teams.
- Kills or captures enemy in the kill zone.
- Upon reaching the limit of advance, halts and establishes security.
- ACE reports will be submitted through the chain of command.

6. The PL will submit an initial contact report to higher.

7. The PL directs special teams enemy prisoner of war (EPW) search, aid and litter, and demo to accomplish their assigned tasks once the assault element has established its LOA. Bodies that have been searched should be marked to ensure the area is thoroughly covered.

8. Once the kill zone is cleared, the PL directs any EPWs be collected and secured and moved out of the kill zone. If the patrol has EPWs, the PL may coordinate for an EPW exchange point to link up with higher to extract them. The PL will ensure that EPWs are treated in accordance with the five Ss: Search, Silence, Segregate, Safeguard, Speed to the rear, and Tag. EPWs should be searched from one side to the other.

9. The PL ensures EPW and search teams identify, collect, and prepare all equipment to be carried back or destroyed.

10. Any friendly casualties will be evacuated and treated first, then enemy wounded, time permitting.

11. The PL ensures demolition teams prepare dual primed explosives or incendiary grenades and await his signal to initiate.

12. The PL directs the unit's withdrawal from the ambush site. Elements normally withdraw in the reverse order that they established their positions. The security elements are the last to withdrawal. The elements may return to the RP or directly to the ORP, depending on the distance between elements.

13. If possible, all elements should return to the location at which they separated from the main body. This location usually is the RP.

14. The APL directs actions at the RP, to include accountability of personnel and equipment and recovery of rucksacks and other equipment.

15. The patrol departs the objective area and moves to a safe location (no less than one kilometer or one terrain feature away from the objective) and disseminates information.

16. If planned or required, the PL executes indirect fires to cover the patrol's withdrawal.

Raid Patrols

A raid is a surprise attack which involves a swift entry into hostile territory to destroy installations, gather intelligence, liberate captured personnel, and to kill or capture personnel. Raid patrols retain terrain just long enough to accomplish the intent, and are governed by four fundamentals: surprise and speed, coordinated fires, violence of action, and a planned withdrawal.[5] The patrol initiates the raid NLT the time specified in the order, surprises the enemy, assaults the objective, and accomplishes its assigned mission within the commander's intent. The patrol does not become decisively engaged enroute to the objective, obtains all available PIR and continues follow on operations.

Raid Sequence of Events – The patrol moves to and occupies the ORP IAW the patrol SOP. The patrol prepares for the leader's recon. The PL, squad leaders, and selected personnel conduct a leader's recon. Normally, the security element accompanies the PL and is emplaced during the leaders' reconnaissance of the objective. The following sequence of events chronologically outline a raid:

1. PL leaves a five-point contingency plan with the PSG.

2. PL establishes the RP, pinpoints the objective, contacts the PSG to prep men, weapons, and equipment, emplaces the surveillance team to observe the objective, and verifies and updates intelligence information. Upon emplacing the surveillance team, the PL will provide a five-point contingency plan.

---

[5] FM 3-21.10, 8-40.

3. Leader's recon verifies location of and routes to security, support, and assault positions.

4. Security teams are brought forward on the leader's reconnaissance and emplaced before the leader's recon leaves the RP.

5. Leaders conduct the recon without compromising the patrol.

6. Leaders normally recon support-by-fire position first, then the assault position.

Based upon the leader's recon, the PL confirms, denies, or modifies his plan and issues instructions to his squad leaders. Additionally, the PL assigns positions and withdrawal routes to all elements, and designates control measures on the objective (element objectives, assault lanes, limits of advance, target reference points, restrictive fire line, and assault line).

Emplacement – the PL directs security elements to occupy designated positions, moving undetected into positions that provide early warning and can seal off the objective from outside support or reinforcement. A technique is for the PL to take the security element with him on the leader's recon to be emplaced sometime during or after the recon.

7. The PL / support element leader (usually the Weapons Squad Leader) moves the support element to designated positions. The support element leader ensures his element can place well aimed fire on the objective (See Figure 13-14; see SHIFT FIRE acronym on page 502).

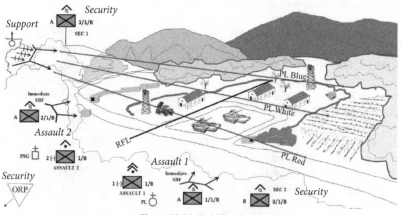

Figure 13-14. Raid Emplaced.

8. The PL moves with the assault element into the assault position. The assault position is normally the last covered and concealed position before reaching the objective (See RAID acronym on page 502). As it occupies the assault position the assault element deploys into its assault formation; that is, its squads and fire teams deploy in order to place the bulk of their firepower to the front during the assault of the objective.

9. The PL checks with SO, ensures that the assault position is close enough for immediate assault if the assault element is detected early.

Raid Commencement – Element leaders inform the PL when their elements are in position and ready. The raid will commence either on a time hack, the PL's command, or on some other means such as commencement of preplanned indirect fires.

10. The PL directs the support element to fire (destruction raid).

11. Upon gaining fire superiority, the PL directs the assault elements (Assault 1 and 2) to move toward the objective.

12. Breaching team moves forward to conduct breach if necessary (SOSRA: Suppress, Obscure, Secure, Reduce, Assault).

13. Assault element holds fire until engaged, or until ready to penetrate the objective.

14. PL signals the support element to "shift, lift, and/or cease fires." The support element lifts or shifts fires as directed, shifting fire to the flanks of targets or areas as directed in the FRAGO (See Figure 13-15).

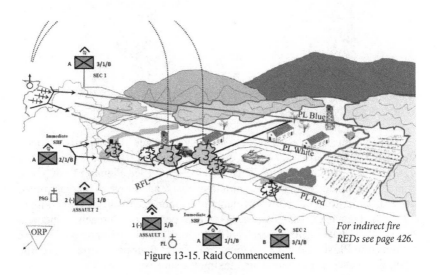

Figure 13-15. Raid Commencement.

Actions at Breach Points (SOSRA) – The following sequence is a technique for conducting a simultaneous breach on a wire obstacle: upon support's initiation, breach teams move to emplace charges; using the acronym SOSRA: Suppress, Obscure, Secure, Reduce, and Assault. Local SBF teams overwatch the breach team's approach and fire if necessary –Suppress (See Figure 13-16 A through E), only if breach team is fired upon, so as to retain surprise.

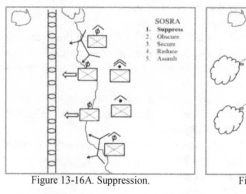

Figure 13-16A. Suppression.

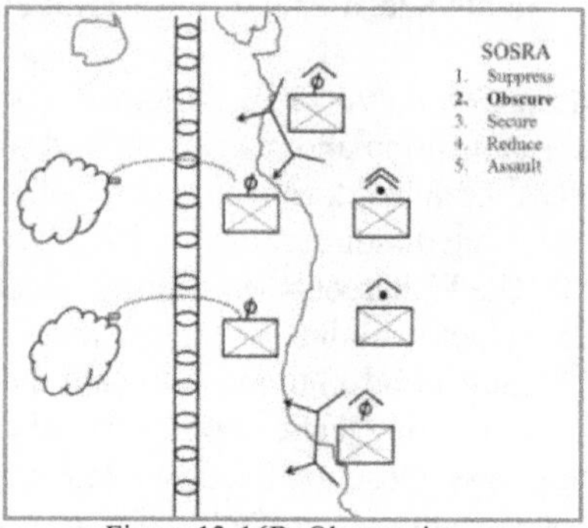

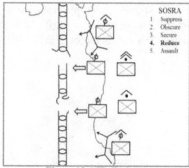

Figure 13-16B. Obscuration.

Figure 13-16C. Secure.

Figure 13-16D. Reduce.

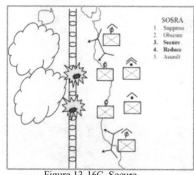

Breach teams then deploy smoke grenades inside the objective's outer defensive wire in order to obscure enemy observation – Obscure (See Figure 13-16B), and emplace explosive charges –Secure (See Figure 13-16C), and if possible initiate firing devices simultaneously, and move to predetermined cover in order to avoid blast fragmentation. Upon the explosion (See Figure 13-16D), breach teams move back to their perspective breach points and ensure they have affected entry (Reduce). If the SBF position's SDZ permits, the PL should have the guns shift fire to their next target/phase line upon the breach explosion. This maximizes surprise, as well as provides a definitive shift fire command.

401

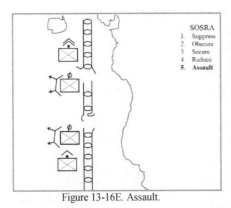

Figure 13-16E. Assault.

If a squad has a failed breach, it flows through the other breach point (See Figure 13-16E). The first two men through the breach points gain a foot hold inside the wire and fire cyclic to enable the assault element's entry. Assault squad leaders will then conduct fire and maneuver through the objective.

15. As the platoon, or its assault element, moves onto the objective, it must increase the volume and accuracy of fires.

16. Squad leaders assign specific targets or objectives for their fire teams. Only when these direct fires keep the enemy suppressed can the rest of the unit maneuver.

17. The support element continues to lift or shift fires as directed as the assault elements fire and maneuver through the objective (Figure 13-17).

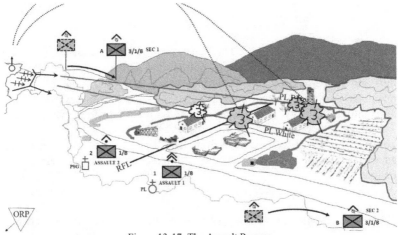

Figure 13-17. The Assault Process.

Assaulting Through the Objective – As the assault element gets closer to the enemy, there is more emphasis on suppression and less on maneuver. Ultimately, all but one fire team may be suppressing to allow that one fire team to break into the enemy position. Throughout the assault, proper

402

individual movement techniques are used, and fire teams retain, as much as possible, their basic shallow wedge formation.

18. Assault element assaults through the objective to the designated limit of advance (LOA).

19. Assault element leaders establish local security along the LOA, and consolidate and reorganize as necessary. They provide ACE reports to the PL and PSG.

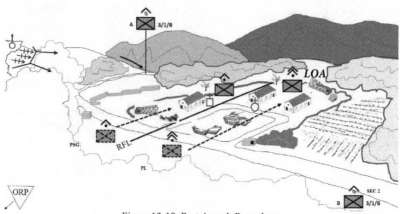

Figure 13-18. Post Assault Procedures.

Post Assault Procedures – The platoon establishes security positions, operates key weapons, redistribute ammunition and supplies, provides first aid, and prepares wounded personnel for MEDEVAC. The PL adjusts positions to ensure mutual support. The squad and team leaders provide ammunition, casualty, and equipment (ACE) reports to the platoon leader. The PL/PSG reorganizes the patrol if necessary.

20. On order, special teams accomplish all assigned tasks under the supervision of the PL, who positions himself where he can best control actions.

21. Special team leaders report to PL when assigned tasks are complete.

Withdrawal Sequence – On order from the PL, the assault element withdraws from the objective using prearranged signals. Platoon leadership ensures an organized withdrawal that maintains control and security is conducted. In the event of casualties, POWs, and EPWs, the PL will ensure they are evacuated prior to the withdrawal and with adequate security. PSG will ensure casualties are treated and will initiate MEDEVAC procedures (9 Line).

22. PL calls "Fire-in-the-hole-one," the assault one element bounds back near the original assault line, and forms a single file withdrawal through the PSG's choke point. All assaulters must move through the choke point for an accurate count.

23. Once the assault one element is a safe distance from the objective and the headcount is confirmed, the PL calls "Fire-in-the-hole-two," and assault two withdraws in the same manner as assault one. If the support elements were a part of the assault line, they withdraw together, then security is signaled to withdraw.

24. Once assault two is a safe distance off the objective, the PL calls "Fire-in-the-hole-three," at which time the demolition team(s) and the PL with his party withdraw through the choke point.

25. The PL ensures all "Fire-in-the-hole" calls are simultaneously delivered over the radio for the security elements situational awareness.

26. Technique dependent, the support may continue to occupy their position until all assault elements have withdrawn or upon a time standard, i.e., remain in place until two minutes following "Fire-in-the-hole-three."

27. Security teams withdraw as per base order, i.e., "Fire-in-the-hole-three" plus a certain time limit (3-5 minutes). All security teams link up at the RP and notify the platoon leader before moving to the ORP.

28. Personnel returning to the ORP immediately secure their equipment and establish all round security. Once the security element returns, the platoon moves out of the objective area as soon as possible, normally in two to three minutes. Leaders report updated accountability and status (ACE report) to the PL and PSG.

29. Squads withdraw from the RP as directed in the operations order. Once at the ORP, leaders account for personnel and equipment, then prepare to move quickly, as a platoon, to the security halt to disseminate information where they will redistribute ammunition and equipment as required and report mission accomplishment to higher along with any IR/PIR gathered and continue the mission. The security halt to disseminate information ought to be no less than one major terrain feature away or one kilometer from the objective.

Security Patrols

A third type of combat patrols that a unit may employ, security patrols, are used in proximity to defensive positions, on the flanks of advancing units or in rear areas. The purpose for security patrols are to detect infiltration by the enemy, destroy infiltrators, and protect against surprise and ambush. Security patrols prevent surprise of the main body by screening to the front, flank, and rear of the main body and detecting and destroying enemy forces in the local area. Security patrols do not operate beyond the range of communication and supporting fires from the main body; especially mortar fires, because they normally operate for limited periods of time, and are combat oriented.

All of the procedures presented in previous sections are to be used in security patrols. Security patrols are employed both when the main body is stationary and when it is moving. When the main body is stationary, the security patrol prevents enemy infiltration, reconnaissance, or attacks. When the main body is moving, the security patrol prevents the unit from being ambushed or coming into surprise chance contact. Within rear areas, an irregular pattern of patrol is established and changed daily. Outside of friendly lines it would be prudent to establish a definite preplanned route for the patrol, of which all adjacent units know the route. The parent unit commander establishes frequent checkpoints for control. If check points are designated, the patrol leader treats them as individual objectives to be searched and cleared.[6]

Conclusion

The intent of this chapter was to provide the SF soldier with a thorough understanding of ambush and raid patrols. In combat, the risks that are undertaken are accepted in proportion to what is understood of the importance of the undertaking. And combat patrols seek to cripple the enemy by harassing, destroying, or capturing enemy troops, equipment, or installations.

---

[6] MCWP 3-11.3 Scouting and Patrolling, 13-8.

Chapter 14 Patrol Bases

"Before you leave your encampment, send out small parties to scout round it, to see if there be any appearance or track of an enemy that might have been near you during the night." – Rogers' 28 Rules of Ranging #17

A patrol base (PB) is a position set up when the patrol unit halts for an extended period. When the unit must halt for a long time in a place not protected by friendly troops, it takes active and passive security measures. The time the patrol base may be occupied depends on the need for secrecy. It should be occupied only as long as necessary, but not for more than 24 hours – except in an emergency. The unit should not use the same patrol base more than once. Patrol bases are typically used:

- To avoid detection by eliminating movement.
- To hide a unit during a long detailed reconnaissance.
- To perform maintenance on weapons, equipment, to eat and rest.
- To plan and issue orders.
- To reorganize after infiltrating an enemy area.
- To establish a base from which to execute several consecutive or concurrent operations.

Site Selection – The PL selects the tentative site from a map or by aerial reconnaissance. The site's suitability must be confirmed and secured before the unit moves into the area. Plans to establish a patrol base must include selecting an alternate patrol base site. The alternate site is used if the first site is unsuitable or if the patrol must unexpectedly evacuate the first patrol base.

Leaders planning for a patrol base must consider the mission and passive and active security measures that will be employed. A patrol base (PB) must be located so it allows the unit to accomplish its mission.
Selection criteria should include: **COOLANT**

C – Cover and concealment.
O – Off natural lines of drift.
O – Out of sight, sound, and small arms fire range of objective.
L – Large enough to accommodate the entire patrol.
A – Affords a defense for a short period of time.
N – Near a source of water.
T – Tough terrain that impedes maneuver/movement.

Additional PB selection criteria includes:
- Avoid known or suspected enemy positions.

- Avoid built up areas.
- Avoid ridges and hilltops, except as needed for maintaining communications.
- Avoid small valleys.
- Avoid roads and trails.

Patrols conduct patrol base activities in two phases, occupation and operation.

Reconnaissance and Occupation of Patrol Base – The PL conducts a leader's recon for the tentative PB. It is reconnoitered and occupied in the same manner as an ORP, with the exception that the patrol will typically plan to enter at a 90 degree turn. The PL leaves a two-man OP at the turn, and the patrol covers any tracks from the turn to the PB (Figure 14-1).

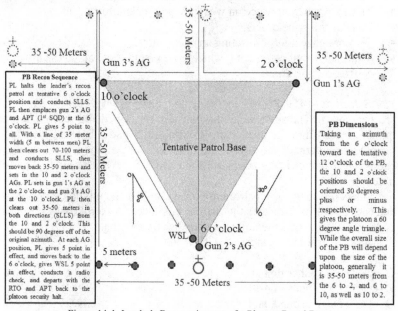

Figure 14-1. Leader's Reconnaissance of a Platoon Patrol Base.

The platoon moves into the PB. Squad sized patrols will generally occupy a circle shaped perimeter; platoon sized patrols will generally occupy a triangle shaped perimeter (Figure 14-2). The PL and another designated leader inspect and adjust the entire perimeter as necessary.

407

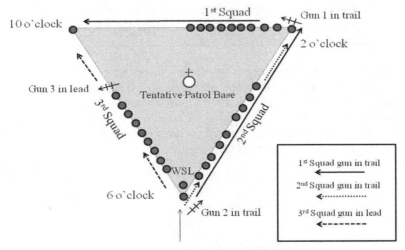

Figure 14-2. Occupation of Platoon Patrol Base.

After the PL has checked each team/squad sector, each TL/SL sends a two-man RS team to the PL at the CP. The PL issues the three RS teams a contingency plan, reconnaissance method, and detailed guidance on what to look for (enemy, water, built up areas or human habitat, roads, trails, or possible rally points).

Where each RS team departs is based on the PLs guidance. Each RS team moves a prescribed distance and direction, and reenters where the PL dictates. Squad sized patrols do not normally send out an RS team at night. RS teams will prepare a sketch of the area to the squad front if possible. When the RS teams are outside the perimeter, the rest of the patrol remains at 100% alert status.

If the PL feels the patrol was tracked or followed, he may elect to wait in silence at 100% alert before sending out RS teams. The RS teams may use methods such as the "I," the "Box," or the "T." Regardless of the method chosen, the RS teams must be able to provide the PL with the same information.

Security – Upon completion of RS, the PL confirms or denies the patrol base location, and either moves the patrol or begins establishing security. The six steps of security are:

- R&S (if not conducted at occupation, at first light)
- Fire Plan (sector sketches & range cards)
- Alert Plan (how to get PB to 100% security)

408

- Evacuation Plan (rendezvous points & alternate PB)
- Communications (w/ higher, jungle antenna?)
- Camouflage (passive security measure)

Fire Plan – The PL prepares to use all passive and active measures to cover the entire perimeter all the time, regardless of the percentage of weapons used to cover all of the terrain. The PL will employ all elements, weapons, and personnel to meet conditions of the terrain, enemy, and situation. The PL will confirm location of fighting positions for cover, concealment, and observation and fields of fire (Figure 14-3).

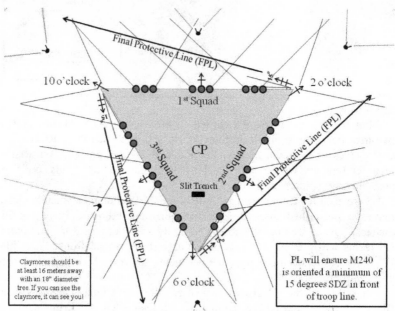

Figure 14-3. Platoon Patrol Base Fire Plan.

The PSG along with SLs/TLs supervise placement of aiming stakes and claymores. The PL and PSG will develop a platoon fire plan based on squad sector sketches and the assigned sectors of fire to all personnel and weapons. The PL will ensure:

- Interlocking sectors of fire 35 meters out.
- Range cards are prepared for the crew served weapons.
- Claymores are emplaced to cover dead space and/or likely avenues of enemy approach and included in the fire plan.
- M203s cover dead space and are included in the fire plan (Figure 8-54).

409

The PSG will ensure that only one point of entry and exit is used for the PB, and will keep an accurate count of personnel in and out of the PB at all times. Everyone is challenged IAW the unit SOP. Hasty fighting positions are prepared at least 18 inches deep (at the front), and sloping gently from front to rear, with a grenade sump if possible.

Evacuation/Withdrawal Plan – The PL designates the signal for evacuation, order of withdrawal, and the patrol rendezvous point (RV), and the alternate patrol base. RVs and the alternate PB should be at least a terrain feature away. They are used in the event the patrol has to displace from its PB location; whether under pressure or not.[1] The PL ensures:

- The alert plan is understood by all.
- Rendezvous points (RVs) are issued.
- The alternate PB grid (six digit) is issued.

Communication Plan – Communications must be maintained with higher headquarters, OPs, and within the unit at all times. Radio watch ought to be rotated with at least two alert personnel to allow for the successful accomplishment of continuous monitoring, radio maintenance, and to act as runners for the PL, and to conduct priorities of work.

Operation of a PB: Priorities of Work – Once the PL has established security, priorities of work commence. Priorities of work are not a laundry list of tasks to be completed. To be effective, priorities of work must consist of a task, a given time, and a measurable performance standard. For each priority of work, a *clear standard* must be issued to guide the element in the successful accomplishment of each task. It must also be designated whether the work will be controlled in a centralized or decentralized manner. Priorities of work are determined IAW METT-TC.

Priorities of work may include, but are not limited to the following tasks:
- Improvement to Hasty Fighting Positions.
- Weapons and Equipment Maintenance.
- Mission Preparation.
- Water Resupply.
- Mess Plan.
- Personal Hygiene.

---

[1] The PL designates two RVs at opposite directions from one another (black and gold) with a single alt PB that can be accessed from either black or gold. Example: RV1 (black) 270° for 500 meters to a draw; RV2 (gold) 90° for 450 meters to a draw. PL then designates an Alt PB (a 6 digit grid coordinate) either due north or due south, accessible from either RV.

- Rest Plan.
- Regardless of priority of work, the patrol will go to 100% when:
- Personnel are entering or exiting PB.
- 1 Belt-fed weapon in down.
- Stand to occurs (1 hour during BMNT & EENT).[2]

Weapons and Equipment Maintenance – The PL ensures that machine guns, weapon systems, communications equipment, and night vision devices (as well as other equipment) are maintained. These items are not disassembled at the same time for maintenance (no more than 33 percent at a time), and weapons are not disassembled at night. If one machine gun is down, then security for all remaining systems is raised.

Water Resupply – The PSG organizes watering parties as necessary. The watering party carries canteens in an empty rucksack or duffel bag, and must have communications and a contingency plan prior to departure.

Mess and Rest Plan – As a rule, weapons and equipment maintenance is performed prior to mess. Normally no more than half the platoon eats at one time. Patrol members typically eat 1 to 3 meters behind their fighting positions. The patrol conducts rest as necessary to prepare for future operations. Additionally, the PL will state the alert posture and the stand-to time. He develops the plan to ensure all positions are checked periodically, OPs are relieved periodically, and at least one leader is always alert. The patrol typically conducts stand-to at a time specified by unit SOP such as 30 minutes before and after BMNT and EENT.

Resupply and Hygiene – The PSG will distribute or cross load ammunition, meals, equipment, and so on. The PSG and medic ensure a slit trench is prepared and marked. The patrol never leaves trash behind.

Squad Size Patrol Bases - When conducting a squad size patrol base, the SL should consider using tough terrain, such as draws, to improve security. The machine gun team is positioned at a cardinal clock direction (3, 6, 9, or 12) and can be quickly repositioned based on enemy contact. The squad perimeter must have interlocking sectors of fire without including the gun team's sector (See Figure 14-4).

---

[2] Following the requisite critical tasks of establishing a PB, the priorities of work are not necessarily done in order but are determined by METT-TC.

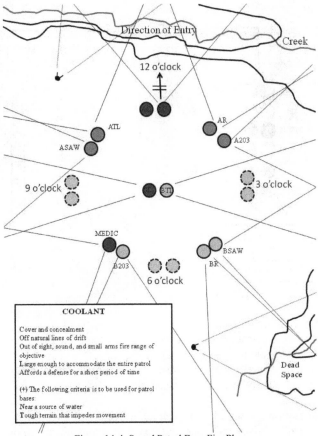

Figure 14-4. Squad Patrol Base Fire Plan.

Clandestine Patrol Base (Squad) – The purpose of a passive patrol base is primarily for the rest of a squad or smaller size element. The patrol moves as a whole and occupies in force (see Figure 14-5).

1. The SL ensures that the unit moves in at a 90° angle to the order of movement.
2. A claymore mine is emplaced on the route entering into the patrol base.
3. The squad sits back to back facing outward, ensuring that at least two individuals are alert and providing security.
4. Generally, the radio hand set and claymore firing device are passed along to those individuals alert and providing security.

412

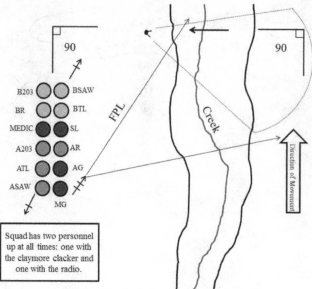

Figure 14-5. Squad Clandestine Patrol Base.

Patrol Base Critical Tasks:

- PL halts the patrol 200-400 meters from the tentative PB.
- PL selects a site that provides: COOLANT.
- PL establishes PB: security, sectors, claymores, range cards, etc. The PB never falls below 33 1/3 % security (100 % when anyone is outside perimeter).
- PL disseminates withdrawal plan (Black and Gold, ALT PB location 6 digit grid) – gives guidance and conducts status checks. You only get what you check up on.
- PL calls higher HQ (commo plan).
- Weapons maintenance, water resupply, mess, hygiene, rest, etc.
- Stand-to.

Conclusion

A unit proficient in patrol base operations can sustain itself for extended periods of time. In this chapter we discussed how PB site selection is key, and a good map reconnaissance can save valuable time. However, nothing can replace a good leader's reconnaissance, as it can preserve time and man hours required to relocate. Further, once a PB is established, the leader only gets what he checks up on. Therefore, it's imperative that he give clear and concise instructions.

Chapter 15 Urban Combat

"In war, the will is directed at an animate object that reacts."
– Clausewitz

During Operation Market Garden (17-25 Sept 1944), the 2nd Parachute Battalion (British 1st Airborne Division) doggedly defended their objective on the north side of the Arnhem bridge. They fought street to street, building to building, floor to floor, and room to room with the II SS Panzer Corps. Colonel Frost and his beleaguered 740 men, fortified themselves and held out against withering German fire within the confines of about a five block urban environment, and withstood repeated assaults for five days; the plan was to hold for three. The point is, although the British Paras were defeated at Arnhem, they demonstrated how an elite unit in urban terrain may operate successfully against a superior force for an extended period of time with a force disproportionate to the enemy who is attacking them.[1] Likewise, Operation Gothic Serpent (Mogadishu, Somalia 1993) highlights the risk one must assume in conducting a daylight raid in a densely populated urban area, as well as the importance of being familiar with one's battlespace.

This chapter will discuss urban combat. Urban combat collectively describes offensive and defensive operations conducted to defeat an enemy in an urban area both during high-intensity combat and during stability operations.[2] Urban combat presents an extraordinary blend of horizontal, vertical, interior, exterior, and subterranean forms superimposed on the natural relief, drainage, and vegetation.[3] Additionally, the vertical dimension must be considered, as the elevation of buildings provides a threat not normally encountered in tactical operations. These elevated positions offer good observation and fields of fire plus cover and concealment, particularly effective for snipers. This chapter is geared toward the company and platoon level urban operations. It will discuss the fundamentals of urban combat and will consist of the following:

1. Control Measures.
2. Urban Assault Task Organization.
3. Principles of Urban Assault.
4. Principles of Close Quarters Battle.
5. Urban Assault Planning.

---

[1] The British Paras of 2nd Battalion, 1st Airborne Division ran out of ammunition not perserverance.
[2] FM 3-21.10, 12-2.
[3] FM 3-06 Urban Operations, 2-2.

Control Measures – In an urban environment, tactical planners use control measures in order to focus operations as well as mitigate fratricide and collateral damage. These control measures include: building numbering, phase lines, RFLs (restrictive fire lines), LDs (line of departure) and LOAs (limit of advance).

Building Numbering – Tactical planners use building numbering in order to simplify assigning objectives and reporting. Buildings can be numbered either left to right and up and down sequentially or in a spiral clockwise pattern (Figure 15-1).

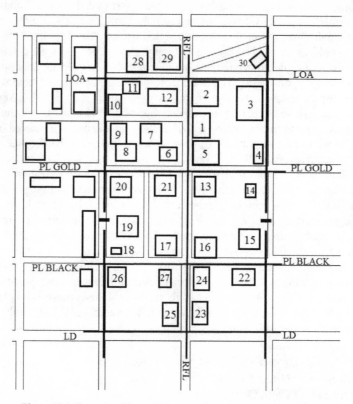

Figure 15-1. Example of Control Measures for a Company Urban Assault.

Phase Lines – Phase lines are used to control the advance of attacking units or to report progress. Principal streets, rivers, and railroad lines are easily identifiable and are suitable phase lines. Phase lines are shown on the near side of the street or open area (See Figure 15-1). In systematic clearing, a

415

unit may have the mission to clear its zone up to a phase line. In that case, the assault force leader chooses his own objectives when assigning missions to his subordinate units.

When using phase lines the assault force leader will set unit boundaries within blocks, so that it is clear whether streets are included in a sub element zone. These boundaries are placed to ensure both sides of a street are in the zone of one unit. Additional considerations include:

- Plan checkpoints and contact points at street corners, buildings, railway crossings, bridges, or any other easily identifiable urban feature.
- Forward units may occupy an attack position for last-minute preparation and coordination. The attack position is often behind or inside the last covered and concealed position (LCC), such as a large building, before crossing the LD. The LD should be the near side of a street or rail line.
- A unit's assigned frontage for the attack of a built-up area depends on the size of buildings and the resistance anticipated. For example, based on city blocks averaging 175 meters wide, a company normally attacks on a one- to two-block front. A battalion attacks on a two-to four-block front.

Restrictive fire line (RFL) – An RFL is a fire control measure which is used to reduce the risk of fratricide. An RFL is a line established between converging friendly forces (one or both might be moving) that prohibit fires and effects across the line without coordination with the affected force. For example, in the offense, the leader may designate an RFL to prevent a base of fire element from firing into the area where an assaulting element is maneuvering.

Line of Departure (LD) and Limit of Advance (LOA) – Additionally, the leader uses LDs and LOAs to control both the marshaling of his forces and the farthest limit of their advance (See Figure 15-1).

Urban Assault Task Organization – The assault force leader normally task-organizes his unit into three elements: an assault force, a support force, and security. Additionally, a reserve force should be used if available.

Assault Force – The purpose of the assault force is to destroy/capture the enemy, or force the withdrawal of the enemy from any urban objective. The assault force of a unit may consist of two or more squads or platoons usually reinforced with attachments. Building clearing and room clearing are normally conducted at platoon and squad levels.

Support Force – The purpose of the support force is to overwatch the assault process and provide any support that might be required by the assault force. The support force may include organic assets, such as mortars, and weapons squads. These assets are under the operational control of the assault force leader. The support force may provide the following:

- Suppressing or obscuring the enemy within the objective building(s) and adjacent structures.
- Isolating the objective building(s) to prevent enemy withdrawal, reinforcement, or counterattack.
- Breaching walls enroute to and in the objective structure.
- Destroying or suppressing enemy positions with direct fire weapons.
- Securing cleared portions of the objective.
- Providing resupply of ammunition, explosives, and personnel.
- Evacuating casualties, EPW, and civilians.

Security Force – The purpose of the security force is to isolate the objective area and enabling the assault force freedom of movement. The security force may include a cordon force, and might be called upon to perform one or more of the following tasks:

- Isolating the objective building(s) to prevent enemy withdrawal, reinforcement, or counterattack.
- Clear bypassed enemy positions.
- Secure the rear or a flank.
- Maintain contact with adjacent units.
- Support or counterattack by fire.

Breaching – All elements may conduct breaching, however, a separate breaching force might be created, or platoons might be given this task and organized accordingly. The purpose of breaching is to provide the assault force with access to an urban objective, using explosive, ballistic, or mechanical methods.

Principles of Urban Assault – A unit's urban movement should focus on the fundamentals of the offense: *speed, concentration, audacity, and tempo.* Additionally, a rapid advance and quick decision making ability are key because, as has been said, an enemy force in urban terrain may withstand repeated assaults and successfully defend itself against a superior force. Enemy actions against the unit might consist of ambushes, enfilade fire down streets, sniper fire, fire from rooftops and from within buildings, or artillery or mortar fire. The Tactician may minimize the effects of enemy fire during the assault by using the following principles of urban movement:

417

US Army Small Unit Tactics Handbook

URBAN

U – Use cover when possible.
R – Reduce your target size while in a static position.
B – By-pass: doors, windows, and corners enroute to target building with security.
A – Avoid bogging down and maintain dispersion.
N – Navigate in low percentage areas.

1. Use cover when possible.
- The leader should use covered routes, to include moving through buildings if possible.
- Select routes that will not mask friendly suppressive fires.
- Crossing streets and spaces between buildings quickly under the concealment of smoke with suppression provided by supporting forces. Move only after enemy fires have been suppressed or obscured.
- Consider the use of cover provided by armored vehicles if available.

2. Reduce your target size while in a static position.
- Avoid silhouetting yourself.
- Avoid standing in front of doorways or windows.
- Use concealment provided by shaded areas.
- Take a knee or a prone position while waiting to move.

3. By-pass: windows, doors, and corners enroute to target building with security.
- Cover likely threats by plugging holes: the unit moves in file along one or both sides of the street with overwatching fires from supporting weapons.
- As the lead man comes to a window, door, or corner of a building, he places himself in that void pulling security while ensuring his muzzles doesn't pass beyond the threshold of the void (See Figure 15-2).

4. Avoid bogging down and maintain dispersion.
- Bogging down typically occurs when leaders can't make a decision or during enemy contact.
- It's imperative that the assault force not remain in a static position too long as this may allow the enemy to gain the initiative and converge on the assault element.

- Additionally, the assault force should avoid bunching up as this normally decreases security and situational awareness as well as increases the potential for enemy fires to have a devastating effect.

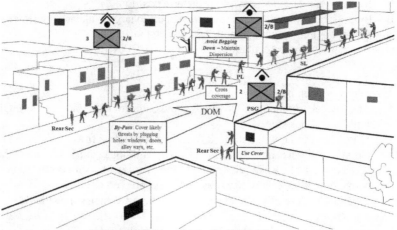

Figure 15-2. Platoon Conducting Urban Movement.

5. Navigate in low percentage areas.
- Leaders should select a route to the objective that is less traveled and less lighted.
- If possible, leaders should plan to move at night or during other periods of limited visibility.

An assault may not always be able to use the inside of buildings as routes of advance and must move on the outside of the buildings. Smoke, suppressive fires, and cover and concealment may also be used to hide movement. Assaulters move parallel to the side of the building (maintaining at least 12 inches of separation between himself and the wall to avoid rabbit rounds, ricochets and rubbing or bumping the wall), stays in the shadow, presents a low silhouette, and moves rapidly to his next position.

Infiltration of the Assault Force – Urban movement is made rapidly and without sacrificing security. The assault force moves along covered and concealed routes which may involve; moving through buildings, down streets, subsurface areas, or a combination of all three.[4]

---

[4] FM 3-21.10, 12-41.

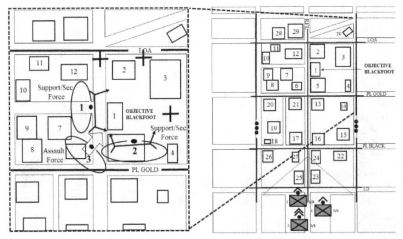

Figure 15-3. Platoon Urban Movement Plan.

In the example above (Figure 15-3), the 2nd Platoon isolates the objective by seizing terrain that dominates the area – occupies strong points around the target structure.[5] When the assault force (3rd Squad) arrives at their LCC, they will prep charges, and conduct a final communications check with the assault force commander (PL) and recon element if employed. If a cordon force (outer ring security) is available it will greatly enhance security during the operation, as well as post assault, MEDEVAC, and the recovery of the recon element. The assault force will wait in place until the PL gives notification to move to breach point(s).

In the example (Figure 15-4), B Company conducts a raid. 1st Platoon is assault 1 – the decisive operation (DO), 3rd Platoon is assault 2 – shaping operation 1 (SO1), Weapons Squad is SBF1 and 2 – shaping operation 2 (SO2), and 2nd Platoon is security – shaping operation 3 (SO3). As the assaults 1 and 2 depart from the LD, the SBF positions overwatch, and bound forward, keeping pace with the assault process, maintaining a 15 degree SDZ in front of advancing elements. During the assault process, the raiding force by-passes, if possible, outlaying buildings enroute to the objective. In this case, buildings 5 and 8. 2nd Squad/2nd Platoon provides rear security while 1st and 3rd Squads provide flank security (The east-west road is determined to be the most likely enemy avenue of approach). Flank security squads move along with the assault process depositing a fire team

---

[5] Examples of key terrain are bridges, building complexes, public utilities or services, and parks. The population of a built-up area may also be considered key terrain. The identification of key terrain allows the defender to select his defensive positions and helps in determining the enemy's objectives (FM 3-21.10).

420

each along the roads leading to the objective both north and south with a fire team each at the western end of the objective as their front line trace.

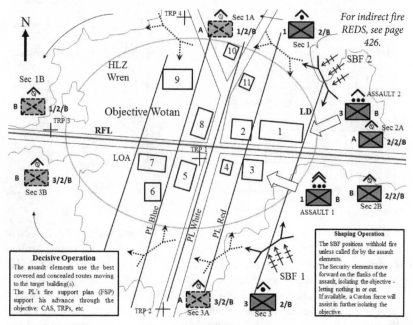

Figure 15-4. Company Raid.

The assault force commander is the up and out continuity with all elements, to include a cordon force, CAS, MEDEVAC, etc. To assist him, the platoon sergeant or troop sergeant will coordinate the unit's assault process, as well as post assault procedures; site exploitation, tactical questioning, MEDEVAC, combatant handling, etc. Once the assault force has isolated the objective, on order it conducts close quarters battle through the objective.[6]

Close Quarters Battle (CQB) – Close quarters battle (CQB) is a technique of fire and maneuver that utilizes the rapid, methodical application of surgical firepower combined with surprise, speed and violence of action in order to seize a room, or a series of rooms, and all of its inhabitants (both

---

[6] As has been said, a raid is a limited-objective form of attack which involves a swift entry into hostile territory to destroy installations, gather intelligence, liberate captured personnel, and to kill or capture personnel. When conducting raids to liberate captured personnel or kill or capture high value individuals (HVIs), i.e., be less kinetic, then the focus should be on isolation and time permitting, systematic clearing.

hostile and other) by dominating the room, eliminating the threat, and controlling the situation. The assault may begin from the top or bottom of a building, however, entering at the top and fighting downward is the preferred method.

Principles of CQB – There are three principles of CQB: *surprise, speed, and violence of Action*. Surprise is the concealment of the assault force's intentions until the initiation of the assault at a time most advantageous. Speed is initiative, both operational and individual, plus flexibility. Upon initial entry, assaulters move quickly and deliberately, to flood the target building, while eliminating the threat. The principle, violence of action, is both mental and physical, and is characterized by aggressive, explosive force.

CQB is governed by five fundamentals which are:
- *Dominate*. Flood the room, rapidly moving to points of domination.
- *Eliminate*. Eliminate the threat with surgical discriminatory fire. Continue to engage threats until they are eliminated. Shot placement is key.
- *Control*. Search the dead; dead check and clear away weapons. Search the living; control unknowns, move them away from doors and windows. Search the room and mark it according to SOP.
- Exfil on Command.
- Be prepared to conduct follow on operations.

Situational awareness is paramount to CQB. Here are some basics to remember:
- Be close to but not touching the wall.
- Maintain muzzle awareness and have muzzle up on entry.
- Engage the immediate threat.
- Rapidly clear the fatal funnel.
- Go opposite of the man in front of you.
- Positively identify the threat – surgical discrimination.
- Shot placement is key: eye orbital area / upper thoracic chest.
- Engage the threat until elimination.
- Move to the point of domination.
- Clear your primary then secondary sectors.

Entering and Clearing a Room - is a battle drill and relies upon speed, surprise and violence of action. As they say, slow is smooth and smooth is fast. That is true in many ways except CQB where slow is dead. CQB is also methodical, that each member of the team must know his sector of fire and how his sector overlaps and links with the sectors of the other team members (See Figure 15-5).

Center-Fed Room Clearing

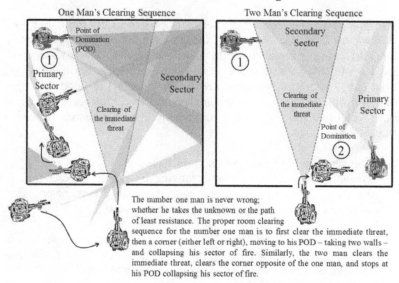

One Man's Clearing Sequence

Two Man's Clearing Sequence

The number one man is never wrong; whether he takes the unknown or the path of least resistance. The proper room clearing sequence for the number one man is to first clear the immediate threat, then a corner (either left or right), moving to his POD – taking two walls – and collapsing his sector of fire. Similarly, the two man clears the immediate threat, clears the corner opposite of the one man, and stops at his POD collapsing his sector of fire.

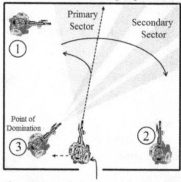

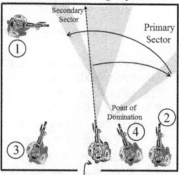

Three Man's Clearing Sequence

Four Man's Clearing Sequence

The proper room clearing sequence for the number three man is first, toward the number one man (remaining 1 meter off his barrel) and than over toward the number two man to within one meter off the number four man's barrel.

The proper room clearing sequence for the number four man is first, toward the number two man (remaining 1 meter off his barrel) and than over toward the number one man to within one meter off his barrel.

Figure 15-5. Center-Fed Room Clearing.

423

Corner-Fed Room Clearing

One Man's Clearing Sequence

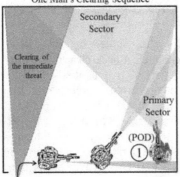

Two Man's Clearing Sequence

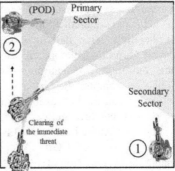

The number one man is never wrong; whether he takes the unknown or the path of least resistance. The proper room clearing sequence for the number one man is to first clear the immediate threat, then a corner (either left or right), moving to his POD – taking one wall – and collapsing his sector of fire. Similarly, the two man clears the immediate threat, clears the corner opposite of the one man, and stops at his POD collapsing his sector of fire.

Three Man's Clearing Sequence

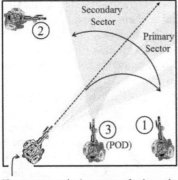

Four Man's Clearing Sequence

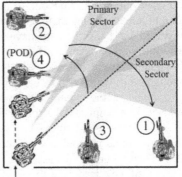

The proper room clearing sequence for the number three man is first, toward the number one man (remaining 1 meter off his barrel) and than over toward the number two man to within one meter off the number four man's barrel.

The proper room clearing sequence for the number four man is first, toward the number two man (remaining 1 meter off his barrel) and than over toward the number one man to within one meter off his barrel.

Figure 15-6. Corner-Fed Room Clearing.

Post Assault Procedures – Once the room has been dominated and the threats eliminated, announce "room clear." This allows personnel to safely move deep within the room and begin priorities of work, which are: *dead, room, living. Dead* – search the dead; ensure eliminated threats are dead (dead check) and clear away weapons. *Room* – search the room. This is not a detailed search. Look for additional doors leading into another room or trap doors, as well as explosive devices, etc. *Living* – control non-threats, move them away from doors and windows. Before departing a room during an assault, a man must be left behind to control non-threats (non-threats can be assembled at post assault). The cleared room is then marked according to SOP as the assault element leaves.

If the high value individual remains unaccounted for, with time and situation permitting, the assault force conducts a back clear (re-clearing all rooms and buildings) – an area is clear only as long as it's held. After the building or complex has been secured, the assault force begins its post assault procedures. For example, one assault team may assume security, another may conduct tactical questioning, while a third may conduct site exploitation (detailed search). Assault team leaders will give their ACE report to the assault NCOIC. Additional considerations should be made for designating a room for casualty collection (CCP). All elements must be prepared to conduct follow-on operations and Exfil on command.

Urban Assault Planning – Leaders should bear in mind that the situation will always have an effect on the particular planning sequence as time will always be dependent on receiving more intel. During course of action (COA) development, find out what subordinate leaders think, find some different ideas among them and designate them to develop those ideas. However, don't tell them to develop COAs that they do not show some ownership of. For example, if no one voiced an opinion for a vehicle option, don't tell someone to create a vehicle option so we have three different options, one of which will be a thrown away.

Additionally, the assault force commander should avoid giving generic guidance like emphasize surprise. This will cause the COA to focus on achieving surprise and not the end state of the mission. Generally speed and surprise go hand in hand. As the situation develops, the importance of both will fluctuate. Further, the assault force commander should brief COA to an audience of key leaders only. This makes arbitration easier and doesn't confuse the assault force by hearing three different plans. It further frees them up to concentrate on other tasks (1/3, 2/3 rule).

Different COAs – There are always options; we don't all see the same ones. This is why it is so critical to solicit the COAs without being too specific on what you want to hear. "I want the site cleared and secured and I want the high value individual (HVI) intact, I don't care if you sneak up to the site or come screeching up in a vehicle. I don't care if you breach in two places or five." All COAs must accomplish the end state. The assault force commander will then assess which one has the best chance of success (See Figure 15-7).

Generally, COAs are distinguishable from each other by task organization and method. Same task org, same approach, same breach points, with a different internal flow are not three COAs. Finally, the assault force commander should choose a COA in private. No explanation for the commander's choice is required, but all the leaders emerge with one voice and one plan to prepare. While the commander has veto power and the last say, the assault leadership needs to have about 51% of the vote on a final plan. This is simply because his force will conduct the actions on the objective and he trained them and best knows their capabilities.

CONSIDERATION Weight:	COA 1	COA 2	COA3	COA 4
SPEED - RP to crisis site (breach point)				
SURPRISE				
VIOLENCE OF ACTION				
COMPROMISE - how far from breach point				
FLEXABILITY- ability to alter plan (FRAGO)				
COVER and CONCEALMENT				
MANEUVER				
SNIPER OBSERVER SUPPORT				
FIRE SUPPORT				
COMMAND AND CONTROL				
SUSTAINMENT				
1= Bad 5 = Best TOTAL				

Additional considerations: QRF, MEDEVAC, sensitive structures, etc.

Figure 15-7. Assault Plan COA Matrix.

Breach points – Choose where you want to effect the structure based on intel and shape of the structure. Don't simply choose a breach point based on how assessable it is. It's better to have a difficult breach into an area that dominates the site, then a smooth breach into a useless bathroom. Similarly, don't let the good breach points decide where you will affect the target. Most importantly, don't put all your eggs in one basket. Attack from multiple directions and multiple floors if possible. The safest and most systematic assault plan might not achieve the objective. You have to assume some reasonable risk. Expect that at least one entry / breach point will not work and the force will have to adjust to the missing assaulters.

Assault Brief

Introduction and Task Organization
I. Situation
A. AI/AO
 1. Unit starting point and movement route/means.
 2. Condensed intelligence summary (see page 301).
B. Target Orientation
 1. *Crisis area:* Immediate area around the crisis point.
 a. Surrounding Terrain: OACOK (see page 299).
 2. *Crisis site:* Specific location within the crisis area.
 a. Location and description: Building 1 (give general information).
 3. *Crisis point:* Pinpoint location within the crisis site.
 a. Location and description: Second floor, 3rd room from the left on the south side.
 4. *Cordon force:* Location, size, capabilities, POC, etc.
C. Enemy Situation
 CAR - CAS, artillery, reactionary Force.
 1. Size, personalities, activity to date, weapons, reinforcements, and probable COA.
 D. Hostages: Number, nationality, language, description, known medical problems, location.
II. Mission
A. Mission statement x 2
III. Execution
A. Scheme of maneuver
 1. Assault team leader brief
 a. Team composition
 - Number of men in the team, number of charges, shotguns, mechanical tools, etc.
 b. Movement from LCC to breach point
 c. Location of breach point
 d. Actions at breach point: Primary/alternate breach, and failed breach.
 e. Actions on target: "We'll clear from N to S in a clockwise manner, secure the stairs, etc.
 2. Phase lines: Show sector boundaries, actions at phase lines, etc.
 3. Coordination points: Tentative/known coordination point, actions/marking at each.
 4. Post assault procedures: Site exploitation, assembly and exfiltration plan.
 5. Contingencies: IEDs, casualties, chemical agents, structure fire, COC, bump plan, etc.
 6. Fires and CAS plan
IV. Medical support plan
V. Communications plan

Conclusion

The purpose of this chapter was to indoctrinate the student of war to the basics of urban combat. Urban combat focuses on closing with and destroying the enemy in close quarters battle. Tactical planners should weigh the risks of friendly fires, ricochets, and fratricide. The enclosed nature of close quarters battle means that weapons' effects, SDZs and shoulder-fired weapons' back-blast, must be considered. Additionally, care in planning should be made to minimize civilian casualties and overkill weapons' effects. During the planning phase, leaders should make every use of control measures to lower these risks.

Chapter 16 Fire Support

"The effective functioning of the infantry-artillery team depends upon the intelligent and unremitting efforts of both members to solve the difficult problem of liaison."
– Infantry in Battle

Fire support is the collective and coordinated use of indirect fire weapons and armed aircraft in support of the battle plan.[1] The leader includes fire support in his planning to achieve decisive results. Planning should always include fire support in all its forms even if the leader thinks it unnecessary. Fires can suppress enemy observation, create distractions, achieve immediate suppression, cover a withdrawal off of an objective, or assist in breaking contact. This chapter will discuss the following:

1. Fire Support Planning
2. Indirect Fire Capabilities.
3. Risk Estimate Distance (RED).
4. Types of Indirect Fire Missions.
5. Example Call for Fire (CFF) Missions.

Fire Support Planning – A clearly defined maneuver purpose enables the patrol leader to determine how he wants fire support to affect the enemy during his mission. Fires may be planned as scheduled or on-call. The leader should plan fires:

▪ On key terrain features along the route. These can serve as navigational aids or to deceive, harass, or destroy the enemy.
▪ On known enemy positions.
▪ On known or suspected ambush sites.
▪ On the flanks of identified danger areas.
▪ Wherever a diversion appears desirable. For example, if the unit must pass near an identified enemy position, artillery or mortar fires on the position may distract the enemy and permit the unit to pass undetected.
▪ At intervals along the route, every 500 to 1000 meters for example. With fires so planned, the unit is never far from a plotted concentration from which a shift can be quickly made.

---

[1] FM 3-21.20 The Infantry Battalion, 10-1.

Indirect Weapons Capabilities

Weapon	Max Range	Min Range	Max Rate	Burst Radius	Sustained Rate
60mm Mortar	3500m	70m	30 for 4min	30m	20r/min
81mm Mortar	5600m	70m	25 for 2min	40m	8r/min
120mm Mortar	7200m	180m	15 for 1min	60m	5r/min
105mm Howitzer	14000m	0m	6 for 2min	35m	3rnds for 30min, then 1r/min
155mm Howitzer	18000m	0m	4 for 3min	50m	1r/min temp dependent
155 DPICM	18000m	0m	4 for 3min	50m	1rnd for 60min, 1r/min

Figure 16-1. Indirect Weapons Capabilities. Reference FM 3-21.8.

Blasting Areas – When mortar and artillery rounds impact they throw fragments in a pattern that is never truly circular, and may even travel irregular, based on the round's angle of fall, the slope of the terrain, and the type of soil. However, for planning purposes, each high explosive (HE) round is considered to have a circular lethal bursting area (See Figure 16-2).

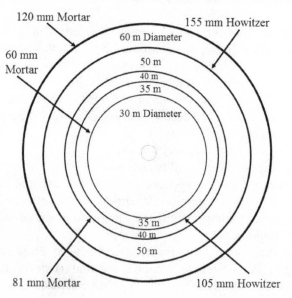

Figure 16-2. Artillery and Mortar Blast Radii.

Risk Estimate Distance (RED) – Risk estimate distance (RED) is defined as the minimum distance friendly troops can approach the effects of friendly fires without suffering appreciable casualties of 0.1 percent injury PI or higher.[2] RED applies to combat only. RED takes into account the bursting radius of particular munitions and the characteristics of the delivery system. It associates this combination with a percentage representing the likelihood of becoming a casualty, that is, the percentage of risk.

RISK ESTIMATE DISTANCES (0.1% PI)			
SYSTEM	1/3 RANGE	2/3 RANGE	MAX RANGE
60mm Mortar	100 meters	150 meters	175 meters
81 mm Mortar	165 meters	185 meters	230 meters
120mm Mortar	150 meters	300 meters	400 meters
105mm Howitzer	175 meters	200 meters	275 meters
155mm Howitzer	200 meters	280 meters	450 meters
155 DPICM	280 meters	300 meters	475 meters
RISK ESTIMATE DISTANCES (10% PI)			
SYSTEM	1/3 RANGE	2/3 RANGE	MAX RANGE
60mm Mortar	60 meters	65 meters	65 meters
81 mm Mortar	75 meters	80 meters	80 meters
120mm Mortar	100 meters	100 meters	100 meters
105mm Howitzer	85 meters	85 meters	90 meters
155mm Howitzer	100 meters	100 meters	125 meters
155 DPICM	150 meters	180 meters	200 meters

Figure 16-3. Risk Estimate Distance. Reference FM 3-21.20, 10-9.

Danger Close – is announced when applicable. Include the term danger close in the method-of-engagement portion of the call for fire when the target is within 600 meters of any friendly elements for both mortars and field artillery. When adjusting naval gunfire, announce DANGER CLOSE when the target is located within 750 meters and naval guns 5 inches or smaller are in use. For naval guns larger than 5 inches, announce DANGER CLOSE when the target is within 1,000 meters. The creeping method of adjustment will be used exclusively during danger close missions. The

---

[2] FM 3-21.20, 10-9.

forward observer makes range changes by creeping the rounds to the target using corrections of less than 100 meters.[3]

Types of Indirect Fire Missions

Adjust fire – This type of fire mission is used when the observer is not sure if the round(s) will have effect on the target. The observer may use grid, polar, or shift missions.

Fire for Effect – This type of fire mission is used when the observer is reasonably sure that the round(s) will have effect.

Suppression Mission – This type of fire mission is used for a rapid delivery of fires normally against pre-planned targets with a duration.

Immediate Suppression – This type of fire mission is used for a rapid delivery of fire against targets that have taken friendly elements under fire.

Additional fire missions include: suppression of enemy air defense (SEAD), illumination, and smoke.

Call for Fire (CFF)

A Call for Fire (CFF) is a concise message prepared by the observer. It contains all the information needed by the FDC to determine the method of TGT attack. It is a request for fire not an order. It must be sent quickly and clearly so that it is understood, recorded, and read back without error by the FDC recorder.

There are three parts consisting of six elements in a CFF:

1. Observer Identification.
2. Warning Order.   Part One

3. Target Location.   Part Two

4. Target Description.
5. Method of Engagement.   Part Three
6. Method of Fire and Control.

---

[3] FM 3-21.8, 2-32.

Method of Fire and Control – The method of fire and control indicates the desired manner of attacking the target, whether the observer wants to control the time or delivery of fire, and whether he can observe the target. The observer announces the appropriate method of fire and control.[4] Methods of Control include:

- When ready (standard)
- At my command (time of flight?)
- By round, shell, piece, section, platoon
- Do not load/ "Cancel do not load"
- Cannot observe (for a "Fire for Effect" FFE on known target)
- Time on target/ Time to target
- Continuous Illumination
- Coordinated Illumination
- Continuous
- Repeat
- Followed By

Adjust Fire Missions

Grid Method – Requires a map and compass. There are three initial steps to an adjust fire grid mission. These are:

1. The observer locates the target on the map.
2. The observer sends FDC an eight digit grid.
3. The observer needs to determine the observer-target (OT) direction in mils. The OT direction normally will be sent after the initial CFF, since it's not needed by the FDC to locate the target. However, direction must be sent before the first correction is made. The following is an example of a grid CFF:

Observer:"Q8Z this is Y6N, adjust fire, over."
FDC: "Adjust fire, out."
Observer:"Grid PU 347 689, over."
FDC: "Grid PU 347 689, out."
Observer:"Four trucks in the open, VT in effect, over."
FDC: "Four trucks in the open, VT in effect, out."
FDC: "Shot, over."
Observer:"Shot, out."
FDC: "Splash, over."
Observer:"Splash, out." "Add 400, over."

---

[4] FM 3-21.8, 2-33.

432

FDC: "Add 400, out."
Observer:"Drop 200, over."
FDC: "Drop 200, out."
Observer:"Fire for effect, over."
FDC: "Fire for effect, out."
Observer:"End of mission, four trucks destroyed, over."

Polar Method – Using this method the observer doesn't need a map, however the FDC must know the observer's location. There are three key elements to an adjust fire polar mission. These are:

1. The observer sends FDC a direction to the target expressed in mils (to nearest 10 mils).
2. The observer sends FDC a distance to the target expressed in meters (to nearest 100m).
3. The observer sends FDC a vertical shift in 5 meter increments (to nearest 5m).
* Observer must report his location prior to sending CFF.

The following is an example of a polar CFF:

Observer: "Q8Z this is Y6N, adjust fire, polar, over."
FDC: "Adjust fire polar, out"
Observer: "Direction 1240, Distance 600, down 30, over."
FDC: "Direction 1240, Distance 600, down 30, out."
Observer: "Infantry Platoon in the open, danger close, over."
FDC: "Infantry Platoon in the open, danger close, out."
FDC: "Shot, over."
Observer: "Shot, out."
FDC: "Splash, over."
Observer: "Splash, out."
            "End of mission, 10 casualties, platoon dispersed, over."

Shift from a Known Point Method – Using this method the observer doesn't need a map, however the observer must have one known point also known by the FDC. Shift from a Know Point is reasonably accurate but is the slowest of the three methods. There are four key elements to an adjust fire shift mission. These are:

1. The observer sends FDC an OT direction expressed in mils (to nearest 10 mils).
2. The observer sends FDC a lateral shift (left/right) expressed in meters (to nearest 10m).
3. The observer sends FDC a range shift expressed in meters.

4. The observer sends FDC a vertical shift in 5M increments.
*Direction is from observer to target, all other data is from known point to target.

Hand Mils Measurements
1 finger: 30mils
2 fingers: 70mils
3 fingers: 100 mils
4 fingers: 125 mils
Fist: 180 mils
5 fingers spread: 300 mils

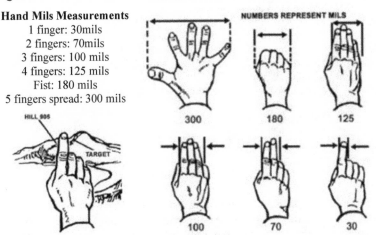

The following diagram visually demonstrates the steps involved with the shift method:

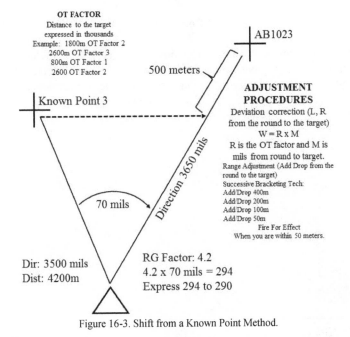

Figure 16-3. Shift from a Known Point Method.

The following is an example of a shift CFF:

Observer:	"Q8Z this is Y6N, fire for effect, shift from AB1023, over."
FDC:	"FFE, Shift from AB 1023, Out"
Observer:	"Direction 3650, right 70, add 500, down 10 over."
FDC:	"Direction 3650, right 70, add 500, down 10 over."
Observer:	"Machine gun position, converged sheaf, at my command, over."
FDC:	"Machine gun position, converged sheaf, at my command, out."
FDC:	"Shot, over."
Observer:	"Shot, out."
FDC:	"Splash, over."
Observer:	"Splash, out."
	"End of mission, target destroyed, over."

Adjust Fire by Sound – For adjusting fire in jungle environments, estimate the distance to the explosion of the round by counting the number of seconds from the impact of the projectile until you hear the explosion. Multiply the number of seconds by the speed of sound (350 meters/second). Add or drop the resulting distance, as appropriate.[5]

Conclusion

The goal of this chapter was to gain a basic working knowledge of the capabilities, planning particulars, and control measures associated with fire support. Special Forces soldiers plan and coordinate fire support in order to achieve decisive results. Planning should always include fire support in all its forms even if the leader thinks it's unnecessary.

---

[5] FM 90-5, I-2.

Chapter 17 Air Operations

Special Forces soldiers must be able to plan, organize, and operate helicopter landing zones (HLZs). This chapter will discuss the basics regarding this critical task.

Helicopter Landing Zones (HLZs) – Leaders must consider the following when selecting an LZ for day and night operations:

- Type of helicopter.
- Security.
- Clearing size.
- Surface conditions.
- Ground slope.
- Obstacles on approach and departure.
- Approach and departure paths.
- Prevailing winds.

Aircraft Touchdown Point (TDP) Sizes – A minimal circular landing point separation from other aircraft and obstacles is needed (See data below). The size of the LZ will be decided by the aviation unit commander based on size/type of aircraft, pilot/unit proficiency, whether the operation will take place during the day or at night, and atmospheric conditions. Avoid potential hazards such as blowing sand and snow, tree stumps, or large rocks.

Type of AC:	Diameter of Touchdown Point (TDP)
1. MH-6 / AH-6	10 Meters
2. UH-72A / OH-58D	15 Meters
3. AH-1W /AH-1Z / AH-64 / UH-1Y / UH-1N	20 Meters
4. UH-60A / UH-60L / UH-60M / SH-60	25 Meters
5. MV-22B / CV-22B	30 Meters
6. CH-47(D/F) / CH-53(E/K)	35 Meters
7. Desert/Snow Landing Zones and	100 Meters
Sling Load Aircraft (Day)	100 Meters
8. Sling Load Long Lines	125 Meters
9. Sling Load Aircraft (Night)	150 Meters[1]

Note: The surface conditions at the site should be firm enough to support the weight of the aircraft and free of loose sand, snow, or debris (brown-out or white-out conditions).[2]

---

[1] Distance between centers of TDP is 1.5 times the size of the touch point used for sizes 1-6.
[2] All obstacles will be removed, reduced or marked. A landing point will never contain an obstacle. (Obstacles are anything that is 18" high, wide or deep).

Chapter 17 Air Operations

Ground Slope – A patrol leader should choose an LZ site with relatively level ground. Ground slope can be considered an obstacle. In general, for the helicopter to land safely, the slope should not exceed 7 degrees. Whenever possible, direct pilots to land upslope rather than downslope. All helicopters can land where ground slope measures 7 degrees or less and no advisory is required. When the slope exceeds minimum restriction, observation and utility helicopters that utilize skids for landing must terminate at a hover to load or off-load personnel or supplies (See Figure 17-1).

Type of AC:	UH-1/CH-53	OH-58/MH-6/AH-6	MV/CV-22	UH-60/CH-47
Max Slope	6	8	9	15

Figure 17-1. Maximum Slope.

Note: When the slope exceeds 15 degrees, all helicopters must be issued an advisory and terminate at a hover to load or off-load personnel or supplies. Never land an aircraft facing downslope if at all possible.[3]

Calculating Ground Slope – The approximate ground slope angle may be calculated by multiplying the gradient by 57.3. This method is reasonably accurate for slope angles under 20 degrees (See Figure 17-2).

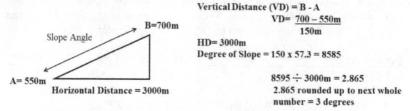

Figure 17-2. Ground Slope Computation.

Obstacles on Approach or Departure – For LZs that are bordered on the approach and departure ends by tall obstacles such as trees, power lines, or steep mountains, planners figure an obstacle ratio of 10 to 1. That is, if a helicopter must approach or depart directly over a 10-foot tall tree, then the landing point must have 100 feet of horizontal clearance. A 50 meter buffer or a 5:1 Obstacle Ratio (whichever is greater) will be given on approach and

---

[3] FM 3-21.38, 4-5. To determine slope in percentage or degrees, express all measurements in either feet or meters, but not both. If the map sheet expresses elevation in meters, multiply by three to convert into feet. If the map sheet expresses elevation in feet, divide by three to convert to meters.

departure ends of the LZ.[4] Left and Right sides of the site: A 10 meter buffer will be given to both sides of the site.

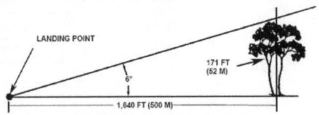

Figure 17-3. Maximum Angle of Approach.

Approach and Departure Paths – Ideally, approaches and departures are made along the long axis of the LZ over the lowest obstacle, and into the wind. Always attempt to land aircraft into a head wind. Wind direction of 45 degrees left or right of land heading considered a head wind (Figure 17-4).

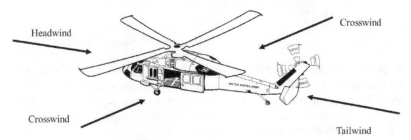

Figure 17-4. Prevailing Wind at LZ.

Crosswind and tailwinds for each aircraft are listed in below (Figure 17-5).

Type of AC:	UH-1N/UH-60/CH-53/MH/AH-6	MV/CV-22	OH-58	UH-1Y	CH-46/47	AH-64
Crosswind	15	30	35	40	45	45
Tailwind	15	10	20	40	10	45

Figure 17-5. Maximum Crosswind and Tailwind Allowance.

Marking of LZs – Use NATO "Y" and "T" landing zone markings systems to designate the touchdown point (TDP). When using a Nato "T" you must add 20 meters to the total length of the site. LZs may be marked with various methods: VS-17 panels, omni-directional visible lighting systems, and strobe lights or virtually any type of overt lighting or marking system.

---

[4] FM 3-21.38, 4-7.

Regardless of the type of marking device used, the patrol identifies the TDP (See figure 17-6).

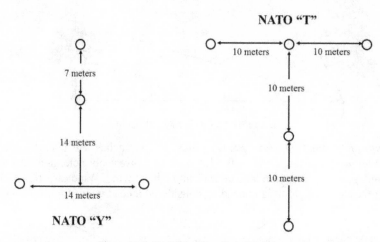

Figure 17-6. NATO Landing Zone Markings.

Night Operations – A lighted (inverted) "Y" indicates the landing point of the lead aircraft. At night, all landing lights should be placed in directional holes that can only be seen from the direction of approach and from above, but not from the ground. If this is not possible, keep all lights off for security purposes until the last practical moment.

When pilots are using NVGs, ground personnel mark the LZ with infrared (IR) chemlights in the NATO pattern. Ground personnel mark the reception committee leader's (RCL) position by IR buzz-saw (tying an IR chemlight to 3-foot of 550 cord and swinging it in a vertical circle).

Night Emergency Landing – Vehicle headlights offer one kind of emergency night lighting. Place two vehicles about 35 meters apart and 35 meters downwind of the landing point. They shine their headlights so that their beams intersect at the center of the landing point. The helicopter approaches into the wind, passes between the vehicles, and lands in the lighted area. This method does not work well for large helicopters.

Establish a Landing Zone – The patrol leader halts his element in the vicinity of the tentative LZ. This distance is METT-TC dependent. The PL then conducts a leaders' recon of the tentative LZ, and occupies the site by establishing security, and sets the remainder of his element in chalk order.
1. PL then sets up the LZ marking system by determining the land heading which is regulated by the following:

- Long axis of the site.
- Wind direction and speed.
- Slope at the site.

2. PL will ensures there is 360 degree security/observation of the site.
3. PL will then determine the obstacle ratio at the approach and departure ends of the site and establish the location of TDP.
4. PL will then call the marking party forward and ensure the marking system is either tied or staked down. If the situation permits, the patrol recovers the markings before exfil.

Note: the marking can be sucked into the engine intakes if not secured.

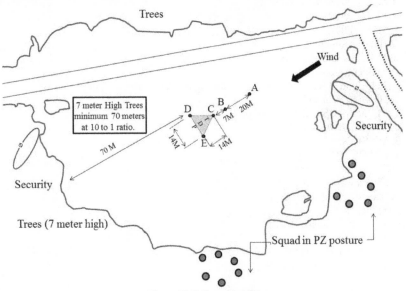

Figure 17-7. One-sided LZ.

Approaching the Aircraft – Once the HLZ is occupied and secured, the patrol leader:
1. Readies personnel and equipment for loading.
2. Ensures personnel move toward the aircraft only after it has landed.
3. Approach the aircraft at a crouch. Be aware of items such as antennas.
4. If the aircraft has landed on a slope, approach it from the down slope side.
5. Approach the following types of aircraft as indicated:
- UH-1 helicopter: Approach from 45 degrees off the front of the aircraft.

- UH-60 helicopter: Approach directly from the sides. Use this same approach for OH- 58, OH-6 and cargo helicopters when using the forward troop doors.
- For cargo helicopters (CH-47, CH-46, and MV-22B) when using the rear ramp: Approach from 45 degrees off the rear of the aircraft.
- CH-53 helicopter: Approach only from the right rear in order to avoid the tail rotor.

Note: Never approach utility or light observation helicopters (Other than the UH-72A) from the rear due to the tail rotor hazard. The UH-72A is a right side as well as a tail loading Medevac A/C.

Air Movement Checklist:

1. SITUATION.
  a. Enemy Situation.
  (1) Enemy air capability.
  (2) Enemy ADA capability.
  (3) Include in weather: % Illum, illum angle, NVG window, ceiling, and visibility.
  b. Friendly Situation.
  (1) Unit(s) supporting operation.
  (2) Friendly ADA status.
2. MISSION.
3. EXECUTION.
  a. Concept of Operation.
  b. Subunit Missions.
  c. Coordinating instructions.
  (1) Pickup Zone.
    (a) Name/Number.
    (b) Coordinates.
    (c) Load Time.
    (d) Takeoff Time.
    (e) Markings.
    (f) Control.
    (g) Landing Formation.
    (h) Approach/Departure Direction.
    (i) Alternate PZ Name/Number.
    (j) Penetration Points.
    (k) Extraction Points.
  (2) Landing Zone.
    (a) Name/Number.
    (b) Coordinates.
    (c) H-Hour.
    (d) Markings.
    (e) Control.
    (f) Landing Formation/Direction.

(g) Alt LZ Name/Number.
(h) Deception Plan.
(i) Extraction LZ.
(3) Laager Site.
 (a) Communications.
 (b) Security Force.
(4) Flight Routes and Alternates.
(5) Abort Criteria.
(6) Down Aircraft/Crew (designated area of recovery [DAR]).
(7) Special Instructions.
(8) Cross-FLOT Considerations.
(9) Aircraft Speed.

Conclusion

The purpose of this chapter was to gain an understanding of what is required to plan, organize, and operate helicopter landing zones (HLZs). The goal is develop a basic knowledge of the minmal requirements required to safely conduct a HLZ operation – knowledge of potential hazards, slope calculation, ground clearance, wind allowance, standard markings, as well as particularities of night air operations. Additionally, the selection of the HLZ must satisfy the requirements of both the aircrew and ground force.

Part Five: Common Skills

Chapter 18 Weapons

"When the crap hits the fan you won't rise to the occasion, you'll default to your level of training." – Barrett Tillman

In order to excel, it is imperative that every Special Forces soldier have expertise with the following weapon systems that are covered in this chapter. This chapter will discuss the following:
- Cardinal Rules of Weapons Safety.
- M4 Carbine.
- M203 Grenade Launcher.
- M249 Squad Automatic Weapon (SAW).
- M240 Machinegun.
- M136 AT4.

The Four Cardinal Rules of Weapons Safety

1. Always treat every weapon as if it's loaded.
2. Don't point your weapon at anything you're not willing to destroy.
3. Keep your finger off the trigger until you are ready to engage.
4. Always be sure of your target, and what is behind and in front of it.

M4 Carbine

The M4 carbine is a gas-operated, magazine-fed, shoulder-fired weapon with a telescoping stock. The M4 is a variant of the original AR-15 rifle designed by Eugene Stoner and made by ArmaLite. As a shortened variant of the M16A2 rifle, the M4 has a 14.5 in (370 mm) barrel, which allows its user to better operate in close quarters combat. This section will discuss the loading, clearing and functions check of the M4 Carbine (Figure 18-1).

Figure 18-1. M4 Carbine.

M4 / M16 Carbine General Data

Weight:
Carbine, M4A1, w/sling and loaded magazine..8.63 lb
Rifle, M16A2, w/sling and loaded magazine ....8.81 lb
Rifle, M16A3, M16A4, w/sling and loaded magazine ....9.13 lb

Length:
Carbine with compensator, buttstock extended ....33.0 in.
Carbine with compensator, buttstock closed ....29.75 in.
Barrel (M4)... 14.5 in.
Barrel (M16) .... 20 in.
Mechanical Features:
Rifling...Right-hand twist 6 grooves, 1 turn in 7 in.
Trigger pull (M16A2, M16A4, & M4) .... 5.5 to 9.5 lb
Trigger pull (M16A3 & M4A1).. 5.5 to 8.5 lb
Ammunition:
Caliber.. 5.56mm
Muzzle velocity (M4) .... 2,970 fps
Muzzle velocity (M16) .... 3,100 fps

Ranges:
Maximum range... 11,814 ft (approximately 3,600 m)
Maximum effective range:
Individual/point targets (M16A3/M16A4 Rifles & Carbines)...... 1,641 ft (500 m)
Individual/point targets (M16A2 Rifle) .... 1,806 ft (550 m)
Area targets (M16A3/M16A4 Rifles & Carbines)....................... 1,950 ft (594 m)
Area targets (M16A2 Rifle).. 2,625 ft (800 m)

Rates of Fire:
Cyclic rate of fire (Carbines) (approximate)................................700 to 970 rds/m
Cyclic rate of fire (Rifles) (approximate) ....700 to 900 rds/m
Maximum rate of fire:
Semiautomatic.. 45 rds/m
Burst .... 90 rds/m
Sustained rate of fire ....12 to 15 rds/m[1]

---

[1] Technical information from TM 9-1005-319-23&P, 28 Nov 2008.

Loading the M4 Carbine – The following sequence is to be used when loading the M4 Carbine:

1. Point the muzzle in a Safe direction (work space). Attempt to place selector lever on SAFE. If weapon is not cocked, lever cannot be placed on SAFE.

2. Lock the bolt open by pulling the charging handle to the rear. Press bottom of bolt catch and allow bolt to move forward until it engages bolt catch. Return charging handle to full forward position. If you have not done so before, place the selector lever on SAFE.

3.Conduct a three-point check by visually inspecting the chamber, the magazine well, and the bolt face to ensure these areas contain no ammo.

4. Inspect the loaded magazine and insert it pushing it into the magazine housing until the magazine catch engages and holds the magazine in place (press/pull).

446

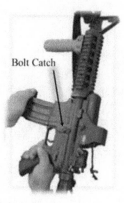

Bolt Catch

5. With the selector lever on SAFE, allow the bolt to go forward by pressing the upper portion of the bolt catch.

6. Tap the forward assist.

7. Close the dust cover.

Dust Cover

Forward Assist

Clearing of the M4 Carbine – The following sequence is to be used when clearing the M4 Carbine:

1. Point the muzzle in a Safe direction (work space). Attempt to place selector lever on SAFE. If weapon is not cocked, lever cannot be placed on SAFE.

SAFE

2. Remove the magazine by depressing the magazine catch button and pulling the magazine down (drop the source of feed).

PRESS CATCH BUTTON

PULL MAGAZINE DOWN

3. To lock the bolt open pull the charging handle to the rear. Observe the ejection of the round. Press bottom of bolt catch and allow bolt to move forward until it engages bolt catch. Return charging handle to full forward position. If you have not done so before, place the selector lever on SAFE.

4. Conduct a three-point check by visually inspecting the chamber, the magazine well, and the bolt face to ensure these areas contain no ammo.

5. With the selector lever on SAFE, allow the bolt to go forward by pressing the upper portion of the bolt catch.

6. While pointing the rifle in a safe direction, place the selector lever on SEMI and squeeze the trigger.

7. Pull the charging handle fully rearward and release it, allowing the bolt to return to the full forward position.

8. Place the selector lever on SAFE.

9. Close the ejection port cover.

M203 Grenade Launcher

The M203 grenade launcher is a lightweight, single-shot, breech-loaded, pump action (sliding barrel), shoulder-fired weapon that is attached to an M16 rifle series, or the M4 carbine series with the M203A1, and M4 carbine series with the rail system (Figure 18-2).[2]

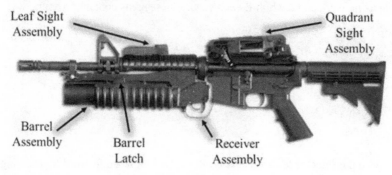

Leaf Sight Assembly

Quadrant Sight Assembly

Barrel Assembly

Barrel Latch

Receiver Assembly

Figure 18-2. M203 Grenade Launcher.

The M203 has the following capabilities:

- Maximum range is 400 meters.
- Maximum effective range for an area target is 350 meters.
- Maximum effective range for a point target is 150 meters.
- The minimum arming range of the 40 mm round is 14 to 38 meters.
- The rate of fire is 5 to 7 rounds per minute.
- The casualty radius of an M203 40 mm HE round is 5 meters.

Loading the M203 – The following sequence is to be used when loading the M203:

1. To load the weapon, first press the barrel latch and slide the barrel forward.

2. Once the barrel is in the forward position place the weapon on SAFE and visually inspect the barrel to ensure it is clear.

Barrel Latch

On

Safe

---

[2] FM 3-22.31, 3-3.

3. Then insert ammunition into the chamber and slide the barrel rearward until it locks with an audible click.

Unloading the M203 - To unload the grenade launcher, first depress the barrel latch and move the barrel forward. The cartridge case or round should automatically eject. If the case is stuck, tap it with a cleaning rod to remove it (Figure 18-3). Then place the weapon on SAFE, slide the barrel rearward, locking it to the breech.

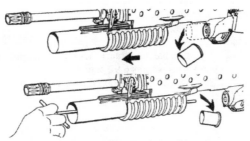

Figure 18-3. M203 Stuck Cartridge.

M249 SAW

The M249 machine gun is a gas-operated, air-cooled, belt or magazine-fed, automatic weapon that fires from the open-bolt position. It has a maximum rate of fire of 850 rounds per minute. Primarily, ammunition is fed into the weapon from a 200-round ammunition box containing a disintegrating metallic split-link belt. As an emergency means of feeding, the M249 machine gun can use a 20- or 30-round M16 rifle magazine but increases the chance of stoppages. This gun can be fired from the shoulder, hip, or underarm position; from the bipod-steadied position; or from the tripod-mounted position (Figure 18-4).

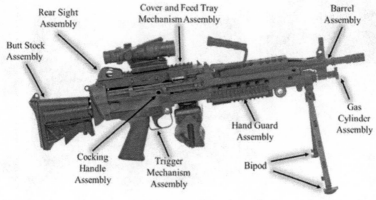

Figure 18-4. M249 SAW.

M249 Squad Automatic Weapon General Data

Specifications:
Length of Weapon.. 40.87 inches
Height of Weapon (on Tripod).. 16.00 inches
M249.. 16.41 pounds
M122 Tripod Mount with T&E, pintle .... 16.00 pounds
Ammunition.............. 5.56-mm ball and tracer (4:1 mix) ammunition-delivered in 200-round drums, each of which weighs 6.92 pounds.
Basic load .... 1,000 rounds in five 200-round drums
Tracer burnout .... 900 meters (+)
Ranges:
Maximum .... 3,600 meters
Maximum effective .... 1,000 meters with the tripod and T&E
Maximum for grazing fire overuniformly sloping terrain...............600 meters

Area Target:
On tripod .... 1,000 meters
On bipod .... 800 meters
Point Target:
On tripod .... 800 meters
On bipod .... 600 meters
Rates of Fire:
Sustained............................ 50 rounds a minute in 3- to 5-round bursts, with 4 to 5 seconds between bursts (barrel change every 10 minutes).
Rapid .... 100 rounds per minute, fired in 8- to 10-round bursts, 2 to 3 seconds between bursts (barrel change every 2 minutes).

451

Cyclic .... 650 to 850 rounds per minute, continuous burst, barrel changed every minute.[3]

Clearing the M249 SAW

Always assume the M249 machine gun is loaded. To clear the M249, perform the following procedures:

A. Move the safety to the fire position by pushing it to the left until the red ring is visible.

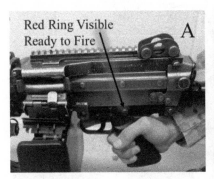

B. With the right hand, palm up, pull the cocking handle to the rear, locking the bolt in place.

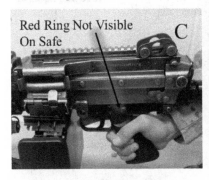

C. While holding the resistance on the cocking handle, move the safety to the SAFE position by pushing it to the right until the red ring is not visible. (The weapon cannot be placed on safe unless the bolt is locked to the rear.)

---

[3] Technical data taken from FM 3-22.68 Crew-Served Machineguns, July 2006.

D. Return and lock the cocking handle in the forward position.

E. Raise the cover and feed mechanism assembly, and conduct the *five-point safety check* for brass, links, or ammunition:
(1) Check the feed pawl assembly under the feed cover.
(2) Check the feed tray assembly.
(3) Lift the feed tray assembly and inspect the chamber.
(4) Check the space between the bolt assembly and the chamber.
(5) Insert two fingers of your left hand in the magazine well to extract any ammunition or brass (See Figure 18-5).

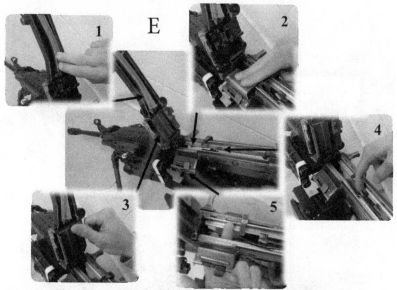

Figure 18-5. Conducting a Five-Point Inspection of the M249 SAW.

F. Close the cover and feed mechanism assembly.

G. Move the safety to the "F" position. With the right hand, palm up, return the cocking handle to the rear position. Press the trigger and at the same time ease the bolt forward by manually riding the cocking handle forward.

453

Load an M249 SAW

To load the M249, the weapon must be cleared as described. With the feed cover raised, the gunner makes sure his face is not exposed to the open chamber area while loading.

Belt – When loading belted ammunition, always cant the weapon to the right. Make sure the open side of the links is facing down, and place the lead link tab or first round of the belt in the tray groove against the cartridge stop. The rounds should be placed flat across the feed tray (See Figure 18-6).

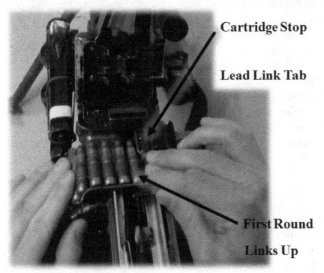

Figure 18-6. Loading an M249 SAW.

With your left hand, count five to six rounds down to hold ammunition in place on the feed tray, while at the same time closing the feed cover with your right hand. When closing the feed cover, always place your hand in front of the rear sight to prevent accidentally changing the sight adjustment.

Magazine – Load the 20 or 30 round magazine by inserting it into the magazine well on the left side of the receiver. Push the magazine firmly into the well until it seats and the release tab clicks into the recess on the magazine.

Functions Check on the M249 SAW

A function check must be performed to ensure that the M249 machinegun has been assembled correctly. The procedures, in order, are as follows:
1. Grasp the cocking handle with the right hand, palm up, and pull the bolt to the rear, locking it in place.
2. While continuing to hold the resistance on the cocking handle, use the left hand to move the safety to the SAFE position.
3. Push the cocking handle forward into the forward lock position.
4. Pull the trigger (The weapon should not fire).
5. Grasp the cocking handle with the right hand, palm up, and pull and hold it to the rear.
6. Move the safety to the FIRE position.
7. While continuing to hold resistance on the cocking handle, use the left hand to pull the trigger and ease the bolt forward to prevent it from slamming into the chamber area and damaging the face of the bolt.
8. If the weapon fails the function check, check for missing parts or repeat the reassembly procedures. Before disassembling the weapon, make sure it is positioned where the guide rod and spring cannot cause bodily harm if the bolt is locked to the rear. The cover and feed mechanism assembly can be closed with the bolt in either the forward or the rearward position.

M249 SAW Immediate Action

Immediate action is action taken to *reduce a stoppage without looking for the cause.* Immediate action should be taken in the event of a misfire or a cook off. A misfire is the failure of a chambered round to fire. Such failure can be due to an ammunition defect or faulty firing mechanism. A cook off is the firing of a round due to the heat of a hot barrel and not to the firing mechanism.

Cook offs can be avoided by applying immediate action within 10 seconds of a failure to fire. The gunner keeps the M249 on his shoulder while performing immediate action procedures. If the M249 stops firing, he takes the following immediate actions. An effective memory aid is POPP, which stands for Pull, Observe, Push, and Press:

1. Pull and lock the cocking handle to the rear while observing the ejection port to see if a cartridge case, belt link, or round is ejected. Ensure that the bolt remains to the rear to prevent double feeding if a round or cartridge case is not ejected.
2. If a cartridge case, belt link, or round is ejected, push the cocking handle to its forward position, take aim on the target, and press the trigger. If the

455

weapon does not fire, take remedial action. If a cartridge case, belt link, or round is not ejected, take remedial action.

M249 SAW Remedial Action

Remedial action is any action taken to determine the cause of a stoppage and to restore the weapon to an operational condition. This action is taken only after immediate action does not remedy the problem.

Cold Weapon Procedures – When a stoppage occurs with a cold weapon, and if immediate action has failed, use the following procedures:
(1) While the weapon is on your shoulder, grasp the cocking handle with the right hand, palm up; pull the cocking handle to the rear, locking the bolt. While holding the resistance on the cocking handle, move the safety to SAFE and return the cocking handle.
(2) Place the weapon on the ground or away from your face. Open the feed cover and perform the five-point safety check. Reload and continue to fire.
(3) If the weapon does not fire, clear the weapon and inspect it and the ammunition.

Hot Weapon Procedures – If the stoppage occurs with a hot weapon (200 or more rounds in less than 2 minutes, or as noted previously for training), move the safety to SAFE, wait 5 seconds (during training, let the weapon cool for 15 minutes), and use the same procedures as outlined for cold weapon procedures.

Jammed Cocking Handle – If a stoppage occurs, and if the cocking handle cannot be pulled to the rear by hand (the bolt may be fully forward and locked or only partially forward), the gunner takes the following steps:

(1) Tries once again to pull the cocking handle *by hand.*
(2) If the weapon is hot enough to cause a cook off, moves all soldiers a safe distance from the weapon and keeps them away for 15 minutes.
(3) After the gun has cooled, opens the cover and disassembles the gun. Ensures rearward pressure is kept on the cocking handle until the buffer is removed. (The assistant gunner helps the gunner do this.)
(4) Removes the round or fired cartridge. Uses cleaning rod or ruptured cartridge extractor if necessary.
(a) In a training situation, after completing the remedial action procedures, do not fire the gun until an ordnance specialist has conducted an inspection.

(b) In a combat situation, after the stoppage has been corrected, the gunner changes the barrel and tries to fire. If the weapon fails to function properly, he sends it to the unit armorer.

M240B Machinegun

The M240B is a general-purpose machinegun that can be mounted on a bipod, tripod, aircraft, or vehicle. The M240B is a belt-fed, air-cooled, gas-operated, fully automatic machine gun that fires from the open bolt position.[4]

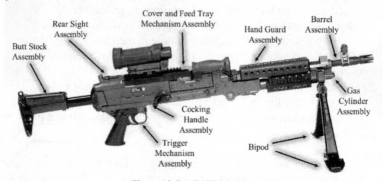

Figure 18-7. M240B Machinegun.

M240B Machinegun General Data

Specifications:

Length of the M240B .... 49 inches
Weight of the M240B .... 27.6 pounds
Weight of tripod-mount M122A1 .... 20 pounds
(tripod with/flex-mount, complete)
Ammunition.. 7.62-mm
Basic load (three-man crew) .... 900 to 1,200 rounds.
Tracer burnout .... 900 meters

Ranges:

Maximum range... 3,725 meters
Maximum effective range area target:
M122A1 Tripod .... 1,100 meters with tripod and T&E
M122A1 Bipod .... 800 meters

---

[4] FM 3-21.68, 3-1.

Maximum effective range point:

Tripod..800 meters

Bipod..600 meters

Suppression...1,800 meters

Maximum range of grazing fire over uniformly sloping terrain...........600 meters

Height of the M240B on the tripod mount M122A1.....................17.5 inches

Rates of fire:

Sustained..................................100 rounds per minute, 6- to 9-round bursts 4 to 5 seconds apart, barrel change every 10 minutes.

Rapid ....200 rounds per minute, 10- to 13-round bursts 2 to 3 seconds apart, barrel change every 2 minutes.

Cyclic ....650 to 950 rounds per minute in continuous bursts (barrel change every minute).[5]

Clearing the M240B Machinegun

A. Unload the M240B by pulling and locking the bolt to the rear position, if it is not already there.

B. Manually return the cocking handle to its forward position.

C. Place the weapon on safe by moving the selector switch to the "S" position.

Safety is Placed in the "S" position – to the right.

D. Raise the cover and feed mechanism assembly, and conduct the five-point safety check for brass, links, or ammunition:

---

[5] Technical data taken from FM 3-22.68 Crew-Served Machineguns, July 2006.

(1) Check the feed pawl assembly under the feed cover.
(2) Check the feed tray assembly.
(3) Lift the feed tray assembly and inspect the chamber.
(4) Check the space between the bolt assembly and the chamber.
(5) Insert two fingers in the ejection port to extract any ammunition or brass (See Figure 18-8).

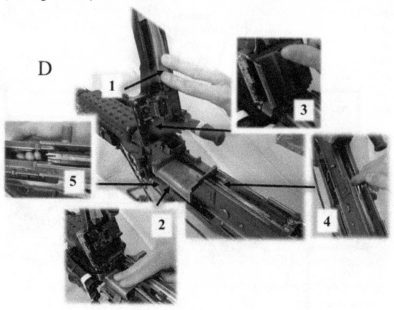

Figure 18-8. M240B Clearing Procedure.

E. Close the cover and feed mechanism assembly.

F. Move the safety to the "F" position. With the right hand, palm up, return the cocking handle to the rear position. Press the trigger and at the same time ease the bolt forward by manually riding the cocking handle forward.

Load a M240B Machinegun

To load the M240B, the weapon must be cleared as described above. To load the weapon lower the feed tray, place the safety on "F," and pull the cocking handle to the rear. Then put the weapon on "S," and ease the cocking handle forward. When loading, always cant the weapon to the right. Place the first round of the belt in the feed tray groove, double link leading, with open side of links face down. Hold the belt about six rounds from the

459

loading end, while closing the cover assembly. Ensure that the round remains in the feed tray groove, and close the cover assembly (Figure 18-9).

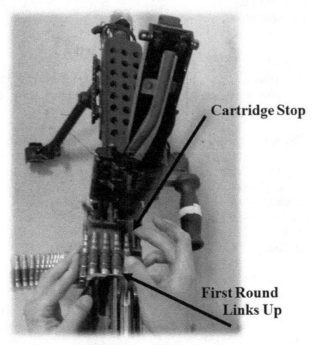

Cartridge Stop

First Round
Links Up

Figure 18-9. Loading the M240B Machinegun.

M240B Immediate Action

Immediate action is action taken to *reduce a stoppage without looking for the cause*. Immediate action should be taken in the event of either a misfire or a cook off. A *misfire* is the failure of a chambered round to fire. Such failure can be due to an ammunition defect or faulty firing mechanism. A *cook off* is the firing of a round by the heat of a hot barrel and not by the firing mechanism. Cookoffs can be avoided by applying immediate action within 10 seconds after a failure to fire. If the M240B stops firing, the perform the following immediate action: (An effective memory aid is POPP, which stands for pull, observe, push, and press.)

a. Pull and lock the cocking handle to the rear while observing the ejection port to see if a cartridge case, belt link, or round is ejected. Ensure that the bolt remains to the rear to prevent double feeding if a round or cartridge case is not ejected.

b. If a cartridge case, belt link, or a round is ejected, return cocking handle to forward position, aim at the target, and presse the trigger. If the weapon still does not fire, or if a cartridge case, belt link, or round is not ejected, take remedial action.

M240B Remedial Action

Remedial action is any action taken to determine the cause of a stoppage and to restore the weapon to an operational condition. This action is taken only after immediate action did not remedy the problem.

Cold Weapon Procedures – When a stoppage occurs with a cold weapon and immediate action has failed, the use the following procedures:
(1) Pull the cocking handle to the rear, locking the bolt. Return the cocking handle and place the safety to SAFE.
(2) Place the weapon on the ground or away from face and open the cover, perform the five-point safety check. Reload and continue to fire.
(3) If the weapon does not fire, clear the weapon and inspect it and the ammunition.

Hot Weapon Procedures – If the stoppage occurs with a hot weapon (200 rounds or more in 2 minutes or as noted above for training), the gunner moves the safety to SAFE, waits 5 seconds (during training, lets the weapon cool for 15 minutes), uses the same procedures as outlined for cold weapon procedures.

Jammed Cocking Handle – If a stoppage occurs and the cocking handle cannot be pulled to the rear by hand (the bolt may be fully forward and locked or only partially forward), take the following steps.
(1) Try once again to pull the cocking handle *by hand*.
(2) If the weapon is hot enough to cause a cook off, move all soldiers a safe distance from the weapon and keep them away for 15 minutes.
(3) After the gun has cooled, the pull the cocking handle to the rear. Ensure rearward pressure is kept on the cocking handle until the driving spring rod assembly is removed. Open the cover and disassemble the gun. (The assistant gunner helps the gunner do this.)
(4) Remove the round or fired cartridge. Use cleaning rod or ruptured cartridge extractor if necessary.
(a) In a training situation, after completing the remedial action procedures, the gun should not be fired until an inspection by an ordnance specialist has been made.

461

(b) In a combat situation, after the stoppage has been corrected, change the barrel and attempt to fire. If the weapon fails to function properly, the send it to the unit armorer.

Machinegun Employment

The following terms should be understood with regard to machinegun employment:

Sector of Fire – This is a target area assigned to an individual, a weapon, or a unit. Leaders normally assign each gunner a primary and a secondary sector of fire.

Final Protective Fire (FPF) – An FPF is an immediately available, prearranged barrier of fire. It is used to stop enemy movement across defensive lines or areas.

Final Protective Line (FPL) – An FPL is a predetermined line along which grazing fire is placed to stop an enemy assault. If an FPL is assigned, the machinegun sights along it, except when engaging other targets. An FPL becomes the machinegun's part of the unit's final protective fire. Although an FPL is fixed in direction and elevation, the gunner must make a small shift for searching. This keeps the enemy from crawling under the FPL, and compensates for terrain irregularities or the sinking of tripod legs in soft soil.

Principle Direction of Fire (PDF) – A PDF is just what it sounds like; the main direction of fire, usually into an area with good fields of fire or with a likely dismounted avenue of approach. Gunners firing a PDF may also provide fire support to an adjacent unit. Machineguns are sighted on the PDF only in the absence of an assigned FPL. If a PDF is assigned and other targets are unengaged, machineguns continue to sight on the PDF. A PDF has the following characteristics:
- It is used only if an FPL is not assigned; it then becomes the machine gun's part of the unit's final protective fires.
- Gunners determine the direction to wide targets by aiming on one edge of the target area and noting the amount of traverse needed to cover the entire target.
- The gunner covers the entire wedge-shaped area from the muzzle of the weapon to the target, although elevation might start out set for a priority portion of the target.

462

Grazing Fire – A good FPL covers the maximum area with grazing fire, which is effective over various types of terrain out to 600 meters. To graze fire as far out as possible over level or uniformly sloping terrain, the gunner sets the rear sight at 600 meters; selects a point on the ground that he estimates to be 600 meters from the machinegun; aims, fires, and adjusts on that point. To prevent enemy troops from crawling under grazing fire, he searches (downward) by lowering the muzzle of the weapon. To do this, he must separate his elbows.

Dead Space – The extent of grazing fire and dead space is determined in two ways. Ideally, the gunner adjusts the machinegun for elevation and direction. A member of the squad then walks along the FPL, while the gunner aims through the sights. Any place that the soldier's waist (midsection) falls below the gunner's point of aim is dead space.

Primary Sector of Fire – The primary sector of fire is the area to be covered by an individual gunner or unit.

Secondary Sector of Fire – The secondary sector of fire is a separate area covered by the same gun team. To establish a secondary sector of fire, the soldier or unit moves the gun to an alternate firing platform. He does this by removing the gun from the tripod, and firing the secondary sector from the bipod-supported position.

Lift Fire – The "lift fire" command is commonly used mistakenly as a "cease fire" command. However, this is not the proper definition or use of this command. "Lift fire" is used in conjunction with overhead fire which can be used against targets at ranges from 350-850 meters from a tripod mounted machinegun when it is advantageous for friendly soldiers to move beneath the cone of fire while simultaneously engaging the target(s) with the machinegun.

Surface Danger Zone (SDZ) – The ground and airspace for vertical and lateral containment of projectiles, fragments, debris, and components resulting from the firing, launching, or detonation of weapon systems to include explosives and demolitions. Department of the Army Pamphlet 385-63 (Range Safety) establishes SDZs for virtually all types of weapon systems. The SDZ for the M240 machinegun is 15 degrees (DA Pam 385-63, April 2014, Table 4-14).

M136 Anti-Tank 4 (84mm)

The M136 AT4 is a lightweight, self-contained, shoulder-launched munition (SLM) designed for use against the improved armor of light armored vehicles. It provides lethal fire against light armored vehicles, and has some effect on most enemy field fortifications. The AT4 is a round of ammunition with an integral, rocket-type cartridge. The cartridge consists of a fin assembly with tracer element; a point detonating fuze; and a high-explosive antitank (HEAT) warhead. The AT4 weighs 14.8 lbs, has a maximum range of 2100 meters, maximum effective range of 300 meters, and a minimum arming range of 10 meters.[6]

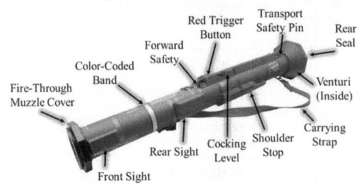

Figure 18-9. M136 AT4 Inspection Points.

Prepare for Firing

Use the following steps when preparing the M136 AT4 for firing:
1. Remove the M136 AT4 from its carrying position, and cradle it in your left arm.
2. Keeping the munition's muzzle pointed toward the target area.
3. With your right hand, pull and release the transport safety pin (See Figure 18-10).
4. Unsnap, unfold, and hold the shoulder stop with your right hand.
5. Grip the base of the sling on the front of the launcher with your left hand continuing to hold the shoulder stop with your right hand.
6. Raise the munition out and away from your body. While keeping the munition pointed at the target, pivot your body 90° to face the target. Place the munition on your right shoulder. The carrying strap may be used to steady the munition.

---

[6] FM 3-21.8, B-2; FM 3-23.25, 1-2.

7. Reach forward with your right hand, and grasp the front sight cover. Press down, and slide it rearward. With your right hand, grasp the rear sight cover. Press down, and slide it forward.

8. Ensure the backblast area is clear of personnel (Figure 18-11).

9. Unfold the cocking lever with your right hand. Place your thumb under it and, with the support of your fingers in front of the firing mechanism, push it forward, rotate it downward and to the right, and let it slide backward.

10. Adjust the rear sight to the correct range, using the following: When opening the rear sight cover, the range is preset at the 200-meter battlesight range setting. To adjust the rear sight range setting to more than 200 meters, turn the range knob clockwise (toward the muzzle). To decrease the range, turn the range knob counterclockwise (toward the firer). There is an audible clicking sound at each 50-meter increment; this sound aids you during limited visibility.

11. Place the first two fingers of your right hand on the red safety release catch, and extend the thumb. While keeping the thumb extended, press the red safety release catch down, and hold.

12. Pull back on the sling with your left hand to seat the shoulder stop firmly against your shoulder.

13. Aim the launcher. The rear sight should be no less than 2 1/2 inches and no more than 3 inches from your eyes.

14. Press the red trigger button with the thumb of your right hand to fire the launcher, and hold until the munition fires.

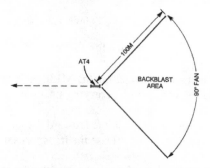

Figure 18-11. M136 AT4 Backblast Area. Reference FM 3-23-25, A-2.

Conclusion

The purpose of this chapter was to gain proficiency with the above basic weapon systems in order to effectively employ them in combat. The goal is to develop subconscious weapons handling skills. While handling weapons, the cardinal rules of weapons safety should always be stressed.

465

Chapter 19 Demolitions

The purpose of this chapter is to provide the SF soldier with a basic understanding of the characteristics of explosives used by US forces and will discuss the following: *nonelectric firing systems, calculation of time fuse, basic detonation cord knots, charge characteristics and formulas and the M18 Claymore Mine.*

Nonelectric Firing Systems – The two types of systems for firing explosives are electric and nonelectric.[1] Both systems may use detonation cord to increase efficiency. Nonelectric systems use a nonelectric blasting cap as the initiator. The initiation set consists of a fuse igniter (M60/81), the time blasting fuse (M700), and a nonelectric blasting cap (M7). When combined with detonating cord, a single initiation set can fire multiple charges (See Figure 19-1).

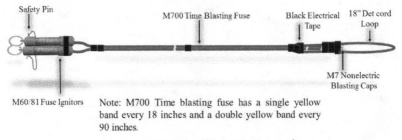

Safety Pin

M700 Time Blasting Fuse

Black Electrical Tape

18" Det cord Loop

M60/81 Fuse Ignitors

M7 Nonelectric Blasting Caps

Note: M700 Time blasting fuse has a single yellow band every 18 inches and a double yellow band every 90 inches.

Figure 19-1. Dual-Primed Nonelectric Firing System.

Calculate Time Fuse – Fuse length is dictated by time-space mission requirements, such as minimum safe distance (MSD) and the time needed for evacuation. To begin, conduct a test burn to determine the average burn rate. Start by cutting off six inches from the roll and discard it (cut should be made squarely across the time fuse). This ensures that any moisture the time fuse may have been exposed to will not affect the test of the burn rate. Next, measure and cut 3' feet of time fuse. The yellow bands will assist you (See Figure 19-1). You will now need to ignite one end of the fuse to determine the amount of time it takes to burn three feet using your stop watch. Once the time fuse burn is complete, take the total time and convert it into seconds. Then divide that number by three. This is getting an average burn rate per foot, which will be your final burn rate. If the number has a decimal,

---

[1] Additionally, modernized demolition initiators (MDI) may be used which consist of precrimped blasting caps onto premature lengths of shock tube and time fuse with an environmental seal at the other end. MDIs are beyond the scope of this book. See FM 3-34.214.

round to the nearest 100th. Remember, your burn rate should be 40 seconds per foot with a tolerance of plus or minus five seconds per foot (See below).

$$\frac{\text{Time required (min) x 60 (sec/min)}}{\text{Burning rate (sec/ft)}} = \text{Fuse length (ft)}$$

Detonating cord – consists of a core of pentaerythrite tetranitrate (PETN) wrapped in a reinforced and waterproof, olive drab plastic coating. Det cord explodes at a rate of approximately 28,000 feet per second. To prime plastic explosives with detonating cord, use the following det cord knots:

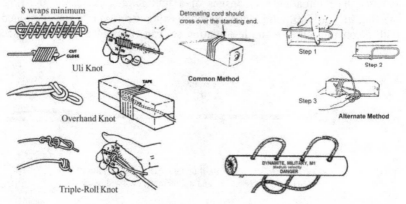

Figure 19-2. Priming Explosives with Detonation Cord.

To prime explosives with det cord, form either a uli knot, a double overhand knot, or a triple-roll knot as shown in Figure 19-2. Cut an L-shaped portion of explosive, leaving it connected to the explosive. Ensure that the space is large enough to insert the formed knot. CAUTION: Use a sharp, nonsparking knife on a nonsparking surface to cut explosives. Personal injury or damage to equipment may result from long-term failure to follow correct procedures. Place the knot in the L-shaped cut. Push the explosive from the L-shaped cut over the knot. Ensure that there is at least 1/2 inch of explosive on all sides of the knot. Strengthen the primed area by wrapping it with tape.[2]

Branch lines - is a length of detonating cord between the charge and the firing system. Branchlines should be attached to a det cord ring or line main to fire multiple charges. Combining the branchline with an initiating set

---

[2] FM 3-34.214 Exposives and Demolitions 2007, 2-14.

allows a single branchline to be fired. A branchline should be fastened to a line main with either a det cord clip, a girth hitch with an extra turn, or a Gregory knot (See Figure 19-3).

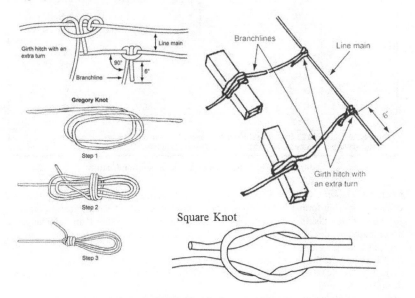

Figure 19-3. Connecting a Branchline to a Line/Ring Main.

The connections of branchlines and line or ring mains should intersect at right angles. If these connections are not at right angles, the branchline may be blown off the line main without complete detonation. To prevent moisture contamination and to ensure positive detonation, leave at least 6 inches of the running end of the branchline beyond the tie. It does not matter which side of the knot the 6-inch tail is on; at the connection of the line or ring main.[3] To splice det cord from the branch line to the firing system use a square knot (See Figure 19-4).

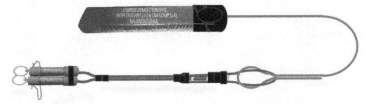

Figure 19-4. Primed Explosive Charge and Firing System.

---

[3] FM 3-34.214 Exposives and Demolitions 2007, 2-28.

Explosive	Unit (Pounds)	Size (Inches)	Detonation Velocity		RE Factor	Packaging/ Weight[2]
			M/Sec	Ft/Sec		
TNT	0.25	1½ D x 3½ L	6,900	22,600	1.00	200 per Box/55 Lb
	0.50	1¾ x 1¾ x 3¾	6,900	22,600	1.00	96 per Box/53 Lb
	1.00	1¾ x 1¾ x 7	6,900	22,600	1.00	48 per Box/53 Lb
M112 Block[1]	1.25	1 x 2 x 10	8,040	26,400	1.34	30 per Box/40 Lb
M118 Block	2.00	1 x 3 x 12	7,300	24,000	1.14	4 Sheets per Block;
M118 Sheet[1]	0.50	¼ x 3 x 12	7,300	24,000	1.14	20 per Box/ 42 Lb
M186 Roll	25.00	¼ x 3 x 50 ft	7,300	24,000	1.14	3 per Box/80 Lb
Ammonium Nitrate	43.00	7 x 24	3,400	11,000	0.42	1 per Box/52 Lb
M1 Dynamite	0.50	1¼ D x 8 L	6,100	20,000	0.92	100 per Box/62 Lb

[1]The volume of M112 is 20 cubic inches. The volume of one sheet of M118 is 9 cubic inches.
[2]Packaging weights include packaging material and weight of container.

Figure 19-5. Characteristics of Block Demolition Charges.

Charge Calculations – Use the six-step, problem-solving format below for all charge calculations. This format is used to determine the weight (P) of the explosives required for a demolition task in pounds of TNT. If using an explosive other than TNT, adjust P accordingly by dividing P for TNT by the relative effectiveness (RE) factor of the explosive you plan to use.

Step 1. Determine the critical dimensions of the target.

Step 2. Calculate the weight of a single charge of TNT by using the appropriate demolition formula.

Step 3. Divide the quantity of explosive by the RE factor. Skip this step if using TNT.

Step 4. Determine the number of packages of explosive for a single charge by dividing the individual charge weight by the standard package weight of the chosen explosive. Round this result to the next higher, whole package. Use volumes instead of weights for special-purpose charges (ribbon, diamond, saddle, and similar charges).

Step 5. Determine the number of charges based on the targets.

Step 6. Determine the total quantity of explosives required to destroy the target by multiplying the number of charges (step 5) by the number of packages required per charge (step 4).[4]

Internal Charges $\quad P = \dfrac{D^2}{250}$

Steel Cutting Charges $\quad P = 3/8$ x area of cross section
(I Beams)

External Charges $\quad P = \dfrac{D^2}{40}$

Steel Cutting Charges $\quad P = D^2$
(Cables, rods, and bars)

Abatis $\quad P = \dfrac{D^2}{40}$

Breaching Charges $\quad P = R^3 KC$

$$N = \dfrac{W \text{ (width)}}{2R \text{ (breaching radius)}}$$

---

[4] FM 3-34.214 Exposives and Demolitions 2007, 3-4.

M18A1 Anti-Personnel Mine

The M18A1 antipersonnel mine (Claymore), is a directional fragmentation mine that may be employed with obstacles or on the approaches, forward edges, flanks and rear edges of protective minefields as close-in protection against a dismounted Infantry attack. The Claymore projects a fan-shaped pattern of 700 steel balls in a 60-degree horizontal arc, at a maximum height of 2 meters, and covers a casualty radius of 100 meters. The optimum effective range is 50 meters. The forward danger radius for friendly forces is 250 meters. The backblast area is 16 meters to the rear and sides of the munition (Figure 19-6).

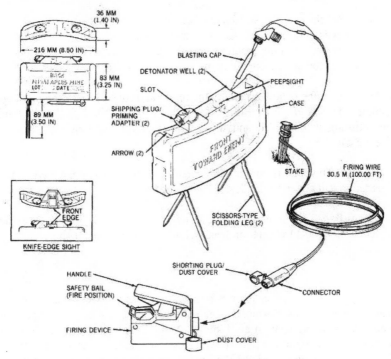

Figure 19-6. M18A1 Antipersonnel Mine Components.

Emplace M18A1 Claymore

The mine should be inspected prior to use, i.e., in ORP or PB. The following steps detail the emplacement of the mine using the acronym **ATARC – Aim, Tie, Arm, Re-aim, Camouflage**.

Chapter 19 Demolitions

1. The man emplacing the mine takes every component of the mine with him, especially the firing device. He begins by tying the firing end of the wire to a fixed object i.e., tree or tripod and paying out the wire to the emplacement site. A recon of the emplacement site should be conducted prior to emplacement.

2. **Aim**. At the emplacement site the legs of the mine are elongated and the mine is aimed. The mine requires a minimum back-blast of 16 meters with a sufficiently sized tree (18" diameter) or similar tamping material. The mine is aimed so that the 60 degree arc of the blast fan is covering the desired section of the kill zone or deadspace.

3. **Tie**. After the mine is sufficiently aimed, the wire is tied to the nearest semi-immovable object, such as the emplacement tree. The wire should be as close as possible to the ground surface so as to avoid detection. Tying the wire prevents the mine from being moved by foot traffic.

4. **Arm**. The mine is now armed by the removal of one of the shipping plug-priming adapters and a careful placement of the wire through the shipping plug-priming adapter slit, and the insertion of the blasting cap into the blasting cap well.

5. **Re-Aim**. The mine is now re-aimed to ensure that the 60 degree arc of the blast fan is still covering the desired section of the kill zone or deadspace.

6. **Camouflage**. The mine is now sufficiently camouflaged in order to avoid detection using local vegetation from behind the emplacement site.

Conclusion

The purpose of this chapter was to gain a basic understanding of the characteristics of basic explosives, nonelectric firing systems, calculation of time fuse, basic detonation cord knots, charge characteristics and formulas and the M18 Claymore Mine. The reader is directed to the GTA 5-10-33 Demolition Card and FM 3-34.214 for further basic demolition information.

Additionally, here are some notes on safety: explosives should be handled carefully; as a general rule transport firing systems and explosives separately; observe minimum safe distances (MSD); and investigate and clear misfires with minimum personnel.

Chapter 20 Basic Tactical Combat Casualty Care

Tactical combat casualty care (TCCC) is the pre-hospital care rendered to a casualty in a tactical, combat environment.[1] The intent of this chapter is to give an understanding of the basics of TCCC, and will cover the three phases of TCCC: (1) *care under fire,* (2) *tactical field care,* and (3) *tactical evacuation care* (CASEVAC/MEDEVAC). Use the **MARCH** acronym to help you remember important steps in TCCC:

M – Massive Bleeding.
A – Airway.
R – Respiration.
C – Circulation.
H – Hypothermia.

1. Care Under Fire (eliminate the threat and treat casualties) –

- Return fire and take cover.
- Direct casualty to remain engaged as a combatant if appropriate.
- Direct casualty to move to cover and apply self-aid if able.
- Try to keep the casualty from sustaining additional wounds.
- Move casualty from burning vehicles or buildings.
- Airway management is generally best deferred until the tactical field care phase.
- Stop life-threatening extremity hemorrhage if tactically feasible. The number one cause of preventable battlefield deaths is hemorrhage from extremity wounds. Preventable deaths percentage wise is 60% from extremity wounds, 23% from tension pressure, and the remaining 7% from loss of airway.

M – Massive Bleeding.

Apply a Tourniquet –
A. Place the wounded extremity through the loop of the band. Position the tourniquet about 2 inches above the injury site. Route the self-adhering band through both sides of the friction adapter buckle. Feed the self-adhering band tight around the extremity and securely fasten it back on itself.

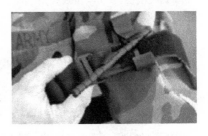

---

[1] Tactical Combat Casualty Care Handbook, 1.

B. Twist windlass rod until arterial (bright red) bleeding has stopped. Lock rod in place with windlass clip.

C. Secure rod with windlass strap and secure self-adhering band under windlass strap. Then secure windlass strap to Velcro on windlass clip.

D. Write a "T" and the time of application on the casualty's forehead with a pen, the casualty's blood, mud, or other substance.

If the tactical situation permits, check for a distal pulse. If a distal pulse is still present, apply a second tourniquet side by side and proximal (closer to the heart) to the first. Tighten this tourniquet and recheck the distal pulse.

Note: During self-application of the tourniquet to an upper extremity wound, defer routing the self-adhering band through both sides of the frictionadapter buckle.

2. Tactical Field Care – This is the care given once the fight is over or the patient and provider are no longer threatened by hostile forces. This phase involves a more detailed examination of the patient to find and treat wounds and a recheck of any interventions.[2]

A – Airway.

Airway management – If the casualty appears to be unconscious, check for responsiveness – "Are you okay?" Gently shake or tap. If no response,

---

[2] In combat medicine during hours of limited visibility, use Pain, Blood, and Deformity (PBD). The care provider checks from head to toe, feeling for PBD. The backside is simply raked using both hands and then inspecting his own hands after each rake of the backside from top of torso to the bottom of the buttocks.

position the casualty and open the airway (Recheck every 15 minutes). Use the acronym **AVPU**:

A – The casualty is *alert*, knows who he is and where he is, etc.
V –The casualty is not alert, but does respond to *verbal* commands.
P – The casualty responds to *pain*, but not verbal commands.
U – The casualty is *unresponsive* (unconscious).

A. If the casualty is unconscious without an airway obstruction, use:
- Place the casualty in the recovery position.[3]
- Head-tilt/Chin-lift or jaw thrust maneuver.
- Nasopharyngeal airway.

Head-tilt / chin lift or jaw thrust maneuver – The tongue is the most common cause of an airway obstruction. When a casualty is unconscious, muscles relax. This relaxation may cause the tongue to slip to the back of the mouth and block the airway. Do not use this technique for suspected neck or spinal injury – surgical cricothroidotomy.

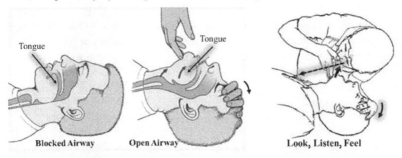

Use your fingers to remove anything that could block the casualty's airway such as loose teeth, facial bone or vomitus. Perform rescue breathing if necessary.

Mouth and nasal airways – For respiration rate less than normal (less than two in 15 seconds) – snoring or gurgling sounds – use either mouth or nasal (oral or nasal pharyngeal) airway. Do not use an oralpharyngeal airway (OPA) on a patient with a gage reflex. Do not use the nasopharyngeal airway (NPA) if the roof of the casualty's mouth is fractured, brain matter is exposed, or if clear fluid is coming from the ears or nose (Leaking cerebrospinal fluid may indicate a skull fracture).

---

[3] This is the patient's left side with left arm extended and knees slightly bent. The thought being blood flows from patient's right through the heart and out the left side.

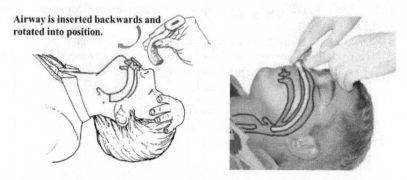

Airway is inserted backwards and rotated into position.

Place the casualty on his back (face up). Ensure patient is unconscious. Remove airway and lubricant from aid bag. Lubricate the tube and expose the opening of the casualty's nostril. Insert the tip of the airway into right nostril with bevel facing septum. Advance until the flange rests against the nostril.

Note: An NPA is preferred to an OPA for several reasons: (1) the NPA will probably be more tolerated by the patient if they become conscious; (2) an OPA could become dislodged during movement, becoming an obstruction; (3) using an OPA may induce vomiting.

Hemorrhage control –
A. Apply an emergency trauma bandage, hemostatic dressings (HemCon) or hemostatic powder (QuikClot), and direct pressure to a severely bleeding wound. Apply directly to bleeding site and hold in place 3-5 minutes. If dressing is not effective in stopping bleeding after 4

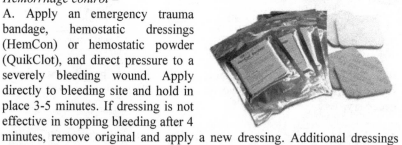

minutes, remove original and apply a new dressing. Additional dressings cannot be applied over ineffective dressing. Hemostatic dressings should only be removed by responsible persons after evacuation to the next level of care.

B. Once bleeding is controlled, apply outer bandage (Ace wrap or emergency dressing) to secure the hemostatic dressing in place. 1. Place pad on wound

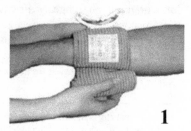

1

475

and wrap elastic band around limb or body part.

2. Insert elastic bandage into pressure bar. Tighten elastic bandage.

3. Pull back, forcing pressure bar down onto pad.

4. Wrap elastic bandage tightly over pressure bar and wrap over all edges of pad. Then secure hooking ends of closure bar into elastic bandage.

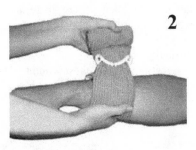

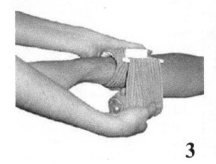

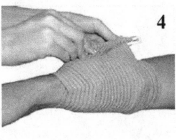

C. Tourniquets – Reassess prior tourniquet application. Expose wound and determine if tourniquet is needed. If so, move tourniquet from over uniform and apply directly to skin 2 to 3 inches above the wound. If a tourniquet is not needed, use other techniques to control the bleeding.

When time and the tactical situation permit, a distal pulse check should be accomplished. If a distal pulse is still present, consider additional tightening of the tourniquet or the use of a second tourniquet, side by side and proximal to the first, to eliminate the distal pulse.[4]

R – Respiration.

Rescue breathing – Maintain head-tilt/chin-lift or jaw thrust, pinch nostrils closed and administer two full breaths (2 seconds). Check carotid pulse. If pulse is present, administer mouth-to-mouth ventilations at 1 per 5 seconds. Check for breathing and pulse after one minute.

Open / Sucking Chest Wound – All open and/or sucking chest wounds should be treated by immediately applying an occlusive material to cover

---

[4] Tactical Combat Casualty Care Handbook, 24.

the defect. Then secure material in place. Signs of chest open/sucking wounds include: sucking or hissing sounds from wound; casualty coughing up blood; frothy blood coming from wound; and/or shortness of breath/ difficulty breathing.

Locate the open chest wound. Check for entry and exit wound (look and feel). If no vented chest seal is available, occlude both wounds (entry and exit) with airtight material, taping all four sides; decompress as required (See diagram below).

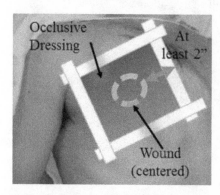

Expose the wound by removing, cutting, or tearing the clothing covering the wound. Use scissors from aid bag, a knife, or a bayonet. Do not remove clothing stuck to the wound. Do not clean the wound or remove objects stuck in the wound. Since air can pass through dressings and bandages, you must place airtight material over the chest wound before you dress and bandage the wound. Plastic from a field dressing is one source of airtight material. Expose the wound. Place occlusive bandage on exhale. Place inside surface of plastic wrapper directly over the hole. If conscious, tell the casualty to resume normal breathing. Dress and bandage the wound to protect the airtight material from damage and protect the wound. Place the casualty in the recovery position with the injured side to the ground.

Needle "D" (decompression) – A needle "D" is performed only if the casualty has a penetrating wound to the chest and increased difficulty breathing. Tracheal deviation, a shift of wind pipe, is a late sign of tension pneumothorax (PTX).[5] Insert a 14-guage 3.25 inch needle/catheter unit in the second intercostal space at the midclavicular line (See Figure 20-1). Ensure that the needle entry into the chest is not medial to the nipple line and is not directed towards the heart. An acceptable alternate site is the fourth or fifth intercostal space at the anterior axillary line. Caution: Avoid puncturing the lung. Always use the superior margin of the rib to avoid the intercostal nerves and vessels.

---

[5] A casualty with penetrating chest trauma will generally have some degree of hemothorax or PTX as a result of his primary wound.

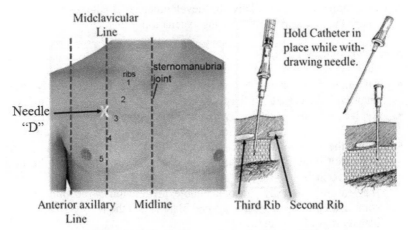

Figure 20-1. Needle Decompression for Tension PTX.

C – Circulation.

Any bleeding site not previously controlled should now be addressed. Conduct a full body search for additional injuries. Only the absolute minimum of clothing should be removed.

Vascular access – Obtain IV access at this point during the tactical field care phase. While in training, a 14- or 16-gauge IV catheters is normally used. However, the use of a single 18-gauge catheter is preferred in the tactical setting as it is more adequate for rapid delivery of resuscitation fluids and medication. Additionally, a saline lock should be used, and medics should not start an IV on an extremity that may have a significant wound proximal to the IV insertion site.[6]

H – Hypothermia.

Combat casualties are at a high risk for hypothermia, which is defined as a whole body temperature below 95 F (35 C). Hypothermia can occur regardless of the ambient temperature. The blood loss typically associated with combat trauma results in peripheral vasoconstriction, which contributes to the development of hypothermia. In addition, the longer a casualty is exposed to the environment during treatment and evacuation, especially in

---

[6] Tactical Combat Casualty Care Handbook, 11.

wet conditions, the more likely the development of hypothermia. This is even more the case during rotary-wing evacuation.

Prevention of hypothermia –

- Minimize the casualty's exposure to the elements. Keep protective gear on or with the casualty if feasible.
- Replace wet clothing with dry clothing if possible. Get the casualty onto an insulated surface as soon as possible.
- Apply the Ready-Heat blanket from the HPMK to the casualty's torso (not directly on the skin) and cover the casualty with the heat reflective shell.
- If a heat-reflective shell is not available, the previously recommended combination of the blizzard survival blanket and the Ready-Heat blanket may also be used.
- If the items mentioned above are not available, use dry blankets, poncho liners, sleeping bags, or anything that will retain heat and keep the casualty dry.
- Warm fluids are preferred if IV fluids are required.

3. Tactical Evacuation Care – Evacuation care is the care rendered once the casualty has been picked up by an aircraft, vehicle, or boat for transportation to a higher echelon of care. In preparation for MEDEVAC, consider the following:

- The casualty should remain wrapped in the Ready-Heat blanket, heat reflective shell, or blizzard blanket.
- If these items were not available in the other phases of care, check with evacuation personnel to see if they have them or any other items that can be used to prevent heat loss.
- Wrap the casualty in dry blankets and, during helicopter transport, try to keep the wind from open doors from blowing over or under the casualty.
- Use a portable fluid warmer on all IV sites, if available.

MEDEVAC Request – As soon as the situation permits, collect all applicable information needed for MEDEVAC request and determine: Grid coordinates for the PZ; radio frequency, call sign, and suffix; number of patients and precedence; type of special equipment required; and how the pickup site will be marked.[7]

9 Line MEDEVAC

LINE ITEM	EXPLANATION
1. Location of Pickup Site.	Encrypt grid coordinates. When using *DRYAD Numeral Cipher, the same SET line* will be used to encrypt grid zone letters and coordinates. To preclude misunderstanding, a statement is made that grid zone letters are included in the message (unless unit SOP specifies its use at all times).
2. Radio Frequency, Call Sign, Suffix.	Encrypt the frequency of the radio at the pickup site, *not a* relay frequency. The call sign (and suffix if used) of person to be contacted at the pickup site may be transmitted in the clear.
3. No. of Patients by Precedence.	Report only applicable info & encrypt brevity codes. A = Urgent, B = Urgent-Surg, C = Priority, D = Routine, E = Convenience. (If 2 or more categories reported in same request, insert the word "break" btwn. each category.)
4. Spec Equipment.	Encrypt applicable brevity codes. A = None, B = Hoist, C = Extraction equipment, D = Ventilator.
5. No. of Patients by Type.	Report only applicable information and encrypt brevity code. If requesting MEDEVAC for both types, insert the word "break" between the litter entry and ambulatory entry: L + # of Pnt -Litter; A + # of Pnt - Ambul (sitting).
6. Security Pickup Site (Wartime).	N = No enemy troops in area. P = Possibly enemy troops in area (approach with caution), E = Enemy troops in area (approach with caution), X = Enemy troops in area (armed escort required).
6. Number and type of Wound, Injury, Illness (Peacetime).	Specific information regarding patient wounds by type (gunshot or shrapnel). Report serious bleeding, along with patient blood type, if known.
7. Method of Marking Pickup Site.	Encrypt the brevity codes. A = Panels, B = Pyrotechnic signal, C = Smoke Signal, D = None, E = Other.
8. Patient Nationality and Status.	Number of patients in each category need not be transmitted. Encrypt only applicable brevity codes. A = US military, B = US civilian, C = Non-US mil, D = Non-US civilian, E = EPW.
9. NBC Contamination, (Wartime).	Include this line only when applicable. Encrypt the applicable brevity codes. N = nuclear, B = biological, C = chemical.
9. Terrain Description (Peacetime).	Include details of terrain features in and around proposed landing site. If possible, describe the relationship of site to a prominent terrain feature (lake, mountain, tower).

Reference: FM 8-10-6, *Medical Evacuation in a Theater of Operations, pages 7-7 through 7-9.*

Conclusion

Many battlefield fatalities are preventable.[8] The purpose of this chapter was to gain a knowledge of basic life-saving techniques to provide the best trauma care available on the battlefield – tactical combat casualty care (TCCC). At a minimum, the goal is to understand the three phases of TCCC, memorize the MARCH acronym, and be able to apply a pressure dressing, tourniquet, and chest seal, along with a needle decompression. Along with airway management, this constitutes the core basics every SF soldier should know.

---

[7] Evacuation Categories: Urgent – evacuate to save life, limb, or eye sight within 1 hour. Urgent surgical – evacuated within 2 hours to the nearest surgical unit. Priority – medical condition could deteriorate (4 hours). Routine – within 24 hours. convenient – whenever possible.
[8] Studies show that some 25% of all combat fatalities in Iraq and Afghanistan between 2001 and 2011 (4,596) were potentially survivable (60% from extremity wounds).

Chapter 21 Communications

"The basic requirement of combat communications is to provide rapid, reliable, and secure interchange of information." – RHB

To be successful in a tactical environment, Special Forces soldiers must be able to install, operate, and maintain communications equipment in order to command and control, send and receive instructions, request logistics or fire support, and gather and disseminate information. This purpose of this chapter is to provide a basic understanding of tactical radio communications equipment and will discuss the following:

1. Introduction to Combat Net Radios (CNR).
2. Radio Troubleshooting.
3. Type-292 Jungle Antenna.

Radios operate on various frequency bands (See Figure 21-1). The radio's range depends greatly on the terrain. The approximate range assumes a clear line of sight (LOS) with little to no interference. Ranges are drastically reduced in urban areas.

Band	Frequency
VLF (Very low freq.)	3 – 30 kHz
LF (Low freq.)	30 – 300 kHz
MF (Medium freq.)	300 kHz – 3 MHz
HF (High freq.)	3 – 30 MHz
VHF (Very high freq.)	30 – 300 MHz
UHF (Ultra high freq.)	300 MHz – 3,000 GHz
SHF (Super high freq.)	3,000 – 30,000 GHz
EHF (extremely high freq.)	30,000 – 300,000 GHz

Figure 21-1. Radio Frequency Bands (FM 6-02.53, B-4).

Combat Net Radios (CNR) – The family of combat net radios is comprised of intra-squad radios, single-channel ground and airborne radio system (SINCGARS) radios, and single-channel tactical satellite radios. This chapter will introduce the following radios:

- RT-1523 SINCGARS ASIP Radio.
- AN/PRC-148 Multiband Inter/Intra Team Radio (MBITR).
- AN/PRC-152 Multiband Handheld Radio.

RT-1523 SINCGARS ASIP Radio – is a vehicle-mount, backpack, and airborne, battery operated transceiver that has a total of 2320 programmable channels and is tunable over a frequency range of 30.000 to 87.975 MHz. It weighs 7.8 lbs. with battery, and its 12-14 volt battery has an approx. life of 20 hours (Figure 21-2).

Figure 21-2. RT-1523 SINCGARS ASIP Radio.

AN/PRC-148 – The MBITR is a portable, battery operated transceiver that has a total of 100 programmable channels and is tunable over a frequency range of 30–512 MHz.[1] It weighs 2.6 lbs. with battery, and has a battery life of approx. 12 hours (Figure 21-3).

Figure 21-3. AN/PRC-148 MBITR.

AN/PRC-152 – Similar to the MBITR, the AN/PRC-152 is a SC multiband handheld, battery operated transceiver that has a total of 100 programmable channels and is tunable over a frequency range of 30–512 MHz.

---

[1] FM 6-02.53, 4-23.

Additionally, it has an embedded GPS receiver to display local position. It weighs 2.7 lbs. with battery, and has a battery life of approx. 8 hours (Figure 21-4).

Figure 21-4. AN/PRC-152.

AN/PRC-152 Load a Single Channel:

1. Determine the proper FREQ.

2. Rotate the CIPHER knob to PT and the function knob to F. The radio will initialize.

3. Press PGM (the 8 button on the keypad), select SYSTEM PRESETS, press ENTER, then select SYSTEM PRESETS CONFIG, and press ENTER.

SYSTEM PRESET NUMBER will be displayed with the cursor on the preset number identifier.

4. Enter the appropriate number (1–99) by pressing the keypad number and press ENTER. The number is entered as the preset identifier, and the cursor is moved to the channel description.

5. Use the keypad to enter a text description of the preset channel, and press ENTER. The text description is saved, and the enable preset option is displayed.

6. Select YES. Preset is enabled.

7. Use the buttons until LOS is displayed, and press ENTER. The VULOS CONFIG menu is displayed.

8. Select FREQ and press ENTER. The FREQ programming screen is displayed.

9. Select RX FREQ and press ENTER. The receive FREQ can be loaded.

10. Use the key pad to enter the desired FREQ, and press ENTER. The FREQ is loaded, and the FREQ menu is displayed.

11. Select TX FREQ and press ENTER.

12. Select USE RX and press ENTER. The SC is loaded and set for transmitting and receiving.

483

Radio Troubleshooting – The majority of radio communication problems may be solved by the ABCs of basic troubleshooting:

A – Antenna: Check fitting, consider long whip or field expedient.
B – Battery: Clean, dry, and charged.
C – Connection: Clean connection with an eraser.

Typical radio communication problems:
1. No power – check battery, check function switch.
2. High pitch in handset – clean connection with an eraser.
3. Will not transmit – check antenna, check, connection, check frequency.
4. Will not receive – check antenna, check connection, check frequency.
5. Will not key – press push to talk (PTT).
6. Continuous keying – press PTT, change handset.

General rules for radios:
1. Protect handsets and microphones with plastic bags.
2. When radios are protected by plastic bags, make sure the battery vent is not obstructed. Radios protected in this manner must be constantly checked to insure moisture does not build up in the bag.
3. When not in use, remove batteries and pack in waterproof container.
4. Clean radios as frequently as individual and crewserved weapons are cleaned.

General rules for batteries:
1. Turn off radio power before changing the battery (its bad for the radio and you'll dump the fill).
2. Keep batteries as dry and warm as possible – batteries perform best at moderate temperatures and generally have a shorter life at very cold temperatures.

General rules regarding antennas:
1. Keep whip antenna vertical when transmitting.
2. Insure antenna is not grounded by being in contact with foreign object.
3. Position antennas to achieve the best line-of-sight possible between stations (such as on top of a hill) – the higher the antenna the greater the range the radio transmission will have.

Antennas – Antennas are classified by the directions in which they can radiate energy. The three classifications include omnidirectional (all directions), bidirectional (two directions), or directional (one direction).

Type-292 Jungle Antenna – Developed for jungle use, the 292 is an omnidirectional antenna that consists of one radiating wire and three ground plane wires having lengths corresponding to the desired frequency.

1. Use the planning considerations discussed in the next paragraph to determine the length of the elements (one radiating wire and three ground plane wires) for the desired frequency (See Figure 21-5).
2. Cut these elements from claymore or similar wire. The heavier the gauge, the better, but insulated copper core wire works best.
3. Cut spacing sticks the same length as the ground plane wires. Place the sticks in a triangle and tie their ends together with wire, tape, or rope.
4. Attach an insulator to each corner and one end of each ground-plane wire to each insulator.
5. Bring the loose ends of the ground-plane wires together, attach them to an insulator, and tie securely.
6. Strip about 3 inches of insulation from each wire and twist them together.
7. Tie one end of the radiating element wire to the other side of insulator and the other end to another insulator.
8. Strip about 3 inches of insulation from the radiating element.
9. Cut enough wire to reach from the proposed location of the antenna to the radio set. Keep this line as short as possible, because excess length reduces the efficiency of the system. Tie a knot at each end to identify it as the "hot" lead. Remove insulation from the "hot" wire and tie it to the radiating element wire at insulator.
10. Remove insulation from the other wire and attach it to the bare ground plane element wires at insulator.
11. Tape all connections and do not allow the radiating element wire to touch the ground plane wires.
12. Attach a rope to the insulator on the free end of the radiating element and toss the rope over the branches of a tree. Pull the antenna as high as possible, keeping the lead in routed down through the triangle. Secure the rope to hold the antenna in place.
13. At the radio set, remove about 1 inch of insulation from each end of the wire. Connect the ends to the positive side of the cobra head connector. Be sure the connections are tight or secure.
14. Set up correct frequency, turn on the set, and proceed with communications.

Antenna Length Calculation – The length of an antenna must be considered in the construction of field expedients. At a minimum, a quarter of the frequency wavelength should be used as the length of the antenna.

Operating Frequency In MHz	Element Length (Radiating Elements and Ground-Plane Elements)	
30	2.38 m	(7 ft 10 in)
32	2.23 m	(7 ft 4 in)
34	2.1 m	(6 ft 11 in)
36	1.98 m	(6 ft 6 in)
38	1.87 m	(6 ft 2 in)
40	1.78 m	(5 ft 10 in)
43	1.66 m	(5 ft 5 in)
46	1.55 m	(5 ft 1 in)
49	1.46 m	(4 ft 9 in)
52	1.37 m	(4 ft 6 in)
55	1.3 m	(4 ft 3 in)
58	1.23 m	(4 ft 0 in)
61	1.17 m	(3 ft 10 in)
64	1.12 m	(3 ft 8 in)
68	1.05 m	(3 ft 5 in)
72	0.99 m	(3 ft 3 in)
76	0.94 m	(3 ft 1 in)

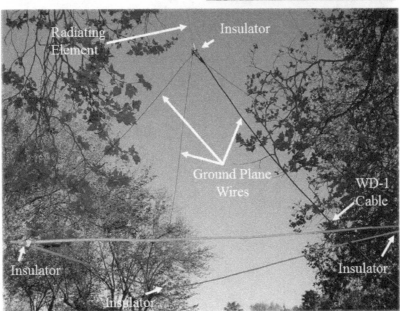

Figure 22-5. 292 Jungle Antenna.

To calculate the physical length of an antenna in feet, use the following equation. It will give you the antenna length in feet for a 1/ 4 wavelength of the frequency. To determine the antenna length in feet for a full wavelength antenna, multiply the antenna length by 4:

$$X = 234/ Freq$$

(X = the length of the antenna in feet; Freq = the radio frequency used)

Example

234/ 38.950 = 6.01 feet (Quarter Wavelength Antenna)
6.01 feet x 2 = 12.02 feet (Half Wavelength Antenna)
6.01 feet x 4 = 24.04 feet (Full Wavelength Antenna)

Conclusion

This purpose of this chapter was to gain a basic understanding of tactical radios, troubleshooting (A,B,Cs), antennas and general rules of thumb. Prevention is the best cure. Care in the field ensures communications equipment works effectively. The goal is to communicate timely and decisively to accomplish any mission.

Chapter 22 Fieldcraft

To be effective, a Special Forces soldier must be good in the field. Not only must he understand the basics of land navigation (be able to locate his position on a map using terrain association, and plot a course from one point to another), but he must possess a basic knowledge of rope knots, field-expedient methods of acquiring food and water and fire-starting techniques. The chapter presupposes a basic knowledge of land navigation and will discuss the following:

- Terrain Features.
- Supplemental Land Navigation Techniques.
- Navigating Without a Compass.
- Basic Knots.
- Field Expedient Water Procurement.
- Fire-Staring Techniques.

Terrain Features –Below are the ten basic terrain features (Figure 22-1).

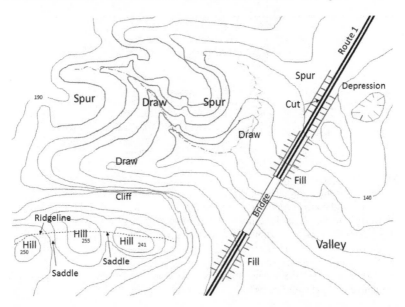

Figure 22-1. Basic Terrian Features: Major terrain features are hills, saddles, valleys, ridges, and depressions. Minor terrain features are draws, spurs, and cliffs. Supplementary terrain feautures are cuts and fills.[1]

---

[1] FM 3-25.26 Map Reading and Land Navigation, 10-11. A map is a graphic representation of a portion of the earth's surface drawn to scale, as seen from above.

Supplemental Land Navigation Techniques

Intersection – is the location of an unknown point by successively occupying at least two (preferably three) known positions on the ground and then map sighting on the unknown location. It is used to locate distant or inaccessible points or objects such as enemy targets and danger areas. There are two methods of intersection: the map and compass method and the straightedge method (See Figure 22-2).[2]

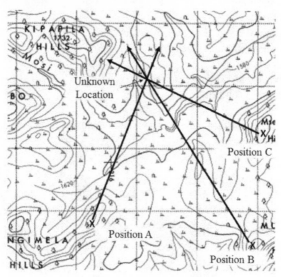

Figure 22-2. Intersection Technique.

Map and compass method:
(1) Orient the map using the compass.
(2) Locate and mark your position on the map,
(3) Determine the magnetic azimuth to the unknown position using the compass.
(4) Convert the magnetic azimuth to grid azimuth.
(5) Draw a line on the map from your position on this grid azimuth.
(6) Move to a second known point and repeat steps 1, 2, 3, 4, and 5.
(7) The location of the unknown position is where the lines cross on the map. Determine the grid coordinates to the desired accuracy.

Straight edge method (compass not available):
(1) Orient the map on a flat surface by the terrain association method.
(2) Locate and mark your position on the map.

---

[2] FM 3-25.26, 6-13.

(3) Lay a straight edge on the map with one end at the user's position (A) as a pivot point; then, rotate
the straightedge until the unkown point is sighted along the edge.
(4) Draw a line along the straight edge
(5) Repeat the above steps at position (B) and check for accuracy.
(6) The intersection of the lines on the map is the location of the unknown point. Determine the grid coordinates to the desired accuracy.

Resection – is the method of locating one's position on a map by determining the grid azimuth to at least two welldefined locations that can be pinpointed on the map. For greater accuracy, the desired method of resection would be to use three or more well-defined locations (Fig 22-3).

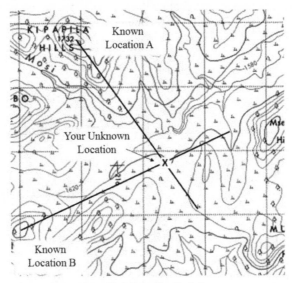

Figure 22-3. Resection Technique.

(1) Orient the map using the compass.
(2) Identify two or three known distant locations on the ground and mark them on the map.
(3) Measure the magnetic azimuth to one of the known positions from your location using a compass.
(4) Convert the magnetic azimuth to a grid azimuth.
(5) Convert the grid azimuth to a back azimuth. Using a protractor, draw a line for the back azimuth on
the map from the known position back toward your unknown position.
(6) Repeat 3, 4, and 5 for a second position and a third position, if desired.

(7) The intersection of the lines is your location. Determine the grid coordinates to the desired accuracy.

Navigating Without a Compass – You can determine your location by using the earth's relationship to either celestial bodies. Here are a few methods:

Shadow-tip method – (1) Place a stick that is at least 3 feet long upright in the ground so you can see its shadow. Ensure the shadow is cast on a level ground that is free of leaves and brush. Mark the tip of the shadow it casts. (2) Wait approximately 15 minutes, then mark the new position of the shadow's tip with another small object. (3) Draw a line between the two marks. This is an approximate east-west line. Stand with your left foot on the first mark and your right foot on the second – you are now facing north (See Figure 22-1). Note: If in the Southern Hemisphere, you would be facing south.

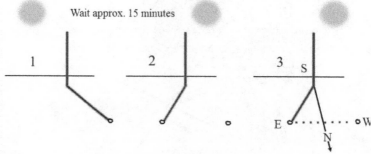

Figure 22-1. Shadow Tip Method.

Watch method - In the northern hemisphere, hold the watch horizontal and point the hour hand at the sun. Bisect the angle between the hour hand and the 12 o'clock mark to get the north-south line (See Figure 22-2).
If there is any doubt as to which end of the line is north, remember that the sun rises in the east, sets in the west, and is due south at noon. The sun is in the east before noon and in the west after noon.

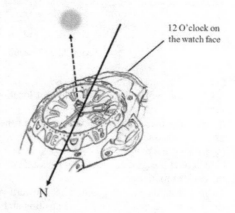

Figure 22-2. Watch Method 1.

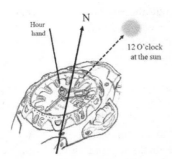

Figure 22-3. Watch Method 2.

In the southern hemisphere, hold the watch and point the 12 o'clock mark at the sun. Bisect the angle between the 12 o'clock mark and the hour hand the to get the north-south line (See Figure 22-3).

Using the Moon – the moon, having no light of its own, orbits the earth on a 28-day circuit, and reflects light according to its position (new moon, full moon, etc.). If the moon rises before the sun has set, the illuminated side will be the west. If the moon rises after midnight, the illuminated side will be the east. This obvious discovery provides us with a rough east-west reference during the night.

Navigating with Stars – When using constellations to determine direction, identify your location's Temperate Zone.[3] For example, the North Star provides an excellent nighttime navigational aid in the North Temperate Zone. In order to locate it, find the the Big Dipper constellation, made up of seven fairly bright stars in the shape of a dipper with a long curved handle (See Figure 22-4).

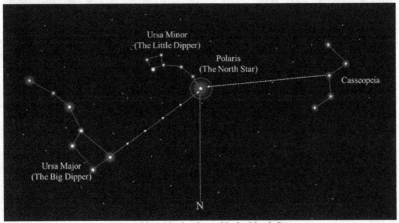

Figure 22-4. Navigating with the North Star.

The the two stars that form the side of the cup farthest from the handle, used as pointers, are situated in the direction of The North Star which is about five times the distance between the two stars of the dipper cup. For

---

[3] Temperate Zone is the area between the tropics and the polar circles.

additional help, the North Star is located about midway between the central star of Cassiopeia and the Big Dipper. Once you've found the North Star, draw an imaginary line straight down from it to the ground. This direction is true north, and if you can find a landmark in the distance at this point, you can use it to guide yourself.

In the Southern Hemisphere, true south is determined in relation to the Southern Cross, a constellation composed of five stars. The four brightest stars of form a cross. Identify the two stars that make up the long axis of the cross. These stars form a line which 'points' to an imaginary point in the sky which is above the South Pole. Follow the imaginary line down from the two stars five times the distance between them. Draw an imaginary line from this point to the ground, and try to identify a corresponding landmark to aid you navigationally (See Figure 22-5).

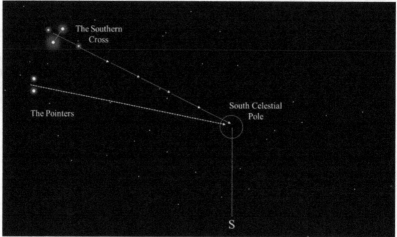

Figure 22-5. Navigating with the Southern Cross.

Improvised compass – You can construct improvised compasses with: (1) a needle or some other wire-like piece of steel such as a straightened paper clip, double-edged razor blade, etc. and (2) something small that floats such as a piece of cork, the bottom of a styrofoam coffee cup, a piece of plastic, a leaf, or the cap from a milk jug, etc. Once you've got both implements you'll need to magnetize or polarize the metal by slowly stroking it in one direction on a piece of silk or carefully through your hair using deliberate strokes. A magnet also works well (only stroke one end and in one direction). Next, find some standing water, place the magnetized metal on a float and it will align itself with a north-south line.

Basic Knots – the following knots are useful in securing yourself and your equipment: (1) *Square knot (below)*– is a joing knot that is used to tie two ends together.

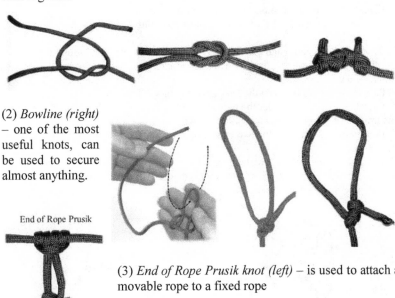

(2) *Bowline (right)* – one of the most useful knots, can be used to secure almost anything.

End of Rope Prusik

(3) *End of Rope Prusik knot (left)* – is used to attach a movable rope to a fixed rope

(4) *Rerouted Figure Eight (below left)*– is an anchor knot which may be used to secure a climber.

(5) *Water Knot (below right)* – joins two ends of tubual nylon which is commonly used for a security harness.

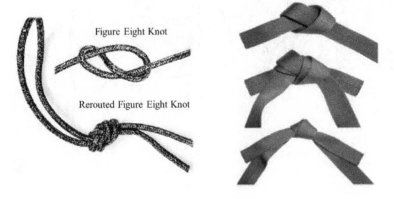

Figure Eight Knot

Rerouted Figure Eight Knot

Rappel Seat – is an improvised rappel harness made of rope which usually requires a sling rope 14 feet or longer (See Figure 22-6). Use the following steps when tying the knot:
1. Find the middle of the sling rope and make a bight.
2. Decide which hand will be used as the brake hand and place the bight on the opposite hip.
3. Reach around behind and grab a single strand of rope. Bring it around the waist to the front and tie two overhands on the other strand of rope, thus creating a loop around the waist.
4. Pass the two ends between the legs, ensuring they do not cross.
5. Pass the two ends up under the loop around the waist, bisecting the pocket flaps on the trousers. Pull up on the ropes, tightening the seat.
6. From rear to front, pass the two ends through the leg loops creating a half hitch on both hips.
7. Bring the longer of the two ends across the front to the nonbrake hand hip and secure the two ends with a square knot safetied with overhand knots. Tuck any excess rope in the pocket below the square knot.

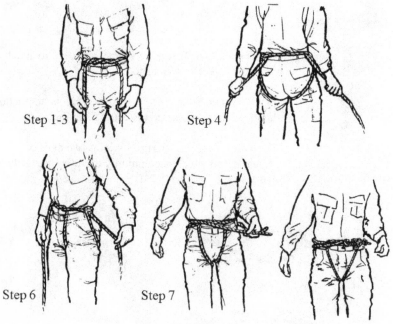

Figure 22-6. Rappel Seat.

495

Field Expedient Water Procurement – field skills of foraging are perishable. There are two basic senarios in which one would need to forage: One in which you end up on your own (survival); and another, in which you are operating as a member of a patrol.

Water Procurement – you can't live long without it. Even in cold areas, you need a minimum of 2 quarts of water a day (As a basic rule, the maximum amount of water per day is 10-12 quarts). Purify all water before drinking. Either boil it for at least one minute (plus 1 more minute for each additional 1,000 feet above sea level) or for a maximum of 10 minutes anywhere. Use water purification tablets. Almost any environment has water present to some degree. Figure 22-7 lists possible sources of water in various environments.

Environment	Source	Procurement Method
Desert	Cacti	Cut off the top and squeeze the pulp. Do not eat the pulp (Suck the juice out of the pulp and discard).
Desert	Ground	(Wherever you find green vegetation, low areas or damp surface sand). Dig hole deep enough to allow water to seep in.
Desert	Fissures in rock	Insert flexible tube and siphon water. Lower a container if fissure is large enough.
	Condensation on metal	Use cloth to absorb water, then wring water from cloth.
Beach	Ground	Dig hole deep enough to allow water to seep in (use container if available); obtain rocks, build fire, heat rocks; drop hot rocks in water, hold cloth over hole to absorb steam; wring water from cloth.
At Sea	Rain	Catch rain in tarp or container.
Jungle	Tropical Vine	Cut a notch in the vine as high as you can reach, then cut the vine off close to the ground. Catch the dropping liquid in a container or in your mouth
Jungle	Banana Tree	Cut down the tree, leaving about a 30-centimeter stump, and scoop out the center of the stump so that the hollow is bowl-shaped. Water from the roots will immediately start to fill the hollow.
Jungle	Rain	Rainwater collected in clean containers or in plants is usually safe for drinking.
	Lakes, ponds, etc.	Purify water from lakes, ponds, swamps, springs, or streams, especially the water near human settlements or in the tropics.

* When possible, purify all water you get by using iodine or chlorine, or by boiling.

Figure 22-7. Water Procurement in Various Environments (FM 21-76 Survival).

Fire-Starting Techniques – Understanding the concept of the fire triangle is very important in correctly constructing and maintaining a fire. The three sides of the triangle represent air, heat, and fuel. If you remove any of these, the fire will go out (FM 21-76). You need three types of materials to build a fire – tinder, kindling, and fuel. Tinder is dry material that ignites with little heat – a spark starts a fire. The tinder must be absolutely dry to be sure just a spark will ignite it. If you only have a device that generates sparks, charred cloth will be almost essential. It holds a spark for long periods, allowing you to put tinder on the hot area to generate a small flame.

You can make charred cloth by heating cotton cloth until it turns black, but does not burn. Once it is black, you must keep it in an airtight container to keep it dry. Prepare this cloth well in advance of any survival situation. Add it to your individual survival kit. Kindling is readily combustible material that you add to the burning tinder. Again, this material should be absolutely dry to ensure rapid burning. Kindling increases the fire's temperature so that it will ignite less combustible material. Fuel is less combustible material that burns slowly and steadily once ignited. Figure 22-8 lists types of fire-starting materials.

Laying a fire – There are several methods for laying a fire, each of which has advantages. The situation you find yourself in will determine which fire to use (See Figure 22-9). Always light your fire from the upwind side. Make sure to lay your tinder, kindling, and fuel so that your fire will burn as long as you need it. Igniters provide the initial heat required to start the tinder burning.

Tinder	Kindling	Fuel
Bark	Small twigs	Dry standing wood
Dead grass	Cardboard	Dead branches
Moss	Strips of wood	Animal fats
Straw		Coal
	Cattail	
Sawdust	fluff	Dried animal dung
Dead evergreen Needles		Dry peat
Cotton		
Waxed paper		
Lint		
Dried Vegetable fibers		
Fatwood (Pine resin)		
Steel wool		
Gunpowder		

Figure 22-8. Fire-Starting Material.

497

Site Selection – When selecting a site to build a fire, you should consider the following: Where (terrain and climate) you are operating, what materials and tools are available, how much time you have, why you need a fire, and where is the enemy–how near is he?

Preparation – If you are in a wooded or brush covered area, clear brush away and scrape the surface soil from the spot you selected. The cleared circle should be at least 3 feet (1 meter) in diameter so that there is little chance of the fire spreading. To prepare the site for a fire, ensure that it is dry and that it look for a dry spot that offers: Protection from the wind; is suitably placed in relation to your shelter (if any); concentrates the heat in the direction you desire; and has a supply of wood or other fire burning material.

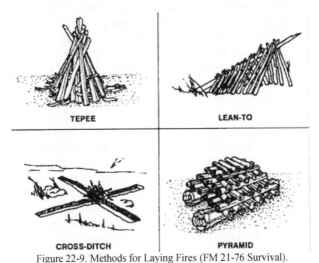

TEPEE   LEAN-TO

CROSS-DITCH   PYRAMID

Figure 22-9. Methods for Laying Fires (FM 21-76 Survival).

Conclusion

The purpose of this chapter was to discuss the basics of fieldcraft. For additional information, such as food procurement, the reader is directed to FM 21-76 Survival. Every member of a patrol must be ready to operate for extended periods alone. For this reason each man should possess a survival kit which should include the following: First aid items; water purification tablets; signal mirror; fish hooks; 550 cord; lighter, metal match, waterproof matches; snare wire, etc. For the case, you might want to use a Band-Aid box, a first aid case, an ammunition pouch, or another suitable waterproof case.

SUT Handbook Conclusion

Learning is being able to profit from experience. Thus, the goal of this book was to develop a theoretical knowledge from history, particularly mistakes to avoid, as well as a practical method of applying sound doctrine, tactics, techniques, and procedures pertinent to small unit tactics. Likewise, because light infantry tactics are highly perishable, it's imperative that the Special Forces soldier place a high premium on the technical and tactical aspects of his profession; so as to live up to the reputation that has been hard earned.

Duty is the privilege of service. It's the honor of having your fellow countrymen depend on you. Duty is, "your word is your bond." And you'd rather sacrifice your life than your word. This is duty, over against a mere cause. Everything else in your career is but corollary to this vital distinction. And it's of utmost importance for you, as the future of the Special Forces Regiment, to realize that the eyes of our 'beloved land of culture and ancient descent' are upon you; depending upon your expertise in tactics, decisive leadership of men in battle, and quiet professionalism. If this high ideal has led you to seek comradely in the ranks of the Special Forces Regiment, then you, like me, place a high premium on it – duty. Duty is not living for ourselves alone but something greater than ourselves. It's a sort of annihilation of the self – as well as a fulfillment of it. We serve with the memory of those who have gone before us. And may we never fail those with whom we serve.

Today as America continues to face challenges, you as the man in the arena, the custodian of our nation's defense, will be 'called upon to perform tasks in isolation, far from familiar faces and voices,' to take a stand for truth and liberty; to defend the defenseless and liberate the oppressed; to prove your worth in the test of arms under the eyes of God; to guard our country and our way of life, and to be prepared and willing to give your life in their defense. This is love of God, Country and truth, lived out in steadfast faith, duteous selfless service, confidence, and undaunted courage, with no thought of personal advancement, ambition or applause. This privileged duty is ours.

Truth, strength, and honor!

Annex A Code of Conduct

Article I: I am an American, fighting in the armed forces which guard my country and our way of life. I am prepared to give my life in their defense.

Article II: I will never surrender of my own free will. If in command I will never surrender the members of my command while they still have the means to resist.

Article III: If I am captured, I will continue to resist by all means available. I will make every effort to escape and aid others to escape. I will accept neither parole nor special favors from the enemy.

Article IV: If I become a prisoner of war, I will keep faith with my fellow prisoners. I will give no information nor take part in any action which might be harmful to my comrades. If I am senior, I will take command. If not, I will obey the lawful orders of those appointed over me and will back them up in every way.

Article V: When questioned, should I become a prisoner of war, I am required to give name, rank, service, number, and date of birth. I will evade answering further questions to the utmost of my ability. I will make no oral or written statements disloyal to my country and its allies or harmful to their cause.

Article VI: I will never forget that I am an American, responsible for my actions, and dedicated to the principles which made my country free. I will trust in my God and in the United States of America.

Annex B Robert Rogers' 28 Rules of Ranging

1.All Rangers are to be subject to the rules and articles of war; to appear at roll-call every evening, on their own parade, equipped, each with a firelock, sixty rounds of powder and ball, and a hatchet, at which time an officer from each company is to inspect the same, to see they are in order, so as to be ready on any emergency to march at a minute's warning; and before they are dismissed, the necessary guards are to be draughted, and scouts for the next day appointed.[1]

2.Whenever you are ordered out to the enemies forts or frontiers for discoveries, if your number be small, march in a single file, keeping at such a distance from each other as to prevent one shot from killing two men, sending one man, or more, forward, and the like on each side, at the distance of twenty yards from the main body, if the ground you march over will admit of it, to give the signal to the officer of the approach of an enemy, and of their number, etc.

3.If you march over marshes or soft ground, change your position, and march abreast of each other to prevent the enemy from tracking you (as they would do if you marched in a single file) till you get over such ground, and then resume your former order, and march till it is quite dark before you encamp, which do, if possible, on a piece of ground which that may afford your sentries the advantage of seeing or hearing the enemy some considerable distance, keeping one half of your whole party awake alternately through the night.

4.Some time before you come to the place you would reconnoitre, make a stand, and send one or two men in whom you can confide, to look out the best ground for making your observations.

5.If you have the good fortune to take any prisoners, keep them separate, till they are examined, and in your return take a different route from that in which you went out, that you may the better discover any party in your rear, and have an opportunity, if their strength be superior to yours, to alter your course, or disperse, as circumstances may require.

6.If you march in a large body of three or four hundred, with a design to attack the enemy, divide your party into three columns, each headed by a proper officer, and let those columns march in single files, the columns to the right and left keeping at twenty yards distance or more from that of the center, if the ground will admit, and let proper guards be kept in the front and rear, and suitable flanking parties at a due distance as before directed, with orders to halt on all eminences, to take a view of the surrounding ground, to prevent your being ambuscaded, and to notify the approach or retreat of the enemy, that proper dispositions may be made for attacking, defending, And if the enemy approach in your front on level ground, form a front of your three columns or main body with the advanced guard, keeping out your

---

[1] Rogers, Journals of Major Robert Rogers, 82-86.

flanking parties, as if you were marching under the command of trusty officers, to prevent the enemy from pressing hard on either of your wings, or surrounding you, which is the usual method of the savages, if their number will admit of it, and be careful likewise to support and strengthen your rear-guard.

7.If you are obliged to receive the enemy's fire, fall, or squat down, till it is over; then rise and discharge at them. If their main body is equal to yours, extend yourselves occasionally; but if superior, be careful to support and strengthen your flanking parties, to make them equal to theirs, that if possible you may repulse them to their main body, in which case push upon them with the greatest resolution with equal force in each flank and in the center, observing to keep at a due distance from each other, and advance from tree to tree, with one half of the party before the other ten or twelve yards. If the enemy push upon you, let your front fire and fall down, and then let your rear advance thro' them and do the like, by which time those who before were in front will be ready to discharge again, and repeat the same alternately, as occasion shall require; by this means you will keep up such a constant fire, that the enemy will not be able easily to break your order, or gain your ground.

8.If you oblige the enemy to retreat, be careful, in your pursuit of them, to keep out your flanking parties, and prevent them from gaining eminences, or rising grounds, in which case they would perhaps be able to rally and repulse you in their turn.

9.If you are obliged to retreat, let the front of your whole party fire and fall back, till the rear hath done the same, making for the best ground you can; by this means you will oblige the enemy to pursue you, if they do it at all, in the face of a constant fire.

10.If the enemy is so superior that you are in danger of being surrounded by them, let the whole body disperse, and every one take a different road to the place of rendezvous appointed for that evening, which must every morning be altered and fixed for the evening ensuing, in order to bring the whole party, or as many of them as possible, together, after any separation that may happen in the day; but if you should happen to be actually surrounded, form yourselves into a square, or if in the woods, a circle is best, and, if possible, make a stand till the darkness of the night favours your escape.

11.If your rear is attacked, the main body and flankers must face about to the right or left, as occasion shall require, and form themselves to oppose the enemy, as before directed; and the same method must be observed, if attacked in either of your flanks, by which means you will always make a rear of one of your flank-guards.

12.If you determine to rally after a retreat, in order to make a fresh stand against the enemy, by all means endeavour to do it on the most rising ground you come at, which will give you greatly the advantage in point of situation, and enable you to repulse superior numbers.

13.In general, when pushed upon by the enemy, reserve your fire till they approach very near, which will then put them into the greatest surprise and consternation, and give you an opportunity of rushing upon them with your hatchets and cutlasses to the better advantage.

14.When you encamp at night, fix your sentries in such a manner as not to be relieved from the main body till morning, profound secrecy and silence being often of the last importance in these cases. Each sentry therefore should consist of six men, two of whom must be constantly alert, and when relieved by their fellows, it should be done without noise; and in case those on duty see or hear any thing, which alarms them, they are not to speak, but one of them is silently to retreat, and acquaint the commanding officer thereof, that proper dispositions may be made; and all occasional sentries should be fixed in like manner.

15.At the first dawn of day, awake your whole detachment; that being the time when the savages choose to fall upon their enemies, you should by all means be in readiness to receive them.

16.If the enemy should be discovered by your detachments in the morning, and their numbers are superior to yours, and a victory doubtful, you should not attack them till the evening, as then they will not know your numbers, and if you are repulsed, your retreat will be favoured by the darkness of the night.

17.Before you leave your encampment, send out small parties to scout round it, to see if there be any appearance or track of an enemy that might have been near you during the night.

18.When you stop for refreshment, choose some spring or rivulet if you can, and dispose your party so as not to be surprised, posting proper guards and sentries at a due distance, and let a small party waylay the path you came in, lest the enemy should be pursuing.

19.If, in your return, you have to cross rivers, avoid the usual fords as much as possible, lest the enemy should have discovered, and be there expecting you.

20.If you have to pass by lakes, keep at some distance from the edge of the water, lest, in case of an ambuscade or an attack from the enemy, when in that situation, your retreat should be cut off.

21.If the enemy pursue your rear, take a circle till you come to your own tracks, and there form an ambush to receive them, and give them the first fire.

22.When you return from a scout, and come near our forts, avoid the usual roads, and avenues thereto, lest the enemy should have headed you, and lay in ambush to receive you, when almost exhausted with fatigues.

23.When you pursue any party that has been near our forts or encampments, follow not directly in their tracks, lest they should be discovered by their rear guards, who, at such a time, would be most alert; but endeavour, by a different route, to head and meet them in some narrow pass, or lay in ambush to receive them when and where they least expect it.

24.If you are to embark in canoes, battoes, or otherwise, by water, choose the evening for the time of your embarkation, as you will then have the whole night before you, to pass undiscovered by any parties of the enemy, on hills, or other places, which command a prospect of the lake or river you are upon.

25.In paddling or rowing, give orders that the boat or canoe next the sternmost, wait for her, and the third for the second, and the fourth for the third, and so on, to prevent separation, and that you may be ready to assist each other on any emergency.

26.Appoint one man in each boat to look out for fires, on the adjacent shores, from the numbers and size of which you may form some judgment of the number that kindled them, and whether you are able to attack them or not.

27.If you find the enemy encamped near the banks of a river or lake, which you imagine they will attempt to cross for their security upon being attacked, leave a detachment of your party on the opposite shore to receive them, while, with the remainder, you surprise them, having them between you and the lake or river.

28.If you cannot satisfy yourself as to the enemy's number and strength, from their fire, conceal your boats at some distance, and ascertain their number by a reconnoitering party, when they embark, or march, in the morning, marking the course they steer, when you may pursue, ambush, and attack them, or let them pass, as prudence shall direct you. In general, however, that you may not be discovered by the enemy upon the lakes and rivers at a great distance, it is safest to lay by, with your boats and party concealed all day, without noise or shew; and to pursue your intended route by night; and whether you go by land or water, give out parole and countersigns, in order to know one another in the dark, and likewise appoint a station every man to repair to, in case of any accident that may separate you.

– Major Robert Rogers, 1759

Annex C   Small Unit Tactics Taxonomy

ACE
1. Ammunition
2. Casualties
3. Equipment

5 Ss + T
1. Search
2. Silence
3. Segregate
4. Safeguard
5. Speed
6. Tag

SLLS
1. Stop
2. Look
3. Listen
4. Smell

METT-TC
1. Mission
2. Enemy
3. Terrain
4. Troops
5. Time
6. Civil consider.

SALUTE
1. Size
2. Activity
3. Location
4. Unit / uniform
5. Time
6. Equipment

5 Paragraphs of an OPORD
1. Situation
2. Mission
3. Execution
4. Sustainment
5. Comd. and Control

Troop Leading Procedures
1. Receive the mission
2. Issue a WARNO
3. Make a tentative plan
4. Initiate movement
5. Conduct a recon
6. Complete the plan
7. Issue an OPORD
8. Supervise and refine

GOTWA
1. Where the leader is GOING
2. OTHERS he is taking with him
3. TIME he will be gone
4. WHAT to do if he doesn't return in time
5. ACTIONS on contact – you and me

Principles of Patrolling
1. Planning
2. Reconnaissance
3. Security
4. Control
5. Common Sense

9 Line MEDEVAC
1. Location
2. Frequency and call sign
3. Number of patients by precedence
4. Special equipment needed
5. Number of patients by type
6. Security of pickup site
7. Method of marking at pickup site
8. Patient nationality
9. NBC

OCOKA
1. Observ. & Fields of Fire
2. Cover and Concealment
3. Obstacles
4. Key Terrain
5. Avenues of Approach

Movement Techniques
1. Traveling
2. Traveling Overwatch – contact likely
3. Bounding Overwatch – contact imminent

Ambush Categories
1. Hasty
2. Deliberate

Ambush Types
1. Point
2. Area

Ambush Fundamentals
1. Surprise and Speed
2. Coordinated Fires
3. Violence of Action

Reconnaissance Fundamentals
1. Gain the Information
2. Avoid Detection
3. Task Organize
4. Employ Security Measures

Raid Fundamentals
1. Surprise and speed
2. Coordinated fires
3. Violence of action
4. Planned withdrawal

Types of Recons
1. Route
2. Zone
3. Area

Six Forms of Manuever
1. Envelopment
2. Turning Movement
3. Infiltration
4. Penetration
5. Frontal Attack
6. Flank Attack

505

Annex D Small Unit Tactics Acronyms

Leader's Recon of the OBJ (Ambush)   PINPOINT
Pinpoint OBJ and verify overall suitability: 35-50 meters
Identify left, right, and center of kill zone
No obstacles from near side to the LOA
Point out 2 claymore trees (18" diameter)
Overall clear fields of fire
Identify support and then assault positions
No dead space
Travel to identify left and right-side security positions

Security Brief   EWAC
Engagement criteria.
Withdrawal.
Abort criteria.
Compromise.

Assault Line Brief   SPARC
Sector of fire.
Priority of targets.
Assault lane.
Rate of fire.
Conceal position.

Leader's Recon of Assault on a Raid OBJ   RAID
RFL (Restricted fire line)
Assign LOA
Identify Primary and Alternate Breach Points
Determine LCC

Leader's Recon of Support on a Raid OBJ   SHIFT FIRE
Stand-off clear fields of fire.
Hard sectors of fire: give azimuths.
Initiation PACE.
Fire control measures: Shifts/Lift.
Talk the guns.

Find targets for each gun.
Implied security tasks.
Rates of fire.
Egress plan.

Rally Points   COOLANT
Cover and concealment.
Off natural lines of drift.
Out of sight and sound.
Large enough.
Affords a defense for a short period.
Near a source of water (Patrol base).
Tough terrain (Patrol base).

Breach   SOSRA
Suppress
Obscure
Secure
Reduce
Assault

Urban Operations   URBAN
Use cover when possible.
Reduce your target size while in a static position.
By-pass: doors, windows, and corners enroute to target building with security.
Avoid bogging down and maintain dispersion.
Navigate in low percentage areas.

Annex E Small Unit Tactics Practice Exam

1. What are the nine principles of war (FM 3-0)?
A. Mass, Objective, Offensive, Security, Economy of Force, Maneuver, Unity of Command, Surprise and Simplicity.
B. Mass, Objective, Offensive, Security, Execution, Mission, Unity of Command, Surprise and Synchronization.
C. Mission, Offensive, Attack, Defense, Retrograde, Maneuver, Command, Coordination and Synchronization.
D. Mass, Objective, Offensive, Synchronization, Speed, Surprise, Violence of Action, Control and Command & Signal.

2. What does METT-TC stand for (FM 3-0, 5-5)?
A. Mission, Equipment, Time, Troops, Terrain, and Civilian Considerations.
B. Maneuver, Enemy, Terrain, Time, Topography, and Casualties.
C. Mission, Enemy, Terrain & Weather, Troops & Support Available, Time Available, and Civil Considerations.
D. Movement, Enemy, Task, Troops, Time, and Control.

3. What are the three levels of war (FM 3-0, 6-2)?
A. Global, National, and Tactical.
B. Theatre, National, and Tactical.
C. Strategic, Conventional, and Unconventional.
D. Strategic, Operational, and Tactical.

4. What are the six war-fighting functions (FM 3-0)?
A. Maneuver, Service and Support, Command & Signal, Intelligence, Security, and Fire Control.
B. Sustainment, Command & Control, Fire Support, Security, Intelligence, and Movement.
C. Intelligence, Command & Signal, Maneuver, Fires, Security, and Support.
D. Movement & Maneuver, Intelligence, Fires, Sustainment, Command & Control, and Protection.

5. What is leadership (FM 3-21.8, 1-24)?

6. What are the three principles of leadership (SH 21-76, 1-1)?
A. Be, Know, and Do
B. Lead, Follow, or Get out of the way.
C. Direct, Take Charge, Execute.

7. What are the four major factors of leadership (SH 21- 76, 1-1)?
A. Leader, Follower, Situation, and Execution.
B. Lead by example, Know yourself, Seek self-improvement, and Be technically and tactically proficient.
C. Leader, Led, Situation, and Communications.

8. What four factors determine the method of infiltration (FM 3-21.8, 9-7)?
A. Mission, Weather, Terrain, and Enemy.
B. Enemy Situation, Mission, Weather, and Topography.
C. Obstacles, Enemy, Service Support, and Mission.

9. What are the three types of combat patrols (FM 3-21.8, 9-7)?
A. Raid, Ambush, and Security.
B. Raid, Recon, and Ambush.
C. Ambush, Recon, and Presence.
D. Ambush, Movement to Contact, and Raid.

10. True or False. The TLP begins when the leader receives the first indication of an upcoming mission. (FM 3-21.8, 5-6)?

11. What is the last step of the TLP (FM 3-21.8, 5-6)?
A. Execution.
B. Complete the Plan.
C. Supervise and Refine.

12. What is the sixth step of the TLP (FM 3-21.8, 5-6)?
A. Conduct Reconnaissance.
B. Complete the plan.
C. Issue an Operations Order.

13. What are the three movement techniques (FM 3-21.8, 3-19)?
A. Traveling, Traveling Overwatch, and Bounding Overwatch.
B. File, Modified Wedge, and Fire Team Wedge.
C. Column, Wedge, and Vee.

14. Which squad movement technique should be utilized when enemy contact is expected (FM 3-21.8, 3-20)?
A. Travelling Overwatch.
B. Alternating Bounds.
C. Successive Bounds.
D. Bounding Overwatch.

15. What is the correct distance from the lead squad to the Platoon leader for a Platoon moving in traveling overwatch (FM 3-21.8, 3-25)?
A. 200 Meters
B. 50-100 Meters
C. 75 Meters
D. 25 Meters

16. What is given during paragraph two of the Operations Order?

17. Identity the purpose of the following mission statement?

508

A CO, 2/75 IN, attacks at 190600 NOV 07 to seize high ground vicinity NB 459270 (OBJ DOG) IOT prevent the enemy from disrupting 3/75 IN (BN decisive operation) attack.

A. To seize high ground vicinity NB 459270.
B. To attack at 190600 NOV 96.
C. To prevent the enemy from disrupting 3/75 IN's attack.
D. To support the BN main effort.
E. To destroy the enemy on OBJ DOG.

18. What do the letters in the acronym OCOKA stand for?
A. Obstacles, Concealment, Overhead Cover, Key Avenues of Approach, and Areas of Interest.
B. Observation and Fields of Fire, Cover and Concealment, Obstacles, Key Terrain, and Avenues of Approach.
C. Obstructive Terrain, Cover, Obstacles, Key Avenues of Approach, and Available Time.

19. You are the BTL of a 12 man squad on an ambush patrol. Your squad has just received indirect fire and your SL is dead. Your squad has moved 600 meters to a draw away from enemy contact and FOs. List five tasks you need to accomplish in order to effectively reorganize following the contact (SH 21-76, 1-7).

20. During Paragraph 3(B) Task to Maneuver units the squad leader must give what to each individual or special teams that he gives a specific task to accomplish?
A. Task and Purpose.
B. Direction and Motivation.
C. Task and Standard.
D. Specified and Implied.
E. All of the above.

21. In what paragraph would you find Medical evacuation and hospitalization and method of evacuating dead and wounded?

22. In Paragraph one, what does (Composition) and (Disposition) of Enemy Forces tell you?
A. The identification of that enemy force, and the location of those forces in the general area.
B. The location of the enemy force, and their actions.
C. The amount of enemy personnel and their location.

23. Movement, step four of the TLP, can occur when?
A. If movement is necessary, at any time during the TLP.
B. Only after receiving the OPORD.
C. Once the tentative plan has been made and not before.
D. Once rehearsals have been conducted and refined.

24. Where do you find your Squad Mission statement in the higher OPORDER?

25. Troop Leading Procedures refer to which of the following?
A. Process by which changes are made to an existing order.
B. Dynamic process, used by small unit leaders, to analyze a mission, develop a plan, and prepare for an operation.
C. Process to provide advance notice of operations that are to come.
D. Essential information needed to carry out an operation.
E. All of the above.

26. What are the four fundamentals of raid?
A. Security, Support, Assault, and a Planned Withdrawal.
B. Firepower, Speed, Control, and Violence of Action.
C. Surprise and Speed, Coordinated Fires, Violence of Action, and a Planned Withdrawal.

27. Which order is used to make timely changes to an existing order?
A. Fragmentary Order.
B. Operations Order.
C. Warning Order.

28. Which of the following best defines Economy of Force?
A. To strike the enemy at a time, place or in a manner for which he is unprepared.
B. To mass the effects of overwhelming combat power at the decisive place and time.
C. To employ all combat power available, in the most effective way possible, allocating minimal essential combat power to secondary efforts.
D. To allow the commander to identify where and when to take risks without jeopardizing the security of the entire force.

29. What is the definition of a battle drill (SH 21-76, 6-1)?

30. What are the five principles of the breach?
A. Suppress, Seize, Destroy, Mark, Assault.
B. Suppress, Obscure, Secure, Reduce, Assault..
C. Suppress, Smoke, Breach, Secure, Assault.

31. What are the three types of recon patrols used during patrolling?

32. The task organization of the recon patrol is made up of what three elements or combination of the three elements?
A. Surveillance, Security, and R/S.
B. Patrol HQ, Recon Element, and Security Element.
C. Security, R/S, and ORP Security.

33. What are the four fundamentals of reconnaissance?

34. What is the acronym used to report all gathered Priority Information Requirements (PIR)?

35. What are the four reasons during the conduct of the recon that each R&S team might return to the release point?

36. What are the two types of information directed from higher to be gathered on a recon patrol?
A. (PIR) Priority information requirements, and (IR) information requirements
B. Specified tasks, and implied tasks.

37. In what order are the elements of the ambush emplaced?

38. At what point do the security elements move to their alternate positions and why?
A. Upon the cease fire command.
B. Upon fire-in-the-hole-one.
C. Upon initiation and to seal off the objective.
D. Upon arrival of a QRF.
E. All of the above.

39. How long is a patrol base used for?
A. 12 hours.
B. 18 hours.
C. No more than 24 hours unless an emergency arises.

40. For selection criteria, name four of the five things you look for in a patrol base.

41. Under normal conditions what is the last priority of work?
A. Rest.
B. Chow.

42. The claymore mine projects a fan shaped pattern of steel balls in a horizontal arc of how many degrees?
A. 90 degrees.
B. 60 degrees.
C. 30 degrees.

43. What is the normal PACE plan for initiation?

44. If the claymore mine is placed in front of sufficient cover, how far back should you be to meet the minimum safe distance?
A. 33 meters.
B. 35 meters.
C. 18 meters.
D. 16 Meters.

45. What is the optimum effective range for the claymore mine?
A. 50 meters.
B. 250 meters.
C. 150 meters.

46. The M240B fires what type of round?
A. 7.62 x 51 mm.
B. 7.62 x 39 mm.
C. 7.62 x 54 mm.
D. All of the above.

47. You are firing your M4 and experience a double feed. What actions should you take to clear this malfunction?

48. What is the effective range for the M240B on a tripod for a point target?
A. 600 meters.
B. 800 meters.
C. 1100 meters.

49. Who was the father of the US Army Special Forces?
A. Dick Meadows.
B. Charlie Beckwith.
C. Russell Volckmann.
D. Aaron Bank.

50. Who was the father of the OSS?
A. Audie Murphy.
B. Robert Howard.
C. William Donovan.
D. Douglas MacArthur.

Annex F SUT Practice Exam Answer Key

1. A.

2. C.

3. D.

4. D.

5. Leadership is influencing people by providing purpose, direction, and motivation while operating to accomplish the mission and improve the organization.

6. A.

7. C.

8. B.

9. A.

10. True

11.C.

12. B.

13. A.

14. D.

15. B.

16. Mission Statement

17. C.

18. B.

19. Call Higher, Check Security, Check crew-served weapons, Pinpoint Location, and Check Equipment.

20. A.

21. Paragraph 4, Service and support

22. A.

23. A.

24. Paragraph 3, Sub Paragraph A, Line 1

25. B.

26. C.

27. A.

28. C.

29. A battle drill is a collective action rapidly executed without applying a deliberate decision making process.

30. B.

31. Area, Zone, and Route

32. B.

33. Gain all required information, Avoid detection by the enemy, Task organize, and Employ security measures.

34. SALUTE

35. They have gathered all PIR, they reached the limit of advance, their allocated time to conduct recon has elapsed, or they made contact with the enemy.

36. A.

37. Security, Support, and Assault

38. C.

39. C.

40. Cover and concealment, off natural lines of drift, out of sight/sound/small arms range of enemy/objective/roads, large enough for the entire element, easily defendable for a short period of time, near a source of water, difficult terrain that impedes foot movement.

41. A.

42. B.

43. Claymore, M240B, Squad Leader's M4, and AG's M4.

44. D.

45. A.

46. A.

47. Lock the bolt to the rear, remove the source of feed, use your fingers to work the rounds loose, load a fresh magazine, fire.

48. B.

49. D.

50. C.

Annex G Soviet Weapon Capabilities[1]

AK-47 Assault Rifle:
Cartridge..7.62 x 39mm
Maximum range.. 1000 meters
Maximum effective range (area)................................... 300 meters

AK-74 Assault Rifle:
Cartridge..5.45 x 39mm
Maximum range.. 1000 meters
Maximum effective range (area)................................... 300 meters

RPK Machinegun:
Cartridge..7.62 x 39mm
Maximum range..2500 meters
Maximum effective range (area)................................... 800 meters

RPK-74 Machinegun:
Cartridge..5.45 x 39mm
Maximum range..2500 meters
Maximum effective range (area)...................................800 meters

PKM Machinegun:
Cartridge..7.62 x 54mm
Maximum range.. 3800 meters
Maximum effective range (area)................................... 1000 meters

SVD Sniper Rifle:
Cartridge..7.62 x 54mm
Maximum range.. 1300 meters
Maximum effective range with 4 x power telescopic sight........................ 800 meters

DShK 1938 Heavy Machinegun:
Cartridge.. 12.7 x 108mm
Maximum range..7000 meters
Maximum effective range (area)................................... 1000 meters

KPV Heavy Machinegun:
Cartridge.. 14.5 x 114mm
Maximum range..4000 meters
Maximum effective range (area)................................... 1000 meters

BG-15 (GP-25/30) Rifle-Mounted Grenade Launcher:
Projectile.. 40mm
Maximum range..400 meters
Maximum effective range .... 100 meters

AGS-17 Automatic Grenade Launcher:
Projectile.. 30mm
Maximum range..1700 meters
Maximum effective range .... 700 meters

RPG 7 Shoulder-fired Rocket:
Projectile...85 mm shaped-charged,
rocket, which will penetrate up to 330 mm (12") of armor.
Maximum range.. 920 meters
Maximum effective range (stationary target)........................... 500 meters

---

[1] Technical data extracted from FM 100-2-3 The Soviet Army, June 1991.

515

Maximum effective range (moving target)... 300 meters
Projectile self-destructs approx. 4.5 seconds after firing.

RPG 16 Shoulder-fired Rocket:

Projectile... 58.3 mm shaped-charged, rocket,
which will penetrate up to 375 mm (15") of armor.

Maximum range.. 920 meters
Maximum effective range (stationary target)...................................... 800 meters
Maximum effective range (moving target)... 500 meters

82mm Recoiless Rifle :

Projectile... 82mm HEAT round
Maximum effective range..450 meters
Rate of fire.. 6 rpm

2B9 82mm Mortar:

Projectile..82 mm
Maximum range...5000 meters
Minimum range ....100 meters

2B11 120mm Mortar:

Projectile..120 mm
Maximum range...7200 meters
Minimum range ....460 meters

M1943 (M160) Mortar:

Projectile.. 160 mm
Maximum range...5700 meters
Minimum range ....500 meters

D30 122 mm Artillery:

Projectile..122 mm
Maximum range...15300 meters

T72/80 MBT:

Projectile..125 mm
Maximum range...4500 meters

Annex H   Tactical Symbols

A military symbol is a graphic representation of units, equipment, installations, control measures, and other elements relevant to military operations. A unit symbol is composed of a frame, color (fill), branch (an arm of service of the Army/Marine Corps) or functional symbols (icon), and text and/or other symbol modifiers (Figure H-1).

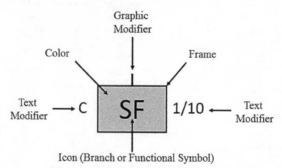

Figure H-1. Components of a Military Symbol.

Purpose. The purpose of military symbology is to allow commanders and staffs to graphically display certain elements of the operational picture. Situation maps, overlays, and annotated aerial photographs are used to express an operation plan or order, concept, or friendly or hostile (enemy) situation. The combination of unit and equipment symbols and control measures, as well as other military symbols, creates an indispensable tool for quickly portraying military operations.

Status of Symbol. Status refers to whether a unit is known to be present at the location identified or whether it is a planned or suspected location. Regardless of affiliation, present status is indicated by a solid line and planned or suspected status is indicated by a dashed line (see Figure H-2).

Status	Friendly			Hostile	Neutral	Unknown
	Unit	Equipment	Installation			
Present	☐	◯	☐	◇	☐	✧
Planned or Suspected	☐	◯	☐	◇	☐	✧

Figure H-2. Status of Symbol.

US Army Small Unit Tactics Handbook

Unit and Equipment Symbols Guide

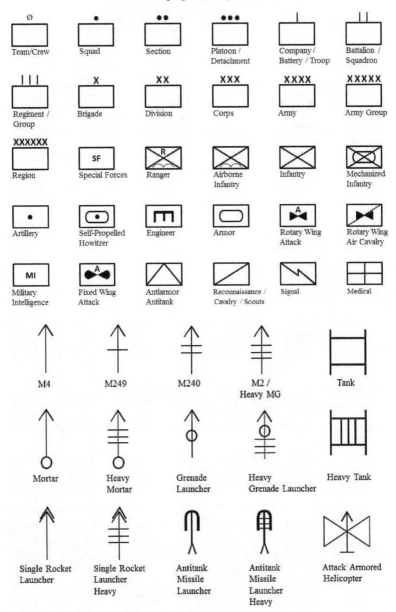

Figure H-3. Equipment Symbols.

Tactical Mission Tasks

ATTACK BY FIRE: Uses direct fires, supported by indirect fires, to engage an enemy without closing with him to destroy, suppress, fix or deceive him.	CLEAR: Remove all enemy forces and eliminate organized resistance in an assigned area.
BLOCK: Task that denies the enemy access to an area. Or, may be an effect that integrates fire planning and obstacle effort to stop an attacker or prevent him from passing.	CONTAIN: To stop, hold, or surround an enemy or to cause the enemy to center activity on a given front and to prevent the withdrawal of any part of the enemy's force.
BREACH: Employs all available means to break through or secure a passage through enemy defense, obstacle, minefield, or fortification.	DEFEAT: Occurs when an enemy has temporarily or permanently lost the physical means or the will to fight.
BYPASS: Directs a unit to maneuver around an obstacle, avoiding combat with an enemy force.	DESTROY: Physically renders an enemy force combat-ineffective until it is reconstituted.
CANALIZE: Restricts enemy movement to a narrow zone by exploiting terrain coupled with the use of obstacles, fires, or friendly maneuver.	DISRUPT: Integrates direct and indirect fires, terrain, and obstacles to upset an enemy's formation, tempo, timetable or cause his forces to commit prematurely.
EXFILTRATE: Remove personnel or units from areas under enemy control by stealth, deception, surprise, or clandestine means.	ISOLATE: Seal off - both physically and psychologically - an enemy from his sources of support, deny freedom of movement, and from having contact with other enemy forces.
FIX: Prevent the enemy from moving any part of his force from a specific location for a specific period of time.	NEUTRALIZE: Render enemy personnel or material incapable of interfering with a particular operation.
FOLLOW & ASSUME: A second committed force follows a force conducting an offensive operation and is prepared to continue the mission if the lead force is fixed, attrited or unable to continue.	OCCUPY: Move into an area so that the force can control the entire area. Both movement to and occupation of the area occur without enemy opposition.
FOLLOW & SUPPORT: A second committed force follows and supports a lead force conducting an offensive operation.	REDUCE: The destruction of an encircled or bypassed enemy force. There is no tactical mission graphic for this task. No Graphic Symbol
INTERDICT: Prevent, disrupt, or delay the enemy's use of an area or route.	RETAIN: Ensure that a terrain feature already controlled by a friendly force remains free of enemy occupation or use.
SECURE: Prevent a unit, facility, or geographical location from being damaged or destroyed as a result of enemy action.	SUPPORT BY FIRE: A maneuver force moves to a position where it can engage the enemy by direct fire in support of another maneuvering force.

Figure H-4. Tactical Mission Tasks.

519

Graphic Control Measures and Fire Support Graphics

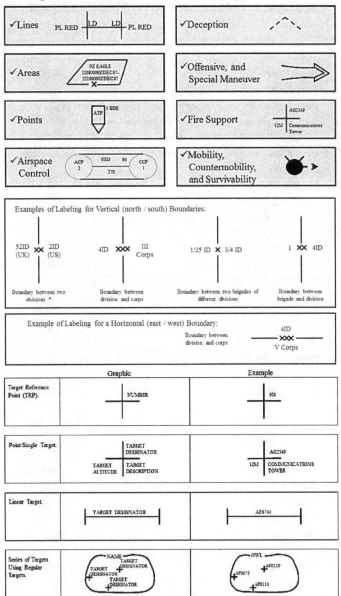

H-5. Graphic Control Measures and Fire Support Graphics.

520

Annex I Recommended Reading List

"The task of the educated mind is simply put: read to lead." – Cicero

1. Bank, Aaron *From OSS to Green Beret: The Birth of Special Forces.* Presidio Press: Novato, 1975.
2. Beavan, Colin *Operation Jedburgh.* Penguin Books: NY, 2006.
3. Clausewitz, Carl Von *On War.* Barnes and Nobles: NY, 2004.
4. Hart, B. H. Liddell *Strategy.* Meridian: New York, 1991.
5. Hoe, Alan *The Quiet Professional.* University Press of Kentucky: Lexington, 2011.
6. Infantry Journal *Infantry in Battle.* Marine Corps Association: Quantico, 1986.
7. Kilcullen, David *Counterinsurgency.* Oxford: NY, 2010.
8. Kolenda, Christopher *Leadership: The Warrior Art.* Army War College Foundation Press: Carlisle, 2001.
9. Malcolm, Ben S. *White Tigers: My Secret War in North Korea.* Brassey's: DC, 1996.
10. Marshall, S.L.A. *Men Against Fire.* University of Oklahoma Press: Norman, 2000.
11. McRaven, William H. *Spec Ops. Case Studies in Special Operations Warfare: Theory and Practice.* Presidio Press: NY, 1995.
12. Paddock, Alfred H. *US Army Special Warfare: Its Origins.* University Press: Lawrence, 2002.
13. Plaster, John L. *SOG: The Secret Wars of America's Commandos in Vietnam.* Nal Caliber: New York, 1997.
14. Schemmer, Benjamin F. *The Raid.* Harper & Row: NY, 1976.
15. Shelby Stanton, Green Berets at War: U. S. Army Special Forces in Southeast Asia 1956-1975, Novato, CA: Presidio Press,   1985.
16. Simpson, Charles M. III *Inside the Green Berets.* Presidio Press: NY, 1983.
17. Summers, Harry G. *On Strategy: A Critical Analysis of the Vietnam War.* Presidio: NY, 1982.
18. Taber, Robert *The War of the Flea.* Potomac: Dulles, 2002.
19. Wood, W.J. *Leaders and Battles.* Presidio Press: Novato, 1984.
20. Volckmann, Russell *We Remained: Three Years Behind the Enemy Lines in the Philippines.* New York: W. W. Norton, 1954.

Index

Index

523

*"I have pursued my enemies and overtaken them; neither
did I turn back again till they were destroyed."
– King David, Psalm 18:37*

CPSIA information can be obtained
at www.ICGtesting.com
Printed in the USA
LVHW101640230723
752882LV00015BA/116/J